AMERICAN LEGACY

AMERICAN LEGACY

The Story of
John & Caroline Kennedy

———❖———

C. DAVID HEYMANN

ATRIA BOOKS
New York   London   Toronto   Sydney

ATRIA BOOKS

A Division of Simon & Schuster, Inc.
1230 Avenue of the Americas
New York, NY 10020

First Atria Books hardcover edition July 2007

ATRIA BOOKS and colophon are trademarks
of Simon & Schuster, Inc.

Designed by Dana Sloan

Manufactured in the United States of America

ISBN-13: 978-0-7434-9738-1
ISBN-10:   0-7434-9738-4

For Beatrice Schwartz,
friend, lover, companion, confidante,
domestic partner, muse, and more

You just keep going along.
You just keep going along or you're left behind.

—Caroline Kennedy

People keep telling me I can be a great man.
I'd rather be a good one.

—John F. Kennedy Jr.

CONTENTS

◆

AUTHOR'S NOTE

◆————————————————◆

AFTER THE assassination of President John F. Kennedy on November 22, 1963, his widow, Jacqueline Bouvier Kennedy, took it upon herself to raise their two children, John Jr. and Caroline, in as normal an atmosphere as their celebrity would allow. As a single parent, Jackie gave them her love and her time, and supported them in their daily activities and life decisions. Her strong commitment to her children and her fervent desire to keep them out of the glare of the spotlight—not always successfully—were nevertheless a testimonial to her diligence, a true sign of her devotion. The results of her efforts were (and are) clearly visible. Unlike so many of the other Kennedys of their generation, John and Caroline were centered and successful. For all their losses and travails, they managed to avoid the pitfalls and scandals that beset so many of their cousins. Their values reflected the better part of their heritage. They were humble, modest, and refined—rare attributes in any individual regardless of background.

What makes John and Caroline's story unique is that from the moment of their births, they occupied a central position in what is generally regarded as the most famous family in the United States, if not the world. Even as young children growing up in the White House, their most subtle gestures and actions made headlines. As they grew older, their fame derived less from their accomplishments than from what each came to represent in historic terms. As the children of arguably the most famous American couple of the second half of the twentieth century, they were destined to live their lives in the public domain, the subject of countless magazine articles, television specials, and newspaper reports. Yet until now they have not been the subject of a dual biography. In that sense, this volume represents a first.

In good times and bad, John and his sister, Caroline, were unusually close, bound together not only by common heritage and circumstance but by a series of traumas and tragedies that ultimately altered the course of their lives. Yet what seems particularly unique about them is that despite their shared intimacy, the two were vastly different in personality and temperament. A wife and mother, Caroline has always been introverted and intensely private. She possesses her father's appearance but her mother's strength of will. She is as devoted to her own children as her mother was to hers. Like her mother, she is something of a mystery, difficult to read, hard to interpret. John looked more like his Bouvier mother but boasted his father's debonair charm, outgoing conviviality, and sense of humor. Caroline has always been reticent, whereas her brother shone in public. Had he lived, it is likely he would have followed in his father's footsteps and entered the political arena. Given the opportunity—and with a bit of Irish luck—he might well have gone all the way.

In several respects, this book is more about John than it is about Caroline. His life is complete. For better or worse, his tragic (and untimely) end allows us to examine him in a fuller, more definitive vein. Many of his friends and acquaintances were willing to speak on the record for the first time. Caroline's life continues to evolve. In this regard, she remains very much a work in progress. While generally cooperative, her friends and associates were less forthcoming and more protective. Approaching the age of fifty, she is still an open book, a volume with an ending yet to be written. What emerges is a portrait of two siblings, a brother and sister—one perspective drawn in full color, the other limned in shades of black and white. This, then, is their story.

Part I

Chapter 1

———◆———

THE FALL OF ICARUS (1)

O N NOVEMBER 17, 2002, Caroline Kennedy, accompanied by her
uncle Senator Edward M. Kennedy, flew from New York to Paris,
France, to celebrate the opening at the Louvre of "Jacqueline Kennedy:
The White House Years," an exhibition of Jackie's Camelot-period fashions, featuring formal attire, travel outfits, sportswear, riding clothes, and
personal favorites. On loan from the John F. Kennedy Presidential Library and Museum in Boston, Massachusetts, the exhibit had been
shown the year before at New York's Metropolitan Museum of Art, opposite the Fifth Avenue apartment building where Jackie had resided the
last thirty years of her life, until her death in May 1994 at age sixty-four.

In flawless French, Caroline addressed an overflowing audience, including French government officials and members of the European press,
at the Louvre's Musée de la Mode et du Textile, telling them that Jacqueline Kennedy's élan and trendsetting flair were born of the French capital. "While a student at Vassar," said Caroline, "my mother spent her
junior year abroad, studying at the Sorbonne. She took courses in French
art and literature. Her passion for French history guided and informed
her work in the White House. Paris is the city my mother loved best and
that inspired her the most. And so it is fitting that this exhibit should
come to the Louvre."

Caroline continued in the same vein for another five minutes. As she concluded her speech, the audience rose and gave her a resounding ovation. The next speaker was Ted Kennedy. Standing at the podium, the Massachusetts senator, hale and hearty looking if a bit overweight, observed that the exhibit represented a milestone for the Kennedy clan. "The Kennedys have come full circle," he remarked. "Jackie has returned to Paris, and this visit will be remembered and cherished in both our countries."

On November 20 Ted and Caroline boarded a commercial airliner and flew back to the United States. Thurston Gauleiter, an investment banker from Los Angeles, sat behind them in first class. "I couldn't help but overhear snippets of conversation," he said. "For the most part, they discussed Caroline's late brother, John F. Kennedy Jr. Caroline admitted that since the day of John's death in 1999, when his plane plunged into the dark waters of the Atlantic, she'd been afraid to fly. 'Not an hour passes when I don't think of him,' she said. 'For many months after his death, I kept expecting the phone to ring and for John to be at the other end. I kept thinking the door to my apartment would open, and he'd come bounding into the room.' Teddy responded by comparing John Jr. to his brothers Jack and Bobby Kennedy. 'I remember,' he said, 'how as teenagers in Florida, your father and Bobby, on even the roughest of days, would swim miles out into the ocean. They had an insatiable appetite for adventure. The storm-warning flags would be flapping furiously in the wind and rain, and they'd be frolicking in the surf like a couple of polar bears. Your brother was cut from the same cloth. He loved a challenge. He'd kayak in the most turbulent of seas and fly under conditions that grounded even the most experienced of pilots. Like Bobby and your father, he had the desire to live life to the fullest.'

"Later in the flight," continued Gauleiter, "Ted Kennedy again brought up his nephew. 'John could've gone all the way,' he told Caroline. 'He was still becoming the person he would be. He had just begun. There was in him a great promise of things to come.'"

What Kennedy presumably meant was that John had a brilliant political career ahead of him. He had the appearance, the background, the legacy. He had proven skill as a public speaker. He had panache and

charisma. He had integrity. He had a sense of justice. More than anything, he had humility. What other person of his renown made himself
so available? His family possessed great wealth and power, but he came
off like "one of the guys." He represented the clan's greatest hope for the
future. He was the crown prince, rightful heir to the throne. The one
thing he didn't have was time.

After the airliner transporting Teddy and Caroline landed in New
York, the senator switched planes and flew on to Washington, D.C. The
following weekend he visited Caroline, her husband, Edwin Schlossberg,
and their three children—Rose, fourteen, Tatiana, twelve, and nine-year-
old John—at their three-acre weekend home in Sagaponack, Long Island. It marked his first trip to the area since those unbearable days
following the July 16, 1999, disappearance at sea of John Jr.'s high-
performance Piper Saratoga II HP airplane as it made its way from Essex
County Airport in Caldwell, New Jersey, to Martha's Vineyard, Massachusetts.

On that occasion, Ted Kennedy drove past a half-dozen state troop-
ers, several squad cars, yards of yellow police tape, and a caravan of reporters and television cameras posted at the foot of the tree-shrouded
Schlossberg driveway. Maria Shriver and William Kennedy Smith, Caroline's cousins, had arrived earlier. Teddy spent an hour playing basketball
with the Schlossberg children, and another hour manning the telephones, anxiously awaiting news of a breakthrough from the Kennedy
compound in Hyannis Port, Massachusetts. The family had gathered at
the beachfront compound that weekend in anticipation of a wedding between prizewinning documentary filmmaker Rory Kennedy, Ethel and
Robert F. Kennedy's youngest child, and her longtime sweetheart Mark
Bailey. A large tent had been erected on the lawn in front of Ethel's
house, where the bride and groom planned on hosting their reception. A
wedding rehearsal dinner had been scheduled for Friday evening, July
16, the actual ceremony to begin at noon on Saturday. Instead of the
much-anticipated weekend festivities, the Kennedy clan found itself immersed in yet another tragedy.

The missing plane, carrying thirty-eight-year-old John Jr., his thirty-
three-year-old wife, Carolyn, and thirty-four-year-old sister-in-law Lau-

ren, had seemed to vanish into thin air. John had planned to head first for Martha's Vineyard to drop off Lauren, then loop around and fly the short distance to the airport in Hyannis, where he and Carolyn would be picked up and driven to the Kennedy compound to join the wedding party. Vague hope and optimism remained alive among the members of a clan whose painful history had for decades been chronicled in a plethora of books, magazines, and newspaper headlines. "If anyone can make it, it's John," Robert F. Kennedy Jr. assured a reporter. "My guess is that he's probably marooned with the others on some small, uncharted island off the Massachusetts coast." What RFK Jr. didn't realize—and couldn't know—is that John hadn't bothered to store life vests aboard his plane, claiming that he had no use for them. The chances that he or any of the others had reached land after crashing at sea were slim at best.

For all his nonchalance and joie de vivre, John had taken his aviation lessons seriously. His instructors may have detected in him a certain daredevil streak, but they also acknowledged that when it came to piloting, John had always behaved in a conscientious manner. Several months earlier, flying his previous plane, a 1977 five-seat, single-engine Cessna 182, JFK Jr. had discovered an electrical problem shortly after takeoff from Essex County Airport and had immediately turned back. Harold Anderson, a pilot who had often flown with Kennedy, observed that the student pilot had more than once canceled flights because of inclement weather. Yet after fulfilling the Federal Aviation Administration (FAA) requirements for his pilot's license on April 22, 1998, John boldly admitted to the press that the only person willing to fly with him was his wife. "And even she has her doubts," he said. "Let's face it, I'm no Charles Lindbergh—not yet, anyway." His tongue-in-cheek attitude repeated itself when he presented one of his flight instructors with a photograph of himself, inscribed as follows: "To the bravest person in aviation, because people will only care who trained me if I crash. Best wishes, John Kennedy." And on May 27 of the same year, he appended a humorous (but eerily prophetic) postscript to a letter sent to fashion designer Tommy Hilfiger, owner of a vacation retreat on Nantucket, an island not far from Martha's Vineyard: "I finally got my pilot's license. Beware the skies over Nantucket, they'll never be safe again."

Meanwhile, in the wake of the Saratoga's disappearance, President Bill Clinton, weekending at Camp David with wife Hillary, took it upon himself to issue a presidential order authorizing an intensive, wide-reaching, and very costly land-sea-and-air search and rescue mission involving coast guard, naval, and air force planes, helicopters, vehicles, and vessels. Additionally, the Massachusetts State Police dispatched more than two dozen officers to Martha's Vineyard and Woods Hole, Massachusetts, where a temporary command post had been established, involving representatives from the National Transportation Safety Board (NTSB), the FAA, the U.S. Department of Transportation, the National Oceanic and Atmospheric Administration, the Department of Defense, and a variety of state agencies. Within the first twenty-four hours, members of the Air National Guard and Civil Air Patrol were ordered to join the search team. Remaining in contact with Senator Ted Kennedy throughout the crisis, President Clinton also spoke by telephone with Caroline Kennedy, assuring her that everything would be done that could be done. Caroline and her husband had partied on Martha's Vineyard with actors Ted Danson and Mary Steenburgen at a celebration of Clinton's fifty-first birthday in 1997. During the conversation with Caroline, the president fondly recalled a February 1998 visit when he took John Jr. and his wife on a personal tour of the White House, following a dinner in honor of British prime minister Tony Blair. It was President Clinton who later informed the Kennedy clan that the search and rescue operation had been downgraded to a search and recovery mission. After several days and no word from the passengers, it became a matter of pinpointing the submerged aircraft's exact location and bringing the three bodies to the surface.

For Caroline Kennedy, the nightmare began on Saturday, July 17, at 4:30 a.m. She and her husband had decided to celebrate their thirteenth wedding anniversary and Ed's fifty-fourth birthday (on July 19) by going white-water rafting for a week on the Salmon River ("the River of No Return") in the foothills of Idaho's Sawtooth Mountain range. Arrangements for the trip had been completed well before the announcement of Rory Kennedy's wedding ceremony. The Schlossbergs were bringing along their children, and because John Jr. wanted his nephew and nieces to enjoy their vacation, he and Carolyn Bessette had volunteered to represent the JFK branch of the family tree at Hyannis Port.

On the morning of July 16, the Schlossbergs flew from JFK International Airport in New York to Sun Valley, where they hired a car service to take them sixty miles north to the Mountain Village Resort in Stanley, a quiet Idaho town surrounded by rolling green fields, forests, and meadows. They were greeted at the front desk by resort employee Ken Nedeau, who registered the family before showing them to a two-bedroom suite on the second floor of the wood-frame three-story hotel.

"We have all the amenities," Nedeau informed the Schlossbergs, "but we're more like a hunting lodge than a ritzy resort. Everything is very modest and down to earth. We don't even have cellular-phone service in Stanley. A lot of people come up here to get away from it all."

Nedeau told them that besides white-water rafting, there were a number of other activities: mountain biking, horseback riding, backpacking, swimming, hunting, and fishing. In the winter they had downhill and cross-country skiing. In the spring the fields were filled with wildflowers. They were open year-round.

That afternoon the Schlossbergs, informally attired in Levi's, work shirts, and sneakers, walked around and took in the scenery—dazzling views of distant mountain peaks rising high above the Salmon River. They ate an early dinner in the family-style restaurant located next door to the lodge, the walls of the room adorned with deer and moose heads. They then put their children to bed and went for drinks at the nearby Mountain Village Saloon. By 11:00 p.m. Ed and Caroline were asleep in one bedroom, their children in the other.

Five hours later, Phil Enright, chief of police in Stanley, awoke to a ringing telephone. After apologizing for the lateness of the hour, the caller identified himself as Anthony Radziwill and explained that he'd been trying to reach his cousin, Caroline Kennedy, at the Mountain Village Resort. "I'm calling," he said, "because something seems to have happened to Caroline's brother, John F. Kennedy Jr. His plane is missing. There's no answer at the resort—their telephone doesn't appear to be working."

Anthony Radziwill, the nearly forty-year-old son of Prince Stanislas (Stas) and Lee Radziwill, the younger sister of Jacqueline Kennedy, had problems of his own, unrelated to John's mysterious disappearance. For the past five years he had suffered from a rare and debilitating strain of cancer that had required numerous operations and chemotherapy sessions. The disease had ravaged his body, reducing his once trim and athletic frame to skin and bone, leaving him tethered to oxygen tanks and portable kidney dialysis machines. Although he had recently embarked on an experimental treatment program developed by physicians at Staten Island University Hospital in New York, the prognosis was not good. His life expectancy was measurable not in years but in days.

Anthony and John Jr. were not only first cousins but the best of friends. In 1994, when Radziwill married Carole Ann DiFalco, a reporter (and later a producer) for ABC-TV News—the same organization for which Radziwill had also been a producer—JFK Jr. served as best man; two years later Radziwill returned the favor, standing up for John at his wedding to Carolyn Bessette. Because of their inextricable ties and Radziwill's terminal illness, John had offered him the use of Red Gate Farm, Jackie Kennedy's 474-acre oceanfront estate at Gay Head, on Martha's Vineyard. On a medical leave of absence from his latest position as a freelance producer at HBO, Anthony (and Carole) had moved into the house over the Fourth of July weekend and anticipated spending the rest of the month there.

On Friday evening, July 16, after eating dinner and watching television, the couple fell asleep only to be roused about midnight by a telephone call from a Kennedy family friend. The friend, nicknamed "Pinky," had volunteered to meet JFK Jr.'s plane at Hyannis and to drive John and his wife to the Kennedy compound at Hyannis Port. The plane hadn't arrived, and Pinky wanted to know if the Radziwills knew anything.

Alarmed by the call, Carole Radziwill rose, sat down at the kitchen table with a pad and pen, and spent the next three hours placing telephone calls in an effort to trace the missing aircraft. Among others, she called Carolyn Bessette's mother in Connecticut, who, until that moment, had been unaware that Lauren Bessette had joined her sister and brother-in-law on the same flight. It was at this juncture that Anthony Radziwill walked into the kitchen, saw Carole's hastily scribbled notes, broke down in tears, but then pulled himself together and began making his own telephone inquiries.

Alerted to the situation, Senator Ted Kennedy likewise became involved. The senator telephoned JFK Jr.'s TriBeCa loft at 20 North Moore Street, where he spoke with Pat Manocchia, John's former classmate at Brown University and now the owner of La Palestra, the exclusive Manhattan exercise studio located in the Hotel des Artistes building on West 67th Street. Manocchia, whose air conditioner wasn't working, had been invited by John to spend the weekend as his houseguest. Manocchia told the senator that so far as he knew, John and Carolyn were in the air and on their way to the Cape.

Teddy also telephoned Efigenio Pinheiro, Jackie Kennedy's longtime Portuguese butler. Pinheiro, who began working for JFK Jr. after Jackie's death, often looked after Friday, John's American Kennel Club–registered black-and-white Canaan dog. Pinheiro had retrieved the dog from John's apartment the day before but had heard nothing further from either John or Carolyn.

Additional calls by the senator revealed that the Coast Guard Operations Center at Woods Hole had already been placed on alert (by Carole Radziwill, among others) and, in turn, had notified FAA headquarters in Washington, D.C., which had referred the matter to the FAA's command center in Herndon, Virginia. Determining that John had landed neither at Martha's Vineyard nor Hyannis, the FAA investigated the possibility that he had set down at some other airfield in the region. When no such landing site could be found, the FAA turned to the Air Force Rescue Communication Center at Virginia's Langley Air Force Base. The Rescue Center contacted the White House, and by early Saturday morning the massive search operation had gotten under way, covering an initial area of nine thousand square miles.

In light of these developments, Anthony Radziwill decided to reach out to Caroline Kennedy in Idaho. After several futile attempts on his own, he dialed a long-distance operator. When the operator failed to get through to the Mountain Village Resort, Radziwill telephoned the Sun

Valley Police Department. A sympathetic desk sergeant referred him to Phil Enright and provided the law enforcement officer's home phone number.

Enright lived ten minutes from the resort. Following his conversation with Anthony Radziwill, the police chief donned his uniform and drove over in his patrol car. The hotel switchboard had been shut down for the night. Enright reached Caroline on the house phone. The clock over the front desk read 4:30 a.m. "Somebody named Anthony Radziwill has been trying to reach you," he told her. "I'll have them reconnect the switchboard, and you can call him back."

Caroline Kennedy must have known that a telephone call from her cousin at such an ungodly hour could only be related to her brother. She and John had last spoken on Thursday, July 15, a day before the Schlossbergs left for Idaho. They had bantered back and forth as they always did in their daily telephone conversations. At the end, Caroline made her brother promise that he would fly to Massachusetts only with a certified flight instructor at his side and only during daylight hours.

Although he had logged some thirty-six hours in his new Saratoga, John had little experience flying solo—3.3 hours, to be exact. And on only one occasion had he flown the plane alone at night, a forty-eight-minute flight to Martha's Vineyard during which he had made his only solo nighttime landing. It was true, on the other hand, that over the past few months he had made seventeen round-trip flights between Caldwell, New Jersey, and Martha's Vineyard, with stopovers up and down the Massachusetts coastline. Yet these journeys, according to his logbooks, had taken place in company with either an instructor or a seasoned copilot. He was what automobile owners refer to as a "Sunday driver." He knew just enough to be considered dangerous.

Caroline Kennedy's phone conversation with Anthony Radziwill lasted less than five minutes. When they were done, she rang up Ted Kennedy, who had already arrived in Hyannis Port for the wedding. Kennedy confirmed that John's plane had gone astray but cautioned his niece not to act precipitously. Until they knew more, she and Ed would do well to stay put. Chances were good, he said, that they were all worrying for naught. Other family members reflected a similar sentiment.

With his well-earned reputation for tardiness, John would no doubt turn up in a matter of hours, and the incident would be totally forgotten.

Despite her uncle's assurances, Caroline wanted to fly home. Ed Schlossberg canceled the rafting expedition and made arrangements for a chartered plane to transport them to New York. Friends of the family arrived by car from Sun Valley to drive them to the airport.

"I helped them with their luggage," recalled Ken Nedeau. "Few words were exchanged, but you could see the panic in Caroline's eyes. The news had pulverized her. She wasn't the same person who'd arrived the day before when she appeared relaxed and carefree. She had struck me then as extremely laid back and easygoing. If you didn't know her by name or photograph, you'd never have guessed that she was Caroline Kennedy, daughter of the late president and Jackie Kennedy, arguably the most famous woman in the world."

For the sake of privacy, the Schlossbergs chose to wait for more news at their home in Sagaponack. Ted Kennedy flew down on Sunday morning, July 18. The news from Martha's Vineyard wasn't promising. A swimmer had recovered a small suitcase bearing a business card with Lauren Bessette's name on it. The suitcase contained her bathing suit, hair dryer, and makeup kit. The Coast Guard reported finding sections of the aircraft's left landing gear, a leather seat, and a pedal cover. Carolyn Bessette's cosmetic case and a bottle of her prescription medication washed ashore. Additional pieces of airplane wreckage continued to materialize, including cushions, carpeting, a rubber pedal, and the Piper Saratoga's right landing gear. The discovery of these and other items bolstered Caroline's conviction that a tragic accident had taken place, killing her brother and his two passengers.

To help relieve his wife's growing anxiety, Ed Schlossberg suggested they leave the children with Uncle Ted and go for a quiet bike ride. For the next ninety minutes, the couple pedaled along Sagaponack's bucolic back roads, Caroline's face shielded behind a pair of sunglasses. When they returned, she lowered their American flag to half-mast. Spotting a pair of newspaper photographers crawling around in the bushes, Caroline jumped into a car with Maria Shriver and William Kennedy Smith and took off. After the car ride, she seemed even more agitated.

Thoroughly exhausted, Caroline skipped dinner that evening and went straight to her bedroom. A few hours later when Ted Kennedy looked in on her, he found her red-eyed from crying. Surrounded by hundreds of photographs, she was sitting up in bed examining family snapshots through a magnifying glass. She began to sob. Teddy cradled her in his arms. "I should've stopped John long ago," she said. "He had no business flying his own plane."

Caroline's misgivings concerning the vagaries and perils of flight had been instilled in her by a catalog of Kennedy family airplane disasters. The uncle she had never known, Joe Kennedy Jr., eldest son of family patriarch Joseph P. Kennedy, perished in 1944 when his World War II bomber blew up halfway across the English Channel. Her aunt Kathleen (Kick) Kennedy died in an airplane crash four years later while flying from Paris to Cannes. In 1964 a small plane transporting Ted Kennedy from Washington to Springfield, Massachusetts, slammed into an apple orchard, killing the pilot and one of Ted's senatorial aides; Kennedy spent ten weeks in the hospital, recuperating from a broken back and other serious injuries. Ethel Kennedy's parents and one of her brothers, George Skakel Jr., were killed in separate plane crashes. In 1973 Caroline's stepbrother, Alexander Onassis, Aristotle Onassis's only son, died while piloting a plane in Athens, Greece.

Despite her evident concern for her brother's safety, Caroline went only so far in trying to dissuade him from continuing his flight training. Having started in flight school on an occasional basis as early as 1982, John discontinued the lessons (after logging roughly fifty hours of flight time) in 1988 when his mother intervened, threatening to disinherit him if he persisted. He resumed his training two and a half years after her death, enrolling at FlightSafety International, an aviation school in Vero Beach, Florida, as well as Million Air, a flight academy in Teterboro, New Jersey. He interrupted the lessons once again following the December 1997 death of his cousin Michael Kennedy, then re-enrolled in both programs some three months later. Christopher Benway, his main instructor at FlightSafety International, considered John a diligent student with average abilities. According to an FBI interview with Benway following JFK Jr.'s death, his greatest deficit was his inability to multitask, an essential attribute for any accomplished pilot.

To protect John's privacy while he took lessons, FlightSafety International registered him under the pseudonym John F. Kane. For a time, he remained FlightSafety International's only part-time student, a concession the school made to accommodate his personal needs. In total, including his earlier training, JFK Jr. amassed approximately 310 hours of flight time, less than 10 percent of that total while flying solo without benefit of an experienced trainer.

In signing up for the flight programs, John ignored Ted Kennedy's admonition that he honor his mother's deathbed plea—under no circumstances did she want him to take aviation lessons. Maurice Tempelsman, Jackie's domestic partner for the last fifteen years of her life (and the co-executor of her estate), fared no better than the Massachusetts senator in trying to convince John to give up piloting lessons. Several of John's friends offered similar advice. Richard Wiese, a fraternity brother at Brown, felt that John didn't pay enough attention to details and hadn't completed a rigorous enough pilot-training program to justify taking the kind of risks he sometimes took. "My father's a retired commercial airplane pilot," said Wiese, "and I know what meticulous preparations he made before every flight, among other things studying weather- and atmospheric-condition reports. John had little patience for that kind of information. He may have been overconfident about his piloting skills. He had developed a false sense of security based on his safe flying record, but almost always he had flown with an experienced instructor in the cockpit. When I warned him of the possible consequences, he accused me of being 'like all the others—you just don't want me to fly.'"

Even as unlikely a figure as Mike Tyson, the former heavyweight boxing champion, berated John for flying his own plane. An avid boxing fan, John visited Tyson on March 1, 1999, at the Montgomery County Detention Center in Maryland, where the pugilist was serving a one-year sentence for assaulting two motorists after a minor traffic accident. Placed in a locked room with Tyson, John began talking boxing history, only to have the fighter turn the conversation to the subject of aviation. "You're nuts to fly," Tyson told his visitor. "Flying a small plane like that is crazy." Kennedy countered by citing a serious motorcycle accident Tyson had suffered in 1997. "And you're not about to give up your Harley, are you?" asked John. "No," said Tyson, "but that's different—at least you're on good old terra firma." "Well," responded Kennedy, "you can't imagine how beautiful it is up there in the wild blue yonder." "Listen, man," said Tyson. "Promise me one thing—next time you go up there, swear to me you won't bring along somebody you love."

George Plimpton, who'd known Jackie Kennedy since her junior year at the Sorbonne and had maintained close relations with her children, called Caroline Kennedy on Monday morning, July 19, three days after the Saratoga's disappearance. "Caroline was understandably upset," said Plimpton. "From family and friends she ascertained that her brother had made the flight not only without a certified instructor or copilot, but that he'd flown at night under questionable weather conditions. Had she known all this in advance, she would never have condoned the flight.

"Caroline knew that her brother had passed a written exam in instrument flying, but she also knew he hadn't completed his training and wasn't instrument rated. He lacked instrument flying experience, which meant that under FAA regulations he could pilot his own plane without having to file a flight plan, but only during daylight hours and under rigidly specified visual flight rules. He had no business—or even the legal right—to fly solo at night, especially under conditions that demanded instrument certification."

John had originally planned on making the flight that weekend with Jay Biederman, a young pilot he'd known since the late 1980s and who usually accompanied him on his airplane travels to Massachusetts. Biederman, however, announced that he wouldn't be available on July 16, having agreed to join his parents on a two-week vacation in Switzerland. A friend of Jay's volunteered to replace him, but by this time John had decided to make the flight on his own.

In the days immediately following JFK Jr.'s fatal flight, Caroline Kennedy placed the blame for her brother's misjudgment on their cousins, particularly Robert F. Kennedy's children, long known for their boisterous, scandal-mongering antics. Bobby's sons, she told friends, lacked common sense. With their machismo attitude, they would no doubt have chided John had he opted to put off the flight until the following day.

When Caroline expressed these sentiments to George Plimpton, he took exception. "I disagreed with her argument," remarked Plimpton. "It sounded like the kind of rationale Jackie might have offered. Bobby's brood may have demonstrated too much bravado at times, but the bottom line is that John was somebody who enjoyed taking chances. He was a thrill seeker. He loved all that physical stuff—windsurfing, skateboarding, Rollerblading, scuba diving, skiing, even hang gliding. You name it, he did it. He felt a need to push himself to the limit. It was the same trait that motivated his father to drive around Dallas on November 22, 1963, without the bubbletop roof on the presidential limousine, or that compelled Bobby Kennedy to wade through potentially dangerous crowds without Secret Service protection during his 1968 political campaign. I'm not suggesting that they had a death wish—they didn't—but they did share a common desire to live dangerously. On the very day John acquired his Piper Saratoga, he started talking about wanting to invest in a Learjet."

Jackie's cousin John Davis attributed JFK Jr.'s fascination with aviation to the "overly strict" manner in which his mother brought him up. "The result," suggested Davis, "is that John felt a constant need to prove himself. It was his way of breaking loose from his mother's shackles. The Saratoga represented a means of escape. John spent countless hours at Essex County Airport, where he kept his plane, hosing it down, polishing it, vacuuming the cabin, giving it the kind of tender, loving care you'd ordinarily bestow upon your first new car.

"The fact of the matter is that neither Caroline Kennedy nor anybody else could have prevented the accident. If Jackie had been alive, she wouldn't have allowed him to take piloting lessons. But nobody else, Caroline included, had that kind of influence over John. He was accommodating but also very strong willed. He had a mind of his own. His heroes were men of action. As a young kid, he had wanted to become an astronaut. His passion for flying overrode every other consideration. Flying defined him—it set him free."

John F. Kennedy Jr.'s last days prior to his final flight were fraught with difficulty. His most pressing dilemma was the financial future of *George,* the glossy political magazine he had cofounded with Michael Berman in September 1995. After a promising beginning, based primarily on JFK Jr.'s heightened celebrity and undeniable charisma, the periodical suffered considerable setbacks both in circulation and advertising revenues. Since its inception, it had gone some $30 million in the red and was currently losing more than $1 million per month, a tidy sum even by egregious New York publishing standards. Hachette Filipacchi, the French media consortium, had become the magazine's sole financial backer. According to publishing insiders, Hachette had begun to lose faith in the publication's ability to survive, at least in its present form. Starting in early June 1999, Jack Kliger, Hachette's newly appointed CEO, successor to the position previously held by David Pecker, had been conducting weekly meetings with John to determine *George'*s future.

"The magazine didn't have a very clear plan," said Kliger. "John was working hard and doing as good a job as he could. He needed a business executive to work with him, to help develop a different direction. By 1999 *George* had lost some of its initial vitality, so we were exploring ways to get it back on track."

Uncertain of Hachette's long-term commitment to *George,* John began to investigate other potential backers and financial opportunities. He pleaded his case before a number of investment bankers and high-rolling venture capitalists. Hollywood superstar (and future politician) Arnold Schwarzenegger, the husband of Maria Shriver, became an unofficial financial adviser to John. The two would meet whenever Schwarzenegger, a sage businessman, visited New York.

On Monday, July 12, with Jay Biederman (soon to leave for Switzerland) at the controls of the Saratoga, JFK Jr. flew from Martha's Vineyard to Toronto for talks with Keith Stein and Belinda Stronach, a pair of enterprising Canadians who hoped to organize a syndicate of investors to take over for Hachette. The meeting, which had been arranged by Leslie Marshall, an editor at *In Style* magazine, lasted for several hours. Keith Stein emerged from the conference convinced that it had gone well. John Jr. came away certain that the Canadians were eager to move forward but only if he agreed to surrender editorial control of the publication.

"He wouldn't have it," said TriBeCa photographer Jacques Lowe, a devoted former friend of John's parents. Lowe and John had both attended a Tuesday evening advertising agency cocktail party in TriBeCa. Afterward they had a bite to eat at a neighborhood coffee shop. John seemed on edge. "Hachette's contract with John was scheduled to lapse at the end of the year," continued Lowe. "Unless Hachette reneged, John would be forced to find a new sponsor. But the Canadians weren't the answer. 'They're interested,' John told me, 'but only if they can run the show. I'm not about to relinquish my role in the venture. I'll shut it down before I do that.'"

Another matter that weighed on John's mind was the state of his marriage to Carolyn Bessette. "They were very close and very much in love," remarked George Plimpton. "Still, as with most marriages, they had their issues. Their fundamental point of difference involved children. Carolyn wanted to wait before starting a family. Her parents had gone through a difficult and bitter divorce, which had almost certainly left a scar. In addition, Carolyn never grew accustomed to being in the limelight. She once said, 'Can you imagine me having to wheel a baby carriage around Manhattan and being chased by all those blood-sucking paparazzi?' She didn't want to raise a family in New York, but she also didn't want to move permanently to Red Gate Farm. Jackie's house was too large and impersonal. Consequently, she and John spent nearly every weekend that summer on the Cape looking at prospective properties."

The subject of children, when and where to have them, came up repeatedly in the Kennedy-Bessette household. On the last weekend before the crash, JFK Jr. and Carolyn played host at Red Gate Farm to CNN television correspondent Christiane Amanpour and her husband, former U.S. State Department spokesman James Rubin. John and Christiane, although never romantically involved, had shared a house (with several others) in Providence, Rhode Island, when John attended Brown University and Christiane was an undergraduate majoring in journalism at the University of Rhode Island. After dinner on Saturday night, July 10, the two couples rode off in John's 1969 Pontiac GTO convertible, a car he lovingly called "the Goat." Despite its hypercharged engine, he and Carolyn used the Goat predominantly to tool around traffic-engorged Martha's Vineyard. That night they ended up at the Lamppost, a popular Vineyard hangout. Over drinks, John asked Christiane if she and James were planning on having children at any time in the near future. "We are," she said. "We've been trying to get pregnant." On this note, Carolyn broke into the conversation. "Oh, please don't say that," she remarked. "If you get pregnant, John will want us to get pregnant, too."

John looked annoyed at his wife's offhand remark. Although uttered in a humorous tone, the comment was not dissimilar to others Carolyn had made in the past. Childbearing remained a sensitive issue for her. During one particularly trying period, whenever the theme arose, she refused to sleep with her husband. Since March 1999, Carolyn and John had been consulting with a well-known New York marriage counselor, at the same time attending individual weekly therapy sessions with psychiatrists of their own. Carolyn's therapist, whom she'd been seeing since late 1997, prescribed antidepressants; John's therapist advised his patient to make certain his wife took her medication.

"John and Carolyn weren't exactly headed for divorce court," said Richard Wiese, "but they'd reached what you might call a pivotal moment in their marriage. Carolyn had never become inured to the tabloid frenzy that constantly buzzed around her head. She could only imagine what having children would do to exacerbate the situation. Being the focus of the media was second nature to John. He'd grown up with it. He not only survived the attention of the press, he thrived on it."

Public relations expert R. Couri Hay felt that Carolyn "was in way above her head. She had married up—way up. She was no Jacqueline Kennedy—and she knew it. Had Jackie been alive, the marriage would never have taken place. Carolyn didn't have the background or education that it took to be married to a future president. Her depression, frustration, anger, and refusal to bear children all stemmed from their basic incompatibility."

Beyond his professional and personal worries, JFK Jr. had to contend with yet another hardship. Over Memorial Day weekend, six weeks before his death, he suffered an aggravated fracture of the left ankle. The accident took place at Red Gate Farm, when he flew his $6,500 two-seat Buckeye ultralight powered parachute into a tree. The delicate flying machine consisted of a triangular metal tube frame set on two wheels, two seats in the front and a piston motor, fan, and removable foil parachute to the rear. As the Buckeye rolled along the ground, air currents were propelled from the fan into the parachute, gradually lifting the Buckeye into the air. Capable of remaining airborne for three hours at an altitude of up to twelve thousand feet, its engine sputtering like an electric lawn mower, the Buckeye would soar high over Gay Head's jagged cliffs, drift out to sea, then along the shoreline as John swung it back toward the makeshift landing strip he had devised in the sand dunes not far from his mother's house. Designed for use by the most ardent of extreme-sport enthusiasts, the Buckeye was such an odd-looking apparatus that observers on the ground frequently mistook it for an unidentified flying object—and reported it as such to the authorities. Although operating the "flying lawn mower" required a certain amount of training, no license was needed or issued. Wanting to share his toy with his friends, John urged everyone he knew to try it out. There were few takers.

Friends inside the house heard the Buckeye smash into a thicket of Scotch pines, clipping branches and uprooting one of the trees, which the resident caretaker left on the ground as a reminder to John of his carelessness. Carolyn Bessette watched in disbelief as her husband extricated himself from the wreckage and hopped toward her on his right leg. X-rays at the local hospital revealed that John had fractured two bones in his left ankle. The ankle was temporarily set and swaddled in protective padding. John and Carolyn returned to New York early the following morning, June 2, and surgery was performed at Lenox Hill Hospital that afternoon. Initially harnessed into a bulky splint, the ankle (reinforced by several pins) was later placed in a plaster cast. After two days at Lenox Hill, John spent another week recuperating at home, his injured left leg propped up on a stack of pillows to reduce pain and swelling. At the beginning of July, John's orthopedist removed the cast and placed the limb in a CAM Walker, an open-toed, heavily fortified boot that rose to just below the left knee. Held in place by Velcro straps, the boot could be loosened and removed when the patient bathed or went to bed.

Hot, itchy, and cumbersome, the splint, cast, and CAM Walker in succession prevented John from participating in any of the physical activities he so much enjoyed. He could neither Rollerblade nor ride his bike. He found it difficult to work out at any of the four Manhattan exercise studios to which he belonged. Unable at first to get to the office, he communicated with his magazine staff via telephone. For a short duration, he rented a wheelchair with a raised footrest, but returned it because he abhorred the idea of being dependent on others to wheel him around. Because the broken ankle prevented him from operating the foot pedals on his plane, he had no choice but to take along an instructor whenever he flew.

Five weeks after the surgery, during Christiane Amanpour's visit to Martha's Vineyard, John railed against the inconvenience of his injury. It soon dawned on his visitors that his broken ankle caused him considerable pain and that he was probably overexerting himself. His personal physician refused to prescribe a potent pain medication, so John sought relief from another doctor who promptly put him on Vicodin extra strength. He was still taking pain medication the day he died, as well as Ritalin for attention deficit disorder and PTU (propylthiouracil) for Graves' disease, a thyroid condition that sporadically drained him of energy. He had been afflicted with ADD since early childhood and had suffered from Graves' disease since 1990.

JFK Jr. was still in the CAM Walker on Wednesday morning, July 14, when he and Carolyn summoned Empire Executive Car and Limousine service of Manhattan to pick them up at home and deliver them to the Paramount Plaza Building, 1633 Broadway, where *George* maintained office space on the forty-first floor; Hachette's corporate offices were located in the same building. The magazine had agreed to hold a breakfast reception for the executive board of the Robin Hood Foundation, a fund-raising organization that sponsored worthy projects in low-income New York neighborhoods. John had belonged to the group since 1991.

Members of the board who had never been exposed to the charms of Carolyn Bessette marveled at the ease with which she moved from one person to the next, gazing at each in turn through hypnotic aquamarine eyes, asking questions and reacting as if their answers truly mattered. "Carolyn Bessette Kennedy cast a spell," said one board member. "She had intelligence, allure, wit, and style. Tall, svelte, and blond, Mrs. Kennedy bordered on the beautiful. She and John made a formidable team. Although I didn't experience it that day, I'd heard that she could be standoffish and remote. She valued her privacy and resented the press. But, of course, these were traits that we also associated with Jackie Kennedy, so it's easy to see how John Jr. could be deeply attracted to his wife."

As so often happened at gatherings that he attended, John became the focus of attention. Members of the Robin Hood board besieged him with questions and comments regarding his political intentions. His pat answer while editor in chief and president of *George* had always been the same: "I'm happy with what I'm doing now." In his more private moments, he expressed a desire to move on, to explore the possibility of running for political office. In 1992 Bill Clinton, for whom JFK Jr. had campaigned, asked John to join his presidential cabinet. He declined the offer, telling Richard Wiese that if Clinton gave him a top cabinet position, it would be construed as an attempt on Clinton's part to capitalize on the Kennedy family name; if it turned out to be a cabinet post of minor significance, it would only hinder John's political possibilities for the future.

When asked by Richard Wiese in early 1999 whether he might oppose Hillary Clinton in New York's upcoming senatorial race, John admitted that he had given the matter serious thought. His unstated reason for not undertaking such a challenge was his fear that Carolyn would buckle under the pressure. He would exercise patience and make his run for office at a later date.

Following the Robin Hood breakfast, Carolyn went shopping for a blouse at Bergdorf Goodman, then picked up her sister Lauren at the midtown Manhattan offices of Morgan Stanley Dean Witter, where she worked as a financial analyst and senior executive in its Asian department. A Wharton business school graduate, conversant in Mandarin

Chinese, Lauren had joined the investment firm seven years earlier as a trainee in its Hong Kong division. She had returned to the States in 1998 and purchased a luxurious TriBeCa loft two blocks from John and Carolyn. Living in such close proximity, Carolyn and Lauren were frequent guests in each other's homes. "They were extremely devoted to each other, even though Lauren had a twin sister to whom she was even closer," said William Peter Owen, a friend of the Bessette family. "Lauren was a rising star on Wall Street, and Carolyn had become the wife of John F. Kennedy Jr. Theirs was an unmitigated success story."

The Empire car assigned to Carolyn that morning dropped off the Bessette sisters at the Stanhope Hotel, Fifth Avenue and 83rd Street. *George* used the hotel to house out-of-town visitors and for occasional staff meetings and photo shoots. At 1:30 p.m. John joined his wife and sister-in-law for lunch in the hotel café. They occupied a rear banquette and for the first ten minutes discussed Lauren's twin sister, Lisa, a Renaissance art major who had just earned her graduate degree at a university in Germany. The conversation soon shifted to the coming weekend and Rory Kennedy's wedding. Lauren, currently dating John's cousin Robert (Bobby) Sargent Shriver III, planned to meet up with him on Martha's Vineyard. Not entirely convinced that she wanted to fly with John, she had reserved round-trip shuttle tickets for herself aboard Continental, one of a handful of commercial airlines that made regularly scheduled flights to and from the Vineyard.

To Martin Nordquist, an engineering consultant seated with his wife Nora at an adjacent table, it was evident that Lauren had serious misgivings about making the flight with John and Carolyn, particularly since John had decided to pilot the aircraft himself. "It was widely known and reported in the press," said Nordquist, "that John was unreliable. A recent article claimed he'd nearly landed his plane on the Massachusetts Turnpike, mistaking it for a runway at Boston's Logan Airport." John also tended to lose things. Strangers were forever finding his house keys and credit cards in taxicabs and restaurants and returning them to him. It reached the point where John had asked his tailor to sew a special flap into his trouser pocket to secure his wallet.

According to Nordquist, Carolyn quickly came to her husband's defense, pointing out that they'd flown to Martha's Vineyard and the Cape on numerous occasions that summer. When Lauren argued that they'd always had a certified flight instructor aboard, Carolyn grew short-tempered and told her sister that they were doing her a favor to fly her to the Vineyard. After a point Lauren relented—she understood John's desire to pilot his own plane and agreed to accompany them.

Having hashed out the details of the flight, John and Carolyn began to smooch a bit. They were holding hands and kissing. But then something strange happened. Toward the end of their meal, John and Carolyn became embroiled in an argument of their own. It had to do with Carolyn having made a Sunday morning appointment with a Cape Cod real estate agent to go house hunting. This was apparently the first John had heard of it. "Not this weekend," he said. "We're going up there to attend a wedding, and then we're supposed to join Anthony and Carole at Gay Head." "There's plenty of time to look at real estate," responded Carolyn. Suddenly they were off and running, trading barbs through clenched teeth. "They were still haggling when they stood up to leave," said Nordquist.

John returned to the office and spent the remainder of the afternoon perusing a stack of financial papers, intermittently fielding his angry wife's telephone calls. He spoke by phone with his sister and entertained several business-related calls. At 4:00 p.m. he received a telephone call from U.S. attorney general Janet Reno's office. John had written Reno in late June, requesting an interview with her for the January 2000 issue of *George*. Her personal assistant informed John that Reno had agreed and would be in touch the following week to set up an appointment.

At five o'clock John telephoned Jacques Lowe and recounted details of his latest altercation with Carolyn. He told the photographer that he intended to spend the next night or two at the Stanhope Hotel. Lowe sensed that JFK Jr. appeared to enjoy the bickering—he relished the thought that Carolyn wasn't afraid to stand up for herself.

"I kidded him about staying at the Stanhope," recalled Lowe. "I told him it was fortuitous that *George* maintained a corporate account at the hotel—that way he always had a place to stay when Carolyn kicked him out of the house."

John had slept at the Stanhope during other dark moments with Carolyn, isolated occasions when he wanted to avoid a head-on emotional collision. Aside from the question of children, one of their recurring differences, though of a less serious note, involved Carolyn's not feeling comfortable in John's sparsely appointed TriBeCa loft. It was too cold, too spare. It had all the makings of a graduate student's apartment, albeit in a building where even the smallest loft went for well over hundreds of thousands of dollars. Nor did Carolyn particularly care for the neighborhood. TriBeCa, for all its upscale restaurants, boutiques, and art galleries, had too few trees and too many boarded-up warehouses. If they had to live in New York, she preferred the charm of Greenwich Village or, better yet, the opulence of the Upper East Side, where John's sister resided. Carolyn constantly reminded him that with his personal assets worth in excess of $150 million, they could live anywhere.

John returned to the Stanhope after work and checked into room 1511. He ordered a light supper from room service and ate while watching the evening news on television. Several hours later he received a visit from Julie Baker, a statuesque thirty-five-year-old brunette model and jewelry designer he had known for years and dated for several months in 1994, at the same time he was breaking off his much publicized on-and-off five-year relationship with actress Daryl Hannah. "Jules," as he called her, bore a striking physical resemblance to Jacqueline Kennedy, a likeness that didn't go unnoticed by several of John's friends, some of whom kidded him about it. After they terminated their romantic relationship, Jules became a confidante, one of the few women outside his marriage he trusted implicitly and with whom he could explore the most intimate of privacies.

Jules remained with John until half past twelve, listening to him vent about his wife, his work, his life in general. He wanted to start a family, but until recently whenever he broached the subject with Carolyn, she dismissed him by turning away—usually in bed. John admired strong-willed women, like his mother, but Carolyn was often more than strong willed.

John and Julie met again early the following morning. Over breakfast in the Stanhope's dining room, they completed their previous night's conversation. "Don't worry," Julie told her companion. "Carolyn will come around. If she doesn't, I'll have a talk with her."

After breakfast, JFK Jr. taxied to Lenox Hill Hospital, where his orthopedist removed the CAM Walker, outfitting him with a walking cane and a new pair of lightweight metal crutches. He was told to wean himself off the crutches and begin using the cane. In several weeks he could rid himself of the cane. The doctor encouraged him to continue the physical therapy sessions he'd already begun in order to regain enough flexibility in his left ankle to bear the full weight of his six-foot-one-inch, 190-pound, tightly muscled frame. He cautioned John not to pilot his plane until he was able to walk without pain. John made no mention of his intention to fly to his cousin's wedding the following day, a decision no doubt fueled in part by his pent-up restlessness, and frustration at having been grounded from all activity for the past six weeks.

From the hospital, he went to his North Moore Street loft to change from a black-and-white striped T-shirt and tan cotton slacks into a blue pin-striped business suit, then hastily packed a weekend bag to take back with him to the hotel. On the way uptown, he stopped at the Kennedy family offices on the seventeenth floor of 500 Fifth Avenue to retrieve his quarterly financial statement. On the way out, he bumped into his cousin Christopher Kennedy Lawford, whom he'd last seen several months earlier at a party in the Village. John lunched that day with Peter Jay Russo, a former magazine publisher with whom he hoped to discuss *George*'s future. They ate at San Domenico on Central Park South, where John frequently entertained pals and business associates. (His sister, Caroline, regularly dined there with her husband, and sometimes alone with John.) Kennedy told Russo that even though Condé Nast Publications had originally hesitated to back *George,* he'd recently met with Steve Florio, a friend and the firm's CEO, who'd expressed an interest in taking over for Hachette. "That seemed a viable plan," said Russo. "I told John that we ought to regroup and discuss the matter further once Hachette made its intentions known."

Later that afternoon John showed up at La Palestra and handed studio owner Pat Manocchia a set of keys to his loft, so Manocchia could spend the weekend. He then got together with Gary Ginsberg, a lawyer-turned-journalist who worked for John at *George,* and the pair were driven by car service to Yankee Stadium to attend an interleague night game between the Yanks and the Atlanta Braves. George Steinbrenner, owner of the Yankees and a friend of Ted Kennedy's, often gave John complimentary box seats next to the Yankees dugout. John's appearance at the game caused the usual hubbub, dozens of baseball fans—young and old—queuing up for his autograph. John obligingly signed score-cards until a Yankee Stadium security guard chased the crowd back to their seats.

Following the game and a midnight snack with Ginsberg, John returned to the Stanhope, arriving shortly after 1:00 a.m. "He was limping uneasily on his crutches and in obvious pain," said Jeffrey Jones, the hotel's night clerk. "He stopped to chat and said he was leaving in the morning. He mentioned that he planned to fly to Martha's Vineyard and was looking forward to the trip, because he hadn't been able to pilot his plane in weeks. I wished him well."

At 9:00 a.m. the next morning, Friday, July 16, John checked out of the Stanhope and ate breakfast at the hotel Carlyle on Madison Avenue between 76th and 77th Streets. "It's ironic that JFK Jr. should have returned to the Carlyle on that particular morning," said Tommy Rowles, a bartender at Bemelmans, the Carlyle bistro situated off the hotel's main lobby. "I'd been at Bemelmans for forty-five years. I served his father, who always stayed at the Carlyle, and I served the son as well. John Jr. enjoyed hearing stories about his father. After his mother moved to New York following JFK's assassination, she used to bring the boy to the Carlyle for haircuts. He was just a tot in those days. But he continued to drop in from time to time as he grew up, usually for a glass of wine, occasionally with a date. He'd lived in the area and felt safe here."

John spent the remainder of the morning in his office, chatting with staff members about forthcoming issues of *George* and preparing for an afternoon appointment with Hachette CEO Jack Kliger. The previous day's business section of the *New York Post* had predicted *George's* imminent demise. Anticipating the worst, John had arranged meetings for the following week with several financial institutions, including Chase Manhattan Bank, to discuss the prospect of raising funds to keep the publication afloat.

At about noon, John received a telephone call from Brian Calcagne, director of sales for Air Bound Aviation, the company at Essex County Airport that had sold him the Saratoga. He continued to use Air Bound to house and service the plane. Calcagne, who eventually bought John's first plane from him, the Cessna 182, wondered if he planned on flying the Saratoga later that day. Confirming the flight, John asked the caller to have the aircraft ready for departure by early evening. Next he heard from Robert Merena, a flight instructor for Million Air with whom John had flown on a number of occasions. Merena wanted to know if Kennedy needed somebody to accompany him to Martha's Vineyard. John told the instructor that having just been liberated from his CAM Walker, he wanted to fly the plane himself.

"Are you sure?" inquired Merena.

"I'm sure," said JFK Jr.

At 1:00 p.m. John took *George*'s executive editor, Richard Blow, to lunch at Trionfo Ristorante, on the ground floor of the Paramount Plaza Building. They sat at John's usual table, one of four in a private back room. The other three tables were empty. Kennedy pulled over a chair and rested his left leg on it. They discussed the financial future of the magazine. Although outwardly optimistic that *George* would find a substitute backer should Hachette decline, Kennedy struck Blow as quieter and more contemplative than usual. Aware that John had political aspirations and had considered running for the New York senatorial seat currently sought by Hillary Clinton, Blow felt reassured by his boss's insistence that he intended to continue with the magazine, even if it meant cutting back on a staff overpopulated with editors and writers he'd kept on board simply because he found them fun to have around.

By 3:00 p.m., the time John usually left the office on Friday afternoons, he was again seated at his desk and on the telephone with his friend William (Billy) Sylvester Noonan, canceling a long-standing dinner appointment the two had set up for that Friday night, which another friend, Dan Samson, had also planned to attend. He told Noonan, a summer resident of Nantucket and someone he'd known since their teenage years, that his sister-in-law had to work late and that after work he had to drop her off at Martha's Vineyard.

The conference with Kliger ran an hour, from 4:00 p.m. to 5:00 p.m., without any definitive resolution. "We met, as we always did, in John's office," said Kliger. "Most of the staff had already checked out for the weekend. Hobbling about on his crutches, John seemed moderately uncomfortable. Although nothing was permanently decided, I think John understood that we were willing to commit to *George* for another year, provided we could bring in a financial expert to help sort things out. That was the game plan, and we agreed to move ahead with the arrangement and to meet again upon his return."

Feeling a sense of relief—or so he told Kliger—Kennedy took care of some lingering business. He telephoned New York literary agent Sterling Lord, who'd sent *George* an unpublished poem by the late Jack Kerouac, and thanked him for the submission, though, regrettably, it didn't fit the magazine's format. He spent forty-five minutes reviewing lists of story ideas compiled by his editors. He called Lauren Bessette at Morgan Stanley and agreed to meet her at six-thirty in front of his office building. He turned on his IBM computer and went to Weather Service International's aviation website to determine the current weather conditions for Martha's Vineyard and the rest of Massachusetts. The forecast was favorable: four to ten miles of visibility, mild winds, moderate haze, no summer rainstorms in the vicinity. The conditions fully complied with the FAA's visual flight rules as they applied to pilots without an instrument rating. Minimal visibility requirements for noninstrument pilots called for daylight-hour flights and a visibility range of three miles or more. JFK Jr. felt confident in his decision to make the flight without the services of a certified instructor.

Carolyn Bessette Kennedy had spent the day preparing for the trip, making a quick run to Saks Fifth Avenue and then on to her East Side beauty salon, where John finally reached her on her cell phone. She was in the process of having a pedicurist match her toenails to a swatch of the material she hoped to wear to the wedding. Dissatisfied with the results, she asked the pedicurist to repeat the process, not once but twice. By 6:45 p.m. she was seated in the back of a Lincoln Town Car en route to

Essex County Airport, where she would join John and her sister aboard the Saratoga.

Jessica Bruno, a Bessette family friend, had spoken with Carolyn earlier in the day and determined that she and John had overcome their differences. "Carolyn sounded rather chipper," noted Bruno. "Having made up over the phone, she said that they were looking forward to spending the weekend together. They'd decided to leave the city a little later than usual to avoid traffic. Friday afternoons in the summer can be deadly. As fate would have it, there was a great deal of traffic that day. John, Carolyn, and Lauren arrived at the airport later than expected."

Creeping through Times Square gridlock in John's leased car, a white 1997 two-door Hyundai sports coupe convertible (with New Jersey plates), Lauren may have wondered if she had made a wise choice after all in agreeing to fly with her sister and brother-in-law. Jane Dawson, a friend of hers, described Lauren as "the kind of person who rarely changed her mind once she decided on something. She was loyal to the end. But she also told me that the one thing she didn't want was to end up making the flight with John at night."

A night flight seemed inevitable. Having finally broken through the Times Square gridlock, John and Lauren found themselves hopelessly mired in bumper-to-bumper Lincoln Tunnel traffic. And Route 3, on the New Jersey side of the Hudson River, was no better. Carolyn Bessette's driver, having opted for the Holland Tunnel, faced the same impediment. The drive from Manhattan to Caldwell, New Jersey, which on a traffic-free day can be negotiated in forty-five minutes, took nearly twice as long on the evening of July 16.

It was 7:50 p.m. by the time John pulled the Hyundai into Jack's Friendly Service Station, a few hundred yards from the entrance to Essex County Airport. Using a single crutch for support, he struggled out of the car and into the small convenience store attached to the service station. There he paid the cashier, Mesfin Gebreegziabher, for a banana, a bottle of Evian water, and a four-pack of triple-A batteries. On his way out, he ran into Roy Stoppard, a business executive with a private pilot's license and many years of flying experience. "I knew John from other airport convenience stops," said Stoppard, who'd just flown in from Boston.

"He was exiting, and I was entering, so we stopped to chat just outside the store's front door, near the gas pumps. He asked me what he could expect weather-wise en route to the Vineyard, and I told him I'd run into some thick haze on the way down. The weather conditions were shifting, so I told him he might want to wait awhile before leaving. 'No chance,' he said. 'I'm already late.'

"He was carrying two plastic bags in his left hand, a crutch tucked under his right arm. As we stood there talking, I noticed that one of the bags contained what looked like a bottle of white wine, which he'd presumably brought with him from New York—they don't sell wine at Jack's. On closer examination, I could see that the bottle had been opened, because the seal was broken and the cork jammed back into place. In light of what happened that night, I often wonder what role, if any, can be attributed to that ominous-looking bottle of wine. I don't know if John had been drinking that evening, but I wouldn't bet against it.

"As he turned to leave, I wished him luck. 'Thanks,' he said, 'I'll need it.'"

Chapter 2

◆

THE FALL OF ICARUS (2)

MOVING GINGERLY ON a single crutch, John F. Kennedy Jr. transferred the luggage from his Hyundai into the twin, 100-pound capacity cargo holds on either side of the Saratoga. It was 8:10 p.m., and John had parked his car alongside the plane in front of the Air Bound Aviation hangar at Essex County Airport. Ten minutes later, following Carolyn Bessette's arrival in the Lincoln Town Car, he did the same with her luggage. Carolyn helped by toting her own garment bag as well as a stack of fashion magazines she had bought to read on the flight. With both holds filled, John gave Lauren a brief tour of the aircraft. At twenty-seven feet, nine inches in length and with a thirty-six-foot wing span, it seemed extremely compact. Built in 1995, bearing the identification number N9253N stenciled in large numerals across its fusillade, the 300-horsepower, single-engine, red-and-white Piper Saratoga II came equipped with retractable landing gear, refreshment console, executive writing table, carpeting, and six tan leather seats (including the pilot's and right-front passenger's). The remaining four seats were arranged "club-style" in two rows facing each other and were located directly behind the pilot's seat.

John purchased the plane on April 28, 1999, from Air Bound Aviation for $225,000. Air Bound had acquired it several months earlier from international businessman Muir Hussain, who told a reporter that the Saratoga's seating arrangement was "confining and uncomfortable." John, however, considered it "cramped but cozy," a sentiment shared by his wife. Andy Ferguson, president of Air Bound Aviation, asserted that Carolyn Bessette "loved the plane and loved flying in it. Contrary to popular opinion, she wasn't the least bit afraid to fly with John. John brimmed with confidence; one might even say overconfidence. Flying one of these small planes is like riding a roller coaster without the rails. If there's trouble up there, the pilot has to depend on his own skills to land the plane safely."

JFK Jr.'s determination to become a pilot had a practical component to it that may have transcended the pleasure factor. In the past, when forced to resort to commercial air travel, he found himself, like everyone else, waiting for hours at ticket counters, security checkpoints, and departure gates. Once on the airliner, he was at the mercy of fellow passengers and curiosity seekers. The less considerate passenger thought nothing of bombarding him with questions or demanding his autograph. While he understood (and even enjoyed) the human element of the dilemma—the endless fascination that most people maintain for celebrity—being the object of such scrutiny left him with a feeling of vulnerability. In 1990, when flying to Palm Beach, Florida, he had been unable to book a first-class seat. To avoid having to sit next to a stranger, he purchased an extra tourist-class seat and traveled with his guitar on it. The press attacked him for the tactic, labeling him "a poor little rich boy." In 1991, on an American Airlines flight to Los Angeles, a passenger seated nearby suddenly whipped out his video camera and started filming John until a flight attendant forced the intruder to return to his seat. Reporters booked on the same flights as John routinely took advantage of the situation, engaging him in idle conversation, then writing up the encounter as if it had been a prearranged formal interview, often inventing dialogue to fit the occasion. Chartering his own plane and pilot worked no better for John. Too many charter flight pilots, in an effort to drum up business, leaked the names and travel plans of their most famous clients. In January 1992, JFK Jr. had barely stepped off a charter flight to St. Louis when a swarm of reporters and photographers descended upon him. One of the photographers later admitted that they'd been tipped off to his arrival by the pilot.

Not that life in the media fishbowl was exactly a foreign concept to John. Even as he finished packing up the Saratoga, a British freelance photographer named George Exley Smith lurked in the shadows of the Air Bound hangar, snapping pictures of the scene. "I'd flown into Essex County Airport from Long Island with a pilot friend of mine," Smith explained. "Somebody at the airport mentioned that JFK Jr. and his wife were expected to fly out of there later that afternoon. Hoping for a photo op, I decided to hang around. They didn't arrive until after eight. John and his sister-in-law drove up first, followed by Carolyn a few minutes later. I remember how fresh and vibrant the two sisters looked, Carolyn in a black sleeveless blouse and black pedal-pushers, Lauren in a stylish pearl gray dress. John dragged himself around on a crutch while conversing on his cell phone. He then began circling the plane, manually checking the flaps and inspecting the twin fuel tanks (located against the front edge of both wings) to make sure they were full. It's a hop, skip, and jump from Caldwell to the airport at Vineyard Haven, on Martha's Vineyard, approximately forty-five minutes to an hour, depending on weather conditions. The Piper Saratoga has a fuel capacity of slightly over a hundred gallons. It burns roughly sixteen gallons of fuel per flight hour. The hundred gallons that John's plane supposedly carried that day would've kept them going for a good six hours."

Reflecting further, Smith recalled thinking it odd that a novice pilot like John, with his bad leg and lack of instrument rating, would want to make the flight alone at night, particularly given the rapidly changing weather picture. The air was so viscous and the haze so pervasive by this time that Smith's photographs were rendered practically unusable. Other pilots at the same airport were abandoning their flight plans and rescheduling for the morning.

On July 6, 2000, nearly a year after JFK Jr.'s fatal flight, the National Transportation Safety Board, an independent federal agency that investigates the causes of aviation, nautical, and railroad accidents, issued its final report on the Kennedy crash. In preparing the document, which was supplemented by lengthy operational files and field reports, the NTSB sought the cooperation of both the FAA and the FBI. Agents for the Federal Bureau of Investigation conducted dozens of interviews with aviation experts, including four veteran pilots who for years had flown the same route as John—from New Jersey to either Martha's Vineyard or Nantucket. All four reported low visibility due to fog and haze on the night of the accident. Three of them, having flown earlier on the same day, recalled that while flying over water they were forced to utilize their instrument training. "It was pretty bad out there," said one of the three. "There were no discernible reference points and no sign of a horizon." The fourth pilot, having flown into Essex County Airport just as John was leaving, had earlier come within three miles of Martha's Vineyard and described the night sky over the Vineyard as "inky black and filled with haze." He could see nothing, he said, "not a single light." He thought at first that there had been a vast power outage. It was as if the entire island had been sucked up by the sea.

For his part, John Jr. remained unaware of any last-minute weather changes. He had failed, either by choice or oversight, to update the information he'd gleaned from the Weather Service International website before leaving his office. Nor did he avail himself of what are known as "pre-ops," or pilot reports, filed by fliers already airborne. Pre-ops usually contain late-breaking data on existing atmospheric conditions such as wind velocity, haze, rain, and cloud configurations. Even the most cursory review would have revealed that fog and haze had closed in over Martha's Vineyard, rendering the airport at Vineyard Haven virtually unattainable to anyone but the most experienced, instrument-trained pilot.

Sunset that Friday began at 8:14 p.m. and ended at 8:47 p.m. The maximum visibility at Essex County Airport at the time of John's departure had been reduced to "between three and four miles." The airport itself was steeped in an eerie, purplish day-ending light, the sky partially enveloped by a thick overlay of haze. Cellular phone records for the pilot and his two passengers reveal that Carolyn placed two last calls while the plane was still on the ground, the first to Carole Radziwill at Martha's Vineyard to confirm that she and John would arrive at Gay Head the following evening after Rory Kennedy's wedding, the second to Jenny (Jean) Messina, Carolyn and Lauren's high-spirited, eighty-six-year-old maternal grandmother. According to the NTSB report (and confirmed by cell phone records), no further calls were made or received after takeoff.

Carolyn and Lauren had buckled themselves side by side into the second row of seats, facing the rear of the plane, back to back with the pilot seat. John tested the engine by gunning it, triggering the nose propeller and sending up a gray cloud of grit and exhaust. The plane's vibrations set off the Hyundai's antitheft alarm. Carolyn unbuckled herself, clambered off the plane, shut off the alarm, and returned to her seat. John rolled the aircraft out of the Air Bound lot into position on runway 22, revved the engine again, and, after receiving clearance from air traffic control, took off at 8:38 p.m., heading south for a short distance before banking gently to the right and turning the plane to the northeast. At 8:40 p.m. he radioed air traffic control that he was "north of Teterboro . . . headed eastward."

Tracing the events that ensued over the next hour, the NTSB report details a cascade of questionable pilot decisions and insurmountable problems that would ultimately lead to the destruction of the Saratoga and those aboard. While no single element of the journey proved truly decisive, they quickly piled up on each other like an unsteady stack of dominoes. The first of these took place at 8:49 p.m., eleven minutes into the flight, when John accidentally tripped a Traffic Alert and Collision Avoidance System (TCAS) alarm in the air traffic control tower at Westchester County Airport, in White Plains, New York. American Airlines flight 1484, a commercial jetliner carrying 120 passengers and six crew members, had leveled off at three thousand feet in anticipation of a final approach and landing. Three miles away, climbing into a direct collision course with the inbound jetliner, was the much smaller Saratoga. Unable to reach John over his radio transmitter, the air traffic controller immediately contacted the pilot of the jetliner, alerting him to the situation and instructing him to make a course adjustment.

Excerpts of the radio transmissions between the White Plains air traffic controller and the pilot of American Airlines flight 1484 (as reproduced in the NTSB report) reveal the air controller's frustration over John's failure to respond. After several frantic calls to the Saratoga, the air traffic controller gave up and concentrated his efforts on guiding the commercial jetliner out of harm's way. At 8:53 p.m., four minutes after the onset of the alarm, the American Airlines pilot radioed the controller: "Yes, we have him. I think we have him." The pilot had spotted the Saratoga off his right wing, dangerously close but now at a slightly higher altitude than the jetliner. It is clear from the Saratoga's flight pattern that John never saw the other aircraft and had no idea that he had violated its air space, nearly causing a catastrophic midair collision.

The most bizarre aspect of the event, aside from the fact that it was never reported in the press, had to be JFK Jr.'s failure to respond to the air traffic controller's radio transmissions. Interviewed by the FBI for the NTSB report, Christopher Benway, John's instructor at FlightSafety International, disclosed that his pupil had experienced profound difficulty with lesson eleven of the instrument training course he'd begun but never completed. The lesson tested a flight student's knowledge of high-frequency radio ranges and transmissions. According to Benway, it took John four attempts to complete the lesson and another three—seven in all—before the instructor felt comfortable with Kennedy's performance. On the night of July 16, JFK Jr. appears to have regressed, possibly because it had been nearly two months since his last solo flight. The NTSB report mentions in passing that in the course of his flight, with the exception of his curtailed message following takeoff, John made no attempt to use his radio transmitter, not even during the tense moments preceding the crash.

Following the near collision over Westchester County Airport, JFK Jr. continued to climb to 5,500 feet, flying on a straight line in the direction of Martha's Vineyard. For one brief span, a period lasting no more than thirty minutes, as he pushed on into the night, John must have experienced the feeling of serenity and well-being, elation and exhilaration that came to him whenever he sat at the controls of his plane. "It's euphoric," he once said of flying. "There's nothing like it and there are no words to describe it." He could feel the Saratoga quiver and throb as it cut through the darkness, the night air lifting the plane's riveted aluminum wings, propelling it forward at an average cruising speed of 175 miles per hour. The syrupy haze that blanketed New Jersey had gradually thinned. As he flew over the coastline of Connecticut, he could make out the twinkling lights of Bridgeport and New Haven. The moon and stars were dim but visible. The horizon, a fine line dividing sea from sky, was discernible in the distance.

It might have been at this stage that John would have wanted to utilize the autopilot function in his plane, a device that could have steered the plane to its destination. According to the operational files compiled by the NTSB, the Saratoga's autopilot wasn't engaged during the aircraft's final journey. The same files reveal that on several previous trips undertaken by John in company with a certified flight instructor, the autopilot had malfunctioned and had to be reset mid-flight. But even had the device been in perfect operating order, the fact remains that he had never been trained to operate the autopilot and therefore could not have deployed it on his own.

Ted Stanley, a Martha's Vineyard charter pilot who maintained a friendship with JFK Jr., observed that "John wasn't acquainted with the operation of the autopilot because at that time the FAA didn't require a private pilot to be familiar with its use. As a result, flight training programs rarely included the autopilot in their curriculum for beginning pilots. After John's death, I began corresponding with the FAA to try to rectify this situation. I don't know if there have been any regulatory changes about learning to fly in autopilot, but it seems to me it should be featured in any program devoted to basic pilot training."

Ted Stanley went on. "There are several flight adages that apply to John," he noted. "One of them is: 'Judgment comes from experience, and experience comes from bad judgment.' In other words, John found himself in a predicament he hadn't encountered before. Had he somehow come through it, he would have known better what to do the second time around. Another saying has it that 'There are old pilots and bold pilots, but there are no old, bold pilots.' In undertaking the flight, John may have been too bold for his own good."

At 9:29 p.m.—fifty-one minutes after takeoff—as the Saratoga approached Point Judith, Rhode Island, on the last leg of its flight, the haze suddenly kicked in again. The white lights of towns and villages below abruptly vanished. The moon and stars were gone as well, their light bleached into invisibility. Only the horizon remained, a vague, unwavering line that now seemed to be covered by a porous swatch of white gauze.

At this point, a more advanced pilot would have shifted from visual flight rules to instrument flight rules, an option unavailable to John. A more prudent pilot might have turned inland and sought permission to land at an alternate site, lay over, and continue once the weather cleared. Another possible route—one that John occasionally flew—would have taken him farther along the coastline of Rhode Island, heading northwest, thus reducing the time the plane would have to fly over open water. Instead JFK Jr. chose to maintain his bearing, turning east at Point Judith and flying the last thirty miles over the Atlantic. As soon as he completed the turn, he must have realized he had made a mistake. The blinding fog and haze, worse at sea than over land, had obscured everything, including the horizon. Sea and sky blended into one impenetrable black mass, and John soon found himself in the middle of it.

In preparing for his pilot's license, JFK Jr. had familiarized himself with the FAA's various pamphlets and circulars, not least of which were those devoted to the subject of spatial disorientation. One in particular, FAA Advisory Circular 61-27C, "Instrument Flying: Coping with Illusions in Flight," stated that illusions or false impressions occur when information provided by sensory organs is misinterpreted or inadequate, and that illusions in flight can be caused by complex motions and certain visual scenes imagined under adverse weather conditions and at night.

The advisory circular further maintained that some illusions might lead to spatial disorientation or the inability to determine accurately the attitude or motion of the aircraft in relation to the earth's surface. The advisory circular concluded that spatial disorientation, as a result of continued reliance on visual flight rules under conditions better suited to instrument flight rules, is regularly near the top of the cause/factor list in annual statistics on fatal aircraft accidents.

Without radioing ahead, immersed in a monochromatic void, staring at the complex display of dials and instruments on the control panel before him, John initiated a gradual descent of the Saratoga that varied between 400 and 800 feet per minute. Besides preparing for a final approach and clearance to land, he may have hoped to drop the plane far enough below the haze to catch sight of the Gay Head Lighthouse beacon or to reestablish a view of the horizon. Only minutes from the rapidly approaching shore, having descended from 5,500 to 2,200 feet, John began a right turn. Squinting into the darkness for some telltale sign, he could make out neither the horizon nor the lighthouse beacon. He may have then searched in vain for the navigational beacon that sits on the Vineyard airfield and is used by pilots to guide themselves to a runway. Inexplicably, he now climbed back to 2,600 feet and began to turn left. As the plane turned left, it began to descend again, the speed of descent increasing to 900 feet per minute. The Saratoga's airspeed also increased. In an effort to slow the plane and regain control, John attempted to raise the Saratoga's nose by pulling back the yoke, a tactic that might have worked had the plane's wings been level. Under the circumstances, with the aircraft descending at an angle, the maneuver only added to the pilot's problems. Without visual reference points, John could no longer differentiate between up and down, right and left. His mind and inner ear told him one thing, his eyes and a wildly whirling altimeter told him something else. Unable to process the conflicting strands of information, he became even more confused. Thirty seconds after trying to raise the plane's nose, he attempted still another right turn. At 1,500 feet, the Saratoga entered what aviators call a "graveyard spiral," spinning like a top as it plummeted downward (for about fifteen seconds) at a rate that exceeded 5,000 feet per minute. The plane struck the water in a nose-down attitude, the force of impact equivalent to an automobile plowing into a cement wall at 200 miles per hour. The pilot and his two passengers died instantly. The recorded time was 9:41 p.m. Air control at Martha's Vineyard had the plane on its radar screen when it vanished, but didn't realize it was Kennedy (since he had filed no flight plan) until days later when they reviewed radar screen tapes. The last sound the aircraft's occupants heard as they fell, their bodies crushed into their seats, must have been the wind screaming past the plane's windows.

The Saratoga's propeller, wings, and tail were sheared away in the crash and sank to the bottom, not far from the twisted fuselage, which came to rest in an upside-down position. Every window in the aircraft had been broken or blown out. The plane's supposedly indestructible flight data recorder ("little black box"), more vulnerable than the type used in commercial airliners, shattered in the crash and proved useless to NTSB investigators. Despite an exhaustive search for the missing plane, it took until Tuesday morning, July 20, before sonar readings pointed the way to a possible wreckage site on a cold (52 degrees Fahrenheit) patch of ocean bottom, 116 feet below the choppy surface, 7.5 miles southwest of Gay Head. Shortly before midnight on the same day, a remote-operated submersible craft equipped with a camera spotted the wreckage, ending all speculation as to the fate of the Saratoga and those aboard.

Two and a half hours later, at 2:15 a.m., Wednesday, July 21, a team of U.S. Navy divers approached the wreckage. A grisly scene awaited them. John's body, his head and upper torso protruding from a broken cockpit window, was badly decomposed. His right arm washed back and forth in the brisk underwater current, as though beckoning the divers to his side. At ten in the morning another dive team returned to the wreckage to search for the bodies of Carolyn and Lauren Bessette. They were found on the ocean floor less than ten yards from what remained of the plane, still strapped side by side into their seats, their bodies as waterlogged and ravaged by the sea as John's. In addition to devastating internal injuries, all three had suffered massive cuts and lacerations to the head, face, and torso, enabling their bodily fluids to escape and their remains to putrefy. Sharks and other sea creatures had gnawed away at their flesh, adding to the carnage.

Senator Ted Kennedy had departed the Schlossberg house at Sagaponack on Monday afternoon and rejoined the clan at the Kennedy compound in Hyannis Port. Coast Guard officials reached him there with news of the latest developments. Teddy notified Caroline Kennedy as well as the mother of Carolyn and Lauren Bessette. Realizing that all was lost, Ted had already issued a public statement: "We are all filled with unspeakable grief and sadness. John was a shining light in all our lives, and in the lives of the nation and the world that first came to know him as a little boy. He was a devoted husband to Carolyn, a loving brother to Caroline, an amazing uncle to her children, a close and dear friend to his cousins, and a beloved nephew to my sisters and me. He was the adored son of two proud parents whom he now joins with God. We loved him deeply."

Despite his outward calm, a stance he adopted for the sake of his family, Ted Kennedy felt utterly stricken. How many more Kennedys, young and old, could he be expected to bury? To add to his misery, July 19 marked the thirtieth anniversary of the Chappaquiddick scandal.

At 12:15 p.m. on Wednesday, a Navy helicopter delivered Ted and his two sons, Edward Jr. and Patrick, to the USS *Grasp,* a navy salvage ship, to witness the recovery operation. Two teams of divers descended in steel cages that were attached to the salvage vessel by wires and cables and worked like elevators. Ted Kennedy watched grimly as one by one, starting with John, the three cadavers were hoisted out of the murky depths and placed in white metallic caskets on the deck of the ship.

In Washington, D.C., President Clinton held a press conference in which he addressed various topics. When asked to comment on his authorization, at considerable taxpayer expense, of an extended search for JFK Jr.'s Saratoga, he replied: "Because of the role of the Kennedy family in our national lives, and because of the enormous losses that they have sustained in our lifetimes, I thought it appropriate to give the search a few more days. If anyone believes that this was wrong, the Coast Guard is not at fault—I am . . ." A day after the recovery of the plane and the bodies, Clinton ordered all American flags at the White House to be flown at half-mast.

At 7:00 p.m. on Wednesday, the salvage vessel arrived at the U.S. Coast Guard Station in Falmouth, Massachusetts. The three metallic caskets were transferred to a pair of coroner vans, John in one and the Bessette sisters in the other. Escorted by Massachusetts State Police cars on yet another dark Kennedy motorcade, the vans drove the bodies to Barnstable County Hospital in Pocasset. There Dr. Richard J. Evans, chief medical examiner for the Commonwealth of Massachusetts, assisted by Dr. James Weiner, performed a state- and FAA-mandated autopsy on JFK Jr., followed by complete physical examinations (including X-rays) of Carolyn and Lauren Bessette. Photographs of the three corpses were taken at various stages of the process, but to avoid unwanted publicity, the Kennedy and Bessette families requested that the film not be developed. The entire procedure took just under four hours and ended close to midnight. The cause of death on all three death certificates was "multiple traumatic injuries." At Caroline Kennedy's behest, her brother's autopsy report remained permanently sealed.

Under the headline "JFK Autopsy Rushed," *The Boston Globe* published an article (July 29, 1999) accusing the medical examiner's office of hurrying the autopsy as an accommodation to the Kennedy family. The article questioned the haste and secrecy with which the autopsy was performed and the fact that it was conducted at night, immediately following the recovery of the bodies. Even more dismaying, it would seem, was the alacrity with which the three cadavers were then cremated. The moment the autopsy ended, the corpses were taken to the Duxbury Crematory, in Duxbury, Massachusetts. By early Thursday morning, July 22, the ashes of all three were turned over to attorneys for both families.

Carolyn and Lauren Bessette's mother, Ann Freeman, their orthopedist stepfather, Dr. Richard Freeman, and Lauren's twin sister, Lisa, drove to Woods Hole from the Freeman residence in Greenwich, Connecticut, to attend the funeral services with seventeen members of the Kennedy family. The Freemans issued a public statement of their own; it began: "Nothing in life is preparation for the loss of a child . . ." They had lost two children.

At nine-thirty, Thursday morning, a Coast Guard vessel ferried the Bessettes and Kennedys to the USS *Briscoe,* a guided-missile destroyer made available for the funeral by then Defense Secretary William S. Cohen. Coast Guard officers helped the bereaved to board the Navy destroyer. Among those in the Kennedy contingent were John's sister, Caroline, Uncle Ted, Maria Shriver, William Kennedy Smith, and Patrick Kennedy. Also present, seated pensively in a wheelchair, was Anthony Radziwill.

Cruising to a point midway between the beach at Gay Head and the spot where the Saratoga went down, the destroyer stopped and dropped anchor. Along the shoreline of southwestern Martha's Vineyard, vacationers and local residents, gripped for days by news of the plane's disappearance, strained to watch the drama from afar. They saw little. An armada of Coast Guard ships had been carefully placed to block the view and protect the privacy of the funeral guests. A strictly enforced security zone of ten nautical miles had been imposed by the FAA to keep the news media—in chartered boats and helicopters—at a respectful distance.

The half-hour ceremony began at noon and was conducted by two Navy chaplains and a Roman Catholic priest. A quintet of Navy musicians played softly in the background while members of both families stepped forward to cast the ashes of the dead into the sea. Caroline spoke to the group of her brother's desire to be buried at sea. Farther out in the Atlantic, the USS *Grasp* continued to salvage pieces of the Saratoga, lifting to the surface the badly damaged control panel and a nine-foot section of fuselage. These and other airplane parts would be carefully examined by FAA and NTSB inspectors in an effort to determine the cause of the crash.

The mourners arrived back in Woods Hole at three-thirty in the afternoon. The Bessettes returned to Connecticut, and the Kennedys proceeded to Hyannis Port for a private reception. At the reception, Ted Kennedy attempted to convince Caroline to hold a larger, more public memorial service in John's honor than the one she'd arranged for the following day at the Church of St. Thomas More on East 89th Street in Manhattan. He suggested, "rather forcefully," claimed one witness, that it be held at the Washington National Cathedral in the nation's capital, and that television cameras be allowed into the cathedral. Caroline stood her ground—she had no intention of politicizing her brother's death.

On Friday morning, July 23, President Clinton—accompanied by Hillary and their daughter, Chelsea—waded through a maze of police barricades and a mass of spectators to reach the entranceway to the church. Invitations to the memorial service were extended to only 150 handpicked guests, including Muhammad Ali, John Kenneth Galbraith, and Arthur M. Schlesinger Jr. The altar had been decorated with hundreds of white roses. Caroline Kennedy read from Shakespeare's *The Tempest*. Anthony Radziwill, who would survive his cousin by a mere three weeks, read Psalm 23. Wyclef Jean, one of John Jr.'s favorite recording artists, sang a haunting rendition of "Many Rivers to Cross." A gospel choir sang "Swing Low, Sweet Chariot." Reverend Charles O'Byrne, who had presided over John and Carolyn's wedding, gave the homily, and Ted Kennedy delivered the eulogy, comparing John's virtues with those of President Kennedy: "We had to think that this John Kennedy would live to comb gray hair, with his beloved Carolyn by his side. But like his father, he had every gift but length in years." At the end, President Clinton presented Caroline Kennedy, Ted Kennedy, and the Bessettes with identical photo albums of John and Carolyn's visit to the White House.

A day later, many of the same invitees gathered again at a memorial ceremony for Carolyn and Lauren Bessette. Organized by their uncle, Florida surgeon Jack Messina, the event was held at Christ Church in Greenwich. Ed and Caroline Schlossberg, Ethel Kennedy, Jean Kennedy Smith, and Kathleen Kennedy Townsend represented the Kennedy camp. Notably absent from the proceedings was Carolyn and Lauren's father, William J. Bessette, a cabinet store owner and former engineer from White Plains, New York. No longer on cordial terms with his ex-wife, Bessette had been left to mourn the loss of his daughters in his own fashion.

Other memorial services were held in cities and towns across the country. More than one newspaper editorial compared John Jr.'s untimely death to the earlier demise of Princess Diana. "It marks the end of an era," proclaimed *Newsweek*. John and Carolyn's apartment building in TriBeCa became a shrine for thousands of New Yorkers who left behind flowers, letters, drawings, balloons, and posters in such abundance that many of the tenants in the building had trouble gaining access to their lofts.

Meanwhile, the investigation by the FAA and NTSB into the cause or causes of the accident had just begun. The four-hour-long autopsy performed on John by the chief medical examiner of Massachusetts (less than the time it took to examine and X-ray the bodies of Carolyn and Lauren Bessette) established a probable cause of death without addressing a more compelling question: What were the culminating circumstances and events that contributed to JFK Jr.'s cataclysmic end?

The answer to this and other pertinent questions can be found not in the autopsy report or in the NTSB's final report of July 6, 2000, but in a joint NTSB/FAA document, "Final Forensic Toxicology Fatal Accident Report," a five-page summation of contributing factors long withheld from public scrutiny but currently available under the Freedom of Information Act (FOIA). The document, dated August 6, 1999, and signed by NTSB medical investigator Dennis Canfield, Ph.D., is based on an examination of muscle and organ samples extracted from JFK Jr.'s body during the July 21 autopsy and flown to the FAA's Mike Monroney Aeronautical Center in Oklahoma City, Oklahoma. After extensive testing in the FAA's medical laboratories, it was determined that the deceased's lung and muscle samples were laced with unusually high traces of ethanol (alcohol). John's lung sample contained 36 milligrams of ethanol per deciliter (mg/dL); the ethanol reading for his muscle sample was 55 mg/dL. While these figures mean little to the layman, they are significant when interpreted by a toxicologist.

From the wording of the August 6, 1999, report, Dennis Canfield seems to imply what the high ethanol readings in JFK Jr.'s body may have suggested. Canfield writes: "The ethanol found in this case may *potentially* be from postmortem ethanol formation and not from the ingestion of alcohol." Despite Canfield's conclusion, the NTSB's final report (which was not prepared by Canfield but by nameless officials) categorically states: "The toxicological tests are *negative* for alcohol and drugs of abuse." It is clear from the FAA's report that the toxicological tests were *positive* with respect to the presence of alcohol (or ethanol) in JFK Jr.'s body. The single detail the FAA could not determine—or did not want to determine—was whether the high ethanol readings were the result of postmortem alcohol formation or the result of alcohol ingestion, an act that by definition would have had to take place prior to the subject's death. At the very least, it is obvious that the NTSB's final report is nothing less than a misrepresentation of the facts.

In determining the primary cause of JFK Jr.'s high alcohol reading, it is important to note that the readings were based on tests performed on the subject's lung and muscle samples and not on his liver, which for some unknown reason was never tested. According to experts in the field, postmortem formation of alcohol deposits almost always takes place in the liver and not in the muscular system.

Dr. James C. Garriott, arguably the best-known toxicologist in the United States, left little doubt that the alcohol readings in JFK Jr.'s body samples are "a valid indicator of ingested alcohol *prior* to death." To this contention, he added: "It's not an extremely high reading, but under certain circumstances it might be considered high. It's the equivalent of two to three glasses of wine imbibed in close succession. Kennedy's alcohol reading was twice the legal level established by FAA regulations as the standard for licensed commercial airplane pilots. Moreover, it's entirely possible that because the subject's body was submerged in salt water for so many days prior to recovery and testing, the original reading might have been significantly higher." Garriott also found it "strange" that the subject's liver sample was never tested for alcoholic content, as a countermeasure to the ethanol readings in his other body samples. "As unlikely as it seems," he said, "it's possible the liver couldn't be accurately tested because of its advanced state of decay."

While by no means an alcoholic—"He far preferred pot to booze," said JFK Jr.'s friend John Perry Barlow—John did enjoy an occasional glass of wine or bottle of beer, and periodically was known to drink far more than that. He'd been spotted less than an hour before the start of his last flight carrying what appeared to be an uncorked bottle of wine. That he wasn't an extreme or habitual drinker could possibly have heightened the effect of what alcohol he did imbibe prior to the flight. Then there were John's medications, the pharmaceuticals he'd been prescribed for attention deficit disorder and Graves' disease, as well as the pain pills he took for his ankle injury. While none of these was mentioned in the NTSB's final report—tests were simply not conducted for these particular medications—there is no question that they too could have increased the effect of any alcohol he might have consumed.

Given the NTSB's apparent obfuscation of the record, it is easy to understand why their operational files on JFK Jr. are incomplete. A separate document of some three hundred pages, these files normally include a section titled "Human Performance." Listed in the index to the operational files, the "human performance" section is not only missing but, according to an NTSB spokesperson, "was never begun." Had it been included, it would have had to deal with the subject's state of mind and degree of inebriation (if any) on the day of the crash. It would help to explain, among other things, John's failure to obtain a weather update prior to takeoff, his inability (or unwillingness) to either receive or initiate radio transmissions, and his near collision with a commercial jetliner over Westchester County Airport.

Although the NTSB's final report attributes the Saratoga's crash to "pilot error," its summary of probable cause fails to address the underlying issues. Having eliminated the possibility of "mechanical failure," the report blames the accident on "the pilot's failure to maintain control of the airplane during a descent over water at night, which was the result of spatial disorientation. Factors in the accident were haze and the dark night." The report makes little or no reference to those factors that led up to the final scene, such as alcohol, pharmaceuticals, a broken ankle, and an overall lack of knowledge, judgment, and experience, to say nothing of youth, folly, and overconfidence.

Of course nobody can ever know exactly what happened in that airplane on that particular night. John could have momentarily dozed off, or he could have been in an argument with his wife—or his wife and sister-in-law could have been arguing in the back of the plane, and he became distracted. Or possibly it had been, on a metaphysical level, merely the confluence of a series of unfortunate events over which John had no control.

John Perry Barlow recalled receiving an e-mail from JFK Jr. that had been sent on July 16, the last day of Kennedy's life. The e-mail consisted of a letter from John commiserating with his friend over the recent death of his mother. "I'd been with my mother," said Barlow, "during her last days, much as John had been with his mother toward the end of her life. After my mother died, I wrote to John. He responded by e-mail and said he was grateful that I'd been able to see my mother through to the end, just as he had done. 'Now we both know that death is not so macabre,' he wrote. What was macabre is that I read the e-mail only after John's death. He spoke to me from the grave.

"From time to time, John and I talked about the meaning of life," continued Barlow. "He had a fairly strong idea that sooner or later something unexpected might happen to him. He was a fatalist. He believed that someday his number would come up, and there wasn't a hell of a lot he could do about it. He wanted to experience as much as he could in his life. He loved to fly. He needed to fly. If he had to choose a way to die, it would have happened just as it did—with John at the controls of his plane."

JFK Jr. also explored the subject of death with his sister Caroline, discussing with her not only his desire to be buried at sea but the circumstances that had robbed them of both parents, a much loved uncle, several young cousins, and a cluster of close friends. Death seemed a kind of common denominator, uniting the siblings, binding them together. "We aren't exactly cursed," John had once said of the Kennedys, "but we're pretty damn close to it. Yes, we've had our share of luck. We've been to the mountaintop. But there have been entirely too many tragedies, mostly of our own making." So untimely and unjust had been his own tragic end that it seemed, well after the fact, almost incomprehensible. Never had Caroline Kennedy imagined that at age forty-one, she would become the keeper of the flame, the sole survivor of a family that in its heyday appeared to be all but immortal.

Part II

———◆———

Chapter 3

◆

"GOOD MORNING, MR. PRESIDENT"

A PATCHWORK OF GARDENS, meandering tree-lined lanes, and red-brick Federal and Victorian town houses, Georgetown was not so much a place as a state of mind. Cozily nestled in the oldest section of Washington, D.C., the tiny, picturesque village was home to the great, the near great, and the once great in government and the media. One of the most visible young couples in Georgetown in 1954 was the Kennedys. Senator John F. Kennedy of Massachusetts, thirty-six, a three-term former Democratic congressman, had married twenty-four-year-old Jacqueline Lee Bouvier in Newport, Rhode Island, on September 12, 1953. With 1,200 guests present at their reception, the event became known among society columnists as "the wedding of the decade." He was the son of Joseph P. Kennedy, the first Irish Catholic ambassador from the United States to England, and Rose Fitzgerald Kennedy, whose father, John Francis (Honey Fitz) Fitzgerald, had served as mayor of Boston. One of the wealthiest men in America, Joe Kennedy struck it rich during Prohibition by importing vast shipments of gin and whiskey from England, Scotland, and Canada, storing the illegal provisions in a Palm Beach prison, investing the profits in an array of enterprises, including real estate, oil, utilities, shipping, movie theaters, racetracks, gambling casinos, and, his most valuable asset, the Chicago Merchandise Mart. Often depicted as brilliant but ruthless, he doubled his bankroll while serving as chairman of the U.S. Securities and Exchange Commission, taking advantage of investment loopholes he would soon declare illegal. To avoid paying taxes both during his lifetime and after, he established a series of nonprofit corporations and interlocking trusts that skirted the law but effectively preserved a family fortune variously estimated at between 650 million and several billion dollars.

Jacqueline Kennedy, the senator's wife, was the daughter of Janet Lee, an accomplished equestrienne and New York City club woman, and John Vernou Bouvier III, an independent Wall Street investment broker otherwise known as "Black Jack" because of his darkly masculine features and rampant womanizing. Several years after their 1940 divorce, when Jackie was eleven, Janet married another stockbroker, Hugh Dudley (Hughdie) Auchincloss Jr., and with her daughters, Jackie and Lee (four years Jackie's junior), moved into his spacious estates: Hammersmith Farm, at Newport, where they spent their summers, and Merrywood, at McLean, Virginia, only minutes from downtown Washington. Jacqueline's background as a Miss Porter's School debutante and honors student at Vassar and the Sorbonne, as well as her fashionable position as inquiring photographer at the *Washington Times-Herald,* provided John F. Kennedy with what he needed most to secure his political future: social acceptability. Jackie's East Coast finishing-school polish, French Catholic heritage, and Hollywood-star good looks matched JFK's most celebrated qualities—his urbane sophistication, youthful vitality, and quick wit.

After honeymooning in Acapulco and San Francisco, Jack and Jackie returned to Washington and took up temporary residence with the Auchinclosses at Merrywood. They split their weekends between the Kennedy compound in Hyannis Port and the Kennedy mansion on North Ocean Boulevard in Palm Beach. By the beginning of 1954, the newlyweds had taken a six-month sublet at 3321 Dent Place, a three-story Georgetown residence. To keep up with her husband's political interests, Jackie enrolled in an American history seminar at nearby Georgetown University. Lorraine Rowan, the future wife of Republican senator John Sherman

Cooper of Kentucky, and a close Georgetown friend of Mrs. Kennedy, noticed that "Jacqueline began to infuse her dinner-table conversations with tidbits about Thomas Jefferson and John Quincy Adams, among others. In her spare time she produced a book of very clever political cartoons, which she decided not to submit for publication. Otherwise she spoke a lot about redecorating her new home. I said to her, 'What's the point of spending money on somebody else's house?' She couldn't stand the decor. 'Jack wants to start entertaining in it,' she said, 'but it's such a dreary little place.'"

Once their half-year lease ran out, the Kennedys again found themselves drifting back and forth between the homes of in-laws. In general, it was a difficult time for them. Jack underwent a year of very painful spinal fusions at the Hospital for Special Surgery in New York. Finally, after what must have been a good deal of pressure from Jackie, he paid $125,000 for Hickory Hill, a stately white brick Georgian residence on six acres of woodland in McLean, not far from the Auchinclosses. The grounds, featuring stables and a swimming pool, were ideally suited for Kennedy-style softball and touch football games. Jackie, whose leg had been injured during a football scrimmage, soon gave up the sport and retired to the sidelines.

"Jackie couldn't stomach all that boisterous rah-rah business," said Langdon Marvin, a political aide to JFK. "The Kennedys, on the other hand, couldn't get enough of it. When it came to leisure activities, they tended to be loud, obtrusive, and ultracompetitive."

In the summer of 1956, Jackie, nearly seven months pregnant, accompanied Jack to the National Democratic Convention in Chicago, where he narrowly missed being selected as Adlai Stevenson's vice-presidential running mate. When it ended, JFK, in need of a vacation, sought his wife's permission to travel to Europe with his brother Teddy and Florida senator George Smathers. Jackie agreed, and the three men set off for the south of France, where they chartered a forty-foot sloop complete with a captain and galley cook for a cruise of the Mediterranean. The captain of the vessel, in an interview with a French journalist, let it be known that his passengers had brought along a trio of young women. The story reached Jackie at Hammersmith Farm in Newport, where she had decided to stay during her husband's absence.

On August 23, while resting on the front lawn, she suffered a wave of nausea followed by severe abdominal cramps. By the time she reached her bedroom, she had begun to hemorrhage. An ambulance rushed her to Newport Hospital. In an effort to save the baby, doctors performed an emergency cesarean. The infant, an unnamed girl, died before drawing her first breath. It marked Jackie's second failed attempt to have a child. Her first, the year before, had terminated in a miscarriage.

When Jackie regained consciousness following the surgery, the first person she saw was Bobby Kennedy, who had rushed to the hospital to take his brother's place. It was Bobby who informed his sister-in-law of the infant's death. It was also Bobby who arranged for the baby's burial.

Not until August 26, when he reached Genoa, Italy, did JFK speak directly with his wife. His initial reaction to Jackie's request that he return as soon as possible was one of mild annoyance. George Smathers set him straight. "If you ever want to run for president," he told him, "you'd better haul ass back to your wife." Jack flew home the next day.

"That was the closest they ever came to a divorce," said Pierre Salinger, JFK's future White House press secretary. "When he got back, Jackie read him the riot act. Rumor had it that the old man, Joe Kennedy, offered Jackie a million dollars to stay with his son. As far as I know, no such transaction ever took place. Nevertheless, Jackie felt strongly that Jack should have been there for her. It wasn't the womanizing that bothered her. Her father and father-in-law were both ladies' men. She didn't like it, but it wasn't enough to drive them apart. What bothered her was all that family business—if you were with one Kennedy, you were with all of them. Jackie wasn't a team player. She resented Rose, Ethel, and several of Jack's sisters, accusing them of wanting to monopolize his time. 'What about me, what about my happiness?' she asked him."

After the stillbirth of her child, Jackie had little desire to return to Hickory Hill, which she had planned and decorated with a baby in mind. Its emptiness only reinforced her sadness and disappointment. To her sister, Lee, Jackie confessed that she suspected she was incapable of childbearing. Lee, who had just separated from her first husband, publishing heir Michael Canfield, invited her sister to visit her in New York. It was during this trip that Jackie decided to sell Hickory Hill to Bobby and Ethel Kennedy.

With five children and six more to come, Bobby and Ethel jumped at the opportunity to acquire the spacious McLean estate. After transferring the deed to his brother, JFK suggested to Jackie that they return to Georgetown. In May 1957 they purchased a redbrick, slant-set Federal town house at 3307 N Street. Built in 1812, it contained four bedrooms, a long, high-ceilinged drawing room with two fireplaces, a dining room, kitchen, and pantry. The back windows of the house looked out on a brick-paved backyard shaded by magnolia trees.

Jackie loved the house and soon brought in the high-priced New York decorator Mrs. Henry (Sister) Parrish to refurbish the interior. "No more moving around," Jackie told John White, a former colleague at the Washington *Times-Herald*. "I'm tired of living like a gypsy." White noted that the Kennedys lived like anything but gypsies. Among other amenities, including rare French antiques and tapestries, they had a residential staff of three: a maid, valet, and cook. "Jackie could set a mean dinner table," acknowledged White, "but she couldn't boil an egg."

In late May 1957 LeMoyne (Lem) Billings, JFK's great friend from their boarding school days at Choate, attended a roundtable discussion in Hyannis Port, where the main topic was whether or not to seek the presidency in 1960. The final decision depended in large measure on Jack's reelection in 1958 to the seat he presently occupied as senator. Billings recalled that while the others debated Jack's political future, Jackie sat apart mixing and matching various fabric patterns she hoped to use in her new Georgetown home. When Joe Kennedy noticed that his daughter-in-law wasn't participating, he grumbled, "Come on, Jackie. We're making some important decisions here, and we need your input." Reluctantly, she joined the group.

"By the end of the meeting," said Billings, "it was decided that not only would Jack pursue the presidency but Jackie would play an important role in the campaign. She agreed to do whatever she could to help."

That same month, Jackie discovered that she was again pregnant. Exhilarated by the prospect of giving birth to a healthy infant, she telephoned her father in New York to share the news. Her happiness was short-lived. In the course of their conversation, she learned that sixty-six-year-old

Black Jack Bouvier hadn't felt well in months. Her concerns were reinforced by a telephone call she received from her stepbrother Hugh Dudley (Yusha) Auchincloss III, whose Manhattan apartment was ten minutes from Black Jack's residential hotel. Yusha had dropped in on Black Jack. The once vibrant bon vivant looked drawn and had lost weight. He was in constant pain and could no longer hold down his food.

Jackie flew to New York to be with her father. While there, she conferred with his personal physician, who disclosed that Black Jack had liver cancer but had agreed to undergo chemotherapy. Jackie returned to Washington. On July 27, the eve of her twenty-eighth birthday, her father checked into Lenox Hill Hospital but assured his daughter that there was no cause for alarm. A week later he lapsed into a coma. Jack and Jackie flew into LaGuardia Airport the same day and took a taxi to Lenox Hill. They arrived an hour too late. Black Jack's last word, according to a nurse, had been "Jackie."

Saddened by her failure to see him again before his death, Jackie arranged her father's funeral and burial in the Roman Catholic cemetery at East Hampton, Long Island, where the Bouviers maintained a family plot. Back at 3307 N Street, she focused her attention on her pregnancy. A heavy smoker, she temporarily gave up cigarettes and started a high-protein diet recommended at that time for expectant mothers. She perused books on infant care and began a modified exercise program. Her obstetrician, Dr. John Walsh, affiliated with Lying in Hospital, the neonatal and pediatrics division of New York Hospital–Cornell Medical Center, devised a daily regimen that she followed to the letter.

On November 26, 1957—two days before Thanksgiving—Jackie settled into her Manhattan hospital room. Her pregnancy had been uneventful, but because of her previous cesarean, Dr. Walsh had no choice but to repeat the procedure. While JFK and Janet Auchincloss paced nervously in a nearby waiting room, Jackie gave birth on November 27 to a seven-pound, two-ounce baby girl. The infant, Caroline Bouvier Kennedy, bore the same first name as Jackie's sister, Lee, whose actual name was Caroline Lee. Both Caroline Kennedy and her aunt were named after Black Jack Bouvier's grandmother Caroline Ewing of Philadelphia, the spirit behind the creation of the New York Foundling hospital. The gesture represented Jackie Kennedy's final homage to her late father.

One of the first family friends to see Caroline was Lem Billings, who visited the hospital the day after Thanksgiving. "Because of the holidays," said Billings, "the maternity ward had only a skeleton staff on hand. As a result, Jack was running around playing nursemaid to Jackie. It was a far cry from his calloused reaction to her previous pregnancy. When I arrived, he led me to the nursery. There must have been a dozen babies in the window. 'Now, Lem,' he said, 'which one of those babies do you think is the cutest?' Not knowing what Caroline looked like, I pointed to somebody else's baby. Jack wouldn't speak to me for days."

JFK took great delight in the new addition to his family, pronouncing his daughter "fit as a fiddle and robust as a sumo wrestler." Jackie's mother noticed that whenever her son-in-law looked at Caroline, "he radiated with happiness." Kennedy family nurse Luella Hennessey arrived at the hospital a day after Caroline's birth and proceeded to instruct the forty-year-old father in the fine art of bottle feeding and diaper changing. "I can govern a state and maybe run the country," JFK later told his friend Charles (Chuck) Spalding, "but I can't seem to change a diaper."

While still in the hospital, Jackie hired a full-time English nanny, Maud Shaw, a short, stout, energetic woman in her mid-sixties with gray hair and a clipped British accent. Shaw's 1965 memoir, *White House Nanny*, characterized Jack and Jackie as typical parents, overly protective and concerned mainly with Caroline's health and eating habits. An earlier, unexpurgated draft of her memoir, more candid than the published version, appraised Jack and Jackie's parenting skills: "The moment Caroline whimpered or wet her diaper, they would turn the infant over to me. Mrs. Kennedy refused to breast-feed the baby as an alternative to the bottle. Senator Kennedy lacked patience. Shoving the bottle into Caroline's mouth, he would invariably look at me and say, 'This is your department, Miss Shaw, not mine. I'd rather you do it.' He would turn the baby over to me as if handing off a football."

On December 13, Caroline Kennedy, sixteen days old, wearing the same baptismal gown first worn by her great-grandfather James T. Lee, was anointed with holy water by Boston archbishop Richard Cushing at

New York's St. Patrick's Cathedral. Jackie's sister, Lee, the infant's god-mother, clad in mink, cradled Caroline in her arms during the christening ceremony, while her godfather, Bobby Kennedy, a somber expression on his face, looked on. Immediately following the event, Caroline sat for her first portrait and assumed what her father termed "the proper pose: she shut her eyes and fell asleep."

Maud Shaw joined the rest of the domestic staff at the Kennedy home in Georgetown. The household now included the original live-in team plus a part-time laundress and a Spanish-speaking maid, Providencia ("Provi") Paredes. Occupying a third-floor bedroom next to Caroline's nursery, Shaw soon noticed the bond that seemed to grow between the infant and her father. "He wasn't around very much," she wrote in the first draft of her memoir, "but whenever the senator did come home, he headed straight for the nursery. Caroline would coo and smile for him, which she did for nobody else, not even her mother. The two of them—father and daughter—appeared to communicate almost telepathically."

Back in the fold, Lem Billings also took note of their tender connection and the beneficial effect it had on his relationship with Jackie. "Jack adored the baby," he said. "He talked about her incessantly. And Jackie encouraged his participation in Caroline's life. Caroline helped stabilize Jack and Jackie's marriage, if only temporarily. Having the baby brought them closer together. It gave new meaning to the marriage and helped restore Jackie's self-image. The Kennedy women were all but expected to have children, and now that she had a child, Jackie could count herself among their select ranks.

"Just as pleased as Jack and Jackie by the birth of Caroline was Joe Kennedy, whose overriding interest had always been JFK's political career. 'Don't underestimate the importance of having a wife and kids if you want to become the first Catholic president,' he used to say to Jack. It looked good on paper. It rounded out JFK's qualifications, which included a Harvard diploma, wartime service as naval captain of PT-109, three terms in the House, membership in the U.S. Senate, and a Pulitzer Prize for *Profiles in Courage*. He could now add 'husband and father' to the list."

In March 1958, with JFK set to run again for the Senate, *Life* magazine asked him to agree to a cover story dealing with his family life, the article to include the first published photographs of his daughter. "I'm not going to allow Caroline to be used like some campaign mascot," said Jackie when he approached her with the offer. "I don't care how many votes it costs you."

Bobby Kennedy, currently chief counsel to Senator John L. McClellan's select committee on racketeering, attempted to convince Jackie that the article would put Jack over the top in the Massachusetts senatorial race. Ted Kennedy, having taken over for Bobby as JFK's campaign manager, likewise coaxed Jackie. "*Life*," he pointed out, "has the highest circulation of any magazine in America. It reaches millions of readers. You can't buy that kind of publicity." Jackie finally relented, but only when Joe Kennedy, a friend of Henry Luce, the publisher of *Life*, promised that if she consented to the article, Jack would take a break from campaigning to take a vacation with her in Paris that summer.

The April 21 cover of the magazine featured Jack and Jackie in the nursery at 3307 N Street, Caroline ensconced in her father's lap, staring at a stuffed toy in a corner of the room. The article itself included a photograph of Caroline playing peekaboo with her father and another of Caroline wistfully peering over her bassinet at both her parents. "I'm not home much," Kennedy is quoted as saying, "but when I am, Caroline seems to like me."

Despite Jackie's seeming indifference to certain aspects of early child care—like Jack, she couldn't stand to change the baby's diapers—Jackie did spend quality time with her daughter. Early that summer an inflatable wading pool was set up in the backyard, and every afternoon following Caroline's nap, mother and daughter splashed around together. Jacques Lowe, one of the few photographers whose presence the future First Lady welcomed, recalled that "Jackie always addressed Caroline as though speaking to an adult. There was none of that cloying baby talk, and she urged others to do the same. She read poems and stories to the infant, which I doubt Caroline understood at such a tender age, though she listened attentively and laughed at all the appropriate spots."

Lorraine Rowan Cooper and Evangeline (Vangie) Bruce, the wife of David K. E. Bruce, U.S. ambassador to England, France, and West Germany, would on occasion visit Jackie for high tea and conversation. A Georgetown neighbor of the Kennedys, Vangie remembered that Caroline and Maud Shaw sometimes joined them. "It seemed quite remarkable," she said. "Caroline would sit in her high chair and sip lukewarm tea mixed with milk out of a baby bottle. Instead of a pastry or finger sandwich, the nanny fed her a jar of Gerber baby food. She used a tiny silver spoon from Tiffany with her initials inscribed on the back of the handle. Every Georgetown baby had one."

Vangie Bruce recalled a visit she paid to Jackie in the late summer of 1958. "I happened to be in Washington," she said, "checking on our Georgetown residence, which we'd rented out for the year. Jackie phoned and asked me to come over. She seemed upset. Jack was stepping out on her, seeing other women, and she wanted to know how to handle the situation. I told her that David and I had what they call a European marriage. From time to time, there might be a short-lived involvement with somebody else. It didn't count for much. A lover isn't a spouse, and an affair isn't a marriage. The important thing is discretion. Nobody wants to be held up to public ridicule.

"Jackie understood the concept very well but felt embarrassed because Jack wasn't exercising discretion. He'd been using the hotel Carlyle in New York for his trysts. Friends of hers knew about it, and if they knew, everyone would know, including the press. I listened for a while. Finally I said, 'Jackie, why don't you campaign with Jack? He's running for reelection in Massachusetts. He'll welcome your participation. And that way you can keep an eye on him.'"

Jackie might have remembered the roundtable strategy session she'd attended at Hyannis Port the year before, when she agreed to campaign with Jack in the 1960 presidential race. There would be no presidential campaign for JFK if he didn't win big in Massachusetts. With this in mind—coupled with Vangie Bruce's advice—she sent Maud Shaw and Caroline to Newport to stay with her mother and stepfather. She then joined Jack on the campaign trail, crisscrossing Massachusetts from one end of the state to the other.

In most instances the public turned out in greater numbers for a peek at the candidate's wife than they did for the candidate. "Surprisingly," observed Jacques Lowe, "the crowds stood five deep on street corners whenever Jackie appeared. John F. Kennedy came from a wealthy family, but to the ordinary voter Jackie represented something greater. She was an American aristocrat, the closest thing we had in this country to the Queen of England. People were endlessly curious about her. She wasn't your run-of-the-mill politician's squaw. Even her voice, breathless and whispery, was different."

Thanks in large measure to his wife, John F. Kennedy won the 1958 senatorial race in Massachusetts by a landslide, thereby establishing himself as the Democratic Party's front-running hopeful for the top spot in the 1960 presidential contest.

It wasn't until January 20, 1960, that John F. Kennedy officially announced his run for the presidency. But long before that date, with Bobby Kennedy as national campaign manager, Joe Kennedy set the race in motion, purchasing a twelve-passenger, twin-engine Convair plane with a sitting area, sleeping quarters, dining nook, and galley fully stocked with New England clam chowder, French wines, and Cuban cigars. An experienced pilot and copilot were hired to fly the plane, which JFK named the *Caroline.*

During most of 1959, the presidential aspirant, often accompanied by his wife, logged thousands of miles in all kinds of weather on what must have seemed an endless voyage. In what was surely a demonstration of utter devotion, Jackie showed herself to be as courageous and vigorous as her husband. Politics came to play so vital a role in the Kennedy household during this period that Caroline's first spoken words, her father jokingly claimed, were "New Hampshire," "Wisconsin," and "West Virginia." To this Jackie added: "I'm sorry so few states have primaries, or we would have a daughter with the greatest vocabulary of any toddler in the country."

Jackie's dedication to the cause was bolstered by Joe Kennedy, who confided in his daughter-in-law that he had set aside $30 million of his own money to help ensure his son's victory. Micromanaging the fiscal end of the campaign from "the dugout," his outdoor poolside "office" in Palm Beach, the family patriarch took Jackie under his wing. "He became her mentor," said Pierre Salinger. "He taught her the ropes. He told her how important it was to portray the family as well-to-do but not prodigiously wealthy, which is why he banned reporters and photographers from his Florida estate. He felt it was too opulent for public consumption. In the same vein, he kept family retainers out of view. No pictures of Maud Shaw ever appeared in the press. He wanted to convey the impression that Jack and Jackie were raising their daughter themselves. In a country where the average coal miner earned twenty-five dollars a week, it wouldn't do to have it known that Caroline's nanny made sixteen times that figure."

In August 1959 Jack and Jackie took Caroline to the Kennedy compound in Hyannis Port on an all too brief five-day family vacation. With Jackie's consent, a photographer from *Look* and another from *The Saturday Evening Post* snapped pictures of JFK and Caroline playing in the sand and strolling along the beach at sunset. Additional photographs of Caroline in the same magazines showed her in a variety of poses: hugging her mother, holding a stuffed animal, gathering flowers in a field. Joe Kennedy rewarded Jackie for allowing Caroline to be photographed by showering her with gifts, including (appropriately enough) a $3,000 Leica camera.

Jackie needed little prodding. She not only allowed the photographers to take pictures of Caroline—a partial reversal of her former policy—she also became her husband's number one public defender. The journalist Peter Lisagor never forgot her reaction following his grilling of JFK on a segment of *Face the Nation*. "When it was over," he said, "Mrs. Kennedy looked at me as though I'd crawled out of some hole and had struck with fangs and poison at the heel of her husband." Jackie berated Lisagor for asking Jack such "absolutely horrible questions." When historian James MacGregor Burns wrote an early biography of JFK, he made the mistake of sending Jackie a copy of the manuscript for her editorial comments. She read it, then responded with a long and angry letter criticizing Burns for his "political bias," recommending that he not publish the biography until after the 1960 election.

"Now that I'm on the stump with Jack, I might as well make a few concessions," Jackie wrote to Vangie Bruce in February 1960. Despite her declaration and newfound devotion to the campaign, she hated the idea of being separated from Caroline. "Whenever we leave," she told Maud Shaw, "I get this awful feeling that Caroline must think it's because we don't want to be with her." Jackie asked the nanny to reassure Caroline as often as possible that her mommy and daddy loved her very much.

Then, in mid-May 1960, Jackie learned that she was again pregnant and could expect to have the baby in December. Cutting back on her campaign travels, she nevertheless remained involved, sponsoring a series of weekly at-home luncheons for women in politics. She joined forces with her mother to throw a $50-per-person fund-raiser at Merrywood, bringing Caroline along to meet the guests. Jackie, Ethel, and Joan Kennedy (Teddy's wife) coordinated efforts to conduct an ongoing national telephone campaign. She and Lady Bird Johnson—wife of Texas senator Lyndon Johnson—accompanied each other to several ladies' club luncheons in New York, Washington, and Boston. On the few scattered occasions that Jack came home for a visit, she brought Caroline along to the airport, well aware that it provided the press with an excellent photo opportunity. The black-and-white image of a mother and her young daughter embracing the weary warrior became a sure vote-getter. The press reported that whenever the candidate clapped his hands twice, Caroline raced to him and jumped into his arms. The press further reported that JFK had a nickname for Caroline; he called her "Buttons."

One of Jack's home visits coincided with *Newsweek*'s publication of a major cover story on the candidate. Noticing the magazine on a hallway table, Caroline grabbed it and rushed off in search of her father. She found him in an upstairs bathroom lounging in the tub. "Daddy!" she squealed, pointing a tiny finger at his picture on the front cover of the periodical. JFK looked up just as she tossed the magazine into the tub. Kennedy watched helplessly as it began to sink beneath the water's surface.

Caroline's playful antics enchanted JFK's ever-expanding voter base. Encouraged by her mother, she memorized two Edna St. Vincent Millay poems, "First Fig" and "Second Fig," and surprised her father one evening by reciting them for him. She interrupted a JFK press conference in Palm Beach by clomping loudly into the room in her pajamas and a pair of her mother's high heels, causing the press corps to burst into laughter. Using Jackie's favorite shade of lipstick, she drew what bore a vague resemblance to a horse on her parents' bedroom wall.

For the most part, Caroline displayed a levelheadedness rarely found in someone so young. A trifle remote and a bit shy at times, she was also remarkably unspoiled. "Caroline wasn't like other children of privilege," wrote Maud Shaw. "She wasn't at all like her Kennedy cousins. Not once in my presence did she ever throw a temper tantrum. You could reason with her. Her even temperament and inner calm made her a great favorite of Rose Kennedy's, whose reputation as a strict disciplinarian was well deserved. And even though Rose never particularly liked Jacqueline Kennedy, she gave her daughter-in-law high marks for the job she did with Caroline."

In July 1960, while John F. Kennedy attended the Democratic National Convention in Los Angeles, Jackie and Caroline remained behind at Hyannis Port, content to watch the proceedings on television. What the daily broadcasts didn't discuss or reveal were Kennedy's after-hour meanderings, his voracious sexual appetite for women outside the domain of marriage. It seemed that the closer he came to the presidency, the more frenetic became his random search for such encounters.

The FBI files on JFK at this time make reference to "a pair of stewardesses the subject has been seeing in Los Angeles," as well as such Hollywood sirens as Jean Simmons, Larraine Day, and Angie Dickinson. Also on the Bureau's list was Judith Campbell (Exner), a Las Vegas showgirl and girlfriend of Mafia crime boss Sam Giancana; in addition to Marilyn Monroe, whom Kennedy had met through his sister Pat and her husband, actor Peter Lawford. A lifelong Democrat, she contributed $25,000 to JFK's campaign fund. Abundantly documented in countless books and articles, the future president's affair with Monroe culminated in her slithering rendition of "Happy Birthday to You" in his honor at New York's Madison Square Garden and her apparent suicide from an overdose of sleeping pills in August 1962.

Seemingly impervious to the perils of exposure, JFK carried on with reckless abandon. "It was a learned trait," said Langdon Marvin. "He was the son of a man who thought nothing of bringing his mistresses home to the dinner table, Gloria Swanson among them." Truman Capote put it in more graphic terms. Over lunch one day with film producer Lester Persky, he said, "Those Kennedy men are like dogs. They have to stop and piss on every fire hydrant."

The gossip surrounding JFK's extracurricular activities at the convention reached Jackie at Hyannis Port. She walked around in a daze, doing her best to hide her emotions, especially in front of Caroline. If she wasn't yet cynical about the institution of marriage, she soon would be. With one child in the picture and another on the way, she had probably allowed herself to believe that Jack would have changed. He hadn't.

There was concern among several of JFK's advisers that Kennedy's womanizing, public as it was, would be used by the Republicans should he become the Democratic Party's presidential candidate. Ken O'Donnell, JFK's future White House chief of staff, warned his boss of the possible repercussions. "I told him," said O'Donnell, "that nobody would elect for president a man known to be cheating on his wife and humiliating his family. He wasn't the least bit concerned."

Aside from the selection of Lyndon Johnson as his running mate, John F. Kennedy's first-ballot victory on July 13, 1960, afforded few surprises. Bobby Kennedy had arrived in Los Angeles a week early and established a command post in a four-room suite at the Biltmore Hotel. Joe and Rose Kennedy moved into the former Marion Davies estate in Santa Monica, given to her by her longtime lover William Randolph Hearst. Joe installed a battery of telephones in the house but otherwise maintained a low profile, sending Rose to the convention center in his stead. As for JFK, he reserved his own suite at the Biltmore, adding to it by taking a short-term lease on actor Jack Haley's penthouse apartment on North Rossmore, a ten-minute drive from the convention site. It was there that he entertained his various female friends.

Jackie's sister, Lee, attended the convention with Stas Radziwill, the roly-poly, mustachioed, Polish-born nobleman she had married in March 1959. Twenty years Lee's senior, Stas lived in London, where he owned a real estate firm. Like other members of the extended family, the Radziwills were recruited to campaign for Jack. They gave speeches in a number of cities, including Boston, San Francisco, and Milwaukee. Lee's other function was to keep Jackie apprised of Jack's nonpolitical activities. In so doing, she spared her sister few details.

Jackie and Caroline watched in Hyannis Port as the state of Wyoming cast the deciding vote, establishing John F. Kennedy as his party's candidate and placing him on a collision course with Vice President Richard M. Nixon, soon to be named the Republican Party's choice for president. After telephoning his father, Jack called his wife and daughter. "We won!" he announced. "I know," said Jackie. "Caroline and I watched it on television." Not wanting to diminish JFK's first-ballot victory, Jackie never mentioned the thought uppermost on her mind—her husband's philandering. She preferred to save the thought for another day.

The following morning, July 14, against the strenuous objections of Bobby Kennedy and a number of JFK advisers, Jack offered Lyndon Johnson the vice-presidential slot on the ticket. At Hyannis Port, a horde of photographers and reporters appeared on Jackie's doorstep, clamoring for an interview. While Caroline scampered about on the front lawn, her mother informed the press that because of her pregnancy she would be playing a lesser role in what remained of the campaign. Still, she said, she planned on doing her share. "I believe," she remarked, "I should be with Jack when he's engaged in such a monumental struggle."

Jackie adjusted her schedule to include what she considered only the most essential events. She made personal appearances with Jack in Maine, Rhode Island, and Delaware. She gave newspaper and magazine interviews. On September 20 she joined JFK for a sixty-minute CBS-TV interview conducted in their Georgetown home by Charles Collingwood. One of the high points of the prime-time program was a brief appearance by Caroline Kennedy. Dressed in a fluffy pink frock and white slippers, she made her national television debut, revealing to the host and an audience of fifty million Americans that her favorite bedtime story was *Goldilocks and the Three Bears*. Asked why her daughter preferred *Goldilocks* to all other fairy tales, Jackie replied, "It's the longest story in her book, Charles, so when we read it to her she gets to stay up later."

A few days after the Collingwood broadcast, Jackie received a visit from journalist Joe Alsop, a close friend to JFK. Alsop found Jackie in an agitated mood, worried not only about her pregnancy but about the recent onslaught of publicity. She railed against the press for revealing that she had bought her maternity wardrobe at Bloomingdale's and had paid $34.95 for a new silk tea dress off the rack at Lord & Taylor.

"I can't imagine what it'll be like if Jack beats Nixon, and we have to move into the White House," she said, adding that she was appalled at some of the personal questions posed by reporters. The press photographers were no better. "I permitted a few of them to take pictures of Caroline at the airport and when we visited Hyannis Port, but it's never enough for them," she said. "They chase the poor child around from morning to night, wanting to make her into some kind of ghastly little Shirley Temple clone."

Alsop reminded Jackie that she'd once been a journalist herself and ought to have more understanding.

"Joe," said Jackie, "I worked as an inquiring photographer. I didn't report the news. I didn't go around prying into people's private lives. Even now, I write an occasional piece on what it's like to be a candidate's wife. But when I do, I don't give away any state secrets."

Alsop was on the verge of launching into a lengthy diatribe on Jackie's responsibilities as the candidate's wife when Caroline meandered into the room, dragging a large Raggedy Ann doll behind her. Sensing Alsop's intentions, Jackie pulled her daughter into her lap. "Mr. Alsop was just leaving, sweetheart," she said. "You and I can play with Raggedy Ann."

Whatever the extent of her commitment to the campaign, Jackie spent as much time as possible with Caroline. When she ran errands in the neighborhood, she usually had her daughter in tow along with Maud Shaw to push the stroller. They started at Scheele's, a small Georgetown market with a large food inventory. The proprietor of the store often slipped the child a slice of salami or roast beef while Jackie placed the day's order. From Scheele's they made their way to P Street and Morgan's Pharmacy with its gleaming marble-top soda fountain, where they would each have a glass of freshly squeezed orange juice. Then, it was on to Stambuck's Saddle Shop for a look at the latest in riding gear, fashions, and accessories. Stambuck's was Jack Kennedy's least favorite Georgetown store, because it was there that Jackie spent the most amount of money.

JFK's advisers soon became convinced that New York, with its large electoral vote, could be pivotal in the election. Bobby Kennedy attempted to pressure Jackie into agreeing to put in an appearance. Dr. Walsh advised against it, insisting that it would be strenuous and could jeopardize her pregnancy. "If I don't go, and Jack loses," she told her obstetrician, "I'll never forgive myself."

She went. Once again putting her facility with languages to good use, she addressed immigrant audiences. She spoke Spanish in Spanish Harlem, Italian in Little Italy, French in a Haitian neighborhood in Brooklyn. She joined Jack in a ticker tape parade through a vast ocean of people in the financial district and later accompanied him to a campaign luncheon at the Waldorf-Astoria. Seated at a separate table from JFK, she leaned over and told her good friend, artist Bill Walton, a few chairs away, that this was the closest she'd come in months to dining with her husband.

The climax of the campaign, particularly because it had evolved into such a close contest, were the four nationally televised one-hour debates between JFK and Nixon in September and October 1960. In conjunction with the debates, Jackie hosted a series of parties attended by national committeewomen and their husbands and the state chairmen and cochairmen of Citizens for Kennedy-Johnson, as well as friends, relatives, and members of the press. In mid-October actor Henry Fonda interviewed Jack and Jackie for NBC-TV, the couple trotting out their "cutesy" daughter (Fonda's word) for a fleeting appearance.

On November 8, Election Day, Jack and Jacqueline (whose pregnancy had caused her to vote by absentee ballot) went together to the polling section at the West End Library in Boston. As they left the polls, a reporter asked her what she thought of her husband's chances. "It will be close," she predicted, "but Jack will certainly defeat Milhous." Stunned by his wife's colloquial use of Nixon's middle name, Jack nevertheless managed a broad smile. The photograph that ran the following day on the front page of *The Boston Globe* showed the couple walking hand in hand to a waiting car.

Jackie described the period between the closing of the polls and the moment of victory as "the longest night in history." She and Jack, Ben and Tony Bradlee, and Bill Walton had a quiet dinner at home in Hyannis Port. After dinner they settled in front of the television to watch the returns come in. They were joined by Ted Sorensen, presidential speechwriter and White House special counsel under JFK, and Caroline, who'd been given permission by her parents to stay up. Next door at Bobby's house, JFK's aides and advisers gathered reports by telephone from campaign leaders in states where the polls hadn't yet closed.

At 10:30 p.m., when the first returns indicated a substantial lead for Kennedy, Jackie whispered, "Oh, Bunny, you're president now."

Her pronouncement came too soon. Within an hour, Nixon had pulled even and then slightly ahead. Caroline went to bed at 11:30, and Jackie followed thirty minutes later. JFK waited until 3:30 a.m. before turning in. At that hour, the election was still undecided. But at 5:45 that morning, the Secret Service moved to establish security and surround the Hyannis Port house and compound.

Jackie woke up at 6:30 a.m., heard the news—Kennedy had won by less than 115,000 popular votes (49.7 percent) out of the nearly 70 million cast—and went to rouse Maud Shaw and Caroline. At 7:00 a.m., prompted by her mother, Caroline marched to her father's bed, poked him on the shoulder, received a hug and a kiss, and, her eyes sparkling with delight, said, "Good morning, Mr. President."

Chapter 4

———◆———

1600 PENNSYLVANIA AVENUE

JACQUELINE KENNEDY HAD come to think of the N Street house in Georgetown as a final destination. "This is it!" she repeatedly informed friends. "This is where I'll raise my family." Of course, she'd offered the same commentary on moving into Hickory Hill. But 3307 N Street was different. Too often she and Jack had moved from place to place. It had given their marriage, already laden with problems, a kind of transitory quality, a sense of "nothing is permanent." "It sometimes has the feeling," she told her friend Joan Braden, "of a one-night stand."

Moving again, even into so grand a setting as the White House, brought back some unpleasant memories for Jackie. Leaving the sanctity of Georgetown for the uncertainty of the executive mansion created new trepidations. A few days after the election, Jackie overheard a conversation between her husband and a member of the president-elect's Secret Service detail. Jack asked the agent how difficult it would be for "somebody with a grudge" to "take out" a president. "Well," the agent responded, "there are always loopholes in the system. We're pretty good at what we do, but if somebody out there is determined enough to do it, he'll do it—or at least he'll try."

A week later, Hearst newspaper columnist Igor Cassini, a trusted friend of the Kennedys, visited Jackie at Hyannis Port. "It was a crisp day, but the sun felt warm," recalled Cassini. "Jackie and I sat on the lawn talking, while little Caroline ran around chasing squirrels or some such thing. Jackie seemed preoccupied with her family's safety. 'How do you protect the president against the danger of assassination?' she asked. 'All it takes is one lunatic with a loaded gun.' I assured her that the Secret Service used the most sophisticated law enforcement methods and strategies and that she had nothing to fear. Looking back, in light of everything that happened, I realize how empty my words must have sounded to her."

Because of the advanced state of her pregnancy, Jackie decided to celebrate Caroline's third birthday a week early. On November 20, thirty children and twenty adults piled into the Georgetown house to watch the antics of a pair of clowns hired by Jackie for the afternoon. Evelyn Lincoln, JFK's personal assistant both in the Senate and the White House, noticed that although Caroline "appeared to be happy," there was a "hint" of distress, the possible result of her apprehension over the expected arrival of a new member of the family.

On November 25, 1960, with the press camped outside their front door, Jack, Jackie, and Caroline ate their Thanksgiving meal together. After dinner, Kennedy prepared to leave for the airport, where the *Caroline* waited to take him and his aides to Palm Beach for discussions on the transition process and the challenging task of appointing a new presidential cabinet. Jack had flown three-quarters of the way to Florida when an urgent message reached the pilot. Jacqueline Kennedy had gone into early labor and had been whisked by ambulance to Georgetown University Hospital, where she had arranged to have the baby.

At the airport in West Palm Beach, JFK learned his wife was about to undergo an emergency cesarean operation. He immediately boarded the press plane that had accompanied the *Caroline* and made the return flight to Washington. They were still airborne when news crackled through that Dr. Walsh had delivered Jackie of a two-week premature baby boy, John Fitzgerald Kennedy Jr., slightly underweight at six pounds, three ounces, and in need of incubation, but otherwise active and in satisfactory health.

On regaining consciousness, Jackie asked to see the newborn baby. As she was being wheeled to the nursery, a news photographer burst from a storage closet in the hospital corridor and aimed his camera at her. When Jackie saw him, she screamed out, and two Secret Service agents came running. Pouncing on the intruder, they confiscated his camera and exposed the film. At Jackie's request, they released the photographer.

"If you arrest him," she said, "it will only create more unwanted publicity."

Another episode took place three days later, on Sunday, November 28, the potential seriousness of which alarmed even the president-elect. Thomas L. Scudder, then a lieutenant with the seventh precinct of the Washington, D.C., Police Department, was in charge of police security during Jackie's hospitalization.

"That Sunday we posted several policemen in and around Georgetown University Hospital," said Scudder, "but it was a nurse who first spotted this fellow in his late teens or early twenties roaming around on a grassy area under Jackie's window. Her room was on the fifth floor, and her window was unlocked but not open.

"The nurse summoned the police, and a patrol car intercepted him. He was carrying a package containing five sticks of dynamite. When I got there, the package was on the ground, and the guy had been handcuffed and placed in the back of the patrol car.

"I radioed the army bomb squad, and after their people carted off the explosives, I contacted Deputy George Waldrodt, acting chief of police. What did they want me to do with the perpetrator? Waldrodt said he'd get back to me. He called a few minutes later. 'Send him downtown,' he replied. 'We'll want to interrogate him. Then send me a report and forget it ever happened. Don't make any carbons, don't make any copies, don't mention it—now or ever.'

"They swept it up the line and under the rug. They never booked the guy, because that would have created all sorts of paperwork, and that's the last thing they wanted. My guess is that somebody upstairs talked it over with Secret Service, Secret Service discussed it with the president-elect, and the president-elect said something like 'I don't want any unnecessary noise. It'll only frighten Jackie.' And that was the end of it."

Slowly, Jackie regained her strength. For the first six days, she was too exhausted to leave her bed for more than a few minutes and began to recover only when they removed the baby from the oxygen-fed incubator and moved him into her room. JFK visited the hospital three times a day and after the second day began bringing Caroline along. Her blond hair in pigtails, wearing a pair of white tennis sneakers and clutching a small bouquet of black-eyed Susans, she saw her baby brother for the first time on November 27, while he was still in the incubator. To make her feel important so she wouldn't think the new baby was displacing her in any way, JFK told Caroline that John Jr. was her birthday present. "For the longest time, Caroline thought that he belonged to her," Maud Shaw wrote in the first draft of her memoir, "and frequently referred to him as 'my baby.' Later she called him 'my kissing baby.'"

Flowers, baby clothes, and presents from well-wishers around the country poured into the hospital in such abundance that they had to be picked up daily and distributed to other Washington hospitals and charity organizations. When a nurse asked Jackie what she wanted to do with all the cards she'd received in recognition of the new baby, she responded, "Give them to my husband. I wouldn't know what to do with them."

Joe Kennedy had told Jack that as First Lady, Jackie would need her own fashion designer, and to this end Joe sent Igor Cassini's brother, Oleg Cassini, to see her in the hospital. Oleg arrived with a portfolio of fashion suggestions. "What I need from you," she told her visitor, "is protection from the press. I don't want to read about my clothes before I wear them. I don't want to see a lot of fat little old ladies hopping around in my originals. The press will print anything. I just read that I use dye in my hair because it's such a mousy gray. I trust you understand my concern." Cassini assured her that when it came to her wardrobe, he would exercise complete discretion. He kept his promise, and Jackie kept him as her chief designer, supplementing her fashion needs by turning to the leading European couture houses, such as Dior and Givenchy.

On December 2 Jack Kennedy returned to Palm Beach with Caroline in tow, while Jackie, still at Georgetown University Hospital, caught up with a week's backlog of newspapers. When she read in *The Washington Post* that she'd been taken to the hospital only after she'd begun "to hemorrhage," she placed a call to Phil Graham—whose wife, Katharine, owned the newspaper—and voiced her objection to the use of so clinical a phrase. Graham told his wife that the future First Lady was beginning to sound too aristocratic for her own good. Katharine, who had four children of her own, concurred but ordered the *Post* to send Jackie a rare orchid plant accompanied by a letter of apology. Jackie offered the plant to one of her nurses.

Two days later Jackie received a letter from Eleanor Roosevelt congratulating her on the arrival of her new son. The same letter commented on some of the privileges Jackie would enjoy as First Lady, but then made note of several of the difficulties she would face, especially bringing up children in the White House. "I think on the whole," wrote the former First Lady, "life is rather difficult for both the child and the parents in the 'fish bowl' that lies before you."

JFK returned to Washington on December 8 to attend John Jr.'s baptism in the small chapel at Georgetown University Hospital. As he, Jackie, Caroline, and three Secret Service operatives passed through the hospital corridors on their way to the chapel, they were waylaid by a dozen press photographers. "Isn't he the most beautiful baby boy you've ever seen?" Jack said to them, pointing to the small bundle in his wife's arms. John Jr. wore the same christening gown that his father had worn at his baptism back in 1917, forty-three years earlier.

Later that day Jackie kept an appointment with Mamie Eisenhower for the traditional housekeeping briefing of the incoming mistress of the White House. One of her Secret Service agents had phoned ahead and asked that the White House have a wheelchair waiting for Mrs. Kennedy, as she was still subject to spells of dizziness and exhaustion. Envisioning herself having to push her successor around the mansion, Mrs. Eisenhower instructed her staff to keep the wheelchair out of sight in a closet, and make it available only if asked.

Jackie didn't ask. She felt ill-at-ease in the presence of her less-than-gracious hostess. When she left, she looked not only weary but upset. She informed Letitia (Tish) Baldrige, her White House social secretary (who, after an altercation with Jackie, was replaced by Nancy Tuckerman), that the place looked "like an emporium that had been decorated by a wholesale furniture store during a January clearance." The private living quarters were in even worse shape than the official rooms—stains on the carpets, falling plaster, fingerprints on the doors, peeling wallpaper, filthy drapes. The floorboards were covered with cleat marks—Dwight Eisenhower evidently wore his golf shoes indoors as well as out. Another peculiarity was the two identical television sets that sat side by side in a corridor just outside the residential dining room. Jackie learned that Dwight and Mamie liked to watch different TV programs while eating dinner together seated in adjoining chairs in front of their respective sets. The future First Lady decided on the spot that her pet project in the White House would be a sweeping renovation of both wings of the mansion, replacing the existing contemporary collection of furniture and objets d'art with authentic furnishings and period pieces she planned to acquire predominantly on the basis of donations and privately contributed funds, as well as from a large selection of historical holdings locked away in the White House basement.

The same day she visited the White House, Jackie took her children—John Jr. and three-year-old Caroline—to the Kennedy estate in Palm Beach, determined to remain in seclusion until the January inauguration. White House chief usher J. B. West had supplied her with albums of elaborately annotated photographs of many of the executive mansion's 132 rooms, which she intended to study and analyze until she became familiar with every detail. Over the next few weeks, she hoped to prepare mentally and physically for the arduous days that lay ahead.

The peace of mind that Jackie sought in Palm Beach once again eluded her. For one thing, she discovered that Jack had rekindled his romance with an old flame: Florence (Flo) Pritchett, the wife of Earl E. T. Smith, the former U.S. ambassador to Cuba, whose Palm Beach villa stood next door to the Kennedy estate. "Before Jackie entered his life," said Langdon Marvin, "Jack had wanted to marry Flo. She had everything he ever wanted in a woman, except that she'd been married and divorced once before, and Joe Kennedy wouldn't consider it as a possibility for his son. In those days, marrying a divorced woman, especially for a Catholic presidential candidate, would have been an act of political suicide."

Reconciled to the situation, JFK continued to see Flo from time to time and once again took up with her during Jackie's stay at Georgetown

University Hospital. Ironically, Earl Smith, some twenty-five years Flo's senior, had romanced Jackie's mother, Janet Auchincloss, during the last days of her marriage to Black Jack Bouvier. Learning of Jack's latest fling with Flo, Jackie called Evangeline Bruce from Palm Beach and said, "I can't seem to rid myself of the Earl Smiths—it's enough to give a person an inferiority complex." She had earlier, according to Kennedy family biographer Sally Bedell Smith, consulted with one of her physicians and asked what he suggested she do to "spice up" her sexual relationship with her husband. By way of response, the doctor counseled his patient to engage in more foreplay and to encourage her husband to do the same. Presumably, having followed the doctor's recommendation, Jackie learned that while "more foreplay" might have been a stimulant, it was by no means a deterrent.

While still in Palm Beach, Jackie began to suspect her husband of yet another indiscretion, this one with Pamela Turnure, a twenty-two-year-old Georgetown debutante whose liaison with the future president would, like so many others, come to the attention of the FBI. Jackie's suspicions were further aroused when Jack suggested that Pamela be retained as Jackie's White House press secretary.

When Jackie asked why she needed her own press secretary, JFK responded, "Pierre Salinger can't handle everything by himself—there's too much for one person to do." Initially surprised that Jackie had agreed to the arrangement, Salinger concluded that the First Lady "either had so little regard for Pamela that she didn't care, or more likely felt she could better control the situation if she hired her."

On January 20, 1961, with the dome of the Capitol glowing in the sunlight, a blanket of snow covering the ground, Jackie by his side, and a legion of VIPs in top hats and overcoats looking on, John F. Kennedy took the oath of office to become the thirty-fifth president of the United States. The ceremony, more coronation than inauguration, captured the eye of the American public. What the nation saw on television that bright, shining day was a finely wrought, expertly directed study in presidential showmanship. No one realized that JFK wore long underwear beneath his dark suit so he could take off his topcoat and appear more manly and vigorous, or that he had put on a touch of makeup, or that Dr. Max Jacobson, a New York physician popularly known as "Dr. Feelgood," had shot him up with a syringe of methamphetamines so that his deep Palm Beach tan looked even deeper. No one was aware that Cardinal Richard Cushing slowed his invocation because he spotted a trail of smoke rising from beneath the podium and feared the presence of a bomb meant for Kennedy. No one knew that Jackie Kennedy had helped her husband fashion his inaugural address out of a sheaf of first-draft notes written by Ted Sorensen, or that she had listened to him rehearse the speech dozens of times while they were in Florida. Nor did anyone know that it had been her idea to invite the elderly American poet Robert Frost to read one of his poems at the ceremony, lending it the cultural veneer that would typify Kennedy's days in office.

The inaugural address, in many ways the most stirring and memorable speech JFK would ever deliver, signaled the start of a new age. "Let the word go forth from this time and place," Kennedy intoned, "to friend and foe alike, that the torch has been passed to a new generation of Americans—born in this century, tempered by war, disciplined by a hard and bitter peace, proud of our ancient heritage." Future presidents Richard Nixon, Ronald Reagan, Bill Clinton, and George W. Bush would borrow and steal phrases and lines from Kennedy's address in their inaugural speeches.

More important than Kennedy's words were his mode of presentation, his idealism, and his conviction that he could somehow make the world a better place in which to live. Indeed, America finally had its dream First Family, even if the dream was nine-tenths illusion, a fantasy concocted partially after the fact by Jacqueline Kennedy's designation of the term "Camelot"—a magic moment in time—to define the thousand days of the Kennedy administration.

At the core of the myth were the Kennedy children, Caroline and John-John (as he became known in the press), the youngest occupants of the White House since Grover Cleveland's three offspring roamed the selfsame corridors nearly seventy years before. Remaining behind in Palm Beach until February 4, when preliminary work on the White House living quarters neared completion, Caroline and John, accompanied by Maud Shaw, arrived at Washington National Airport, where they were picked up by their parents and placed in a limousine. Having suffered a brief but worrisome inflammation of the outer membrane of his lungs, a not-uncommon condition among premature babies, John arrived bundled up in a gray army surplus blanket. Too young to appreciate the significance of the moment, he dozed in a portable bassinet as the limo, flanked by police cars and motorcycles, approached 1600 Pennsylvania Avenue. Caroline, on the other hand, couldn't have been more excited. Clasping her father's hand in the backseat, she squealed with delight as they pulled up to the front entrance. "It's so big," she said of the White House. "It looks like a castle." Pierre Salinger fed the throwaway line to a reporter, and a day later it ran in *The Washington Post.*

For all Jackie's efforts to limit their exposure, the children rapidly became (along with their mother) the Kennedy administration's feature attraction. The media were so starved for fresh tidbits on Caroline and John Jr. that one *Chicago Tribune* editor barked at his Washington correspondent, "Never mind the news on Laos. What have Caroline and John-John done lately?"

Playful and unselfconscious, young Caroline provided the press with an unending stream of titillating news items. When a reporter for the *St. Louis Post-Dispatch* questioned her as to the president's whereabouts, she responded, "He's upstairs with his shoes and socks off, doing nothing." Asked about her mother, Caroline said, "She's upstairs in her bathrobe, also doing nothing." At night, when she should have been sleeping, Caroline frequently tiptoed down the stairs to spy on her parents' White House party guests. One evening during a reception for high-ranking members of the State Department, she sat at the bottom of the staircase and listened to the Marine Corps Band strike up "Hail to the Chief," followed by a medley of Broadway show tunes. Catching the eye of the Marine Band conductor through the balusters, she waved at him. He reciprocated by leading the band through a rendition of "Old MacDonald Had a Farm." Caroline began to clap along to the music. When Jackie heard her daughter, she brought the pajama-clad child into the room and introduced her one by one to every guest. Thereafter, whenever the Marine Band encountered Caroline, they played "Old MacDonald Had a Farm."

Another day, dressed in a white winter coat, white leggings, and white wool mittens, the president's daughter spotted a snowman that Secret Service agents had built for her on the expansive White House lawn. The snowman had button eyes, a carrot for a nose, and a Panama hat on top of its head. Running over to the snowman, Caroline pointed at the figure. "Frosty doesn't need a hat," she admonished the agent who'd placed it there. "He needs a warm jacket and a pair of mittens. That's what Mommy makes me wear."

Pierre Salinger remembered that Caroline often accompanied her father to the Oval Office in the morning. In the late afternoon, Maud Shaw would bring her back for a second visit. Perched on her little tricycle, she pedaled into Evelyn Lincoln's office, grabbed a handful of rock candy from a dish on Evelyn's desk, then plopped herself down in front of Evelyn's typewriter. Banging away at the keys, she would write imaginary letters to imaginary friends. "The only problem," said Salinger, "is that the typewriter couldn't stand up to all that punishment, and more than once we had to call in a repairman. Evelyn eventually located an inexpensive secondhand machine in a typewriter shop and set it up for Caroline on a small table next to her desk. After a while, the child learned to type her own name. This excited her to no end. She would rip the paper out of the machine, scamper into the Oval Office and show it to her father. Next she learned to type her brother's name. She would write 'Caroline and John,' then draw a crayon picture of the White House underneath and bring it back to her mother."

Caroline received almost as much fan mail as the First Lady. In a jocular vein, Pierre Salinger told JFK that he ought to consider hiring a private secretary just for Caroline. "Jackie will never approve," Jack replied in his best deadpan, as if the idea actually merited consideration.

Pierre Salinger was present the day that Caroline raced into the president's office, took hold of her father's leg, and implored him to give her a piggyback ride. JFK hoisted the child onto his shoulders and trotted around the room with her. "She was laughing and chattering the whole way," said Salinger. "But it was evident from his facial expression that the president felt pain. He wore a back brace, a kind of corset for his ailing back, but it didn't seem to help much. That was the last time I ever saw him tote Caroline around like that."

Caroline's White House bedroom, which Jacqueline decorated with the help of her sister, Lee, had pink walls, white moldings, and frilly white curtains at the windows. It contained a canopy bed with rosebud linens and matching draperies, a wooden rocking horse, a bed for Caroline's toy poodle, a birdcage for her canary, bookshelves, and the child's favorite dolls and stuffed animals. A Grandma Moses painting and a selection of brightly colored nursery rhyme posters and prints adorned the walls. Her brother's room, adjacent to hers, had been painted white and accented in pale blue trim. It contained a crib and playpen, changing table, mobiles, and toy soldiers. A hot plate in the corner of the room was used to heat up the baby's formula. Both children had their own bathroom. Maud Shaw's sleeping quarters were located across the hall, well within earshot. The ensemble of rooms sat on the second floor, directly over the executive mansion's grand entranceway.

"Caroline adored her baby brother," wrote Maud Shaw. "She used to help me change his diaper. When he cried, she hovered over him like a mother hen. She liked to comb his long, thick locks. She encouraged him to eat his cereal. 'Be a good boy and finish your food,' she used to tell him. When he was little, he had difficulty pronouncing his sister's name—he called her 'Cannon.'"

Caroline regularly telephoned her grandfather Kennedy in Palm Beach and gave him updates on John's activities. This continued even after December 19, 1961, when at age seventy-three, Joe Kennedy suffered a crippling stroke that left him a shadow of his former self. He could no longer speak. The only word he could say—and he said it over and over—was "No!" To her credit, Caroline persevered. She spoke on the phone with him, and he listened. Occasionally they brought him to the White House in a wheelchair, which Caroline helped push, or she and her mother visited the stricken patient in Palm Beach. Caroline couldn't figure out what had happened to her grandfather, why he was paralyzed on his right side and could no longer feed himself, or why he drooled all the time, but she did her best to cheer him up by carrying on a buzzing one-way conversation about herself and her brother, the weather, the scuttlebutt along the beach in Hyannis Port, and the latest doings of her growing collection of dolls. When she ran out of subject matter, she would sit on his bed and sing songs to him. Her comportment revealed an understanding and compassion not commonly found in somebody so young.

During one of Joe Kennedy's visits to the White House, he listened attentively as Caroline told him that her father was concerned because John-John wasn't yet able to talk, and he had asked Miss Shaw when she thought he might begin to speak. "Oh, but he does, Mr. President," Miss Shaw responded. "You just can't understand him."

From their first day in the White House, Jackie felt her children should have as normal and natural a childhood as possible. To prevent Caroline from becoming isolated from other children her age, the First Lady organized a White House play group that met three times a week from nine-thirty to eleven-thirty in the morning. The play group quickly grew into a nursery school program for sixteen youngsters, including Caroline and the children of White House personnel as well as the children of friends and relatives. The school met Monday through Friday in the third-floor executive mansion solarium, with parents sharing the salaries of two teachers (Elizabeth Boyd and Alice Grimes) and the cost of books, blocks, paints, crayons, toys, a sandbox, and other school supplies. The school continued until the end of 1963 as a kindergarten and first grade. The first-grade curriculum consisted of conversational French, elementary math, American history, grammar, and hygiene. The children wore simple uniforms chosen by Jackie in red, white, and blue. During a time of civil rights unrest, Jackie made her position clear by integrating the class. In addition to the school, the First Lady created a playground (featuring a jungle gym, swings, a trampoline, and a tree house with an attached slide) on the South Lawn, which JFK could see from the windows of the Oval Office. When he wanted to take a break from work, he would step outside on the West Wing portico, clap his hands, and the children would come running.

Not long after the completion of the playground, Jackie discovered that it could be seen from the street. The Washington tour bus operators made it a compulsory stop on their daily itinerary. Tourists gawked at the children through the bus windows. Pedestrians frequently paused for a look, peering in at the youngsters between the openings of the cast-iron fence that enclosed the grounds of the White House. When photographs of the play area began to appear in the press, Jackie contacted the chief White House groundskeeper, strongly suggesting that his crew plant a line of rhododendrons and hedges along the interior of the fence to block the view.

When the groundskeeper told Jackie he needed authorization from the president to plant the foliage, she stormed into Pierre Salinger's office. "Pierre," she said, "I want you to inform Jack that the privacy of these children is being violated. It's like living in a zoo, only we're the animals."

It wasn't the first time Jackie had broached the subject with her husband's press secretary. "The rhododendrons and hedges were only the beginning," Salinger recalled. "She wanted to cultivate an entire forest on the property. If she'd been able to get away with it, she would have installed a solid wall of California redwoods. Another time she wanted to landscape the area with several rows of very tall Vermont evergreens. She was quite emphatic about it."

Jackie had additional demands. She told Salinger she didn't want a single picture dealing with the family's private life to appear in any publication without her prior approval. She was still enraged that in 1961 *Newsweek* had run a cover photo of Caroline with an article about her attending a children's ballet school in downtown Washington. The ensuing publicity had forced Jackie to cancel the lessons. She didn't want the playground to suffer the same fate.

"Jackie, you can't control the press," Salinger told her, "and you certainly can't obstruct the public's view of 1600 Pennsylvania Avenue. This is the White House. It belongs to the people. They have an absolute right to the view."

In truth, Jackie's attention to issues of privacy had shifted to a preoccupation with matters of security. Although she claimed that the White House nursery school came about because of her desire to establish a "natural setting" for Caroline, the actual motive had more to do with safety. Jackie didn't want Caroline leaving the White House to attend school in a setting that couldn't be adequately controlled. She had looked into some of the more prestigious private schools in Washington but concluded that to send her daughter off each morning with a pair of armed Secret Service agents, in and of itself no guarantee of absolute security, would only traumatize the child.

Jackie's concern for the safety of her children stemmed not just from past events but from a more recent occurrence. Jack and Jackie took Caroline and John along on a 1961 Easter holiday visit with Joe and Rose Kennedy in Palm Beach. While there, the president and First Lady received an anonymous letter, the contents of which were divulged to Jackie. Evidently written by one or more supporters of Fidel Castro and the new Communist regime in Cuba, the note stipulated that the Kennedy children would be kidnapped and held hostage against any future attack the United States might launch against Cuba.

Playing golf at the Everglades Country Club with Bing Crosby, JFK received word of the letter's arrival and immediately returned to the house, where he told his wife about Operation Zebra, a covert CIA-sponsored plot calling for the invasion of Cuba by Cuban refugees, many of whom currently resided in the greater Miami area. U.S. Special Forces had been training the refugees in paramilitary maneuvers and planned to lend support by providing air coverage during the first phase of the invasion, which would hopefully culminate in the overthrow and elimination of Castro and the existing Cuban government. No doubt word of the pending overthrow had leaked, and it was this eventuality that had led to the threatening kidnap letter.

As a result of the letter, Secret Service protection was doubled around the Palm Beach estate, and at the same time, Caroline and John Jr. were flown to Washington under tight security measures and kept under lock and key at the White House. On April 1, a day after the delivery of the letter, four Miami Cubans were arrested at a West Palm Beach nightspot. Detained for questioning by the FBI, they were released when Bureau officials failed to establish a plausible link between the foursome and the kidnap letter. Plans for Operation Zebra moved ahead, terminating two weeks later in the highly embarrassing fiasco known as the Bay of Pigs invasion. Withdrawing the air support he had initially promised, JFK suffered his first major political setback.

In Washington, Jackie had lunch at the White House with Lorraine Rowan Cooper and Susan Mary Alsop, the wife of Joe Alsop. The First Lady spoke frankly, disclosing her fears, especially for her children.

Over dessert, Jackie brought up the subject of Fidel Castro. She couldn't fathom the reasons behind her husband's deep-seated hatred of the Cuban leader, an antagonism that seemed to transgress the boundaries of political gamesmanship. It approached what could almost be termed a personal vendetta.

"It's exactly that—a vendetta," said Lorraine Rowan Cooper, who'd spent part of World War II as a resident of Cuba. "Papa Joe Kennedy has more money invested in Havana real estate, hotels, and clubs than any American I've ever known. When Castro took over, he seized everything—and he's not about to return it anytime soon."

By mid-1961 Jacqueline Kennedy had imposed an embargo on the press, informing them through Pamela Turnure that she preferred they publish no more than one photograph of either of her children per month. She and Jack argued the point as vehemently as they debated his womanizing and her frequent absences from White House functions. When it came to photographs of the children, Jack didn't always comply with his wife's wishes, inviting the press into the White House whenever Jackie arranged to get away. And when he complied with regard to photographs, he made up for it by supplying the press with a steady stream of anecdotes on one or both of his progeny.

"The minute Jackie left the White House for more than a day," said Pierre Salinger, "the president would instruct me to release some cute little item on John or Caroline to one of the major news agencies. 'Like what do you want me to say?' I'd ask him. And he'd provide me with a long list of story ideas, then tell me to pick something appropriate. It's safe to say that they became the most written-about children in the history of the country."

The stories often involved visiting dignitaries. When former president Harry S. Truman dropped in on JFK to offer advice on how he ought to approach Soviet Premier Nikita Khrushchev at an upcoming European summit, Caroline Kennedy suddenly popped out from behind her father's desk and said, "How are you? You lived here before us, didn't you?" When introduced to Sam Rayburn, former Speaker of the House, she studiously regarded his bald head and asked, "Why won't hair grow for you?" Both stories found their way into print, as did a photograph of Caroline brandishing a toy pistol following a visit to the Georgetown home of her aunt and uncle Jean and Stephen Smith. The appearance of the photo, occurring at the same time as Jackie's discovery that a toy manufacturer had just put on sale a "Caroline doll," aggravated the First Lady to such a degree that she refused to speak to Stephen Smith for more than a month.

Jackie's enmity toward Steve Smith didn't extend to JFK's sister Jean, whose warm and effervescent personality appealed to the First Lady. "Jackie liked Jean better than she liked any of Jack's other sisters," said presidential adviser Larry O'Brien. "She identified with Jean insofar as Steve, like Jack, had a roving eye and a taste for other women. She also cared for Joan Kennedy, Teddy's wife, who turned to Jackie for advice on how to handle her philandering husband. 'Don't worry about it,' Jackie told her. 'It doesn't mean a thing. All the Kennedy men are like that. It's the nature of the beast.'"

Despite the First Lady's lack of enthusiasm for Stephen Smith, it was he who gave Caroline one of her most cherished childhood possessions, a large "talking" doll that had a small tape recorder hidden in its torso. The machine recorded whatever was said and replayed it at the touch of a button. Presented to Caroline on her fourth birthday, the doll accompanied her wherever she went.

One afternoon she forgot it in the Oval Office. It was returned to Maud Shaw that evening. Curious as to what Caroline had been saying, Shaw played the recording device. Instead of Carolyn's little girl voice, the nanny heard the unmistakable strains of John Kennedy berating one of his aides, interspersing his tirade with a choice selection of four-letter words.

Unable to erase the tape, the nanny turned to a Secret Service agent for help. The agent fiddled with the doll for more than an hour but was equally stymied. In an act of desperation, he suggested that they simply remove the cassette and throw it away. The following day, when Caroline wanted to play with the doll, Maud Shaw told her that it had developed a sore throat and couldn't speak. Caroline tucked the doll into bed, where it remained for a day until the Secret Service agent went out and purchased a new tape. The doll made a miraculously quick recovery and was soon talking again.

At age one, John Jr.'s favorite toy was a jack-in-the-box that popped open to the tune of "Pop Goes the Weasel." According to Maud Shaw, John sat on the floor and played with the toy for hours. Depicted as a stubborn child by his nanny, the boy cried whenever anyone tried to take the jack-in-the-box away from him. He cried whenever Maud Shaw had the day off and he was placed in the care of a substitute. "John was as attached to me as I to him," she wrote in the first draft of her memoir.

John and Caroline were the beneficiaries of countless gifts brought or sent to the White House by visiting foreign statesmen and officials. Princess Grace of Monaco, Prince Sukarno of Indonesia, Prime Minister Jawaharlal Nehru and his daughter Indira Gandhi of India, Italian prime minister Amintore Fanfani, and others gave presents to the children; so many that Jackie began sending some to hospitals and orphanages around the country. One present Caroline insisted on keeping was a five-foot-high dollhouse painted white with a red roof and red shutters. A gift from Madam Charles de Gaulle, it came equipped with scale-sized furniture and green flower boxes at the windows. Caroline kept it on the floor next to her bed and made sure to include its miniaturized doll inhabitants in her nightly prayers.

Both children adhered to an extremely strict schedule that Jackie drew up every Sunday for the week to come. For the sake of security, she wanted to know precisely where her children would be—and when they would be there. "It's only after they take the elevator to the second floor and are away from it all in their own little kingdom that I feel safe," Jackie confided to the nanny. The First Lady developed her own set of rules for raising the children but too often communicated her regulations in a manner that many on her staff found dictatorial. "I want the children in bed no later than 8:00 p.m., and I don't want them taking their afternoon nap on the Truman balcony," she told Miss Shaw, referring to the veranda that President Truman installed overlooking the South Lawn. "But the fresh air is good for them," the nanny protested. "Miss Shaw," said Jackie, "when I want your opinion I'll ask for it. In the interim, just do what I say. They're to nap in their respective rooms, not on the balcony."

The First Lady provided Maud Shaw with a written list of demands. She didn't want the children's detail of the Secret Service to "cater" to John and Caroline or to pick up after them. She didn't like the idea of grown men "serving" two children, giving them the impression that they were privileged or entitled. "Let them pick up after themselves," noted Jackie, "especially Caroline, who's old enough to know she can't just drop everything on the floor. Her bedroom is always a mess." Jackie reiterated her request to the Secret Service chief, who followed up with a memo to agents mandating that they keep their distance from the children. Regarding John, she wanted his hair left to grow long—"He looks much cuter that way." When the nanny pointed out that the president insisted his son's hair be cut short, Jackie responded, "Let the president concern himself with affairs of state, and I'll worry about the length of John's hair."

Although the First Lady didn't want the Secret Service to "smother" her children, she upbraided them the day John Jr. tripped in the tree house and knocked out one of his front teeth. The agent on duty at the time of the accident tried to reassure Jackie. "It's only a baby tooth," he said. "I know," she retorted. "But until his second set of teeth grow in, he'll have an ugly gap in his mouth. Where are you guys when you're needed?"

The episode brought to mind a second incident that had greatly distressed Jackie. At a birthday party for Ivan Steers, the three-year-old son of Nina Auchincloss Steers, Jackie's stepsister, Caroline fell off a rubber float at the deep end of the Steerses' swimming pool and had been rescued not by a member of her Secret Service detail but by Mrs. William Saltonstall, daughter-in-law of Senator Leverett Saltonstall. Mrs. Saltonstall, seven months pregnant at the time, saw Caroline struggling in the water and jumped into the pool with all her clothes on. She pulled the child to safety. "What was that nice lady doing in the pool with all her clothes on?" Caroline inquired of her mother. Jackie asked the Secret Service chief why a guest at the party had taken action, while the agent on duty merely looked on.

Coupled with Jackie's dictums concerning the welfare of her children were the orders she dispensed regarding her own comfort level, not least of which was a demand that her bed linens be changed three times a day: in the morning, at midafternoon (following her nap), and at night before she went to sleep. "Not even the Queen of England takes such liberties," wrote Maud Shaw.

Another of Jackie's demands angered White House Chief of Protocol Angier Biddle Duke, to whom she sent a memo criticizing the playing of "Hail to the Chief" at every executive mansion function. "It's fine to have the Marine Band play 'Hail to the Chief' when the dinner is political in nature," she wrote, "but is it really necessary when the guest of honor is a major artist or performer, such as Pablo Casals, Igor Stravinsky, or Rudolf Nureyev?" "And who decides," Duke wrote back, "which artists are 'major' and which are not?" The First Lady sent Duke a brusque follow-up: "If you don't know who's major and who's not, Angie, then perhaps you should find yourself another position."

Overbearing as Jackie sometimes seemed, there were few on the White House staff who questioned her prowess as a mother. J. B. West often went home at the end of a work day and boasted to his wife what an admirable job Jackie was doing with her children. "She may have relegated responsibility to others when they were infants," he said, "but once they began to walk and talk she took over. She reads to each of them for forty-five minutes every night. When time permits, she dines with them in the 'highchair room,' as she calls it. All the other Kennedy children are allowed to do pretty much what they want. Not Caroline and John. The result is that they're not in any way spoiled."

At a certain point, Jackie began to complain about the children's meals. They were being given the same thing to eat every day: hot dogs for lunch and hamburgers for dinner. She assigned Mary Gallagher, her personal secretary, the job of discussing the menu with the White House kitchen staff. The meals soon became more varied and nutritious.

Mary, herself the mother of two young children, talked Jackie into contacting the Baltimore Zoo and inquiring about Suzy, a trained three-year-old chimpanzee whose performances—in a little girl's dress—had charmed many a young audience. Suzy was brought to the White House for a children's party. The event proved immensely successful. John-John clamored to see Suzy again, so Jackie arranged to have her son visit the zoo with several of his young playmates. The zookeepers offered children the opportunity to feed Suzy with baby bottles that for a dollar they filled with warm milk. Despite the monkey's gentle disposition, it somehow managed to break the skin on the back of John's arm, for which he received a tetanus shot. By the time the story made the press, Suzy had metamorphosed into King Kong, and the nick on John's arm had grown into a gaping chest wound. "My kids can't go anywhere or do anything," Jackie told Pierre Salinger, "without it becoming a lurid newspaper story. Growing up in the White House is like living in a house of glass. Nothing is sacred. Everything the children do or say is open to public scrutiny and comment. I'm surprised that *The New York Times* and *The Washington Post* don't run detailed weekly reports on John's potty training."

Like most little girls, Caroline enjoyed throwing tea parties for her dolls and stuffed animals. After her brother turned one and a half, she started inviting him to join her as she "poured" tea and read stories to her "little friends." Finding his sister's teatime "readings" less exhilarating than the latest addition to his toy bin, a foot-long, scale-model fire engine that clanged and banged as he pulled it from room to room, John disrupted one tea party by colliding with a tray containing Caroline's collection of doll-sized cups and saucers, knocking it over and breaking everything in sight.

Caroline retaliated by writing her grandmother Rose a letter, describing John as "a loud, squeaky boy . . . with a very bad temper." In the same letter she reported that her brother had spit in their mother's Coca-Cola and that Jackie had made him drink it. In a second letter to Rose, Caroline mentioned that Miss Shaw had taught her to curtsy and John to bow for a forthcoming visit to the White House by Charlotte, the grand duchess of Luxembourg. But, the letter continued, when Jackie introduced John to the duchess, he threw "a terrible tantrum" and had to be taken away. She ended the letter by saying, "He's a very naughty boy."

Caroline must have soon forgiven her brother, because a short while later she approached their father and asked if he could put her in touch with Santa Claus in his workshop at the North Pole; she wanted to give Santa a Christmas gift wish list for herself and John. JFK, though burdened by events no less weighty than the Cuban Missile Crisis and the construction of the Berlin Wall, took time to contact one of the White House telephone operators and asked her to play along. He then called his daughter from the Oval Office and told her to ask for the White House switchboard. Caroline did as instructed and soon found herself on the line with Santa's workshop. Her face fell when she heard that Santa wasn't home, but she brightened again when the person at the other end identified herself as Mrs. Santa Claus. Mrs. Claus agreed to take Caroline's order and promised to give it to Santa when he returned. Caroline reeled off a lengthy list of toys for herself and an even longer list for John.

From the beginning, Caroline played the role of big sister to the hilt. An early and prodigious reader, she used to read children's books to her brother. She collected Democratic Party memorabilia, such as stickers and buttons, which members of the White House staff would save for her. She would request that a duplicate of each item she received also be given to John. When one of the Secret Service agents berated her brother for making too much noise, Caroline came to his defense and said, "My, we *are* grumpy today, aren't we, Mr. Jones?"

Not that Caroline was always the epitome of model behavior. Her obstreperous side, more in evidence during her formative days in Georgetown, occasionally made itself felt. A story that fortunately never appeared in print involved Pushinka, the Soviet-born dog that Nikita Khrushchev gave the First Family as a gift. The daughter of Strelka, the famous Russian canine that orbited the planet aboard the Sputnik-5 spacecraft in 1960, Pushinka had a somewhat temperamental nature. Strolling along the front lawn of the White House one autumn evening in 1962, Caroline and Maud Shaw encountered Pushinka. The dog was in the process of being walked by the White House kennel keeper. As Caroline reached out to pet the animal, Pushinka growled at her. Instead of recoiling, Caroline stepped behind the dog and gave it a swift kick to the rear end. Emitting a howl, Pushinka turned tail and raced off into the night. When Miss Shaw related the story to JFK, the president smiled at his daughter and said, "That's giving it to those damn Russians!"

In a CNN television interview with Larry King on September 28, 1995, a much older John Kennedy Jr., reflecting on his toddler days, traced his first (and perhaps only) White House memory to Pushinka:

"We trained the dog to go down the slide in the playground behind the White House. And that—sending the dog down the slide—is probably my earliest memory." On Sundays in the White House, he often took baths with Pushinka and Shannon, a cocker spaniel. Other White House canines included a German shepherd named Clipper; Charlie, a wire-haired Welsh terrier; and a gray Russian wolfhound appropriately enough named Wolf.

Once he became more independent, John, like his sister, had the run of the White House. Wearing a short-sleeved white linen shirt and plaid shorts, he could be seen careening up and down the mansion's marble corridors. In his pajamas, bathrobe, and slippers, he would race into the Oval Office, where his father would gratefully interrupt a meeting to play and talk with him.

"Hello, Sam," the president would say.

"No, no, no," the little boy protested. "My name is John." He would then squirrel himself away in the crawl space underneath his father's desk and play with a toy truck or helicopter he'd brought along for the occasion.

Taking their cue from the boss, President Kennedy's staffers were no less indulgent of the child's meanderings. McGeorge Bundy, special assistant to Kennedy on national security affairs, once halted a meeting to taste a mock serving of John-John's cherry vanilla pie. Secretary of State Dean Rusk played hide-and-seek with John. Attorney General Robert Kennedy lunched alone with his nephew in his Department of Justice office, then took him on a tour of the FBI Building. John's favorite exhibit was the room containing the "Ten Most Wanted" posters, replete with mug shots and physical descriptions.

John was even more fascinated by the White House helicopter, which he pronounced "helpercop"—Pierre Salinger solved the problem by teaching him to call it a "chopper." The boy loved to take it on family outings to Camp David or Glen Ora, a house in the rolling foothills of Virginia's horse country, which Jack had rented for Jackie to use as a weekend getaway. When they traveled by helicopter, John was allowed to sit next to the pilot at the controls. Whenever the president returned from an office-related trip and landed on the South Lawn by helicopter, John would be there to greet him. JFK's friend and special assistant Dave

Powers had shown John how to salute the president as he disembarked and stepped onto the White House landing pad. So pronounced was John's love of helicopters and airplanes that his mother decorated the walls of his room with photographs and renderings of both. The child began to collect airplane models, most of them provided by Godfrey McHugh, Air Force aide to Kennedy.

"I first met John Jr. during a military policy meeting with the president in his office," said McHugh. "The boy had sequestered himself in the space behind a panel in JFK's desk. He suddenly shouted, 'I'm a big bear and I'm hungry.' Then he appeared from beneath the desk, holding a metal windup helicopter. His father said something like, 'John's in charge around here.' So he and I became pals, and I recall waiting with him on the South Lawn when the president of Argentina arrived by helicopter. 'Here comes the chopper, here comes the chopper!' he started yelling. Some years after the assassination of Kennedy, I received a telephone call from Jackie. She said her husband had promised to buy John an airplane when he grew up. He was maybe ten or eleven at this point, and she wanted to know whether I could help. I arranged for a transfer of ownership (to Jackie) of a 1940 World War II observation plane that had been deactivated, and we had it repainted its original olive green with the latest Air Force insignia embossed on both wings. Jackie paid to have it moved to her backyard at the Kennedy compound in Massachusetts. I understand John used to spend hours at the controls of the plane, pretending to be a World War II fighter pilot about to engage in a dogfight with a squadron of German dive bombers. In the mid-1980s I bumped into him at some Democratic Party function in New York. John was now about twenty-five years of age. 'John,' I said, 'I heard you were some kind of war hero, taking down all those German dive bombers.' He laughed. He knew exactly what I meant."

Caroline's counterpart to John's airplanes and helicopters were her ponies. In June 1961, Vice President Lyndon Johnson gave her a calico pony, which she named John Jr., after her brother. She had a second pony, Macaroni, which she sometimes rode around the grounds of the White House. One day while meeting with Pierre Salinger, JFK peered out his window and spotted his daughter and the pony in the distance.

Opening the window, he called her name. Caroline rode Macaroni through the Rose Garden, trampling flowers as she went, onto the portico and straight into the Oval Office. "Well, well," proclaimed the president, "if it isn't Hopalong Cassidy in the flesh." And with these words, as Pierre Salinger recalled, "Caroline's pony did what ponies are prone to do—it took a huge dump on the Oval Office carpet."

John Jr. had an allergy to horses, although he too had a pony, Leprechaun, he would occasionally ride. His mother, hopeful he would become an accomplished horseman, ignored the allergy at first and saw to it that he and Caroline both took riding lessons. John's constant refrain during his lessons, according to Maud Shaw, was a shrill "I wanna get off!" Jackie eventually capitulated, discontinued her son's lessons, and gave Leprechaun to Caroline.

Between them, the children possessed more than a dozen pets, including guinea pigs, hamsters, dogs, birds, a lamb, a cat called Tom Kitten (to which President Kennedy proved allergic), and a beer-swilling white rabbit named Zsa Zsa. It turned out that John had a strong attraction to snakes. "One of his best loved places," wrote Maud Shaw, "was a snake farm located not far from Camp David. John insisted on visiting the farm whenever his family spent the weekend at Camp David. He was particularly fond of a giant cobra named George. One Sunday his father took him to the farm, and they returned with a box containing some variety of rare water snake. Mrs. Kennedy let out a scream when she saw it crawling across the living room floor. That evening she said to me, 'Miss Shaw, as soon as John falls asleep, box up that snake and return it to its natural habitat. In other words, take it into the woods and let it loose near one of the ponds. If John asks about it in the morning, tell him the snake missed his mommy and daddy and went home to be with them.'"

One of Jackie's fonder White House moments took place on a snowy winter day when her friend Rachel (Bunny) Mellon, the wife of industrialist Paul Mellon, transported Macaroni from its Virginia stable and helped hitch it to an old-fashioned sleigh found abandoned in an executive mansion warehouse. Wrapped in blankets, Jackie, Caroline, and John Jr. spent an hour being towed around the lawns of the White House. An equally enjoyable event transpired in the spring of 1962 when Jamie Auchincloss, the First Lady's half-brother, took Jackie and the children in his sailboat to the historic village of Jamestown, Virginia. "Jackie wore a head scarf and sunglasses, and to her delight and my amazement, nobody recognized us as we walked around," said Auchincloss. "That is, until we stopped at an ice-cream stand. The man scooping the ice-cream recognized Jackie at once and managed to break four cones for every one he produced."

The expedition nevertheless encouraged Jackie to take other chances. Dressed in faded blue jeans, frayed sweater, and an old maroon overcoat, she piled the children into her blue Pontiac station wagon and drove them to the circus and the theater. One afternoon she and John Jr. went to the same playground on Q Street where she had often taken Caroline when they lived in Georgetown. Jackie shopped for children's clothing with Caroline and spent several weeks alone with her, first at Glen Ora and then at the Kennedy compound in Hyannis Port. They went horseback riding, hiking, and took picnic cruises on Joe Kennedy's boat, the *Marlin.* On weekends they were joined in Hyannis Port by Jack and John-John. Not to be outdone by his wife, the president would cram John, Caroline, and three or four of their Kennedy cousins into an electric golf cart for wild rides to the local candy store. He enjoyed playing games with "C and J," as he sometimes called them, particularly in the family swimming pool. At noon the children would accompany him to the beach. John Jr. loved to build sand castles and then demolish them with furious gusto, lashing out if anyone else tampered with them. JFK delighted in telling his children stories. Franklin D. Roosevelt Jr., undersecretary of commerce during the Kennedy administration, went yachting with the president and Caroline one afternoon and recalled Kennedy telling his daughter the tale of a huge white whale with a voracious appetite for "old, smelly sweat socks." To Caroline's immense joy, the president reached over and removed Roosevelt's shoes and socks. He then tossed the socks overboard. "It's dinnertime," JFK announced as the socks disappeared into the sea. "Caroline howled with laughter," said Roosevelt. "She couldn't get over it. And I lost a perfectly good pair of socks to a half-starved white whale."

JFK went so far in his devotion to Caroline and John that at the height of the Cuban Missile Crisis, he took time off from key strategy meetings to carve a pumpkin and celebrate Halloween with them. He later returned to the conference table to discuss a course of action that could have easily led to a major conflagration with the Russians.

Later that night Jackie and her sister, Lee, took Caroline, dressed like a witch, and Anthony Radziwill, in a skeleton costume, trick-or-treating in Georgetown. Like the children, Jackie and Lee wore masks to protect their anonymity. The ploy worked for about an hour until they reached the home of presidential adviser Arthur Schlesinger Jr. "Hi, Jackie," he said as he opened his front door. "How did you know?" the First Lady asked. "Who else goes trick-or-treating accompanied by a pair of Secret Service operatives?" responded Schlesinger. The agents, clearly visible in their London Fog trench coats, stood under a streetlamp only yards away, ready to pounce at the first sign of danger.

When the president and First Lady took trips together out of the country, as they did to France and Latin America, Jackie wrote the children every day. On a solo journey to India and Pakistan in 1962, she kept in constant telephone contact with them. John Kenneth Galbraith, Kennedy's ambassador to India, recalled that during her visit, the First Lady "chattered nonstop about her children. I had the sense that they meant more to her than anything else in life." On her return, Jackie consented to an interview with White House correspondent Helen Thomas. Asked to comment on raising her children, Jackie observed that Caroline and John were at an age where it was imperative that their parents be with them as much as possible.

On August 6, 1962, while John-John remained behind with Maud Shaw and his father at the White House, Jackie and Caroline embarked on a monthlong vacation in Ravello, Italy, staying with Stas and Lee Radziwill and their two young children at Villa Episcopia, a nine-hundred-year-old villa perched on a cliff high above the Bay of Salerno. To welcome the visitors, the mayor ordered the town square strung with hundreds of multicolored lights. The Radziwills had invited several other houseguests, among them Gianni and Marella Agnelli, owners of the Fiat Automobile Corporation. Leaving Caroline behind, Jackie accompanied the two couples on a brief sojourn to Capri aboard the Agnelli yacht. In the course of the First Lady's absence, the paparazzi descended on her

daughter, snapping pictures of Caroline on the beach and in the villa garden. Expressing her discomfort, she made faces and, in one memorable
shot, is shown sticking out her tongue at the photographer. Jackie's attitude toward the press had finally begun to rub off on her daughter.

Unlike his sister, John Jr. genuinely enjoyed being photographed.
Whenever he spotted Cecil Stoughton, the official White House photog-
rapher and a captain in the Army Signal Corps, he would call out to him,
"Take my picture, Taptain [sic] Stoughton."

On Memorial Day 1962, John F. Kennedy took Caroline along to the
Tomb of the Unknown Soldier at Arlington National Cemetery. Pointing to a mansion overlooking the site, Caroline asked her father the name
of the person who lived in it.

"His name is Robert E. Lee," said Kennedy. "He was a famous Con-
federate general in the Civil War."

"It's beautiful," said Caroline, referring to the Lee mansion.

"It is," agreed JFK. "And so is this cemetery. It's very tranquil, almost
restful. You know, Buttons, I think I could linger here forever."

The Kennedy administration proceeded in almost haphazard fashion,
the president leading the nation from one crisis to the next. Vietnam and
Cambodia, the Cold War and civil rights were all unresolved issues that
Kennedy inherited from Eisenhower, and which in turn he would pass
on to Lyndon Johnson. Although Kennedy's popularity with the voting
public continued to rise, he had managed to alienate himself from powerful factions within both the CIA and the FBI. J. Edgar Hoover, director of the FBI, added frequent notations on JFK's personal comportment
to the president's already bulging files, at one point summoning Attorney
General Robert F. Kennedy into his office to caution him that his
brother's sexual forays with women other than his wife were practically
common knowledge.

Another matter on Hoover's mind were Dr. Max Jacobson's recurrent
visits to the White House and Kennedy's growing dependence on Jacobson's amphetamine injections. Not even Hoover realized the full extent of
Kennedy's involvement with Jacobson, who was also treating Jackie and
the Radziwills. In the spring of 1962 JFK asked the doctor to become his

official White House physician in lieu of Dr. Janet Travell. Although Jacobson continued to treat Kennedy, even accompanying him on presidential trips abroad, he declined the offer, citing the necessity of having to attend to his large New York following. In the years following Kennedy's assassination, Jacobson's license to practice medicine was permanently revoked. President Kennedy's name was invoked only once during the monthlong medical hearings.

Hoover's warning made little impression on JFK. Unable or perhaps unwilling to modify his compartmentalized lifestyle, the president refused to waver. "This administration is going to do for sex what the last one did for golf," said a derisive Ted Sorensen. Actress Jayne Mansfield, Kennedy's latest Hollywood escort, defended the president, contending that she preferred a leader "who will do it to a woman rather than to the nation."

In the midst of all this, within weeks of John Jr.'s second birthday and Caroline's fifth, at the end of November 1962, Jack and Jackie conceived another child. Determined to keep her pregnancy under wraps as long as possible, the First Lady prohibited the White House from making a public announcement. If nothing else, the pregnancy helped strengthen Jackie's resolve to keep her marriage intact despite its shortcomings.

Another factor that added to Jackie's resolve was the way Jack doted on his children. "Before the kids came along," said Chuck Spalding, "Jack was as cold-blooded as a lizard. After the birth of Caroline and John, he changed for the better. He learned how to show affection for people, especially Jackie. If they hadn't had children, the marriage might not have lasted. Even with the kids, there were grave problems, but because of the children, Jackie appeared willing to work at the marriage."

At Glen Ora one weekend, Caroline disappeared from sight. When Lynn Meredith, the new head of the children's Secret Service detail, informed Maud Shaw and Jackie that they were going to have to dredge the pond at the bottom of a nearby hill, the First Lady panicked. Imagining the worst, she telephoned Jack at the White House. JFK attempted to calm his wife, but the longer he spoke the more she worried. Cognizant of Jackie's growing desperation, JFK put aside his work and hurried to a waiting helicopter to be flown to his wife's side. By the time he arrived at

Glen Ora, Caroline had reappeared. She'd been playing with some of her dolls, including a Raggedy Ann, in a chicken coop on the periphery of the property. Furious but at the same time relieved, Jackie scolded her daughter: "Don't you ever disappear like that without telling anyone where you're going." She then fell into Jack's arms. For perhaps the first time, he'd been there when she needed him.

Early in 1963, Jacqueline told Lee Radziwill that she was expecting another baby later in the year and would soon be cutting back on her activities. She waited until April to announce her pregnancy to the press, by which point her attendance at White House functions was limited to state dinners and intimate luncheons with visiting VIPs. Eilene Slocum, a prominent Newport social arbiter, recalled arriving at the White House during Jackie's pregnancy only to find that the tea party she'd been invited to attend was being given by Jackie's mother. "Jackie was out with the children walking the dogs," said Mrs. Slocum. "If you can walk the dogs, you can presumably attend a tea party. It was a slap in the face."

If Eilene Slocum seemed disenchanted with Jackie, others were even more disillusioned. The First Lady's place at White House luncheon and dinner parties had been usurped predominantly by Lady Bird Johnson and Ethel Kennedy. Frances Parkinson Keyes, a member of the Ladies of the Senate, noted that "even when John Kennedy served as senator, Jackie took little interest in our meetings. As the president's wife, she wanted absolutely nothing to do with us. She refused to attend our annual luncheon, even though she was the guest of honor. She couldn't come, she said in 1963, because of her pregnancy. A White House party without the First Lady is a bit like *Hamlet* without the Prince of Denmark."

Jackie's pregnancy and her as yet unresolved feelings toward both politics and her husband's hyperactive libido made her increasingly difficult to be around at times. More intolerant than ever of lapses on the part of her staff, Jackie frequently lost her temper, stamping her feet with impatience, her slow, deliberate whisper all too readily hardening into a sneer. Only her children escaped the full force of her anger.

On Wednesday morning, August 7, Jackie took Caroline from Squaw Island (a mile from the Kennedy compound in Hyannis Port) to her horseback riding lesson in Osterville, twenty minutes away. They had just arrived at the stable when Jackie felt the first stabs of labor pain. Her Secret Service agent turned the car around and sped back to Squaw Island, where the First Lady called Dr. John Walsh and told him she thought she was about to have her baby—nearly four weeks early.

Although Jackie had originally planned on giving birth at Walter Reed Army Medical Center in Washington, alternate plans had been made with the hospital at Otis Air Force Base, in Cataumet, Massachusetts, where an entire wing had been renovated and set aside for the First Lady's eventual use. Flown by helicopter, Jackie arrived at Otis at 12:30 p.m. Aided by a team of Air Force medics, Walsh performed a C-section on his patient and delivered Patrick Bouvier Kennedy, a premature baby boy weighing only four pounds, ten and a half ounces. Suffering from acute hyaline membrane disease, the infant (named after the first member of the JFK family to arrive in America) was immediately placed in an incubator and taken to the postnatal intensive care unit.

The president was called away from a conference at the White House and informed that his wife had been taken to Otis. Twenty-five minutes later, accompanied by Pierre Salinger, Pamela Turnure, and Nancy Tuckerman, he boarded an eight-passenger Lockheed Jetstar to be flown directly to the base.

"Dr. Walsh was waiting for us," said Salinger. "JFK drilled him with questions on Patrick's health. Apparently his lungs weren't developed enough to function properly. Walsh wanted to transfer Patrick to the Children's Hospital in Boston, where they were better equipped to handle cases of this sort. Kennedy agreed, and Walsh suggested that the president might want to have the baby baptized before we moved him. So they sent for the Roman Catholic priest at Otis. Afterward we wheeled the incubator to the ambulance, passing Jackie's hospital room en route. She caught only a glimpse of the baby but never got to hold him."

JFK and Pierre Salinger followed Patrick to the hospital in Boston. "All these Harvard doctors were crowded around the baby's incubator trying to decide what steps to take," continued Salinger. "They looked concerned but uncertain what to do. 'I hate hospitals, don't you?' Kennedy whispered to me. Patrick looked like a tiny sparrow trapped in a large plastic cage."

After consulting with the president, the doctors performed a tracheotomy, inserting a thin metal tube into the baby's throat to prevent his lungs from collapsing. They then placed the infant in a larger incubator and moved it into a hyperbaric chamber in the basement of an adjacent medical building. They converted a fourth-floor waiting room into makeshift living quarters for the president, with beds, a rocking chair, and newly installed telephone lines. The Secret Service posted itself outside the room. For the next day and a half, JFK and Salinger, joined by Dave Powers and Bobby Kennedy, spent hours in the basement standing vigil over Patrick.

At 2:00 a.m. on Friday, August 9, the doctors informed JFK that his newborn son's condition had declined. Kennedy and Powers returned to the basement chamber where they had placed the baby. They donned surgical gowns and caps and sat waiting. Every few minutes Jack rose and moved to the door of the chamber. Peering in through a small window in the door, he watched as doctors and nurses attended to the infant.

At 4:00 a.m., when it became clear that the situation was hopeless, the team lifted Patrick out of the incubator and brought him to the president. A doctor gently set the tiny infant in JFK's arms. Three minutes later the baby drew its last breath. "He put up quite a fight," Kennedy said to Dave Powers. Jack returned to his temporary quarters on the fourth floor, shut the door behind him, sat down on the bed, and wept.

Later that morning the president flew back to Otis Air Force Base to be with Jackie in her hospital room. Caroline went with him, carrying a small flower arrangement, as she'd done following the birth of her brother John. When Jack and Jackie were finally alone behind closed doors, she told him that great as the loss of Patrick had been, "the one blow I could not bear would be to lose you."

Chapter 5

◆

CAMELOT AT DUSK

It was left to John F. Kennedy to tell Caroline and John-John that their new baby brother would not be coming home with them to the White House. Jacqueline Kennedy, still recuperating at Otis, also left it to Jack to bury Patrick. The private funeral Mass led by Cardinal Cushing was attended by the president, Lee Radziwill, and Jackie's half-brother and half-sister, Jamie and Janet Jennings Auchincloss, named after her mother. JFK placed a St. Christopher's medal, designed as a money clip—a wedding present from Jackie—in the tiny white coffin before it was buried in the Kennedy family plot at Holyhood Cemetery in Brookline, Massachusetts. In time, Patrick's body would be exhumed and reinterred with his parents at Arlington National Cemetery, as was the Kennedys' unnamed baby girl, stillborn in 1956.

On September 12, 1963, approximately four weeks after Patrick's death, Jack and Jackie took their children to Hammersmith Farm, where they spent the weekend celebrating their tenth wedding anniversary with the Auchinclosses. On Saturday night, the Auchinclosses gave a dinner party for the Kennedys, at which Jamie Auchincloss toasted the couple, thanking Jackie for making the president a member of the family. Yusha Auchincloss recalled that as an anniversary present, Jack gave Jackie a catalog from J. J. Klejman, the New York antiques dealer, and told her to select whatever she wanted. "JFK read the items aloud," said Yusha, "and though he didn't read the prices, whenever he came to an expensive item he would stage whisper, 'Got to steer her away from that one.' It was very humorous. She finally selected a simple coiled serpent bracelet. Her gift to him was a gold St. Christopher's medal to replace the one he'd placed in little Patrick's coffin and a red-and-gold leather scrapbook containing before-and-after photographs of the White House rose garden, which she and Bunny Mellon had redesigned. Each photo was accompanied by a quotation from *Bartlett's* which Jackie had written out by hand."

The following morning Jack, Jackie, and the children went sailing in Narragansett Bay. Afterward, the president took John Jr. for a visit with Rhode Island senator Claiborne Pell, who had been negotiating a Newport summer rental for the Kennedys for August and September of 1964. "Jack didn't care for Virginia during the summer months," said Pell. "There were too many horses, and it was too hot, although he'd recently given up his lease on Glen Ora and instead built Wexford, a weekend retreat at Atoka in the Middleburg hunt country of Virginia. Wexford was Jackie's domain, a place where she could eventually board and ride horses. They bought the place with monies derived from the sale of their Georgetown home."

While Jack met with Pell, Jackie and Caroline got together with the senator's wife, Nuala, and Sylvia Blake, who'd known Jackie since their teenage years. Blake had always found Jackie "very private and difficult to read." Nuala Pell termed Jacqueline "a true hieroglyphic, a complete mystery." Both agreed that what differentiated her from others, aside from these considerations, was the closeness of her relationship with her children. "She was the greatest mother I ever knew," said Nuala Pell. "That weekend, for example, she totally involved Caroline in her conversations with us. She had the ability to interest her children, even at a young age, in what interested her. The result is that Caroline seemed much older, much more mature than her years. What was remarkable about that weekend, however, was that Jackie seemed to be completely at ease, unmarked by the recent death of the baby. Most women would have been devastated. I couldn't tell if she was merely putting on an act for our benefit, or if she'd simply gotten over it."

In reality, Jackie was more distraught than she was willing or able to admit. Her sister, Lee, presently in England, sensed as much. Having developed a close friendship and sometime romance with Greek shipping tycoon Aristotle Onassis, Lee told Ari of her sister's loss. Onassis suggested that Jackie and Lee, whose marriage to Stas Radziwill was currently on shaky ground, visit Greece and cruise the Greek isles aboard the *Christina,* his 325-foot luxury yacht. They could bring along friends and travel wherever they wanted. He would remain ashore or travel with them but maintain his distance, whichever they preferred. Lee thought the cruise would help revitalize Jackie. She telephoned her sister and made the suggestion, adding that Onassis need not accompany them on the voyage.

Jacqueline accepted the invitation but insisted that Onassis come along. "I can't possibly accept Ari's hospitality and then not let him join us," she said. Jack and Bobby Kennedy were somewhat less than enthusiastic about the idea. They were concerned with the kind of press such a venture might engender and its possible effect on the 1964 presidential election. Aristotle Onassis was not only a foreigner but a jet-setter, the worst possible combination from the point of view of the average American. In addition, Onassis had been the target of a number of criminal probes and investigations by the Justice Department and the defendant in several legal skirmishes with the U.S. Maritime Commission. The most publicized of these involved the purchase by Onassis of fourteen vessels from the commission with the understanding that they would sail under the American flag. Onassis, who prided himself on his astute business acumen, transferred the ships to a foreign registry and saved more than $20 million in taxes. He was indicted by the Justice Department and forced to pay $7 million to avoid criminal prosecution.

"Jackie, do you know what you're doing?" asked the president. "Are you aware of this man's reputation? It's enough that your sister's involved with him."

JFK had heard that Lee planned to have her present marriage to Stas Radziwill annulled in order to marry Onassis. This would make "the Greek," as JFK called him, a brother-in-law to the president of the United States. When Bobby Kennedy learned of this possibility, he let it be known that any such maneuver on Lee's part would have to wait until after the next presidential election.

When Jack realized that Jackie intended to go on the cruise with or without his consent, he requested that Stas Radziwill also go along and that a second chaperone should be included as well—for the sake of appearances, if for no other reason. Onassis had been divorced from his wife Tina since the advent of opera diva Maria Callas, who had divorced her husband and become Ari's constant companion—that is, until Lee Radziwill entered the picture. In JFK's eyes, it would hardly do for the First Lady and her sister to be seen in close company with a divorced man renowned as a connoisseur of beautiful women.

Jackie agreed to her husband's conditions, and the president subsequently turned to Franklin Roosevelt Jr. and his wife, Suzanne, and asked if they would be willing to act as chaperones.

"I'm not certain 'asked' is the correct term," said Roosevelt. "We were *ordered* to go on the cruise. The president wanted someone he could trust, or so he said. What he really wanted was somebody to babysit Jackie, make sure she and Onassis didn't get too chummy. I'd known Jackie for years, and I admired her tremendously. She was Jack's equal at conversation and repartee. She was his equal intellectually and one of the best-looking girls in America. I also knew Onassis. I first met him on Long Island in early 1942. We maintained a friendship of sorts, which I imagine played a part in Kennedy's wanting me to go along on the cruise."

Jackie's final words to Jack before leaving for Greece were "Don't let Caroline and John eat too many sweets—they'll develop cavities." She had made arrangements to have the children taken to Hyannis Port on weekends, where they stayed with Bobby and Ethel's children, playing miniature golf and going for cookouts at the homes of neighbors. On October 4 Jackie joined Lee and Stas Radziwill and Franklin Roosevelt Jr. and his wife, Suzanne, in Piraeus, the ancient harbor of Athens. It was there that they boarded the *Christina*. On their first night aboard ship, Onassis—who had invited his sister Artemis along—gave a dinner party in Jackie's honor followed by a midnight dance on the mosaic dance floor-cum-swimming pool located on deck. In the morning, the yacht, bedecked with hundreds of red roses and pink gladioli, carrying a crew of sixty, including a band, a masseuse, two hair stylists, and two chefs (one Greek, one French), lifted anchor and powered into the Aegean Sea.

"Onassis was on his best behavior," said FDR Jr. "While not formally educated, he was well read and well informed on a number of subjects, including world affairs. In certain respects, one might even call him brilliant. He spoke five languages and could be extremely charming. Although by no means a handsome man, there was something very attractive and manly about him. Then there was the *Christina*. Named for his daughter, it contained a dozen lapis lazuli fireplaces, gold-plated bathroom fixtures, forty-two telephones, a beauty salon, doctor's offices, a movie theater, and an ivory-topped bar. There were nine luxury staterooms. Jackie's stateroom had been previously inhabited by the likes of Sir Winston Churchill and Greta Garbo."

Ari entertained his guests with stories of life in Smyrna, the city of his birth. He spoke of his early struggles, of how he had been a telephone operator in Argentina earning 25¢ an hour, how he had married the daughter of a powerful Greek shipping magnate, slowly working his way to his present station. Often Ari and Jackie sat together on the poop deck under a wildly starlit sky long after the others had gone to bed. They became friends, attending small portside dinner parties and late-night bouzouki dances in Greek nightclubs. They visited Istanbul, Lesbos, Crete, Ithaca, and Skorpios, an island of cypress trees and rocky hillsides that Onassis had acquired from the Greek government in the early 1950s for $5 million.

Franklin Roosevelt Jr. noted that while "Jackie and Ari may have flirted a little, there was nothing going on between them. Everyone knew by then that something was going on between Lee and Ari. Maria Callas wasn't there, and Stas Radziwill left halfway through the trip. We were beginning to look like a boatload of love-struck vagabonds. JFK wasn't pleased, despite the fact that Jackie had written him a ten-page love letter that began 'My dearest, dearest Jack.' He responded by sending her a wire urging her to return."

Toward the end of the trip, Ari gave Jackie an $80,000 diamond-and-ruby necklace. He gave his other female guests less valuable gifts. Lee complained that Onassis had given her "three dinky little bracelets that Caroline wouldn't wear to her own birthday party." In 1968, the year Ari married Jackie, he purportedly jettisoned Lee by handing her a check for $1 million and the deed to a parcel of land on a promontory near Athens.

Jacqueline returned to Washington with a pile of gifts for the children. The following day the family watched cartoons in the basement of the East Wing, where J. B. West had installed a makeshift movie theater. After a dinner of calf's liver—the children's least favorite meal—the president took Caroline and John for a dip in the White House pool, as he'd done most evenings during the First Lady's absence.

If Jackie felt at all contrite about her trip, she didn't show it. On the other hand, she and JFK both seemed more willing than before to make sacrifices for each other's happiness. Jackie had resumed her participation in the White House's hectic schedule of fall social events and had begun to formulate plans for the coming year. "I knew I was back," said Jackie to Evangeline Bruce, "the morning I came down to breakfast in my wrapper with Caroline, and there were these governors and labor leaders, none of whom I'd ever seen before, smoking cigars and eating scrambled eggs in the family dining room. They were discussing politics. I heard the words, but I had no idea what it all meant. And the sad thing is, I didn't really care."

Shortly after Jackie's return from Greece, JFK asked her if she would be willing to accompany him on a long overdue three-day trip to Texas. The junket had been scheduled for late November. Fully capable of distinguishing between important commitments and those she considered unnecessary, she agreed to go.

"JFK really didn't want to make the trip," said Lem Billings. "Larry O'Brien and several other presidential advisers saw the expedition, which would include appearances in Houston, Fort Worth, Dallas, and Austin, as the first campaign stop in Jack's bid for reelection. But there was more to it. It had to do with internal Texas politics. 'Why can't [Lyndon] Johnson wash his own goddamn laundry?' he said. 'Why do I have to get dragged into it? It's nothing but a fence-mending operation.' Maybe he had a premonition of some impending doom. But at the end he seemed pretty gung ho. 'Jackie will show those Texas broads a thing or two about fashion,' he said. He was all fired up."

The last White House function under President Kennedy, the annual reception for the Supreme Court Justices, took place on the night of November 20. The following morning, Larry O'Brien and Godfrey McHugh joined JFK aboard the presidential helicopter for the short flight to Andrews Air Force Base and Air Force One. "We were sitting on the South Lawn helicopter pad," recalled O'Brien. "The president seemed somewhat anxious. He spoke briefly about the Nuclear Non-Proliferation Treaty he'd worked out with the Soviets. He then asked McHugh about the weather conditions in Texas. McHugh gave him a general report, and the president said, 'Oh gosh, I don't know if Mrs. Kennedy will have the right clothes.'"

Flanked by Maud Shaw and John Jr., Jackie finally appeared, striding briskly toward the chopper. Maud Shaw and John-John joined Mrs. Kennedy and the others for the flight to Andrews. JFK sat next to his son behind the pilot and soon began tapping John's foot with his own. "Don't, Daddy," the little boy said, drawing his foot away. A few minutes later the president began again. "Don't, Daddy," said John Jr., letting out a loud giggle. The president laughed back. At the Air Force base, John received hugs from his mother and father, then waved as they boarded the presidential plane. As they left for Texas, John returned to the White House, via helicopter, with Maud Shaw and a pair of Secret Service agents.

"I remember many of the same things people remember about me as a child living in the White House," Caroline Kennedy remarked in 1993. She cited several examples: playing with her brother under the president's desk in the Oval Office, riding her pony, watching the helicopters take off and land. Ironically, probably because she had willfully banished them from her memory bank, Caroline could summon to mind few details of the events surrounding her father's assassination. Her brother, only three at the time, half his sister's age, often admitted remembering nothing at all of his father or his father's death. Yet the most memorable image of the funeral proceedings had to be that of the little boy, resplendent in blue overcoat and shorts, standing at attention outside St. Matthew's Cathedral and squinting into the sun and raising his hand in a military salute as his father's coffin rolled by.

The first news that Maud Shaw received of the November 22, 1963, shooting came a little after 1:00 p.m. in the form of a telephone call from Nancy Tuckerman. "Something has happened to the president," said Tucky. "They've rushed him to Parkland Hospital in Dallas. I'll call you back as soon as I hear how he is." At the time of the call Shaw had been tending to the children in the sitting room of the family suite. Caroline was curled up in an easy chair reading a book, and John was lying on the floor, crayoning in a coloring book. Shaw decided to have them take their afternoon nap and led them to their respective bedrooms. She retired to her own room to await further word. When nobody came or called her back, she walked out into the corridor and headed toward the dining room. She saw one of the children's Secret Service detail, Bob Foster, leaning against the doorpost at the far end of the hallway. She walked up to him. He looked terrible—ashen and near tears.

"Are you all right?" she asked him.

"The president is dead," he said. "He was shot down."

The words were uttered with such bluntness that the nanny nearly recoiled. Seeing her reaction, Foster took her by the arm and eased her into one of the armchairs in the corridor. She sat there in a stupor, attempting to collect her thoughts, only vaguely aware of her surroundings. When at last the truth began to sink in, she rose and returned to her room.

Miss Shaw subsequently learned that the Secret Service detail had drawn lots to determine who should break the news to her, and Foster had lost. Not knowing what to say, he had simply blurted it out.

The nanny's first thoughts on being told were reserved for Caroline and John. They would never again see their father's face light up and grin, or hear him clap his hands and call their names. They would have to grow up without their father, their lives forever compromised and transposed.

At approximately 4:00 p.m. Bob Foster reappeared, this time at Maud Shaw's door. He informed her that Mrs. Kennedy was on her way back to Washington on Air Force One with the president's body. She wanted the children to be brought to her mother's recently acquired house at 3044 O Street in Georgetown.

"For the record," added Foster, "Lyndon Johnson has been sworn in as president. He recruited some federal judge in Dallas to do the honors just before they took off."

On hearing this pronouncement, Miss Shaw picked up the telephone and placed a call to Jackie's mother to confirm the arrangements.

"We're expecting you," said Mrs. Auchincloss. She paused for several moments, then spoke again. "Miss Shaw, there's something I would like you to do, and my daughter would, too. We feel you should be the one to break the news to the children, at least to Caroline. John is too young to understand, but Caroline isn't."

"Oh, no," replied Shaw. "Please don't ask me to do that. It's the last thing in the world I want to do. I simply can't."

"Please, Miss Shaw," implored Mrs. Auchincloss. "It has to be you. Caroline trusts you more than anyone. Nobody is closer to her than you. You must do it. I'm asking you as a friend."

Shaw agreed to have a chat with Caroline but not until after dinner. This said, she went to rouse the children. Helping them get dressed, she hastily packed a pair of overnight bags with their clothes and some toys. Bob Foster carried the bags into the elevator and placed them in the trunk of a Secret Service vehicle which took them to Georgetown. Hugh and Janet Auchincloss looked shaken, but they received the children warmly, telling them the guest bedroom was being made up. After a hefty dinner of macaroni and cheese, Caroline and John played together in the living room. At one point, John-John asked his grandmother to turn on the television so he could watch cartoons. Afraid that the children would learn of the assassination if she switched on the set, Mrs. Auchincloss told them it was broken.

At 7:30 p.m. a Secret Service car unexpectedly pulled up outside the house. A minute later, Bob Foster stood in the hallway talking quietly to Mrs. Auchincloss. Air Force One had landed at Andrews Air Force Base. Bobby Kennedy had been the first to board the plane, scurrying through the cabin until he located Jackie in the rear of the plane surrounded by Larry O'Brien, Ken O'Donnell, and Dave Powers. The First Lady wore the same hat and pink Schiaparelli suit she had donned that morning for the Dallas motorcade. It was caked with blotches of the president's dried blood and brain matter. She had refused to change. "Let them see what they've done," she said. "I want them to see." Determined to stay with Jack's body, Jackie and Bobby accompanied his casket from the Air Force base to the National Naval Medical Center in Bethesda, Maryland, where the president's autopsy would be performed.

"I've come to take Miss Shaw and the children back to the White House," said Foster. "Mrs. Kennedy wants them there when she returns. She would also like you and your husband to be there, so I've taken the liberty of sending for a second car."

Slightly bewildered but treating it like a big game, Caroline and John clambered back into the car with Maud Shaw. The car drove quickly across the city and through the gates of the White House. Flashbulbs went off as they drove in. Across the street on Pennsylvania Avenue, stretching to Lafayette Square and beyond, stood a crowd of thousands, many in shock and others in tears.

"Why are all those people here?" Caroline asked.

"To see you," said Maud Shaw, thankful only that her young charge didn't probe further.

Inside, the White House seemed a mass of confusion, a blur of bleary-eyed, anguished-looking ushers and staff members rushing about in all directions. J. B. West sat in a chair in the middle of the corridor looking forlorn and lost. A military aide dashing up a hallway collided full-force with a member of the press corps racing in the opposite direction. A long line had formed outside the medical offices of the chief White House physician, whose main job for the next four days entailed dispensing sedatives and tranquilizers to anyone who expressed a need. Even Maud Shaw, a woman not easily shaken, would avail herself of the medication.

With Bob Foster leading the way, Miss Shaw managed to get the children into the elevator and back into their bedrooms. She helped John change into his pajamas, brush his teeth, say his prayers, and climb into bed. He fell asleep almost immediately. Caroline had completed the same rituals on her own. As the child lay in bed, Miss Shaw started reading to her from one of her books, but stopped after a few paragraphs. Sitting on the edge of Caroline's bed, she could feel the tears well up in her eyes and slowly trickle down her cheeks. Caroline looked up at her, her small face etched with concern.

"What's wrong, Miss Shaw? Why are you crying?"

The nanny took the child in her arms. "I can't help crying, Caroline, because there's something very sad I have got to tell you."

She proceeded as best she could, without offering lurid details, to describe what had happened to her father in Dallas earlier that day. The child cried so copiously at first that Miss Shaw was afraid she might choke. She eventually cried herself to sleep, and the nanny retired to her own room, leaving Caroline's door ajar in the event she suddenly awoke and called out for her.

Jackie didn't get back to the White House until 4:30 a.m. Several months later, when Maud Shaw talked to the former First Lady about that horrendous day, Jackie told her that although she had wanted the children near her when she returned from Dallas, she had above all wanted to be the one to tell them of their father's death. Maud Shaw had acted as a surrogate only because Janet Auchincloss had insisted on it. By usurping Jackie's role, the nanny had created a breach that continued to widen over the remaining term of her employment.

Caroline Kennedy awoke early on the morning of November 23. Her first stop was her father's bedroom. Holding a stuffed giraffe, a recent gift from her father, she peered into the darkened room. At the far end, she could make out the still forms of Hugh and Janet Auchincloss, asleep in the president's bed. Their presence confirmed her fear that her father was no longer alive. She shut the door and headed straight for Miss Shaw's bedroom. Along the way she noticed a discarded copy of that morning's *New York Times,* her father's picture shrouded in black on the front page. "Caroline instinctively understood the significance of the photograph,"

Miss Shaw subsequently wrote. "She looked sad and pale as she crawled into bed next to me. I held her tightly for several minutes. Then I told her I'd just learned her mommy had returned to the White House. She wanted to see her immediately, but I suggested we let her get some rest and then visit with her."

It was Bobby Kennedy who imparted the sorrowful news of his father's death to John Jr. "Your daddy has gone to heaven to be with Patrick," he said, referring to the baby Jack and Jackie had lost just two days after his birth. "Patrick was very lonely. He didn't know anybody in heaven. Now he is being taken care of by a great friend."

The explanation, for all its simplicity, passed over John's head. Nor did the handwritten letters that he and Caroline received that day from Lyndon Johnson make an impression on him. Writing the letters—which praised their father's service to the nation and extolled his greatness—had been Johnson's first order of business as Kennedy's successor.

Out of consideration for John, Caroline refrained from mentioning their father in front of her brother. "During the first few days, she asked frequent questions of me," wrote Maud Shaw, "but never in John's presence."

At 9:30 a.m., November 23, Father John Cavanaugh, an old friend of the Kennedys, appeared in Jackie's bedroom. He had been summoned to conduct a private Mass in the East Room for family and intimates of the late president. He had arrived early, he told Jackie, to hear her confession.

"Confession? What am I supposed to confess, Father? That I neglected to watch the calendar and inadvertently ate meat on a Friday some three months ago? Or that over the past year I didn't attend church services every Sunday?" This began a five-minute discourse on Jackie's part that ended with the widow's demand that the clergyman explain her husband's murder. "Why, why? How could God let something like this happen?"

Leaving her room, Jackie arrived at the nursery and after holding her children in her arms for several minutes took them downstairs to the East Room, where they knelt and prayed before the president's coffin. A few minutes later, at 10:00 a.m., Father Cavanaugh led the private Mass.

Caroline and John observed the proceedings with Miss Shaw from the corridor outside the East Room.

"Somehow," wrote Maud Shaw, "the rest of the day dragged through." Jackie passed part of it with R. Sargent Shriver and Angier Biddle Duke, mapping out plans for a four-day period of national mourning, ending with the largest funeral ceremony ever held in the nation's capital. She then spent time with her mother and stepfather as well as members of the Bouvier family. In the late afternoon, accompanied by her mother, she visited with Caroline and John. Changing their clothes for dinner, tears running freely down her cheeks, she said nothing.

Breaking the silence, Maud Shaw said to her, "I'm so sorry, Mrs. Kennedy. I only wish I could do something to help."

Jacqueline tried to smile. "Just keep the children as happy as possible, Miss Shaw. That's all I can ask of you."

That evening, overtired and full of medication (her physician had given her three injections of a sedative), Jackie thrashed around in bed, crying and keening, calling out her husband's name, rolling from her own mattress to the one he used when he slept with her, burrowing into his pillows and into her own until she fell into a troubled sleep. After several hours she awoke. Not able to fall asleep again, she found some blue White House stationery and began writing her husband a letter. Starting "My darling Jack," the letter spoke of their life together, of Caroline and John-John, of Patrick, of their plans and dreams for the future now shattered forever. She began to cry again, the tears staining the page, smudging the ink. She wrote on. After she finished, she folded the letter and placed it in an envelope.

She spent the next hour gathering a few of JFK's favorite articles, including samples of scrimshaw, a gold bracelet he had given her, a set of gold cuff links she had given him. At the autopsy, she had been handed Jack's wedding band and although she considered adding it to the packet, she ultimately decided against it. In the morning she turned up in the nursery and asked her children to write to their father, telling him how much they loved and missed him. John-John, not yet able to write and uncertain as to the reason for the letter, scribbled and colored with a crayon on a blank sheet of paper. His sister printed her message in blue ballpoint. "Dear Daddy," she wrote. "We're all going to miss you. Daddy, I love you very much. Caroline."

Jackie asked Bobby Kennedy to accompany her to the East Room. Waiting for them was Godfrey McHugh, who helped them open the coffin. Jackie placed her letter and those from the children together with the other articles in the coffin. Bobby added a PT-l09 tiepin and an engraved silver rosary to what Jackie had brought. The two men watched as she arranged and then rearranged the items the way she wanted them. She gazed at her husband's face and lovingly stroked his reddish-brown hair. The minutes ticked by as she continued to caress him. Sensing what she wanted, McHugh excused himself and quickly returned with a pair of scissors. Jackie leaned forward and carefully cut a lock of the president's hair. Bobby lowered the lid of the coffin and left the room with his sister-in-law.

Later that morning, following the arrival from London of Stas and Lee Radziwill, JFK's coffin was moved from the White House to the Capitol Rotunda, where for the next twenty-four hours the president would lie in state. During that period some 250,000 mourners filed past the flag-draped coffin. At the White House, Jackie received a visit from Dr. Max Jacobson, Jack's favorite physician, who had flown from New York at the widow's request. After injecting the First Lady with one of his medicinal cocktails, Jacobson turned his attention to Lee Radziwill, a former patient of his, and injected her as well. "I don't know what the shot contained," Jackie told Chuck Spalding, "but it worked. My nerves have finally settled."

Nothing, however, could adequately prepare her for the latest news. Lee Harvey Oswald, a disaffected Marine sharpshooter, had been arrested for the murder of John F. Kennedy. Then, while being transported by a team of Dallas police officers, he was shot at point-blank range by one Jack Ruby, a sometime nightclub owner with ominous underworld connections who told the FBI he had killed Oswald to spare Mrs. Kennedy the agony of having to return to Dallas for Oswald's trial. "One more awful thing," was all Jackie would say about it at the time. She subsequently wrote a letter consoling the widow of Dallas policeman J. D.

Tippit, Oswald's other murder victim. In subsequent years, whenever asked if she felt Oswald had been part of a conspiracy to kill her husband, Jackie's response was always the same: "What difference does it make? Jack is dead—knowing who killed him won't bring him back."

On the night of November 24, Jackie met privately with Pierre Salinger in the family dining room. "She invited me to dinner," recalled Salinger. "She barely touched her food. 'You've got to eat, Jackie,' I told her. 'Your fortitude is all that's holding the country together. Your children need you. We all do.' She finally consumed a bowl of chicken noodle soup."

Over dinner Jackie spoke to Salinger about her children. When they came of age, she didn't want them to read "all that gruesome stuff" on the assassination. "There's only one thing I can do now,' she remarked. "I have to save my children. They have to be able to go through life without constantly looking back at their father's murder. I fear for them. How can I raise them in a normal manner? Can anyone understand how it must feel to have grown up in the White House and then, suddenly, to be living in the shadow of their father's death? There is something so final and sad about it."

Despite her concerns and grievances, Jackie felt it important that John Jr. have the experience of sleeping in his father's bed, if only for a night. "He can't yet comprehend that he will never see his father again," she told Maud Shaw. "Spending a night in the president's bedroom may one day help him to know his father." Although she opposed the idea, Shaw knew enough to keep her thoughts to herself. "I didn't want to further agitate the First Lady," she wrote in the first draft of her memoir. "Mrs. Kennedy wanted to help her son establish a bond with his father, so she insisted he spend the night before the funeral alone in the president's bed. John-John cried so hard that he woke up the entire household. I'm certain he was scared to death."

Rising above her grief, Jackie resolved to impress her husband's place in history on the American consciousness, to remind Americans what had been taken from them. The funeral on Monday, November 25, provided her a means of demonstrating JFK's importance as a global leader, his timeless link with the great presidents of the past. Jackie and her children were joined by Lyndon and Lady Bird Johnson in addition to Bobby Kennedy for the ride from the White House to the Capitol Rotunda, the site of JFK's funeral. According to Lady Bird's published diaries, John Jr. vaulted across seats and from one lap to another until Bobby managed to calm him down. When they reached the Capitol, John was led away by Maud Shaw. Following the eulogies, including a moving presentation by Senator Mike Mansfield, television viewers around the world watched as Jackie and Caroline approached the coffin, knelt and kissed it, then rose and walked slowly away.

Miss Shaw, meanwhile, with several Secret Service agents and a Capitol official as escorts, took John for a walk outside the building. When they were done, the official invited the small group into a large office to wait for Caroline and Mrs. Kennedy. In the office, John's attention was drawn to a mounted board decorated with miniature flags representing each of the 102 nations that had dispatched dignitaries to the funeral. Noticing the boy's interest, the Capitol official asked him if he wanted to have one of the flags as a souvenir.

"Yes, please," said John. "And one for my sister, please."

The official let him choose two flags, after which he paused. Then he said, "Please, may I have one for my daddy?"

The adults exchanged glances. Miss Shaw nodded, and the official invited him to take a third flag. After careful consideration, John-John made his selection and handed the three flags to his nanny for safekeeping. Maud Shaw in turn gave them to Jackie.

After the funeral, the president's coffin was lifted onto a caisson, the same one that had been used to carry Franklin D. Roosevelt's body in 1945. As in Roosevelt's day, the caisson was drawn by six white horses. A riderless horse (ironically named Black Jack), with boots reversed in the stirrups to signify a fallen leader, fell into place behind the caisson as it made its way from the Capitol to St. Matthew's Cathedral for the funeral Mass. The muffled sound of drumrolls playing in the background, Jackie, Bobby, and Ted Kennedy proceeded on foot at the head of a procession that included President Johnson, foreign dignitaries, JFK staffers, and members of the family. Caroline and John were transported in a slow-moving car flanked on all sides by Secret Service agents, also on foot. Along the route, Caroline reached out the window on her side of the car and took hold of Bob Foster's hand. When Caroline's eyes filled with tears, Maud Shaw took her other hand and gave it a reassuring squeeze.

At the black-draped entrance to the cathedral, Mrs. Kennedy and her children were received by Cardinal Cushing, whose ring Jackie kissed upon entering. She and the children exited at the end of the service and it was then, following Jackie's gentle prodding, that John-John stepped forward to salute his father's coffin.

After the burial of the president at Arlington National Cemetery, the widow met privately at the White House with Charles de Gaulle, Emperor Haile Selassie of Ethiopia, Ireland's President Eamon de Valera, and Prince Philip of England. Bobby, Ted, and Jackie then formed a receiving line to greet the other foreign dignitaries. John Davis, having flown from Italy to be with "Cousin Jackie," found her "in a surprisingly elevated mood. She loved being the center of attention and having all these foreign statesmen pay homage to her. The full impact of the assassination hadn't yet hit home. When it did hit, a short time later, she became inconsolable. The reality of the situation was almost too much for her. It amazed me, because I never thought her capable of mustering such deep emotion."

That evening, not wanting to disappoint her son, Jackie celebrated John-John's third birthday with a modest party in the family dining room. (A more elaborate party for both children, their birthdays falling two days apart, took place several days later.) Maud Shaw noticed that while John Jr. seemed to enjoy the party, which featured horns, balloons, and a birthday cake, Caroline appeared to be "miles away." Remote and withdrawn, she sat by herself in a corner of the room, for the most part ignoring her Kennedy cousins. Maud Shaw gave John a picture book on airplanes, but by far his favorite present was the model of Air Force One that Uncle Bobby had ordered for him. Later that night, long after the children had gone to bed, Jackie and Bobby slipped out of the White House and into a Secret Service car that drove them to Arlington, where they visited the president's freshly dug grave. The eternal flame flickered blue in the cool night. They prayed, and Jackie left behind a bouquet of lilies of the valley and the miniature flag John Jr. had chosen for his father.

From the beginning, Jackie worried about where she and the children would live now that the president was gone. Having sold their George-town residence, they had no place to go. Wexford in Virginia was too ru-ral, and Jackie had no desire to move in with either the Auchinclosses or the Kennedys. Lyndon Johnson told her to take as much time as she needed, but she soon realized she couldn't stay in the White House for-ever. John Kenneth Galbraith, home from India, discussed the situation with Averell and Marie Harriman, and they offered Jackie their elegant Georgetown townhouse at 3038 N Street, a three-story, eleven-room Federalist structure of solid brick only three blocks from the house once owned by Jack and Jackie. The Harrimans agreed to move temporarily into the Georgetown Inn, and told Jackie she and the children could stay until they found a more permanent solution.

Ten days after the assassination of President Kennedy, Jackie vacated the White House and with Caroline, John, and Maud Shaw moved into the Harriman residence. The Harrimans welcomed them by throwing a small dinner party for Jackie. Lorraine and John Sherman Cooper did the same. One of Jackie's horseback riding partners, Ambassador Charles Whitehouse, the brother of Sylvia Blake, hosted a cocktail party in Jackie's honor at Washington's F Street Club. Whitehouse would come to see Camelot as "a beautiful sunset before an endlessly bitter night."

In mid-December Bobby and Ethel Kennedy organized a buffet luncheon for Jackie at the Harriman house. Lyndon Johnson, a guest at the same function, found himself shut out by the distinctly pro-Kennedy crowd, many of whom considered him an interloper with no real claim to the throne. Even Jackie, who eventually began to regard Bobby Kennedy as heir presumptive of her husband's position, had taken shots at LBJ, referring to him and Lady Bird as "Colonel Cornpone and his lit-tle Porkchop."

"At this particular buffet," recalled Pierre Salinger, "nobody would go near Johnson. You almost had to feel sorry for the poor fellow. After all, he *was* the president of the United States. Finally Lorraine Cooper broke the ice and joined him on the sidelines. And once that happened, others gradually went over to him and tried to make him feel welcome."

Following the initial spree of parties welcoming her and the children to Georgetown, Jackie suffered a severe setback. Everything in Washington reminded her of Jack. She couldn't drive past the White House without breaking down. Lyndon Johnson invited her to the White House, but she refused—it was far too soon. He signed a bill authorizing ongoing Secret Service protection for the family. He agreed to allow Caroline's White House class to continue meeting until May 1964—the end of the school year.

Over Christmas vacation of 1963, Jackie took Caroline and John to Palm Beach for a visit with Joe and Rose, after which they headed for Aspen, Colorado, for a week of skiing with the rest of the Kennedy clan. When Jackie returned to Washington, she asked John Kenneth Galbraith to go house hunting with her. Restricting her search to Georgetown, the former First Lady eventually paid $195,000 for a fourteen-room, three-story, fawn-colored brick Colonial at 3017 N Street, on the same block as the Harriman house. Built with twelve-inch-thick walls circa 1794, the house was fronted by a small grove of old magnolia trees. Jackie's choice of Georgetown as a place to raise Caroline and John was predicated to a large extent on her past happiness there with Jack. Another benefit was the current presence in Georgetown of Janet Auchincloss, who promised to babysit the grandchildren whenever needed.

One of the problems with 3017 N Street was that it stood on a rise high above the sidewalk and could be reached only by climbing a long flight of stairs. It was easy to see into the first-floor windows from the street below, which meant that the draperies had to be kept drawn at all times. The interior of the house, devoid of sunlight, had a gloomy feel to it. From certain angles one could see into Jackie's second-floor bedroom, making it difficult for her to change without being spied upon. In addition, Jackie and her children had rapidly become Washington's number one tourist attraction. To the dismay of their status-conscious Georgetown neighbors, the family's presence transformed the once peaceful village into a raging casbah. Morning, noon, and night the narrow streets of Georgetown were crammed with strangers eager for a firsthand glimpse of the young widow and/or her two beautiful children. They lined both sides of N Street, climbing trees and standing on the hoods and roofs of cars, double-parking, obstructing traffic, screaming, screeching, chanting Jackie's name like a mantra. They perched on the steps of her house, eating their lunch, tossing the leftovers into the gutter. At night they slept in their cars, buying their meals from street vendors hawking an array of fast-food products. Other vendors sold a line of Kennedy-related souvenirs: T-shirts, postcards, posters, record albums, books, magazines, and Caroline Kennedy "look-alike" dolls. The press likewise camped out in front of Jackie's house. Dozens of reporters and photographers, their pencils poised and cameras cocked, maintained a round-the-clock vigil, as did a battery of television trucks manned by sound technicians and cameramen. Whenever Jackie or her children emerged from the house, the Washington police and Secret Service agents assigned to their detail cordoned off the block and created a path for them. The same procedure applied when any of them returned. But the system didn't always work. Onlookers would break through police lines to grab and embrace the children as they came and went. On one occasion an elderly woman from Florida took hold of Jackie's hair and refused to let go. Professional and amateur photographers thought nothing of popping their flashbulbs in the children's startled faces. The same tour bus company drivers that had so beleaguered Jackie in the White House were at it again, making regular pit stops outside her house, disgorging tourists for a closer look, the buses racing up and down N Street at all hours of the day and night.

"I feel like a freak in a sideshow," Jackie confided to French ambassador Hervé Alphand, and his wife, Nicole. There were days when her desperation and depression, related in part to the constant din and clamor outside her house, simply got the better of her. "It was terribly sad," said Secretary of Defense Robert McNamara. "Here she had been elevated to the position of mythical folk-heroine, yet she remained a prisoner in her own home. It reached the point where she couldn't go out for a walk or a bite to eat without being mobbed. I once took her to a restaurant in Georgetown for lunch. People at neighboring tables stared; even the waiters and waitresses stared. I kept expecting somebody to come to our table and ask her for an autograph."

McNamara had another experience with Jackie. Soon after she moved into her new Georgetown home, he gave her an unfinished oil portrait of JFK that he had bought from a Washington art gallery. The painter had completed the president's face and shoulders. Jackie placed it on the floor of her dining room, leaning against the wall where she intended to mount it. When Caroline first saw the picture, she approached it and began kissing her father's face. "Bob," said Jackie, "I love the painting, but I can't handle Caroline's reaction to it. I had to hide it in a closet, where she can't see it. You'd better come and pick it up." McNamara drove over and retrieved the portrait, eventually hanging it over the fireplace in his own home.

Other friends of the family had their own tales to tell. Franklin Roosevelt Jr. drove Jackie home from a small get-together at his house one evening. As they pulled up in front of the N Street house, he noticed a dozen or so tourists perched on the steps leading to the front door. "I can't take it anymore," said Jackie. "They're like locusts—they're everywhere. I go to the cemetery at night to visit Jack, and they follow me to his grave. I go to St. Matthew's to pray, and they fill up the pews behind me. They're driving me crazy."

"She was in bad shape," said Lem Billings. "She once spoke to a priest about suicide—if it hadn't been for Caroline and John, she might have ended it. She spent entire days in bed, taking antidepressants in the morning and sedatives at night. She convinced herself that somehow she had failed Jack. Her only respite from suffering came from horseback riding. She'd drive to Wexford and spend time with her horses."

Jackie frequently took out her woes on the servants, firing them for the smallest infraction and then rehiring them the following day. She treated some of her friends in much the same fashion, making appointments she didn't keep, throwing dinner parties she didn't attend. When the children started referring to Bob Foster as "Daddy," she had him reassigned. When Evelyn Lincoln, in charge of organizing JFK's presidential papers, complained that she hadn't had a day off in weeks, Jackie rebuked her. "Mrs. Lincoln," she said, "why are you whining? You still have your husband. All I have is the library they're building for Jack."

George Plimpton recalled asking Jackie's permission to publish an ar-

ticle he'd written for *Harper's* magazine on JFK and Caroline attending
the America's Cup yacht race off Newport the year before. "She reacted
to my rather humble request by throwing an absolute fit," said Plimpton.
"I explained that the story was extremely positive, that the sole mention
of her daughter occurred in the description of a foot race at Hammersmith Farm between Caroline and Alice Ormsby Gore, the daughter of
Ambassador David Ormsby Gore. 'I won't have it!' yelled Jackie. 'Under
no circumstances may you publish such an article. I'm sick and tired of
everyone exploiting my children.' 'But Jackie,' I pleaded, 'you're being
completely unreasonable. The piece only makes Caroline look good.'
Jackie wouldn't budge, insisting that either the article be changed or remain unpublished. 'Write anything you want about me,' she said. 'Tell
the world I've gone off my rocker. Just leave my kid out of it.'"

Strangely enough, in the middle of all this, the former First Lady was
capable of the most thoughtful of acts. At a certain point, as Lem Billings
remembered it, when Bobby Kennedy, reaching the depths of his own
depression, expressed doubts as to remaining in Washington and continuing in public service, Jackie sat down and penned him a letter in which
she implored him not to give up, not to quit. She told him she needed
him and that the children, particularly John Jr., needed him as a surrogate father, as somebody they could turn to now that their own father
was gone. Above all, the country needed him. "It is time," she ended the
letter, "to honor Jack's memory—not to continue mourning it. We
would both, myself included, be negligent in our responsibilities to that
memory if we collapse. Jack would want us both to carry on what he
stood for, and died for."

Despite the encouraging tone of her letter, Jackie continued to struggle. The brave, stoic woman of the funeral had given way to an altogether
different persona. Her ongoing grief took its inevitable toll on the children, especially Caroline. Jacqueline Hirsh, an instructor of French at
Caroline's White House school, remembered the effect that the assassination and its aftermath had on the child: "I used to see her privately every
Monday afternoon on N Street. For a while there, it was pretty rough.
After Christmas break, Caroline refused to rejoin her White House class.
The child just looked ghastly, so wan and unhappy. I attributed some of

it to her concern for her mother. Although she almost never complained, she did say, 'My mommy lies in bed all day and can't stop crying.' To get Caroline out of the house, I began taking her and her cousin Sydney Lawford, also a student in the White House class, on outings. If a reporter or photographer approached her in the car and said, 'Hi, Caroline,' she would cower on the floor so she couldn't be seen. 'Please tell me when nobody's looking,' she would say. You could see that her father's death and her mother's collapse were perpetually on her mind."

Caroline disrupted a once-a-week religious training class she had been taking by bringing up her mother's frequent crying jags. "My mother cries all the time," she announced in class. "I get in bed with her and tell her everything is all right and she must stop crying. But she doesn't." The teacher, Sister Joanne Frey, noted how out of character it was for Caroline to vent her worries in public. It seemed to Sister Joanne that this was her way of crying out for help, that the child didn't know what to do about the situation.

William Joyce, a Washington attorney whose daughter had been a classmate of Caroline's during the White House years, bumped into Jackie at another child's birthday party while she was still in deep mourning. "Jackie had on lavender sandals and an old, rumpled pants suit," said Joyce. "She looked terrible. Caroline looked even worse. I felt sorry for the child. She was one of the most miserable looking creatures I've ever seen."

Caroline's unhappiness was heightened by still another development. She had spent the better part of a year posing for an illustrated children's volume, *The Caroline Kennedy First Lady Dress-Up Book,* which was to have been issued in the fall of 1963 by Rolton House, a fledgling publisher of juvenilia that had acquired rights directly from Jacqueline Kennedy by agreeing to contribute a percentage of the book's profits to the charity of Jackie's choice. In the volume, Caroline is depicted in a variety of period outfits and costumes originally worn by such first ladies as Martha Washington, Mary Todd Lincoln, Bess Truman, and Jacqueline Kennedy herself. Because of JFK's death, Jackie canceled the project, and the book, save for a dozen copies (each of which became a collector's item), was pulped. According to Maud Shaw, Caroline was profoundly disappointed. "She had been looking forward to the book so very much," wrote Shaw in the first draft version of her memoir, "and now it too amounted to nothing."

In late December 1963, *Paris Match,* the popular French-language magazine, ran a story claiming that Caroline Kennedy was so upset by her father's violent end that she had begun seeing a child psychiatrist. Not long after the appearance of the article, Philippe de Bausset, an editor and writer for the periodical, received an urgent telephone call from Pierre Salinger. "It was clear that he'd been put up to it by Mrs. Kennedy," said the editor. "He was angry as hell. He called us 'a rag' and threatened a lawsuit if we didn't immediately retract the story. He gave us twenty-four hours to get back to him with an answer. If we didn't comply, the Kennedys would file court papers in both France and the United States—they would sue for millions. We held an emergency editorial meeting with the magazine's chief counsel and the writer of the article to determine a course of action. It turned out we had an impeccable source for the story in the person of Steve Smith, brother-in-law to the president. So I called Salinger back the following morning and informed him that we had a reliable source and were satisfied with the story. 'Who's your source?' demanded Salinger. 'Like any respectable publication,' I told him, 'we protect our sources. I am not going to divulge names. But if the Kennedys pursue legal action, they will soon enough learn the identity of our source.' Needless to say, we never heard from Salinger or the Kennedys again."

Toward the end of January 1964, Jackie roused herself long enough to join Lee Radziwill, Franklin Roosevelt Jr., actor Marlon Brando, and Brando's business manager, George Englund, for a three-hour luncheon at the Jockey Club. "It marked the first occasion since Jack's assassination that I'd seen Jackie truly enjoy herself," said Roosevelt. "She was evidently taken with Brando, who talked with her about India. Jackie told Brando that Nehru had taught her how to stand on her head and meditate. In the middle of the meal, a press photographer somehow gained access to the restaurant and started taking pictures of Jackie, until her Secret Service agent managed to get rid of him. Jackie apologized. 'I can't do anything in this town without being besieged,' she said. 'You ought to move to New York,' Brando told her. 'You'd be much more invisible there than you are here—people won't bother you as much.'"

In mid-February Jackie left the children behind and spent a weekend at the hotel Carlyle in New York. "I felt like a human being for a change," she reported to Franklin Roosevelt Jr. "I walked the streets without being singled out." Two weeks later she again visited New York. She had breakfast with writer Irwin Shaw, lunch with Truman Capote, dinner with producer Leland Hayward and his wife, Pamela (the future wife of Averell Harriman), concluding her stay by accompanying Bobby Kennedy to the Waldorf Towers for a meeting with ex-president Herbert Hoover. Returning to Washington, she phoned Truman Capote and told him that in Manhattan she'd found her mecca, or rediscovered it, since New York was her hometown. "I feel infinitely more relaxed and comfortable in New York than I do in Washington," she said. "Everything about Washington reminds me of Jack."

At Easter Jackie took her children to Stowe, Vermont, for a ski vacation with their Kennedy cousins. Leaving Ted Kennedy in charge of the group, Jackie and Bobby (sans Ethel) set out with Lee Radziwill and Chuck Spalding on a Caribbean holiday at Bunny Mellon's estate in Antigua. It was there that Bobby divulged his intention to resign as attorney general and move to New York, where he planned to make his political stand by running for senator. The idea had taken hold long before Lyndon Johnson's indelicate declaration later in the year that he would bypass all members of his cabinet for the second spot on his ticket in the November 1964 election. "Let's face it," said Bobby, "if Johnson had to choose between Ho Chi Minh and 'yours truly' as a running mate, he'd go with Ho Chi Minh."

RFK's resolve to establish New York as his home base could only have hastened Jackie's decision to do the same. On May 29, 1964, the occasion of JFK's forty-seventh birthday commemoration, she took Caroline and John to Arlington National Cemetery and placed flowers on their father's grave, attended a memorial Mass at St. Matthew's, and went to Hyannis Port, where she talked via television satellite to viewers throughout Europe and the United States. She used the opportunity to transmit a message promoting world peace, thereby declaring herself an early enemy of the war in Vietnam. Back in Georgetown two days later, after eating dinner with her children, she pulled them aside. "Guess what?" she told them. "We're going to move to New York City, and so is Uncle Bobby. We'll all feel better there."

Part III

Chapter 6

NEW YORK, 1964–1968

ANDRÉ MEYER, THE FRENCH-BORN director of Lazard Frères, the New York investment banking firm, had become Jacqueline Kennedy's unofficial financial adviser and occasional escort. Knowing a good real estate offer when he saw one, Meyer encouraged Jackie to pay the $200,000 asking price on a spectacular fifteen-room (five bedroom/ six bath) cooperative apartment on the fifteenth floor of 1040 Fifth Avenue, corner of 85th Street, fourteen of its twenty-three windows overlooking Central Park, the Metropolitan Museum of Art, and the Central Park Reservoir, around which the former First Lady could soon be seen fast-walking for exercise, trailed at a discreet distance by her Secret Service detail. Her annual maintenance on the Manhattan apartment, which included three working fireplaces, totaled $14,000, a figure that rose precipitously over the years, as did the value of the apartment. In addition, she spent approximately $125,000 to have the residence refurbished and redecorated. To pay for the purchase and improvements, Jackie sold her recently acquired N Street townhouse in Georgetown as well as Wexford, which in aggregate brought in more than $600,000. While painters, plumbers, and plasterers readied the Fifth Avenue apartment, Jackie, Maud Shaw, and the children moved temporarily into a large suite at the Carlyle on the same floor as André Meyer, who lived there as well. Michael O'Connell, bell captain at the hotel, remembered John-John always carrying around and hugging an old wooden toy boat. "It was one of the worst little boats I'd ever seen," said O'Connell. The boat had been a birthday gift from his father.

Jackie's resettlement held a number of advantages for both herself and her children. In the first place, they were surrounded in New York by a bevy of friends and relatives, including Bobby Kennedy, who acquired a cooperative apartment at 40 United Nations Plaza. With Jackie's help, he would win a clear-cut victory in the November 1964 New York senatorial race.

Another advantage to New York was the myriad cultural institutions and organizations within close range of 1040 Fifth Avenue. During their first year in New York, while Jackie occupied herself overseeing the work on her apartment and raising funds for the construction of the John F. Kennedy Presidential Library and Museum in Boston, the children were shepherded to various events and activities. Maud Shaw brought them to the Metropolitan Museum of Art, the Museum of Natural History, the Hayden Planetarium, Radio City Music Hall, the Bronx Zoo, and the 42nd Street branch of the New York Public Library. They went rowboating in Central Park, took the Circle Line sightseeing cruise around Manhattan, toured the United Nations, visited the Statue of Liberty and the Empire State Building. They attended the circus at Madison Square Garden, the lighting of the Christmas tree at Rockefeller Center, a children's operetta at Carnegie Hall, a Broadway musical, a Town Hall performance of *The Nutcracker,* and a children's poetry reading at the 92nd Street "Y." They rented horses at Claremont Stables on the Upper West Side, rode their bicycles and went roller-skating on the pedestrian paths of Central Park, and watched the Thanksgiving Day parade on Broadway and the Easter parade along Fifth Avenue. The Central Park Children's Zoo, which now housed several of their White House pets, became one of their favorite Manhattan locations.

"The city rolled out the red carpet for them," wrote Maud Shaw in the first draft of her memoir. "But, in general, we did many of the same things most New Yorkers enjoy doing in their leisure time. Mrs. Kennedy was adamant that Caroline and John not be given special treatment. The only difference between them and children from other affluent house-holds was the constant presence of the Secret Service."

Barbara Deutsch, a neighbor with an apartment at the same address as Jackie, recalled seeing "the Kennedy kids soon after they moved to New York, racing around a nearby Gristede's grocery store on Madison Avenue, while Maud Shaw went food shopping. On this occasion, John-John ran smack into a store clerk precariously balanced atop a stepladder, arranging a floor-to-ceiling, pyramidal display of soup cans. The force of the collision sent clerk and cans flying. Aware that he'd done something wrong, John-John began to cry. Maud Shaw found herself consoling clerk and child at the same time. As the three of them left the store, a press photographer descended upon Caroline, shooting her with his camera. She remained calm, covering her face with her hand until the photographer finally gave up and went away."

Like other curious neighbors, Barbara Deutsch encountered Jackie and her children from time to time in the building elevator. "I'd heard from the Bundys that Mrs. Kennedy had adjusted to her new life in New York," said Deutsch. "Looking at her, it was difficult to say if she'd ad-justed or not. She seemed almost impenetrable. If you smiled at her, she smiled back. If you frowned, she frowned. Engaging with her was like looking into a mirror. I soon determined that Caroline, very definitely her mother's daughter, reacted to strangers in much the same way. That first year she seemed melancholy and withdrawn. She never initiated conversation but if addressed, would politely respond. John-John, on the other hand, struck me as extroverted and ultra-friendly, always chirping away like a little bird. The first time we met, he introduced himself to me. 'Hello, I'm John F. Kennedy Jr.' Whenever we saw each other af-ter that, he'd chat it up, tell me where he'd been and what he'd seen. For all their differences, there appeared to be no competitiveness or sibling rivalry between the two children. They seemed very protective of each other, which was important considering the great loss they had both suffered."

"It was a difficult period for everyone concerned," said Jacques Lowe, a guest at one of Jackie's first New York dinner parties. "There were maybe eight of us around the table on this particular evening, including

Jackie's mother. Caroline and John Jr. were there as well. Jackie served a beautifully prepared roast turkey dish as the main course. Janet Auchincloss and Caroline had dug out the wishbone and were pulling on it. Caroline won. 'Can I wish for anything I want?' she asked. 'Anything,' said her grandmother. 'Then I want to see my daddy again,' said Caroline."

Dave Powers, with whom John Jr. had frequently played soldier when they still lived in Georgetown, flew in one day and joined the family for lunch. "As a starter," said Powers, "Jackie's cook had prepared a large pot of New England clam chowder. John Jr., always a bit finicky when it came to food, refused to touch his soup. Dipping my spoon into the rich, creamy concoction, I said to him, 'Your daddy grew up on clam and fish chowder. You ought to give it a try.' He made a face but finally sampled a spoonful. Finding it to his liking, he went to work on the rest of it. When he was done, he looked me in the eye and asked, 'Do they have clam chowder in heaven?' 'I'm sure they do,' I responded. 'That's good,' said John, 'because then my daddy can have some.' Jackie later told me this was the first time John had verbally acknowledged his father's death."

Maud Shaw had noticed subtle but unmistakable changes in the boy's demeanor. He played and scampered and chatted away as much as (if not more than) usual, but his face would occasionally cloud over as if he were struggling to understand what had happened. He seemed friskier than before, more difficult to handle. He would race ahead of Miss Shaw, reach a street corner, and begin to cross against the light until grabbed from behind and restrained by the nanny. When he came down with the chicken pox (at the same time as Caroline), he refused to stay in bed, jumping up and running madly around the apartment. He developed the habit of approaching strange men on the street and asking them to lift him up, presumably because his own father's bad back had prevented him from performing this task. The family's migration from the White House to Georgetown and then to New York had also left its mark. A number of times, he asked his mother or Miss Shaw why they no longer lived in the "other house—the big white one with all the choppers." When visitors came to Jackie's apartment, John would ask them, "Do you want to hear my daddy speak?" And then he'd lead them to his bedroom where he kept a recording of JFK's speeches near his record player. It proved troubling to more than one guest to have to sit and listen to the dead president in the company of his young son.

In September 1964 Jackie enrolled Caroline in the second grade at the Convent of the Sacred Heart, a prestigious Catholic girls' school housed in a gingerbread mansion on Fifth Avenue and 91st Street. Two of her cousins, Victoria and Sydney Lawford, attended the same school. The staunchly religious Rose Kennedy wrote Jackie a letter complimenting her on sending Caroline to a parochial institution, just as she had done with her daughters. Jackie had her doubts. Moody and listless, Caroline seemed not much better off psychologically than she'd been during the period immediately following her father's assassination. "She no longer lets anyone get close to her," Bobby Kennedy informed Lem Billings. He told Billings that although he saw a good deal of Caroline, it wasn't always easy. "Every time I look at her," said Bobby, "I want to go somewhere and cry."

Terry Gelfenbaum, a student at Sacred Heart at the same time as Caroline, was a close friend of Sydney Lawford. "We had chapel two and sometimes three times a week," she said. "The nuns wore habits and were fairly strict. The classes were small. There was a lot of money at the school. On Friday afternoons the limousines would line up to whisk the kids off to the country for the weekend. Caroline was always quiet and reserved, as if preoccupied with some intensely deep thought."

Although Caroline enjoyed the academic work at Sacred Heart, which boasted a rigorous (if rather conventional) curriculum, she detested the colorless school uniform that students were forced to wear: gray jumper, white blouse, gray jacket, gray socks, red beret, camel topcoat. There were no exceptions. Even Jackie, the product of a progressive private and boarding school education, found Sacred Heart's dress code unnecessarily confining, its rules overly stringent. "Compared to the school Caroline attended at the White House," she wrote to Evangeline Bruce, "the present one seems almost medieval. There are too many regulations, not enough room for individual expression. When they arrive for class in the morning in their various shades of gray, the girls resemble inmates at a penitentiary. Charles Dickens would have had a field day with Sacred Heart."

The most daunting aspect of school for Caroline had to be her inability to make friends. For the first six months, she had practically no after-school playdates and rarely received invitations to her classmates' parties. With the exception of her cousins Victoria and Sydney Lawford, who were frequent dinner guests at 1040 Fifth Avenue, Caroline had few playmates. Intimidated by her background as the daughter of the late president, Caroline's schoolmates maintained their distance, convincing themselves that she wanted as little to do with them as they with her. Cognizant of her daughter's dilemma, Jackie finally called the mother of one of her more popular classmates to ask why Caroline was being socially ostracized. The mother explained that while the Sacred Heart parents all had wanted to invite Caroline, they had thought it presumptuous to ask. "Not at all," said Jackie. "Caroline's just a little girl. She would love to be invited to something, and I will see to it that she goes."

Caroline's social life immediately picked up. She soon had a small circle of friends with whom she congregated after school and on those weekends she remained in town. When she went on a playdate or attended a party, she had to be accompanied by at least one and sometimes a pair of Secret Service agents. The agents posted themselves in the hall outside whatever apartment Caroline happened to be visiting. Whenever she went to the park with her friends, John would invariably be dragged along, leaving his mother with the feeling that her son needed more male companionship. Jackie herself began taking John to Harvard football games. They went to Baker's Field in upper Manhattan to watch Harvard trounce Columbia University; they traveled to Philadelphia for the Harvard-Penn contest, and to Boston to watch Harvard take on Yale. Always on the lookout for manly entertainment for John, she once asked a Central Park patrolman if he would give her young son a ride on the back of his motor scooter. "I wish I could," said the cop, "but it's against police regulations." After a short pause, he again apologized, then asked the former First Lady for her autograph.

When not involved in school activities, Caroline followed her mother's lead by taking part in horse shows and exhibitions. With several of her cousins—Kathleen and Courtney, Bobby and Ethel's daughters, in addition to Maria Shriver—she rode in the young equestrian group of the 4-H horse show, held each year at Barnstable, Massachusetts. She consistently won blue ribbons at horse shows in New Jersey and on Long Island. Then there were the winter ski trips to Sun Valley and Aspen, with Bobby providing instruction to his own children as well as Caroline and John. Caroline turned out to be proficient in the sport. John Jr., a natural daredevil, too often demonstrated more bravado than skill. It was in Aspen, after John slipped on the slope and began to whine, that RFK, long obsessed by a "manly" code of conduct, said to him, "Kennedys never cry"—to which JFK Jr. purportedly retorted, "This Kennedy cries."

Athleticism and a newfound contingent of companions notwithstanding, Caroline continued to suffer episodes of depression and moments of grave self-doubt. She had seen the now-historic Zapruder film on television with its frame-by-frame depiction of JFK's last lurching movements as the assassin's bullets tore through him. In an effort to erase the memory of her father's demise, she collected stamps, coins, magazines, and memorabilia that bore his likeness—anything and everything that showed him at his smiling, handsome best. She struggled to assimilate the picture of the dead hero with the man she had once known and still loved. When her class read and then discussed the story of Joan of Arc, Caroline volunteered an impression, telling her teacher and classmates that "Joan of Arc was killed, just like my father."

"Caroline often walks around with her head down," Jackie informed the well-known psychoanalyst Erik Erikson, before sending Caroline to see him, a continuation of the sessions she'd begun in early 1964 with a Washington therapist. Erikson also took on John Jr. as a patient. If Caroline too frequently seemed lethargic and dour, John was hyperactive and excessively exuberant. John Crouse, a second cousin, recalled young John Jr. "running around Michelle Bouvier Putnam's Park Avenue flat, taking handfuls of bacon fat out of the refrigerator and throwing it at people, basically turning the apartment upside down. Jackie couldn't control him. Nobody could. Caroline was much easier. She would occasionally join in the fun, but she never lost control of herself."

Jackie had set up an easel for both children at a window in the bedroom overlooking the park. Caroline's drawings were full of dead leaves and wilting flowers; John's were violent in nature, consisting of guns, knives, and dead bodies. Erik Erikson consulted with the children once a week on an individual basis. When John first saw him, he complained that his mother was too strict with him, that Caroline could do just about anything, but if he stepped out of line, she would give him a swat. During one of their therapeutic sessions, Erikson provided the youngster with a small rag doll and a set of blocks and instructed him to build a house for the doll. John constructed the house but disposed of the doll by placing it on a bookshelf. When Erikson asked John why he hadn't put the doll inside the house, he replied, "Because the doll went away." "Why did the doll leave?" asked Erikson. "Because he doesn't belong in the house anymore," said John.

The children sustained another loss in the summer of 1965, when Maud Shaw returned to England on what she initially believed would be merely a family trip with Jackie, Caroline, and John. In early March of that year, Jackie informed her that following their visit to England, her services would no longer be needed. On March 22, Shaw wrote to Evelyn Lincoln: "I had planned on going to England with the children in May, but Mrs. Kennedy has just told me she will not need me to return to the States. I must say it was a bit of a shock." Realizing that Caroline and John would be upset, Jackie asked Miss Shaw to say nothing to the children. After seven and a half years with the family, Maud Shaw's going-away present consisted of a gold-embossed leather-bound scrapbook bearing an inscription written by Mrs. Kennedy: "You brought such happiness to all our lives and especially to President Kennedy, because you made his children what they are."

That summer the children went to Britain with their mother and Miss Shaw and spent several days visiting with Shaw's family in Sheerness, England. Jackie, meanwhile, stayed with her sister and her sister's children, Anthony and Anna Christina (Tina), at the Radziwill home in Regents Park, London, where she conducted interviews with prospective nannies. Above all, she wanted to replace Shaw with somebody younger, somebody better able to meet Caroline's and John's present needs. She complained to Evangeline Bruce that Shaw had exercised "too much control over Caroline and not enough over John, especially of late." Jackie was particularly concerned about the feminizing influence that Shaw might have had on John. She told Jacques Lowe, "I'm afraid that without a permanent father figure, John is going to grow up with an identity problem and will want to become a hairdresser." "I doubt it," Lowe responded. "He'll come to know his father through the stories he'll hear from those who were closest to Jack. John Jr. will grow up to become either an astronaut or a politician." In her memoir, Maud Shaw addressed the issue of Jackie's homophobic fears regarding her son, stating that her efforts to "toughen him up" greatly disturbed the young child. "She makes the little mite go through hell," wrote Shaw, pointing out that while John might at times have been emotionally fragile, he showed none of the effeminate signs his mother assigned to him. She provided as an example of his budding masculinity his athletic accomplishments at Bailey's Beach, Newport's most exclusive private club, where since age two he had been jumping off the high board into the deep end of the swimming pool.

Following their visit with Maud Shaw's family, Caroline and John traveled with Shaw and their mother to Runnymede, the site of the signing of the Magna Carta in 1215. It was there that Queen Elizabeth dedicated a national monument in honor of President Kennedy, a ceremony attended by Prime Minister Harold Macmillan as well as Bobby and Ted Kennedy. Afterward, the family had tea with the queen at Windsor Castle. Over the next few days, Jackie, Caroline, and John toured London, visiting Whitehall, Buckingham Palace, and the Tower of London, where John managed to get stuck in the mouth of an old cannon. Fascinated by the executioner's ax shown to the children by Sir Thomas Butler, the tower's governor, John wanted to know everything about the beheadings, how prisoners placed their heads on the block, whether they felt any pain. Less interested than her brother in all the gory details, Caroline seemed more intrigued by the crown jewels.

While still in London, the children posed for the camera of Cecil Beaton. The photographer took a dozen pictures and after developing the roll, sent each child a complete set. Though pleased by the photo-

graphs, years later Jackie would be less enthused by the description offered of her in his multivolume *Diaries* series, in which he called her "an
oversized caricature of herself."

On the return flight to New York, Jackie sat next to actress Bette
Davis, while attempting to keep an eye on the children. Unable to sit
still, JFK Jr. ran up and down the aisle of the plane, until a crew member
invited him to visit the cockpit. "I'm a bit worried," Jackie told Davis.
"You see, John wants to pilot the aircraft."

Jackie's dealings with Maud Shaw did not end in London. When she
learned that the former nanny planned on writing a book about her experiences with the Kennedys, she sent Shaw a letter, reminding her that
she had signed "a pledge of loyalty not to write or give interviews on the
period of your service to the family, an oath required of everyone employed by us." If she persisted, read the letter, Jackie would no longer per-
mit the children to communicate with her.

Having set aside little money toward her retirement and feeling somewhat betrayed by her employer, Maud Shaw wrote the best-selling *White
House Nanny.* When she learned of the memoir's pending release, Jackie
enlisted the help of Sol M. Linowitz, chairman of the board of Xerox
Corporation, to help her draft a letter to the book's publisher, restating
her position that having signed a pledge of loyalty, Shaw needed her permission to publish anything predicated on her service to the Kennedys.
Rejecting Jackie's claim on grounds that the document had been signed
under duress, the publisher's attorney nevertheless encouraged Shaw,
who had worked on the project with a ghostwriter, to tone down the
more contentious sections of the manuscript, including an inflammatory
passage describing Jackie's increased dependence on alcohol in the weeks
and months following the assassination. "In order to get through it,"
Shaw had written, "Mrs. Kennedy drank heavily and all the time." Having made a number of last-minute changes, Shaw once again wrote to
Evelyn Lincoln: "I feel I have done nothing out of place by pattering
about the president and his children. I hope she [Mrs. Kennedy] will
continue to let the children write to me."

Despite several unflattering comments on Jackie in the published version of the memoir, the former First Lady ultimately allowed (and even encouraged) her children to correspond with Miss Shaw. "To do otherwise," Jackie told Jacques Lowe, "would have been unconscionable."

One morning in mid-October 1965, the telephone rang in the office of Peter Clifton, assistant headmaster at St. David's School, 12 East 89th Street, in Manhattan. "Hello, Mr. Clifton," said a soft voice on the other end of the phone. "This is Jacqueline Kennedy. I wonder if I could make an appointment to come in and see the school."

Jackie evidently found the school to her liking. Five-year-old John Jr. was signed up for a prekindergarten program that began in February 1966. A Catholic school for boys, St. David's was run by a lay board of trustees and had no formal affiliation with the Archdiocese of New York. Although it catered to the sons of old, moneyed New York families, the school's roughly three hundred students included a healthy mix of boys on scholarship from a diversity of backgrounds. The heterogeneous educational environment at the school—different races, different religions, different economic circumstances—appealed to Jackie. She didn't want John (or Caroline, for that matter) to become an overindulged, spoiled child. Several of John's cousins attended the school as well, among them Christopher Lawford, Steve and Willie Smith, and Anthony Radziwill. A year ahead of John Jr. in school, Anthony had recently transferred to St. David's from the Lycée Français in London.

Although generally well liked by his teachers, John went through an initial period of adjustment. To be sure, his arrival at St. David's created a stir. During his second week in school, he became involved in a minor fracas. As one of the school's administrators remembered it, John lost his temper because a classmate insisted on calling him John-John, a name he felt he'd outgrown. "Don't call me that—my name is John," he warned his tormentor. When the fellow persisted, John threw a punch. More startled than hurt, the name caller began to cry. John was sent to the headmaster's office, where he waited for his mother to pick him up. Appropriately apologetic, Jackie told the headmaster that the episode was as much her fault as her son's—in an effort to bolster John's self-confidence she had asked Jack Walsh, the six-foot-six-inch chief of their Secret Service detail, to give JFK Jr. boxing lessons. John hadn't yet learned, she said, "to talk with his mouth and not with his fists."

"Nobody knew what to expect when Mrs. Kennedy first enrolled John at St. David's," said Peter Clifton. "We were all on pins and needles." As it turned out, John's presence in the school created fewer problems than anticipated. The most serious dilemma involved the Secret Service detail that accompanied the boy to school in the morning, waited outside his classroom, then saw him home or to his next activity after school. The school board wanted the Secret Service to wait for John in front of the building rather than in the hallway outside his classroom. They refused, pointing out that their proximity to the subject afforded maximum security.

"Mrs. Kennedy was sympathetic," said Peter Clifton, "but there wasn't much she could do to change the arrangement. So we made the best of it. As for John, he was with us for two and a half years, prekindergarten through first grade. He was a very sweet fellow, totally without guile, a quality he exhibited throughout his life. I have to give his mother credit for that. She wasn't active in the Parents Association, but she was involved in everything having to do with her son. She was extremely gracious to the various members of the faculty. She kept in close touch with John's teachers and with me. She was enormously thankful whenever anyone gave John extra attention."

Jackie paid equal attention to the education and rearing of both children. When Caroline's class at Sacred Heart put on a musical that they repeated three or four times for different audiences, Jackie attended each performance. When Caroline had homework she couldn't complete, it remained for her mother to guide her through the assignment. On "Father's Visiting Day" at Caroline's school, Jacqueline stood in for her late husband. When Caroline took a course in conversational French, her mother assumed the role of tutor. The only participatory activity Jackie came to regret was encouraging Caroline to bring home a field mouse from biology class. Within a week, she called the biology teacher and asked her if she could return the mouse to school. The tiny creature insisted on dropping its pellets all over her apartment.

Whenever Jackie went to see Kenneth, the New York hairdresser she had frequently flown to the White House during her term as First Lady, she would bring Caroline along for a styling or cut. She put her foot down only once when Caroline expressed the desire to have her blond tresses colored the same shade as her mother's.

Recognizing that Caroline and John would gain strength from their relationship with aunts and uncles, grandparents, and cousins, Jackie understood as well that growing up with the feeling of belonging to their own small family unit would give them stability. For a long time she attempted to combine both elements. In mid-June 1966 she and Peter Lawford brought their children to Hawaii for a leisurely vacation. Leasing a secluded Japanese-style house in Kahala, Jackie signed up the boys—John Jr. and Christopher—for a series of introductory surfing lessons, while the girls—Caroline, Victoria, and Sydney—received private instruction in the hula. During a camping trip on the beach, John Jr. toppled backward into a campfire but was quickly pulled out by Secret Service agent Jack Walsh.

After a brief stopover in San Francisco, Jackie, Caroline, and John spent the end of July and most of August visiting family members at Newport and Hyannis Port. Ted Kennedy, another father figure to Caroline and John, would take them sailing in their father's boat. Neighbors spotted Teddy walking along the beach with his niece and nephew, talking and skipping stones on the water. Toward the end of summer, Caroline served as flower girl and John as ring bearer for the wedding of Lewis Rutherfurd Jr. and Janet Jennings Auchincloss at St. Mary's Roman Catholic Church in Newport, the site of Jacqueline and John F. Kennedy's marriage ceremony thirteen years earlier. The bride was so upstaged by half-sister Jackie at her own wedding that she broke down in tears.

"I don't want Caroline and John to be just two kids growing up on Fifth Avenue and going to nice schools," Jackie wrote to Evangeline Bruce in the fall of 1966. Vangie wrote back that with a mother like Jackie, she couldn't imagine "Caroline and John ever being just two kids growing up on Fifth Avenue."

"I had just read in the paper that coming home from school with her

mother, Caroline had been knocked down by a press photographer trying to take her picture," said Bruce. "It's obvious that this sort of thing
doesn't happen to just anyone. Jackie's kids had experiences, both good
and bad, that were unique to their place in the world as the offspring of
Jacqueline Kennedy and the fallen president."

On November 22, the anniversary of JFK's death, Jackie picked up
John after school and started walking home with him along Fifth Avenue
when she noticed that they were being followed by a group of children,
some of them from John's class. One of the children began jeering in a
loud voice, "Your father's dead . . . your father's dead!" The rest of them
joined in. John listened to the chorus of voices but didn't say a word. Instead he drew close to his mother, took her hand and squeezed it, as if to
reassure her that things were all right. And so they walked home together,
with the children following and calling out after them.

Despite the many challenges of parenthood, Jackie's greatest pleasure (and
pain) came from being with her children. Fashion designer and boutique
owner Lilly Pulitzer noted that Jackie had been bringing her daughter
into her Manhattan and Hyannis Port clothing stores for several years.
"Jackie would wait patiently while Caroline tried on a dozen or more
outfits," said Pulitzer. "Unlike other mothers, she allowed her daughter
to make her own final selections, even if they weren't always the best or
most economical selections. Even so, *Women's Wear Daily* ran a photograph of her in one of our tight-waisted junior dresses at the christening
(by Caroline) in Newport News, Virginia, of the $200 million aircraft
carrier USS *John F. Kennedy*, describing her as a budding mini-trendsetter
and predicting that it might mean the beginning of the end of the A-line.
When I mentioned the photo to Jackie, she said, 'I don't mind them taking pictures of my kids at public ceremonies—the ones that bug me are
the photographers that hang around outside our apartment building
waiting for them to come home after school.'

"I might add that Caroline loved to shop for clothes in those days,
probably because she hated having to wear her school uniform every day.
It was only later when she became a teenager and somewhat rebellious

that she turned against high fashion in favor of blue jeans and sweat-shirts."

Long before exercise salons and the sport of jogging became popular, Jackie joined Nicholas Kounovsky's exclusive gym on West 57th Street. Her personal trainer there, Ivo Lupis, devised a strenuous exercise regimen that she followed with religious ferocity. Because of a scheduling conflict, she soon began bringing John along to her sessions and was surprised to find that he enjoyed using the gym equipment, inventing his own exercise routine. Little did she realize that "working out" would become a lifelong preoccupation with John.

During one of their school holidays, Jackie took the children to Córdoba, Argentina, to stay on the cattle ranch of Miguel A. Carcona, whose daughters had long before been best friends with Joe Kennedy's sons. Carcona regaled Caroline and John Jr. with stories about their father as a young man. He took them to a tall oak tree on his property under which JFK, while still in his twenties, had placed a large stone. John Jr. wandered off and returned with a stone of his own. "Place it on top of your father's stone," said Carcona, "and then one day when you have a son, you'll bring him here and he'll place a stone on top of yours." Delighted with their host's suggestion, Jackie said, "That's a wonderful idea, Miguel. We'll start a family tradition."

Over another holiday, Jackie, Caroline, and John Jr. flew to Acapulco, where Jack and Jacqueline had spent their honeymoon. They were joined on their vacation by Lee Radziwill and her two children. At one point during their stay, a powerboat carrying a horde of Mexican photographers caused Jackie's sailboat to capsize. Journalists seemed to be everywhere in Acapulco, and their presence unnerved the Secret Service detail assigned to guard the Kennedys. Only John Jr. seemed unperturbed, smiling and waving at reporters whenever they turned up.

In the summer of 1967, in an effort to expose Caroline and John even further to their heritage, Jackie took them on a six-week "sentimental journey" to Ireland, which included a meeting with President Eamon de Valera, the Irish Sweepstakes, and a visit to the Kennedy ancestral home at Dunganstown. They spent most of their time with family friends, the

Murray McDonnells, and their eight offspring at their summer retreat, Woodstown House, a fifty-three-room mansion at Waterford. On one occasion, Caroline and John were splashing in a nearby pond with the McDonnell children when some fifty press photographers showed up and began taking pictures. Caroline and John's Secret Service escort quickly rounded up the children and drove them back to the McDonnell estate. Unsettled by the incident, Jackie telephoned Ireland's Department of External Affairs and asked them to issue a statement that neither she nor the children wanted anything but to be left in peace. A few days later when a handful of photographers appeared and began to mill around the children, they were placed under arrest by the local police and carted off to jail.

John's education outside the narrow confines of the schoolhouse far exceeded what he managed to absorb in class. Unlike Caroline, who excelled in school and always found herself near the top of her class, John struggled to keep up with his contemporaries at St. David's. He was bright, but he found it difficult to focus. Erik Erikson attributed John's early learning disability to attention deficit disorder, a not-uncommon ailment among children his age. Erikson prescribed Ritalin, a relatively new medication that helped curb John's tendency toward hyperactivity but did little to enhance his power of concentration. It came as no surprise to Jackie when school officials notified her that if she wished to keep her son at St. David's, he would have to repeat the first grade. He lacked, they said, the skills and maturity to move ahead. Fearful that being left back at such a tender age could prove humiliating to John, his mother withdrew him from St. David's in favor of Collegiate, the oldest all-boys private school in New York. Founded in 1628 and located at West 77th Street and West End Avenue, Collegiate had one of the finest college admissions programs in the city.

To help prepare John for enrollment in the second grade at Collegiate, Jackie hired a private tutor named Kent Cunow. A recent graduate in English literature from Columbia University, Cunow recalled working with John "for about six months. We used to meet at his mother's Fifth Avenue apartment, a unique and inviting environment accented in yellows, greens, and golds, containing Regency and Louis XIV furniture with Chippendale and a touch of Oriental and Middle Eastern. The rooms were large and airy and scented with herbal and lavender potpourri contained in hand-decorated porcelain bowls scattered about the apartment. Vases of freshly cut flowers and hanging plants filled the rooms. Rare scattered rugs, paintings, and tapestries added to the decor. There was a magnificent library full of first editions and leather-bound volumes, which is where John and I usually worked. His main problem was spelling. The simplest words—dog, cat, boy, girl—gave him trouble. Mrs. Kennedy was extremely supportive. 'Don't worry about it,' she'd say. 'Your father couldn't spell, and he graduated from Harvard.'

"Actually, John struck me as a pretty average learner for his age. I had the feeling that St. David's threatened to hold him back in the first grade simply because they wanted him out of the school. All those Secret Service agents scurrying about was more than they'd bargained for. I'd been hired, I think, primarily to serve as a big brother figure to John."

The question of finances became problematic at this juncture. President Kennedy's last will and testament, completed in 1954 but never updated, made inadequate provisions for his widow, forcing her to confront and petition the family whenever she wanted to purchase anything out of the ordinary. Although JFK had left behind an estate valued at $15 million, most of it was tied up in trusts for Caroline and John. The sole trust in Jackie's name yielded $150,000 per year to cover living expenses; if she remarried, the trust reverted to her children. Jackie had no intention of attempting to invade her children's trusts or using their inheritance to augment her own income. In addition, she received an incidental monthly widow's pension from the government amounting to $10,000 per annum, hardly enough to make a difference. (This, too, would be forfeited if she remarried.) The problem was that in return for the Kennedy family's ongoing patronage, she was expected to do the clan's bidding. Everything she did was carefully scrutinized. Everything she said was weighed as to whether or not it seemed advantageous to the family's ambitions. In essence, the Kennedys treated her as they would a political prisoner.

"Jackie had her problems with the Kennedys," remarked French journalist Paul Mathias, a friend of Lee Radziwill's. "With the exception of Bobby Kennedy, who allotted her an extra $50,000 per year, the Kennedys were unsympathetic to Jackie's financial needs. For instance, after JFK's death she invested in a customized trailer and had it installed in back of her house at Hyannis Port to be used by the Secret Service. She didn't want them hanging out inside her house, because she found them intrusive. Ethel Kennedy accused her of being spoiled. She couldn't for a moment understand the necessity of acquiring a trailer to accommodate the Secret Service.

The Kennedys were likewise taken aback by Jackie's expenditures on costly personal possessions. She adored beautiful objects. She thought nothing of spending $60,000 at A La Vieille Russie on a snuffbox or a flowerpot that had once belonged to Catherine the Great. The Kennedys didn't care a whit about snuffboxes or Fabergé eggs or Persian rugs. They didn't go in for great art or furniture or porcelain. They were interested in power, in politics. From their perspective, if Jackie couldn't make it on $200,000 a year, she had to be doing something wrong.

Because of the delicate balance that existed between Jacqueline and the rest of the Kennedy family, her love life similarly became an issue open to scrutiny. In March 1968, the same month that RFK announced his candidacy in the forthcoming presidential race, the Kennedys were surprised to learn that Jackie had left the children in New York with their nanny and gone off on a trip to see the Mayan ruins of Mexico with Roswell Gilpatric. Born in New York in 1906, Gilpatric had a law degree from Yale, a wife, and had served as deputy secretary of defense during the Kennedy administration. Until their departure for Mexico, their affair had remained so low-key that nobody knew about it.

"I'd known JFK since his days as a congressman," said Gilpatric. "I met Jackie when she became First Lady. They had many informal dinners and social gatherings, which seemed to be the style they both preferred. I also spoke with Jackie at several of the Hickory Hill seminars given by Robert Kennedy, those peculiar functions at which he and Ethel would sneak up on their guests and shove them into the swimming pool. Then during the White House years, Jackie visited me once at a house I owned on the Eastern Shore of Maryland. The First Lady and I were only friends at that point. The relationship evolved slowly after JFK's assassination. As a matter of fact, just prior to the beginning of our involvement, Jackie ended a low-profile romance with John Warnecke, the architect she'd commissioned to design the Kennedy memorial at Arlington National Cemetery."

Covering the Yucatán (Mexico) trip for *Women's Wear Daily*, staff writer Agnes Ash recalled that "there was a lot of smooching and hand holding between Jackie and Gilpatric. It took place in full view of the press . . . Jackie didn't mind the Mexican press because they wrote glowing reports about her and made no mention of her public displays of affection. But she felt the American papers were insulting toward her . . . She was especially down on *WWD* because we reported how much she spent on her wardrobe every year and went into considerable detail on her social activities."

Somehow Rose Kennedy got hold of an advance copy of Ash's final article on the trip with all the juicy tidbits on the flirtation between Jackie and Gilpatric. "Rose telephoned John Fairchild, editorial director of *WWD*," said Ash. "She asked him to kill the piece—it would have an adverse effect on the children, which was a strange excuse considering that Jackie's children were too young to read the publication. I thought it had more to do with RFK's run for the presidency. To Fairchild's everlasting credit, he ran the piece intact."

If the article made it seem as though Jackie and Gilpatric were in love and on the verge of marriage, the fact of the matter is that their relationship was on the verge of collapse. "The weird thing about the Yucatán trip," said Gilpatric, "is that by then I realized we weren't going to work out. While we were on the trip, Jackie alluded several times to Aristotle Onassis and told me her intentions. She was very straightforward. She hadn't entirely decided to pursue Onassis—or encourage him to pursue her—but she seemed to be leaning that way."

Jackie's ties to Onassis had grown stronger in recent months. She had visited him not only at Skorpios but at his Avenue Foch townhouse in Paris. They were seen together in New York, once at El Morocco, another time at Le Perigord Park. With his seventeen-year-old daughter, Christina, in tow, Onassis squired Jackie to Dionysius and Mykonos, a pair of plain but authentic Greek restaurants in Manhattan. She had joined Onassis on a cruise of the Virgin Islands. In mid-April 1968, shortly after the assassination of Martin Luther King Jr., Jackie, Caroline, and John Jr. flew with Onassis to Palm Beach aboard an Olympic Airways jetliner. Olympic, one of a number of corporations controlled by the Onassis family, placed its fleet at its owner's disposal whenever he traveled. In Palm Beach, they stayed at the home of socialite Jayne Wrightsman. Jackie introduced Onassis to Rose Kennedy; despite the Kennedy family's predisposition against Onassis, Rose found him surprisingly amusing, even gracious, particularly so when Ari gave her a $50,000 check as a contribution to Robert Kennedy's presidential campaign fund. Another connection was established by Dr. Henry Lax, Jackie's Hungarian-born internist, whose patient list included both Ari Onassis and André Meyer. In late April the physician invited all three to a dinner party at his East Side apartment. Photographer Ron Galella, whose candid snapshots of Jackie—in restaurants, at nightclubs, and on the street—graced the pages of newspapers around the world, took a picture that night of Ari and Jackie emerging together from Lax's apartment building. The picture ran the following morning on the front page of the New York *Daily News*.

Bobby Kennedy found the photograph disconcerting. Telephoning his sister-in-law from the campaign trail, he was told that she and Onassis had discussed marriage but had made no decisions. "He's a family weakness," said Bobby. "First your sister and now you." According to Pierre Salinger, Jackie informed Bobby that marriage to Onassis would at least guarantee that she and the children could breathe easier, a major consideration in light of her diminished financial situation.

"Several days later," said Salinger, "Jackie received a visit at home from both Ethel and Joan Kennedy. Dispatched by Bobby, they begged her not to marry Onassis; such an action with all the negative publicity attached to it would irrevocably damage the family name and Bobby's chances to become president."

Bobby was the next visitor. He understood Jackie's monetary concerns but entreated her to wait until after the election before announcing her intention to marry "the Greek." He wanted to avoid damage to his reputation. Although Onassis "might be the sweetest fellow on earth," said Bobby, "it would be taken the wrong way. And I won't get a second chance."

"Jackie agreed to compromise," said Pierre Salinger. "She would go along with the Kennedys for the moment at any rate. She would make a final decision after the election. Bobby said that win or lose, he hoped she ultimately decided against marrying Onassis—such a union would make life even more difficult for Caroline and John. 'If anything,' Jackie responded, 'it will make my life more difficult—their existence will be far more agreeable.'"

✦

Chapter 7

RICH AS CROESUS

"I CAN'T EMPHASIZE ENOUGH how important Bobby Kennedy became in the lives of Caroline and John Jr. following the assassination of their father," said Franklin D. Roosevelt Jr. "He was there for them. He paid more attention to those kids than he did to his own. In those difficult days, he helped fill the role created by their father's absence. On an almost daily basis, he played with the kids, took them for walks, spoke to them about their 'martyred' father. He included them in every family gathering and outing. For Caroline, who remembered and even worshipped her father, he remained a surrogate dad. For John Jr., who had no memory, he represented a more vivid presence."

Bobby's run for the presidency carried with it the promise of returning the Kennedy family, including Caroline and John Jr., to a position at the center of power that they felt was theirs practically by right of succession. Surrounding himself with a group of advisers such as Ed Guthman, Burke Marshall, John Seigenthaler, Frank Mankiewicz, and Richard Goodwin, many of whom had been with him during his terms as attorney general and New York Democratic senator, RFK entered the race as his party's sentimental favorite. "I can't wait till we're back in the White House," Jackie told him, a comment calculated to irritate the ever irascible Ethel Kennedy. "What does she mean by when *'we're'* back in the White House?" said the candidate's wife. "Jackie has already been First Lady—it's my turn."

On a more earnest occasion, during a New York dinner party at which she encountered Arthur Schlesinger Jr., Jackie told JFK's former adviser: "Do you know what I think will happen to Bobby? The same thing that happened to Jack. There is too much hatred in this country, and more people hate Bobby than hated Jack."

On June 1, 1968, Roswell Gilpatric had dinner with Jackie at the Colony Club in Manhattan. During their meal she reiterated her dire prediction. "I didn't take her very seriously," admitted Gilpatric. "Three days later I heard from her by phone. 'Bobby's been shot!' she said. He'd been mortally wounded only minutes after his victory in the California Democratic primary. I took her to JFK Airport and put her aboard a private jet owned by IBM president Thomas Watson Jr. I remained behind, but they were joined by Stas Radziwill for the flight to Los Angeles, where they were met by Chuck Spalding, who took Jackie aside and told her straight out that Bobby was dying."

At Good Samaritan Hospital, Jacqueline listened as Ethel described the sequence of events that had led Bobby and his entourage through the swinging doors of the Ambassador Hotel's pantry into the gun-toting hands of a young Palestinian Arab, Sirhan Sirhan, bent on revenge for the Arab defeat by the Israelis in the previous June's Six Day War. She covered her face with her hands as Ethel recounted the morbid details of a succession of gunshots and Bobby lying faceup on the floor, blood spurting from bullet wounds to the head, the confusion and screaming, the apprehension of the hollow-eyed assailant as three members of Bobby's entourage struggled to wrestle the gun out of his hand.

For hours Jackie waited in the hospital, standing watch over her dying brother-in-law. When the end appeared near, she told Bobby's press secretary Frank Mankiewicz: "The Catholic Church is best only at the time of death. The rest of the time it's composed of rather silly little men running around in their black suits. But the Church understands death. I'll tell you who else understands death—the black churches. They see it all the time, and they're ready for it . . . in the same way a good Catholic is ready. We know death. As a matter of fact, if it weren't for the children, we'd welcome it."

Robert F. Kennedy died at 1:44 a.m., June 6, 1968. Having forged a temporary peace, Ethel and Jackie accompanied the body back to New York aboard Air Force One. The funeral took place on June 8 at St. Patrick's Cathedral on Fifth Avenue, after which a twenty-one-car train filled with relatives, associates, and friends transported the coffin to Washington, D.C., while hundreds of thousands of mourners lined the tracks along the way. Bobby was laid to rest next to his brother at Arlington National Cemetery.

Despite an almost frosty exterior, Jackie was overcome by sadness and fear, the same emotions and impulses that had motivated her nearly five years before in the wake of her husband's assassination. In the case of RFK's death, sadness and fear quickly gave way to bitterness, to anger. If America ever had a claim on Jacqueline Kennedy after Jack's death, that claim had now been forfeited. If she felt any doubt or obligation to consider the impact of her actions on the political prospects of the remaining Kennedys, they were resolved by the shots that ended Bobby's life.

"I hate this country," Jackie told Pierre Salinger. "I despise America, and I don't want my children to live here anymore. If they're killing Kennedys, my kids are number one targets. I want to get my children out of this country."

Although she later modified her position, Jackie's emotional outburst indicated the degree of her distress. Her personal intentions could not have been more blatant had she placed a marriage announcement on the front page of *The New York Times.* In a sense, her decision to follow through on her intention to wed Aristotle Onassis had been made at the foot of Bobby's grave. It was reinforced by a conversation between Rose Kennedy and Janet Auchincloss, when Rose informed Jackie's mother that her daughter would have to cut down on her expenses and on her personal staff. "This can't go on," Rose said to Mrs. Auchincloss in a poorly timed declaration of her own. "Now that Jack and Bobby aren't here to provide for Jackie, she will have to learn how to survive on less. My husband's business office can't continue to finance every whim of hers."

Aristotle Onassis represented a means of escape for Jackie as well as the financial independence—for herself and her children—she had so long sought. She needed security, and she craved luxury, and Onassis offered both. She wanted an authoritative male figure in her young son's life and a kindly father figure for her daughter. Above all, she wanted to evade what she so aptly described as "America's obsession" with her and her children.

Jackie spent the rest of June shuttling back and forth between Newport and Hyannis Port, where she was soon joined by Onassis. She wanted Caroline and John to become better acquainted with him and, at the same time, hoped to introduce him to those members of the Auchincloss and Kennedy families he hadn't yet met. At the beginning of July, she sent Caroline to the Aegean isle of Mykonos to vacation with the Radziwills. Not surprisingly, Lee Radziwill had nothing complimentary to say about Onassis or her sister's plan to marry the man. She told Caroline that Ari reminded her of "a Turkish rug merchant." Thereafter, until Jackie set her straight, Caroline referred to Onassis as "my Turkish stepfather."

On July 20, Jackie and her nearly eight-year-old son visited Onassis at Skorpios and were met there by Caroline. Onassis attempted to win favor with the children by showering them with gifts and affection. He sat John Jr. on his knee and explained the Greek myths to him. He went fishing with John off a neighboring island and gave the boy a hundred dollars in Greek currency with which to buy bait. When JFK Jr. offered to return the change, Onassis waved him off. "Keep it," he said. He then reached in his pocket and produced several bills of large denomination. Handing them to the boy, he said, "Now you have enough money to buy yourself a new fishing rod." Amused by the incident, Jackie told Onassis, "Maybe you can woo me with money, Ari, but not my children."

Whatever shortcomings the sixty-two-year-old Greek billionaire might have had, they were outweighed by his advantages. Jackie, at thirty-nine, saw her suitor as a prodigiously successful and resourceful man who believed in himself and believed in living life to the fullest. She felt she could count on him. One of the things she sought for herself and her children was privacy—not always being in the public eye—and he could afford to give them that commodity. There were other factors that went into her decision to join forces with Onassis. With his wealth and domineering personality, he was one of the few men she could marry who would not become Mr. Jacqueline Kennedy. "I can't very well marry a dentist from New Jersey," she once told Truman Capote, a statement that while somewhat elitist carried with it the essence of truth. When Bunny Mellon said to her, "Jackie, if you marry that man, you'll fall off your pedestal," her response said it all: "I'd rather fall off than get frozen there forever."

Although the practical-minded Rose Kennedy voiced concern over the religious question (Onassis was both divorced and a member of the Greek Orthodox Church), she genuinely liked him. His driving force and astute business acumen reminded her of Joe Kennedy. She recognized that Jackie's children would benefit from his presence in their lives. His presence in Jackie's life had the decided benefit of permanently eliminating her daughter-in-law as a drain on the family fortune. Rose's positive reaction to Onassis was not shared by Jackie's mother. Janet Auchincloss thought Jackie's beau vulgar and crude, both in appearance and manner. He didn't have the air of elegance Jackie deserved. Although Janet conceded that Onassis possessed energy and a certain kind of magnetism, she found him singularly unattractive. "He looks," she said, "like a toad." Two to three inches shorter than the former First Lady, he tended to wear the same black business suit day after day. His table manners were lamentable. He treated women shabbily. He hated horses and loved spending long hours in loud Greek nightclubs, whereas Jackie liked small dinner parties and curling up at night with a good book. "They have nothing in common," Janet told her majordomo Jonathan Tapper.

Never one to pay particular attention to her mother's advice, Jackie brought Ted Kennedy to Skorpios in August to help hammer out a prenuptial arrangement with Onassis, whose twenty-year-old son, Alexander, was also present. Onassis's children had always been irreconcilably hostile toward the women in their father's life, particularly Maria Callas, whom they blamed for breaking up Ari's marriage to their mother, Athina (Tina), whose older sister Eugenie Livanos was currently married to Greek shipping magnate Stavros Niarchos, Ari's lifelong nemesis and archrival. The word in Athens was that Onassis wanted to marry Jackie simply to show the world, as well as Niarchos, that he could buy anything or anybody.

Alexander and Christina were no more accepting of Jacqueline Kennedy than of Maria Callas. Although distantly polite, neither of them warmed up to Jackie or gave the slightest indication they ever would. If the Kennedys had dubbed Onassis "the Greek," his immediate family (including his elder sister Artemis Garoufalidis) referred to Jackie as "the Black Widow." Behind closed doors, they counseled their father against going through with the marriage. Jackie's motives, they claimed, were purely monetary. Besides, Ari was far too old to take on the burden of becoming a father to Caroline and John Jr.

Alexander Onassis, an aviator with several years of experience piloting helicopters and executive jets, borrowed his father's chopper and flew Jackie and her children from Skorpios to Athens. During the trip he encouraged John Jr. to sit next to him at the control panel, a practice he repeated whenever he flew with the Kennedys. Although Alexander saw John only periodically in the years to come, their shared interest in aviation created a kind of big brother–little brother bond that endured until Alexander's untimely death in an airplane crash. John's magnanimous personality, already much in evidence, also endeared him to Ari. For a while at least, Onassis filled the role Jackie had chosen for him as an acceptable father figure. If Ari and John got along famously, Caroline proved far more resistant. "It was a difficult situation for Caroline," said Jamie Auchincloss. "She worshipped her father, and Bobby's death was still too recent. It was a lot to dump on a sensitive kid. To Jackie's credit, she never coerced or pushed Caroline. She allowed events to take their inevitable course. The result was that Caroline never grew as close to Onassis as did her brother. If anything, Caroline remained at odds with the old man."

The prospective bride returned to Skorpios weighted down with dozens of items she'd charged to Onassis in Athens, including ten new pairs of shoes and matching handbags, fall wardrobes for her children, and multiple sets of Pratesi sheets, coverlets, and pillowcases. Onassis gave a series of parties for her aboard the *Christina*. He taught Caroline and John how to dance the *syrtaki*. After Labor Day, Jackie and the children returned to New York. John entered Collegiate, and Caroline continued at Sacred Heart.

In late September, after conducting business meetings in Athens with Greek junta leader George Papadopoulos, involving a ten-year, $400 million investment project called Omega, Onassis arrived in New York and checked into his usual suite at the Hotel Pierre. On September 25 and 26 he met with André Meyer to finalize the financial discussions he and Ted Kennedy had commenced at Skorpios. Despite their friendship, Meyer and Onassis had words over the terms of the prenuptial agreement. Meyer wanted Ari to pay Jackie outright the sum of $20 million, more than ten times the figure that Teddy had negotiated with him at Skorpios. After much screaming and shouting, Onassis agreed to give Jackie the lump sum of $3 million, plus the annual interest on two $1 million trusts to be established for each of her children until they reached the age of twenty-one, at which point the trusts would be turned over to them. The written agreement further stipulated that Onassis would give Jackie a $30,000 per month allowance to cover her living expenses. In the event of a divorce or death (his), Jackie would receive an additional $250,000 per year for life. In return she would relinquish her hereditary rights, which under Greek law meant she surrendered her claim to one-fourth of her husband's estate.

Another issue taken up by Meyer had to do with the fact that although Caroline and John Jr. retained their Secret Service coverage until each reached the age of sixteen, Jackie's would cease once she remarried. Meyer insisted that Onassis hire private security guards to protect his future wife. "Don't worry," Onassis responded, "she will be well looked after." The two men shook hands to cement the agreement.

"At first, Onassis felt he had made a pretty decent deal for Jackie," said his personal secretary Lynn Alpha Smith, who worked out of his New York offices in the Olympic Towers on Fifth Avenue. " 'Do you think $3 million is too much?' he asked me. 'Absolutely not,' I said. 'You can buy a supertanker for that, but then you have to pay for fuel, maintenance, and insurance—and you have to pay the crew's salary.'

"We used to call Jackie 'supertanker' around the office. Onassis didn't mind. It made him laugh. 'It's supertanker on the line,' I'd announce whenever she called."

There were added bonuses. Jackie had found a benefactor in Onassis, and he had secured somebody to bolster his personal image, especially in the United States, where he had been blacklisted since World War II, the subject of numerous investigations by the CIA. The KGB, Scotland Yard, French intelligence, and the Mossad in Israel had likewise focused on his myriad international business dealings. Because of his reputation, Onassis had been unable to secure bank loans in America as well as certain countries in Europe. Jackie was about to change all that. She introduced Onassis to Robert McNamara, soon to become director of the World Bank, and to David Rockefeller, head of Chase Manhattan Bank. Doors, previously closed to Onassis, would soon open.

On October 15, 1968, *The Boston Globe* ran a front-page article confirming that Jacqueline Kennedy would soon marry Greek shipping magnate Aristotle Socrates Onassis. The article went on to say that although the Vatican would not recognize the union, Richard Cardinal Cushing (with whom Jackie had recently met) had given the future bride his personal blessing. As soon as Jackie read the story, she telephoned Onassis at his Glyfada villa outside Athens to tell him that their little secret had transcended the rumor stage. To avoid making a circus of their wedding, she suggested they move as quickly as possible. It was wishful thinking on Jackie's part. Within twenty-four hours of the *Globe*'s report, the story had been picked up by every news agency in Europe and North America.

On the evening of October 17, an Olympic Airways Boeing 707 flew Jackie, Caroline, John Jr., Pat Lawford, Jean Smith, Hugh and Janet Auchincloss, Nancy Tuckerman, and the remainder of the bride's wedding party, in addition to a half-dozen Secret Service agents, to the remote airport of Andravida, 192 miles west of Athens. In the course of the flight, Jackie told her children of her intended marriage, stressing that nobody could ever replace their father but that Ari was a good and kind man—in time, they would come to love him. Onassis soon proved his worth, at least monetarily. On Jackie's arrival in Greece, he presented her with a $1.25 million heart-shaped ruby-and-diamond ring from Zolotas, his favorite jewelry store in Athens. He also bought her diamond earrings and a ruby-encrusted gold bracelet, a small sampling of the more than $5 million worth of jewelry he would drop in her lap over the term of their marriage. When Jackie first showed her $1.25 million ring to Caroline, the child playfully tossed it in the air and caught it.

Onassis didn't stop there. He purchased matching diamond clips for Lee Radziwill and Janet Auchincloss and an assortment of watches, leather wallets, and engraved cigarette cases as party favors for the remaining wedding guests. Caroline Kennedy received a Shetland pony and a twenty-eight-foot sailboat emblazoned with her name; her brother was given a red two-seat speedboat with John stenciled in white paint on the stern. To make the children feel at home, he flew in a supply of Coney Island hot dogs and had one of his Olympic Airways pilots personally transport JFK Jr.'s rabbit, one of several house pets the boy kept in New York. After that, John brought the rabbit back and forth with him whenever he visited Greece. During one crossing, when a flight attendant informed him that the rabbit would have to travel in the baggage hold, Jackie intervened. "My husband owns this airline," she said. "The rabbit flies first class with us."

The day Onassis revealed his marriage plans to his children, Christina threw a temper tantrum, while Alexander drank too much and spent the afternoon careening around Athens in his Alfa Romeo. Both threatened to boycott the ceremony. Alexander (like Truman Capote before him) called Jackie "an American geisha." It took considerable diplomacy on the part of Onassis's advisers to convince his children to attend the wedding. In the end, they yielded only because they realized that nothing could forestall the marriage or divert their father from what he had come to believe was his manifest destiny.

The Greek Orthodox wedding took place at 5:15 p.m., October 20, 1968, in the tiny whitewashed Chapel of Panayitsa ("the Little Virgin") on the island of Skorpios. A cold, driving rain buffeted Skorpios and the surrounding sea. Jackie, according to a press report, "looked drawn and concerned" in a long-sleeved, two-piece dress designed by Valentino. Her hair was secured with an ivory ribbon. The groom wore a dark blue double-breasted business suit. Caroline appeared dazzled and wan; John Jr. kept his head down throughout the ceremony. Repeatedly, Jackie glanced anxiously in the direction of her children. Ari's children both appeared nervous and grim. Replete with hymns, chants, and prayers, in Greek and English, the thirty-minute ceremony concluded on a positive note, the newlyweds sipping red wine from a silver chalice. They then participated in the "Dance of Isaiah," circling the candle-lit altar three times with a white-robed priest, followed by Caroline and John. They held their reception aboard the *Christina,* and it was there in the master bedroom suite that they spent their wedding night. Thereafter Jackie occupied a smaller suite that had once been used exclusively by Maria Callas.

Public reaction to the marriage came quickly. The day after the ceremony, a Fleet Street tabloid ran the headline "Jackie Weds Blank Check." Another British publication put it in equally blunt terms: "Jackie Kennedy Sells Her Soul to the Devil." "The Reaction Here Is Anger, Shock, and Dismay," said *The New York Times.* "America Has Lost a Saint," headlined the West German *Bild-Zeitung.* "JFK Dies a Second Time," roared Rome's *Il Messaggero.* Paris's *Le Monde* said, "The Bitter End of Camelot."

Criticism of the union came in a variety of forms and from a wide spectrum of sources, the most damaging of which, from a public relations point of view, emanated from the Vatican. Monsignor Fausto Velaine, chief of the Vatican press office, released a statement that read in part: "It is clear that when a Catholic marries a divorced man, she knowingly violates the law of the Church. This woman now lives in a state of spiritual degradation, a public sinner."

Each day for weeks, her children's Secret Service agents sifted through bundles of hate mail that arrived at Skorpios and at Jackie's Fifth Avenue apartment in New York. Television commentators condemned her for her greed. Editorials appeared describing the former First Lady as a traitor to her country. Comedienne Joan Rivers stood before a Las Vegas nightclub audience and said, "You don't think she actually sleeps with that old fart, do you? I guess she does. She has the time. How many hours a day can you shop at Bergdorf's?" Still distraught over losing Onassis,

Maria Callas told the London *Sunday Times,* "Jackie did well to secure a wealthy grandfather for her children." Charlotte Curtis, women's page editor of *The New York Times,* wrote, "Both parties obviously had something the other wanted. Onassis wanted a social showpiece, and Jackie wanted financial security." Even Alexander Onassis had his say, telling a *Washington Post* correspondent, "My father may need a wife, but I don't need a stepmother."

Jacqueline's major concern over the onslaught of bad press was the overall effect it might have on her children. "I could care less what they think of me," she wrote to Bill Walton. "I just don't want Caroline and John to suffer—they've gone through enough." On October 24 she bid a tearful farewell to her children and packed them off to New York with Hugh and Janet Auchincloss. Remaining behind with her new husband, Jackie invited Billy Baldwin to Greece to have him render advice on the decoration of an eight-bedroom villa currently being constructed on Skorpios to replace the smaller dwelling that Onassis had built years before. Particularly appalling to Baldwin was the gauche interior of the *Christina,* with its pink marble bathrooms, elaborate sitting rooms and salons, plus a drawing room whose walls were covered with murals of naked nymphets depicting the four seasons. To Ari's dismay, his wife insisted on redecorating the entire yacht. The sole exception was Ari's book-lined study, which contained an El Greco and a priceless jade Buddha. Before she finished, Jackie also redid the estate at Glyfada and the town house in Paris, expending millions of dollars of her husband's money in the process.

The notoriety of his mother's recent remarriage was not overlooked by John Jr.'s new classmates at Collegiate. "When he first arrived at school in the fall of 1968, he was an object of great curiosity to the rest of us," said Jim Balinson. An attorney today, Balinson recalled that whenever John Jr. used the school bathroom, his classmates would follow and gawk at him. "He never complained about it," noted Balinson. "He took it all in stride. He wasn't the brightest bulb on the block, but he became extremely popular. He made friends easily and kept them. Considering his background and who he was, John seemed remarkably grounded. He was impulsive and imaginative. For all his renown, he never lorded it over anybody."

Another Collegiate student, Steven Johnson, remembered John for his generosity. "During his first year at Collegiate, one of his classmates came down with a serious illness and had to be hospitalized. John visited him in the hospital. He owned a football signed by Joe Namath. Knowing that his classmate was a huge New York Jets fan, he brought along the football and gave it to him as a present. He used to do things like that all the time."

During his initial year at Collegiate, John rode a New York City subway for the first time when his class took a field trip to the Cloisters museum in upper Manhattan. To reach the site, they boarded the IRT at Broadway and 79th Street and took it to the 207th Street station. John raced back and forth through the subway car in a frenzy of excitement. On the way back, he stood at the front of the first car and stared out the window as the train careened down the track. "Since moving to New York," said Steven Johnson, "he'd always traveled by limousine or taxi and never on a bus or train. He found the metro experience so liberating that he began asking his mother to take him by subway whenever they went anywhere, which of course she couldn't do because they would've been mobbed. But when he went out with friends, he insisted on taking the train. The habit stuck with him. In later years, he seemed to prefer public transportation over taxis and limos."

By prior arrangement—no doubt because of the friction created at St. David's—John's Secret Service detail remained as much out of sight as possible, hanging out in Collegiate's lobby rather than in front of John's classroom. Always the prankster, John Jr. took pleasure in losing the agents, ducking out the side door of Collegiate after school, or disappearing from sight while visiting the homes of friends. He later developed other, more complicated ploys. Bruce Breimer, an American history teacher at Collegiate, described John in high school switching cars with friends so that the Secret Service agents tailing him in their car no longer knew whose vehicle to follow.

Looking back on this period, John would say, "You had to feel sorry for those guys. It couldn't have been very interesting to sit around school all day waiting for me. After a while, they'd doze off. They'd wake up and find out that the class had gone off someplace. 'Where's John?' they'd ask. 'His class went to the museum,' somebody would say. So they'd race over to the museum and look for me there."

Lurking in the background, the agents were a constant presence in the early lives of the country's two most publicized presidential offspring. A new agent, James Kalafatis, had been added to the detail because he spoke Greek and could be of help when the children found themselves at Skorpios. During these years, the agents—including Kalafatis—were faced with countless kidnapping threats against the children. Anonymous letters arrived regularly at 1040 Fifth Avenue, some taken more seriously than others. There were other forms of potential danger as well. Not long after Jackie's marriage to Aristotle Onassis, an anonymous telephone call to Collegiate warned that a bomb had been planted on the premises and was about to be detonated. Jim Balinson recalled the incident. "The school had to be evacuated," he said. "The bomb squad arrived. With the help of Secret Service agents, they scrubbed the building while students and faculty members were secured at a safe distance from the school. I suspect it had to do with John's presence in the school. This sort of thing happened two or three times during his years at Collegiate."

At the beginning, John attracted a contingent of bag ladies who were always around the school, harmless old biddies in sneakers with their hair in curlers, and they would ask people, "Do you know John-John?" They once approached John himself. "'Do you happen to know John-John?'" they asked him. "Yes," he said, "I do." "Really? What's he like?" "He's a great guy," said John with a big smile.

One of John's best friends at Collegiate was a future professional actor named Jason Beghe. Like John, Beghe had a keen sense of humor. Like John, he loved practical jokes and had a precocious gift for mimicry. Both boys entertained their classmates with hilarious imitations of their favorite entertainers. JFK Jr.'s list included Elvis Presley, John Lennon, and Mick Jagger. Both told jokes and stories in a variety of brogues and accents. Starting in the fourth grade, the two boys would sit for hours on the steps of the Metropolitan Museum of Art, hatching their future plans to become stars of the stage and screen. Beghe took guitar lessons once a week after school, while John took up the drums. Jackie put her foot down when John announced his intention to start a rock band. "You'd better rent out a recital hall," she told him, "because your band isn't going to rehearse in this apartment."

Influenced by Beghe, John, at age ten, became active in Collegiate's theater program. Jim Balinson remembered seeing Jackie and Aristotle Onassis at some of the plays in which John performed. "They tried to blend in as much as possible," he said. "They'd sit quietly in the back of the auditorium. Jackie wore those famous oval sunglasses. Of course everyone recognized them, and there was always a bit of staring among the other parents in the audience."

In 1970 Jackie and Ari attended Field Day at Collegiate to watch John participate in various athletic events. Carol Rosenwald, an author and restaurant owner whose son went to Collegiate, remembered the whispering that went around because Jackie looked so unkempt on that particular day. "She looked like she'd just climbed out of bed," said Rosenwald. "She had unwashed, stringy hair, and her sweater had a run in it. Here was this incredible fashion plate with the world's richest man, and she looked more like an impoverished waif than a former First Lady. Had she been anyone other than Jacqueline Kennedy Onassis, it might have gone unnoticed. But given the circumstances, it created a buzz. For that matter, Onassis also looked pretty grimy in an old baggy suit that looked like it had been bought in a thrift shop."

The couple received better grades from Sally Bitterman, whose son, Brooks, was a classmate and a friend of John Jr.'s. Encountering them at several Parents Association meetings, Bitterman remarked that "they were quiet and dignified, never threw their weight around to elicit special favors for John. Once, after Brooks had a playdate with John at the Fifth Avenue apartment, Jackie and Ari called up to make sure he'd gotten home all right. It was very thoughtful of them. None of the other parents did that sort of thing."

Besides the Parents Association, which Jackie hadn't joined at St. David's, she attended meetings of Collegiate's education committee, which had been formed to discuss the question of enrollment expansion and the construction of a new building next to the one that already existed. Marjorie Housepian Dobkin, an associate dean at Barnard College whose three sons attended Collegiate, recalled that at one meeting Jackie asked the group of approximately forty parents whether it was "appropriate for her son to do his homework with the stereo blasting. Given the reason for the committee's existence, the question seemed completely out of place. Nevertheless, people answered it. Some said yes, some no." Aware that she'd been invited to join the committee for financial reasons, Jackie once brought Onassis along. When the issue arose of raising funds for the new building's construction, the Greek entrepreneur produced his checkbook and wrote out a check to Collegiate for $50,000.

Onassis played his role to the hilt. When John's homeroom teacher at Collegiate gave him a failing grade in penmanship, Ari took it upon himself to sit down with the boy and help him improve his almost indecipherable scrawl. When he performed poorly in a geography course, Onassis bought him an atlas and a globe and made him memorize the capitals of every state and country. Never an academe, John proved to be a social star. Friendly, polite, and kind, he received more invitations to parties than anybody else in his class. In what spare time Onassis could muster, he took John to football, basketball, and baseball games. Attending a New York Mets game, JFK Jr. tried explaining the rules of the sport to Onassis. Although Onassis found baseball an absolutely dull endeavor, he stuck out the games just to be with his stepson. An avid soccer fan, Onassis took John to several international matches on Randall's Island and attended John's intramural soccer games at Collegiate.

Ari frequently accompanied Caroline and John to the Central Park tennis courts on West 94th Street, where for several years the two took private lessons. Pat Fenton, their tennis instructor, remarked that while neither was outstanding at the sport, they stuck with it. "Of the two," said Fenton, "Caroline was by far the more serious. She studied tennis and applied herself. John just had a good time. He used to roll around the courts. He hit balls every which way. After their lesson, they would spend time in the grass that surrounded the courts collecting the balls that John had hit over the fence."

Onassis endeavored to give of himself to both of Jackie's children, to become their friend and adviser—not, he insisted, a replacement for their father. On weekends when he found himself in the States, he went with them to his wife's vacation home in Bernardsville, New Jersey, a property she had purchased in 1966. Following one such visit, he complained to Lynn Alpha Smith that he'd ruined his shoes and pants "standing knee-deep in muck and manure, watching Jackie and Caroline ride their horses round and round in endless circles." Although he didn't like horses, he put himself through the ordeal because he wanted to "be supportive." His "supportive" efforts failed to impress Caroline. She resented him for what she perceived as his attempt to usurp her father's position. No matter what he did, he could never please her. She refused to call him "Dad," referring to him instead as "Mr. Onassis." "I liked him, but my sister didn't," JFK Jr. would one day tell Larry King. Another time he said, "To me, Aristotle Onassis was a father. After the first few years, we established a closeness that he never enjoyed with my mother."

Despite Caroline's resistance, Onassis persevered. One weekend in New Jersey, shortly after having new braces put on her teeth, Caroline got into an accident while riding her horse. She collided with a tree branch, sustaining a deep cut on her forehead. Onassis lifted her in his arms, placed her in the backseat of his car, and drove her to the local hospital for stitches. A few days later, he arranged a consultation for her with a leading plastic surgeon to make certain she wouldn't be left with a permanent scar. Although Jackie expressed her gratitude, Caroline refused. She changed her mind only when her mother threatened to suspend her weekly allowance if she didn't properly thank Onassis.

Onassis was noticeably absent on November 21, 1969, at the funeral in Hyannis Port of Joseph P. Kennedy, whose death at age eighty-one marked one more gathering of the tribe. Jackie, Caroline, and John flew up from New York to attend the burial, which by sad coincidence took place one day before the sixth anniversary of President Kennedy's assassination. When asked by her cousin David Kennedy about her feelings toward Aristotle Onassis, Caroline rolled her eyes and muttered, "I don't like him."

Unable to charm Caroline, Ari continued to concentrate his efforts on John. On his way to the office in the morning, he often dropped John off at Collegiate. On pleasant fall or spring days, they walked across Cen-

tral Park together, then cut south to West 77th Street. He occasionally
collected John after school and took him to Trader Vic's for spareribs. Or
he would go with him to Serendipity for hamburgers and ice-cream so-
das, warning him not to tell his mother, lest she accuse him of "feeding
John junk food before dinner."

School holidays and summer vacations were spent at Skorpios, where
John and Caroline swam, snorkeled, and learned to navigate the boats
Onassis had given them as presents. He would take the children on walking tours of the island, introducing them to the birds, insects, and vegeta-
tion that prospered there, occasionally interjecting stories of his youth.
When Onassis traveled from Skorpios to Athens on business, he often
took John along. During the meetings, Onassis would send John off with
his Secret Service detail on walks around the city, or he would give him
money to play pinball machines at the penny arcade. Afterward the two
always went to the movies, attending a cinema in Athens that showed
only English-language films. In 1970 cousins Maria and Timothy Shriver
joined them there for part of the summer, along with Rose Kennedy, Lee
Radziwill, and Martin Luther King III, the ten-year-old son of the slain
civil rights leader. Maria, whose father, Sargent Shriver, had been named
American ambassador to France, became Caroline's most trusted confidante. For hours she listened to her cousin complain about her elderly
stepfather—how difficult she found it to relate to Onassis; how she
couldn't comprehend why her mother had ever married the fellow. When
Onassis, piqued and frustrated by Jackie's increasing absences from Skorpios, resumed his very public romance with Maria Callas, Caroline's feelings for him eroded even further. Unable to fully express herself to her
mother, Caroline turned to her cousin Maria for consolation. As young
teenagers, the two girls spoke by telephone on an almost daily basis.

One of the lighter moments that summer took place on July 28,
Jackie's birthday, when John, Caroline, and the other children donned
costumes and performed an act from a Molière play for the adults, including the captain and crew of the *Christina*. What Jackie particularly
enjoyed about it was that they spoke their parts in French.

Although Onassis's children didn't get along with Jackie—Alexander
refused to sleep under the same roof as his stepmother, moving out

whenever she arrived—they were fond of their two stepsiblings. Despite
the difference in age between the two sets of children, Alexander and
Christina made an effort to spend time with Caroline and John. They
played with them, protected them, taught them how to water ski, and
took them on day trips in Alexander's Chris-Craft to the islands around
Skorpios. "They were utterly patient with Caroline and John, forever answering their questions about Greece," said Pierre Salinger, who made
several visits to Skorpios. "In other words, they acted like a big brother
and sister. I was with them in Athens when a group of paparazzi began
hounding Caroline and John on the street. They kept snapping pictures
until Christina finally grabbed one of their cameras and chased them off.
Although they avoided Jackie, Alexander and Christina would show up
at Skorpios from time to time to eat dinner with Caroline and John. Under better circumstances, they might have grown quite close."

Salinger recalled an incident that played itself out during one of his
visits, which indicated a growing rift between Ari and Jackie. "Onassis
gave a dinner party aboard the *Christina*," said President Kennedy's former press secretary, "at which John Jr. became bored and began running
around squirting the guests with a water pistol. Onassis told him to stop.
When he continued, Onassis jumped up, grabbed the toy, threw it overboard, and ordered him to his cabin. Now Jackie became enraged. She
picked up Onassis's camera, a rather expensive piece of equipment, and
threw it into the sea where he'd tossed the water pistol. She then left the
party to console John. After the guests left, she and Onassis had words.
'John is completely undisciplined,' he told her. 'You worry about your
children,' she snapped back, 'and I'll worry about mine.' To make up to
John, Onassis bought him a jukebox and a mini-jeep to ride around the
rough terrain of Skorpios. He later bought Caroline an identical vehicle.
They were both replicas of a jeep owned by Onassis, the chief difference
being that their maximum speed was ten miles per hour."

When Jackie returned to the States with Caroline and John at the end
of August 1970, Onassis complained to his sister Artemis that his wife
spent more time with her children than she did with him, and that he
didn't feel welcome when he visited with her in New York. Contacted by
Artemis, Jackie contended that one of her primary obligations was to her

children. She and Onassis had debated this very point several months earlier at Maxim's in Paris, and again over lunch at Alfredo's in Rome. His wife's absences became a bone of contention that stuck in Onassis's throat. He didn't expect his interests to supersede those of her children, but he did expect to be placed on an equal footing. Ari had hoped to become Emperor of the High Seas, with Jackie as his Cleopatra—instead she remained a figurehead whose main domicile was located thousands of miles away.

Another Onassis complaint, one that increased in timbre with the passage of time, involved Jackie's exorbitant "shop-till-you-drop" sprees. Costa Gratsos, a trusted Onassis executive, recalled his employer looking over his monthly credit card statements and noting that three-quarters of the charges had been made by his wife. "He'd rant and rave that Jackie averaged twice her monthly allowance in clothing expenditures alone," said Gratsos. " 'What the hell does she do with all those clothes she buys?' he asked. 'The only apparel she wears when I'm around are T-shirts and jeans.' On Ari's orders, I looked into the matter and discovered that she would purchase several dozen silk blouses or entire collections of designer fashions at a time, then dump them off in consignment shops simply to raise cash. She was particularly fond of a place called Encore on Madison and 84th Street, which is where she did most of her business, often using other people's names to cover up her own involvement in the scheme. Moreover, the lady was a speed shopper. She could be in and out of any store in the world in ten minutes or less, having run through fifty thousand dollars or more. She didn't bother with such formalities as price; just pointed, gave them an address, and walked out. She never even wore the clothes, merely sent them away with her maid to collect the resale value. She did the same with accessories, shoes, fur coats, towels, bedding, tablecloths, what have you. On one evening at a party, somebody's pet dog chewed up Lee Radziwill's sable coat. The next day Jackie went out and charged a new sable coat to Ari and gave it to her sister. When I reported all this to my boss, he went nuts. I must have heard every four-letter expletive in existence, and then some. Infuriated, he confronted Jackie. By way of response, she shrugged her shoulders and attributed her actions to never having any hard currency on hand. 'I can't even pay for a cab,' she told him. He instructed his bookkeeper to increase her stipend by ten thousand dollars, bringing her allowance to a hefty forty thousand dollars per month. Even with the raise, the credit card charges continued to come. If anything, they increased each month.

"I didn't want to say anything to Ari, but my thoughts were, 'Do you think she married you for your good looks or for your bankroll?' I remember that for their second Christmas together, she did a small pen-and-ink sketch of the *Christina* and had it made into a bookplate to glue into his book collection aboard the yacht. 'How do you like that?' he said to me. 'I give her millions of dollars, and she gives me a fucking sketch.'"

Gratsos recalled another Jackie gift to Onassis, this one for his sixty-fifth birthday: "She kept telling him what a lousy dresser he was, so for his birthday she went to Christian Dior in Paris and ordered him 365 new ties, one for each day of the year. The problem is she never paid for the ties, simply charged them to his account. He ended up paying more than $25,000 for his own birthday present."

One of the irreconcilable differences between Jackie and Ari, according to those who knew him, was that while he had money and knew luxury, he was a man of simple tastes. He liked nightclubs and discos but had no stomach for the ballet, theater, or opera. He once boasted to Jackie that he'd never attended any of Maria Callas's performances. His favorite dish was pot roast. He preferred knockwurst and beer to filet mignon and champagne. He enjoyed eating in cafés and taverns as opposed to rarefied five-star restaurants. On Skorpios he wore slacks but almost never a shirt. Jackie, on the other hand, loved luxury and adored money. But until Onassis entered her life, the latter commodity had never been available to her in great abundance. Now that she had sampled the "good life," she couldn't get enough of it.

In September 1970 Caroline Kennedy departed Sacred Heart, where she had always earned straight As, and entered eighth grade at Brearley, an academically rigorous private school for girls on East 83rd Street in Manhattan. Although Brearley maintained a dress code, it was more lenient than Sacred Heart's. There were days when the uniform was optional. On those occasions Caroline attended school in a polo sweater, boots, and blue jeans. Although there were no rules about cosmetics, she never wore makeup. Brearley's motto "By Truth and Toil" adorned a seal showing an open book, a triad of beavers, and the lighted lamp of knowledge. Attended predominantly by the children of the elite, the secular institution emphasized self-reliance and self-discipline.

Mary Nelson, a classmate at Brearley, described Caroline as "highly intelligent and studious." She had passed Brearley's difficult entrance exam with flying colors and had qualified for an advanced course in French literature. Her other courses during her first two years at Brearley included English, current affairs, Latin, algebra, physical science, music, and art. In true Kennedy fashion, her first-year gym teacher rated her as "highly competitive." To enhance her fluency in French, Jackie hired a female tutor to go on outings with her daughter and converse only in French. Their excursions around New York frequently took them to the teenager's favorite eateries. Caroline had a more-than-healthy appetite for waffles and scrambled eggs, Phoebe's Whamburgers, Schrafft's ice-cream cones, and Blum's sundaes.

At times she could be impetuous, even rude. Entering a crowded East Side ice cream parlor, she pushed her way to the front; when told she would have to "take a number and wait, just like everyone else," she angrily responded, "But I'm not like everyone else—I'm Caroline Kennedy." The store manager ignored her request.

She tried the same tactic with the same lack of success in a First National City Bank while attempting to avoid a long Friday morning line. Rushing to the head of the line, she said, "I'm Caroline Kennedy, and I'm late for a doctor appointment." When informed she would have to wait her turn, she stormed out of the bank.

Caroline's bedroom at 1040 Fifth Avenue reflected her current state of mind. Bunny Mellon had given her a large canopied bed and a sturdy made-to-order wooden desk. Books of all kinds—some in French—were strewn everywhere. A collection of rock tapes and records sat in a corner of the room. Horse show trophies and ribbons were neatly arranged on a pair of matching bookshelves. On her dressing table stood a custom-made gold-and-silver jewelry box and dresser set presented to her by the officers and crew of the aircraft carrier *John F. Kennedy*.

Of her mother's friends, the one she seemed to prefer was George Plimpton. When Plimpton married in 1968, Jackie was unavailable; instead he invited Caroline to his wedding. When Caroline turned thirteen, she invited Plimpton to her birthday party. "I was the only male there," he said. "A week later I accompanied Caroline to her ballet class. It turned out to be her last class. She loved ballet but preferred horses and didn't have time for both." According to Plimpton, Caroline had developed into a vibrant, well-rounded, sophisticated teen. Her favorite expression was "Really, Mother!" She enjoyed going to football and basketball games. She exhibited distinct leadership qualities and felt most secure in the privacy of privilege among her own kind. "In other words," said Plimpton, "she could be a bit of a snob. But then what would you expect of the daughter of Jack and Jackie Kennedy? She had her father's eyes and his walk. She had a firm handshake and a politician's direct gaze. She also had JFK's sense of curiosity. She was a ceaseless question asker. She kept in touch with Rose Kennedy and felt close to Eunice Shriver, her father's favorite sister."

Caroline's public image—quiet and demure—differed from the teenage persona observed by those closest to her. She enjoyed throwing spaghetti-and-meatball get-togethers for friends. She and her chums indulged in frequent sleepovers at each other's homes. She talked her mother into hiring a dozen Hungarian fiddlers to play during one of the family's traditional Christmas Eve parties. She was quick, smart, and observant. She reverted to her shier self primarily in the company of Aristotle Onassis, partially the result of the nonstop negative publicity generated by her mother's second marriage. Reading the headlines in the *National Enquirer* and other tabloids, she couldn't help but be exposed to reports about her mother's outrageous shopping sprees and her stepfather's drunken outbursts in European nightspots. One particularly heinous story suggested that Onassis had been the evil force behind the assassination of Bobby Kennedy, an unconfirmed and seemingly ludicrous rumor that for years continued to surface in the press, finally giving rise to a poorly received 2004 book on the subject by British journalist Peter Evans.

On October 16, 1970, the London *Daily Mail* published an article on the Onassis marriage based largely on an interview with Greta Nilson, a former parlor maid at 1040 Fifth. According to Nilson, Caroline never seemed particularly happy to see Onassis when he visited with the family in New York. "She lapsed into silence when he was around and insisted on having her dinner served in her bedroom," remarked Nilson. The article noted that although Jackie often took her daughter to the opera and ballet, Onassis never accompanied them. The same could be said for plays, movies, and shopping expeditions as well as dentist and doctor visits. Jackie ate breakfast with her children every morning and then walked her daughter to school. While Onassis went out in the evening, she remained at home with the kids, keeping them away from the television set and helping them with their homework. Onassis once took his new family to dinner at the Four Seasons, where he proceeded to attempt conversation with Caroline. She responded to his questions, claimed the *Daily Mail,* with nods and shakes of her head or, at most, one-word answers. When he finally departed New York, Onassis received a "polite" peck on the cheek from Caroline but with no emotion behind it.

Jackie blamed Onassis for his failed relationship with her daughter, telling George Plimpton that in Greek society "women are considered second-class citizens, relegated to the kitchen and bedroom." While Onassis doted on Alexander, he tended to treat his own daughter, Christina, like an appendage. "He's not really interested in Caroline or anything she has to say," Jackie told Plimpton.

As an example of her claim, Jackie cited an experience Caroline had gone through shortly after transferring to Brearley. When Caroline attended a school-sponsored carnival with several of her classmates, Ron Galella showed up and began running around taking pictures of her. Caroline felt humiliated in front of her friends. Relating the incident to Onassis, Jackie's daughter was stunned by his indifference. "The man's only doing his job," he told her. "Don't make more of it than it's worth." Elaborating on the subject, Onassis told Jackie, "When you're soaking wet, what difference do a few drops more make? If you go after that fellow, you'll be perceived as vindictive and mean-spirited."

Onassis's failure to intercede resulted in further intrusions on Galella's part. He turned up mornings in front of 1040 Fifth Avenue and followed

Jackie and Caroline to school, taking photographs of the child at close range, then waited for her to emerge at the end of the school day. In the summer of 1970, aided by a Greek fisherman, he managed to sneak onto Skorpios and snap pictures of the family through a telephoto lens. That same summer, he followed them on trips to Corfu and Capri. The final outrage, as far as Jackie was concerned, took place in the fall of 1970. John Jr. and his mother were riding their bicycles in Central Park when Galella leaped out at them from behind a clump of bushes with his camera, causing John to swerve and crash. Ordering the Secret Service agents on duty to apprehend the photographer, Jackie demanded that he be placed under arrest and booked at the Central Park police precinct. Claiming that his relentless pursuit caused her and her children "grievous mental anguish," she forced John to swear out a deposition and on the basis of the document sought a permanent injunction to keep Galella two hundred yards from the entrance to her Fifth Avenue apartment building and one hundred yards from her and her children. Galella counterclaimed, seeking $1.3 million in punitive damages for false arrest, wrongful prosecution, and interference with his livelihood as a photographer. Ignoring her husband's admonition to drop the proceedings, Jackie persevered, accruing nearly $600,000 in legal fees, all of it charged to her husband. Refusing to pay, Onassis retained attorney Roy Cohn—a sworn enemy of the Kennedys—to negotiate a settlement with Jackie's lawyer, Simon Rifkind. Onassis wound up paying a total of $285,000. Although Jackie eventually won the case, the injunction against Galella proved all but useless. Hiring other lensmen to do the actual picture taking, Galella continued as before to stalk his prey.

◆

Chapter 8

RITES OF PASSAGE

IN EARLY NOVEMBER 1970, Caroline Kennedy and several of her cousins stood on a reception line at a fund-raiser for Senator Ted Kennedy at Boston Symphony Hall. More than a year had elapsed since Senator Kennedy's involvement in the Chappaquiddick affair, resulting in the death by drowning of twenty-eight-year-old Mary Jo Kopechne, Bobby Kennedy's former personal secretary. At the time of the tragedy, Jackie wrote Teddy a letter of support, encouraging him to put the "terrible accident" in perspective and get on with his political career. The letter went on to say that Caroline had been without a godfather since her uncle Bobby's death and that she (Jackie) would very much like to have Uncle Teddy fill the vacancy.

Moved by the note, Teddy began making regular trips from Washington to New York to see Caroline. In the spring of 1971, he invited his niece to join his family on a white-water rafting trip to Colorado. Thereafter, up to a point, he played an increasingly vital role in Caroline's life. If he failed to engage with Caroline as fully as Bobby once had done, Teddy nevertheless remained constant in his attentions to her upbringing.

Whenever problems arose during Caroline's teenage years, Jackie turned to Ted Kennedy for helpful advice. When Caroline gained too much weight and developed a case of acne, Teddy suggested she be taken to a doctor. Jackie dragged her daughter to see Dr. Henry Lax, who promptly prescribed diet pills. Through her college years, Caroline periodically took diet pills, subjecting herself to punishing starvation diets, intermittently breaking out to gorge on milkshakes and cheeseburgers, regaining whatever weight she had previously lost and then some. It reached the point where Jackie, unbeknownst to her daughter, forewarned the proprietor of a neighborhood dessert shop not to serve Caroline.

Caroline wasn't the only one on whom Jackie fastened her hypercritical eye. According to Costa Gratsos, she was always very aware of Christina Onassis's appearance. "From Jackie's point of view," said Gratsos, "Christina was too fat, too hirsute, not fashionable enough. She encouraged her stepdaughter to go for electrolysis treatments, took her shopping, sent her to Dr. Lax, induced her to exercise, took her to a dermatologist and to a beauty salon. None of this helped cement their already tenuous relationship. After several months, Christina rebelled and angrily told Jackie that she didn't want to look like one more 'vapid American high-fashion model.'"

An important new member of the extended Jackie-Ari household was a woman named Marta Sgubin, who'd been engaged by Jackie in the summer of 1969 as governess to her two children.

"After Maud Shaw's departure," said Sgubin, "Caroline and John Jr. had been subjected to a series of part-time nannies and full-time au pair girls. The au pairs came and went. They worked a year and then went home. I'd worked for a French diplomatic family in Washington and Paris for fifteen years, helping to raise three children. While in Washington, I happened to meet Janet Auchincloss. Mrs. Auchincloss felt her grandchildren would be better served by a more permanent arrangement. I was first interviewed for the job by Aristotle Onassis, who'd come to Paris on business. Born in Italy and raised in France, I spoke both Italian and French with him. He was a real charmer, very Mediterranean, very spontaneous and easygoing, which explains why he and John Jr. got along so well. They shared the same personality traits. After my meeting with Mr. Onassis, his wife came to Paris and offered me the position."

Like Maud Shaw, Marta Sgubin felt a strong attraction to the children. At the same time, she was acutely aware of the complex nature of her assignment. "John could be a little rascal," she recalled.

"Caroline, being older, was the more mature of the two. When she didn't get her way, she would sometimes pout. Both could be enormously stubborn at times. They were strong-willed and enterprising. John was an exceedingly generous little fellow. I remember, for example, that he loved strawberries as a child, but always insisted on sharing them with everyone else. The older he grew, the more generous he became. He thought nothing of giving away his toys to friends.

"What set Caroline and John apart was the closeness that existed between them. They rarely argued or fought with each other. They were also both very attached to their mother. Their thinking must have been, 'If something happens to her, what is going to happen to us?'"

The most vital factor in Jackie's relationship with her children was her desire to provide them with a solid foundation for adulthood.

"She was extremely attentive to their needs, keeping them apprised of her whereabouts at all times," said Sgubin. "She returned their telephone calls, answered their questions, and planned their schedules so that their days were productive. She exposed them to the arts. Mrs. Onassis herself painted and wrote. She wrote poems, short stories, and corresponded regularly with friends and family members. She infused her children with the same love for the written word. Above all, she made certain that they remained a closely knit family unit. It was always the three of them, and this may well have worked to the detriment of her marriage to Aristotle Onassis."

On February 3, 1971, on the basis of an invitation from Richard Nixon, Jackie and her children returned to the White House for the first time since JFK's death to view the soon-to-be-unveiled official portraits of the former president and First Lady. Created by New York artist Aaron Shikler, the portrait of Jackie succeeded in capturing what he called her "extraordinary, almost spooky, beauty."

The portrait of JFK showed the president in a moment of dejection, his head bowed and arms crossed. After viewing the portraits, Jackie and her children joined President and Mrs. Nixon and their two daughters,

Tricia and Julie, for a private supper, during which John Jr. accidentally spilled a glass of milk in the president's lap.

They talked in general terms about all the changes that had taken place in the White House in the years since Jackie's renovation project. The Nixons were determined to steer the conversation away from anything that might upset their guests or make them regret their visit. At one point, Jackie looked at Nixon and said, "When we were in the White House, I always lived in a dream world." After the threesome returned to New York, Jackie telephoned Aaron Shikler and remarked, "Nothing has changed in Washington—nothing! It's the same malicious town it always was." Although Caroline and John Jr. revisited the White House from time to time over the course of their lives, the 1971 expedition marked Jackie's final farewell to the executive mansion.

This period proved difficult for everyone, particularly Aristotle Onassis. By the spring of 1969, his son had fallen deeply in love with Fiona Campbell-Walter Thyssen, a New Zealand–born model formerly married into one of Europe's wealthiest industrial families. Convinced that she was little more than a financial opportunist, Ari became panic-struck when Alexander announced his desire to marry the woman. At Onassis's request, Jackie spoke with Fiona and somehow succeeded in convincing her to cancel their wedding plans. Her intervention alienated Jackie even further from Alexander. In the summer of 1970, Ari's former sister-in-law, Eugenie, was found dead at her home on Spetsopoula, a Greek island that belonged to her husband, Stavros Niarchos. Although an autopsy indicated that she had died of self-inflicted barbiturate poisoning, Onassis had his suspicions that Niarchos was inadvertently involved; his suspicions were bolstered by his ex-wife Tina's proclamation that she intended to succeed her sister as Niarchos's wife.

Another dismaying disclosure came with twenty-year-old Christina's revelation that she planned to marry forty-eight-year-old Joseph R. Bolker, a twice-divorced Los Angeles real estate developer whom she'd recently met at a Monte Carlo resort. After conferring with family members, lawyers, and department chiefs—and after a failed attempt on Jackie's part to dissuade Christina—Ari warned his daughter that if she married Bolker, he would consider disinheriting her. The threat seemed only to spur his daughter on. Joe Bolker and Christina Onassis were married in Las Vegas on July 29, 1971. Their union, the first in a series of short-lived marriages undertaken by Christina in the years to come, lasted nine months.

Wildlife photographer Peter Beard, Lee Radziwill's latest paramour (ultimately identified as a reason for the 1974 breakup of her marriage to Stas Radziwill), spent part of the summer at Skorpios "babysitting" Jackie's children. In July Caroline was sent away to a four-week Austrian sports camp to improve her tennis, leaving Beard to look after her brother. Before returning to Skorpios, Caroline visited Madrid and attended her first bullfight, followed by a side trip to the ranch of Palomo Linares, one of Spain's leading matadors.

During her absence, Pierre Salinger also stopped off at Skorpios. Salinger noted that Beard frequently "ran off with John to avoid exposing him to loud altercations between Onassis and Jackie." Beset by personal family problems, Onassis took out his worries on Jackie, screaming and yelling at her, humiliating her at every opportunity. In front of his wife, he ordered his chauffeur to accompany Jackie on a shopping trip to Athens so that he could go and see a particularly attractive young girl who had made several advances to him. Another time, during a conversation in the presence of guests, Jackie corrected some factual error on Ari's part—he incorrectly cited the capital city of an emerging African nation. Onassis turned beet red. "Don't ever correct me in front of others!" he thundered. "Maybe that sort of behavior flies with an American husband, but not with me!" Jackie barely spoke to him for the rest of the week.

The following summer came to an inglorious close when an enterprising group of Italian photographers wearing diving suits managed to snap pictures of Jackie and Ari sunbathing in the nude on Skorpios. The photographs appeared in a number of European tabloids as well as *Hustler* and *Screw* in the States. Jackie blamed Onassis for the incident. Her mounting fury boiled over yet again a few days later when a team of paparazzi tailed her and her children around Athens. As they emerged from

Family patriarch Joseph P. Kennedy and his wife, Rose Fitzgerald Kennedy, forebears of the Kennedy dynasty and paternal grandparents of Caroline and John Jr. (National Museum of Photography, Film & Television/SSPL)

Janet Lee Bouvier and John (Black Jack) Vernou Bouvier III with daughter Jackie. Caroline and John Jr.'s maternal grandparents were later divorced. (Bettmann/CORBIS)

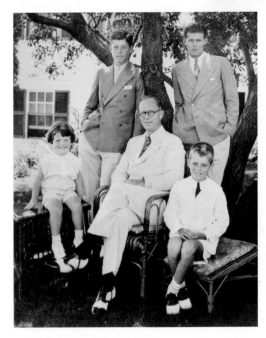

Joseph P. Kennedy and sons (clockwise from top left) John, Joe Jr., Bobby, and Ted. (Fabian Bachrach/ John F. Kennedy Library)

Jackie reads to her daughter, Caroline. (CORBIS)

Senator John F. Kennedy and Jacqueline Bouvier Kennedy at the family compound in Hyannis Port, 1959. (Bettmann/CORBIS)

The president poses with Kennedy clan children at a family reunion. John Jr. is in the foreground, and Caroline stands to the left of her father. (Cecil Stoughton/John F. Kennedy Library)

John Jr. fell in love with flying at an early age. Here he sits at the controls of a presidential helicopter. (Robert Knudson/John F. Kennedy Library)

Caroline on Macaroni and preceded by her father, the president. (Robert Knudson/John F. Kennedy Library)

Jackie with Caroline and John Jr., rowing in New York's Central Park. (CSU Archives/Everett Collection)

Jackie, Caroline, and John Jr. at Robert F. Kennedy's funeral at St. Patrick's Cathedral in New York on June 8, 1968. Immediately following the Mass, his body was transported on a funeral train procession from Penn Station to Washington, D.C., where he was buried beside his brother John at Arlington National Cemetery. (AP/Wideworld Photos)

Jackie with John Jr. and Caroline. She married Aristotle Onassis on the Greek island of Skorpios on October 20, 1968. (Bettmann/CORBIS)

Cousin Anthony Radziwill, Caroline, and John Jr. in a motorboat at Skorpios. JFK Jr. and Anthony were extremely close. Anthony died of cancer three weeks after the death of John Jr. (Ron Galella)

John Jr. with Aristotle Onassis in front of the Plaza Hotel, where they often went for snacks at Trader Vic's. Unlike his sister, John Jr. had a warm relationship with his stepfather. (AP/Wideworld Photos)

A family outing. (Ron Galella)

Caroline attending a party in London for Andy Warhol with boyfriend Mark Shand, brother of Camilla Parker Bowles (current wife of Prince Charles). (A. Botella/Globe Photos, Inc.)

Caroline in London, where she spent a carefree year studying art at Sotheby's. (Express/Express/Getty Images)

Caroline at her high school graduation in 1975 from Concord Academy with John Jr., Jackie, grandmother Rose, and uncle Ted. (Bettmann/CORBIS)

John Jr., Caroline, and her cousin/confidante Maria Shriver. (Russell Turiak)

Caroline with performer Sterling St. Jacques at Studio 54, where she often partied. (Bettmann/CORBIS)

Widely admired as an attentive mother, Jackie often accompanied her children to events and performances. (Getty Images)

John Jr. on his eighteenth birthday, brawling with paparazzi outside of Le Club in New York. Normally cooperative with photographers, he broke his finger during the altercation. (Ron Galella)

John Jr. with girlfriend Jenny Christian at his graduation from Phillips Andover in 1979. (Ron Galella)

John Jr. skates through the streets of New York. (Russell Turiak)

Caroline with beau Tom Carney, whom she had hoped to marry. He broke off the romance because of unwanted publicity. (Russell Turiak)

a store, Jackie confronted one of the photographers and threatened to have them all arrested unless they left her and the children alone.

"The European paparazzi were much worse than their American counterparts," said Secret Service agent James Kalafatis. "Ron Galella was mild by comparison. The Europeans moved in swarms, twenty to thirty to a pack, and they often became very physical—pushing, shoving, screaming, taunting. Jackie wanted me to arrest them, and she wanted Onassis to sue them. The problem is that being part of a Secret Service detail in a foreign country doesn't count for much. Our options were limited. You couldn't just arrest these guys. We lacked jurisdiction over there. The most I could do was hope to get the local authorities to act, which wasn't very likely because in those days the Greeks weren't crazy about Americans."

When Rose Kennedy heard about the nude photographs, she wrote to Jackie, asking how something like this could have happened. If not for herself, had she no concern for the children? And where was that highly touted security team Onassis had promised to provide prior to their marriage?

Whether Onassis recognized it or not, his marriage to Jackie had reached a low point. His New York sojourns gradually decreased in frequency and duration. When he did visit, Jackie made it perfectly clear that he wasn't welcome to stay in the Fifth Avenue apartment and would be better off at the Pierre. "She always had some handy excuse," said Costa Gratsos. "'The decorators are in,' she'd tell him. I never saw an apartment undergo so many decorating changes. It was an upper-class variation on the working-class woman's mania for cleaning house. Or she'd tell him that the children had their Kennedy cousins in for the weekend. On the few occasions she permitted him to sleep over, she demeaned him by placing him in a guest room that contained pink floral wallpaper and white wicker furniture. She refused to redecorate the room, though it was more suitable for a little girl than a shipping impresario."

Onassis would go to his wife's house for dinner, but mainly when she gave dinner parties, and even then he wasn't always invited. The problem, Jackie said, was that he didn't get along with her New York friends.

"And the reason for that," Onassis told Costa Gratsos, "is that half of them are fags and the rest are phonies."

One weekend he accompanied Jackie and the children to Hammersmith Farm, complaining afterward about what poor treatment he'd been accorded by Jackie's mother. An additional sore point was his "sudden" realization that he'd married a total prima donna. Jackie and Ari spent the weekend arguing, carrying on in front of the children. When they returned to New York, Onassis told his wife that her mother was "the most boring woman" he'd ever met.

The couple disagreed on any number of subjects, including child rearing. "The greatest form of child abuse," he told her, "is overindulgence—and that's exactly what you do, especially with respect to Caroline." By way of rejoinder, Jackie pointed out that Christina was far more spoiled than Caroline. "Only in Christina's case," she added, "you overindulge her with money rather than love."

Rather than join Onassis in Paris over the Christmas holidays, Jackie took her children to Washington. One morning as she and John went shopping for Christmas presents, they passed a street vendor selling model cars. JFK Jr. asked his mother to buy him one. When she heard the price, she turned and walked away. "What's wrong?" asked John. "It's too expensive," said Jackie. "Too expensive?" he roared. "I thought you were married to the world's wealthiest man!"

During this period, Jackie, Caroline, and John also began spending less time than usual at Skorpios, opting instead for a month in Montauk, Long Island, where Lee Radziwill had rented Andy Warhol's oceanfront estate. There they were reunited with Peter Beard, hard at work with filmmaker Jonas Mekas on what Beard claimed to be a documentary about the Long Island of Jackie's youth. The film, never completed, contained scenes of Caroline and John Jr. romping in the surf, waterskiing, riding their bicycles, playing Frisbee, sitting on top of a station wagon, and spraying each other with a garden hose. Other scenes incorporated Jackie, Lee, and Lee's two children. The project seemed to have less to do with Jackie's past than with her current lifestyle. Included were segments on Edith and Edie Beale, Jackie's aunt and cousin, in their dilapidated home, Grey Gardens, on Lily Pond Road in East Hampton. The house, full of cats, rats, raccoons, debris, and vermin, had been condemned by the Suffolk County Health Department. It (and its inhabitants) eventually became the subject of another film (*Grey Gardens*), an award-winning documentary by the Maysles brothers, which captured the interest of the public not only because of Edith's and Edie's histrionic personalities but because it provided visual confirmation of Jackie's basic indifference toward her impoverished relatives. It was Aristotle Onassis who eventually helped them out financially.

Doris Francisco, a friend of Edith Beale's, recalled a visit to Grey Gardens that summer by Caroline and John Jr. "John insisted on seeing the attic and rummaging through the heaps of junk," said Francisco. "His Secret Service agent took one look at the place and went up there after him. When they came down, John said the attic reminded him of a stage setting. He found a board and an old, rusty roller skate, which Edith let him keep. Presumably he wanted to make a skateboard out of it."

The publicity engendered by the Maysles brothers documentary led to an employment opportunity for Edie Beale, then in her sixties. Appearing nightly at Reno Sweeney, a Manhattan nightclub, she sang, danced, vamped, signed autographs, and answered questions posed by members of the audience. Asked whether Jackie had married Onassis for his money, her typical answer was, "Of course, wouldn't you?" Asked what Jackie's children were *really* like, she responded, "John's a doll, but his sister's spoiled silly." After a few of Edie's controversial performances, Jackie had her attorneys contact the nightclub management and threaten them with a lawsuit unless they terminated Edie's contract. Bored with the arrangement, Edie quit on her own volition.

Peter Beard, meanwhile, continued to cultivate his already burgeoning friendship with both of Jackie's children. In early 1973 he took them to Kenya, where he owned a plantation. While Caroline stayed behind with the local game warden, Beard and JFK Jr. climbed Mount Kenya together. The Kenya trip had been Jackie's idea. "She wanted to toughen John up," said Pierre Salinger. "She once said to me, apropos of nothing, 'I hope he doesn't grow up to be a wimp.' She'd made similar comments about John to others. I believe it had something to do with the fact that he had no real father figure. There was always Teddy, a father of sorts to all those fatherless Kennedy kids. But in reality, most of them considered Uncle Ted an old windbag. He'd take them white-water rafting but then stand on the shoreline swigging martinis with the rest of the adults, while the kids were left to fend for themselves."

In 1974 Peter Beard took Caroline and John on a snake hunting expedition in the Florida Everglades. As usual, the youngsters were trailed by a squadron of journalists. Early one morning they passed a photographer asleep on a couch in the lobby of their hotel. Young John broke into a loud rendition of "Jumpin' Jack Flash," a Rolling Stones number. The photographer woke up and started fumbling for his camera, by which time the performance had ended, and the son of JFK was out the door.

During their sojourn in Kenya, Beard had lent Caroline one of his Leica cameras, and the teenager began taking photographs. When word spread that she had discovered a new hobby, she received a number of inquiries from photo agents eager to represent her work. The Associated Press offered her $10,000 for the exclusive rights to several of her photos. She had spent a month—in the summer of 1973—living with a family in the small Appalachian town of Clairfield in eastern Tennessee, working as a production assistant on a government-sponsored oral history project and documentary on the daily lives of local coal miners, taking her own photographs on the side. Lexington Labs Gallery in Manhattan later expressed an interest in exhibiting some eighty of Caroline's black-and-white Tennessee photographs, an offer Jackie dismissed as a blatant exploitation of her daughter's name. She changed her mind only after eliciting a promise from the gallery owner, Philip Passoni, that he wouldn't advertise the event and that the opening would remain a low-key affair to be attended primarily by friends of the family. Included in the exhibit were two personal photographs: one of John Jr. holding his nose while jumping into the Aegean Sea off the deck of the *Christina;* the other a self-portrait of Caroline in a Gypsy costume, clutching a cigarette and sporting a temporary nose ring. When Jackie spotted the two photographs, she insisted they be removed from the show.

The two photographs wound up in Jackie's library at 1040 Fifth Avenue. "I saw them there," said Andy Warhol, "sitting on an eighteenth-century table in the vicinity of several landscapes Caroline had taken of

Skorpios. Many of Caroline's photographs found their way into a set of family photo albums compiled by Jackie, which also included photos of Greece taken by John Jr. The albums were neatly stacked on another table in her library next to Greek worry beads of blue glass, a Cambodian ring, a small earthen jug from Mexico, a jade trinket from China, a Rigaud candle, a bowl of fruit, and a vase with flowers. At heart, Jackie seemed a rather sentimental creature. A pack rat if ever there was one, she saved everything. She had an album in which she kept work by her favorite poets that her children copied and gave her as a gift whenever she celebrated a birthday.

"Jackie and Caroline had similar personalities. They tended to bury their emotions. They were like icebergs. They revealed only a small portion of themselves—everything else was deeply submerged."

In September 1972 Caroline Kennedy had once again switched schools, this time entering tenth grade at Concord Academy in Concord, Massachusetts, less than forty-five minutes by car from downtown Boston. Chartered in 1922 as an all-girls boarding and day school, Concord had begun admitting boys the year before Caroline's arrival. Progressive and liberal, the college preparatory school with its 325 students had no dress code and included in its curriculum such courses as Japanese and studies in utopian societies. The town of Concord, best known as the historic residence of Louisa May Alcott, Nathaniel Hawthorne, and Ralph Waldo Emerson, was also the locale where Henry David Thoreau had penned *Walden*. A number of Concord's white Colonial houses served as school dormitories and administration offices. A small village cemetery, which Caroline often strolled past on her way to class, boasted headstones dating back to the 1600s. A quintessential New England hamlet, Concord consisted largely of quaint shops and cafés where students and faculty members congregated after class and on weekends. None of the buildings or houses rose above four stories. Monument Square, located at the end of Concord's aptly named Main Street, contained a collection of monuments dedicated to those whose lives had been lost in various wars. Beyond the square stood the Colonial Inn, built in 1716, where Jacqueline Kennedy rented rooms when she first visited Caroline at school. She subsequently leased a small house in town, often bringing John along on weekend stays.

With its small classes and heavy concentration in the arts, Concord Academy proved an ideal setting for Caroline. "No longer under the direct aegis of her larger-than-life mother," said George Plimpton, "Caroline felt free to become her own person. Jackie would visit, but Caroline was substantially on her own. It gave her a much-needed sense of independence. It also helped that when she turned sixteen, she lost her Secret Service privileges. This added immeasurably to Caroline's joyous new state."

Continuing to receive high grades, Caroline demonstrated a particular aptitude for writing, philosophy, and art history. She took courses in photography, let her hair grow out, stopped taking diet pills and put on weight, started chewing bubble gum, and entertained herself by playing practical jokes on her schoolmates. On one occasion she emptied a box of detergent in the school fountain and watched as the basin overflowed with soap suds. At night she would turn up her stereo and dance solo to the latest rock albums. She once went on a wild car ride with a few boys from Middlesex, a nearby prep school, which violated a regulation prohibiting Concord students from leaving campus without permission from school authorities. Alerted to the incident, Russell Mead, Concord's headmaster, called Caroline in for a talk. She defended her action on grounds that her mother had given her permission to leave the area whenever she wanted. "You need permission from the school, not from your mother," replied Mead. "If it happens again, you'll be suspended."

It didn't happen again, but Caroline discovered other ways to assert her independence, often sleeping through breakfast, skipping classes, and sneaking back into her dorm long after curfew. She liked dirty jokes, cursed like a sailor, once belly-danced down the aisle of a local coffee shop, and occasionally smoked pot with friends. She drank too much beer, indulged her fetish for chocolate, smoked cigarettes in her dorm room—another infraction of school rules—resorting to a spray can of Lysol to disguise the odor. Her greatest break with convention came when she informed her mother that she had no intention of "coming out" as a debutante, as Jackie had done. "People already think of me as an effete snob," she said. "I don't want to give them more ammunition." Although originally opposed to her daughter's decision, Jackie eventually capitulated, telling acquaintances that she admired Caroline's strong will and self-determination.

One of Caroline's roommates at Concord was Carrie Minot, whose sister Susan, a future writer, she befriended as well. "Caroline preferred the more intellectual set," remarked a classmate. "These girls would stay up all hours of the night discussing politics and philosophy. I recall that Caroline supported George McGovern for president in 1972. After attending a McGovern fund-raiser in Boston, she returned to school in a rather depressed mood. Much as she admired him, she recognized that McGovern didn't stand a chance against Richard Nixon."

The same classmate remembered times when Caroline seemed embarrassed by stories in the press regarding her family: "There was an article about her mother flying to Providence, Rhode Island, with Frank Sinatra to attend one of his concerts. Another night she accompanied him to the Uris Theatre in New York to watch him perform and afterward joined him for dinner in his hotel suite. Then there were the endless gossip items about Jackie's shopping sprees at Henri Bendel, Artbag Creations, Hammacher Schlemmer, Gucci, Hermès, FAO Schwarz, and so forth. Shopping—for almost anything—appeared to be her main preoccupation, and the press made as much of it as they could. And then there were all these stories about how impecunious she was. I once read an article about this carpenter who'd built her some bookshelves, and afterward she asked him if he'd rather be paid or have an autographed photograph. He said he'd prefer an autographed check."

"Caroline was well aware of these stories, as well as those involving Aristotle Onassis. There was one about Onassis and the actress Elizabeth Taylor lunching together in Rome, along with several friends, when a diner at another table came over and began annoying Taylor. He refused to leave. Finally, Onassis splashed a glass of champagne in the fellow's face. Caroline saw the news account—as did everyone else—and it upset her. For obvious reasons she was similarly upset in November 1973, on the tenth anniversary of her father's assassination, when every newspaper in the country ran a barrage of articles on JFK, not all of them complimentary. It no doubt brought back terrible memories. Caroline had an intense sense of privacy. It was as though she walked around with a 'No Trespassing' sign plastered to her forehead."

Despite everything, Caroline enjoyed living away from home. Like many of the other coeds at Concord, she dressed informally in clogs, baggy sweaters, and formless skirts. After one of her visits to the campus, Jackie encouraged her daughter to "dress up a bit more" and began shopping for her at the same New York stores she frequented for her own clothes. The new apparel arrived at Concord via United Parcel Service, only to be relegated—unused and unworn—to the back of Caroline's closet, eventually to be given away to friends and classmates.

For all their minor differences—Jackie once complained that she "could no longer communicate" with Caroline—mother and daughter remained close. Jackie joined the Municipal Art Society of New York and helped lead the fight to save Grand Central Terminal from demolition. Caroline traveled down from school to support her mother at meetings. Although Caroline rejected Jackie's suggestion that she take a ballet class in school to lose weight, she sat next to her at a series of energy hearings conducted by Ted Kennedy in the John F. Kennedy Federal Building in Boston. Caroline and her mother attended the annual Robert F. Kennedy Pro-Celebrity Tennis Tournament at Forest Hills, New York, the proceeds of which were distributed among various philanthropies and charities. And whenever Caroline happened to be in New York, her mother accompanied her to the allergist's office, where she received injections against dust, pollen, and ragweed.

By way of contrast, John Jr.'s academic performance at Collegiate never measured up to his sister's accomplishments at Concord Academy. During his junior high school years, he failed several courses outright, earning Cs and Ds in others. Convinced that John had developed a learning block, his mother sent him to still another child psychiatrist, whose name she had been given by her own twice-a-week psychoanalyst. The psychiatrist determined that John was mildly dyslexic and recommended that Jackie hire a reading disability specialist to work with him. The specialist, Susan Frances Ober, improved John's reading skills by introducing him to *Profiles in Courage*. "We read it together word by word," said Ober. "The fact that his father had written the book—and that it had won a Pulitzer Prize—gave him renewed faith in his own abilities. When we were done, he said that one day he hoped to pursue a career in journalism, which is what his father had originally planned to do."

Jackie had wanted to spend the Christmas holidays of 1972 at Skorpios with Caroline and John. But in late November of that year, she learned that a group of eight terrorists, members of the New Left in Greece, had been arrested in Athens for plotting to abduct government officials, diplomats, business leaders, and celebrities. Their list of potential victims included a wealthy Greek-American industrialist named Thomas Pappas, the Greek minister of labor, and John F. Kennedy Jr. Five of the eight were given prison sentences ranging from seven to thirty months; the other three were found not guilty and released.

Fearing for her son's safety, Jackie sought to cancel their trip. John protested, pointing out that the terrorists had all been apprehended and the danger averted. Jackie agreed to go but only provided they remain aboard the *Christina* and not visit Greece. They spent several days off Sardinia's Emerald Coast and another week anchored off Monte Carlo, where Onassis had invested millions of dollars over the years and had recently established business offices to take advantage of Monaco's tax-free status.

In mid-January 1973 Onassis arrived in New York to complete a long-pending business transaction. An argument ensued between Jackie and Ari over a twenty-five-room Gracie Square mansion that Jackie wanted him to acquire for her. Already enraged by her excessive spending, Onassis flatly refused. The situation was exacerbated by Jackie's discovery that John Jr. had hidden a half-dozen marijuana joints in his dresser and that he and several of his school chums had raided the liquor cabinet, downing two bottles of Johnnie Walker Black Label, Ari's favorite scotch. Jackie grounded him for a month, two weeks for each offense. To keep a closer eye on him, she resumed her earlier practice of picking him up after school, giving rise to the occasional taunt by classmates that he was a "mama's boy." Jackie's protective presence continued long into John's adult years, making itself felt in a number of domains, not the least of which were his choice of profession and his selection of girlfriends.

• • •

Aristotle Onassis was still in New York when word arrived, on January 21, 1973, that his son, Alexander, had been gravely injured while taking off from an Athens airport in one of his amphibious planes. Suffering from grievous internal injuries, the twenty-four-year-old heir to the Onassis fortune had been taken to the Red Cross Hospital in the center of Athens and placed on life support. The following morning, accompanied by an eminent Boston neurosurgeon, Ari and Jackie flew to Greece. Two cardiologists, one from Dallas and another from London, were also flown to Athens.

By the time Ari, Jackie, and the three physicians reached Alexander's bedside, his condition had worsened. Hospital surgeons informed Ari that his son was clinically dead, his brain having ceased to function although his heart continued to beat. Alexander died two days after the crash. He was buried next to the little chapel on Skorpios. Of the various members of the family in attendance at the afternoon funeral, only Jackie remained composed, as though she could not allow herself to grieve for the young man who had considered her his mortal enemy. By Jackie's choice, neither Caroline nor John Jr. attended the funeral.

Convinced that one or another of his numerous business adversaries had sabotaged the plane, Onassis offered a $5 million reward to anyone who could provide information leading to the arrest and conviction of the would-be murderer. At great expense he hired French journalist Jacques Harvey to conduct an independent investigation into the crash. After an intensive probe, Harvey concluded that the crash had been an accident. "God is responsible," the journalist told Onassis.

"Ari remained adamant in his conviction that somebody had planted a bomb on the plane," said Costa Gratsos, "and nothing could divert him from this idea. The more Jackie tried to talk him out of his obsession, the angrier he became at her. In this instance I sided with Jackie, and I told Ari as much. He said to me, 'This woman refuses to believe that John F. Kennedy was the victim of a conspiracy, when the entire world knows that he was.' 'No, Ari,' I replied. 'Jackie never denied the possibility of a conspiracy. She said only that the knowledge of such a conspiracy would do no good, since it wouldn't restore JFK to life. The woman has her faults, but you can't blame her for not wanting to pursue the assassination.'"

Alexander's death soured Onassis's feelings for Olympic Airways and for flying in general, and he initiated negotiations to sell the airline to the Greek government. The government took advantage of his weakened state. The Tarzan of the boardroom had grown as meek as a mouse. Acting on behalf of his family, he surrendered the airline at a fraction of its worth. In the wake of his personal tragedy, he was faced with a number of financial setbacks: a rise in oil prices, reduction of fuel consumption and overproduction of tankers, and escalating interest rates. He lost money when plans for a new fleet of supertankers and an oil refinery he wanted to build in New Hampshire fell through. He blamed Jackie for these (and other) failures.

In addition, he felt Jackie was taking him for every penny. Her monthly credit card statements continued to flood his New York offices; they included thousands of dollars of charges for incidentals such as personal messenger services, the care and feeding of her horses, a car service, pharmaceutical and beauty products, hairdressers, interior decorators, personal trainers, a yoga instructor, fresh floral arrangements, even a shiatsu acupuncturist from Malaysia, Lillian Biko, whom she saw regularly to help reduce tension and anxiety. She had also added to her already high household payroll by hiring a Portuguese butler named Efigenio Pinheiro. She spent $5,000 of her husband's money on a high-powered telescope through which she enjoyed watching people in the park. Onassis accused her of withholding her affection whenever he questioned her expenditures and attacked her for criticizing him in front of her children, which served only to further alienate him from them. His resentment was compounded by the feeling that she didn't share his grief, his despair, over Alexander's death. His perceptions, whether justified or not, produced friction and ill will on both sides. Their basic difference was that Jackie had always sought to suppress pain, whereas Onassis, with his dark passions, tended to immerse himself in it.

To assuage his anguish, Onassis swam, gardened, drank ouzo, and sang the nostalgic Greek songs he so much loved. In mid-February, with

Pierre Salinger by their side, Jackie and Ari flew to Dakar, Senegal, and there boarded the *Christina* for a ten-day cruise to Trinidad, where they remained for another week. "Although Onassis kept his deepest, darkest thoughts to himself," said Salinger, "it was clear that he was desperately unhappy. He seemed heartbroken. I had the distinct feeling that his son's death marked the beginning of his own demise as well."

Alexander's death gave rise to one further postscript. Ironically, despite John Jr.'s great interest in helicopters and airplanes, it was Caroline who first decided to take flying lessons. Registering as a student pilot, she signed on for ten hour-long lessons at Hanscom Airfield outside Concord. Flying with an instructor, she had completed five sessions at the controls of a Cessna 150 two-seater. Opposed from the start, Jackie used Alexander's crash as an excuse to end the lessons. Dropping in at the airfield, she ordered Caroline's flight instructor to remove her daughter from the program.

John Jr.'s teen years were an odd admixture of outright privilege coupled with the realization that in New York, at least, he was susceptible to the same hardships accorded any young man coming of age. Willie Mays showed him how to swing a bat prior to a New York Mets baseball game that he attended with a classmate from Collegiate. He clowned around with his idol Muhammad Ali, pretending to punch the former (and future) heavyweight champion in the nose, before the second of Ali's three bouts with Joe Frazier. By the same token, in the spring of 1974, young John was the victim of a Central Park mugging.

Riding his Italian-made ten-speed racer along the bike path to the Central Park tennis courts, where a late-afternoon lesson had been scheduled with Pat Fenton, he was suddenly confronted by a tall, muscular thug wielding a tree branch. With no Secret Service agent in sight, the assailant relieved John of both his bicycle and tennis racket. Because of the victim's renown and the overt media attention caused by the event, the police went out of their way to make an arrest. The mugger, picked out of a police lineup by John, turned out to be a twenty-year-old heroin addict who lived in Spanish Harlem with his sixteen-year-old bride and two-month-old son. Although John testified before a grand jury, Jackie feared that a trial would only lead to further publicity. The charges were eventually dropped.

Like his sister, John continued to be a perpetual press magnet. It was impossible for him to go anywhere or do anything and not be noticed. In November 1974 his mother threw a surprise birthday party for him at Manhattan's Le Club, after which he and several of his Kennedy cousins engaged in a pushing and shoving match with reporters. In December, while skiing with Ted Kennedy's family in the Berkshires, he heaved a Pepsi bottle over the heads of news photographers, and the incident became a front-page story in the *New York Post*. Another article in a spring 1975 issue of *Paris Match* specified that John had become a prolific abuser of pot. Being disciplined by his mother for his earlier use of the substance hardly seemed to matter. An anonymous source, presumably a schoolmate at Collegiate, informed the French periodical that Kennedy had been caught smoking pot in an empty classroom and had received a ten-day suspension. The article went on to say that John frequently smoked marijuana at home. He used it in the building's stairwell and on the roof. According to friends, including John Perry Barlow and a schoolmate named Wilson McCray from Collegiate, getting high on pot became a major preoccupation with John, particularly during his mid-teenage years.

Drugs and alcohol were a common means of escape among other members of the younger generation of the Kennedy family. Anger and rebellion were another. These remained the most convenient modes of response to the harrowing burden of being born into a clan whose every dream had been fulfilled and then forever crushed.

In 1970, at age sixteen, Robert F. Kennedy Jr. was arrested in Barnstable, Massachusetts, for possession of marijuana. He and his cousin Bobby Shriver, also busted for possession, were both placed on probation. Unable to cope with his emotional problems, Bobby Jr. soon graduated to cocaine and heroin. Some years later he was found unconscious in an airport men's room with a heroin needle stuck in his arm. Arrested for the possession of 6.2 grams of heroin, he received a suspended sentence in exchange for entering a drug rehabilitation center and working in a community service program.

Equally (if not more) under the influence was Christopher Lawford who, by his own admission, spent his adolescence and early adult years on an endless alcohol and near-fatal drug binge as he shuttled back and forth between the trendy Hollywood world of his "Rat Pack" father, Peter Lawford, and the extravagant northeastern society existence of his mother, Patricia Kennedy Lawford. Then there was David Kennedy, RFK and Ethel Kennedy's fourth child, whose life seemed darkly shadowed by the assassinations of his uncle and father and the attendant family difficulties that followed. After stints of varying lengths at an assortment of tony prep schools, David was admitted to Harvard. Very likely the brightest and most sensitive member of the third generation, he was also the most troubled. The perpetual outsider, unable to fit in, he gathered wildflowers in a field while his siblings played brutal games of touch football on the sloping lawn of their Hyannis Port compound. Busted in a Harlem hotel for the purchase of narcotics, David received a suspended sentence and spent time in a series of treatment centers. His internment in such programs served only to stimulate his addictions. In his autobiography, *Symptoms of Withdrawal,* Christopher Lawford reveals that after unsuccessfully petitioning the Kennedy trust-fund administrator for cash, he and David took to panhandling for drug money in Grand Central Terminal. Although Lawford and RFK Jr. eventually righted themselves, earning law degrees and establishing reasonably successful careers, David did not. Alone and lonely, he died in 1984 in a Palm Beach hotel room from an overdose of cocaine and Demerol.

There were other afflicted members of the clan. Kara Kennedy, the daughter of Ted and Joan, at age thirteen ran away from home and wound up in a halfway house for drug-addicted teenagers. Joseph Patrick Kennedy II, Bobby and Ethel's eldest son, suffered from violent outbursts of rage. Easily provoked, he regularly beat up his younger brothers and male cousins.

In the summer of 1973, at the age of twenty-one, Joe overturned a jeep on Nantucket while driving his brother David and David's then-girlfriend, Pam Kelley, to the ferry. The accident, caused by Joe's recklessness (according to a police report), had dire results. Paralyzed from the waist down, Pam Kelley would never walk again.

Added to these calamities were the problems encountered by Joan and Ethel Kennedy. Incapable of dealing with Ted's womanizing, never able to fulfill the family's ambitious expectations, Joan found solace in alcohol and barbiturates. "She'd be passed out in the backseat of her car for days at a clip," said Ken O'Donnell. "She wanted to do the family's bidding but couldn't. In November 1973, when Ted Kennedy Jr. had his cancerous right leg amputated, Joan came apart at the seams. She absolutely couldn't deal with her son's illness."

Ethel Kennedy's situation, in many respects attributable to RFK's assassination, led to a breakdown in communication with her children. "The Big E.," as she became known, revealed herself to be what Jackie Kennedy termed "a weird and wacky parent." "She resides in a perpetual stupor," Jackie told friends. "She's dysfunctional." Ethel's children lacked both supervision and discipline. "Hickory Hill," said Larry O'Brien, "began to resemble an insane asylum. There were rats in the kitchen and bats in the attic. The family pets excreted all over the house. The place smelled like a fucking zoo. When any of the kids had problems—even if drug- or alcohol-related—Ethel would ship them out to friends and relatives. She couldn't handle the responsibility."

One of those Ethel turned to for help was Lem Billings, whose Manhattan apartment soon became a home away from home for several younger members of the tribe, among them RFK Jr., David Kennedy, and Christopher Lawford. A periodic abuser of drugs and pharmaceuticals, Lem's involvement in the upbringing of the three teens only made matters worse. Instead of elevating them to a higher level, he allowed himself to descend to theirs. Lawrence J. Quirk, a friend of Billings, observed that "Lem's apartment had all the makings of what in street vernacular is known as 'the corner candy store'—an LSD, hash, pot, speed, coke, and heroin den. Lem often plied the kids with drugs, which is exactly what they didn't need. He became an enabler rather than a savior. In addition, he was gay, which further complicated his relationship with the kids."

Jackie Kennedy was all too aware of the disturbing events that had befallen various members of the family. Similarly aware of Lem's growing dependence on drugs and his complicated relations with at least three members of the third generation, she began to distance herself (and her children) from her late husband's dearest friend. Against all odds, she was determined to mold Caroline and John into well-adjusted, serious, and successful adults, and she had come to regard Billings as a detriment to that end. "She dropped me, just as she'd dropped so many others," said Billings. "I'd call and invite her to lunch, but she was always busy. One evening I received a telephone call at home from Caroline Kennedy. She didn't identify herself, merely asked to speak to David [Kennedy]. Overhearing David's conversation with her, it became clear that it was Caroline at the other end. I took the phone from David and said to her, 'You call my house, and when I answer, you don't even take the time to say hello. What's that all about?' She mumbled something and then hung up. I never heard from her again—and only rarely from her mother."

Jackie also gradually distanced Caroline and John from Ethel Kennedy and the rest of Bobby's brood. Harrison Rainie, a Washington correspondent for the New York *Daily News* and a Kennedy family biographer, felt "Jackie tended to resist the enforced togetherness embraced by the rest of the family. She was never one of those relentless buffs, like Bobby and Ethel, constantly clamoring for family reunions. She was particularly wary of Ethel's household, which was more important to the children's generation than any of the others. She didn't want Caroline and John to play second fiddle and didn't want them to be exposed to an environment that she considered unstructured and untamed."

The major exceptions to Jackie's rule were the family get-togethers that took place during various holidays at Rose Kennedy's homes in Hyannis Port and Palm Beach, long after Joe Kennedy's 1969 death. Ultimately, despite Jackie's reluctance to allow her children to socialize with Ethel's offspring, she encouraged Caroline and John to honor their rightful legacy. Caroline particularly enjoyed the Fourth of July family reunions at the Kennedy compound. One year Rose sent every grandchild a copy of Henry Wadsworth Longfellow's poem on the ride of Paul Revere. The children were expected to memorize the poem and then recite it if they wanted a second helping at their Independence Day picnic. Another year she sent each grandchild a copy of the Declaration of Independence. In so doing, she hoped to inspire the kind of dinner table conversation on current affairs and American history that had prevailed when Joe Kennedy sat at the head of the table.

Of all her grandchildren, Rose Kennedy probably remained closest to Caroline. Barbara Gibson, Mrs. Kennedy's personal secretary, vouched for the fact that Rose and Caroline maintained a lively correspondence throughout the latter's high school and college years. Rose frequently wrote to Caroline, complaining about the deportment of her other grandchildren. She once castigated John Jr. in a letter to his sister, accusing him of having left her Hyannis Port kitchen a mess after making brownies with Victoria Lawford. Another common theme in Rose's letters to Caroline was mention of the inordinate amount of coverage that she and John garnered in the press. The least mention of either of them in a magazine or newspaper invariably resulted in a sympathetic note from Rose. She referred to journalists as "mythmakers interested in exploiting the tribal rites of our family," at the same time questioning the American public's "seemingly insatiable appetite for gossip." In a separate letter, this one to John Jr., she wrote: "Everyone speaks about you, but nobody speaks to you."

The only truly angry letter Rose ever wrote to Caroline came in response to the discovery by a police officer of several marijuana plants growing in Jackie's backyard at Hyannis Port. Although David Kennedy had harvested the plants, Caroline, attempting to protect her cousin, took the blame. Unaware that her favorite grandchild had nothing to do with it, Rose excoriated her for the incident. A likewise unsuspecting Jackie turned to Abraham Ribicoff, the Connecticut ex-senator and a former supporter of President Kennedy, and invited him to her Fifth Avenue apartment to discuss the issue of drugs with both her children.

"I went down to New York and met with the kids," recalled Ribicoff. "Jackie had asked me to lecture them on the danger of becoming addicted to drugs. I spoke with them, but in truth the subject of drugs never came up. Instead I reminisced about their father and my memories of him as a young man. I must have laid it on pretty thick, because after a while we were all in tears. Talking with those two youngsters that afternoon was one of the most moving experiences I ever had."

Chapter 9

———◆———

A GREEK TRAGEDY

IN EARLY 1974 ARISTOTLE ONASSIS was diagnosed as suffering from myasthenia gravis, a crippling neuromuscular disease about which physicians knew relatively little. In Ari's case, the illness initially manifested itself in slurred speech patterns, discoloration of the skin, swollen jowls, and the drooping of his eyelids. Jackie suggested that a week in Acapulco might help relieve some of the symptoms and bolster his sagging spirits. The couple flew down in his private Learjet. Once there, they began to haggle. Jackie expressed a wish to own a villa in Acapulco. It reminded Ari of their dispute over the Gracie Square house she had wanted him to buy for her in New York. He insisted that he neither needed nor wanted a new home in Mexico. He said he'd been generous enough, especially considering her attitude following Alexander's death. They were still bickering the day they returned to the States. Jackie lost her temper, called Ari an ingrate, and said she "neither needed nor wanted" his "damn" money.

"In that case you won't be disappointed," he snapped.

It was in this frame of mind, while winging their way back to New York, that Onassis chose to rewrite his will. Removing himself to a seat at the rear of the plane, he wrote out by hand (in compliance with Greek law) a document intended to serve as his last will and testament. He interrupted the job only long enough to eat lunch with Jackie in the Miami airport, while the plane was being refueled. Ari's hastily composed document named Christina Onassis as prime beneficiary and set up a foundation in memory of Alexander, at the same time establishing strictures that prohibited Jackie and her children from inheriting anything beyond what had been indicated in the original premarital agreement. Onassis's sole concession to his wife encompassed the allocation of one-quarter ownership rights in both his private island and yacht, the remainder of each to go to Christina. As a final insult to Jackie, he named Tina, "the mother of my son," chief executrix of his estate. One problem with the document was that while seemingly valid under Greek statutes, it failed to meet all the requirements of the New York State probate system, leaving the will open to invasion in the United States, where Onassis had major holdings. The same applied to probate courts in France and England, countries in which the Greek tycoon possessed considerable assets and real estate.

Although convinced that Jackie had become more an enemy than an ally, Onassis was content, at least for the moment, to maintain distant but cordial relations with her. When articles began to crop up in British and American tabloids uncovering the extensive extramarital sexual activities of Jack Kennedy, Jackie felt comfortable enough to turn to Ari for help. "I would pay a king's ransom to keep this away from Caroline and John," she told him. Janet Auchincloss advised her daughter to "take the high road" and refuse to acknowledge the contents of the articles. Onassis suggested another tack, one which Jackie ultimately adopted. She purposely discussed the subject of their father's infidelities with her children, assuring them that these affairs never affected his love for his family. Without going into specifics, she imparted the same general philosophy she had once offered to Joan Kennedy, namely that some Kennedy men were self-avowed players, but that it meant nothing.

In late May 1974, Jackie joined Ari and Christina for a brief sojourn in Madrid. Costa Gratsos, also vacationing in Spain, recalled that Jackie began needling Christina, accusing her of wasting her life, flitting from place to place and from playboy to playboy. "Christina finally walked out on Jackie," said Gratsos. "She was enraged. Privately she confessed that if she thought she could get away with it, she'd drown Jackie at sea."

In September, when her mother, Tina, died in Paris from edema of the lung, Christina convinced herself that Jackie was somehow to blame. Some superstitious strain out of her family's peasant past suggested to her that a malevolent force of untold ferocity had to be connected to the deaths not only of her mother but also of her aunt and brother. She told Costa Gratsos that she suspected Jackie of having brought all these misfortunes down upon her, killing everyone she had ever loved. "She's the Angel of Death," said Christina.

On February 9, 1975, Jackie received a telephone call from Johnny Meyer, Ari's personal assistant, saying that Onassis had collapsed in Athens with excruciating pain in his chest. He'd been transported to the same hospital where Alexander had been taken following his fatal airplane crash. Jackie flew to Athens, at the same time that Ari's sister Artemis arrived from London. Christina cut short a vacation in Switzerland and also flew to Athens. They were soon joined by Dr. Jean Caroli, Ari's longtime Paris-based physician, who convinced the patient to fly back with him to be placed in the American Hospital at Neuilly-sur-Seine on the outskirts of Paris. As they were about to land, Onassis turned to Caroli and said, "Professor, do you know the meaning of the Greek word *thanatos*? It means a merciful death. You know perfectly well I will never come out of the hospital alive. You must promise to practice *thanatos* on me. I do not want to suffer. I would rather be dead."

Haggard and gray, forty pounds underweight, the Greek shipping magnate refused a wheelchair and, on February 12, entered the hospital under his own power. Jackie spent the week at their Avenue Foch townhouse in Paris. Caroline Kennedy, presently in her last year at Concord Academy, arrived in Paris shortly after her mother. In lieu of a senior thesis, she had landed a part-time, nonpaying trainee's job with NBC-TV's *Weekend* series, and had been assigned to work with producer Karen Lerner on a documentary about international arms dealer Adnan Khashoggi. While Jackie spent part of each day visiting her nearly estranged husband at the American Hospital, Caroline went off with Lerner and the rest of the camera crew to conduct interviews for the documentary. To complete the project, she and the crew accompanied Khashoggi on a trip to the Middle East with stops in Lebanon and Saudi Arabia.

One evening—in Paris—Christina Onassis took Caroline, Jackie,

Karen Lerner, and several members of the film crew to dinner at L'Orangerie. After the main course, when Caroline asked to see the dessert menu, her mother said in a voice loud enough to be heard by diners at a neighboring table, "You're not going to order dessert, Caroline. You're much too fat. Nobody will ever want to marry you."

Caroline, who stood five feet seven and weighed a pudgy 150 pounds, gave her mother a defiant look.

"If you don't stop picking on your daughter," Christina chimed in, "you'll give her an inferiority complex. Believe me, I speak from personal experience."

After a brief negotiation, Jackie allowed Caroline to order a serving of cherry-flavored Jell-O, without the usual whipped cream topping.

Jackie's ongoing battle with Caroline over the latter's tendency toward avoirdupois had a corollary in the former's unoriginal theory that it was impossible to be either too rich or too thin. She had given her daughter a credit card for individual purchases under $100. Checking the itemized invoices, Jackie noticed that whenever Caroline visited New York from boarding school, she charged such items as cheesecake from Miss Grimble's, brownies from William Greenberg's, and chocolate truffles at $20 a pound from Krön. One day she saw a charge for two pounds of barbecued spareribs at Mr. Chow. After lecturing her daughter on the perils of excessive poundage, she canceled the credit card but reactivated it when Caroline agreed to join her mother on jaunts around the Central Park Reservoir. Caroline eventually signed on for an aerobics class at the fifteen-story Vertical Club on East 61st Street in Manhattan.

"It's strange," said George Plimpton. "Jackie didn't like it when John drank or did drugs, but she didn't seem to care if Caroline got smashed on beer or stoned on grass. It was only when Caroline gained a pound or two that Jackie reacted."

On February 16 surgeons removed Ari's gallbladder. Three days later, assured by doctors that Onassis was on the road to recovery, Jackie returned to New York. She was accompanied on the flight by Johnny Meyer, who noted that "Under the circumstances, Jackie seemed rather chipper. She told me how proud she was of Caroline and John. The subject of Onassis never came up. Toward the end of the flight, I raised the question of his health. 'Don't worry,' said Jackie, 'Ari's indestructible.' I couldn't tell whether she believed it or simply didn't give a damn."

For the next two weeks, Jackie kept in touch with Artemis and Christina by telephone. Neither of them divulged that Maria Callas had been permitted to visit Onassis in the hospital. All that Artemis would say was that Ari seemed unchanged. Still in great pain, he drifted in and out of consciousness.

At the beginning of March 1975, Jackie embarked on a New Hampshire ski trip with John Jr. and Bunny Mellon. Ari's condition took a turn for the worse, but Jackie could not be reached. She and John were back in New York on Saturday, March 15—the day Onassis died, with only his daughter by his bedside.

The funeral took place on March 18 on Skorpios. A half-dozen pall-bearers, led by a Greek Orthodox priest, carried Ari's coffin past wreaths and flowers to the small chapel where his son lay buried. In accordance with the deceased's wishes, the half-hour service was simple and without eulogy. During the ceremony, Jackie kissed the coffin but showed no outward emotion. Nor did Caroline. John placed a small bouquet of flowers on top of the coffin before it was lowered into the earth.

Two days after the burial, Jackie, Caroline, and John returned to Paris to attend the presentation by French president Valéry Giscard d'Estaing of the Legion of Honor—France's cherished civilian award—to Eunice Kennedy Shriver for her charitable work as the wife of the American ambassador. While there, Jackie released a statement to the press, noting that Aristotle Onassis had "rescued" her and her children at a moment when their lives were "engulfed in shadows." Asked whether she anticipated a protracted legal battle with Christina Onassis over Ari's billion-dollar estate, she remarked, "I'll answer with something my husband often told me: 'Throughout the world, people love fairy tales and especially those related to the lives of the rich. You must learn to understand this and accept it.'"

Still in Paris, John Jr. rented a moped to get around and spent time with Christos Kartamos, a wealthy Greek teenager he had met soon after his mother's marriage to Onassis six and a half years earlier. According to JFK Jr. biographer Elaine Landau, the two boys carried on the tradition

John had initiated in New York, smoking pot and drinking alcohol, mostly wine. Rather than raid Ari's liquor supply at the Avenue Foch townhouse, John would give the somewhat older Kartamos money to buy the wine, thus evading Jackie's suspicions.

Jackie had more on her mind at this stage than her son's recreational pursuits. *The New York Times* had published an article alleging that shortly before his death, Onassis had set in motion divorce proceedings against his wife. Jackie became violently upset and called upon Christina to deny the story. Fearful of what Jackie might do or say if she didn't, Christina complied. The *Times* ran another story stipulating that Ari and Jackie were "happily married" and had never considered divorce. "My father adored Jackie," Christina told the newspaper.

On April 28, exactly forty days after Ari's death, Christina and Jackie flew separately to Skorpios for the traditional Greek Orthodox service in memory of the deceased. Christina had already seen to it that Jackie's personal belongings and those of her children were gathered together and shipped to her at Ari's apartment in Paris. Before leaving Skorpios for the last time, Jackie boarded the *Christina* and removed a precious jade Buddha she insisted Onassis had promised to give her. The Buddha, valued at $250,000, had actually been promised to Maria Callas. Christina allowed her stepmother to keep the statue and instead sent Callas an ancient Greek urn worth approximately the same amount of money.

Caroline Kennedy graduated from Concord Academy on June 15, 1975, three months after Ari's death. Attending the ceremony were Jackie and John, Janet Auchincloss, Rose Kennedy, Lee Radziwill, and Uncle Ted, who told the press, "I'm as thrilled for Caroline as the president would have been." With her taste for irreverence and her distaste for formal occasions, Caroline popped bubble gum during the headmaster's graduation address, discarding it only when newspaper photographers gathered around to take pictures of the happy graduate and her family. Twenty years after her graduation, Caroline gave Concord a hefty contribution and joined the school's board of trustees. One board member described her as "arch and demanding," though others cited her creative intelligence in helping reformulate an outdated school curriculum and in providing invaluable ideas for the purpose of raising much-needed funds.

In an effort to show family unity, Jackie, Caroline, and John traveled to Greece that July to attend the wedding at Glyfada of Christina and her most recent flame, Alexander Andreadis, heir to a Greek banking and industrial fortune. "I so love that child," Jackie told the press, her voice ringing with sarcasm. "At last I can see happy days ahead for her."

Jackie and the stepdaughter she claimed to love soon became involved in an eighteen-month dispute over the Onassis estate. The gist of the battle hinged on an interpretation of the will Ari had written in anger while flying with his wife from Acapulco to New York. Simon Rifkind, Jackie's attorney, sought to overthrow the document on the grounds that it was invalid, Greek law ordaining that a last testament had to be written "in a single sitting in a single location." Rifkin pointed out that Onassis had violated both requirements. First, he had executed the will in two sittings, not one, having interrupted the process to eat lunch at the airport in Miami. Additionally, the will had been written in a number of locations as the plane flew from one country to another and from one state to the next—a plane, while airborne, didn't technically qualify as a place.

Far-fetched as Rifkind's argument seemed, Christina's lawyers were reluctant to test its merit in a court of law. Anticipating a bitter legal altercation on at least four fronts (Greece, England, France, and the United States), and not wanting to further alienate Senator Ted Kennedy (the Onassis empire still needed influential friends in Washington), Christina's financial advisers finally offered the widow the flat sum of $20 million, provided she relinquish all further claims to the estate, including her one-quarter share in both Skorpios and the *Christina*. Because of stiff U.S. inheritance taxes, Rifkind demanded—and received—a settlement of $26 million for his famous client. Taking into account the prenuptial payment, monthly allowance, jewelry, clothes, and other gifts, Jackie's gross for the period of her marriage came to roughly $50 million, or nearly $8 million for each year they were married.

The settlement afforded Jackie security for life plus the knowledge that she would be able to provide for her children even beyond the millions they were slated to inherit from their father's (and grandfather's) estate, the first payments of which came due when Caroline and John turned eighteen. It gave Christina the assurance she would never have to speak to her dreaded stepmother again. It also left Christina an enormous share of her father's wealth, to say nothing of the $270 million she had already inherited upon her mother's death.

What the money and the settlement didn't bring Christina was peace of mind. Addicted to alcohol and pharmaceuticals, drifting aimlessly through the world, she continued to excoriate Jackie at every opportunity. "She thinks, talks, and dreams of nothing but money," she told film producer Lester Persky. "What Jackie doesn't realize is that I would have given her fifty times what I gave her for the pleasure of never having to see or talk to her again. I would have paid any price. What amazes me is that she survives while everybody around her drops. She's dangerous. She's deadly. She has decimated at least two families—the Kennedys and mine. If I never see her again as long as I live it will be too soon."

Christina remained in contact with both of Jackie's children, especially John. Each year she sent him a card on his birthday and another at Christmas. In the summer of 1982, they bumped into each other at Studio 54 and spent the evening catching up on old times. Two years later, about to marry her fourth husband, French businessman Thierry Roussel, she invited John to the wedding. He declined, but in 1985, when Christina gave birth to her only child, a daughter named Athina (after her mother), John mailed the infant a silver music box from Tiffany inscribed with the baby's name and date of birth. In 1987, after three years of marriage, Roussel left Christina for a high-fashion model from Switzerland; the divorce settlement cost the thirty-six-year-old Greek heiress an estimated $75 million. Heartbroken and heavily addicted to barbiturates, Christina gradually faded into oblivion. On November 19, 1988, while staying with friends in Buenos Aires, Argentina, she suffered a fatal heart attack. JFK Jr. sent a wreath to be placed at her grave in the family plot at Skorpios, next to her brother and father. The attached note read simply: "To Christina from John."

Part IV

---◆---

Chapter 10

———◆———

FIRST LOVE

Although Caroline Kennedy had been accepted for admission to Radcliffe College in September 1975, she arranged to matriculate the following year and spend the intervening period in London, taking a nine-month art course at Sotheby's auction house. The program, designed to accommodate fifty students, featured a lengthy reading list of books on art history. Students were expected to attend auctions and study the prices of art objects up for sale. Jackie seconded her daughter's decision and agreed to give her a monthly allowance of $250 to cover expenses. Having launched her own career in publishing by accepting a $10,000-a-year position as a consulting editor at Viking Press, the former First Lady hoped that the London sabbatical would allow Caroline to mature in the same way that she'd matured during her college year at the Sorbonne. Her daughter's absence also provided Jackie the opportunity to concentrate her parenting skills on John Jr., who once again lacked an essential father figure, a role Aristotle Onassis had tried to fill. Ted Kennedy, consumed by a quickly collapsing marriage and his own children's problems, was less accessible than he'd been in previous years. Jackie attempted to fill the paternal void in John's life by calling on an assortment of male friends, as she'd often done in the past.

Roosevelt (Rosey) Grier, the former New York Giants football player, a gargantuan figure of a man who'd campaigned with Bobby Kennedy in 1968, was only the latest in a long line of candidates. "Over time," he said, "I grew close to John. In the fall of 1975, I accompanied him to Carnival Day at the Collegiate School. We won a silver dollar together in some event, and I placed him in charge of it, the sole stipulation being that he couldn't spend it without my permission."

John Jr. evidently didn't spend it. The silver dollar that he and Grier had won was later found in a small Collegiate School case tucked away in a desk drawer in his TriBeCa loft at the time of his death.

Other candidates for the surrogate dad title included Peter Beard and George Plimpton. "I saw more of John in the months following Ari's death than I'd seen of him in years," said Plimpton. "I used to take him to New York Knicks basketball games at Madison Square Garden. We went to movies together. I remember Sarge Shriver running for president in 1976 and wanting John to pose with him for photographers. As usual, Jackie opposed the notion. I finally talked her into it. John and I went up to Boston one weekend, and he appeared at a fund-raiser for Sarge. When the press got wind of JFK Jr.'s presence at the event, they turned out en masse. Even as a teenager, John had drawing power."

George Plimpton further recalled that when John was fifteen and in the ninth grade at Collegiate, he had a girlfriend named Christina (Chris) Goodman, whom he'd met the previous summer while attending a monthlong program at the Chase Golf and Tennis Camp in Bethlehem, New Hampshire. Founded by Neil Chase, of Chase Manhattan Bank fame, the camp catered to boys and girls born to the manor, attracting its clientele by advertising in magazines such as *Forbes* and *Fortune*. The camp's popularity among the privileged stemmed from its requirement that campers perform daily tasks and chores, including sweeping the dining hall and cleaning the latrine, in addition to the usual choice of activities. A kind of suburban boot camp for the elite, it had been conceived as a means of instilling discipline among the undisciplined.

"John and Chris met their first day at Chase," said Conrad Rehling, director of the camp. "It was a typical teenage romance. Chris was very pretty, very popular, very socially inclined, and very athletic. She attended the Spence School in Manhattan. John went out with her for about a year. It ended when he left New York and enrolled in boarding school at Phillips Andover, which is where Neil Chase had also gone."

In London, meanwhile, Caroline was staying in Campden Hill Square in the two-story Victorian home of Hugh Fraser, a Tory member of Parliament and a Kennedy family friend who had recently separated from his wife, prolific author Antonia Fraser. Their daughters, Flora and Rebecca, both close to Caroline in age, introduced her to their extensive circle of social acquaintances, among them Adam Carr, whose father was warden of St. Anthony's College, Oxford University; Lord Hesketh, a motor racing enthusiast; Jonathan Guinness, scion to the brewery family; John Boswith, a leading soccer player; and Nicholas Soames, a grandson of Winston Churchill and a close friend of Prince Charles. Shy at first, Caroline soon warmed to the scene. According to Sarah Bradford, a British biographer of Jacqueline Kennedy, Caroline enjoyed dancing the night away at Annabel's and Tramp, dining in the group's restaurants of choice, Morton's and Meridiana, spending weekends with her new friends in the English countryside. She once went hot air ballooning with Bobby Hesketh, Lord Hesketh's younger brother, entertaining him by doing imitations of her mother's stylized, whispery voice, using Jackie's favorite expression—"Oh yeah?"—as a refrain. "Can you believe that woman's voice?" she asked Hesketh. She liked going to museums and lectures. Other features of London's profuse and varied cultural milieu that appealed to her were the theater, the underground cinema, and the occasional rock concert. On the whole, she experienced the same freewheeling lifestyle she had first sampled at Concord Academy, but which would not have been so readily available to her in either New York or Cambridge, Massachusetts. Basically, Caroline could come and go as she pleased. She could drink, smoke pot, party with boys. She could feast on junk food, appear in public with scraggly, unwashed hair, and dress as informally as she wanted without arousing her mother's ire.

Then an incident occurred that catapulted her onto the front page of every European and American newspaper. On October 23, 1975, at 8:40 a.m., Hugh Fraser was preparing to leave his house for the day. He planned to drop off Caroline at Sotheby's before heading for his office. At the same time, Gordon Fairley, an oncologist and next-door neighbor, was walking his two French poodles past Fraser's green Jaguar XJ6 sedan. The phone rang inside the Fraser home. Fraser took the call. He was still on the phone when an enormous explosion was heard. A bomb had been placed and gone off underneath the Jaguar, destroying the car and dismembering Fairley, whose corpse landed in Fraser's front yard. Fraser was slightly injured when shards of glass from a shattered window hit his face. Caroline, still in her upstairs bedroom waiting for the housekeeper to bring her a coat, was knocked onto the bed. Shaken but otherwise intact, she ran downstairs to assess the damage.

"Thank God for the telephone," Fraser told the press. "If it hadn't been for the call, we would all have died."

Scotland Yard investigators suspected the Irish Republican Army of masterminding the bomb in retaliation for life sentences handed down the day before to four IRA terrorists convicted of blowing up an English pub and killing five British civilians. Fraser, an outspoken supporter of the death penalty for violent acts of terrorism, had been the intended target.

In the aftermath of the explosion, Caroline was whisked off to the nearby home of Jackie's friend Lord Harlech (David Ormsby Gore), former British ambassador to the United States. Within hours, she received a telephone call from American ambassador Elliot Richardson—on whose order a security guard from the embassy was dispatched to stay with Caroline for several days—and a visit from British Home Secretary Roy Jenkins, who immediately contacted Jackie and Ted Kennedy in the States to assure them that Caroline was safe. When she finally reached her daughter, Jackie attempted to talk her into leaving London and returning to New York. As obstinate as her mother, Caroline insisted on staying and completing her studies. After several days in a Grosvenor Square apartment owned by Artemis Onassis—at times occupied by Christina—Caroline moved into Lee Radziwill's London dwelling. Instead of using cars to get around, she resorted to the underground.

One reason Caroline wanted to remain in London was twenty-seven-year-old Mark Shand, a tall, tweedy, blond-haired Brit whose father was an English lord and whose family had amassed a fortune in the construction business. Shand's brother-in-law, Andrew Parker Bowles, had courted

Princess Anne before marrying Shand's sister Camilla, best known as the longtime mistress (and eventual wife) of Prince Charles. Mark and Caroline first met in the Bahamas in 1972, when she and Jackie vacationed there with Lee Radziwill and her children. It was Shand, then an art dealer (he would later become an author and wildlife conservationist), who told Caroline about Sotheby's fine-arts program. Not long after she arrived in London, they began to date. He escorted her to a number of parties, including the country wedding of Kim Fraser, Hugh's nephew, into a well-known Devonshire family.

"There were five hundred guests at the reception," said Peter Tollington, a friend of the bride. "We went through five hundred bottles of champagne, served by forty female attendants wearing tartan kilts. Caroline remarked that she'd never seen so many Rolls-Royces gathered in one place at one time. Although she danced with several partners, she kept returning to Mark Shand. She was clearly in love with him. I don't know if he felt the same way. Even then, he was a renowned ladies' man. He ditched his previous girlfriend, an actress named Barbara Trentham, to be able to date Caroline. Did they have a full-blown affair? I'm not sure, but they were obviously heavily involved. For all her glamorous trappings, Caroline struck me as less sexually experienced than many girls her age."

Tollington thought Caroline more attractive in person than in the photographs he'd seen of her. "She was slightly overweight, but she certainly wasn't fat," he said. "She had an interesting face with strong features. She had some freckles and those famous Kennedy buckteeth, but that was all part of the image. Her face had character. She looked like her father."

Mark Shand and Caroline soon became the talk of British society. They attended a small get-together with Prince Charles, and a few weeks later a big "do" in honor of Andy Warhol, whom Shand had previously known in New York. The Warhol gathering took place at the London home of Lord and Lady Lambton, friends of the artist. Rampant with royals and swells, the guest list—which had been drawn up jointly by Anne Lambton and Lee Radziwill—featured the likes of Lady Diana Cooper, the Marquess and Marchioness of Dufferin and Ava, Lord Patrick Lichfield (a cousin of the Queen), Prince Rupert of Prussia, Princess Elizabeth of Yugoslavia, Bianca Jagger, Lucian Freud, Keith Moon, Gunther Sachs, Martin Amis, J. Paul Getty III, and Vivienne Westwood, the owner of the King's Road boutique Sex, a woman clad in head-to-toe black leather who operated at the center of the punk fashion scene.

Author Bob Colacello, Warhol's assistant, remembered that "at five in the morning, the belle of the ball, Caroline Kennedy, in an unassuming but tasteful floor-length skirt and high-necked silk blouse, was still dancing with Mark Shand. 'They look lovely together,' Andy whispered. 'But if this gets in the press, I just know Jackie's going to blame it all on me.' And, of course, it did hit the press. A photographer took a picture of Caroline and Mark leaving the party, and it made page one of all the London tabloids. Jackie, who had spies everywhere, called Andy the day we got back to New York, demanding to know what was going on. 'You should never have invited Caroline to a party like that,' she told him. 'But I didn't invite anybody,' Andy responded. 'Your sister put together the guest list with Anne. I had nothing to do with it.'"

Jackie berated Lee, then telephoned Caroline and warned her to "keep away from the press." But after the bomb scare and with the recent publicity surrounding her romance with Mark Shand, the press wouldn't leave her alone. When she arrived at Sotheby's on the Monday morning following the Warhol party, the entrance to the auction house was clogged with reporters and photographers. She tried to evade them by hurrying to a nearby sandwich bar. The press followed. Frustrated by her inability to lose them, Caroline chucked a glass of water in the general direction of one of the photographers. A write-up of the incident ran in the next day's papers.

The former First Lady again contacted her daughter. "You must think you're Aristotle Onassis," she said. "Or maybe you think you're Christina. When you throw water at a news photographer, you only invite trouble."

A few days later as Mark Shand and Caroline were about to step into Annabel's, they were accosted by a mob of photographers. Shoving the club's doorman aside, the camera-toting crew chased the couple into the discotheque, snapping pictures as they went. On the verge of tears, Caroline darted out the door and onto the sidewalk. Shand went after her and managed to flag down a cab. Snapshots of the harried-looking couple, accompanied by a caption suggesting that they were contemplating marriage, graced the front page of the *Daily Mail.*

The ongoing press barrage became an obstacle that could no longer be ignored. Shand valued his privacy. He informed his friend, society columnist Nigel Dempster, he and Caroline were no longer together. "We're only buddies," he said. A cover story on Caroline by Willi Frischauer in the February 1976 issue of *Ladies' Home Journal* detailed her stay in London but barely mentioned the breakup of her relationship with Shand or the suffering that followed.

"Mark Shand was Caroline's first love," said Andy Warhol. "He swept her off her feet, then dropped her without a second thought. He was the object of her affections, even if she wasn't exactly the object of his. According to Jackie, Caroline was in way over her head. Most of the members of that group were on average five to ten years older than Caroline. They were experienced and sophisticated, whereas she was young and impressionable. What probably scared Shand off was all that unwanted publicity. Like most British aristocrats, he thrived on maintaining a low profile."

In May 1976, having completed her course work at Sotheby's, Caroline flew home. "She'd lost a considerable amount of weight," said Pierre Salinger, who at the time was visiting New York. "She looked terrible. She complained of chronic stomach cramps. Her mother attributed the problem to her breakup with Mark Shand. 'She's having a meltdown,' said Jackie. She had to be hospitalized, but her mother didn't want the press breathing down Caroline's throat. So they brought her up to Boston and checked her into New England Baptist Hospital, where she received treatment for her stomach ailment and some much-needed rest."

Working as an off-camera summer intern at NBC-TV in Washington, Maria Shriver convinced Caroline to become active in Uncle Teddy's 1976 campaign for reelection to the Senate. Hopeful that it would help her forget Mark Shand, she agreed. She had just begun when word arrived, in late June, that Stas Radziwill had died in London of a heart attack. Although he and Lee were divorced, they had remained on friendly terms. Jackie, Caroline, and John joined the rest of the family for the funeral. Staying at the Ritz Hotel in London, Caroline took the opportunity to contact her former boyfriend. She and Mark Shand met for lunch. Still smarting from the unceremonious manner in which he'd disposed of her, Caroline had no desire to rekindle the romance. She only wanted to test herself. She wanted to test her emotions. Had she gotten over Mark Shand? After dining with him, she told George Plimpton that while Mark Shand was a "terrific" person, she was relieved to be back in the States.

In September 1976 Caroline entered Radcliffe College, Harvard's sister school in Cambridge, Massachusetts, eventually taking up residence in Winthrop House, where Jack, Bobby, and Teddy Kennedy had lived during their undergraduate years at Harvard. "She looked like every other Radcliffe student," said a classmate. "She wore faded blue jeans and black turtlenecks. We all dressed alike because we all frequented the same Cambridge clothing stores. But in Caroline's case, the press paid attention to what she wore. In 1975 Earl Blackwell placed her at the top of his annual Worst Dressed list. At Radcliffe, that kind of dubious achievement made her an enviable figure, more so than her mother being named each year to the Best Dressed List."

Unlike most of the other freshmen, Caroline had her own car, a red BMW sports car—the same model her mother owned—that she drove around Boston when she wasn't walking or riding her bike. The reigning celebrity at Radcliffe, she would often be followed around "the Coop" by fellow students as she shopped for schoolbooks and supplies. Within her first month at college, she attended a banquet at Harvard's recently founded John F. Kennedy School of Government. She occasionally drove out to Columbia Point to survey the progress in the construction of the JFK Presidential Library, designed by architect I. M. Pei. After the official opening of the library, in October 1979, Caroline frequently went to peruse the various collections of letters and manuscripts. According to Christopher Andersen, an early Caroline Kennedy biographer, she was a poor tipper but made generous contributions to charities. A Harvard dropout panhandling in Harvard Square once received several hundred dollars in cash from Caroline. She reportedly told a schoolmate: "I wish

I could wake up one morning and not be Caroline Kennedy. Just for one day, I'd like to be somebody else."

A reluctant celebrity, she kept to herself at first. In classrooms and lecture halls, she customarily occupied a corner seat. At house parties, she did her utmost not to draw attention to herself. A common lament among residents of Winthrop House was that nobody truly knew her—she was too private, too guarded. Her quest for privacy seemed to be a quest for survival. When embarrassed, she often broke into a nervous laugh. She went on dates but only sporadically. One escort described her as looking like "a shaggy dog in trousers" and of possessing the "darkest sense of humor since Hamlet." Yet, as in the case of her mother and brother, heads turned when she entered a room. Caroline couldn't help but be noticed. She surrounded herself with a small group of friends, ones she felt she could trust. Not above participating in school activities, she joined other freshmen in climbing the bell tower of Harvard's Memorial Hall. When she descended the structure, a reporter approached her. Why, he wondered, had she climbed to the top of Memorial Hall? "Because it's there," she said. "It's a school tradition." The same journalist then asked her: "Where's Macaroni?" "My pony," she responded, "died years ago."

Little that Caroline said or did during this period proved particularly newsworthy, yet her name repeatedly appeared in the press. Every minor incident became an event, and every event found its way into print. When *The Greek Tycoon,* a film about Aristotle and Jackie Onassis, aired on network television, a reporter for *The Washington Post* asked Caroline for a comment. "I have none," she said. "I didn't watch it." Liz Smith ran an item on an intimate dinner party Caroline attended with her mother at the home of *New York Times* art critic John Russell for the British poet Stephen Spender. In November 1976 the press reported on Caroline's trip to Newport for the funeral of Hugh Auchincloss. Three months later, they reported that she had driven to East Hampton for the funeral of Edith Beale. During the same week—according to *Women's Wear Daily*—she dined at fashion doyenne Diana Vreeland's house and received a private lecture on poise and style. The day after Jackie's announcement that she was leaving Viking Press in favor of an editorial position at Doubleday Books, a journalist reached Caroline at college and inquired as to the reason for the change. "You'll have to ask my mother," she replied. The *New York Post*'s Page Six ran stories on Caroline's purchase of a new dress at Ungaro's on Madison Avenue, followed by her visit to Zitomer's, a pharmacy on East 75th Street, where she charged a 25¢ pack of chewing gum to her mother's account. *The Boston Globe* published an eyewitness account of an argument between Caroline and a bank teller at the Harvard Trust Company in Cambridge. A group of paparazzi surrounded her at Studio 54 as she danced first with Jamaican performer Sterling St. Jacques, then with Hong Kong fashion designer Willie Woo.

The most "sensational" newspaper saga to emerge in the course of Caroline's college career involved a speeding summons she received on her way from Manhattan to East Hampton in the late spring of 1977. Pulled over in her BMW by a Suffolk County (Long Island) Highway Patrolman, she was charged with driving twenty-seven miles an hour over the speed limit. When she failed to appear in court to answer the summons, she received a warning notice. When she again failed to appear, a second notice was sent. After she ignored the second notice, a bench warrant was issued for her arrest. On January 13, 1978, *The New York Times* reported the incident. A day later, three high-priced lawyers marched into the First District Court to enter a plea of not guilty on behalf of their twenty-year-old client, presently on a midsemester trip to China with her mother and uncle, Senator Ted Kennedy. Informed by the attorneys as to Caroline's whereabouts, Judge Paul Creditor withdrew the arrest warrant. "It's hard to believe," he said, "that for a twenty-five-dollar fine, she sends in three thousand dollars' worth of attorneys." The quotation appeared in a follow-up article in the *Times*.

(Caroline wasn't the only family member cited for "moving violations." In 1983, having received more than three speeding summonses in a twelve-month period, JFK Jr.'s Massachusetts driver's license was suspended for ninety days.)

Prior to the arrest warrant, in the summer of 1977, Caroline Kennedy had signed on to work as a copygirl at the New York *Daily News*. Pete Hamill, a short-lived beau of Jackie's, had arranged the position, which entailed little more than fetching coffee for the editors, answering telephones, changing typewriter ribbons, and delivering messages. The old-time editors would send her out to the nearest grocery to bring back six-packs. Rick Leicata, a young reporter at the *Daily News* whom she dated that summer, recalled taking a walk with Caroline when a man came up to her and said, "They should have shot your whole family!" Caroline took it in stride and said to Leicata, "I get that all the time, but there are just as many people who tell me how wonderful my father was and how much he did for the country. And that helps make up for it."

As nonchalant as she sometimes appeared, Caroline's fear of notoriety and exposure sometimes got the better of her. She habitually bolted from theaters just before the curtain dropped lest someone recognize her when the lights went on. To avoid being seen, she entered movie theaters only after the film had started. Seated with a group of *Daily News* reporters in a restaurant that summer, Caroline suddenly rose and headed for the ladies' room. When she didn't return, one of the reporters sent a waitress to look for her.

"She's not coming out," said the waitress.

"Why not?" the journalist inquired.

"She thinks people are staring at her," responded the waitress.

On another public outing with reporters, Caroline seemed somewhat less observant of her surroundings. According to one of the reporters, she "got absolutely smashed on beer and grass. She went home drunk out of her face." When the reporter called her at home the next day, Jackie answered the phone. The caller "couldn't believe it when she said in that sweet little-girl voice of hers, 'I heard all about last night, and I want to know why you didn't invite me to come along. You better take me with you next time because I don't want to miss out on any of the fun.'"

When Elvis Presley died that August, Caroline accompanied reporters to Memphis to attend the funeral. Prior to her departure, her mother contacted Jann Wenner at *Rolling Stone* and asked if he would allow Caroline to cover the funeral for his periodical. Seeing the commercial benefit of having Caroline Kennedy's name associated with *Rolling Stone* and being friendly with Jackie, Wenner agreed. The featured piece ran that October, netting Caroline a literary following among some of her Radcliffe peers.

Despite Caroline's brief exposure to the workings of the fourth estate,

she resisted all efforts on the part of the press to pin her down. Mimi Kazon, a columnist for the now-defunct *Manhattan Express,* tried several
times to interview her for the newspaper. "She didn't just say 'No,'" remarked Kazon. "It was the way she said it. She made a big deal about it.
I found her brother much more gracious and outgoing. He understood I
was only doing my job and tried to make it easier for me."

Jacqueline Kennedy had in mind the same kind of educational experience for John that she had devised and implemented for Caroline. In
September 1976, just as Caroline was entering Radcliffe, John enrolled
as a tenth grader at Phillips Andover Academy in Andover, Massachusetts, twenty-one miles north of Boston. Having withdrawn in good
standing from Collegiate, his end-of-year report indicated strengths in
American history and current affairs, weaknesses in practically every
other subject. With his departure from New York, his former governess,
Marta Sgubin, discovered a new role for herself as Jackie's personal chef,
though she continued to take care of John's needs whenever he returned
to Manhattan. "Every time he visited," she said, "he'd arrive with several
bundles of dirty laundry slung over his shoulder. He'd also turn up with
all sorts of news about his latest adventures at Andover."

Founded in 1778, Phillips Andover Academy had the distinction of
being the nation's oldest incorporated boarding school. Paul Revere designed the school's seal, and John Hancock signed its Act of Incorpora-
tion. The school motto, *"Non Sibi,"* meant "Not for Self." Alumni
included Oliver Wendell Holmes, Edgar Rice Burroughs, Jack Lemmon,
and future presidents George Herbert Walker Bush and his son George W.
Bush. By 1976 Andover had gone the way of Concord Academy, Caroline's alma mater, by becoming a coeducational institution. Within three
months of his arrival, John turned sixteen and shed the Secret Service detail that had shadowed him from birth. "I'm emancipated," he told a
friend. Along with twenty other boys, he spent his first year in Stearns
Hall, otherwise known as Stearns House. His roommate, Tommy
Dodge, shared John's interest in athletics, and the two frequently played
ultimate Frisbee. Their quarters, like everyone else's, contained two single beds, two desks, two bookshelves, and two dressers, but it also in-

cluded an attached common room, which served as a kind of den. John kept a small framed photograph of his father on his desk. To add to the decor, John mounted travel posters and antique maps on the walls. What differentiated JFK Jr.'s living area from others in the dorm was that it overlooked Rabbit Pond, into which (rumor had it) Humphrey Bogart tossed his English teacher before being permanently expelled. During his last two years at Andover, John roomed at Day Hall and spent time hanging out at the Senior Pub in the basement of the Andover Inn, where his mother stayed when she visited. John was permitted to drink alcoholic beverages in the pub only after he turned eighteen.

A familiar figure on campus and in downtown Andover, JFK Jr. donned the de rigueur school outfit of deck shoes (no socks), khaki slacks, and rumpled Brooks Brothers Oxford shirts. He would often skateboard around campus and frequently took lunch (a cheese sandwich and a container of yogurt) while perched atop the old stone wall that enclosed the five-hundred-acre campus. He let his curly hair grow long and shaggy. For quiet reflection, he liked to take walks through a sixty-five-acre bird sanctuary that abutted the campus. He received frequent care packages from home and happily shared them with his dorm mates. Marta Sgubin's brownies went faster than any other item.

The student body at Andover consisted essentially of four distinct groups: jocks, intellectuals, preppies, and the social elite. Nonjudgmental in his acceptance of all, John established friendships with a wide cross section of students, both male and female. "He never carried cash with him," said one of his cronies, "and he was forever borrowing from friends. We used to joke about it, because he never paid anyone back. It was apparently a Kennedy trait. I remember reading about his father's early years, and he too never had any money in his wallet. Despite John Jr.'s habitual lack of funds, everyone liked him. You couldn't help it. He was a lovable character. He had no enemies." Meredith Price, John's first-year housemaster, recalled how "reporters from *Star* and other publications would try to bribe the kids in the dorm to come up with something unsavory about John. They offered them dinner at the Andover Inn provided they disclose something new about the *real* John Kennedy Jr. To my knowledge, nobody ever took them up on it."

Price's other memory of John had to do with his mother. "Jacqueline Onassis," he said, "couldn't have been a more loving and supportive boarding school parent. She made frequent visits, which was not all that common at Andover, where parents were more likely to drop off their kids at the dorm and say, 'See you at Thanksgiving,' or something like that. Jackie visited on a regular basis. She called all the time. It astonished me how extraordinarily interested she was in John's activities."

The Phillipian, Andover's student newspaper, ran a lengthy article during John's initial year discussing the marijuana problem on campus— first-time offenders were customarily placed on probation; second-time offenders faced expulsion. A regular user of pot, John restricted its use primarily to off-campus parties. A security guard once caught him with a joint in the men's room of the school library but never reported him. He did get turned in on one occasion for smoking pot at night on one of the school's many athletic fields, but received nothing more than an official warning.

As small and charming as Concord, the town of Andover boasted its own Main Street, lined on both sides by an array of coffee shops, restaurants, clothing stores, a pharmacy, and a century-old bookshop with a blazing fireplace and comfortable armchairs. Like other students, John would pedal into town on a bicycle he kept at school. He used the downtown railroad station whenever he visited Boston, a trip he often made to see his sister in Cambridge. Although their paths had diverged, they remained extremely close. Every May 29, the date of their father's birthday, they traveled to Washington together to pay homage at JFK's grave. Jackie, in fact, had sent John to Phillips Andover so that Caroline, at nearby Cambridge, could keep a motherly eye on him.

Task-oriented and overly ambitious, Jackie remained convinced that she had been too easygoing on her fatherless son. Whereas Caroline racked up a series of As at Radcliffe, JFK Jr.'s first-year grades at Andover placed him in the bottom fifth of his class. He had flunked a compulsory math course, which he had to repeat—his mother hired a Phillips Academy math teacher to get him through the course on his second attempt. With the summer approaching, she sought new ways to inspire and toughen him up. She had made such efforts in the past, at one juncture packing him off—along with Anthony Radziwill—to the Drake Island Adventure Center in Plymouth, England, for what had been billed as a weeklong course in "sailing, canoeing, rock climbing, and character building." Then there was the program sponsored by the National Outdoor Leadership School, which took John to Kenya, where he and an accompanying band of six—three boys and three girls—were sent into the snake-infested African bush on a madcap trek to nowhere. At one point the group got lost, and a search party of Masai warriors was dispatched to find them. Now, in early June 1977, following his graduation from the tenth grade, Jackie sent him on an Outward Bound survival trip, during which he spent several days on Hurricane Island, a craggy, isolated outcrop off the coast of Maine, where he was deposited with a gallon of water, two wooden matches, and a pamphlet on outdoor living. In mid-June he and his cousin Timothy Shriver traveled to Rabinal, a Guatemalan village that had been devastated five months earlier by a major earthquake. Subsisting on a diet of yellow rice and red beans, sleeping in tents, transporting themselves by donkey, and washing in a cold mountain stream, they joined a group of Peace Corps volunteers in an effort to resuscitate the town and its 20,000-plus inhabitants. Their duties included hauling sandbags, digging trenches, and helping to distribute food and medical supplies. On those nights he wasn't exhausted, John picked up his guitar and accompanied local villagers as they sang their native folk songs.

After his return from Guatemala, John served as an usher at the Robert F. Kennedy Tennis Tournament. Wearing a white linen suit and dirty sneakers, he was photographed at a post-tournament party in the Rainbow Room, walking hand in hand with Meg Anzioni, a cuddly brunette junior miss model whom he dated once or twice that summer. A few days later he attended a party in the Hamptons at which guests passed around cocaine in silver spoons and on a silver tray. Bombed on booze and high on coke, JFK Jr. was driven back to 1040 Fifth Avenue. The following day, as a prank, he poured a bottle of glue down the apartment building's mail chute. To repair the damage, the apparatus had to be completely torn out and replaced. The job, which the co-op board made Jackie pay, cost her in excess of twelve thousand dollars.

"He was just driving his mother crazy," said John Perry Barlow, who'd inherited his father's cattle ranch near Pinedale, Wyoming, but who was perhaps best known as a lyricist for the Grateful Dead. "He was a lot of trouble. He was like a rather large young dog in too small an apartment. She wanted to get him out of the house. And she also wanted him to test his wings a little bit, without intense supervision. For a change of scenery, she sent him to some youth conservation encampment in Yellowstone National Park, but that didn't work out either. The press had direct access to him there. These character-enrichment programs—Outward Bound, the Guatemalan Peace Corps, the Yellowstone experiment—all had their limitations. So she contacted Teno Roncalio, a political friend of hers from Wyoming, who promptly steered her in my direction. She called me and in that breathy voice of hers said: 'This is Jacqueline Onassis.' And I said: 'In the extremely unlikely case this isn't a joke, what can I do for you?' And three days later, in the middle of July, John F. Kennedy Jr. was standing in my front yard. My job was to transform him into a ranch hand for about a month. He dug holes for fence posts and looked after some of the animals."

Fourteen years older than John, Barlow expected the young man to be something of a spoiled brat. "But he wasn't at all," said Barlow. "He was rambunctious and at that point a bit directionless. But he was full of good juice and amiability and that wonderful alert curiosity he had about everything all of the time. Everything was interesting to him. He wasn't afraid to ask questions. It was one of those moments you have in your life every now and again when you meet someone and you know you're going to be friends for life."

Barlow understood that while John was "a great kid," it was difficult for him in the sense that he was always being watched, and probably always would be. Also, no matter what he did in his lifetime, he would very likely never accomplish all that his martyred father had accomplished, a father he never even knew. These were burdens he would have to learn to bear.

John returned to Phillips Andover that fall and although he didn't start, he succeeded in making the varsity soccer squad, scoring a goal in the annual game against Exeter. Holly Owen, Andover's soccer coach, doubled as the director of the school's theater department. Owen, who was well aware of John's pot habit, encouraged him to take a course in stagecraft and to become involved in some of the school's extracurricular theater productions. In addition, he had befriended the future actor James Spader, a classmate with as little interest in academics as John. During his junior year at Andover, Spader dropped out and moved to New York to work odd jobs and study acting. Before leaving, he too became an instrumental force in John's decision to get involved in the theater.

Gordon "Diz" Bensley, whose photography course JFK Jr. took during the second semester of his sophomore year, remembered that John had some reservations about becoming actively involved in the drama department. "I believe he felt his mother wouldn't approve," said Bensley, "especially because he wasn't doing well academically. He enjoyed the work in my course, but at times he seemed a little absentminded. He was the only student I ever had who developed his film with the lights on. Other than that, he was fine. At the end of the semester when he informed me that he intended to take theater courses and perform in school plays, I told him I thought acting was probably an art form better suited to his personality than photography."

In November 1977 John appeared in *Comings and Goings*, a play by Megan Terry about the changing roles of men and women in modern-day society. A year later he acted in a school production of Shakespeare's *Comedy of Errors*. In the second term of his senior year, he played the lead in a stage rendition of Ken Kesey's *One Flew Over the Cuckoo's Nest*. Although Jackie never fully sanctioned her son's participation in the theater, she attended each of his performances, as did Caroline.

"I understood John's intoxication with the stage," said John Perry Barlow. "It gave him an opportunity to climb out of his own skin and assume the personality of whatever character or role he happened to be playing. He could be appreciated for reasons other than merely being John F. Kennedy Jr. All his life, he had been President Kennedy's son first and foremost and 'just John' second. On stage he could be recognized and celebrated for a talent of his own making."

Through his involvement in Andover's theater program, John established two notable friendships. The first, purely platonic, was with Alex-

andra (Sasha) Chermayeff, a native New Yorker with considerable talent
as an artist. Sasha remained a friend of John's long after her graduation
from Andover, her four years at the University of Vermont, and her subsequent marriage to sculptor Phil Howie. Faithfully attending their respective gallery openings, John bought their works of art and displayed
them in his TriBeCa loft. They, in turn, helped him develop an interest
in art even to the extent that they worked with him on several mobiles
(made up of small whale bones) that he later hung from his dining room
ceiling. Sasha and Phil named John godfather to their two children,
Phineas and Olivia, both of whom loved it when he dropped in on them.
In a final moving tribute, he remembered Sasha's youngsters by leaving
them a sizable inheritance, which they received in trust after his death.

The other friendship—of even greater import in terms of John's development—was with Jenny Christian, an exceedingly attractive Phillips
Academy student who played opposite John in *Comings and Goings.* The
daughter of a New York surgeon, Jenny was John's age but a year ahead
of him in school. By consensus, she was one of the most interesting and
sought-after girls on campus. Although John had his pick of Phillips
Academy coeds, he chose Jenny. She became his first major girlfriend.
Christina Goodman had been a playmate of sorts, whereas John's friendship with Jenny blossomed into a full-blown relationship, a deeply felt
romance.

In an interview with JFK Jr. biographer Wendy Leigh, Jenny is
quoted as saying, "If John had fallen out of a pickup truck, he still would
have been irresistible to me. He was extremely handsome, nice, and
sweet. It was a great romance."

Easygoing and self-assured, Jenny seemed impervious to the notion
that John was both a Kennedy and a celebrity in his own right. His
renown, whether earned or inherited, was never more evident than when
Jenny accompanied him, over the Christmas recess of 1977, to the New
York premiere of *Saturday Night Fever.* John Travolta, the star of the film,
had arrived at the theater and was waving to a huge gathering of fans and
photographers when John and Jenny emerged from the limousine behind Travolta's. Suddenly the crowd surged toward John, screaming and
squealing, leaving Travolta alone on the red carpet. His mouth agape, the

star turned to see who had upstaged him. Chagrined that he had stolen Travolta's glory, John gave an embarrassed smile as he and Jenny rushed into the theater.

Warmly welcomed into the Kennedy fold, Jenny nevertheless liked John for John rather than for what he represented, a distinction that even John's mother could appreciate. Jackie's acceptance of her son's girlfriend extended to being included in family functions and resulted in her being invited along on family vacations.

In September 1978 John began his final year at Phillips Academy. Jenny had graduated and gone on to Harvard, where she would major in psychology. The two were still heavily involved. In late November, when Jackie threw a combined birthday party for John and Caroline at Le Club—his eighteenth, her twenty-first—Jenny attended as JFK Jr.'s date. Spotting a *National Enquirer* reporter in the crowd, John began to fight the party crasher and wound up with a broken finger incurred when he slipped and fell. Socialite Richard duPont, a friend of John and a guest at the party, noted that it wasn't the first time the Kennedys had brawled at Le Club. "It was probably all that pot and alcohol," he said. "Half the people there were stoned." A more notable detail about the occasion was Caroline's inheritance of a $1 million trust fund established years earlier by Joseph P. Kennedy for each of his grandchildren; by the time Caroline reached the age of twenty-one, the value of the trust had more than tripled. "You'd never have known she just hit the jackpot," said Richard duPont. "She was extremely unfriendly that night."

In an ironic twist, Jenny Christian was also present in December when John first met an eighteen-year-old actress named Daryl Hannah, the woman with whom he would one day have his most publicized relationship. Jenny had joined John, Jackie, and the Radziwills on a winter vacation in St. Martin. There they checked into the exclusive La Samanna resort. By coincidence, Daryl was also staying at the Caribbean retreat. Carrying a teddy bear around the property, Daryl had all the markings of still another eccentric Hollywood newcomer. With the exception of the stuffed animal, John barely noticed the starlet.

John's grades that semester were so low that Jackie decided to place him in the care of Ted Becker, a New York psychiatrist noted for his intervention in the lives of troubled teenagers. For several months, the Andover senior traveled to Manhattan once a week to confer with Becker. Jackie's concerns, as expressed to Becker, were manifold. She worried about John's poor academic performance in school. She opposed an expressed wish on her son's part to become an actor. In spite of her efforts to toughen him up, she detected an inherent "weakness" in his character. She feared the unhappy and negative influence on him of other young members of the Kennedy clan, particularly David Kennedy and Chris Lawford, who were addicted to hard drugs despite repeated courses of treatment in detoxification centers. John himself, she told the psychiatrist, had become quite the pothead, which may well have contributed to his seeming inability to concentrate in school.

"The trouble with John," said Ken O'Donnell, "was simply that he matured later than most. I also think the death of Aristotle Onassis hit him harder than people realized. He didn't know his own father and didn't remember him except through the stories he heard from those who did. He and Caroline collected all sorts of JFK memorabilia, but this was hardly a replacement for the father he never had. So although he rarely spoke about Onassis, he probably felt closer to him than he did to any of the other father figures that entered and then exited his life."

According to O'Donnell, Jackie compounded John's difficulties by pushing too hard, threatening him with what can only be described as a kind of "emotional blackmail." If he behaved himself and did what she wanted, she rewarded him. But she was just as quick in turning the cold shoulder. If he did something she didn't like, she waved the whip.

"For example," said O'Donnell, "she absolutely hit the ceiling when she learned of his interest in acting. She told him point-blank that it couldn't be, that he would have to pursue a 'more noble' calling. This was when he attended Andover and appeared in several school plays. It happened again when he went to Brown and acted in productions there. I remember hearing that Robert Stigwood, the Hollywood producer, approached John about playing the role of his father in a motion picture based on John F. Kennedy's younger years. John was intrigued, but Jackie wouldn't hear of it. She wanted him to proceed with his studies, finish high school, finish college—and then do what he wanted with his life, so long as it didn't involve acting."

In a true sense, or so it seemed, John Jr. was indentured to his legacy. His capitulation to his mother's wishes lost him, at least for a while, the respect of his Kennedy cousins. People like Warren Beatty and Rudolf Nureyev—as well as other friends of his mother—encouraged him to go into acting. But it wasn't that simple. The whole experience proved so frustrating and schismatic that at a later juncture, discussing his future with a friend, he put his fist through a wall.

Larry O'Brien recalled having dinner at Jackie's home in the spring of 1979. Her mother had recently married a retired banker named Bingham Morris, and they were staying with Jackie. John Jr. was also visiting. O'Brien asked him whether he might ever consider an acting career. John hesitated and then looked at his mother. Finally he blurted out, "Yes, no . . . well, maybe."

Whatever Jackie's predisposition against John's acting ambitions, Ted Becker served as a convenient intermediary, easing Jackie's immediate worries and helping guide JFK Jr. through his final semester at Andover. Becker also supported John's decision to attend Brown University as opposed to Harvard. On June 7, 1979, JFK Jr. graduated from Phillips Andover with the rest of his 340-member class. Jenny Christian joined John's family at the graduation ceremony, presided over by Theodore Sizer, the school's headmaster. Interviewed by the press following the ceremony, Jackie issued but a single comment. "Raising my children," she said, "is the best thing I've ever done."

John and Jenny continued to date even after he entered Brown in the fall of 1979, but by the beginning of 1980 they had broken up. They nevertheless retained warm feelings for each other, spoke occasionally, and saw each other now and again. It was a matter of pride for John that he attempted to remain on cordial terms with all of his former girlfriends.

In late May 1978, at the end of her sophomore year at Radcliffe, Caroline Kennedy began dating Thomas R. Carney, a sleek, soft-spoken freelance writer whose father, the veteran Hollywood screenwriter Otis

Carney, had become a cattle rancher in Wyoming and Arizona. Having grown up in California and Wyoming—where, among others, he had known John Perry Barlow—Tom Carney later moved to New York and began working as a copywriter at Doubleday Books. At Doubleday he made the acquaintance of coworker Jacqueline Kennedy Onassis. Sensing that her daughter would enjoy Tom's company, Jackie gave a small dinner party at 1040 Fifth Avenue to introduce them. Another guest that evening was Maurice Tempelsman, the wealthy diamond dealer slated to become Jackie's permanent live-in companion.

Caroline liked Carney from the moment they met. An Irish Catholic and a graduate of Yale, he was ten years her senior. Tall and lanky, he bore a strong physical resemblance to David Kennedy. She invited him to Hyannis Port to meet David. They were soon going out together. They went roller-skating in Central Park, dancing at Xenon and Studio 54, horseback riding at Jackie's weekend retreat in New Jersey, museum hopping, and window-shopping along Fifth Avenue. They attended a World Series game at Yankee Stadium and went fishing for blues in Montauk. Tom visited her at Radcliffe, and she went to Wyoming to meet his family. By Christmas, seven months after being introduced to Carney, Caroline had shed thirty pounds. Her blue jeans and turtlenecks had given way to smart skirts and frilly blouses. Her once frizzy, often unruly honey-blond hair now fell evenly and gracefully to her shoulders. Carney similarly underwent a change for the better. Having grown lackadaisical about his writing career, he suddenly whipped off articles for *Esquire* and *Penthouse,* and put the finishing touches on his first novel, *Daylight Moon,* published in 1979. Jackie tried but failed to find a producer for a film script he'd written but was quick to ask him along when she and Caroline vacationed together in the Caribbean, just as she'd previously invited Jenny Christian for John.

Tracey Dewart, a part-time waitress at Ruppert's, an Upper East Side restaurant, found herself waiting on Tom and Caroline in the summer of 1979. "She kept taking pieces of cheese out of his salad," said Dewart. "She had her legs up on another chair at the table. She was acting very obnoxious. I asked if she wanted her own salad, and she said she did. She was demanding and bossy, ordering me to bring this and that—another fork, another knife, an extra glass of water, the works. I suppose it was the way she said it. I was miffed."

However cocky Caroline might have become, her relationship with Tom Carney mellowed her, gave her a sense of purpose and security that had been missing in her romance with Mark Shand. As far as Jackie was concerned, Carney possessed all the qualities she would have wanted in a life partner for her daughter. He was creative, kind, intelligent, and talented. Caroline felt likewise. In January 1980 *Ladies' Home Journal* published an article, "Caroline: A Kennedy in Love," which strongly hinted at the possibility of marriage once Caroline graduated from Radcliffe. Her carefully worded public denial only raised further questions. "I really don't have any plans to get married," she said. "I'm finishing school. I don't know after that."

Maura Moynihan, a Radcliffe classmate and close friend of Caroline—and the daughter of Senator Daniel Patrick Moynihan of New York—detected a palpable change in Caroline after she became involved with Carney. "During her last two years at Radcliffe, Caroline displayed impeccable grace and style," she said. "She became a wonderful friend—warm, bubbly, funny, supportive. If you had a problem, any problem, Caroline would be there for you."

The closeness that she achieved with her writer boyfriend helped obliterate any lingering disappointment she might have retained over the failure of her fling with Mark Shand. She became more carefree. Her circle of friends increased in size. Instead of hitting the books at night, she gathered with her new set of friends at the bars and bistros in and around Harvard Yard. Where before she had always omitted her last name when introducing herself—"Hi, I'm Caroline"—she now used her full name on such occasions. She had begun to come to terms with her status as a Kennedy.

When Caroline graduated from Radcliffe on June 5, 1980 (the same year her cousin Michael Kennedy graduated from Harvard), Tom Carney was notably absent. In August, the month they had chosen to announce their wedding plans, he suddenly broke off with her. "What ended it was the publicity," he said later. "I couldn't see spending the rest of my life with cameras hovering around my head."

"They very nearly married," said John Perry Barlow. "It's a pity they didn't—for both of them."

"Caroline was crushed, just crushed," said George Plimpton.

What made matters more difficult for her was Carney's announcement a few weeks later that he had become engaged to forty-one-year-old Maureen Lambray, a former staff photographer for Bobby Kennedy during his 1968 presidential campaign.

Caroline grieved her loss. "He's the first man I ever dated that my mother really liked," she told a friend. "Stop tormenting yourself," responded the friend. "Half the men in America would give their right testicle to be with you, and the other half would give their left."

She busied herself by going out with men she liked and had known for years but with whom she had no intention of becoming romantically involved. That fall she returned to New York and accepted a part-time position as a researcher in the Office of Film and Television at the Metropolitan Museum of Art, working six hours a day, four days a week. With three friends—two men and another woman—she rented a $1,500-per-month, three-bedroom apartment on the Upper West Side. They transformed a formal library in the flat into a fourth bedroom. Jackie thought the neighborhood unsafe for an unattached young woman. Her fears may have been justified when, six months later, a deranged thirty-five-year-old California law school graduate from Palo Alto turned up at Caroline's front door and began to harass her.

The man, Kevin King, initially approached Caroline at her museum job, conversing with her in a manner she quickly construed as menacing. She asked him to leave. He began telephoning her at home, then somehow gained access to her apartment building, frightening her into staying with her mother for the night. He convinced her neighbors to let him sleep in the hallway. When he reappeared at her building a few days later, Caroline returned to her mother's house. Jackie insisted on hiring a team of private security guards and persuaded her daughter to file an official complaint. The police arrested King in his room at the West Side YMCA, charging him with aggravated harassment. Under his bed, among other incriminating evidence, they found a detailed schedule of Caroline's daily activities, a list of the aliases she and Jackie sometimes used to book reservations, and a *New York* magazine article on Mark David Chapman's 1980 murder of John Lennon.

While at Rikers Island awaiting trial, King sent Caroline love letters in which he proposed marriage. "Why don't you marry me?" read one of his epistles. "We can borrow some rice from your mother's wedding." Another was obscene. "Next time I'll fuck all your relatives unless you marry me."

At the one-day trial, held in Manhattan Criminal Court on October 17, 1981, King acted as his own lawyer, cross-examining Caroline by asking her a series of highly personal questions, none of which seemed relevant to the case. In his summation, King told the court that he had "come to New York on a mission of love." If Caroline had any interest in him, he would still "want to marry her."

Assessed a steep fine and sentenced to a year in jail—in addition to time already served—King continued his letter-writing campaign. His last note to Caroline, written from his cell, reiterated his offer of marriage. "You must give me the chance," he wrote, "to give you the love you deserve." While incarcerated, he told a reporter: "Caroline Kennedy could be a great wife. I would like to support her and protect her from all."

Kevin King wasn't the only stalker in Caroline's life. Over Labor Day weekend in 1981, with the King trial yet to be heard, Caroline traveled to Martha's Vineyard to visit with her mother and brother at Red Gate Farm, Jackie's recently completed thirteen-room Cape Cod–style manse overlooking the cliffs of Gay Head. Financed with moneys derived from Jackie's settlement with the Onassis estate and designed by Hugh Jacobson, a socially prominent Washington architect, the house featured such amenities as oversized brick fireplaces, teak sundecks, private dock, heated towel racks, and hot-water toilet bowls. A five-bedroom "barn" (with bleached wood floors) and an attached silo stood about two hundred feet from the main house. A circular bedroom on the third floor of the silo—with its king-size, heart-shaped bed—served as John's sleeping quarters. Separate cottages had been built for the caretaker, Albert Fisher, and Jackie's Greek houseboy, Vasily Terrionios, formerly employed in the same capacity by Aristotle Onassis. The former First Lady kept a Jeep Wagoneer on the property and docked her boat, a thirty-foot SeaCraft, at Menemsha Pond.

Frank Wangler, head of the construction crew responsible for building the house, recalled how "Jackie would appear at the construction site on weekends, often with Bunny Mellon, to check on the progress of the house and plan the landscaping. From time to time she also brought Caroline and John. I used to sit and shoot the breeze with John. You couldn't do that with his sister. Caroline was friendly but not sociable. I had the feeling she looked on the construction crew as if we were servants."

Wangler further remembered that while Caroline wasn't on close terms with members of the crew, she frequently invited her own friends to Red Gate Farm. On that particular Labor Day weekend, she'd asked David Michaelis, a longtime pal, to join her. She and Michaelis were riding bicycles on the paved road in front of the 2,000-foot private driveway that led into Jackie's property, when all of a sudden a car approached from the opposite direction and headed straight for them. As it drew near, Caroline could see that it was filled with news photographers. Of the four paparazzi in the vehicle, she recognized only one: Ron Galella. "Hi, Caroline," he said, leaning out the window. "It's me! How are you?"

The car pulled up on the shoulder of the road and out popped three of its passengers, each armed with a camera. Surrounding Caroline and Michaelis, they began shooting away. Galella, who'd remained in the car, presently joined the others. As Caroline turned her bicycle into the driveway and headed for the house, Galella chased after her, the lens of his camera practically touching the back of her head.

Galella had violated an existing court order prohibiting him from coming within a certain distance of Caroline. Jackie pressed her daughter to take legal action. Galella hired the famed palimony attorney Marvin Mitchelson to represent him at trial. While being cross-examined by Mitchelson, Caroline testified that the confrontation had frightened her, making her heart beat fast. "I've been frightened by Mr. Galella before," she added. "I didn't know what he planned to do."

"Doesn't your heart often beat fast when you're riding a bicycle?" asked Mitchelson.

"Only when I'm trying to get away," said Caroline.

"Why were you so afraid?"

"I didn't want to fall off my bike," she said.

"You were angry, weren't you?"

"I was scared."

The judge ordered Galella to pay Jacqueline Onassis and Caroline $10,000 in damages and issued a permanent injunction forbidding the photographer to take any further pictures of Jackie or her children.

One of the few hopeful moments for Caroline during the two years following her graduation from Radcliffe took place in early December 1981 when, while working at the Metropolitan Museum of Art, she met her future husband, Edwin Schlossberg. George Plimpton recalled seeing Ed for the first time at Jackie's candlelit Christmas party that year. "Tom Wolfe and costume designer William Ivey Long were there," said Plimpton. "Long had known Caroline since Concord Academy and was one of her closest friends. Another guest was international diamond merchant Maurice Tempelsman. Jackie took Schlossberg by the hand and introduced him around. 'This is Caroline's new friend, Ed Schlossberg,' she said. Schlossberg and Tempelsman had one thing in common—they were both utterly un-Kennedy-like. From Jackie's and Caroline's point of view, that could easily have been an advantage. Ed Schlossberg appeared to be a perfectly swell fellow—cerebral, inventive, and industrious— though none of us could ever figure out exactly what it was he did for a living. Not that it mattered. What mattered is that Caroline seemed to have developed strong feelings for Ed—and vice versa. Thereafter, they were more or less inseparable."

Chapter 11

◆

BROWN

J OHN F. KENNEDY JR.'S paternal grandfather, his father, three of his
uncles, a number of his cousins, and his sister all went to the same
college: Harvard. JFK Jr., no ordinary Kennedy, opted for Brown, although he'd been admitted to Harvard. By breaking with tradition, he
may well have been asserting his individuality, advancing the notion that
the torch had at last been passed.

In a more pragmatic sense, he may have had the good judgment to realize that Brown was on the whole less academically competitive than
Harvard. One feature that surely appealed to him, other than Brown's
wide-reaching, liberally oriented curriculum, was that students couldn't
fail courses. The lowest grade attainable in any course was an NC—"No
Credit"—a designation that didn't get factored into the undergraduate's
overall grade point average. It was more difficult to "bust out" of Brown
than almost any other Ivy League institution. John probably felt he
couldn't cut the mustard at Harvard, whereas at Brown, with its more lenient academic regulations, he would have an easier time of it. Indeed,
despite weak spots in his record—he spent his junior year on academic
probation—John earned better grades at Brown than at either Collegiate
or Phillips Andover. He completed his studies in May 1983 as an American history major with a "Gentleman's C" average. "You have to be sus-

picious," he once said, "of anyone with a cumulative 4.0 average—students of that caliber too often wind up in mental institutions."

Susan Sklover, a graduate student at Brown during JFK Jr.'s years at the university, made the observation that "Brown represented a happy compromise for John. For one thing, Providence, Rhode Island, is just a hop, skip, and jump from Boston and only a few hours from New York. While not exactly a bustling metropolis, Providence had enough going to satisfy almost anyone's intellectual curiosity. Guest speakers and entertainers frequently visited the campus. Yet the school was isolated enough to afford its students a modicum of privacy, which is exactly what John craved."

Sklover encountered John for the first time in mid-September 1979, soon after the beginning of the school year, ambling along the quad not far from Littlefield Hall, his high-ceilinged, abundantly spacious freshman dorm. Jackie had helped him move in, toting books and personal belongings, including a stereo, to his dorm room on the second floor. "When I initially spotted him," said Sklover, "he was wearing a pair of blue jeans and a loud Hawaiian shirt. He had long hair and was flashing that million-dollar smile of his. I saw him again a few days later, playing a game of pickup Frisbee on the college green. This time he had on a pair of short shorts and tennis sneakers—no shirt. He looked hot. I know he worked out, because every so often I'd see him pumping iron in the weight room. Half the women on campus lusted after him, and while it helped that he was a Kennedy, the main attraction had to be physical. He had an extremely handsome face and a great bod. He had the physique of a quarterback. The term 'tall, dark, and handsome' seemed to have been invented to describe him. He was a hunk and a half, a perfect 10. I heard he used to receive marriage proposals in the mail all the time, and this went on his entire life. Strange women would send him nude photographs of themselves. Coeds on campus would try to find any excuse to meet him. They wanted to date him, invite him to dinner, and bed him. If he'd wanted, he could have gotten laid four times a day, each time with a different woman. It got so intense for a while that he had to take his meals either very early or late. When he ate with everyone else, hordes of women would appear and sit there gawking at him."

Sklover, who came to know John a bit, thought him all the more attractive because he had a self-deprecating sense of humor. "He could laugh at himself," she said. "He used to refer to himself as 'nothing but a low Irishman.' We would meet occasionally for coffee. He'd call me up at the last minute and say, 'We're supposed to meet, but I don't remember where.' He was perpetually late for his appointments, but he had a sweet disposition. I can't remember him ever being depressed. There was something very vital and alive about him. And even though he was the most sought after male on campus, he didn't take advantage of it. He tended to have long-term girlfriends."

According to his friends, girls constantly converged on his dorm with the hope of finding him in. Or they would wait for him to come out and then traipse after him. Whenever he headed for Thayer Street, the school's main drag, it was usually with a couple of coeds trailing in his wake. In warm weather he would appear at an ice-cream truck parked near his dorm; groups of coeds would stand around and watch him order frozen lemonade, then head back to Littlefield Hall, polite but indifferent. When asked by the press if he thought John might someday run for public office, one of his dorm mates put forth the observation that he would probably be "too busy socializing to become involved in a political campaign." By the same token, a faculty member at Brown once inquired of JFK Jr. if he might ever run for office, to which John responded, "Are you kidding—my mother would kill me."

J. Carter Brown, chief curator of the National Gallery of Art in Washington, D.C., made regular trips to Brown University, which had been founded in 1764 and named for his family ancestors. "I'd known Jacqueline Kennedy Onassis for years," he said. "She was aware of my visits to Brown. One day she called and asked me to look in on John during my next trip. I contacted him beforehand and invited him to join me for lunch at the Brown University faculty club. This must have been a month or two into his freshman year. To my utter amazement, he showed up in a pair of shorts. I told him he'd have to wear a tie and jacket, so he ran back to his room and reappeared twenty minutes later, properly attired. He proudly announced that the sport jacket he had on had belonged to his father. I suppose what surprised me most during lunch were his table manners, which bordered on the atrocious, whereas his sister Caroline, whom I'd met, had beautiful manners. John sat hunched over his food, shoveling it into his mouth without so much as a pause. In the middle of it, he suddenly reached over, speared a couple of my French fries with his fork and gobbled them up. He took them right off my plate. It was so bizarre I thought he might be putting me on. As we left the faculty club, I noticed three or four coeds waiting for him. 'You're pretty popular around here,' I said. He regarded the girls with complete indifference. 'Not really,' he responded. 'I don't even know them. They just follow me around the campus all the time.'"

J. Carter Brown happily reported meeting up with John again some ten years later at a New York dinner party and finding his table manners much improved.

JFK Jr. drew more than mere coeds to his side. Tourists frequently arrived on campus in search of Littlefield Hall, planting themselves in front of his dorm, hoping for a glimpse of the man they still sometimes referred to as "John-John." He was a phenomenon, an American prince who was treated as such. John Hare, Brown's top tennis prospect and a future fraternity brother of JFK Jr., met him on the second day of freshman orientation. Hare remembered the time during first semester when the entire audience turned to look as he and John walked into a Providence movie theater. Rick Moody, class of '83 and a budding writer, recalled his first sighting: "It was in the dining hall. There was a commotion at a nearby table. A tall, perfectly handsome guy in jeans [stood up.] An elbow next to me landed in the ribs. 'That's him, that's him.' I saw the most famous teenager on earth get seconds of pizza."

Caroline Kennedy at Radcliffe, though a source of nonstop curiosity to her schoolmates, eventually managed to blend in with the rest of the student body. John was never accorded the same privilege at Brown. Yet through it all, he maintained his composure and equanimity. "He had a way about him that was grace personified," said Jim Barnhill, a theater professor at the university.

As at every other school he'd ever attended, John was a much-coveted media magnet at Brown, particularly among the tabloids. The *National Enquirer* and *Star* regularly dispatched reporters and stringers in a relentless effort to unearth tidbits on the son of the late president. They'd been there waiting for him, along with the legitimate press, from the moment he clambered up College Hill and walked through Brown's front gates to attend freshman orientation week. The only details worth mentioning in the tabloids that first semester were that John enjoyed "slumming" with friends at some of Providence's seedier bars, and that he'd inquired as to the possibility of taking flight instruction instead of intramural sports to fulfill his freshman-year gym requirement. The athletic department refused his request. In his junior year, however, he managed to log some fifty hours of pilot training before his mother intervened, exacting a promise from him that he would cease and desist. Having given up the flight lessons, John took up rugby, acquitting himself admirably on Brown's varsity team. His "rugger" days ended abruptly when a member of the Cornell squad, nearly twice his size, collided with him and cracked two of his ribs. As Brown's team trainer attended to him, John wondered aloud why the college didn't have a water-skiing team.

Robert Reichley, director of Brown's public relations office, had been placed in charge of fielding any media requests that might come in for John. Within days of his arrival, requests began to pour in. A local strip joint offered John $3,000 to appear at the club. A shopping center in a nearby Rhode Island town wanted him to cut the ribbon at the opening of a new hardware store. A leading perfume manufacturer asked John to endorse their latest men's cologne. Laurence Leamer, in *Sons of Camelot,* recounts a series of telephone calls Reichley received from some producer at ABC-TV's *Good Morning America,* requesting that John come on the show. "She got really huffy," said Reichley, "and I called John to my office to talk about it. He came over, and I dialed her phone number. I only heard John's side of the conversation. 'Yes, ma'am . . . yes, ma'am . . . well, ma'am, I'm honored by your invitation, and I want to come on your show, but I don't have anything to say, and some day I may have something to say, and I hope that you'll remember me and ask me back.'" It was the "best kiss-off," said Reichley, he'd ever heard.

John did less well when it came to offering excuses for his lackluster academic achievements. His first college paper, written for Professor Ed Beiser's freshman course in political science, received the equivalent of a failing grade. Nearly in tears, John went to see Beiser in his office. "He was really shaken," remarked the professor. "He said, 'What am I going to tell my mother?' 'You don't have to tell her anything,' I said. 'You just have to write another paper for me.'"

John fulfilled the new assignment and ultimately passed the course, but he also unburdened himself to his mother, admitting his initial failure. "Whatever you decide to do," she responded, "don't follow in your uncle Ted's academic footsteps." The veiled warning referred to Ted Kennedy's undergraduate education at Harvard, when he paid a classmate to take his Spanish final for him. The incident netted the future senator a one-year suspension and provided his future political enemies with still another example of the man's lack of character.

Unusually close to his mother, John called her from Brown on an almost daily basis, inundating her with his latest slew of problems. Never very adept at balancing his budget, he rarely had money for extras. When he failed to pay several consecutive telephone bills, the phone company shut down his private line. Jackie paid the overdue amount and his telephone service was reinstated. She came to his rescue again when the campus police towed his car (a used Honda) because of unpaid parking violations. In mid-October of his freshman year, she sent up his father's Oval Office rocking chair and a published volume of JFK's presidential speeches. Dorm mates recall John sitting in the chair—which remained in his possession throughout his college career—while reading the speeches aloud. Despite his obvious celebrity, his friends considered JFK Jr. "a regular guy"—relaxed, courteous, not the least bit uppity or arrogant. He happily took part in the usual dormitory fun and games—the food fights, shaving cream battles, water-balloon skirmishes, panty raids, and cross-campus streakings. Then there was the time he helped disassemble a Volkswagen, carry it part by part into Littlefield Hall, and reassemble the automobile in the dorm counselor's bedroom suite. When the counselor called John's mother to complain, she sounded sympathetic but only up to a point. "Boys will be boys," she finally said in an effort to rid herself of the caller.

"It was clear they had a wonderful bond," observed John's classmate Charlie King of his friend's relationship with his mother. When King visited JFK Jr. at his mother's Fifth Avenue apartment, she greeted him at the front door. "Hi, I'm John's mother," she said. "It was very endearing," noted King. "In a lot of ways, she was just like any other mom. She would hover for a bit in the room but then go do her other stuff."

Whatever else she might have been, Jackie was hardly "just like any other mom." Over winter break of 1979, John invited Robert (Rob) Littell, one of his closest friends at Brown, to join him in New York at his mother's annual Christmas party. "We met on the beach in Providence during orientation week," said Littell. "I had no idea he was at Brown, or even that he was such a big deal. He came straight over to me and extended his hand. 'Yo, my name's John,' he said. 'What's yours?' It turned out we had a good deal in common, most notably that neither of us had a father. Mine had committed suicide. We were both raised by she-wolves—strong-willed mothers and older, ultraprotective sisters. We had a shared interest in sports and girls. I was on the lacrosse team, and John played some rugby. That first year we hung out together at 'the Ratty' [the student cafeteria], went to parties, swigged beer, played Frisbee and touch football. On Christmas day, my sister and I visited him at his mother's house in New York, and as he led us through the apartment he paused in front of a two-foot-tall Egyptian statuette. 'Original paint,' he mumbled. It was the only comment he made about the decor, which was timeless and quite extraordinary. On the wall of his bedroom, I saw a large frame containing a small portrait and the signature of each U.S. president up to and including his father."

Jackie struck Littell as one of the most "incredible" women he'd ever met. In a most animated fashion she entertained her dinner guests with stories about some of the personages she'd met. "She'd seen and done it all," said Littell. "Years later, after her death, I saw the Egyptian statuette again, this time on exhibit in the Metropolitan Museum of Art with a plaque describing it as 4,500 years old."

Starting in the second semester of his freshman year, John became involved in Brown's Theatre, Speech, and Dance department, auditioning for and procuring the role of Bonario, a foot soldier in Ben Jonson's seventeenth-century *Volpone*. John Emigh, a professor in the department, directed John in the student production. "John was a good actor, a natural actor," he said. "In contrast to his privileged background, he was at his best playing low-life roustabouts. There's little question that had he persevered, he could have had a successful career as an actor. His mother opposed it because she didn't want him trading in on his name. On the other hand, it's an oversimplification to suggest that he didn't go into the field simply because his mother never approved. I think John himself would have wanted to succeed on his own merit, and not because he was the son of John and Jacqueline Kennedy, which became a burden he had to bear regardless of his career choice. If his life had been otherwise—if he hadn't been the Kennedy of Kennedys—he may have chosen theater as his profession. He had the talent, the wherewithal, and the interest to do it."

During rehearsals of *Volpone,* the *National Enquirer* published an apocryphal article contending that JFK Jr. had undergone a gender change at birth. As a joke, members of the *Volpone* cast taped a huge Do Not Enter sign on the men's dressing room door, directing John to use the ladies' dressing room instead.

"John took it with good humor," said Emigh. "He could dole it out, and he could take it. He had no pretensions about himself. He was down-to-earth. He wasn't shallow. People who knew him well were aware that he had depth."

Emigh remembered Jackie's appearance at Brown on the opening night of the play. "It was to her credit that she attended almost all of his performances," said Emigh. "She was there for him. And so was Caroline Kennedy. John was particularly eager to gain their respect. Even if acting professionally wasn't in the cards, he was grateful for their presence."

After the play closed, John thanked Emigh for giving him the opportunity to perform. "He was an immensely humble and honest person," said the theater professor. "I remember him taking a seminar that semester called 'The American Experience in Vietnam,' taught by Professor Charles Neu. The story as I got it was that on the first day of class, Neu went around the room asking the students why they'd signed up for the course. When John's turn came up, he said, 'A lot of people think that what happened in Vietnam was my father's fault. I'd like to find out the truth.' That kind of very direct response epitomized his outlook on life."

Despite his stated intentions, John failed to deliver a term paper for the Vietnam course and received an NC as a final grade. Unimpressed with JFK Jr.'s academic performance, Neu also found that "John had an annoying way of speaking. He did not enunciate all of his words. It had a kind of thickness to it, almost as if to pretend he was a slightly dim-witted athlete." It was a strange assessment considering that elocution had always been one of John's strong points as an actor.

John had spent several days in late 1979—and again in early June of 1980—campaigning for Ted Kennedy in his unsuccessful bid for the Democratic Party presidential nomination. He then traveled to South Africa and the Republic of Zimbabwe, touring the mines, working for Maurice Tempelsman's diamond company, and meeting with government and student leaders, before joining Rob Littell in England for a two-week pub crawl of London and Dublin. Having smuggled an ounce of pot past security guards (and police dogs) at Heathrow Airport, John proceeded to break a window at the Ritz in London, thereafter insisting that he and his travel companion camp out in public parks and church-yards. In Dublin they got together with John's cousin Michael Kennedy and Michael's fiancé, Victoria Gifford, daughter of football great Frank Gifford. In a haze of pot and booze, John managed to lose his passport before returning to the States. Back at Brown that fall, JFK Jr. helped es-tablish the South African Group for Education, a student organization that invited notable speakers to the campus to talk about apartheid and the implementation of regulations prohibiting U.S. corporations from dealing with pro-apartheid South African companies. Maurice Tempels-man financed the group. Among the speakers lined up by John were for-mer U.S. ambassador to the United Nations Andrew Young, and Helen Suzman, an influential South African parliamentarian, both of whom John treated to cheeseburger luncheons at a local diner called Beef 'n' Bun.

John also resumed his involvement in the theater, signing up for Jim Barnhill's undergraduate acting course. Barnhill shared John Emigh's sentiments concerning Kennedy's potential. "The theater was a true love for John, and it's sad that he couldn't pursue it further than he did," said Barnhill. "One day he came to class and told me that he'd been to New York over the weekend and had been approached on the street by a man who told him, 'I'd love to have you come to Hollywood and audition for some films.' John replied, 'I can't do that. I'm John Kennedy.' Dismayed, the man walked away shaking his head. Evidently such encounters happened to him quite frequently.

"I don't know how well he performed in his academic courses, but John had no difficulty learning his lines. He was overwhelmingly handsome and as fine an actor as any of Brown's theater majors. Whenever he appeared in a production, we could count on a full house. People came just to see John Kennedy Jr. And most of them were astounded at how good he was. 'That's John Kennedy?' they'd ask. Then, in the summer of 1981, after working as an intern at the Center for Democratic Studies, a Washington think tank, he joined me on a ten-day group tour of folk theater festivals in India. Although he never took my advanced course in acting, we remained on friendly terms for the duration of his stay at Brown. As I recall, he returned to the campus only once or twice after he graduated. He came back for his tenth-year reunion and attended a student production—on that occasion he brought along Daryl Hannah. Shortly before he died, the university asked him to serve in an advisory capacity on a committee they had convened on communications. But that of course never came to pass."

While still a sophomore, John performed in Shakespeare's *The Tempest* and in *A Matter of Degrees,* a student film in which he played a guitar-strumming Romeo. At the end of March 1981, during rehearsals for *The Tempest,* Ronald Reagan was shot while emerging from the Washington Hilton Hotel. The following day, Laurence Maslon—director of the play— and several cast members sat around making fun of Reagan, "the mediocre actor turned mediocre politician." Evidently reminded of the shooting that had taken his father's life, JFK Jr. took issue with the comments. "Come on, guys—he's the fucking president. And besides that, he's Irish." Several months later, in June 1981, he and his sister attended a White House ceremony at which Reagan presented Ethel Kennedy with an award commemorating the humanitarian contributions of the late Robert F. Kennedy.

At the beginning of his sophomore year, John Jr. joined Phi Kappa Psi. The four-story, redbrick frat house stood next to a half-dozen other on-campus fraternities on Wiston Quad. Its brothers were known to be the best-looking, most popular men at Brown. While not exactly a jock house, Phi Psi catered more to athletes than to scholars or intellectuals. "It was like the fraternity depicted in the film *Animal House*," said Richard Wiese, John's "big brother." "There were a lot of crazy antics, a lot of booze and pot—all the usual and expected vices. It's embarrassing to look back on it, but it was fun at the time." The hazing process for the class of '83 consisted of drinking, streaking, paddling, goldfish swallowing, and retrieving olives from a bucket of ice with one's rear end (before eating the olive). Needless to say, John passed with flying colors.

The center of social activity at Phi Psi was its horseshoe-shaped basement bar located in a large, darkened room that featured a pinball machine, mounted dartboards, and a jukebox that rarely worked and had to be replaced midsemester by a built-in stereo sound system. The walls of the barroom bore hand-designed murals commemorating some of the more notorious past members of the house. A communal television set on the main floor sat amid an array of clunky but durable lounge furniture dating to the sixties. Live rock bands were regularly imported from New York and Boston for marathon weekend social events.

Each dormitory-style bedroom housed two brothers. By prior agreement, JFK Jr. and Rob Littell had decided to live together. They were assigned room 201 on the second floor, just off the staircase that led to the front hall. To create extra floor space for their desks, they constructed matching loft beds. Rob's mother gave them an old green couch, the stuffing of which gradually emerged through cracks and tears in the frayed fabric. They mounted John's twin stereo speakers in windows facing a church across the street and kept them there until parishioners appeared in person to complain about the noise. They replaced the speakers with a decorative item: a real stuffed tiger cub that John had picked up during his second trip to Kenya.

To add to the drama of his presence, John drove out to a farm one afternoon and bought a medium-size pig that he nicknamed after his roommate ("Litpig") and kept in a makeshift pen in the fraternity house basement, next to the bar. He let it roam free during parties and fed it a daily keg of beer. After a few weeks, when the joke grew stale, he drove the animal back to the farm and left it there.

One of John's Phi Psi buddies remembered John telling him that pigs made great pets—they were more intelligent than people realized. "Evidently Aristotle Onassis kept some pigs on Skorpios," said the fraternity brother, "and that's how John learned about them." The same frat brother reminisced about seeing John's mother at a "TGIF"—Thank God It's Friday—Phi Psi cocktail party for parents. "I'm standing there, sipping a brew, minding my own business," he said, "and here comes Jackie O., Queen of the Universe, striding straight at me. And this is in the basement of a goddamn frat house. It was unreal. It was like encountering God."

Richard Wiese recounted another time Jackie came to visit. "John had to deliver a paper to one of his professors," said Wiese, "so he asked me to wait for his mother and keep her occupied until he returned. I'd never met her before. 'You know what she looks like,' he said, 'dark hair, dark sunglasses.' So I'm sitting on the wall outside Phi Psi, and up comes Jackie Onassis. 'Oh, Mrs. Onassis,' I said. Then I explained that her son would be delayed. And she said, 'Can you show me to John's room. I've only been here once before, and I can't remember which one is his. I have to use the phone.' We'd just had a frat party, so the floor was sticky from beer. As I led the way, I could hear her shoes going, *swish, swish.* We reached the room that he shared with Rob Littell, and those two had a well-deserved reputation for being the sloppiest guys in the frat. Indeed, their room was in total disarray. It looked like a bomb had blown it apart—books, clothes, athletic gear, newspapers, towels were scattered everywhere. 'Where's the phone?' she asked. She couldn't find it in the mess. Neither could I. She got on her hands and knees and started following a cord that ended up leading to the stereo. She looked perplexed. I told her she could use my phone. So she came up to my room, which was just up the stairs on the third floor. She made a quick call and then sat down on my couch and chatted with me for about forty-five minutes. I'd done quite a bit of traveling, so we talked about different countries and cultures. John always kidded me afterward that his mother had told him he should be more like me. I seemed more polished and my room was neater. I also seemed more focused in my studies. It became a kind of standing joke between us, but of course no guy likes to hear from his mother that he should be more like some other guy. But I suppose most mothers and fathers pull that number now and again. In that respect, Jackie was no different than any other parent."

Wiese, a Ford model during his summer vacations, possessed an extensive wardrobe. "John and I were approximately the same height and weight," he said, "so it wasn't unusual for him to want to borrow clothes. One day when he couldn't find an appropriate sport jacket for a dinner at Brown, he came around and asked if he could borrow a blue blazer. I had some misgivings. 'Don't worry,' he said, 'you'll be sitting at the same table. I'll give it back to you right after dinner.' So I let him borrow it. As soon as the dinner started, somebody threw a meatball, and it hit the jacket. He could see that I was upset. 'I'll have it dry-cleaned,' he assured me. I didn't see the jacket again until a month later when I went to his room and found it wadded up in a ball behind the couch in the corner of his room."

Despite John's carelessness, Wiese had nothing but affection for him. "John had average Ivy League intelligence," he said, "but he was by far the most modest and unassuming person I ever knew. He had great intuition and great charm. He could sense the mood in a room the moment he walked in. He was an ordinary person with extraordinary qualities. He had more charisma than all his Kennedy cousins combined. He was casual, fun-loving, and unpretentious. My only gripe—and this is a charge levied against all Kennedys—was that he could be a bit of a limousine liberal. For example, every year our fraternity 'adopted' several kids from underprivileged families in the area. We'd invite them to the frat house, give them presents at Christmas, take them on outings, and so forth. In 1980–81, we wound up with a group of three or four white kids. John suggested we add a black kid to the mix. 'What difference does the kid's race make?' I said. 'Wiese,' he snapped, 'why don't you go back to your exclusive all-white enclave?' I didn't respond, but it seemed clear he'd missed my point."

John's comradeship with Richard Wiese—as with Littell—was to a large extent contingent upon their involvement in athletic activities and a love of the outdoors. "He wasn't a tremendous athlete at Brown," said Wiese, "but he got better. Primarily he learned how to concentrate on one activity at a time, whereas previously his attention drifted too easily. He became a good football player. We must have played in a thousand touch football games together. At night we used to go jogging. But it wasn't an ordinary jog. The Smith Center swimming pool at Brown was this modernistic, pyramid-shaped structure. He and I would run up and down the center's roof. It was like running an obstacle course. After graduation we went on numerous expeditions together—hiking, camping, kayaking, rock climbing, skiing. Then, in later years, when he became involved in ultralight aviation, we explored the possibility of starting our own ultralight business on Long Island. John compartmentalized his friendships. As a result, I occupied the niche of outdoorsman, the proverbial Marlboro Man. Almost all of his lifelong friendships grew out of his four years at Brown. We each served a purpose. But none of us knew everything about him. The keeper of the secrets had to be his sister. Caroline Kennedy was the one person who knew it all."

Caroline also happened to be her brother's harshest critic. Taking note of his erratic academic record at Brown, she labeled him "a true underachiever." He defended himself by pointing out that as a dyslexic he saw certain letters backward—"which is the reason I sometimes don't do as well in school as I should."

John's sister was aware as well of his more magnanimous deeds, those that he kept to himself, such as his surprise visit to Massachusetts General Hospital to see his pal Billy Noonan, who was about to undergo surgery for an advanced case of testicular cancer. Arriving at the hospital after visiting hours on his way from Providence to New York at the beginning of a Christmas break, John told Noonan that he couldn't go home without seeing him first. "I couldn't sit down," he said, "and have you facing this thing." Following successful surgery and a lengthy convalescence, Noonan, an undergraduate at Boston College, told John that the visit had meant everything and more than anything had helped him pull through. Noonan would later write *Forever Young*, a memoir based on his long friendship with JFK Jr.

During his sophomore year, following the termination of his relationship with Jenny Christian, John became involved in several short-term romances. His first girlfriend at Brown, Karen Elliot, happened to be Richard Wiese's lab partner in biology. Rob Littell recalled John being "thrown over" by another coed, a ravishing California blonde who returned to school after Christmas vacation only to inform JFK Jr. that she'd met somebody else. "She was probably the first girl to ever dump him," said Littell. "But the real kicker came when he discovered that she'd left him for another woman."

Not that John suffered for lack of female attention. There was the strange case, as Littell related it, of the cute strawberry blonde from Maine whose unsolicited letters began filling John's mailbox. In addition to the usual display of personal photographs, none of them particularly explicit, her mailings included a series of collages made up of newspaper and magazine shots of John she had cut out and pasted to sheets of construction paper.

The postal route wasn't so new to John. What transformed the unanswered letters into a more threatening form of communication was the girl's sudden appearance, suitcase in hand, at Phi Psi. John wasn't around, so she confronted Rob Littell, subjecting him to her latest batch of JFK Jr. collages. When John returned and saw the girl, he called campus security. Fifteen minutes later, they escorted "Miss Crazy"—as Littell called her—out of John's room and away from the fraternity.

Within hours she reappeared. Making her way back into the now empty and unlocked fraternity room, she removed Littell's clothes from his dresser and closet, and replaced them with her own. When Littell returned from lacrosse practice, he found his belongings neatly stacked in piles on the second-floor staircase landing. Entering the room, he asked the young lady, who had changed into a nightgown, what she thought she was doing.

"As of now," she said, "I'm John's new roommate."

Campus security came back and again retrieved the girl, but not before making her put back Littell's clothing. Kennedy and Littell latched themselves in that night. Just before dawn the girl began pounding on their door and kept at it for more than an hour. When nobody answered, she went downstairs and watched television. JFK Jr. eventually got rid of her by asking somebody to drive her back to Maine, where she stayed.

A male classmate of John's recognized the hard way just how powerful JFK Jr.'s presence could be for the average Brown coed. "Back in 1981," he said, "the year John lived at Phi Psi, he did a lot of partying, not just at his own fraternity but at others as well. I attended a number of parties at which he'd show up, usually with an entourage. The entourage often arrived first, and if they deemed the party worthy of John's attendance, he'd follow. John was the Sun King, and the members of his entourage constituted his royal court. If he laughed, they laughed; if he groaned, they groaned. The amazing thing is that chicks would line up at these affairs to get a shot at him. Everybody was auditioning. I was dating a girl from a wealthy family at the time, and she stood right on line with the others. You'd think to yourself, 'I can't match that.' There would be a buzz in the air, like a whisper: 'John . . . John . . . John.' His presence defined the evening. He'd stay maybe an hour and leave. And when he left, half the party left with him."

Chris Overbeck, another Phi Psi brother with whom JFK Jr. forged a lasting friendship, offered a similar point of view. "Being alone with John," he said, "was a vastly different experience than being in a group with him. It was as if all roads led to Rome—and John was Rome. Everybody had his own road into John. At parties, John was like the center of a wheel—all the spokes ended at John, and the individual spokes had little to do with each other. Everybody was focused on communicating with John. This created a social dynamic that had more to do with the spokes than with John."

Reflecting on JFK Jr.'s public persona, John Hare said, "It must have been a terrible burden on some level to always be the center of attention. It's a little like being a movie star. It was just something he had to live with every day."

A number of women made the mistake with John of acting overly sophisticated in his presence. "This was definitely a turnoff for him," said Richard Wiese. "John constantly downplayed his importance and lived in a way that belied his wealth. He owned 'crappy' cars, usually rode a bike or took the subway, dressed down, and loved eating in diners. Even the parties he gave tended to be downscale. This may have been compensatory behavior because he wanted to be a regular guy, but it was so ingrained in him that he actually became a regular guy. He didn't appreciate women—or men, for that matter—who put it on. He could always see through them."

It was during the second half of his sophomore year that John met Sally Munro, a classic New Englander whose old Boston Irish family had long-standing Democratic Party roots and owned a large, multimillion-dollar homestead in Marblehead, Massachusetts. Although John seemed reluctant to acknowledge the resemblance, Sally looked like Caroline Kennedy and was often mistaken for her. Like Caroline, she had graduated from Concord Academy. Also like Caroline, she was smart, solid, and a bit shy. A literature major at Brown, she shared John's interest in the theater. Self-confident and not afraid to voice an opinion, it was she who first pointed out to John that people around him tried too hard to please and impress him. Under her influence, he not only became more studious but also better organized, tidying up both his room and desk.

Her arrival in his life came not a moment too soon. During his sophomore year, John netted so many "Incompletes" in school that he spent his junior year on academic probation. The dean of academic affairs at Brown wrote John, notifying him of this fact. "Even on the scale of our modest requirements regarding scholastic achievement," read the letter, "you are skating on very thin ice, which could shatter at any moment."

On a somewhat lighter note, when Sally wasn't browbeating John in a concerted effort to improve his study habits, the couple entertained themselves by renting and watching X-rated films, a pastime that probably added to what his friends described as a loving and lustful bond. "John far preferred the intensity of a serious relationship to the uncertainty of the single lifestyle," said Rob Littell. Sally and John went out, though not always exclusively, for a period of five years.

"Sally was very sweet," said Richard Wiese. "She seemed to be quiet, especially around the testosterone-driven guys at Phi Psi. She would sit on the sidelines and watch John play touch football. He was into her. When he liked a woman, he gave her his total affection. Sally was no exception."

Although he continued to frequent Phi Psi on party weekends, John spent his junior and senior years living off-campus in a recently renovated five-story, five-bedroom Victorian townhouse at 155 Benefit Street, a short distance from the Rhode Island School of Design and a ten-minute uphill walk to Brown. The residence contained bay windows, a spiral staircase, fireplaces, the original wall molding, and a spacious backyard for sunbathing and barbecuing. "It was a wonderful old Providence house," said Chris Overbeck. "A Pentecostal family owned it. The owner's mother, Mrs. Mulligan, lived next door and watched us like a hawk. Besides John and myself, there were three girls in the house during the first year: Christiane Amanpour (then a student in the journalism department at Rhode Island University), Brown coed Lynne Weinstein, and Christina Haag (a Brown coed and a future JFK Jr. girlfriend, whom JFK Jr. had known since her high school days at Brearley). John and I occupied twin bedrooms on the third floor. The owners of the house didn't want to rent to students, but John and I managed to talk them into it. Whenever we gave a party, Mrs. Mulligan would come over and ask, 'What's going on?' 'Everything's fine, Mrs. Mulligan,' I'd tell her. 'Everything's under control.' The first year we did pretty well with her. The second year, when some of the housemates moved out and others moved in, we fared a little worse. And after that, as I understand it, they refused to rent to students."

Christiane Amanpour, whom everyone called "Kissy," though nobody quite knew why, became a kind of den mother to the group. Raised in London, the daughter of a wealthy Iranian father and an English mother, Amanpour divided the housemates into cooking and cleaning crews. Thrusting a mop into John's hands, she sent him off to clean the toilets. Before long, she had him flipping cheeseburgers for the voracious group. The household chores were rotated each week. A handwritten schedule was affixed to a small bulletin board in the kitchen. "She wasn't hard," John said of Amanpour. "She was just sort of British and determined."

Commenting on JFK Jr., whom she defined as an "ultimately tragic figure," Amanpour said, "I was always stunned watching people humiliate themselves in front of him, whether they were young, whether they were older men and women. Not humiliate—belittle. They constantly belittled themselves around John, so eager were they to be his friends. He fully understood what was going on. Everybody looked at him as the repository of his father and his family's greatness."

John enjoyed the familial atmosphere of the house, particularly the sit-down dinners during which the five invariably locked horns in political debate. "When John knew and trusted you, he could be really out there," said Chris Overbeck. "He'd poke fun at you—anything you felt vulnerable about, especially politics. Playfulness was his way of being affectionate. He was *in your face*. He'd make you laugh at yourself. He understood people and situations very quickly. He had emotional intelligence. He had a way of connecting with people very quickly—all sorts of people. But he also loved to argue."

Overbeck, a staunch Republican, recalled one boisterous altercation with John over the Vietnam War. John, voicing emotions he hadn't been able to express in Professor Neu's course on the subject, became enraged at Chris's contention that the war had been a necessary evil, that it had been fought on political grounds that had long since shifted. Full of righteous indignation, JFK Jr. yelled, "How can you say that? How can you think it? It can't be. That war was all wrong. We should never have been in it." By the following day, with a new subject on the table, the Vietnam War debate had been laid to rest.

John's greatest opportunity for escape remained the world of the theater. In the first half of his junior year he played Big Al in David Rabe's fast-paced *In the Boom Boom Room*. To prepare for the role, he went to a downtown barbershop and emerged with an austere crew cut. He returned to the same down-and-out Providence bars he'd haunted as a freshman, imbibing the blue-collar atmosphere and gleefully reporting to friends that nobody there seemed to recognize him. The play's director, Santina Goodman, an African-American transfer student, would soon become another member of John's ever-expanding circle of confederates.

A former flight attendant, Goodman was ten years John's senior. Starting at Brown—and forever after—JFK Jr. used to kid her. "For an old girl," he'd tell her, "you're still pretty good looking." Like others, she marveled at his uncanny ability to juggle and balance an entire constellation of friends. "Each of us," she said, "had a special and separate relationship with him."

Rick Moody, a fellow member of the *Boom Boom* cast, described John's thespian talents as combining the best of Robert De Niro and Jack Nicholson, interspersed with "maybe a dash of his dad's inaugural pluck." John "delivered his lines with brio, with . . . reserves of charisma," noted Moody. After a few weeks of rehearsal, JFK Jr. began calling Moody by his character's name, "Ralphie," whenever they encountered each other on campus—"Ralphie, what's up, my man?" It turned out that he did the same with all his fellow cast members.

On opening night, toward the end of the first act, as JFK Jr. and Rick Moody stood backstage, they heard "a particularly robust laugh from the audience, singular and confident and warm." Leaning over, John whispered to "Ralphie," "That's my sister. That's Caroline." On closing night, John threw a cast party at 155 Benefit Street. To Moody's surprise, he had gone to the trouble of decorating the house with balloons and streamers. Beyond this, Moody found the place "tastefully" furnished and appointed. "Things matched," observed Moody.

During the second semester of his junior year, John won the lead role of the playboy in J. M. Synge's *The Playboy of the Western World,* an Irish drama about a meek, timid fellow who transforms himself into a virtual dynamo. Cast in the role by Don Wilmeth, the play's director and head of the Department of Theatre, Speech, and Dance, John adopted an Irish brogue so effectively that few members of the audience recognized him. Finding him "talented, with solid instincts, but essentially undisciplined as an actor," Wilmeth had reservations at first, wondering if he hadn't miscast the son of the late president. "Strapping and muscular, he hardly looked like the milquetoast character he was supposed to play," said Wilmeth. "We discussed the role at length and decided it had to do with state of mind—attitude. After he watched it, one of my colleagues, somebody who'd spent a lot of time in Dublin and worked at the Abbey Theatre, rated it the best *Playboy* he'd ever seen. John surpassed all expectations."

Wilmeth admitted being "a bit intimidated by John. It was hard not to be. He was so charismatic. He was such a presence. His mother, sister, and grandmother [Janet Auchincloss] came to see the play—and my goodness! To walk into the lobby of the theater and have Jackie and her family standing there was something else."

John's cousin Timothy (Tim) Perry Shriver, with whom John had roomed the summer before while interning at the Center for Democratic Studies in Washington, had recently been named assistant director of ConPEP (Connecticut Pre-Collegiate Enrichment Program), which anticipated hiring seventeen tutors for its summer 1982 program, to be conducted at the Storrs campus of the University of Connecticut. John volunteered to join the program and for eight weeks that summer tutored a group of disadvantaged teens in English, math, and drama, helping his students mount a play at the end of the session. While at the encampment, he made friends with Dan Samson, a Yale junior whom he insisted on calling Dick. Samson bestowed John with the same nickname. They called each other Dick, a habit they continued for the duration of their friendship.

John returned to Brown in September 1982 to begin his senior year. Christina Haag had graduated, moving to New York to study acting, and was replaced at 155 Benefit Street by Cordelia Richardson, with whom John purportedly enjoyed a brief and clandestine flirtation. Rob Littell, on a leave of absence the previous year because of a lacrosse injury, was once again living with John. JFK Jr.'s frat brother John Hare joined the group for a time. Chris Overbeck, also having graduated, came and went during the course of the school year. Christiane Amanpour returned and quickly resumed her role as Benefit Street den mother.

JFK Jr.'s girlfriend, Sally Munro, having graduated from Brown in June 1982, took an assistant manager's job in a Boston bookstore, commuting weekends to be with John. On those days that she stayed at Benefit Street, she took her turn on the cleaning and cooking crews. On those occasions when John had to complete a paper or study for an exam, she assumed his household responsibilities as well, giving him more time to spend on his schoolwork. The arrangement led one of the housemates to dub her "Cinderella," a nasty but perhaps fitting sobriquet. Her legion of jealous detractors, made up primarily of "wannabe" JFK Jr. girlfriends, described Sally as "nothing out of the ordinary" and wondered just how long she could survive.

In the middle of it all, Chris Overbeck and John's friendship suffered a temporary breakdown. "At a certain point, I became fed up with the dynamic in the house," said Overbeck. "I felt everyone always deferred to John. I wanted to be friends with him but only if we were going to remain on an equal footing. 'I used to think we were pretty good friends, but now I'm not so sure,' I told him. I gave him a list of reasons why I was questioning the friendship. He was so used to getting his way that he'd begun to walk with a swagger. I don't think he was even aware of it. My comments took him by surprise. His entire face dropped as if to say, 'Oh, that's not true.' But he listened, and he took my feelings to heart. Then he changed—he worked on it. He could be selfish, but he was never malicious. It was a natural selfishness, because he was who he was. His positive reaction to my criticism convinced me that he deeply valued his friendships—they meant everything to him."

John Hare concurred that Kennedy had an enormous capacity for making and keeping friends, a trait his father had amply demonstrated before him. "He was very open-minded, had a winning smile, and a good deal of inner self-confidence," said Hare. "He was comfortable spending time and spending his own personal and emotional capital with people of different interests and people with different backgrounds." John continued to make new friends at Brown, both male and female, until the day he graduated. Toni Kotite, two years behind John at Brown, met him during sophomore year and remained his friend for the rest of his life. She went to lunch with him in New York a week before he died.

During his final year in college, John appeared in only one theatrical production, *Short Eyes,* an all-male prison drama by Miguel Piñero. Again directed by Santina Goodman, John played the role of Longshore, whose murder in prison of a child molester represented the most violent moment in a play full of violence. Christina Haag, having driven up from New York to watch the production, declared it one of John's best performances.

In March 1983 Brooke Shields arrived at Brown with her mother, Teri, for a tour of the campus. Jackie Onassis, an acquaintance of Teri Shields, had asked John to help out the sixteen-year-old Calvin Klein model and actress. Don Wilmeth remembered seeing them together on campus. Brooke wore beige corduroy slacks, a brown wool blazer, and brown leather boots; she had a Gucci bag slung over her shoulder. "Talk about heads turning!" said Wilmeth. "The two of them walked across campus as John showed her around. Here was this beautiful, ideal couple." After the tour, John took Brooke and her mother to Thayer Street for pizza. When apprised by his mother that Brooke had chosen to attend Princeton over Brown, he shrugged his shoulders. "I guess she didn't like the pizza joint," he told friends.

Although it was rumored that John received assistance from an unnamed Brown instructor in completing several overdue term papers during his final semester, no proof of this charge has ever emerged. To the contrary, most of the professors whose courses he took during his last two years at Brown praised his junior- and senior-year efforts. Professor Mary Gluck recalled John approaching her to sign up for her fifteen-student final-semester seminar on Europe at the turn of the century. "The year before," she said, "he took my lecture course in European intellectual history and did well enough to earn a B plus. He performed equally well in the senior seminar. Unlike certain myths that I've read, he was really a decent student. He didn't work as hard as some students and wasn't as systematic as some others, but he did care about his studies. We held the last session of the seminar at his off-campus house. I remember him coming to my office shortly after that to turn in his final paper. 'Here it is,' he said, 'hot off the press.' What sticks in my mind about him is that he was extremely adept at fitting in with everyone else. He was just such a nice guy."

On June 6, 1983, John received his bachelor's degree from Brown. The evening before the ceremony, he threw an all-night party at 155 Benefit Street, inviting what seemed like half the graduating class. John and Rob Littell were still drinking beer at eight in the morning when they finally showered, dressed, and met with their respective families before donning the traditional cap and gown. Under his gown JFK Jr. wore jeans and a pair of cowboy boots. Jackie, Caroline, Janet Auchincloss, and Rose and Ted Kennedy were there. The press turned out en masse for an opportunity to capture the graduate on film. So intense was the media focus that it appeared almost as if John represented the entirety of Brown's crop of graduates for 1983, an impression furthered by the appearance above the ceremony of a skywriter's inscription: *Good Gluck, John!* Jackie's deliberately misspelled send-off referred back to a botched birthday cake inscription that for some reason had greatly amused JFK Jr.

The day after graduation, about fifty of John's friends and relatives set out for Hyannis Port, where Ted Kennedy had set up a food tent and hired a band to celebrate his nephew's graduation. In addition he gave John a framed arrangement of the handwritten notes he'd received from President Kennedy during the Cuban Missile Crisis, a gift JFK Jr. later donated to the John F. Kennedy Presidential Library. Following the Hyannis Port party, a smaller group headed for Red Gate Farm on Martha's Vineyard to continue the festivities. Sally Munro attended as John's date. "We stayed for days," noted Rob Littell, "reluctant to let the party end."

Several weeks later, John joined a dive team aboard the *Vast Explorer,* a salvage vessel engaged in a hunt for the *Whydah,* a legendary pirate ship that had gone down in the waters off Cape Cod in 1771 with a treasure estimated to be worth some $200 million. Having mastered the sport of scuba diving during his summers at Skorpios, John actively participated in the search. Todd Murphy, a crewmate on the boat, remembered the expedition. "It was a really salty crowd, and John fit in as well as anybody," he said. "We'd be in the water waiting to dive and freezing and having this crazy fight, squirting water out between our teeth. John was a character." For the record, the *Whydah* was recovered but not until 1985, long after John had gone off in a whole new direction.

Jackie wanted John to get away after his graduation, partially to avoid having to deal with a press reawakened to his presence now that he'd graduated Brown and was back in New York. Accompanied by Sally Munro, he returned to India and registered for a public health course at the University of New Delhi. He also took part in an urban poverty program sponsored by Mother Teresa, helping to organize English lessons for the children in the slums of Delhi. Although he'd rarely experienced such squalor, he immersed himself in the project, lamenting that he couldn't do more to improve the situation. He terminated his stay in India by taking a train to the resort city of Goa, where his mother joined him on a two-week vacation that ended in Jaipur.

Returning to New York, John followed his sister's lead by moving into an apartment on Manhattan's Upper West Side. He and Rob Littell took a sublet on a two-bedroom, two-bath flat at 309 West 86th Street, not far from Riverside Park. The real estate agent responsible for the rental gave them a crystal obelisk from Tiffany when they moved in. John observed that instead of the obelisk, he wished she had given them a better view— the apartment, which belonged to an ABC-TV news producer who had relocated to Paris, looked out on an alleyway.

John agreed to accept a minimal annual salary of $2,000 to work for the New York City Office of Business Development, at the same time serving as acting deputy executive director of the 42nd Street Development Corporation, a nonprofit organization cofounded several years before by Jackie Onassis (with former advertising executive Fred Papert), which since its inception had been lobbying for the construction of a national theater center in Times Square. He also became involved in several charitable projects, including Reaching Up and Exodus House. He spent his evenings either relaxing at home with Sally Munro or cruising Manhattan's trendiest downtown pubs and clubs with Rob Littell and other chums. "Going out with John was like having a key to the city," noted Littell. They were regulars at the China Club, the Roxy, Xenon, and Nell's. "Cocaine and pot were the drugs of choice in the city," added Littell. "We managed to keep our activity limited and recreational. The allure faded over time."

So too, apparently, did John's desire to continue along his present path. In mid-1984, he approached his mother with the suggestion that he apply for admission to the Yale School of Drama in New Haven, Connecticut. The idea didn't take. She recommended that he consider going to law school instead.

Chapter 12

———— ◆ ————

MAURICE AND ED

BY EARLY 1984, "the Kennedy girls"—Jackie and her daughter, Caroline—were both firmly entrenched in their latest domestic relationships, Jackie with Maurice Tempelsman, and Caroline with Ed Schlossberg. In Maurice, Jackie had at last found the equilibrium and peace of mind she had so long sought and failed to find in either of her marriages. A longtime Democratic Party insider, he and his wife, Lily, married since 1949, were frequent guests at the White House during the Kennedy years as well as in subsequent administrations. Initially an acquaintance and sometime financial adviser to Jackie, Maurice gradually won his way into her heart.

Born into an Orthodox Jewish family in Antwerp, Belgium, in 1929 (the same year as Jackie), he, his younger sister, and their parents fled Europe in 1940 to escape the Nazi onslaught. After two years on the Caribbean island of Jamaica, the family arrived in New York. By age fifteen, Maurice was taking night courses in business administration at New York University, working days for his father, a successful raw diamond broker. It was Maurice, at twenty-one, who hitched the family firm, Leon Tempelsman & Son, to the global marketplace by convincing U.S. government officials to buy industrial diamonds for its stockpile of strategic materials maintained for national emergencies. As the middleman in the operation, Maurice made millions. He later acted as the centerpiece in a transaction that brought uranium to the U.S. in exchange for surplus agricultural commodities.

According to U.S. Department of Justice files, Maurice Tempelsman was a key representative and associate of Harry Oppenheimer, the owner-director of Anglo-American Corporation and DeBeers Consolidated Mines, the world's largest miners and distributors of gold and diamonds. It was Tempelsman who introduced Oppenheimer to John F. Kennedy; in 1960, both men made generous contributions to Kennedy's presidential campaign fund. Thanks to Oppenheimer, Tempelsman befriended a number of African potentates, most notably Zaire's President Mobutu Sese Seko, thereby expanding his firm's operations into Zaire, Sierra Leone, Gabon, Zimbabwe, and South Africa. His empire soon included mining interests, diamond and mineral sales, distribution companies, the world's second-largest petroleum drill-bit manufacturing corporation, and an extensive private art collection. In connection with the art collection, Tempelsman was subsequently accused of various improprieties, all of which he denied, and none of which was ever proved.

For all his considerable accomplishments and wealth, Tempelsman remained a shadowy, mysterious figure. He struck many of Jackie's friends and acquaintances as nothing more than a "poor man's Aristotle Onassis." Like Onassis, Tempelsman was short, portly, older looking than his actual years. Both men smoked Dunhill cigars and were fluent in a number of foreign languages. Both were financial wizards. Their other shared passion, besides money and Jackie Kennedy, was the sea. Tempelsman's moderate-size schooner, the *Relemar*—named for his three children (Rema, Leon, and Maurice)—while no match for the *Christina,* nevertheless served its owner well. He and Jackie made good use of the boat, navigating it up and down the eastern seacoast from Florida to Maine and back again.

Although he and his wife had separated in November 1982, it wasn't until 1984 that Tempelsman moved into Jackie's Fifth Avenue apartment, occupying a bedroom adjacent to hers. "Maurice Tempelsman may not have contributed a dime to Jackie's daily living expenses," said Truman Capote, "but you can be sure he gave her a lot of presents.

What's more, not only Jackie but also Lee Radziwill made bundles of cash on the basis of Tempelsman's advice on when to buy and when to sell in the volatile silver and gold markets. Girls like Jackie and Lee don't change—they only grow richer."

Maurice Tempelsman's cousin Rose Schreiber offered a different view, pointing out that if Jackie married her first husband for status and her second for money, then her latest attachment was based on mutual respect and friendship. "Theirs was a mature, comfortable, intimate relationship, one which obviously satisfied both of them," said Schreiber. "In most respects, it was a far better, healthier coupling than any Jackie had experienced before."

Despite his unassuming appearance, Tempelsman was regarded by most of his own friends as a charming and worldly figure. He dressed well, liked to read, and loved to travel and go to the opera. He had savoir faire. He also enjoyed the simple pleasures that nature had to offer, which is something Jackie coveted as well. He could be effervescent and lively. Women were attracted to him. At parties, particularly now that he was involved with Jackie, he practically had to push them aside.

The problem with the Jackie arrangement, at least from a public relations standpoint, was his marriage, which didn't end when he moved in with the former First Lady. Maurice had married Lily, also from Belgium, when he turned twenty. For years they lived and raised their family in a luxury apartment at the Normandy, on Riverside Drive and 86th Street. They enjoyed a close marriage, Lily acting as her husband's adviser on all matters, including business. When the children were older, she went to graduate school to earn her master's degree and started working as a marriage counselor at the Jewish Board of Guardians. Even Lily had to admit the irony in her choice of profession, considering that she entered the field at the very moment her own marriage began to crumble.

A major development in the marriage had to do with religious commitment. "Lily was a very observant Jew, strictly Orthodox," said Rose Schreiber. "As a matter of fact, she told me she didn't enjoy going to the White House with Maurice because he would never ask for kosher meals. His parents kept a kosher home, and so did Lily. Their children had all gone to Ramaz, a Jewish day school in Manhattan. But after a point,

Maurice stopped going to synagogue. Lily would go to pray on Saturday mornings, and he'd go boating. His gradual disaffection disturbed Lily."

According to Schreiber, it was Lily who took the initiative in asking her husband to move out of their apartment. "He would have stayed with her," she said, "but it had reached the point where every time she opened the newspaper, she would come across another photograph of Maurice with Jackie—at museum exhibits, in restaurants, on Martha's Vineyard where they spent their weekends. Maurice moved into a hotel suite on the East Side, spending several nights each week at Jackie's apartment, the number of nights increasing with time until he finally moved in with her."

From all indications, Jackie understood that the chances of formalizing her relationship with Maurice were slim at best. Her standard line became "We can't marry because his wife won't give him a divorce." When she said this to George Plimpton, he responded, "This is 1984, Jackie. You don't have to marry to stay together." More than likely, she preferred it that way—she had long come to appreciate her independence.

Neither Caroline nor John Jr. felt particularly close to Tempelsman, though both liked and respected him, all the more because he made their mother happy. John entertained him by imitating the sounds of a humpback whale; Tempelsman enlightened Caroline by giving her informal lessons on African art, using artifacts from his own collection to drive home his points. "Maurice worships the ground my mother walks on," JFK Jr. said to George Plimpton. "He doesn't try to dominate her, nor she him. They treat each other as equals."

As for Caroline, she had settled comfortably into her third year on the staff of the Office of Film and Television at the Metropolitan Museum of Art. As she approached her twenty-sixth birthday, her responsibilities on the job had increased from part-time researcher to full-time liaison officer between the museum staff and outside producers and directors shooting footage at the museum. She helped coordinate a *Sesame Street* children's special, *Don't Eat the Pictures,* for PBS. Working sixteen-hour days, she dispelled the notion entertained by certain members of the office staff that she was little more than "a rich young lady who lunches." Casting off her usual resistance to all forms of public exposure, she agreed to a cameo role in the production, appearing on-screen as one of the museum's first visitors of the day.

When not working, Caroline could usually be found in the company of Ed Schlossberg. Although she had moved from the Upper West Side into her own apartment on East 78th Street, she spent most of her time at Ed's expensively furnished Wooster Street loft in SoHo. The two went skiing in Aspen, visited museums and art galleries, took in movies and plays, attended dance and jazz concerts, vacationed at Hyannis Port and Martha's Vineyard. Maura Moynihan, among the first of Caroline's friends to be introduced to Ed, described their relationship as "idyllic— they were great together. Every time I saw Caroline after she and Ed began dating, she absolutely beamed. They never argued. They were true soul mates."

Their favorite getaway was a house Ed's parents had given him in Chester, Massachusetts, a tiny and sparsely populated village in the Berkshires, about two and a half hours from New York. The town consisted of a single street lined by a dozen storefronts, among them Carni's (a coffee shop/gas station), an art gallery, a restaurant (open only three days a week), an all-purpose market, and the Blue Note Café—the local honky-tonk. A mile from town, at 15 Johnson Hill Road, half-hidden behind scattered stands of birch trees and conifers, was the Schlossberg residence. At the front of the property stood a caretaker's home, a nondescript circa-1940s white cottage with metal siding and a stone chimney. The main house sat to the rear of the property. A converted barn with a wraparound porch and a high, stone fireplace, it contained a spacious, loft-like living area on the first floor, a series of bedrooms branching off a circular balcony on the next floor. The house looked out on a small yard and an even smaller vegetable garden. Several mortarless stone walls separated the property from the one next to it. The wraparound deck was covered with groupings of Adirondack chairs and large potted plants. Ed's Harry Ferguson tractor sat in the middle of a nearby field.

Ed Carrington, the nearest neighbor, recalled that the couple "kept pretty much to themselves, although if you bumped into them, they were always cordial." Their only friend in the area, William Ivey Long, also owned a house in Chester. Ed Schlossberg and Caroline were often seen

walking to town together or riding their bikes. Each year they participated in Railroad Day, a local festival that drew crowds from neighboring towns and villages. They enjoyed visiting a sugarhouse, where
maple syrup was made. They watched plays performed by the Chester
Theatre Company in the auditorium of Chester Town Hall. Summers
they drove to Jacob's Pillow for open-air concerts and dance performances, or they went hiking in the Chester-Blandford State Forest. They
gardened, picnicked, swam, and went horseback riding. Winters they
skied in the Berkshire woods and ice-skated on a frozen pond a few miles
from the house. One of their favorite activities was to write poetry together, in blank and sometimes rhymed verse, then read the final product aloud.

Eleanor Doyle, the town's postmaster, remarked that Ed and Caroline
"were like everyone else. They walked around in blue jeans and blended
in. They were just normal people. They took part in local activities, frequented the village's eateries, and contributed financially to the Chester
Historical Society, now located in what was formerly our minuscule town
jail. You'd never have known they were rich and famous city people, or
flatlanders as we call them today."

The most generous compliment bestowed upon Ed Schlossberg by
his neighbors, none of whom seemed to know him very well though he'd
been visiting the area since the 1960s, was that he was indistinguishable
from the other thousand or so residents of Chester. From all indications,
Edwin Alfred Schlossberg, born July 19, 1945, remained an unknown
quantity, as shadowy and mysterious a figure as Maurice Tempelsman.
Twelve years older than Caroline—the same age difference that separated
her parents—Schlossberg has been variously labeled (or labels himself)
an author, poet, scholar, conceptual artist, designer, architect, city plan-
ner, businessman, philosopher, Renaissance man, sage, and visionary. He
was also apparently a screenwriter, having at one time penned a screen-
play—never produced—based on Virginia Woolf's 1931 novel *The Waves*.

Like Maurice Tempelsman, Ed Schlossberg came from a devout Orthodox Jewish family. All four of his great-grandparents were Ellis Island
immigrants who were born within fifty miles of one another in the vicinity of Poltava, Russia. His parents, Alfred and Mae Schlossberg, were

members of the Park East Synagogue on New York's Upper East Side, where Ed attended Hebrew school and was then bar mitzvahed. Schlossberg's father, founder of Alfred Schlossberg, Inc., a Manhattan textile-manufacturing firm, had served as president of the synagogue and had supported various Jewish and Zionist causes. As in the case of other newly rich Jewish families, the Alfred Schlossbergs purchased a vacation home in Palm Beach and socialized with the upwardly mobile, sending Edwin to the progressive Birch Wathen Lenox School in New York (where his older sister Maryann had gone before him), then on to Columbia University, from which he graduated in 1967. He returned to Columbia as a graduate student, receiving a master's in English literature in 1969 and a PhD in science and literature two years later. Although often praised for his intelligence and resourcefulness, Schlossberg amassed his share of detractors. If Maurice Tempelsman had a reputation as being a kind of minister without portfolio, Ed Schlossberg gave the impression to some of being a social climber without a rope.

Following the completion of his doctorate, Schlossberg began producing novelty and instructional manuals such as *The Kids' Pocket Calculator Game Book* and *The Home Computer Handbook,* neither of which sold in significant numbers. Most likely supported by his parents, he turned out sophomoric, supposedly avant-garde poetry, designed high-tech T-shirts, and experimented by printing fragments of poems against sheets of aluminum and Plexiglas. A follower of the downtown art scene, he befriended the likes of John Cage, Robert Rauschenberg, and Jasper Johns. Larry Rivers, the celebrated conceptual artist, met Schlossberg at the West Islip, Long Island, home of Maurice and Tatyana Grosman. Tatyana, founder of Universal Limited Art Editions, a small but successful handpress publishing venture, thought Schlossberg's work invigorating enough to put out twenty-five copies of *Wordswordswords,* a high-priced collection of Ed's poetic ruminations on language and ideas. Larry Rivers remained skeptical of Schlossberg's abilities. "I liked Ed, but I wasn't as convinced as Tatyana was of his genius," said Rivers. "One of his early mentors was R. Buckminster Fuller. He used to parrot Bucky all the time, throwing around phrases like 'human inter-creativity' and 'Spaceship Earth.' He talked a good game, but his artwork didn't bowl me over.

It was highly derivative and not very good. He had several one-man shows at the Ronald Feldman Gallery in SoHo. Feldman was apparently a friend of his. An art critic I know called the work 'gentrified graffiti.' Not surprisingly, it began to sell only after it became known that Ed and Caroline Kennedy were about to get married."

Having failed to make a substantial impression in the world of art, Schlossberg started his own firm, Edwin A. Schlossberg, Inc., advertising himself as a multimedia designer of museum and educational installations and environments. One of his first major commissions—the Brooklyn Children's Museum—was soon taken over by another specialty designer, Brent Saville, who described his predecessor as a self-serving, egomaniacal individual with more moxie than understanding, more luck than insight. Others involved in the same project thought Schlossberg opportunistic, shallow, and insincere.

Despite his evident failure to follow through on the Brooklyn Children's Museum project, Schlossberg succeeded in picking up new commissions. In 1979, after submitting a winning bid, he was selected by the Massachusetts Society for the Prevention of Cruelty to Animals (MSPCA) to help design a barnyard zoo—with interactive exhibits—on forty-five acres at Farmington, about twenty-five miles west of Boston. Judy Golden, then assistant director of education for the MSPCA, recalled that Schlossberg received $1 million and toiled for three years on his end of the project. "He worked with his design group," said Golden, "and made a number of trips to the area. He came up with a variety of interactive games and devices directed at schoolchildren, from videos to fiber-optic face masks through which visitors could see the world from the animal's perspective. For example, a chicken has eyes on the sides of its head and sees upward to protect itself against predators, since it's low to the ground. Besides chickens, there were masks for pigs, horses, cows, sheep, cats, and dogs. In the stable, where the horses were kept, he built something resembling a treadmill—when you stood on the machine, it mimicked the different gaits of a horse, from a walk to a gallop. In 1982, when he completed the project, he brought Caroline up to have a look around. Until then, none of us knew that they were going out."

As innovative as Schlossberg's devices seemed, there were unforeseen problems. "Most of the exhibits he designed, particularly those with moving parts, demanded modification and needed constant repair," said Golden. "He hadn't anticipated that dust and tiny hay particles in the barns would jam the equipment. Some of the exhibits just didn't work." For unknown reasons, the zoo shut down in 1986, never to reopen.

Despite his professional follies and an uncertain career, Ed Schlossberg appealed to Caroline Kennedy. Tall, husky, and prematurely gray, he made a fine impression on those that met him for the first time. A friend of Caroline's insisted that although quiet, "Ed has a great sense of humor. He and Caroline have a chemical attraction to each other. In that sense, they were quite a bit like Jackie and Maurice Tempelsman. I remember a gathering at which Tempelsman held forth on ancient Egyptian art, while Ed Schlossberg gave somebody a quick brushup on conceptual art. It made for an interesting juxtaposition."

Ed Schlossberg represented a new direction for Caroline. To her, he appeared loyal, witty, bright, warm, kind, and supportive. In early 1984, when she received a letter at the Metropolitan Museum of Art from one Herbert Randall Gefvert threatening to kill her, she turned to Ed Schlossberg for help. Several days later she received another communication from her newest correspondent, this one stating that "twenty hit men" were "going to get" Caroline, while he—Gefvert—intended to blow up the museum. Caroline and Ed approached the museum's security division, which in turn brought in the FBI. Federal agents learned that Gefvert, a former mental patient, had rented a room in a small midtown transient hotel. Gefvert was apprehended and sent to Bellevue Hospital for observation before being placed in a more secure out-of-state mental institution.

Then, in late April 1984, Rose Kennedy suffered a stroke. Caroline flew to Palm Beach to spend spring vacation with her grandmother and several of her Kennedy cousins. It was during this visit that David Kennedy also turned up in Palm Beach, having just been released from a drug rehabilitation program at the Mayo Clinic in Rochester, Minnesota. When Rose refused to let him stay at the Kennedy estate, he checked into room 107 at the Brazilian Court Hotel, where he embarked on a twenty-four-hour drug-and-alcohol binge. At some point during this period he went to Rose's house and raided her medicine cabinet, making off with a vial of Demerol. Rose Kennedy's nurse reported the theft to Caroline Kennedy.

On April 25 the switchboard operator at the Brazilian Court, unable to reach David in his room, asked a desk clerk to look in on him. Gaining access to the room with a passkey, the clerk found David lying facedown on the floor next to his bed. Paramedics were summoned to the hotel. It was too late. The twenty-eight-year-old son of Robert F. Kennedy had expired several hours earlier. The autopsy revealed excessive amounts of drugs and pharmaceuticals in his digestive tract. In the course of an investigation into David's death, Palm Beach police officers interviewed Caroline Kennedy. According to a preliminary police report, Caroline claimed she had no knowledge that David was "suffering from any illness or taking any drugs." It was not the first time she had rushed to his defense. Authorities later arrested two bellhops at the Brazilian Court in connection with the sale of cocaine to the deceased.

On April 27, accompanied by Caroline and several Kennedy cousins, David's body was flown from Palm Beach to Boston's Logan Airport. Burial services were held that day at Holyhood Cemetery in Brookline. Struggling to comprehend the implications of David's death, Caroline again turned to Ed Schlossberg. "Ed saw her through it," said Maura Moynihan. "It sounds trite, but he was her Rock of Gibraltar."

"On the other side," said journalist Harrison Rainie, "being with an almost middle-aged man meant having to give up several long-standing friends of her own age and background. It was one more little act of rebellion on Caroline's part, a way of getting out from under the family boot. One reason Caroline undoubtedly liked Ed Schlossberg was that he was so different from her Kennedy cousins. He was artsy, intellectual, and Jewish. He came from a prosperous family, but they weren't in the same fiscal class as the Kennedys. All that mattered to Caroline in terms of her family was that her mother approved of him—and she did."

Schlossberg's attentions and her own growing maturity were decisive factors in Caroline's desire to finally upgrade her overall appearance and lifestyle. It was a period of transition for her. Whereas previously she had always lost weight to satisfy either her mother or the latest man in her life, she now dieted to satisfy herself. She didn't so much diet as alter her eating habits. Gone were the cheeseburgers, spareribs, and ice-cream sundaes of her youth, replaced as they were by a more spartan fruit and vegetable regimen. Inspired by Schlossberg's close, almost paternal interest in the minutiae of her life, she tossed out her well-worn collection of sweaters and corduroy Levi's, replacing them with selections from the top designer fashion houses. She acquired Gucci handbags and a $6,000 Cartier watch. She spent money on jewelry. She became a client of hair stylist Thomas Morrissey, a former Kenneth employee. She attended benefits hosted by Literary Lions, a fund-raising faction of the New York Public Library. At her twenty-seventh birthday party, she wore a flimsy black-and-yellow silk pajama suit chosen for her by Ed Schlossberg. She told admirers of the ensemble that he had helped select a number of her new outfits, pointing out that for himself he preferred op-art ties, linen jackets, and calfskin ankle boots. She had likewise gained new responsibilities, including an appointment to the board of the John F. Kennedy Library. She received still another promotion in her division at the Metropolitan Museum of Art, currently serving as department manager and coordinating producer. Then, in 1985, she surprised fellow staff members and friends by resigning her museum position to enroll at the Columbia University School of Law. Her mother was ecstatic that Caroline had opted for a legal career.

Rumors of an Ed-and-Caroline marriage began to surface as early as January 1984, at which time it was also said that there was interfamilial opposition to such a union. The rumors most often cited had to do with Schlossberg's supposed refusal to sign a prenuptial agreement drawn up by Kennedy family lawyers to protect Caroline's inheritance; there was also the sticky religious issue. The Kennedys were regarded, at least publicly, as one of the leading Irish-Catholic clans in America, and the fact that Schlossberg was Jewish raised questions in the minds of certain family members. Having recovered from her stroke, Rose Kennedy confided to a family friend that she couldn't understand what Jacqueline and Caroline saw in Jewish men that they were "unable to find in men of their own faith."

A parallel situation arose with regard to Maria Shriver's long-term ro-

mance with bodybuilder-turned-actor Arnold Schwarzenegger. While
not Jewish, Schwarzenegger was an outspoken celebrity, a middle-of-the-
road Republican, and an Austrian with a pronounced, almost embarrassing German accent. It wasn't so much how he spoke, though, but what
he said. Arnold tended to sound too much like the warmongering mechanical men he so often portrayed on the silver screen. In addition, he
had discussed (in at least one widely published interview) his lustful appetite for the opposite sex—hardly the kind of information that would
have thrilled the distaff members of the Kennedy tribe. Even worse, ge-
nealogical researchers subsequently discovered that Schwarzenegger's father, Gustav, had been a card-carrying member of the Nazi Party both
before and during World War II.

The impediments and obstacles to both Caroline's and Maria's relationships were gradually overcome. Ed Schlossberg, it turned out, had no
difficulty signing a prenuptial agreement. Nor did he voice objection to
the proposition that any children he and Caroline might beget be
brought up according to the tenets of the Catholic Church. Maria
Shriver's plans to marry an actor also gained acceptance, the more so because she, herself, had become a highly visible television news commen-
tator and thus a public personality in her own right. Moreover, although
a foreigner and an avowed Republican, Schwarzenegger possessed a keen
understanding of the political process in America.

JFK Jr.'s friend Richard Wiese recalled visiting John at the Kennedy
compound in Hyannis Port during the mid-1980s and encountering
Arnold Schwarzenegger, who was also visiting. "This was long before the
Terminator became involved with government," said Wiese. "At some
point during the weekend, he became involved in a political debate with
Ted Kennedy and several other high-ranking Democratic Party politicos.
Schwarzenegger took the Republican side. To everyone's amazement, including Ted Kennedy's, he more than held his own. He was quite knowl-
edgeable and adept at defending his position."

The weekend in question represented a turning point. Impressed by
Schwarzenegger's mental capabilities, the Kennedys smiled favorably
upon his romance with Maria Shriver. And if the Kennedys were about
to embrace the Terminator, could Edwin Schlossberg be far behind? In a

quiet statement in *The New York Times* at the beginning of March 1986, Jacqueline Onassis announced her daughter's engagement to Schlossberg and plans for a July 19 Hyannis Port wedding. Caroline had informed her family that she wanted a "small, subdued" ceremony. The date might have been more carefully chosen: July 19, 1986, happened to be the seventeenth anniversary of Chappaquiddick. On the other hand, it also marked Ed Schlossberg's forty-first birthday.

Chapter 13

◆

WINNERS AND LOSERS

A FTER SOME EIGHTEEN MONTHS with Rob Littell in their West 86th Street sublet, John Kennedy Jr. moved into a place of his own. Using Feathered Nest Realtors, he acquired a comfortable one-bedroom flat on Manhattan's Upper East Side, within walking distance of his mother's apartment at 1040 Fifth Avenue. As a parting gesture, he and Littell threw a going-away party. When the owner of the 86th Street residence returned from Europe, he found his apartment in a state of disrepair. "It looked like a herd of yaks had lived in it," said a friend of John's. There were nicks in the walls, burn marks on the area rugs, stains on the hardwood flooring, mildew and mold on the bathroom doors. The owner threatened to sue John unless he agreed to pay for repairs. Jackie visited the apartment and surveyed the damage. To avoid the unpleasant publicity that a lawsuit might bring, she cut the landlord a check, thereby ending the matter.

The wasted condition of the apartment suggested that Sally Munro had been jettisoned from John's life and that he was dating again. One of his occasional companions was Catherine Oxenberg, the ABC-TV *Dynasty* star whose mother, Princess Elizabeth of Yugoslavia, had been a lover of President Kennedy and a frequent guest at the Kennedy White House. One evening in early 1985, John took Catherine to the Madison

Avenue Pub, on Madison and 81st Street. "He came in all the time," said one of the Pub's bartenders. "Not long before he brought Oxenberg around, he stopped by with a rowdy bunch of his Kennedy cousins. They started tossing a football back and forth, making a lot of noise, disturbing our regular patrons. After a while, John grabbed the football and led the group back onto the street. The following day he returned by himself and apologized for their behavior, which I thought damn decent of him. When he came in with Catherine Oxenberg, they sat at a small rear booth and ordered French onion soup and burgers from the kitchen, and bottles of Heineken from the bar. They stayed about an hour. I'm no expert, but their body language suggested that they were merely buddies, nothing more than that."

Chuck Freed, a part-time bartender at Zanzibar and Grill, a popular hangout on East 36th Street, remembered John rolling in on one occasion about three in the morning with a statuesque blonde. "They had drinks at the bar," he recalled. "The girl seemed pretty familiar with John. She kept leaning her head on his shoulder, laughing at his jokes, running her hand through his hair. Another guy at the bar recognized John and began riding him about Ted Kennedy—how he'd been trounced by Jimmy Carter in the Democratic Party primaries in 1980, what a womanizing drunken bastard he was, how he'd murdered that poor girl at Chappaquiddick. I imagine this sort of thing happened every time John wandered into a bar. I don't know how he did it, but he somehow managed to mollify the fellow. They ended up the best of friends. John and his date left about four in the morning, no doubt headed for a quieter, more conducive location—like John's bedroom, for example."

Tony Smith, a Manhattan liquor store proprietor who paid his monthly rent at the 42nd Street Development Corporation, where John worked, recalled walking in and finding John reclining in a chair, feet up on the desk and a "knockout redhead" sprawled all over him. As soon as he saw Smith, he stood up. "Can I be of help?" he asked. Smith handed him the check, and they chatted for a while. "John was very cordial," said Smith. "There wasn't a trace of arrogance in him. If anything, he seemed embarrassed that I'd caught him fooling around with the girl."

Mark Padnos, a library administrator and literary translator in the City University of New York (CUNY) system, met John at a roller-skating benefit for disadvantaged children. "It happened that we lived no more than a block apart in Manhattan," said Padnos. "Consequently, we'd run into each other on the street from time to time, and to my amazement he actually remembered my name. He'd stop and say something like, 'Mark, my man, how's it hanging?' As often as not, he'd have a date on his arm. I once took a date of my own to Keens Steakhouse on West 36th Street. It was our first date. Suddenly in the middle of dinner, heads began to turn. In walked John Kennedy accompanied by somebody who looked exactly like actress Melanie Griffith. It might've been her, for all I know. They were being led to a table by the maître d'. When he saw me, he stopped in his tracks. 'Mark,' he said, 'what're you doing in these parts?' We exchanged niceties, and he continued on his way. My date appeared more than a little impressed. 'Wow!' she exclaimed. 'You know John Kennedy?' To make a long story short, my brief encounter with John that evening culminated in my date dragging me back to her apartment and insisting that I spend the night."

Peter Blanchard, a former television executive, recalled seeing JFK Jr. in the VIP lounge at the Palladium disco in downtown Manhattan on the occasion of Greek tycoon Stavros Niarchos's seventy-sixth birthday bash. "As photogenic as he happened to be, as handsome as he appeared in press photographs, JFK Jr. looked even better in person," said Blanchard. "Besides John, one of the guests at the party was the Brazilian actress Sonia Braga. The minute she spotted John, she threw herself at him. I mean she wrapped herself around him like a serpent coiled around a tree. She wouldn't let go. To say that John looked uncomfortable is an understatement. Such aggressive behavior on the part of a woman obviously distressed him. After a few minutes, he managed to extricate himself. He congratulated Niarchos, stood next to him for the house photographer, and quickly made his exit."

Only slightly less aggressive was Madonna, whose desire to reenact the Marilyn Monroe myth had led her to lighten her hair color and pose as Marilyn for the pages of *Life* and other magazines. Well aware of President Kennedy's affair with the late actress, she got hold of JFK Jr.'s private telephone number and invited him to her upcoming concert at Madison Square Garden. Following the concert, John turned up in Madonna's dressing room. While he cooled his heels in a corner of the room, the diva directed her attention in the direction of several less celebrated visitors. Sensing that he might bolt at any moment, she finally sauntered over to John and suggested that they leave together.

A few days later they were photographed jogging in Central Park. They worked out together at the New York Athletic Club and at the Plus One Fitness club in SoHo, which John had joined to the tune of $6,000 a year. Madonna spent a day with him at Hyannis Port. "He was impressed by her talent, and she was impressed with him," said Rob Littell. "They were an almost couple but were stymied by her busy performance schedule. John invited her to his mother's Christmas party, which practically amounted to being welcomed into the family. Because she was giving a concert out of town, she declined. I like to think of them as two media ships passing in the night."

John later asked Madonna to another of his mother's dinner parties. Married at the time, she signed Jackie's guest book as "Mrs. Sean Penn." Having convinced Michael Jackson to publish *Moonwalk* (his personal memoir) with Doubleday, Jackie now went after Madonna, encouraging her to commit her thoughts to paper. The recommendation resulted in *Sex,* an explicit album of photographs and text published in 1992, not by Doubleday but by Warner Books.

Although Jackie admired Madonna's energy and drive, she advised John to sever his friendship with her. In the first place, Madonna was a married woman; second, Jackie regarded Madonna as a media-crazed rock star hungry for the spotlight. To drive home the point, John's mother turned to Ted Kennedy, divorced from Joan in 1982, and asked the senator to speak with John. Teddy complied, but his words had little effect. Despite Ted's and Jackie's warnings, JFK Jr. remained very much in contact with Madonna. When her marriage to Sean Penn began to deteriorate, she called John, then in law school, and asked him for legal advice. He was among the first to learn that she intended to seek a divorce.

"During the summer of 1988, John worked as an intern for a prestigious Los Angeles law firm," said Rob Littell. "As the summer drew to a close, he prepared to head back to New York to resume his law school studies. Madonna again called and suggested that they rendezvous in Chicago. It was all very secretive. So on the way home he stopped off in the Windy City, and they checked into some cheap, dinky motel. John loved to tell this story, because it was so funny. Here he was in a Chicago motel room with the world's hottest chick, the two of them at long last prepared to consummate their relationship. They were working their way around the bases and as they rounded third and headed for home, she asked him if he had any protection. He didn't, so now they began discussing how they were going to get hold of a prophylactic. She was still legally married to Sean Penn, and John had a steady girlfriend. They didn't have any wigs or Groucho Marx glasses, and they were afraid of being busted. They couldn't very well just meander into a pharmacy and ask for a pack of Trojans. They were too well known, too recognizable. To John's great chagrin, the relationship was never completed. Needless to say, every Madonna and JFK Jr. biographer since the beginning of time has described them as having had wild and lurid sex together, but that's simply not the case. Let's just say that John hit a long triple that day."

A postscript to the Madonna saga ensued that fall when John attended a tribute to Robert De Niro at the Museum of the Moving Image in New York. Following the ceremony, he joined Liza Minnelli, Matt Dillon, Jeremy Irons, and other Hollywood notables at a reception in the Tribeca Grill, a restaurant co-owned by De Niro. Sean Penn happened to be there as well. When John approached Penn to introduce himself, the actor said, "I know you—you owe me an apology." John walked away. The next day he received a funeral wreath of white roses with an accompanying note. "Johnny, my deepest sympathy," the card read. "I heard all about last night." It was signed "M."

Although they were never able to re-create the circumstances that had led them to a would-be night of bliss in a run-down Chicago motel room, John and Madonna remained friends. In 1995, at John's request, she contributed a lighthearted essay—"If I Were President"—as well as an original photograph, to the first issue of *George,* JFK Jr.'s new magazine. The photo, a portrait of Madonna in a skimpy blue bikini standing on a diving board, caught John's eye. "My God," he said to one of his editors, "she's better looking than Marilyn Monroe."

Sally Munro's successor as John's girlfriend was the same Christina Haag with whom he'd resided in the Benefit Street house at Brown. The Catholic daughter of a well-to-do New York marketing executive, Christina had known John since her sophomore year at the Brearley School, where she went after attending the Convent of the Sacred Heart. "Manhattan kids run around in packs," she said, "and we met because we were in the same group of friends. We'd known each other since the age of fifteen. John used to joke that our relationship was the longest courtship in history. He said this with a bit of irony because we'd first been friends and then housemates at Brown."

Entering Juilliard after graduating from Brown, Christina studied acting, supporting her thespian ambitions by working as a hatcheck girl at Elio's, an Italian restaurant, and as an assistant to Christine Thomson, a Seventh Avenue fashion designer. A radiant brunette, she was creative, stylish, and serious about her acting career. Her devotion to the stage infused John with the desire to give acting another chance. "John was fascinated by the process of acting," said Haag. "And he was good at it, particularly when it came to character roles. I don't know if being a professional actor could have fulfilled him over the long run, but if he hadn't been born a Kennedy, there's a good chance he would've earnestly pursued it as a career. Like any true actor, he found pleasure and release in being someone else. That's what acting is all about. John had grace, charisma, imagination, and a rare sense of ease. He had a terrific instinct for comedy. In other words, he possessed wonderful natural gifts for the stage."

John and Christina had often discussed the possibility of performing together in a play. Director Robin Saex, a friend of Christina's from Brown but at that time living in New York, encouraged the joint effort. After considering various choices, they settled on Brian Friel's *Winners,* a one-act drama about a seventeen-year-old Irish-Catholic youth engaged to marry his seventeen-year-old pregnant girlfriend. Set in Ireland, the play ends tragically with the death of both characters.

"John and I played around with the script in Robin Saex's apartment," noted Haag. "We all worked well together, so we decided to proceed. Robin contacted Nye Heron, executive director of the seventy-five-seat Irish Arts Center in Manhattan, as well as Kevin Breslin, Jimmy Breslin's son, and they agreed to coproduce the venture."

At first Christina felt she understood far more about acting than her male counterpart. "During rehearsals," she continued, "John began correcting my version of an Irish brogue. 'You poor boy,' I thought. 'What do you know about any of this?' At Juilliard I'd been studying with one of the best dialect coaches, Tim Monich, who coaches Tom Cruise among others. I was convinced I knew everything. I became rather self-righteous about the whole thing. John and I got entrenched and argued about the pronunciation of the vowel in the word *God.* Nye Heron finally stepped in and said, 'Actually, John is right.'"

Winners debuted on August 15, 1985. Neither Jackie nor Caroline went to see John perform, a sure sign that they disapproved of his participation in the play. Family members who showed their support by attending included Kara Kennedy, William Kennedy Smith, Robert F. Kennedy Jr., and Anthony Radziwill. "There were ten performances, one a week," said Nye Heron. "At Mrs. Onassis's request, there were no reviewers or reviews. Admission was by invitation only. I felt John did extremely well with his role, but I also realized he had no intention of making the stage his lifelong profession."

Although drama critics were banned from the show, photographers from *People* and other publications milled around outside the theater waiting for John to arrive on his ten-speed bike. ICM, one of the largest entertainment agencies in the country, sent representatives to scope out the talent. There was talk of moving the play to Broadway after its ten-week run, but John and Christina—romantically involved by now—had made other plans: Christina had another year to go at Juilliard, and John had law school on his mind. "Despite my decision to study law," he told a reporter for *People,* "I don't regret having performed in the play. I enjoyed every moment."

"John and I had been attracted to each other for ten years," said Christina, "and during the period of the play our attraction became irresistible. John was a wonderful person. He was fun. He embraced life. He took risks. He was funny and tender. He was great. He was also unbelievably messy. I'd always thought that I was messy. I forever misplaced things. But compared to John, I was the most organized person in the world. He would lose things all the time. Somehow I would know where those things were. John was trying to grow up. He was maturing, but he retained a certain boyishness—and that, too, was part of the charm."

Christina soon discovered, as others had before her, that it wasn't always easy to be the girlfriend of John Kennedy, primarily because of the vast amount of attention accorded him by press and public alike. Reporters and photographers constantly followed him around. It reached the point where he felt compelled to tote his own camera, using it to photograph the photographers. During the five years of his romantic involvement with Christina (late 1985 to early 1991), he would occasionally be spotted in the company of other women. A report or photo of the sighting would inevitably appear in the press, leading to stormy altercations with Christina. "We had our disagreements," she acknowledged. "He had a temper, but he was never disrespectful." She also had to contend with the public. Strangers routinely approached John for his autograph or, in some cases, to have their picture taken with him. Equally trying were the brazen few who would ask him personal questions about his family. Without appearing to be rude or uncomfortable, he dealt with the intrusions. His partner, however, never quite mastered the art.

A secondary impediment, though one that Christina managed to overcome, were John's ties to his mother and sister. "You had to earn Jackie's fondness," said Haag. "She had to feel that you were going to be good for John, and I guess she felt that way about me. We had a similar sensibility. Apart from John, she was incredibly encouraging and supportive of my acting career. We saw each other frequently. She had a wicked sense of humor and was a wonderful raconteur. I loved hearing her stories. After John and I split up, Jackie and I stayed in touch. She called whenever she saw me on television. She paid a condolence call when my father died. I corresponded with her when she became ill toward the end of her life."

Being present at a number of Kennedy family functions, Christina likewise befriended her boyfriend's sister. "John adored Caroline," she remarked. "He didn't trust a lot of people, but he trusted her. Caroline and I got along. We'd attended two of the same schools [Sacred Heart and Brearley], though at different times. Caroline was a much more analytical and practical person than John, which is one of the reasons he so often consulted with her before making important decisions. He also valued Maurice Tempelsman's advice. Maurice was very bright and wise and had a way of looking at the big picture. He and Jackie both thought law school a sound undertaking for John. But it was ultimately John's decision to go. As adroit and persuasive as Jackie happened to be, she couldn't force John, at age twenty-five or twenty-six, to do anything he didn't want to do. He seriously considered his mother's counsel and the suggestions of Maurice Tempelsman and Caroline, but in the end he made up his own mind."

If Christina Haag had artistic gifts, John brought athleticism and his craving for the outdoors into their relationship. "I learned courage from John," commented Christina. "He pushed me to take chances and showed me I could do certain things I didn't think I could do. I am not a jock, but we would ski together, and he taught me to scuba dive and water-ski. He also taught me how to drive. I was one of those New York girls who never bothered getting a driver's license until he and I became involved. John was a wonderful teacher—he was patient and encouraging. We hiked, backpacked, and Rollerbladed. I tried to ground him a bit with regard to extreme sports, but I understood his need to participate in certain activities. It worried me at times, but John knew what he was doing. For example, he used to go heli-skiing—a helicopter would deposit him at the top of a peak, and he'd shoot down the mountain at full speed. It relaxed him to face and overcome his fears."

Of the women in John's life, none knew him better or more intensely than Christina Haag. "John could sit down with kings, and he could sit down with paupers," she said, "and he could have a great time with all. He had compassion for people. He had his own kind of celebrity. He was more than handsome—he was beautiful. He was also somewhat goofy. Men who are just handsome become less and less so if that's all they possess. You can look at a handsome face only so long. John had much more than that. He had spirit, soul, and humor—he could laugh at himself and at the human condition. I loved him very much."

Rob Littell recalled the day John received a letter of rejection from Harvard Law School. "Well, I guess I won't be going *there*," John had said. Another law school also rejected his application, and he began to wonder whether he'd get in anywhere. "New York University Law School finally accepted him," said Littell, "and we all breathed a deep sigh of relief." Jackie did more than that. "Now I can die happy," she jokingly told friends. "She called me in Washington," said Vangie Bruce. "She was tickled pink that both her children were presently in law school. It seemed to justify all her efforts."

To celebrate, John went camping in New Mexico with Billy Way, a former classmate at Andover and fraternity brother at Brown with whom he'd remained on friendly terms. Aside from their shared education, the two young bons vivants looked a good deal alike. A great athlete—as were most of John's friends—Way excelled at tennis and enjoyed a brief career on the professional tennis circuit. He and John flew to Albuquerque, where they rented an RV and drove in the direction of Taos. They went rock climbing and did some hang-gliding. "At night," said Way, "instead of using the cramped RV kitchenette, we built campfires and prepared our dinner outdoors. One evening over dinner, John revealed that he'd always hoped to open his own restaurant. He wanted to call it The Last Supper.

"Of course, you never knew when John was pulling your chain. So when he suddenly said he thought he saw a pair of dim red eyes peering at us in the darkness, I told him he'd probably had too much to drink. But as I turned my head I saw the same thing he did—a pair of sickly crimson eyes attached to a large mass of fur half-hidden in the bushes. 'What is it?' I whispered. 'It looks like a fucking bear,' John whispered back. 'You're kidding me,' I said. 'I wish I were,' he responded. I asked if he thought we ought to try and make it back to the RV, which was parked maybe fifty yards away. John suggested we stay put and do nothing to alarm the creature. So we sat there like a couple of marble statues frozen in time. There was something funny but also very scary about the experience. After what seemed an eternity, although it was probably more like three minutes, we heard the beast lumber off in the opposite direction, probably as frightened of us as we were of it. At this point, we grabbed our gear, ran to the RV, and sped off in search of a nearby motel."

It wasn't the last time the two went camping together. In early April 1986 they took off for the Florida Keys in John's bright orange Karmann Ghia. "John had brought along his guitar," recalled Way. "We'd polished off a couple of six-packs, when he started singing the Rolling Stones song 'Sympathy for the Devil,' one of the most memorable lyrics of which goes: 'I shouted out, "Who killed the Kennedys?" / When after all it was you and me.' It was a chilling performance, I can assure you. John loved to shock people—he used to sing these lyrics to all his friends."

After the second camping trip, John spent a week sailing and relaxing at the family compound in Hyannis Port, where he'd gone to attend the April 26 nuptials of Maria Shriver and Arnold Schwarzenegger, at which Caroline Kennedy served as maid of honor. A neighbor who'd known JFK Jr. for years remembered seeing him every day that week, walking from his mother's house to the local post office. Bare-chested and wearing only a towel, his muscular frame shimmering in the sunlight, he'd amble along without a care in the world.

His tendency to show off came into play again on the day before the Schwarzenegger wedding at a reception hosted by Sargent and Eunice Shriver aboard a rented yacht. As the yacht sailed along the shoreline, John suddenly stripped down to his briefs, dived overboard, and swam back through the cold, choppy water to the Kennedy compound a mile away. The following day, at the postceremonial festivities, performer Grace Jones danced so provocatively with John that hundreds of guests stood still and watched.

Nearly three months later, on July 19, 1986, twenty-eight-year-old Caroline Kennedy married forty-one-year-old Ed Schlossberg in a ceremony that had all the earmarks of any Kennedy extravaganza, including clambakes, sailboat races, and touch football games. But while the broad outlines were similar, the fine details were somewhat different. The infor-

mal wedding invitations featured a pastel-shaded watercolor rendition of
the Kennedy compound topped by an announcement that the ceremony
would begin at 3:00 p.m. at Our Lady of Victory Roman Catholic
Church in Centerville, Massachusetts. Each invitation went out with a
six-page fact sheet prepared by Nancy Tuckerman. Invitation recipients
were asked *not* to divulge details of the wedding to members of the press.
White-and-gold Cadillac limousines, better suited to the needs of rock
stars, had been leased to deliver the principals to the freshly painted,
flower-studded country church. African-American fashion designer Willi
Smith had bedecked the ushers in violet linen jackets and white slacks;
the bridesmaids in two-piece, ankle-length, lavender and white floral-
patterned dresses; and the bridegroom in a loose-fitting navy blue linen
suit and silver tie. For a more conservative look, Jackie suggested that
Caroline turn to designer Carolina Herrera for her wedding gown. "I am
not going to get involved," Jackie told Herrera, "because Caroline is the
one who will wear it. I want her to be the happiest girl in the world." The
result was a wedding gown of white silk organza with a rounded neckline
and a twenty-five-foot train, the short sleeves and dress bottom ap-
pliquéd with shamrocks. As best man, John Jr. wore white slacks and a
deep violet jacket designed by Perry Ellis.

New York party organizer George Trescher, having successfully engi-
neered the Maria Shriver wedding, had been called back to do the same
for Caroline Kennedy. Two large tents, both filled with flickering Japanese lanterns and fragrant buckets of flowers, were pitched on the lawn
adjacent to Rose Kennedy's Hyannis Port home. One of the tents would
be used for the postceremony reception. The other would become the
site of a sit-down champagne dinner. Between the tents, under white
beach umbrellas, Trescher installed dozens of white wicker chairs and tables where guests could sit and socialize.

Author Christopher Mason, Trescher's assistant at the time, recalled
the day's preparations: "Because ninety-six-year-old Rose Kennedy was
going to watch part of the event from a wheelchair on her front porch,
we went to considerable lengths to make it a success. I had brought a
camera, but we were warned not to photograph Rose. I remember peek-

ing into a room in her house completely filled from floor to ceiling with hundreds of dolls from every nation. Glorious Foods did the food, and Robert Isabell did the flowers. Thanks to Jackie's involvement, the entire affair came off like a royal wedding. It was more elegant than the wedding of Maria Shriver and Arnold Schwarzenegger, which had terminated with the unveiling of a life-size statue of Arnold as Conan the Barbarian (Maria standing in his arms), a wedding present from Kurt Waldheim, the then president of Austria. It didn't help matters that Waldheim had recently been exposed in the press as a former Nazi supporter. There were no such slipups at Caroline's wedding."

An incident did occur, however, that generated a fair amount of speculation. "It was early in the morning on the day of the wedding," continued Mason, "and we were setting up tables and putting the finishing touches on the tents. John Jr. emerged from his mother's house with a towel wrapped around his waist He headed for the compound swimming pool, disposed of the towel, and plunged in. He splashed around for a while. The guys who worked for Glorious Foods and for Robert Isabell weren't exclusively gay, but they were mostly gay, as were many of the sixty or so waiters and the rest of the party staff. There were also a few female staff members present. It's safe to say that all eyes were riveted on John. He emerged from the pool, grabbed the towel, and draped it around his shoulders, not around his waist. Naked as a newborn but far better hung, he made his way past us and headed back to his mother's place—but not before creating a near riot among the help. In retrospect, I can only assume he enjoyed displaying his body for all the world to see."

John had made a speech at the bridal dinner the night before the wedding, offering a toast in which he alluded to how close he, Caroline, and Jackie had always been. "All our lives," he said, looking at Ed Schlossberg, "it has just been the three of us. Now there are four."

The "small, subdued" wedding ceremony that Caroline originally envisioned for herself had escalated into a major media event. Declared the "Wedding of the Year" by the press, it featured a guest list of 425 names, only 21 of them representing Ed Schlossberg's side of the family. Thousands of spectators, hundreds of press photographers and reporters, and a security force of more than a hundred clustered around the Centerville church to welcome the bride and groom. Among the invited guests were a dozen members of the Kennedy administration, including Ted Sorensen, John Kenneth Galbraith, Dave Powers, Arthur Schlesinger Jr., and Richard Goodwin. Although Caroline had never been an archetypal Kennedy off-spring—hyperactive, self-centered, and boisterous—practically every one of her Kennedy cousins had been invited. Also in attendance were many of Caroline's best friends: Maura Moynihan, Susan Minot, Arthur Sulzberger Jr. and his wife, Gail (of *New York Times* fame), and Alexandra Styron (the daughter of author William Styron). Artists Jasper Johns and Robert Rauschenberg had been invited by Ed Schlossberg. Lee Radziwill was there with her most recent suitor, architect Richard Meier, in what became one of their last public appearances together. Excluded from the festivities were the various members of the Bouvier family, most notably Maude Davis and Michelle Putnam, the elderly twin sisters of Jackie Kennedy's father. "Banning my mother and aunt had been Jackie's idea, not Caroline's," said John Davis. "It was a terrible insult, a real slap in the face to two women who'd always been there for her." Ironically, the one relative Jackie would have wanted at the wedding—her half-sister Janet Jennings Rutherford—had died of lung cancer the year before at age thirty-nine. Caroline Kennedy had been named godmother to one of Janet's young children.

Mary Tierney, covering the event for the *Chicago Tribune,* noted that members of the press were excluded from both the ceremony and the re-ception that followed. "We stood around outside the church and waited for the wedding party to emerge," she said. "Ed Schlossberg seemed out of place in his baggy, oversized suit. He looked like a ragbag. Caroline looked ungainly, as if she'd never worn a pair of high heels before. Her train was too long—she looked like she might topple over any moment. The dresses for the bridesmaids were unflattering. Jackie looked good in a fluid, pale lime green sheath, but as somebody said to me, 'If a masseuse pounded on you so many hours a day, you'd look good too.' She exited the church on Ted Kennedy's arm. Teddy had given away the bride. They posed for photographers, Jackie wiping away tears of joy. She looked better than her daughter, though her son was an absolute Adonis. He and his girlfriend, Christina Haag, made a truly fetching picture. Maria

Shriver was maid of honor. The singer Carly Simon, a neighbor of Jackie's on Martha's Vineyard, arrived half an hour late, when the service was nearly over. Mae Schlossberg, Ed's mother, tripped as she came out of the church. Her ankle swelled, and she had to leave the reception early."

Mae Schlossberg's sudden departure may have been her way of protesting what seemed an odd and insulting oversight on the part of the Kennedys. Conducted by the Rev. Donald A. MacMillan of Boston, the wedding service omitted any and all mention (or recognition) of the bridegroom's faith. No rabbi was present at the ceremony. There was no formal nuptial Mass, but that was the only concession the Kennedys made with regard to Ed Schlossberg's religion. "I suppose," commented Mary Tierney, "that this might have been done to satisfy Rose Kennedy, but, then again, Rose didn't even attend the service. In this day and age, one would look for some recognizable sign that this wasn't simply a case of one Catholic marrying another Catholic."

New York attorney Eugene Girden, a friend of Alfred and Mae Schlossberg, confirmed that they were upset by the marital arrangements: "Ed's father had nice things to say about Jackie. He liked her. But there was initial disappointment about the marriage to Caroline because of the religious issue, especially in having a Catholic wedding. It bothered them a great deal."

Film producer Susan Pollock, a Schlossberg family relation who now and then dined with Ed and Caroline, believed that the bridegroom actually converted to Catholicism in order to marry into the Kennedy family. "I know he takes Holy Communion," said Pollock, "which means that he would have had to convert. I also know he promised to bring up their children in the Catholic faith. On a personal level, I never particularly liked Ed. He's haughty and dull. He's very intelligent, but what does he do with it? His disavowal of Judaism must have hurt his parents."

Agnes Ash, at the time editor of the *Palm Beach Daily News,* evidently also thought Ed and Caroline "an odd coupling, not necessarily on religious grounds but because of their social differences. The elder Schlossbergs had a home in Palm Beach, but nobody there had ever heard of them. Knowing Jackie, I was surprised she so wholeheartedly endorsed the marriage. I'd heard that Ed, a self-confessed intellectual, liked giving Caroline electronic gadgets as gifts. He once gave her a VCR, which in those days was still a relatively novel item. It took her weeks to figure out how to operate it. Palm Beach residents weren't impressed by Caroline's choice in a husband. The general feeling was that she could've done better."

As to the broader question of religion, Pierre Salinger summed up the feeling of many when he remarked, "You might say that Ed Schlossberg didn't so much find Jesus Christ—more to the point, he found Caroline Kennedy."

Back at the Kennedy compound following the service, the guests were ushered through the reception line in the first tent, then into the second tent for a dinner of cold pea soup with mint, shrimp and apples, mixed vegetables, roast chicken with rice, cold sirloin of beef, salad, raspberries with ice cream, and a four-tiered wedding cake with chocolate filling and white icing. Ted Kennedy offered four toasts—the first to family matriarch Rose Kennedy, the second to Alfred and Mae Schlossberg, the third to the bride and groom, the last to Jackie Kennedy, "that extraordinarily gallant woman, Jack's only love. He would have been so proud of you today."

After dinner the guests repaired to the manicured compound lawn to listen to a band called Supreme Court. Marc Cohn, the band's lead singer who went on to enjoy a successful recording career, performed several numbers, followed by Carly Simon. At the end of the evening, George Plimpton, standing on the beach and armed with a megaphone, presented the bride and groom with his wedding present: an ornate fireworks display.

"The first part of it," explained Plimpton, "consisted of firework tributes to some of the relatives and guests at the wedding. There were about a dozen of them: a Chinese rose for Rose Kennedy, a sailboat for Teddy, a long column for lanky John Kenneth Galbraith, a bow tie for sartorial Arthur Schlesinger Jr. I wanted the fireworks to suggest the essence of each individual. And then there was the main body of the show, which I called 'What Ed Schlossberg Does.' There was a problem here because by the time this segment of the program took place, a classic Cape Cod fog bank had rolled in off the Atlantic. I'd tried to get the show moved up to beat the cloud cover, but Carly Simon's manager wouldn't allow her to sing earlier than scheduled. So she sang, and then the fog came in. And that's the one thing that kills fireworks. When fireworks go off in a cloud, they fizzle and die. It's like summer lightning. You see the colors but they're usually diffused. I was disappointed, though as it turned out everyone loved it because they felt it typified the theme. It faithfully represented 'What Ed Schlossberg Does.' What he did in life and for a living seemed to be a mystery to everyone. He was a sort of museum display coordinator, a poet, a conceptual artist. He did a little of everything and a lot of nothing. A recorded sound work of his, featured on an album called *Revolutions Per Minute,* was described by a *New York Times* review as 'an exceedingly boring meditation.' So, anyway, the obscuring effect in this case worked to the show's advantage."

The moment the last firework disappeared into the fog, Ed Schlossberg and his bride were off in their rock star limousine for Boston's Ritz-Carlton Hotel and the start of a monthlong honeymoon in Maui and Japan. In Tokyo, when a foreign correspondent asked the bride whether she wanted to be addressed as Caroline Kennedy or Caroline Schlossberg, she responded: "Just call me Caroline." Following their return to New York—Caroline to return to Columbia Law School and Ed to regenerate his career—they paid $2.5 million for a third-floor co-op apartment at 760 Park Avenue, at Park and 78th Street. The press had already begun referring to Schlossberg as "Mr. Caroline Kennedy," a designation he bore with dignity and good humor. Among New York's blue book elite, he was generally regarded as little more than a social climber, a nouveau riche Jewish "kid" who'd abandoned his faith to win the hand of an American princess. It didn't seem to matter that he made Caroline happy. During their five-year courtship, Ed had demonstrated his loyalty, his devotion, his basic decency, and his ability to protect Caroline. Above all, he shared with his bride a deep and abiding desire for a quiet, peaceful, and private existence. The last thing Caroline wanted was to duplicate the painful circumstances her mother had endured by marrying men like John F. Kennedy and Aristotle Onassis, personages of unfathomable power and bottomless wealth. Ed Schlossberg was not an adventurer.

Deeply in love with Caroline and totally monogamous, he offered her the marital constancy and stability Jackie had always sought but never found. If Schlossberg hadn't as yet achieved success in his career, that too would come. His marriage to Caroline legitimized his avant-garde sensibility, increased his commercial viability, and enabled him to gain access to organizations and businesses previously unavailable to him.

Several years into the marriage, Caroline's friend Alexandra Styron would say, "Caroline seems to have come into her own in the last few years. I've never seen her happier than she is now. She and Ed are as much in love as any married people I've ever known. They stick pretty close to home. Caroline is really an extremely unassuming, down-to-earth person."

Maura Moynihan recalled some of the parties at Ed and Caroline's house during their first years of marriage. "Caroline was in law school and studying hard," she said, "but on weekends when they stayed in town, they gave the best parties. Like Jackie, Caroline loved party games. Her favorites were Charades and Personalities. The game of Personalities is like 20 Questions, but you have to identify the names of historic figures. There was always a lot of wit and humor at their parties. I remember a birthday party Jackie threw for Caroline in late November 1986, after she and Ed had been married for several months. Guests were issued handheld silver masks, like an eighteenth-century masquerade ball. It sounds pretentious, but it wasn't. It was just a great deal of fun."

Caroline's marriage notwithstanding, she remained as protective as ever of her privacy. Unlike so many of her Kennedy relations, she doted on maintaining a low profile. Like her mother, she disdained the collective togetherness, the self-serving clannishness that typified the rest of the family. To protect her privacy, she changed her unlisted telephone number at least twice a year and refused to grant interviews to the press. She and Ed were known to banish any associates or employees who spoke about them to the press. When Leon Lobel, owner of Lobel's Prime Meats on the Upper East Side, admitted to a reporter that Caroline was a customer, she switched butchers, returning only after receiving Lobel's assurances that he wouldn't make the same mistake a second time. At Columbia, she frequently ate lunch at the West End on Broadway or at Anna Lee's, a small restaurant on Amsterdam Avenue and 116th Street, but when the press began casing these establishments for a photo op, she stopped going. Caroline's quest for anonymity was so pervasive that she rarely discussed her private life with anyone, even her closest friends. "She has always been extremely wary of people," said George Plimpton. "She fears being cultivated for her cachet rather than her charm."

"She's like her mother," claimed Jamie Auchincloss. "She never reveals anything about herself and finds it difficult to confide in people." Auchincloss had been banished from the inner sanctum for granting interviews to family biographers. John Davis, having suffered the same indignity for writing about the family, compared Caroline to her mother insofar as "both always drew out their companions instead of talking about themselves. Like Jackie, Caroline has the capacity of giving you the most extraordinary attention. She focuses on the person she's talking to with the most brutal intensity. The result is that you tell her everything about yourself, and she tells you nothing."

In late August 1986 John Jr. queued up with other first-year law students to enroll at NYU. On his first day of classes, in early September, he arrived by bike, a helmet on his head and a backpack stretched across his shoulders. Dozens of international news photographers showed up to commemorate the moment. Near the end of his first semester, John treated a half-dozen male classmates to dinner and cigars at the exclusive "21" Club. When one of his law school cronies celebrated a birthday, he hired a stripper to perform her act in the friend's apartment. He invited another classmate to accompany him to Boston to attend the Profile in Courage Awards, an annual ceremony that he and his sister hosted in memory of their father, and for which Ed Schlossberg designed the silver lantern that became the event's official insignia. Despite his privileged upbringing and occasional self-indulgences, John had an appreciation of the everyday, the ordinary. Rather than turn himself into an American icon, he struggled to develop his own identity, that of an active, caring, well-rounded individual.

It wasn't always easy. Con Edison turned off his electricity at one point because he'd neglected to pay his last three bills. Billy Way remembered visiting him just after the lights went out. "Burnt down candles were stuck to the carpeting," said Way. "Candles flickered in the bathroom and kitchen area. Two weeks' worth of dirty dishes were stacked in the sink. Having run out of dish- and silverware, he'd begun using paper plates and plastic utensils. Empty Chinese take-out food containers and pillowcases stuffed with dirty laundry were strewn throughout the apartment, along with dozens of legal textbooks. The amazing thing is that he could've easily afforded a maid. He refused to hire one, he said, because people would accuse him of being spoiled. Of course once his mother got wind of the situation, she stepped in and set the matter straight by bringing in an industrial cleaning crew to sanitize the place."

Riding his bike through a red light at 24th Street and Fifth Avenue one morning on his way to school, he was stopped by a traffic cop. The policeman requested identification, and John fished out his driver's license. Examining the license, the officer asked him, "Are you *the* John F. Kennedy Jr.?" "I suppose I am," he responded. "In that case," said the officer, "you're free to go." Meanwhile, a crowd had gathered on the sidewalk. Aware that they were watching him, he surprised the officer by saying "I broke the law—I'll take the summons." He ended up paying a $50 fine.

Although proud that John had gained entrance to a leading law school, Jackie continued to worry about her son's progress. Far more dedicated and disciplined in her own law school studies, Caroline set an academic pace her brother simply couldn't match. In many respects they were complete opposites. Caroline was closed off to outside stimulation, whereas John was open. Caroline was focused, while John was all over the place. Accident-prone, he seemed always to be suffering from some kind of athletic injury. His attention level, even when it came to the opposite sex, tended to drift.

Although attached to Christina Haag, his name constantly cropped up in the gossip columns in connection with other women. One evening he showed up for dinner at the Russian Tea Room with actress Julia Roberts, then returned later that night with another date. He was once spotted "putting the make" on Sinéad O'Connor. By way of response, the Irish performer broke his pen in two and stuffed the pieces into his pocket. On February 20, 1987, John attended supermodel Cindy Crawford's twenty-first birthday party, after which they went out on a few innocent dates. Maintaining a friendship with John, Cindy later posed for the cover of the first issue of *George*.

John went on several dates with twenty-two-year-old Click model Audra Avizienis. Interviewed by the *New York Post,* Avizienis insisted that she and JFK Jr. were "only friends." "He has a girlfriend," she said. "Or have they broken up?" Asked if she found him sexy, she described him in a way nobody else ever had, insisting that his "sex appeal" emanated from "a quiet sadness." There was "something sad and pensive about John."

Having evidently inherited his father's penchant for models and Hollywood celebrities, John also went out with film and television star Sarah Jessica Parker, who purportedly spent a weekend at Hyannis Port. According to Rob Littell, John used to tell the story of how the actress once met him by limousine at JFK Airport, wearing a mink coat with nothing underneath. "She denied the story," said Littell. "She claimed she never owned a mink coat and that she saw him at a different point in time. All I can say is that maybe it wasn't a mink, but John loved the story and came back all excited that day. He wasn't prone to exaggeration, especially when it came to women. If anything, he tended to underplay his romantic adventures. He didn't have to exaggerate—women constantly threw themselves at his feet."

John and Christina Haag lived together in Washington during the summer of 1987. Christina appeared in a play, and John clerked with the Civil Rights Division of the Justice Department, a plum position his grades didn't merit. Returning to New York in the fall to begin his second year of law school, he vacated his East Side apartment and switched back to the West Side, briefly subletting a two-bedroom apartment on 89th Street and West End Avenue. He took his breakfasts at the Jackson Hole on 85th Street and Columbus Avenue. Alexandra Eno, a waitress at the restaurant, recalled John as "exceedingly polite, never demanding. He sometimes came in with his girlfriend. I'd given birth to a daughter the year before, and he always asked about her—not in a conventional way, but because he truly seemed to care. I once brought her in, and he sat there playing little games with her. He loved children. He used to come in wearing sweats and then depart for NYU either by bike or subway. One day he told me he'd been the victim of a pickpocket on the train, and as a result preferred biking it to the Village. In warmer weather, he'd eat at one of the outdoor tables, oblivious to the stares. For the most part, people left him alone. New Yorkers generally don't make a fuss about celebrities. One morning a homeless guy sat down at his table and began to hassle him. I asked him to leave John alone. 'That's okay,' John said. 'He's not bothering me.' He bought the guy breakfast and chatted with him for a while. When they were done, he took out his wallet, handed the guy a ten-dollar bill, and wished him well. I was amazed."

While John was in his second year of law school, the FBI uncovered a kidnap plot directed at John. He refused the Bureau's offer to provide round-the-clock police protection. Baird Jones, an acquaintance of JFK Jr. and a former student at New York University School of Law, confirmed that such threats were commonplace. "I happened to know the people who ran the mail room at NYU," said Jones. "One day they showed me some of the threatening letters and postcards they'd received for John. His correspondents evidently didn't know his home address, so they'd communicate with him through the university. The cards and letters were addressed to 'John Kennedy Jr., c/o NYU.' It was incredible stuff, totally insane. One card stipulated that unless several million dollars changed hands, John would be kidnapped or killed. It was difficult to take any of these threats seriously, but on the other hand you couldn't very well ignore them. It surprised me that John was able to go about his business—ride his bike around town, get on the subway—without the slightest hesitation. If he harbored any reservations, he certainly never expressed them, at least not to me. Before he arrived at NYU, the security there seemed woefully lax. Anybody could gain access to the law school. After he matriculated, they began taking student ID cards seriously. You had to have one to get in anywhere. Then there were the incessant groupies, mostly women, who'd hang out in front of the law school hoping to meet John. The minute he emerged, they'd start yelling, 'Oh, look, it's John! Hey, John!' And then they'd go running up to him. They weren't dangerous, but they must have been annoying. I don't think it ever occurred to him that something could happen to him. When he biked down to NYU he always took the same route, so it wouldn't have been that difficult to waylay him. I find it notable that he loved those very popular James Bond 007 films. Perhaps he saw himself as James Bond, always able to extricate himself from precarious situations. The 007-syndrome is something he shared with his father. President Kennedy had been an avid reader of Ian Fleming's James Bond novels. The comparison speaks for itself."

Baird Jones and JFK Jr. occasionally saw each other during the latter's NYU Law School phase. "I became a party promoter, and I'd always invite John. There were parties at the Mudd Club, Limelight, and Horatio 113. He often brought Christina Haag. He never used drugs in my presence, but I heard he did a lot of coke and acid in those days. Strangers would come up to him and ask, 'Are you John Kennedy?' He'd deny it at first, but they'd persist and eventually the truth would emerge. People ass-kissed him all the time. The thing is, he was very much in touch with reality, which is more than I can say for a lot of other celebrities I met along the way. I knew Caroline Kennedy as well, though not after she married Ed Schlossberg. Prior to that, she used to hang out at Studio 54 with Peter Beard and other friends. She was a big-time drinker. After she married Schlossberg, she faded from the club scene. I had the feeling that unlike Caroline, John was a fish out of water in law school. I could never figure out why he went. He didn't seem to enjoy it, and he didn't strike me as somebody who wanted to pursue a legal career. My sense is that he was simply killing time, finding his way. He seemed torn between what he really wanted to do and what others expected him to do."

Although John didn't distinguish himself academically in law school the way his sister did, the combination of his name plus his go-with-the-flow, very congenial manner meant that he potentially—more than any other contemporary—was going to make a difference in the world. The "who" he was in tandem with his openness and accessibility would enable him to do great things. Like his father, he had the charisma to carry through an agenda. Being a Kennedy, he had a built-in support system.

Whatever else one might say about the family, they instilled in their progeny a sense of responsibility. And out of the crop of Kennedys of his generation, John Jr. was the one who could do it. His sister may have been steadier and more grounded, but John had the whole package: personality, appearance, and panache. By the age of twenty-seven, not yet quite there, he nevertheless realized he had an important role to play in life.

Chapter 14

———◆———

BABIES, BOOKS, BOYS, AND NEW GIRLFRIENDS

IN 1987 CAROLINE KENNEDY worked as a summer intern at Weiss, Rifkind, Wharton, and Garrison, her mother's longtime Manhattan law firm. In November of the same year, following a visit to her gynecologist, Caroline called her mother and said, "Congratulations, you're going to be a grandmother!" Her pregnancy ran its course without any of the complications that had afflicted Jackie during her childbearing years. "Caroline wasn't sick a day, not one day," Ed Schlossberg proudly informed a writer for *McCall's,* adding that his wife hadn't missed a single law school class or lecture. During her pregnancy, Caroline visited Rose Kennedy at Hyannis Port, her mother on Martha's Vineyard, and with Ed and her brother made several trips to Boston to oversee the design by Massachusetts sculptress Isabel McIlvain of a statue of President Kennedy that would stand in front of the gold-domed Massachusetts State House on Beacon Street. While in Boston, they visited a park near Harvard that had been dedicated to JFK on what would have been his seventieth birthday. And then of course there were the weekend sojourns to the Schlossberg home in Chester, Massachusetts.

In her third and final year at the Columbia University School of

Law, Caroline performed exceedingly well, graduating in the top 10 percent of her 346-member class. She was named a Stone Scholar, in honor of the late U.S. Supreme Court Chief Justice Harlan Fiske Stone, a distinguished law professor and dean at Columbia in the 1930s. Ed Schlossberg, John Jr., Jackie, Ted Kennedy, Nancy Tuckerman, and Marta Sgubin were among the 1,500 spectators at the May 17, 1988, law school graduation ceremony, held under a tent set up on the Columbia campus. Maurice Tempelsman attended as well, though he sat in a separate row from the others to avoid being seen with Jackie. Still a married man, his living arrangement with the former First Lady remained a subject of controversy with the media. A recently published photograph of Tempelsman emerging from Jackie's apartment building at eight in the morning had led Jacqueline to suggest that henceforth they appear separately at certain public events, particularly those involving the children.

Five weeks after receiving her law degree, on the afternoon of June 24, Caroline telephoned her obstetrician, Dr. Frederick W. Martens Jr., to report that she believed she'd gone into labor. Dr. Martens told her to begin timing her contractions and to practice some of the breathing techniques she and Ed had been taught in their Lamaze sessions. Several hours later, Jackie sent Maurice Tempelsman's Lincoln Town Car to 760 Park Avenue to collect Caroline and Ed and take them to New York Hospital–Cornell Medical Center. There, under the assumed name "Mrs. Sylva," Caroline checked into a seventh-floor $720-per-diem private room. A security guard, hired for the occasion by Jackie, was posted in the corridor outside the room with express orders to "keep out" any members of the press and unauthorized hospital personnel that might try to gain entrance.

Wearing her "lucky" double strand of pearls, Jacqueline arrived at the hospital at 10:00 p.m. and was greeted in the waiting room by her son-in-law, who promptly reappeared at his wife's bedside. Dressed in a blue suit, clutching a fistful of cigars, John joined his mother an hour later. When she heard that Caroline had been moved into a prenatal birthing room to be prepped for delivery, Jackie began to panic. Pacing back and forth, she recalled all her own birthing problems, keeping at it until John (according to a waiting room attendant) told her to "sit down and chill out."

At 3:00 a.m. on Saturday, June 25, 1988, Caroline gave birth to Rose Kennedy Schlossberg, a 7-pound, 12-ounce baby girl named after Rose Kennedy, a month short of her ninety-eighth birthday. Caroline had ordered the infant's layette at Cerutti, the same Madison Avenue children's boutique where she herself had been outfitted as a baby. Blankets, towels, shawls, sweaters, nightgowns, stretchies, bottles, and undershirts were delivered to the Schlossberg residence to be put away in the nursery. Calling her friends and relatives, Jackie's favorite refrain following the birth of Rose Schlossberg was: "I'm a grandmother—can you believe it?"

"We want to raise Rose the same way that Mrs. Kennedy brought up Caroline and John," Ed Schlossberg told *McCall's*. In accordance with this pronouncement—and to the immense disappointment of Schlossberg's parents—Rose Kennedy Schlossberg underwent her baptismal rites shortly after leaving the hospital. The ceremony, limited to members of the immediate family, took place at the Church of St. Thomas More with "Granny O"—Jackie's new press moniker—cradling the infant in her arms. Alfred Schlossberg's reaction to the ceremony, expressed to a former business associate, was a terse "Can you imagine a grandchild of mine being baptized? I can't."

At home again, Caroline resumed a strict study regimen in preparation for the New York State bar exam required of all statewide practicing attorneys. She took the test in mid-August and passed on her first attempt. Rudolf Nureyev happened to be at Lee Radziwill's house in East Hampton in late August when Caroline brought Rose for a visit. "Why for God's sakes did you name your baby Rose?" he asked Caroline. "I didn't name her," she responded. "My mother did." Nureyev later told an acquaintance, "I can't understand why Jackie would name her granddaughter after Rose Kennedy—she can't stand the old bat." When Caroline brought the baby to Newport to show her off to Janet Auchincloss, Jackie's mother became confused. Suffering from Alzheimer's disease, Janet at first didn't recognize Caroline and didn't understand whose baby it was. Gradually, according to Jan Pottker, Janet's biographer, "the fog lifted, and she told Caroline, 'She's lovely!'"

The Schlossbergs hired a full-time sleep-in nanny for Rose. Caroline spent an hour each day working out with a personal coach at the Trainer's

Edge on Third Avenue. Ed Schlossberg and Jackie signed up at the same gym. Caroline augmented her exercise program by going for Cyclax facials and blowouts. On nanny's day off, she took the baby for long strolls through Central Park. Once when a news photographer snapped a picture of Caroline pushing the baby carriage, she let loose with a verbal tirade. On seeing the picture in the press, Bouvier Beale, Jackie's cousin, remarked: "If Jacqueline hadn't married that Irishman, we all could have sunk into shabby gentility, and nobody would have been the wiser. I mean, it's distressing to have the focus of publicity placed on a very average situation, and just because of the act of marriage."

"Caroline's attitude regarding the press seemed totally unrealistic," said Andy Warhol. "It reminded me of Greta Garbo—'I want to be left alone!' If you're a bona fide celebrity, you can't very well dictate terms. You can't say, 'Now you can take my picture, and now you can't.' It doesn't work that way."

The full-time nanny freed Caroline to begin research on her first book, *In Our Defense: The Bill of Rights in Action,* which she coauthored with Ellen Alderman, a Columbia University Law School classmate. Published in February 1991 by William Morrow & Co. to coincide with the two hundredth anniversary of the ratification of the Bill of Rights, the book examines seventeen court cases that illustrate the intricacies of the first ten amendments to the Constitution. Research for the project initially took the coauthors from the Hopi Indian Reservation in rural Northern California to death row at Arizona State Penitentiary for a case involving two brothers whose father had been convicted of murdering several members of an Arizona family. Having helped their father to escape from prison, the brothers were themselves wrongfully convicted of first-degree murder. The conviction was eventually overturned. Identifying herself as Caroline Kennedy in her byline on the book (as opposed to Caroline Kennedy Schlossberg), she and Alderman made publicity tour appearances on *Good Morning America* and *Larry King Live.* Interviewers were told in advance *not* to ask Caroline "personal questions." *In Our Defense* enjoyed a run on the *New York Times* nonfiction bestseller list, thanks in part to book jacket testimonials from the likes of media man Bill Moyers and former Texas congresswoman Barbara Jordan.

The birth of a niece, for which John Jr. had flown from Los Angeles to New York, marked the start of an intriguing period in his life. He and Christina Haag had taken a summer (1988) rental on a house in Venice Beach, California. She was appearing in a play, *Sleeping with the Past,* at the Tiffany Theater. He'd been hired as a $1,000-a-week summer associate with the prestigious Los Angeles law firm of Manatt, Phelps, Rosenberg & Phillips, located on Olympic Boulevard in Century City. Senior partner Charles Manatt, former national chairman of the Democratic Party, had been a political supporter of Ted Kennedy. The firm gave a party to welcome their new summer employees, at which John received more than his share of attention from female members of the staff. "The attention continued throughout John's time in the firm," said another summer associate. "The women there—lawyers, recruits, interns, secretaries, receptionists, and paralegals—were eager as hell to gain access to him. They talked about nothing else that summer. Some of them wanted him for his connections, others for his matinee-idol sex appeal. Certain men in the firm resented him for his popularity among the women and grumbled about his inability to handle the most elementary legal assignments. They were mistaken—he did everything asked of him and did it well. That's not to say that he had the makings of another Clarence Darrow, or that he planned on spending the rest of his born days toiling for a corporate law firm. But to his credit, he kept his nose to the grindstone and was always willing to lend a helping hand."

The truth is that John's attention that summer was fully given over to his live-in girlfriend. "John and I talked about spending our lives together, and talked about what that would be like," said Christina Haag. "I'd heard that Jackie thought John and I should marry. I heard from people close to her that she felt we made a good team. But I'm not sure John was ready for marriage, and I probably wasn't either. He had to find his place in the world—and he didn't until he published *George.* If a man's to take marriage seriously, he needs to feel his life is in order. Publishing *George* was something he did for himself—it came about as a result of his own initiative. Legal work wasn't his calling. Law school trained him to think, but it was merely a stepping-stone."

While in Los Angeles, John joined a gym called the Sports Club, playing a lot of racquetball and adhering to an exercise and weightlifting program drawn up for him by Arnold Schwarzenegger. Al Block, a part-time trainer at the gym, recalled that John could press 250 pounds. "After his workout and shower," said Block, "he'd stand around the locker room in the buff and stare at himself in the full-length mirror. He'd spend half an hour combing his hair. He even combed his chest hair. He wasn't the least bit modest. If anything, he seemed a showoff." When John wasn't working out, he and Christina Haag attended Hollywood parties and went dancing at the Flaming Colossus. They went camping and scuba diving. They swam in the Pacific and Rollerbladed along the boardwalk in Venice. They went to film premieres and dinner parties. That summer John developed a taste for tequila. More than once he drank himself into a happy stupor. He liked Dominican cigars and habitually smoked one cigarette a day.

Among the people JFK Jr. occasionally hung out with in Hollywood was Marlee Matlin, the twenty-two-year-old deaf actress who'd won the Academy Award for Best Actress in 1987 for her role in *Children of a Lesser God.* John and his sister Caroline had first met Marlee in New York in the early '80s at Eunice Shriver's Special Olympics. They'd seen her again at a fund-raiser for Jean Kennedy Smith's Very Special Arts, a program founded in 1974 to help promote the interests of the mentally disabled. Jack Jason, a special assistant to the actress, couldn't help but observe that Marlee and John were drawn to each other, though their relationship never blossomed into a romance. "Still," said Jason, "they very much enjoyed each other's company. I was walking with Marlee in New York one day in the early nineties when John, riding by in a car, spotted us and pulled over. He and Marlee began hugging and kissing like long-lost lovers. John had the ability to grab people's attention without trying. He wasn't a great intellect—that was his sister's main characteristic—but he had personality. There was something special about him. He was a really good guy. He was as close to being a mensch as a Catholic could get without being Jewish."

In July John took time off to introduce his uncle Ted Kennedy at the

1988 Democratic National Convention in Atlanta, Georgia. Invoking his father's name, John delivered a short speech that electrified the audience. "Over a quarter of a century ago," he began, "my father stood before you to accept the nomination for the presidency of the United States." Walter Isaacson wrote in *Time* magazine that it felt like the roof of the Omni Auditorium would fall in "from the sudden drop in air pressure caused by the simultaneous sharp intake of so many thousands of breaths." It wasn't so much what John said, but rather how he said it. "I heard that speech," said Pierre Salinger, "and I thought, 'Oh, my God. This guy is going to run for office one day. He's got the style and the look.' I think it occurred to everyone who watched the speech on television or in person that the small boy once called 'John-John' had grown into a man. He stole the show. When he finished, he received a three-minute standing ovation. John had as much charisma as his father, maybe more. I don't know how well he would've performed on a Mensa test, but I subscribe to the theory that there are different kinds of intelligence. John had political intelligence. He understood people and he had showmanship, a quality that probably emanated from his talent as an actor. If I had to compare him to a well-known politician, it would be Ronald Reagan. They had different political beliefs but a similar sensibility."

Actor Alec Baldwin, who later became friendly with John, viewed the speech on television and was sold on JFK Jr.'s prowess as a budding political figure. "Whatever this guy runs for, he's going to win," said Baldwin. "That's what I thought. There was no doubt in my mind that whatever he ran for, senator or governor or whatever, he'd win hands down."

Former senator George Smathers approached JFK Jr. at a postconvention reception and told him, "You ought to enter politics. You've got the goods." Surrounded by reporters, John deflected questions about his political future by providing ambiguous answers. "I wouldn't want to think too far into the future," he ventured. "Going into politics is like going into the military. It takes a certain toll on your personality and on your family life."

While still in Atlanta he went dancing one evening with actors Ally Sheedy and Rob Lowe at a local club called Rupert's. Spotted by a reporter from *The Boston Globe*, he was again asked about his future plans.

"Right now," he said, "I've got to get my law degree. Until then, there's no point in conjecturing. For all I know, I might end up opening a hot-dog stand in front of the Metropolitan Museum of Art."

Despite his seeming reluctance, JFK Jr. became more immersed in the "family business" than he'd ever been. Back in New York that September—following his nocturnal encounter with Madonna in Chicago—John began his last year of law school, taking time off to make several joint campaign appearances in Pennsylvania with Democratic Party presidential candidate Michael Dukakis. "I don't know if he had any political ambitions," said Dukakis, "but John had everything it took to be a success in public life." He next went to Boston to campaign for Joe Kennedy II in his race to regain the congressional seat he'd taken over in 1986. Besides managing Uncle Ted's latest senatorial run, Joe had helped establish the Citizens Energy Corporation, a nonprofit organization that made shrewd business deals in oil sales (much of it Kennedy controlled), and then used the profits to provide inexpensive home-heating fuel to the poor. With his family's backing—including John's—Joe won a convincing victory in 1988.

Instead of parlaying his latest success into a promising political future, Joe made a fatal mistake. In March 1989 he announced that he and his wife of ten years, the socially prominent Sheila Rauch, were separating. "This has been a very painful day for me and my family," he proclaimed. "As a father, my principal obligation and deepest personal desire is to assist my children through the most difficult time in their lives." Joe's compassionate words were washed away by what happened next. Sheila Rauch's subsequent book, *Shattered Faith,* disclosed in convincing detail the manner in which Joe "browbeat and bullied" his wife into agreeing to annul their marriage, paving the way for her now no-longer husband to remarry. Once again Joe had brought embarrassment and dishonor to his very public family.

Unaware of the circumstances surrounding Joe's disintegrating marriage, JFK Jr. traveled from Boston to Providence to campaign on behalf of Ted's son Patrick Kennedy. At twenty-one, while still a junior at Providence College, Patrick had decided to run for a seat in the Rhode Island state legislature. Round shouldered and puffy cheeked, Patrick had two years earlier spent time in a drug- and alcohol-abuse rehabilitation center. An admitted depressive (yet, like Joe Kennedy, given to outbursts of anger), Patrick—often tongue-tied and mystified by syntax—nevertheless had plenty of campaign cash and ready access to the more prominent members of the clan, factors that ultimately outweighed his overall lack of charm and experience.

Independent filmmaker Josh Seftel produced a documentary, *Taking On the Kennedys,* which referred to Patrick's 1988 campaign and covered his successful bid in the Rhode Island congressional race of 1994, for which the 1988 campaign was a mere preliminary. Seftel recalled Caroline Kennedy's participation in both campaigns, her being flown to Providence to give a press conference at which one journalist asked her, "So how does it feel to be Caroline Kennedy?" "She was all business," said Seftel. More noteworthy was John Jr.'s participation, which consisted of sitting outside the polling booths and having his picture taken (by one of Patrick's assistants) with would-be voters. Seftel remembered one woman "hugging John, inhaling his air, sniffing his skin, and departing with a satisfied smile on her face." The Polaroid ploy worked so well in 1988 that Patrick used it again in 1994.

Daryl West, Patrick Kennedy's biographer, recounted a chance meeting in Providence in 1988 between JFK Jr. and Jack Skeffington, who was the incumbent, as well as Patrick's opponent on the ballot. "I'm John Kennedy," JFK Jr. said to Skeffington. "I know who you are, John," replied Skeffington. "Jack, I'm going to tell you something," John continued. "I don't like being here. I don't think it's fair for me to be here. I want you to know the only reason I'm here is for my cousin. But I don't believe in it. I didn't want to be here, and I don't think it's fair. This is your neighborhood." At the end of his brief soliloquy, John extended his hand and said, "Good luck to you, Jack." Amazed by John's candor, Skeffington later commented that what most impressed him about JFK Jr. was his "common touch."

JFK Jr.'s inherent sense of decency encouraged Billy Way to say of him, "If you didn't know who John was, you wouldn't know who he was." Way recalled a time when he and John were walking down Madison Avenue together. "John found a five-dollar bill on the sidewalk," said

Way, "and he went running down the street asking everyone he passed if they'd lost some money. He finally found the guy who'd dropped it."

As for politics, Way felt that John "was still exploring options. When he returned to New York after Patrick Kennedy's victorious 1988 campaign in Rhode Island, he told me how much he disliked posing for photos with strangers just to get their vote. Although he certainly wasn't shy, I think he shared with his father a kind of early reticence about constantly being in the public eye. I remember reading that when President Kennedy first got into the field of politics they practically had to shove him out on stage to give a speech. John Jr. enjoyed being in the spotlight, just not all the time. But John had an amazing talent for getting along with all sorts of people, which is a prerequisite for anyone considering a career in public service. He had law school buddies, pals in the acting profession, friends from his days in college such as myself, Rob Littell, Richard Wiese, John Hare, Dan Samson, Pat Manocchia, Billy Noonan, and Chris Overbeck. And somehow he had the ability to juggle all these different contingents like no one else."

Dave Powers remembered 1988 as the twenty-five-year anniversary of John F. Kennedy's assassination. "To my surprise," said Powers, "Jackie decided that neither she nor her children would participate in any public events surrounding the assassination. She refused to allow the JFK Center for the Performing Arts in conjunction with ABC Television to present a filmed retrospective as a remembrance of the twenty-fifth anniversary. Ted Kennedy and the rest of the family were eager to participate, but Jackie's voice ultimately prevailed, and the project never materialized. We scheduled several events at the JFK Library in Boston and invited Caroline and John Jr. to take part, but Jackie again intervened, and the kids eventually begged off."

Although John Jr. lacked his sister's direct memory of their father, he acquired a composite memory based on what he'd read and been told by those that had known and worked with the late president. "John rarely discussed the subject with me," said Christina Haag, "but he had a lot of curiosity about his father and feelings of longing for him. But he was basically well adjusted. He didn't allow any of this to interfere with his pursuit of happiness."

The same could not be said for Caroline, whose nature was such that she tended to become contemplative and morose at the mere mention of her father's assassination. She—more than John—supported Jackie's decision to commemorate the twenty-fifth anniversary privately. On November 22, 1988, Jackie, Caroline, and John Jr. attended an 8:30 a.m. private Mass at St. Thomas More. They attended no public ceremony and issued no public statement in connection with the occasion.

"Get your eyes off that man's extraordinarily defined thighs . . . ! Measure them three, four feet around . . . They are fantastic . . . Legend has it that if he lived in Tahiti instead of Manhattan, he could crack coconuts with them. Get your eyes off that man's derriere! We saw your gaze wandering back there. It is true that columnist Liz Smith has noted that the boy 'has gorgeous buns,' but you've got to remember: He has a mind too." Thus read the September 12, 1988, issue of *People,* the "Sexiest Man Alive" issue with John F. Kennedy Jr. on the front cover and six pages of interior text and photographs. A year earlier the same magazine anointed him "America's Most Eligible Bachelor," a title similarly conferred by *US* magazine. But it was the "Sexiest Man Alive" accolade—in one of the magazine's most widely distributed issues—that catapulted JFK Jr. from mere supercelebrity status to the very summit of Mt. Olympus.

An exasperated Jacqueline Onassis told friends that by "making John out to be a Hollywood hunk, the magazine has hurt his reputation. Nobody will take him seriously after this." George Plimpton attended a dinner party at Jackie's house in late September and remembered Jackie carrying on about John for more than an hour. "The guest list," said Plimpton, "included poet Mark Strand, Prince Michael and Princess Marina of Greece, Jayne Wrightsman, and the Maharani of Jaipur. Jackie was jabbering away about how potentially damaging the article could be should John ever want to pursue a political career. I think it marked the first time I'd ever heard her mention such a possibility. Suddenly the front door opened, and in walked John Jr. wearing a backpack. Jackie stopped talking. John said to her, 'Are you discussing me again?' Jackie giggled. John stayed for no more than ten minutes. After he went, Jackie picked up where she'd left off."

"Things changed for John after he became the cover story as the 'Sexiest Man Alive,'" said Christina Haag. "He became the subject of even more public attention than he'd received before. He continued to try to live his life as he always had, as if there was nothing special about him, but it became impossible."

That John could ever have lived his life as if "there was nothing special about him" seems doubtful. What might have changed as a result of the article—an article about which his best friends constantly teased him—is that the public now began to recognize him for what he was rather than what he'd been. No longer merely the son of a fallen world leader, he'd begun to forge his own identity, an identity enlivened both by his appearance before the Democratic National Convention and by the fact that he was exceedingly photogenic, that he personified the image of pure and perfect beauty first fostered by the ancient Greeks. In the parlance of Hollywood film agents, "the camera loved him."

"Listen," he told Barbara Walters in the course of a television interview, "people can say a lot worse things about you than you're attractive and you look good in a bathing suit."

In 1987 John attended a Halloween party as "Golden Boy," covered with gold glitter and clad only in a loincloth. In 1989 he attended the same Halloween party as Michelangelo's David, wearing only what looked like a large fig leaf, his torso coated with talcum powder.

New York public relations specialist R. Couri Hay recalled John "proudly strutting around the Aspen Club in Colorado and Plus One in New York in nothing but his birthday suit." Martha's Vineyard resident Stuart Own recalled that John often frequented the nude beach in Gay Head, a half mile from his mother's house. Shelley Shusteroff, a New York travel agent and photographer, captured John on film as he walked around in the buff on the beach at St. Bart's in the French West Indies. The nude photographs, for which she was allegedly offered a six-figure fee, were never published. A photograph that did appear in the press showed a shirtless John strolling around Times Square wearing shorts, sneakers, and a backpack.

One of the people most responsible for helping mold John's physique and keeping him in prime shape was Radu Teodorescu, whose Physical

Culture Studio on West 57th Street in Manhattan soon became JFK Jr.'s second home. A Romanian by birth, Radu's star-studded clientele included such names as Cindy Crawford, Regis Philbin, Matthew Broderick, Vanessa Williams, and Bianca Jagger. With a well-deserved reputation as "the toughest personal trainer in town," Radu gradually established a friendship with John. "I became his personal trainer in 1985," he said, "but we also became friends outside the gym. Through John I met and trained his cousin Tony Radziwill. The three of us did things together. One weekend we went out in East Hampton, where I also had a gym, and climbed the sand dunes. Some of the dunes were fifteen to twenty feet in height. We'd clamber to the top, then jump off. Tony Radziwill hesitated at first, so I told him to slide down the embankment. John, who was fearless and did everything, convinced him to jump, and he did."

Radu observed, as others had before him, that John enjoyed being pushed to extremes. "He had enormous resolve," said Radu. "I had him doing exercises on the rings, the trapeze, the high bar, and on the mat. He didn't exercise simply to enhance his appearance, but because he wanted to learn how to control his body. Mother Nature blessed him with good looks and a strong physique. He wanted to go beyond that, to understand how the body functioned. He was a risk taker, but he didn't undertake dangerous pursuits without first preparing himself for them. He took himself seriously enough to exercise care, so that even when it appeared he was being reckless, he really wasn't. He used to ride his bike through the streets of New York like a madman, weaving in and out of traffic at top speed. He did the same on Rollerblades. But for the most part, he knew what he was doing."

Accident prone, John nevertheless took his spills. He ripped open his knee one day while Rollerblading in Central Park. Bleeding profusely, he called Radu to his apartment to gauge the extent of the damage. When Radu advised him to head for the nearest emergency room to have the wound stitched, John refused. He didn't want to have the accident reported in the press.

"John wanted to enjoy his life fully," said Radu. "Because of his family history—the assassinations of his father and uncle—I would guess that he had the idea in his head that he wouldn't die in a quiet way. He was like a comet. He lived in the moment. He had a sense of his own magnitude, but he had a rudimentary way about him. I once said to him, 'John, does it ever cross your mind that you might be president one day?' 'I'm making no predictions,' he responded. 'We'll see what happens.'"

In looking back on John's life, Radu firmly believed that "Jackie was the only one who could have saved him from his fate. She would have made certain that he was safe. She understood his limitations almost better than he did." It was Jackie who, in the fall of 1988, insisted that John give up the piloting lessons he'd begun to take as early as 1982. Unimpressed by his argument that in six years he'd put in only fifty hours of accumulated flight time, almost all with an instructor by his side, Jackie cited Alexander Onassis's untimely death as an example of the folly of flight.

"In no uncertain terms," said Yusha Auchincloss, "Jackie laid down the law. John wasn't going to take any more aviation lessons, not as long as she could help it."

John withdrew from his part-time flight lessons and threw himself into other adventures. He purchased three kayaks, housing one at Martha's Vineyard, the others at the Hudson River Boathouse in TriBeCa. Jim Wetteroth, president of the boathouse, recalled that John would "sometimes bring a friend along and let him use the second kayak. He would usually go out on his own, mostly in the evening. He was a very competent and vigorous young man. He'd kayak out on the Hudson for an hour, and an hour back. He did it as a kind of workout. He was friendly with the other members of the boathouse, but he didn't go out of his way to make friends. He was our only true celebrity. The rest of us pretty much left him alone. He was just another person who loved to kayak. I suspect that's what he enjoyed most about the sport—being out on the water and not having to put up with the rest of the world."

Fred Davenport, a New York City public school teacher, went kayaking with John in East Hampton on several occasions. "We went kayaking in the ocean," said Davenport, "and on this particular day the waves were pretty rough. They were crashing ashore. When they're that strong they can drag you out of the kayak and you can get hurt. I wanted to quit, but

John pushed ahead. I suddenly realized that he wasn't wearing a life-jacket. It dawned on me how much on the edge he liked to live. I thought to myself, 'This guy is crazy—he's going to get into trouble someday.' And of course he did, but it happened in a plane, not a kayak."

Radu Teodorescu reported a similar incident when he joined John and several of John's friends on a kayak trip along the East River. "There's a spot near Roosevelt Island where the current is very tricky," said Radu. "Anybody who boats in that area knows about it. Sailboats and motorboats always steer clear of this spot, because it's so dangerous. But being the consummate daredevil, John wanted to go straight through it. We followed him that day because we didn't want to desert him. Suddenly our kayaks began spinning around. We came close to hitting each other and capsizing. We were yelling and screaming and paddling like mad to get out of there. I don't mind admitting that I was scared to death, because if you capsize in that kind of situation, you risk getting swept under. We finally succeeded in paddling our way out of the current. Once we hit calm water, somebody said to John, 'Why the hell did you insist on doing that?' 'Because it was fun,' said John, 'wasn't it?' That was so typical of him. He liked to push people just a little further—and himself as well."

Rob Littell admired JFK Jr. for his open-mindedness, his worldliness, and the "mature" way in which he accepted individuals on their own merit. "Here's a guy," he said, "who had a wealth of experiences. He grew up waterskiing behind converted Canadian destroyers in the Greek Isles, kayaked on the Red Sea, and hung out with Mother Teresa, Muhammad Ali, and the Dalai Lama. Later on he got to know Fidel Castro, President Clinton, and various members of the Rockefeller family. All that rubbed off on him. He knew about all sorts of sexual practices at a time when I didn't know how to unhook a girl's bra, for crying out loud. He had great relationships with all kinds of girlfriends. I learned a great deal from him. For example, I was an outspoken homophobe when I first met him at Brown, but John straightened me out. It took me ten years to get over my homophobia, to accept gays for who they are. He had matured on all these levels long before I did. His philosophy was, if you want to love somebody regardless of that person's sexuality, go ahead. But did he ever have sexual experiences with other men? Certainly not on purpose."

Littell's inconclusive determination as to John's apparently complex sexuality doesn't preclude other possibilities, particularly given his "openness" to a variety of experiences. In October 1988, while in Washington to attend a Democratic Party fund-raiser at the Georgetown home of Pamela Harriman—where he'd briefly lived with his mother and sister following JFK's assassination—John visited a Live Sex Live emporium and purchased some two dozen "triple-X" videos. Several of them, according to Marcus Brown, the store's proprietor, were gay films. "He'd just been named 'Sexiest Man Alive,'" said Brown, "so I figured, 'Hey, why not?'"

Cathy Griffin, a West Coast journalist and regular contributor to Liz Smith's nationally syndicated column, spoke with a friend of John's from Brown who'd moved to New York after graduation and transformed himself into a "celebrity" transvestite under the name "Vaginal Cream Davis." According to Griffin, John loved to party with Davis and had more than a passing interest in the New York world of gays, transsexuals, and transvestites. "John was captivated by Davis and his (or her) crowd. He used to hang out with them at Xenon, surrounded by glitterati such as Halston, Liza Minnelli, Jerry Hall, and Mick Jagger. They also did all the gay bars together: Private Eyes, Underground, and Rex. JFK Jr. loved that whole scene." John's mother once gave a party at her Martha's Vineyard estate for twenty-five of her Kennedy nephews and nieces, to which John invited several of his new transvestite acquaintances. "John's guests were so attractive and feminine," said one party attendee, "nobody there realized or even thought about their true gender. For all their supposed sophistication, the Kennedys were straight as a gate and completely unenlightened in terms of contemporary culture. John Jr. was the sole exception."

According to George Wayne, a columnist, photographer, and social arbiter for *Paper* magazine and *Vanity Fair,* "John Kennedy Jr. was one of the most gender-confused personalities of our time. His bisexuality was legendary in nightlife circles up and down the eastern seaboard—in Manhattan, in the Hamptons, on Cape Cod." The late journalist Doris

Lilly had encountered John on several occasions. "I imagine," she said, "that he was fantasized over by gay men and straight women alike. A lot of people projected their subliminal thoughts onto him. I'd always been pretty good friends with billionaire publisher Malcolm Forbes, who'd long before come out of the closet. I once attended a *Forbes* magazine office party, where I met a very attractive young husband and wife team. After the party, Malcolm told me that JFK Jr. had participated in an orgy with the couple—he'd gone to bed with the woman and performed a homosexual act with the man. I don't know if the story's true, but on the other hand I never knew Malcolm Forbes to lie."

More exacting testimony came from Holly Woodlawn, a transsexual and Andy Warhol superstar, whom John first met at Studio 54. "We used to dance together all the time," said Woodlawn. "'You're gorgeous,' he told me. He was tall, and I liked tall men. He looked sexy and sweet. He knew who and what I was. I think he had a proclivity for 'trannies.' I know he was attracted to me because when we danced, he played with my ass and stuff. He kissed me on the dance floor, and I kissed him back. I thought, 'My God, President John F. Kennedy's son is kissing me.' My pussy was aglow, if you know what I mean. It was Studio 54, and all sorts of things were going down in the bathroom. He asked for my telephone number. 'I'm listed,' I told him. The first time he called, I hung up on him, because I didn't believe it was John. He called me back. We frequently talked on the phone, mostly small talk. 'How're you doing, what are you up to?' I got the idea that he liked me and wanted to have sex. He was intrigued by the fact that I was a transsexual. I would've gone to bed with him, but it never came to that. I wanted to put all this in my autobiography, but my publishers were afraid of being sued. It wouldn't have surprised me a bit to learn that John was bisexual."

Jean Christian Massard, a physical therapist from France, encountered John at a New York party in October 1988. "The night after we met, John and I went to a downtown club called Area," said Massard. "As word spread that John F. Kennedy Jr. was in the club, all sorts of girls joined us at the bar. They were pushing and shoving each other to get near us—or should I say, near John. He knew the owner of Area, a fellow named Eric Goode, who saw the mob scene and moved us to a quiet table. Over the next few weeks, we made the rounds together. We became friendly and discussed a number of subjects, including sexuality. I admitted that I was bisexual. He confided—and I believed him—that he'd had several flings with men. One evening he called and invited me to his apartment. I'm quite certain he wanted to have sex, because he made it clear that we'd be alone. As I had a previous engagement that night, I asked him if I could take a rain check. I subsequently misplaced his phone number, and he never called me back, so we never got together. But I'm sure he indulged in gay sex from time to time. He traveled in a fast crowd. He could have had practically any woman on the face of the earth. Women weren't much of a challenge for him, so he took it to the next level. There's nothing wrong or even unusual about it. Rock stars and leading Hollywood men do it all the time."

Richard duPont, who'd known John since the late 1970s, recounted an episode that ensued during roughly the same period. "I wasn't one of John Jr.'s closest pals, but we did see each other occasionally. We both knew Countess Christina 'Titi' Wachtmeister, who'd been married to the King of Sweden, and whose father had been the Swedish ambassador to the United States. She had an apartment in the East 60s and a job doing public relations for Absolut, the vodka manufacturing and distribution company. We used to go up to her place and drink. On one occasion she undressed in front of us and put on some cheesy pink lingerie that Andy Warhol had signed and given her as a birthday present. I had the feeling she wanted to make it with John, but I have no idea if they ever indulged.

"What I do know is that one night a bunch of us went out to Xenon with Fred Hughes, president of Andy Warhol Enterprises. John and Fred knew each other. John—as well as his sister Caroline—attended parties at Fred's house. He owned a brownstone on Lexington Avenue, which I think had once belonged to Andy Warhol. At any rate, the group at Xenon that night included Fred, John, myself, and maybe a half-dozen titled British aristocrats, half of them gay. I hit it off with one of the guys, Lord Something-or-other. At about three in the morning, we all headed back to Fred's house. Fred's bedroom was upstairs. This fellow and I went up there and had sex on Fred's four-poster bed. The room was dark except for a nightlight in the bathroom. Forty or so minutes went by, and we decided to get up and shower after sex. There was a chest of drawers near the bathroom with a chair next to it. As we headed for the bathroom, we discovered that someone was seated in the chair. It was JFK Jr. He'd probably just used the bathroom when we came in and had simply sat down and watched the show. 'Excuse me,' he said, 'I didn't think you'd mind.' The guy I was with thought nothing of it. 'Would you care to join us in the shower?' he asked. 'Oh, no,' said John, 'that's all right.' It's clear that John derived some sort of pleasure from being a voyeur. Andy Warhol was like that. I imagine that for John the entire act was akin to watching a porn flick. Even though I continued to see him now and then, neither of us ever mentioned that freaky night again."

Baird Jones, who'd known John for years, related a somewhat sketchy anecdote about an acquaintance of his, a middle-aged, "very married" European who claimed he'd once—in a fit of passion—"given JFK Jr. a blow job." Considered on its own merit, the story appears to be fanciful. Placed in context with the testimonials of others, the episode begins to ring true (or truer), suggesting that John's interest in sexual experimentation was not simply voyeuristic in nature, although that too seems to have been a major component—if not the *only* component—in his homoerotic makeup. "I know for a fact," said Jones, "that John not only frequented nude beaches but nude gay beaches. Not that this necessarily meant he was bisexual, but it's strange behavior for somebody who's not."

"We live in a pornographic and gossip-ridden age," said David Patrick Columbia, editor in chief of *Quest* magazine and a longtime literary observer of upper-crust social and sexual mores. "The trouble with gossip," he added, "is the professional lack of insight, which makes it appear inauthentic. But based on my own experience, I don't feel the multitude of stories that have circulated over the years regarding John Jr.'s sexual practices are merely the product of the gossip mill. This is not an opinion that's likely to be popular among his closest friends and family members, but it's what I believe. There are simply too many reliable sources out there to totally negate the subject—and if you're going to write a meaningful biography of the man, you have to consider the likelihood that John wasn't just another womanizer, that in fact he was open to other possibilities."

Columbia went on to point out that Jacqueline Kennedy more than once expressed the fear that her son had gay tendencies. "I'm uneasy saying it," observed the editor, "but there's no question John had a very 'ambisexual' sensibility, something that went far beyond what *GQ* refers to as 'metrosexual.' He wasn't just a well-groomed male with feminine undertones. To be honest, I've never seen a more handsome person in my entire life. He was better looking than any movie star. His beauty was transcendent, even intimidating. To point out that he was narcissistic about his looks is only to state the obvious. In John's case, there appeared to be a kind of autoeroticism—he was turned on to himself. That quality alone places him in a separate category."

Columbia proceeded to speak of a friend he'd known for years, "an exceptionally good-looking gay guy who lives in Texas today and is HIV positive. I have to admit that when this person still lived in New York, he did a bit of hustling with older men. But I knew him well enough to say that although he had chutzpah, he wasn't prone to exaggeration. One night he and I went to dinner at Rosa Mexicano on the East Side. On that occasion he told me that John Jr. used to frequent an exclusive club called Au Bar, where he would pick up male models and leave with them. He provided enough details to convince me utterly of the story's veracity.

"As we finished dinner that night, I noticed that the guy sitting at the next table had his hand over his face so as to obscure it from view. Taking a second look, I realized it was John Kennedy Jr. He no doubt overheard us. To avoid further embarrassment, I said to my friend, 'Let's get out of here.' After JFK Jr. died, my friend disclosed that he and John also had a history. They'd gone to bed a few times. It amused him because while jogging around the reservoir in Central Park, he'd sometimes see John's mother running there too. My friend wasn't boastful about the affair. If anything, he seemed deeply remorseful that John had died at such a young age and at such a meaningful point in his life."

In retrospect, it appears that John was fundamentally attracted to women but had the capacity to sleep with men and enjoy it. It is doubtful that he considered himself either gay or bisexual. His experiences with men—whatever they might have been—seemed limited to a specific period in his life, when he still felt free enough to experiment. Given

John's fatalistic approach to life, his expectation that it could end at any time, he very likely regarded sex as one more endeavor he could push to the limit.

As early as the fall of 1988, it must have become clear to him that his relationship with Christina Haag, as much as he cared for her, would not evolve into a permanent situation. Although he still considered her his "full-time" girlfriend, he was spotted darting around town with actress Molly Ringwald. There were others. Never at a loss for women, he attended a dinner party in the Hamptons given by supermodel Christie Brinkley, married at that time to singer Billy Joel. Richard duPont had a friend who attended the same affair and recalled that Christie seemed "overly eager" to have John sit next to her. Wary of the situation—and of Billy Joel's presence—JFK Jr. asked another guest at the party to switch places with him and sit next to the hostess. John passed the evening at a far corner of the table, maintaining a polite but distant exterior.

He maintained even more distance when it came to supermodel Naomi Campbell. According to an article in the June 1996 issue of *Cosmopolitan,* Naomi was having dinner at Café Tabac when she spotted John at another table. Summoning her waitress, she told her to invite John to join her. When the waitress informed John of Naomi's request, he politely declined and continued with his meal. Not accustomed to being rebuffed, Naomi stormed out of the restaurant without paying her bill—and without leaving the waitress a tip.

In late September 1988, in the midst of a tempest of social activity, John attended a wedding reception for his aunt, fifty-five-year-old Lee Radziwill (who'd just overcome a drinking problem), and Lee's new husband, dance choreographer-turned-film director Herbert Ross, whose previous wife, Nora Kaye, a former ballerina, had died the year before. Like Maurice Tempelsman and Ed Schlossberg, Ross was Jewish. The wedding took place in Lee's apartment, after which the bride and groom repaired to 1040 Fifth Avenue to attend a reception and dinner that Jackie Onassis had arranged in their honor. The select guest list of thirty included Rudolf Nureyev, Mark Hampton, Ray Stark, Steve Martin, and Bernadette Peters. Although Anthony Radziwill had gone to Korea, Lee's daughter Anna Christina (Tina) came, as did Ed and Caroline Schlossberg. Caroline wore an Armani dress that Lee had once donned and then bestowed upon her. "Lee was working as a consultant for Giorgio Armani fashions," said George Plimpton. "They remunerated her partially in clothes, which she would hand down to Caroline. Out of politeness, Caroline took the clothes but rarely wore them."

Lee, said Plimpton, "hadn't had it easy. She'd tried her hand at all sorts of professions, including acting, and succeeded at none of them. Imagine living your entire life in Jackie's shadow. Such had been Lee's fate. It gave her an inferiority complex, like the horse that finishes second in the Kentucky Derby. It's a sound horse, but it's not the winner."

Another guest at Jackie's house that evening, twenty-seven-year-old Daryl Hannah, had befriended Herb Ross while appearing in *Steel Magnolias,* a film he'd recently finished directing but which hadn't yet been released. John Jr., who'd watched her performance in *Wall Street,* had last seen the actress some ten years before while vacationing with his mother, the Radziwills, and his then girlfriend, Jenny Christian, in St. Martin. There he'd made fun of the gangly siren—nicknamed "Toothpick" by her teenage pals—for walking around the beach resort with a teddy bear in her arms.

No longer a toothpick, Daryl had metamorphosed into a woman of considerable beauty. In 1984, the year she played a mermaid in *Splash, McCall's* placed her on its list of "10 Best Female Bodies in America." In November 2003 she would pose nude for *Playboy.* Nearly six feet tall, blond, with Teutonic bone structure, she had dropped out of the University of Southern California to launch a successful film career. Her stepfather, a Chicago real estate mogul named Jerry Wexler, had more money than all the Kennedys combined. Though she'd grown up surrounded by luxury, Daryl's chief ambition had always been to make it as a Hollywood star. Her closest allies in the industry were actresses Susan St. James and Rachel Ward. Her stepfather's brother Haskell Wexler was a well-known cinematographer. A strict vegetarian, she shared John Jr.'s enthusiasm for outdoor sports. "Like Jackie, she was a patrician," said gossip columnist Michael Gross. "She was also a film queen, like Marilyn Monroe, so there were facets to her that would have appealed to John's father."

John and Daryl had more in common than familial wealth, good looks, and a penchant for physical thrills. In the first place, they were both paired off. John remained involved with Christina Haag; Daryl and her boyfriend, musician Jackson Browne, lived together (with his son Ethan) in a $2.5 million house in Santa Monica. Over the next twelve months, John and Daryl saw each other only sporadically. They did the same things John had always done with his girlfriends. They played Frisbee and Rollerbladed in Central Park. They went to the movies. They rode their bikes. They went sailing at Martha's Vineyard, boating at Smith Mountain Lake in Virginia, and skiing at Telluride, Colorado, where Daryl owned a cabin, and her stepfather owned a vast estate. Always eager to test his physical prowess and stamina, John had finally met his match. A tomboy's tomboy, Daryl had little difficulty keeping up with John.

Like John, she possessed a giddy sense of humor. Hilary Shepard-Turner, an actress friend of Daryl's since high school, recalled that Hannah used to make fun of John's perfect head of hair by calling him "Helmet Head." "We had him paged in an airport," said Hillary. "We could hear the announcement over the public address system: 'Mr. Head, Mr. Helmet Head.' He answered the page. He thought it was hysterical."

Christina Haag had grown accustomed to reading about John and his various would-be relationships with other women, mostly starlets and models. The occasional gossip items linking John and Daryl constituted a mild annoyance for Christina but little more. For years John had been a tabloid Casanova, the target of wild exaggerations concerning his "lurid" sex life. Jackson Browne, on the other hand, purportedly resented the situation, particularly when Daryl announced her intention to study directing at the NYU Film School. Making the transition from Santa Monica to Manhattan—with frequent trips back and forth—Daryl rented an apartment at Broadway and 72nd Street. It was only then that her liaison with John became a matter of serious consideration.

In March 1989 Jacqueline Onassis slipped into a private room at the New York Eye, Ear and Throat Hospital on East 64th Street in Manhattan to undergo a full frontal face-lift as performed by Dr. Michael Hogan. The plastic surgeon had previously completed cosmetic surgery on Lee Radziwill, who convinced her older sister to follow suit. It had been nearly a decade since Jackie's eye lift. Approaching her sixtieth birthday, she told friends she wanted to be "reborn." While at the hospital, she permitted only her children to visit. Caroline brought young Rose to see her grandmother. John visited by himself and made the mistake of admitting to his mother that he'd become involved with Daryl Hannah. Jackie didn't dislike Daryl—she just didn't like her for John. Although he'd renounced flying lessons at his mother's behest, he had no intention of dropping Daryl.

While Jackie recuperated from her face-lift by vacationing with Maurice Tempelsman in the Bahamas, John submitted to a series of interviews with prospective law firms. "It seemed," said Billy Way, "that whenever John went for an interview with a potential employer, they'd ask him questions about his personal life. They rarely plumbed his legal abilities or intentions."

Ed Schlossberg, meanwhile, had signed on with Olympia & York, a real estate development corporation, to participate in the design of three properties consisting of bars, restaurants, and futuristic game parlors. The first opened in Manhattan in early 1989. One of the games Ed devised for the project was called Food Fight, in which players responded to multiple-choice audio questions about nutrition by slugging one or another of several punching bags. A second game, Beat the System, purported to instruct participants on the ins and outs of stock and commodity market investments. Describing his concept of "entertainment," Ed told *The New York Times* that the process of the interactive computer-driven game was far more engaging than the passive practice of watching a movie "and then going home." In recognition of his claim—and for other contributions to the world of contemporary culture—*Better Homes and Gardens* profiled Schlossberg, dubbing him "the Wiz."

Caroline's family tapped the Wiz's talents by asking him to design a commemorative lantern as part of the official insignia for the newly established John F. Kennedy Profile in Courage Awards, a $25,000 prize presented each year to those in public service who, in one way or another, stand up against the system for the betterment of the country. In keeping with their chosen role as promoters of the Kennedy legacy, Jackie, Maurice, Ed, Caroline, and John Jr. flew to Boston to join the rest of the clan in a JFK Library ceremony to announce the creation of the award. Although the president's widow declined the opportunity to speak, John Jr. offered a few brief but touching remarks. During the press conference that followed, a reporter asked about the constant scrutiny of both the public and private lives of the multifarious members of the family. Senator Ted Kennedy, the event's main speaker—and ever the politician—retorted, "We welcome more scrutiny of John and Caroline. Jackie can take pride in their accomplishments." That evening Maurice Tempelsman—"M.T." to Caroline and John—escorted Jackie to a $1,000-a-plate fund-raiser for the JFK Library.

"Caroline and John spoke highly of Tempelsman," said George Plimpton. "They respected him. They appreciated the way in which he encouraged their mother to be herself, yet at the same time offered guidance in certain select areas. Ed Schlossberg tried to play a similar role vis-à-vis Caroline. Unfortunately, in attempting to protect her from the public, he came across like a prison warden. He tended to smother her—at least that's the perception people had of him. He lacked Maurice Tempelsman's finesse. In addition, he gave the impression of being a curiously humorless fellow. I can count on one hand the times I saw him laugh or even crack a smile. And when he did, it usually seemed forced and unnatural. It's reasonable to assume that Caroline found him amusing—I can only speak for myself."

One benefit Schlossberg derived from being married to Caroline Kennedy involved the connections he managed to establish by virtue of his mother-in-law's international fame. "In order to meet all the right people, Ed made it his business to attend as many of Jackie's dinner parties as possible," noted Plimpton. A typical "sit-down" at Jackie's house brought out the best and the brightest, particularly in the arts. Her "A-list" dinner guests included names such as Diane Sawyer and Mike Nichols, Leonard Bernstein, Isamu Noguchi, Elizabeth de Cuevas, Barbara Walters, Diana Vreeland, Kitty Carlisle Hart, Martha Graham, Gloria Steinem, Philip Johnson, and I. M. Pei. In the annals of twentieth-century New York social evenings, Jackie had few peers. She had both the know-how and the means. By 1989, under Maurice Tempelsman's aegis, she had quadrupled the $26 million settlement received from the

Onassis estate. At the time of Jackie's death in 1994, published reports established her personal wealth at well over $200 million. Exclusive of their Kennedy family inheritance, Jackie's children would emerge with individual fortunes far in excess of those possessed by their twenty-six Kennedy cousins.

JFK Jr.'s wealth, celebrity, and appearance thrust him into the spotlight yet again in mid-May 1989 when he graduated from the NYU School of Law. "We'd all been together for three years," said fellow student Linda Pliskin. "The graduation ceremony was to take place in an adjunct building that belonged to Madison Square Garden. We were informed that John had held a news conference earlier in the day, so the ceremony could proceed without interference from the press. We'd each been issued a card and asked to write our name the way we wanted it read. The way it worked is that you handed the card to the dean; he read your name aloud; you walked across the stage and were handed your diploma. I totally remember what happened when the dean called John's name. He tried to low-key it by writing 'John Kennedy' on his card, rather than 'John F. Kennedy Jr.' It made no difference. When he walked across the stage, the place exploded. There was a blinding flash of light. Every camera in the auditorium went off at once. And this wasn't the press. These were the parents and grandparents, aunts and uncles, and brothers and sisters who'd come to see their own family member graduate. I mean the place lit up like nothing I'd ever seen. So everyone there walked away with a piece of history, a photograph of John Kennedy being handed his law diploma."

Passing the New York State bar exam proved more problematic for John than it had for his sister. To his chagrin—and despite a promise to his mother that he would "buckle down and study"—he failed twice before passing on his third attempt. In reality, John nearly passed the second time around, scoring a 649, falling just short of the required score of 660. His failure may well have been a reflection of his reluctance to commit himself to the possibility of a future legal career. Prominent California attorney Keith Bardellini typified John as "hardly the sharpest blade in the drawer but very popular with the ladies." Bardellini recalled seeing John in Los Angeles in the early summer of 1989. "He certainly didn't look like he was studying for the bar exam. Instead, he and Daryl Hannah amused themselves in a private suite at the top of the Four Seasons Hotel." According to newspaper reports, John spent the summer juggling romances on both coasts. In July, when Daryl decided to take up again with Jackson Browne, John returned to New York.

On July 22, 1989, Jackie's mother, Janet Auchincloss, divorced from her third husband, Bingham Morris, died at the age of eighty-one at Hammersmith Farm. Two days later Jackie and her sister, Lee, led several hundred mourners into Newport's historic white-steepled Trinity Church for the funeral, while hundreds of spectators gathered outside in the ninety-degree heat to gape at the former First Lady and her two children. The simple forty-minute service was followed by a brief grave site ceremony at the Island Cemetery, where Janet's ashes were interred next to those of husband number two, Hugh D. Auchincloss. Jackie embraced Caroline and John at the graveside before all three were driven away in a silver limousine. After a luncheon at Hammersmith Farm, she and her children (together with Maurice Tempelsman and Ed Schlossberg) headed for Jackie's home on Martha's Vineyard. A few days later Jackie flew to Paris and popped in at D. Porthault's Avenue Montaigne store to purchase baby pillows in cases printed with tiny pink ribbons for her granddaughter, Rose.

John spent the first week of August in Los Angeles where, said the *National Enquirer,* he was "having a secret romance with an unknown but simply stunning, willowy, Texas-born blonde model and college student named Stephanie Schmid." To substantiate its claim, the *Enquirer* had gathered exclusive photographs of the couple cuddling on the boardwalk at Venice Beach, the same boardwalk where he and Christina Haag had spent so much time the summer before. His "romance" with Schmid was short-lived. An item in another tabloid, this one unsupported by photographs, placed him in the Polo Lounge a few days later with Princess Stephanie, the androgynously striking daughter of Prince Ranier and Princess Grace of Monaco.

By late August John was back in New York living in a sublet at 71 Hudson Street, one of several apartments he would come to occupy in the area, and after Labor Day weekend he began working as a $29,000-

a-year assistant district attorney in the offices of Manhattan district attorney Robert M. Morgenthau. Prior to joining the criminal justice system, John conveniently paid off $2,300 in outstanding parking violations. *The Village Voice* published an article suggesting that he'd gained employment with Morgenthau as a result of Jackie's influence, not because he merited the position. When he failed the bar exam a second time, the *New York Post* ran a bold front-page headline that read: "The Hunk Flunks." The *Voice* printed a second piece, this one criticizing Morgenthau's office for retaining John's services despite his bar exam failures. Stanley Chess, president of the Bar Review, defended John in a *Newsweek* article, pointing out that the "New York bar is one of the toughest in the nation; more than 50 percent [of the applicants] failed when JFK Jr. sat for the exam."

"The press made far too much of the matter," said Billy Way. "They made John out to be a dunce. Every newspaper in town ran a story on what was essentially a nonstory. The *New York Post* said something like, 'Instead of hitting the books, John spends his evenings at Tatou, a popular East Side nightspot, or at the China Club, hanging out with Wilhelmina model Julie Baker, Christina Haag, and other chicks.' They depicted him as some sex-addicted, girl-crazed playboy freak whose life was spent Rollerblading, jogging, biking, and racing from one discotheque to another. After he failed the bar a second time, he said to me, 'What's the big deal? Judge James Landis, an associate of my grandfather [Joseph P. Kennedy], didn't pass the bar until he was forty-six, when he was dean of the Harvard Law School.'"

The explosion of negative publicity took John's friends by surprise. "Generally speaking," continued Way, "he was popular with journalists. How could he not be? I was always amazed at how charming and debonair he was with those guys. He'd disarm reporters by going up to them and saying something cute. They were putty in his hands. The point is that they're all sharks; they'll write anything to sell newspapers. If he'd been John Doe—some ordinary dude who'd flunked the bar—nobody would've blinked. The stories annoyed him because they upset his mother. Jackie had hoped that his employment with Morgenthau would mark the beginning of a more settled, purposeful turn in his career. She nevertheless remained optimistic. To make certain he passed on his third attempt, she hired a tutor to help him prepare and shelled out a thousand dollars for a bar review course. It worked."

When John at last passed the New York bar exam in late 1990, he held a press conference in the district attorney's office. "I'm relieved by the news," he said, "very relieved." Jackie and Caroline were no doubt equally pleased.

Part V

———◆———

Chapter 15

———◆———

THE BEST AND WORST
OF TIMES

IN 1990, ANTICIPATING THE BIRTH of their second child, Ed Schlossberg and Caroline Kennedy purchased an even larger co-operative
apartment than the one in which they'd previously lived. The new co-op
on the eleventh floor of 888 Park Avenue, at 78th Street, was a vast
L-shaped apartment with high ceilings and city views. It contained a
picture gallery, library, study, master bedroom suite, living room, dining
room, kitchen and pantry, laundry, storage areas, three additional bedrooms, and a total of four and a half bathrooms. The couple turned one
of the bedrooms into a nursery, soundproofing it by lining its walls with
layers of foam. They spent $11,000 on plumbing and bathroom fixtures.
Ed designed furniture for the apartment and mounted a selection of his
own artworks. The couple filled the apartment with decorative objects
they'd collected over the years, both independently and together. Their
taste in interior design was more suggestive of Ed's modernist vision than
of Jackie's traditionalism. They refused to engage any of the high-end
decorators Jackie and Lee continually sent their way.

Not unlike her brother, Caroline had grave doubts about pursuing a
full-time legal career. After discussing the matter with both her mother

and Uncle Teddy Kennedy, she decided to continue writing books. Raising children and looking after the interests of her husband took precedence over the demands that would have befallen her as a practicing attorney. Despite her status as the daughter of a former president, Caroline fit the description of any youthful, well-off New York City mother. She shopped at the local market for food and was often seen browsing for baby clothes at Cerutti and the more pedestrian Ben's for Kids. With her mother, she attended Carolina Herrera's fashion shows. Once a week Jackie went to Caroline's to have a "roll-around"—a playdate with Rose. And once a week Caroline took Rose to Jackie's house for lunch. Other days she met her own friends for lunch, including *Rolling Stone*'s Jann Wenner and *Saturday Night Live* producer Lorne Michaels, frequently dining with them at E.A.T., a gourmet delicatessen on Madison Avenue. More than once Michaels proposed that she guest host the show. More than once she declined.

She also met regularly for lunch with Maria Shriver. At one of their luncheons, Maria related an amusing anecdote about Caroline's mother. Jackie had approached Maria's husband, Arnold Schwarzenegger, with the possibility of his penning a bodybuilding book for Doubleday. But when he proposed instead to write a tome explicating his then conservative Republican philosophy, Jackie became flustered. Politely declining his offer, she'd said: "Arnold, why not stick to what you know?"

Although Ed and Caroline still visited his country home in the Berkshires on weekends, they spent part of each summer in the Hamptons. With her deep sense of family and legacy, Caroline stayed on as a trustee of the JFK Library's executive board and accepted a similar post with the Kennedy Foundation, which distributed funds to a variety of groups and organizations, a number of them Kennedy-run. She eventually became president of the JFK Library Foundation, an assignment that necessitated frequent trips to Boston. Paying tribute to her mother's interests, she served on the boards of the American Ballet Theatre and the Citizens Committee for New York City. Her political involvement, however, was limited to making monetary contributions to Democratic Party candidates, among them Al Gore, Bill Clinton, Ted Kennedy, and Patrick Kennedy, when the latter ran for Congress in Rhode Island. She also contributed to Emily's List, a group that sponsored a cross section of Democratic Party female political candidates. Fiercely independent, Caroline was unwilling to be involved superficially in political campaigns and organizations just for the sake of the press.

Now that it had gotten off the ground, Ed Schlossberg's design company continued to flourish. His Rolodex was laden with the names and telephone numbers of countless contacts provided him by both Jackie and Caroline. By 1991 he'd taken on a host of new consignments, including a "learning annex" for Atlanta's Ferbank Museum of Natural History, and an "innovation center" for the Henry Ford Museum in Dearborn, Michigan. Having invented and marketed an article of clothing he called a "zipper tie"—a cravat that turned into a scarf—he began work on a collaborative venture with an office furniture manufacturing concern also located in Michigan. *The Boston Globe* described the latest effort as "an interactive computer program to help workers relate their personalities to their office environments." In a burst of hyperbole, *The Washington Post* compared the whimsical innovator to Buckminster Fuller, Steven Spielberg, and Santa Claus. Known to walk to work in the morning (rather than ride a sleigh), Schlossberg maintained multiple business listings, including one at 841 Avenue of the Americas and at 873 Broadway. The lease on the Broadway office space terminated when the landlord instigated an $80,000 lawsuit against Schlossberg for unpaid rent. Claiming that he'd been effectively evicted because of the landlord's failure to make certain repairs, Schlossberg spent four years in court and ultimately settled the claim by paying the landlord $40,000.

On May 5, 1990, Caroline gave birth to her second child, a daughter named Tatiana Celia Kennedy Schlossberg, after Tatyana Grosman, Ed Schlossberg's former mentor. Now whenever Caroline visited her mother, she brought along both children, creating a new bond of intimacy between them. Caroline welcomed her mother's input on child rearing, a remarkable concession considering how trying it must have been at times to be Jackie's daughter. As Dr. Sanford Friedman, a New York cardiologist, put it: "Most girls have problems with their mothers. But being the daughter of Jackie O. must have been impossible. What was it that Norman Mailer said of her? 'She isn't merely a celebrity, but a legend; not a legend, but a myth—no, not a myth, rather a historic arche-type, virtually a demiurge.' I'm not certain, but can one even converse with a demiurge?"

If Caroline's ties to her mother grew tighter, John's began to sever. "He was determined to break out of his cocoon," said Pierre Salinger. "In order to gain his independence, he had to distance himself from his mother. Jackie didn't exactly have to trick him to get him to visit her, but she did have to conjure up all sorts of excuses to lure him up to her apartment."

Jackie had wanted to celebrate her son's thirtieth birthday with a for-mal banquet at either Le Cirque or Mortimer's, but John rejected the of-fer in favor of a smaller, more sedate dinner with his mother, Caroline and Ed Schlossberg, George Plimpton, and about a dozen others at the Grolier Restaurant on East 32nd Street. He then attended a bash thrown in his honor by Santina Goodman and Toni Kotite, two of his Brown University friends, at a tavern on West 18th Street that specialized in chili and chicken wings. Having finally begun to pay attention to his wardrobe, he showed up, said Michael Gross, "in a custom-made ma-roon zoot suit and leopard skin wingtips." Though dateless, he spent most of the night on the dance floor with various female friends. "He wasn't afraid to let loose, have a good time, even make a bit of a fool of himself," remarked Karen Duffy, a writer he'd met in the mid-1980s when she worked as a shucker at a South Street Seaport oyster bar.

Duffy, who became chummy with John, claimed in a 1999 article for *Glamour,* that at the time of his thirtieth birthday he was dating a close friend of hers, a "good-looking, ginger-haired" model named Jenny. Ac-cording to Duffy, Jenny had both a great sense of humor and a good deal of money, not that the latter consideration would ever have mattered to John. Owner of a Manhattan townhouse, Jenny frequently threw dinner parties for ten or more. At one such event, John carried the evening with his charm and reserve. There was something about him, observed Karen Duffy, "that tacitly asked for a bit of distance and respect." The man who walked Duffy home that night was rabid with jealousy. "All the women fall for this guy," he said. "What's so great about him?"

Not long after his thirtieth birthday, John—accompanied by Toni Kotite—attended a party in honor of Robert De Niro at the Tribeca Grill. He also arranged a bachelor party for Rob Littell, just as he'd done for Chris Overbeck several years earlier. The festivities for Littell started on Friday afternoon at Times Square in a rented Winnebago and ended on Sunday at Martha's Vineyard with a marathon game of touch football and a good deal of drinking.

Having reduced her work schedule at Doubleday to a manageable three days a week, Jacqueline busied herself with her grandchildren, especially Rose, the firstborn, who possessed the same broad mouth, oval face, and large round eyes that Jacqueline had at a similar age. Careful not to spoil her grandchildren—they referred to her as "Grand Jackie"—she applied many of the same techniques and principles she'd used in bringing up Caroline and John. She read poetry to her granddaughters, made up nursery rhymes, taught them how to draw. She encouraged Caroline to carry on in the same vein. Determined to maintain as normal a lifestyle as feasible, Caroline eschewed bodyguards and drivers. As her mother had done during her childhood, she celebrated Halloween by going trick-or-treating with her daughters. She took them to Serendipity, the same sweetshop where Jackie had taken Caroline and John as youngsters. Regarding the family tradition of horseback riding, Caroline introduced her children to Paul and Eva Font, who'd started her in a pony club when she was still in kindergarten.

Like Jackie, Caroline cherished the simple, spontaneous pleasures associated with bringing up children. Francine Fromm, a Park Avenue neighbor, remembered seeing Caroline, the nanny, and Caroline's two young daughters in Central Park. "Caroline was like a little kid again," said Fromm. "When she did that Indian whoop to gather the girls, you could see she just loved it. She ignored the stares of other park-goers and did her thing: rode the merry-go-round, visited the zoo, climbed the Hans Christian Andersen statue, rented rowboats, and while the girls enjoyed ice-cream cones, Caroline and the nanny indulged in less fattening sorbets."

Another neighbor, Anne Hickory, spotted Caroline "hailing a taxi on

Park Avenue one afternoon, nimbly balancing young Tatiana in one hand and a stroller in the other. Pedestrians passed and looked, cars honked, and a taxi finally pulled to the curb. Caroline lovingly guided her daughter into the cab, pulled the stroller in behind her, and off they went."

While Caroline spent less time at the family compound in Hyannis Port and at Rose Kennedy's estate in Palm Beach, she nevertheless lent her support to the many public causes espoused by her Kennedy cousins. She backed Kathleen Kennedy Townsend's political campaigns in Maryland and applauded when Kathleen finally became the state's lieutenant governor. When Robert F. Kennedy Jr. sounded a clarion call for environmental issues, including a plan designed to clean up the Hudson River, Caroline attended benefits and contributed funds. She went to Kerry Kennedy Cuomo's fund-raiser for the Robert F. Kennedy Memorial Center for Human Rights, in New York, in January 1991 and, as she brushed past the crowd to reach her family, was overheard saying, "I want to get my points for showing up."

Of all the Kennedy cousins, Caroline was the most centered and well grounded. Despite some experimentation with alcohol and drugs, she had averted the rash of scandals and problems that had beset so many others in the family. Kerry Kennedy, a 1982 graduate of Brown, attributed her cousin's coping skills to her "superior intelligence and iron will." Other cousins were more critical, accusing her of having constructed a psychological wall behind which she too often sought refuge. "If you're her best friend," said Chris Lawford, "there's no better friend. If you're not, she's very conscious of what she says and does. She's nervous in public. She's conscious of people wanting to be close to her simply for her name." Amanda Smith, an adopted sister of William Kennedy Smith, never warmed to Caroline. "She can be quite dreadful, really awful," noted Smith. "She considers herself better than the rest of us."

One cause of Amanda's resentment toward Caroline is probably traceable to a 1991 episode involving thirty-year-old William Kennedy Smith, the second son of Jean Kennedy Smith and the late Stephen Smith. It was charged that in the predawn hours of March 30, after carousing at several Palm Beach nightspots with his uncle Senator Edward M. Kennedy and Teddy's son Patrick, Smith had met and raped a twenty-nine-year-old Florida socialite named Patricia Bowman on the grounds of Rose Kennedy's oceanfront estate, by then little more than a crash pad for Kennedy men and their girlfriends. A fourth-year medical student at Georgetown University, the accused proclaimed his innocence, maintaining that the encounter had been nothing more than a sexual act between two consenting adults. Details soon unfolded in the media of a night of debauchery led by Uncle Ted, a botched investigation by the Palm Beach County Police Department, and the possible obstruction of justice by Kennedy operatives. The incident reverberated with the all-too-familiar Kennedy scandals of yesteryear: drug addiction, philandering husbands, general recklessness, alcoholism, and, yes, Chappaquiddick.

Although Stephen Smith, the family's "spin master," had died of cancer six months before the alleged rape, the Kennedy machine readily rolled into high gear to defend one of their own. Reporting on the Palm Beach trial that December, Dominick Dunne observed in *Vanity Fair* that the Kennedys "gave an unprecedented display of solidarity combined with stardom, waving at the press, smiling at photographers, any one of them capable at any moment of stepping in front of the bank of microphones and addressing the multitudes. 'We're a very close family,' all of them said over and over again. And they are. Or appear to be, judging by the parade of loyal relations who came in and went out of the courtroom." Among those attending the trial were William Kennedy Smith's brother and two adopted sisters (Amanda and Kym Maria), Ethel Kennedy and two of her sons, Sargent and Eunice Kennedy Shriver and two of their sons, Patricia Kennedy Lawford and three of her children, and John F. Kennedy Jr. Caroline Kennedy, while undeniably fond of her accused cousin, did not attend. Her refusal to show up no doubt rankled Amanda Smith as well as other members of the clan.

According to Dominick Dunne, there was much speculation as to whether Jackie Onassis would arrive to do "her stint." At a Palm Beach dinner party, Dunne encountered a childhood friend of Jacqueline's, who contended: "They'll never get Jackie here at this trial." Jackie had never been a team player, after all, and she had always gone out of her way to shield Caroline and John from the so-called sleaze factor that had permeated Kennedy legend since the deaths of the president and attorney general. Although they socialized with some of the Kennedys, both of Jackie's children had been kept at a comfortable distance from the rest of the family, particularly Ethel Kennedy's offspring. Author Leo Damore reported hearing that Alexander Forger, Jackie's sometime Washington attorney, had recommended that she and her kids steer clear of the Smith trial. "Caroline and John were more Jackie's kids than they were Kennedys," said Damore. "Up to a point, they did her bidding and followed her lead, Caroline more so than her brother. They'd both always been on decent terms with William Kennedy Smith. I recall seeing Smith at a Broadway play at some point with John and Christina Haag, and John paid far more attention to Smith than he did to his girlfriend."

Jackie and Caroline were both horrified by the accusations of sexual assault against Smith, but also by Ted Kennedy's irresponsible behavior: how he had gone "cruising" with his son and nephew earlier in the evening; how he had joked with them as they lewdly danced around with tablecloths wrapped around their heads; and how, half-naked and apparently bombed, he had menaced his son's female companion at four in the morning. Agnes Ash summed up what must also have constituted Jackie's and Caroline's reaction to the incident, when she wrote in the *Palm Beach Daily News:* "What kind of person goes out playing and picking up girls with his kids?"

Initially Jackie had tried to remain aloof from the proceedings and privately urged her children to do the same. John Jr. had been a conspicuous no-show at the July 1991 wedding of cousin Max Kennedy, where he was to have been an usher with Willie Smith. Because of his employment in the Manhattan District Attorney's office, his mother didn't want him to be photographed with the accused rapist.

Remembering how strong and effective Jackie had been on other dire occasions, and not willing to forgo her evident powers to evoke sympathy and sway public opinion, the Kennedys turned on the heat, bombarding her with letters and calls imploring her to place family loyalty above everything. According to Leo Damore, Ted Kennedy said to Jackie, "If only I'd taken a long walk on the beach instead of going out with the

boys." The statement meant little considering that the day after the alleged rape, Teddy and Willie were spotted at Chuck and Harold's, a well-
known Palm Beach watering hole. Ethel Kennedy likewise contacted
Jackie, reminding her that should John Jr. one day seek public office, the
family would be needed. At the very least, Jackie could aid the cause by
allowing her children to appear at the impending trial. Even Ethel, long
dismissed by Jackie as an unfit parent, realized the tremendous public relations value manifest in the personalities of both John and Caroline.

Not one to be bullied, Jackie nevertheless felt a deep affection for
Willie's mother. In the early days of her marriage to Jack, while his other
sisters had snubbed her, Jean Kennedy Smith remained a stalwart ally,
constantly defending Jacqueline's remote manner and aristocratic deportment. When the other Kennedys criticized her marriage to Aristotle
Onassis, Jean stood firm in offering unconditional support to her sister-
in-law. Therefore, in deference to Jean, Jackie relented—in her own way.
Three months before the trial began, she and John attended the clan's annual Labor Day gathering in Hyannis Port, where they were amply photographed enjoying themselves with William Smith and other family
members. Jackie also hosted a family barbecue at her Martha's Vineyard
estate, inviting Willie and numerous other cousins to spend the night.

In the end, neither Jackie nor Caroline appeared at the trial. John Jr.,
however, took matters into his own hands. He not only attended the
trial, he aided defense attorney Roy Black by participating in the jury selection process prior to the trial. Black, a high-powered, soft-spoken
criminal attorney from Miami, credited JFK Jr. for having helped make
his job easier. John made certain that he and Willie were photographed
leaving the courthouse together. Surrounded by reporters while having a
late-night snack at a Palm Beach club, John lambasted them by saying, "I
don't think any of you has been too fair to my cousin." Shortly after,
Smith was acquitted of all charges.

Roy Black more than earned the $1 million legal fee he received for
his services. His greatest coup had been his ability to convince Judge
Mary Lupo not to allow the testimony of three other women who
claimed Smith had sexually assaulted them in recent years. Although ex-

onerated in his Palm Beach trial, Smith's reputation continued to dog him. On August 27, 2004, more than five years after John Jr.'s death, *The New York Times* reported that Smith had yet again been charged with rape. The purported victim, twenty-eight-year-old Audra Soulias, of Chicago, filed papers against Smith in Cook County Circuit Court. A former assistant to Smith at his nonprofit Chicago-based Center for International Rehabilitation, Soulias claimed that he had raped her on the occasion of her twenty-third birthday in 1999. She attributed the delay in filing to a prolonged effort to settle the matter out of court. Smith called the charges "outrageous, untrue, and without merit," and referred to Soulias as a "disgruntled employee." Having passed a polygraph test in support of the charge, Soulias sued Smith for more than $3 million. Whatever else the lawsuit accomplished, it left readers of *The New York Times* (and other reporting newspapers) with the indelible impression that William Kennedy Smith was a serial sexual predator. The lawsuit was subsequently dismissed by a Cook County judge, who found the complaint to be without merit.

Although Jackie's immediate family emerged unscathed from the Willie Smith rape trial, the case once again subjected the clan to a good deal of public scrutiny. Caroline and John Jr. were particularly susceptible. While exempt from scandal, everything they said or did, every public appearance, became a newsworthy event. Thus when John was seen having lunch one day at a Manhattan eatery with actress Julia Roberts, whom he'd met for the first time in Los Angeles the summer of 1990, the press immediately assumed that they were dating. The truth is that Roberts was a girlfriend of Pat Manocchia's, John's former fraternity brother at Brown. In 1996 Roberts accompanied Manocchia to Caroline Kennedy's party in celebration of John's marriage to Carolyn Bessette. Otherwise, she and John barely knew each other.

Additional fodder for the press mill came about when John prosecuted his first case as an assistant district attorney. To make certain his initial effort went as seamlessly as possible, his supervisors assigned him what they considered an open-and-shut case: The defendant, a second-story man, had been found asleep in his victim's locked apartment, his pockets stuffed with jewelry. Nervous at first, bumbling his way through the cross-examination, John received generous guidance on the admissibility of certain evidence from Presiding Justice Frederic Berman. To no one's surprise, after less than an hour, the jury found for the prosecution. When asked by a reporter for the New York *Daily News* to explain his apparent difficulty in prosecuting the case, John responded, "I guess I'm not a legal genius."

Manhattan DA Robert Morgenthau was supportive of John's efforts. "I never doubted that he would pass his bar exam," he said, "nor did I doubt that he would make a fine prosecutor." Morgenthau's generous assessment was no doubt offered to deflect public criticism of John's barely adequate performance.

Veteran defense attorney William M. Kunstler recalled the day he received a telephone call from John. "I'd made some facetious remark in the press about his first case," said Kunstler. "It went something like, 'This case would've posed serious problems for any defense.' It wasn't a kind comment. A few days after I made it, John Jr. called and suggested we meet for dinner. We got together at a Chinese restaurant in midtown Manhattan. He told me he'd read my comment and agreed with it. He said he had little interest in practicing law. I was impressed with his candor. I liked him. 'Why don't you run for political office?' I asked him. 'Not yet,' he replied. 'I'm not ready.' After dinner, as we walked toward the subway, we stepped over this homeless guy lying on the sidewalk. He must have recognized John, because he raised his head and said, 'You should be at home preparing for your next case,' to which John replied, 'You're right, I should.' The amusing thing about this brief encounter is that a few days later, the homeless guy was quoted on Page Six of the *New York Post*. He must have called it in."

Assigned to the Special Prosecutions Division of the DA's office, John handled mostly low-level crimes involving petty thieves, con artists, and street hustlers. One of his cases called for the prosecution of a drug-addicted male prostitute who'd beaten up and robbed a prominent out-of-town businessman in his hotel room. In four years as an ADA, he was used sparingly, attaining six convictions out of the six cases he handled. His strength lay in his ability to compel people to open up. "He could judge if somebody was telling the truth," said Michael Gross. Despite his record, he didn't stand out. New York State Supreme Court Judge Richard Lowe, who presided over one of John's trials, said of him: "I don't think he has the potential to be a great trial lawyer. His passion lies elsewhere. But he handles who he is with extreme grace." Nursing a beer one evening at the Madison Avenue Pub, John was approached by a heckler who said, "Hey fellow, I hear you're a pretty lousy lawyer." "No question," agreed John, "I am."

The press frequently offered money to the other assistant district attorneys for stories about John. One paralegal provided a tidbit of how the women in the office were constantly after him, including an elderly cleaning lady who spent hours each night tidying his tiny office. She even cleaned the underside of his desk. Michael Gross reported in *Esquire* that John's mail had to be screened—as in years past, women sent unsolicited pictures of themselves. One admirer sent the "working hunk" a cappuccino machine.

One day a messenger hand-delivered a videotape, photograph, and letter to John from a Brazilian television actress visiting the United States. Known as Xuxa, the actress—whose real name was Maria da Graca Meneghel—claimed she'd seen a picture of John in a magazine and wanted to meet him. Evidently taken with her video and photo, John telephoned Xuxa and agreed to meet her for lunch at the Tribeca Grill. The day of the meeting, Xuxa sent a limousine to the district attorney's office to pick up her date. Refusing to be seen stepping into a limo in front of his place of employment, JFK Jr. walked to the restaurant. The meal went smoothly, and afterward the couple strolled around TriBeCa before going their separate ways. But that wasn't the end of it. A few weeks later, the tabloid TV show *A Current Affair* broadcast video footage of John and Xuxa's entire date. Although Xuxa publicly denied involvement in the plot, it was clear to John that he'd been set up.

Albert R. Khafif, an assistant district attorney in the appeals division of the Manhattan District Attorney's office, saw a good deal of John during this period. "There were ten of us in the appeals division," recalled Khafif. "We had a daily routine. We would all break for lunch at the same time, but first we'd play Frisbee in an open court behind the DA offices. After Frisbee we'd all walk over to Broadway and have lunch together, then return to the office for the afternoon session. Though he was in a different division, JFK Jr. often joined us for Frisbee and lunch. He evidently came and went as he pleased. He had a politician's personality rather than that of a lawyer. He didn't perform brilliantly in the DA's office, but you had the sense that he didn't really care, that he regarded the position as nothing more than a stepping-stone."

Owen Carragher Jr., another officemate of John's, insisted "in ways that are most meaningful, he was just one of us. Except with many more and far better-looking girlfriends."

At one juncture John grew a goatee, kept it a few weeks, then shaved it off. One night, after winning a case, he went to dinner with Oleg Cassini, Jackie's White House fashion designer. "I had a great deal of admiration for John," said Cassini. "He'd become the face of the Kennedy family. People who disliked the Kennedys—and there were many—liked him. That evening he talked about his work in the DA's office. What he enjoyed most about it was the marvelous assembly of characters he encountered on an almost daily basis—police officers, victims, public defenders, and so on. The interplay of conversations he heard reminded him of the theater. What he didn't like were the working conditions—too many crimes, not enough resources. 'Everyone in the office is overwhelmed,' he complained. 'A sense of humor is the only way you can survive.' He also criticized the injustice of the justice system, the fact that those defendants able to afford high-priced lawyers usually 'beat the rap,' whereas the underpriviliged were more or less at the mercy of the courts."

Cassini asked John if he ever wondered about his father's assassination. "I asked him why the Kennedy family had never launched its own investigation of JFK's murder. I asked if he thought there had been a conspiracy. 'Based on the books I've read,' he responded, 'I think it's more than likely that Oswald didn't act alone. But my family is extremely self-protective. There are certain details about the assassination they probably don't want to know. The same applies to Bobby's assassination.'"

John usually rode his bike to and from work and often left early to work out at Plus One. He took time off during his second year to go kayaking with friends in the Red Sea. Accompanied by Uncle Teddy, he made an annual pilgrimage to the Kennedy School of Government at Harvard to meet the new scholars and faculty members. He lent his support to the Kennedy Fellows Program, which each year awarded stipends to seventy-five social workers to further their education. He joined the Robin Hood Foundation, traveling by subway to Harlem and the South Bronx to check on projects the group had agreed to sponsor. Armed with pretzels and a six-pack, he regularly attended New York Yankees night games. He watched Monday night football games at sports bars with his ADA colleagues and college buddies. Saturday afternoons the same group converged in Central Park for their own touch football contests. Once when he saw a press photographer lurking on the sidelines taking pictures, he ran over and invited the shutterbug to join the game. "We're a man short," he said. Billy Way recalled a St. Patrick's Day party that John attended as a leprechaun, dressed from head to toe in green, replete with bell-topped ballet slippers that tinkled with every step. He frequently left "zany" messages on Way's voice mail, imitating the distinctive voices of well-known actors such as Jimmy Stewart and James Cagney. He once left a whispery falsetto message in imitation of Marilyn Monroe. "If Caroline was focused, John was spread out," said Way. "He was all over the place. He was disorganized and forgetful, but it was all part of his charm. One day he called his dry cleaners to ask if he'd left several months' worth of paychecks from the DA's office in a pants pocket."

John had recently been diagnosed with Graves' disease, a thyroid condition that sometimes drained him of energy and for which his physician had prescribed medication. "You'd never have known it," continued Billy Way. "He seemed so full of energy so much of the time. In a way, I suppose Graves' disease helped balance out his more prevalent ailment, attention deficit disorder, from which he'd suffered since childhood. Of the two, the ADD clearly won out."

Alex Siegal, a British freelance photographer, remembered John's penchant for playfulness. "For several days in 1991, I practically stalked the guy," remarked Siegal. "I rented a bike and tailed him as he rode his bike to work each morning. He played this cat-and-mouse game—he'd pedal real slow, let me practically catch up to him, then he'd round a corner and take off like a bat out of hell. We'd dive in and out of traffic like a couple of madmen. After about a week of this, he slowed down long enough to let me pull up next to him. My camera bag was slung over my shoulder. 'What can I do for you?' he asked. I pointed at the camera. 'I'd like a few pictures,' I said. 'Why didn't you say so in the first place?' he answered. He pulled over, climbed off his bike, and let me shoot away."

Caroline Kennedy turned out to be a far less willing photographic subject than her brother. "I prowled around her Upper East Side neighborhood for a couple of days before I finally saw her," said Siegal. "She was walking along on Park Avenue with her head down, avoiding eye contact. She must have seen me, because she suddenly picked up her pace and hurried into her building. I returned the following day and this time I found her seated at the fountain in a coffee shop, reading a book and sipping an ice tea. I sat down next to her and asked what she was reading. She looked at me and stiffened. Obviously aware of my British accent, she said, 'I've learned that every Englishman in America is either a reporter or a photographer. Therefore, I will not enter into a conversation.' With that, she slammed her book shut, asked for the check, paid her bill, and left."

Another freelance photographer, Stanley Witt, had a similar experience. "I saw Caroline shopping for children's clothes at the Gap," said Witt. "I wanted to be polite about it, so I asked her if I could take a picture. 'Absolutely not,' she snapped. She turned and hurriedly headed for the exit. I went after her. She stopped and said, 'If you continue to follow me, I'll call the police.' She evidently hated the press. I have a friend, a photographer for *Time,* who attended a book party in the winter of 1991 at the home of Bill Moyers to celebrate the publication by Doubleday of Elizabeth Crook's *The Raven's Bride.* Based on the life of Sam Houston, the novel interested Jackie Onassis because Houston had been included in John F. Kennedy's *Profiles in Courage.* Jackie was there, and so was Caroline with her husband. My friend wasn't on assignment that day, but he had his camera with him. He took a shot of Jackie and then turned to Caroline. She began to back away, a look of horror on her face. And that's when Ed Schlossberg jumped in. Arms flailing, he stepped between Caroline and the camera. 'Can't you see that my wife doesn't want her picture taken?' he said. It was ludicrous, because book parties are always fair game for the press. It's true my friend wasn't the official party photographer, but Caroline's reaction was way over the top."

She didn't mind being photographed at several elaborate events she attended some months later, one to celebrate the hundredth anniversary of the Municipal Art Society, the other a gala for six hundred guests at Grand Central Terminal. While she didn't stand out in public as much as her mother or brother, Caroline attracted far more attention than she craved. Florinda Arnold, a New York business executive, encountered Caroline and Ed Schlossberg in late 1991 at a Broadway show. "During intermission, people gathered around them in a circle and gawked," said Arnold. "Caroline looked extremely uncomfortable. I saw her again several months later eating lunch with a girlfriend at the Four Seasons Grill. I sat close enough to notice that she ordered a very nonfat lunch—a garden salad followed by broiled sole with a complement of grilled vegetables. There were all sorts of power brokers there that day, including Tina Brown, Barbara Walters, and Henry Kissinger. The only one to create a ripple when she came and went was Caroline Kennedy. It was hard to believe that nearly thirty years after Camelot, Jackie, Caroline, and John were still among the most stellar of stars. If anything, they were of greater interest now than they'd been three decades before."

Reflecting on the question of public exposure, Yusha Auchincloss believed Caroline was even more protective of her privacy than her mother. "The difference between them," said Auchincloss, "is that Jackie didn't care a whit what people thought of her. She accepted the fact that no matter how much she protested, the media would never stop pursuing her. Caroline, on the other hand, believed that if she stuck her head in the sand, she'd no longer be noticed. John Jr. took an altogether different tack. He went out of his way to embrace members of the press. It didn't minimize his exposure, but in general—though not always—they handled him with kid gloves."

· · ·

Tom Bannon, general manager of Island Restaurant on Madison Avenue and 92nd Street, remembered seeing John only once in his establishment. "It was early 1991," said Bannon. "He came in by himself. The place went dead. Nobody talked, nobody moved, nobody breathed. All eyes were on him. After looking around, he took a seat at the bar near the front of the restaurant. He ordered a light meal and a glass of wine. Every young waitress on duty that evening found an excuse to venture to the bar for a closer look. They were all smitten. One of them, a married gal, said to me later that if she were ever to cheat on her husband, it would have to be with John F. Kennedy Jr."

John's appearance at Island occurred about the same time as the termination of his relationship with Christina Haag. "When we broke up, it wasn't over one incident or event," she said. "It was sad and painful. We talked about getting back together for about a year after the breakup. John dated a lot of people before he settled down with Carolyn Bessette. He wasn't yet committed to his life. He wasn't ready for a serious relationship. Although he may have wanted to be with me, the timing wasn't right. Timing is everything. If John had married earlier in life, and if it had failed, it would have been a public failure. He didn't want a public failure. John married only after his mother died, but I don't feel it had anything to do with his seeking her approval. It had to do with his growing up. All I can say is that I loved John very much."

Although Daryl Hannah had gone back with Jackson Browne, she and John continued to see each other whenever she traveled to the East Coast. On August 29, 1990, she accompanied him to Lola's, a downtown Manhattan restaurant, to celebrate Tim Shriver's thirty-first birthday. The following day they did the TriBeCa pub crawl, stopping at a bar called STP to shoot a game of pool. They attended a party at Life, a Bleecker Street club, where they spent forty-five minutes searching for a piece of jewelry Daryl lost while dancing with John. An early September item in *The Boston Globe* claimed they'd been spotted checking into a Boston hotel. Natalie Cross, a Jamaican-born assistant to the actress, was quoted as saying, "Daryl's playing both sides." She was living with Browne, but she was once again dating Kennedy.

In the early fall of 1990, while shooting *At Play in the Fields of the Lord*, Daryl fell ill with a mysterious virus. On location in the rain forest of Brazil, she was taken to a nearby medical clinic, where she spent the next week recuperating from a dangerously high fever. When he heard about her misfortune, John—a true romantic—ordered dozens and dozens of long-stemmed red roses to be delivered to her bedside.

Following his breakup with Christina Haag, John again spent time with Daryl. "She was very sweet," said Rob Littell. "She and John got along famously. They were a great number. The only problem is that they were both flowers. Every decent relationship needs a gardener and a flower. You can't have two gardeners, nor can you have two flowers. I never perceived them as a long-term deal. Neither did John's mother. She'd seen too many of these high-intensity, high-illumination affairs fall apart. They were a wonderful couple, but they weren't marriage material. I don't think they saw themselves walking down the aisle together."

"Jackie didn't like Hollywood actresses," said George Plimpton. "It may have had something to do with Jack Kennedy's lifelong attraction to starlets. I remember Jackie's calling me one day and saying, 'Did you see that photograph of Daryl Hannah in *The New York Times*?' They'd run an advertisement for some film she'd just made, and Daryl appeared in the ad attired in a rather suggestive, diaphanous outfit. I tried to explain to Jackie that Daryl was simply playing a role—it had nothing to do with her true persona. 'Oh, yeah,' said Jackie. 'Well, while she's seeing John here in New York, she's still living with that rocker in California.'"

On May 30, 1991, a day after John attended the annual gathering of the clan at the JFK Library to commemorate President Kennedy's birthday, John Jr. flew to Los Angeles for a scheduled visit with Daryl. Their arrangement had been contingent upon Jackson Browne's plan to be out of town. At the last minute Browne decided to stay put. Ensconced in a room at the Four Seasons and unable to see Daryl, John resorted to an escort service. An hour later a young lady knocked at his hotel room. Tall, lanky, and blond, she bore a strong resemblance to Daryl Hannah. "At first," said April Showers (a pseudonym), "he refused to identify himself. I told him I needed some form of identification—a driver's license, passport, something with his picture on it. That's how we protect ourselves from the police. If a vice cop uses a phony ID, it's considered entrapment, so we always ask to see ID. He balked at first but then dug out his driver's license with the name 'John F. Kennedy' printed on it. Not that I didn't recognize him, but in this business you take nothing for granted."

Like so many of her customers, John spent half the session unburdening his soul. "Men love call girls," said April, "because they know they can talk without incriminating themselves. And that's exactly what he did. Of course I knew all about his illustrious family and his on-again, off-again romance with Daryl Hannah. But I didn't know the fine details, which basically boiled down to his being in love with an insecure woman afraid to give up her boyfriend in return for a more fulfilling relationship with John. I asked him why he didn't give her an ultimatum. 'You're John Kennedy,' I said. 'Anyone in his or her right mind would trade up for you.' 'Yeah,' he said, 'but not this one.'"

Their conversation took place during and between an hour's worth of sexual acrobatics. "He wanted to know what famous Hollywood stars I'd been with," said April. "I told him I couldn't name names. He tried to cajole me. 'Give me a hint,' he said. I refused. Then he inquired whether my professional name—April Showers—had anything to do with my area of expertise. I told him I did yellow and brown showers, but only for an extra fee. 'Want to avail yourself?' I asked. He smiled. 'Yellow showers I can dig,' he said. 'But how do brown showers work?' 'They work,' I said. 'I take an enema, and we retire to the bathtub. Some men like to watch, others like to indulge.' The subject seemed to fascinate him. 'People shit on me all the time,' he quipped. 'I don't have to pay for it.' He had a great sense of humor. I don't remember much about the sexual end of it. I think because he'd flown all the way to Los Angeles and couldn't see Daryl Hannah, he was pretty frustrated and had a good time. He gave me a nice tip. As I was about to leave, he said, 'If I ever run for president, don't pop out of the woodwork on me—you could cost me votes.' 'Don't worry,' I replied, 'my lips are sealed.'"

A week after his return to New York, he showed up at Café des Artistes with three girls in tow. He was playing the field. In his personal memoir about John, Rob Littell relates what he considered one of "the funniest stories he ever told me." John was at home, "in bed with a woman he was dating at the time when the phone rang. And rang, and rang. The caller would hang up, the ringing would stop and then the phone would start ringing again." To "put an end to it," John took the receiver off the hook and placed it on a night table next to the bed. He resumed his lovemaking, evidently with a very loud and amorous young lady. What John didn't realize until he heard a woman's voice screaming at him over the phone is that his caller, another of his lovers, had been privy to the entire scene.

Although John and Christina Haag had broken up, they would go out on a final date. In late 1990 they performed in an independent film, *A Matter of Degrees,* a remake and update of the student film in which John had appeared at Brown. In the remake, JFK Jr. plays the guitar and sings an Elvis Costello song. The number—at John's request—ended up on the cutting-room floor. He appears in the film but only as a ten-second cameo standing in the background of a crowded party scene. He and Christina attended the premiere of the film at the Bleecker Street Cinema in New York on September 13, 1991. Later that night John was seen at the Brasserie restaurant with another girl on his arm.

In early 1992 Caroline Kennedy again teamed up with Ellen Alderman to begin research on their second book, *The Right to Privacy,* an examination—via contemporary case studies—of the first and fourth amendments. Published three years later by Knopf, the book dealt with issues close to Caroline's heart, namely the invasion of an individual's right to privacy versus the public's "right to know." Interviewing plaintiffs and defendants in well-documented invasion of privacy cases, the authors crisscrossed the country with their legal pads and tape recorders. They located a married couple in Iowa whose hotel room had contained a two-way mirror. Another case involved an eighteen-year-old high school girl who had been secretly videotaped by her boyfriend when they were having sex. The volume included cases of ordinary citizens whose identities had been stolen off the Internet, and people whose photos had been taken and then published without their consent. In Los Angeles Caroline interviewed porn magazine impresario Larry Flynt, who had once published a nude snapshot of Jackie Onassis. An ardent first-amendment advocate, Flynt had lost a 1982 lawsuit to a young woman whose unauthorized photograph he'd run in the pages of *Chic*. Seated among life-size statuary of copulating nudes, Caroline later observed, "You wouldn't mistake Mr. Flynt's office for someone else's." Said Flynt of his interviewer: "I found Caroline very charming, very smart."

One of the volume's main shortcomings is its total lack of personal context or anecdote. Book buyers expecting to find illumination into Caroline's lifelong struggle with the media were ultimately disappointed. If anything, *The Right to Privacy* reads like an introductory text better suited to the needs of a law school student than to the interests of a general audience. The tone of the book, like Caroline herself, is formal and remote. Absent from the commentary is an examination of the more intriguing and complex issue of "celebrity and the right to privacy." So wary was Caroline of public exposure, so devoid of introspection is the book, that the authors even removed from their finished manuscript a section titled *Onassis v. Christian Dior*, a 1989 case Jackie won over the use of her likeness in an a print ad by the famed fashion house.

More interesting than anything the authors had to offer—either in the book or on a ten-city national promotion tour (including an appearance on *The Tonight Show* with Jay Leno)—were the comments of the employees at Knopf associated with the volume's publication. Peter Gethers, editor of *The Right to Privacy*, said of Caroline, "She's astonishingly well-adjusted to her fame. Let's face it—Caroline is the star. But they're a good writing team. Ellen is a little overprotective of Caroline because of who she is, and Caroline's protective of Ellen—she doesn't want to be seen as the driving force."

While Caroline worked on her book and attended to the needs of her family, her brother toiled on as an assistant prosecutor and again turned his attention to politics, campaigning in New York and Massachusetts on behalf of Bill Clinton. In July 1992, in company with his mother and Maurice Tempelsman, he went to the Democratic National Convention at Madison Square Garden in New York, where on the last night they viewed a short film showing President John F. Kennedy shaking a young

Bill Clinton's hand on the White House lawn. Clinton, the 1992 Democratic Party presidential candidate, credited JFK with having inspired him to enter politics. Earlier in the week, JFK Jr. attended a party for Bill and Hillary Clinton hosted by Pamela Harriman, the Democratic nominee's chief benefactor. Following Clinton's election to the presidency that fall, he and Hillary joined Ted Kennedy, Ethel, and JFK Jr. on a visit to the graves of John and Robert Kennedy at Arlington National Cemetery. It was shortly after the grave site visit that the president-elect evidently offered John Jr. an unspecified cabinet post in his administration, an offer John ultimately rejected.

During the late summer of 1992, JFK Jr. met and first dated his future wife, Carolyn Bessette. "Carolyn was John's ideal physical type," said John Perry Barlow. "There was immediate attraction on both sides." She was working in the public relations department at Calvin Klein and had been introduced to John by Calvin's then-wife, Kelly Klein, during his visit to the fashion showroom. They went out a few times before John invited her to spend a weekend at Sea Song, a Sagaponack, Long Island, beach house he and Anthony Radziwill had rented each summer since 1990. Radziwill used the house extensively; John appeared infrequently.

The house, not far from where Ed and Caroline Schlossberg would purchase their weekend retreat, was a ten-minute drive from Lee Radziwill's East Hampton residence. In her 2005 memoir, *What Remains,* Anthony's future wife, Carole Radziwill, recalled the weekend John brought Carolyn to Sagaponack: "I was washing dishes, Anthony was running on the beach, and John was reading the paper when she [Carolyn] walked out of the bedroom, blonde and ten stories high, in a white cotton nightgown with yellow trim." After introducing herself to Carole, Carolyn asked if she could borrow a toothbrush. Besides Carolyn's imposing beauty, Carole detected two of her most notable traits: Carolyn talked with her hands and was touchy-feely. "She held my hand when she talked to me or when we walked down the street," wrote Carole. "She played with my hair, absentmindedly, when she was making a point. It took me some time to get used to all the touching. She dismissed the barriers, the walls of politeness, the invisible personal space we protect. There was no awkward embrace with her, no hesitation. She hugged you tight, as if she might never see you again."

As Carole Radziwill mentions in her memoir, John and Carolyn broke up the following weekend. Following a lengthy telephone conversation with Daryl Hannah, John decided to resume his tempestuous romance with the actress. It was, he admitted two years later, a "foolish" move.

Chapter 16

———— ◆ ————

JOHN AND DARYL

IN LATE AUGUST 1992, Daryl Hannah visited John in New York. They spent a few days together at Sagaponack and a few more at Martha's Vineyard, where JFK Jr. put on a daring waterskiing exhibition, prompting the actress's remark that he was "an adrenaline junkie, somebody who loves to live on the edge of disaster." Daryl proved to be an adrenaline junkie of a different kind, one who also enjoyed living on the edge of disaster. In mid-September, with Jackson Browne out of town, she asked John to visit her in Santa Monica. Checking into the Shangri-La Hotel, John spent two days with Daryl at the Santa Monica house. Daryl's former assistant, Natalie Cross, later reported that it wasn't the first time he'd visited the house, nor was it the first time they'd made love in the same bed she shared with her musician boyfriend. They also made love by the pool and at Santa Monica Beach, a block and a half from the house.

It was during John's stay that Daryl apparently admitted she'd wanted to go out with him ever since their first meeting at St. Martin when both were teenagers. Years later, at Daryl's behest, her stepfather had telephoned his friend Ted Kennedy to help arrange her invitation to the Ross-Radziwill wedding reception. John, in turn, admitted that he'd previously flunked the New York State bar exam because Daryl had broken up with him and gone back with Jackson Browne.

A week later, during a trip to New York to see John, Daryl decided she wanted to be with him on a permanent basis. On September 23 she flew back to California to end her relationship with Jackson Browne and retrieve her personal belongings. At this point versions differ as to what actually transpired.

According to an October 22, 1992, article in *People,* a fight broke out between Browne and Hannah. Natalie Cross had witnessed a number of previous battles over Daryl's involvement with JFK Jr. This time, claimed *People* magazine, Daryl emerged with "a black eye, a broken finger, swollen lips, and body bruises." Strangely enough, it was Browne and not Hannah who finally called the police, telling them that "somebody" was "ransacking" his home. When the patrol car arrived, the officers found Browne alone in the house. "Everything's all right," he assured them, neglecting to report that Daryl had barricaded herself in a guest cottage on the property. The officers quickly departed. So did Daryl. Her sister, Page, picked her up and drove her to the hospital, where their mother, Susan Wexler, and uncle Haskell Wexler soon joined them. The actress's spokesperson, Alan Nierob, released a press statement: "Daryl Hannah received serious injuries incurred during a domestic dispute with Jackson Browne for which she sought medical treatment."

In a statement of his own, issued some time after the incident, Browne vehemently denied the allegations: "It is untrue that I was violent, and it is untrue that the argument was about possessions and things she was trying to remove. Daryl's stepfather [Jerry Wexler] was dying. She was under tremendous pressure . . . She was in very fragile shape. We had been breaking up for quite a while. Absolutely no assault occurred."

Since no police report was filed, and because neither Browne nor Hannah turned in an official complaint, celebrity watchers were forced to draw their own conclusions.

The same *People* article included testimony from Daryl's uncle attesting to the assault. "Jackson beat Daryl," said Haskell Wexler. "I was with her in the hospital. I saw ugly bruises on her eye and chin and on her ribs. The examining doctor reported she had blood in her urine. The doctor was shocked by the severity and noted Daryl as a 'badly battered woman.' I photographed her in the hospital."

Daryl's mother, who'd always wanted her daughter to go back with JFK Jr., spoke to a reporter for a *People* cover story that ran on October 16, 1993. "I saw my daughter in the hospital," said Sue Wexler. "I saw the damage that was done to her. The doctor was very concerned. Jackson was a very, very good friend of mine, but when I saw Daryl, I just felt betrayed."

Additional commentary in both the 1992 and 1993 *People* articles suggested that Browne had a history of violent behavior. "This has happened before, but never this bad," ventured one unnamed source. Another remarked that Browne was known to have "an explosive personality." Browne's pals defended him. "He's just not a violent guy," said one friend. A second buddy remarked, "I would bet everything I own that Jackson did not batter Daryl."

A day after the fracas, JFK Jr. arrived in Los Angeles and returned with Daryl (via MGM Grand Air) to New York. They shifted back and forth between his latest Hudson Street rental and an apartment she'd recently acquired in the Althorp, a landmark building at Broadway and 79th Street in Manhattan. Several days later, New York photographer Russell Turiak took a picture of Daryl sporting a black eye and a heavily bandaged finger. "She stopped at a West Side movie theater with another woman to buy tickets," he recalled. "This was shortly after she supposedly got her ass kicked by Jackson Browne. It was a $40,000 photograph. It's not every day you see a movie star walking around with a black eye. And now that she was living with John, her value as a photographic commodity soared. After they bought their tickets, they walked down the street and disappeared into an Indian restaurant. Just before they ducked into the restaurant, I got my shot. The next day I drove down to TriBeCa, near where John had an apartment. I passed a bistro, and there, seated in a window booth, sipping a beer, was Daryl Hannah with a couple of friends. I stopped the car and started taking photos of her through the window. I suppose I could've gone into the bistro, but I had no intention of pissing her off."

During the heightened period of their romance—1992 to 1994—John and Daryl were constantly in the news. "It's Love!" proclaimed the cover of *People.* The *Los Angeles Times* ran a photo of John and Daryl walking arm in arm, underlined by a caption that read: "Two of a Kind." The *Chicago Tribune* featured a shot of John and Daryl at her stepfather's funeral in Chicago. They were photographed nuzzling in Central Park. The *Globe* printed a picture of John and Daryl walking her dog, Blade, an overpampered mixed breed that vomited whenever the actress went off to a film shoot. The international press took an equal interest in the couple. Oblivious to the media, they vacationed in the Philippines, Hong Kong, the Republic of Palau, Tokyo, Switzerland, the South Pacific, Latin America, and various spots around the United States. For a time, John adopted Daryl's stringent vegetarian diet, restricting himself to fresh fruits and vegetables. As often as not, wherever they went, whatever they did, people converged on them like animals at a watering hole. "One advantage to being a movie star," said Pierre Salinger, "is that Daryl was as inured to public exposure as John. It didn't particularly bother her, while the woman John eventually married had real issues with the press."

Speculation that John and Daryl planned to marry reached a high point when Daryl went to a flea market and purchased an antique wedding gown. Novelist Sugar Rautbord, a friend of Daryl's, informed the press, "Daryl really likes John. She's desperate to marry him." Margaret James, a Palm Beach socialite, encountered the couple in an airport in Tokyo. "Daryl was draped all over him, and they looked ecstatic," said Margaret. "They seemed so natural together, almost like newlyweds." Stopped on a street corner by a New York *Daily News* reporter, Caroline Kennedy denied knowledge of any pending marital plans involving her brother.

Rumors nevertheless persisted. Photographer Jacques Lowe recalled asking John if he and Daryl had "any intention of tying the knot." John stared at Lowe but said nothing. "I thought he hadn't heard me," said Lowe, "so I repeated the question. 'How did you know?' John finally responded. But you never knew when John was just being cute. He loved to kid people. In retrospect, my best guess is that he considered the possibility but ultimately decided against it."

Having followed John's career, British journalist Annette Witheridge noted that "many of his friends thought he should marry Daryl. They were such a dynamic duo. His mother didn't like the idea, and that sufficed to prevent the relationship from ending in marriage. It's a pity in a way, because they seemed to have something special."

Photographer Ken Katz agreed. "Daryl had boyish qualities," he said. "She and John used to go gallivanting in the mud after a rainstorm. They loved to dress down. They were like two carefree kids. They would play football and Frisbee in Central Park. Daryl was very easygoing. Carolyn Bessette, JFK Jr.'s future wife, wasn't like that. I always felt John had more in common with Daryl."

In *Sweet Caroline*, Chris Andersen's biography of Caroline Kennedy, the author claims that on two occasions JFK Jr. telephoned his sister to announce that he and Daryl were planning to marry. Andersen further claims that in the summer of 1993, the two procured a marriage license in Santa Monica. In truth, although John and Daryl may have informally discussed marriage, they never planned a wedding and never took out a marriage license. According to Billy Way, "John had no intention of marrying Daryl, the chief reason being that she had an ongoing film career and no intention of giving it up. In the end, John wanted a woman whose career was John. He wanted a woman whose desire it was to become the power *behind* the throne, much as Jackie had been to JFK. That's not to say that John and Daryl didn't have fun together. In many ways, from what I gathered, it was a tremendous relationship—great sex, great times. It just wasn't a marriage."

Larry Zarrow, a TriBeCa neighbor of John's, reported seeing JFK Jr. dancing cheek to cheek with Daryl on the sixth-floor rooftop terrace of an apartment he'd leased on Hudson Street, near Jay Street. "My apartment was in a building opposite his," said Zarrow, "and my windows looked out on his windows. John was wearing his boxer shorts, and she had on a nightgown. It was a Sunday morning. He began tickling her, and she'd run away. He'd chase after her, and they'd begin dancing again. Despite this very entrancing scene, I wasn't surprised to learn that they eventually broke up. Like father, like son. President Kennedy had a yen for sexy actresses, but he ended up marrying Jacqueline Bouvier."

Rob Littell recalled spending a weekend with John, Daryl, and several other friends at Red Gate Farm. The men in the group—JFK Jr., Rob,

Kevin Ward, Kevin Ruff, and Willie Smith—decided to leave their girl-friends behind and go scuba diving after dinner. Weighted down with diving gear, they set out by boat at about 10:00 p.m. and soon found themselves lost in a blinding fog. With John at the helm, his face in the wind, their boat ran aground. Eventually the tide lifted them off the bottom and the fog dissipated. They headed for the Gay Head lighthouse, and with Littell remaining on deck, the others donned their gear and went into the water. Fairly quickly, the moon vanished, and the fog returned. Littell tried alerting the divers by slapping the surface of the water with an oar. Finally the foursome came back up. Returning to the house, they were set upon by an irate crew of women. Daryl Hannah, the angriest of the lot, had already called the Coast Guard. She and John spent the rest of the night locked in heated argument.

A similar episode took place when John, Daryl, and several others vacationed in Baja California. The group watched as John swam out to sea and suddenly vanished. After a half hour, John's companions began to panic. Daryl Hannah summoned a team of lifeguards who motored out in a speedboat and finally located the missing daredevil leisurely floating on his back two miles from shore.

"John grew up with the notion that life has to be lived to the fullest," said Frank Mankiewicz, a Kennedy supporter and RFK's former press secretary. "He didn't shrink or hang back from experience."

Although generally prudent in prepping himself for such escapades, there were moments of pronounced danger for which he wasn't adequately prepared. While living with Daryl, he went on a kayaking trip with several buddies in the Baltic near the Åland archipelago between Sweden and Finland. Inclement weather and a rough sea did little to deflate John's enthusiasm. Caught in swirling waters, John dropped his oar and watched it float out of reach. Two other kayaks in the group capsized. John made little of the incident, telling the press: "We got what we came for: some laughs, some thrills, and a few stories."

There seemed to be a positive correlation between John's misadventures and his relationship with Daryl Hannah. The more dangerous his escapades, the more serious were their arguments. The two were overheard bickering loudly on Fifth Avenue as they approached Jackie Onassis's apartment building. "Make up your mind," JFK Jr. shouted at Daryl. "Where do you want to go?" He stormed into the lobby of the building. Carrying a bag of low-calorie treats from E.A.T., Daryl followed. A moment later they were back on the street, still squabbling. They walked to Madison Avenue and continued their argument in a coffee shop. When they exited, John hailed a cab and jumped in, leaving Daryl behind.

Richard Wiese spent time with John and Daryl. "It was a tough but interesting relationship," he said. "They were both a little spoiled. They were both used to getting their way. Daryl once commented to me that all of John's friends felt sorry for his having to put up with a Hollywood actress. 'But you know,' she said, 'he's no day at the beach.' I suppose she meant that he wasn't easy either."

"By the end of 1993," observed Phil Auburn, an acquaintance of JFK Jr.'s, "John and Daryl seemed to be on the verge of splitting up. They spent most of their time arguing. Everything became a bone of contention between them. I remember when they took out some videos from Blockbuster and forgot to return them. They fought like cats and dogs as to who would pay. In July 1993 John had quit his job in the district attorney's office and was searching for something meaningful to do with his life. Daryl, whose career had peaked, appeared in a bunch of second- and third-rate films. Her focus was John. She hoped to tie the knot with him, but it was all rather hopeless. As promising as the relationship had been, they had no future together. It was the beginning of the end."

On January 19, 1993, Caroline Kennedy gave birth to her third (and last) child, a son named John Bouvier Kennedy Schlossberg, after Caroline's maternal grandfather. Family members called him Jack. In keeping with tradition, Ed and Caroline Schlossberg would soon enroll their daughters—Rose and Tatiana—in the Brearley School. Caroline was there a lot, with the family dog, to pick up her daughters after school. Maude Davis, Jackie's cousin (daughter of Maude Bouvier Davis and sister of John Davis), taught remedial reading at Brearley. "Neither of Caroline's daughters were students of mine," she said, "but I heard a lot about them from my colleagues. Like their mother and grandmother—as well as their father—Rose and Tatiana were extremely private. They never flaunted themselves. They were excellent students. They were gifted writers. I think that's in their genes. And, of course, their father turned them on to computers. Ed Schlossberg designed the school's computer lab. I used to see him around, but I never met him personally. He's supposedly a rather quiet, pensive fellow. Unlike Caroline, her daughters stayed on in the school. The dress code had eased since Caroline's day, and Brearley was no longer as competitive. There's a great deal of emphasis on reading and writing. It's certainly one of the best girls' private schools in the country."

When Rose Schlossberg was in the first grade at Brearley, her class went on a field trip to the American Museum of Natural History. Jackie went along. "She was the only grandparent in the group," said Bambi Mitgang, whose daughter was in the same class. "She wore jeans and loafers and talked kid stuff with the teachers and parents. There were maybe a half-dozen mothers on the trip. They seemed surprised by both Jackie's friendliness and attire. I suppose they expected her to be exceedingly remote and show up in a Dior gown and pillbox hat."

Ed and Caroline Schlossberg were hands-on parents. They spent most of their spare hours with their children, reading to them, watching videos, helping them with homework. The children likewise enjoyed being in the company of "Uncle John." JFK Jr. had all the makings of a devoted dad. One weekend he took Rose and Tatiana skiing in New Hampshire. He played games with baby Jack. The youngsters shared Jackie's and John's love for the genteel simplicity of Martha's Vineyard. During one of their visits, John borrowed his mother's binoculars and led the girls on a nature tour of the island. Another weekend he took them on a sail from Martha's Vineyard to Nantucket, where they spent the day with Jackie at the seaside summer home of Bunny Mellon.

Caroline Kennedy had become a trustee of the immensely wealthy Park Foundation, which (along with the Joseph P. Kennedy Jr. Foundation) controlled the brunt of the Kennedy family's holdings. She secured a trustee position for her husband on the John F. Kennedy Library Foundation, which among other benefits resulted in his participation in several exhibition design projects. In addition, he had started a small foundation of his own (the Edwin Schlossberg Foundation), which awarded limited grants to practicing artists. Professionally, Ed had branched off in multiple directions, procuring commissions from such prestigious corporations as Sony, Pfizer pharmaceuticals, and AOL Time Warner. According to public records, he had founded a number of corporations of his own. Edwin Schlossberg Apparel Inc. had been incorporated in Delaware in 1991 and dissolved two years later. ESL Guide Inc., a learning-tools venture, lasted until 1994. Interainment Inc., a company devoted to the "development, testing, and validation of intellectual properties," similarly came and went, as did another half-dozen of his business concerns, some listed with Dun & Bradstreet, others not.

As for Jackie, she had become independently friendly with Hillary Rodham Clinton. Soon after Bill Clinton's inauguration, she invited the new First Lady to her Fifth Avenue apartment for a long chat on how to raise a well-adjusted child in the White House. Hillary claimed in her autobiography, *Living History,* that Jackie provided sound advice, basically suggesting that Hillary not expose her thirteen-year-old daughter, Chelsea, to too much too soon. Hillary's critics maintained that this, and subsequent meetings, were all part of a carefully orchestrated plot to lure the former First Lady into the Clinton camp. The president even spoke off the record to Jacqueline about the possibility of her accepting an ambassadorship, an offer she flatly declined.

Their next meeting took place in the summer of 1993. While vacationing on Martha's Vineyard, the Clintons—Bill, Hillary, and Chelsea—joined Jackie and Senator Ted Kennedy for a cruise on Maurice Tempelsman's boat. Also on board were Ed and Caroline Schlossberg, Ted's new wife, Victoria Reggie (member of an old Washington political family), and presidential adviser Vernon Jordan and his wife, Ann, in addition to several Secret Service agents. Leaving Menemsha Harbor, the boat anchored off a small island where the group went swimming. Caroline and Chelsea climbed a forty-foot platform on the boat and leaped into the water together. "Caroline is one of the few people in the world who can understand Chelsea's unique experiences," noted Hillary in her autobiography. The group returned to Gay Head for lunch at Jackie's house, then spent the rest of the day on Jackie's private beach. That evening, the president and First Lady took everyone to dinner at a small inn operated by the family of singer James Taylor, a longtime resident of Martha's Vineyard. From that day forward, Chelsea Clinton regarded Caroline Kennedy as a friend and role model. The Clinton visit, complete with Secret Service agents and hordes of reporters and photographers, constituted a rare public intrusion into Jackie's private domain.

A week later, President Clinton repaid Jackie's hospitality by inviting her and Maurice to his forty-seventh birthday party. In October the president attended the rededication of the Kennedy Library in Boston. The star that day was Caroline Kennedy Schlossberg, who received a standing ovation for her remarks. "I remember watching Jackie's face," said writer Doris Kearns Goodwin. "It was Caroline's moment, and you could see the pleasure her mother took in that. It was a sort of passing of the guard."

Jackie took equal pleasure in reading John Jr.'s comments in a 1993 interview published in *Vogue,* with photographs by Annie Leibovitz. Asked about the so-called Kennedy legacy, he said: "It's not for me to talk about a legacy or a mystique. It's my family. It's my mother. It's my sister. It's my father. We're a family like any other. We look out for one another. The fact that there have been difficulties and hardships, or obstacles, makes us closer." In answer to a question concerning the possibility of his entering politics, John remarked: "It's obviously something people ask me occasionally, and having grown up with it, I have to admit it's something I consider a lot . . . If you run for office, you'd better be sure it's something you want to do and that the rest of your life is set up to accommodate that decision. It takes a certain toll on your personality, and on your family life. I've seen it personally. So if I were to do it, I would want to make sure that was what I wanted to do, and that I didn't do it because people thought I should . . ."

Commenting on JFK Jr.'s remarks, actress Suzanna Bowling, the daughter of a William Morris theatrical agent, remarked, "John was very conscious of the fact that people expected him to play a certain role in life. He'd finally begun to understand himself, to break out of the mold into which he'd been cast. For years he catered to the needs of others. People flocked to him. They enjoyed being in his presence—they wanted the connection. He validated their existence. 'If I'm seen with him,' they said to themselves, 'then I'm famous too.' He'd reached the point where he wanted to determine his own future, to be his own boss rather than please others. His sister had found a safe niche for herself; she doted on privacy. John, however, seemed destined for greatness, like his father before him."

Jackie vacillated between granting John his need for independence on the one hand, and her desire to control him on the other. She enjoyed the notion that he continued to make use of Red Gate Farm, affording her the opportunity to keep him within reach. He visited when she was there and also when she wasn't. Although she insisted that her own bedroom be kept spotless, she gave John full run of the house without ever complaining about empty beer cans or overflowing garbage bags. Jackie became annoyed at her son only once. He and several friends, including Daryl Hannah, had spent a weekend at the house and left a mess. "Doesn't your girlfriend believe in helping out?" said Jackie. The house-trashing incident took place a week after the March 14, 1993, theft of JFK Jr.'s Typhoon sport utility vehicle. John had parked his new SUV in TriBeCa and absentmindedly left the keys in the ignition. Three and a half years later, in November 1996, the SUV turned up when police pulled it over on Staten Island and arrested the driver for possession of stolen property.

"John adored his mother and vice versa," said George Plimpton. "They nevertheless had their differences, particularly in the summer of 1993 when he stepped down from his position with the DA's office. 'And do what?' asked Jackie. She was disappointed. She'd just seen a picture of John and Daryl Hannah in one of the tabloids Rollerblading down the street together. He had on a baseball cap turned backward. 'You look like an overgrown frat boy,' she told him, 'and Daryl looks like an unmade bed.' John walked out on his mother and slammed the door in her face. Unquestionably, she tried to influence—or rather inspire—him, without appearing to dictate his future. She never looked very favorably upon his affair with Daryl Hannah. In her eyes, it hardly fit the image of somebody who had a date with destiny."

After the argument, Jackie called Plimpton and asked him to have a heart-to-heart with John. They met for drinks. "I told him," said Plimpton, "that his mother had concerns about his future. Did he have any specific plans? He spoke about wanting to start a kayak business, organizing international kayak excursions. He and a friend were looking into it. He then mentioned journalism. He had a vague notion of wanting to kick off some sort of political magazine. This was evidently the germination of what later evolved into *George.* At the time, however, it all sounded rather nebulous and unformulated."

When Plimpton informed Jackie of their conversation, she seemed confused. "Journalism?" she asked. "I know he reads the newspaper, but I've never seen him so much as look at a magazine."

According to Plimpton, Jackie eventually brought up the subject to John. He told her his father had wanted to go into journalism—he hadn't followed through only because Joe Kennedy Jr. had been killed during World War II, thus placing JFK in the political spotlight. That seemed to satisfy Jackie—she fully understood the connection.

In the late fall of 1993, John received a telephone call from Ken Sunshine, a public relations consultant to David Dinkins, the mayor of New York, currently campaigning for reelection. Aware that Dinkins had been in California with Bobby Kennedy when he was assassinated in the spring of 1968, JFK Jr. called the mayor and volunteered his services. He contributed to the mayor's reelection fund and joined the campaign.

John did a Saturday morning walking tour for Dinkins on the Upper West Side, ending up at Zabar's, the well-known food emporium on Broadway and 80th Street. "There was a horde of cameras outside," said Ken Sunshine, "and when he went in by the fish counter, several old ladies buying lox started screaming, 'John! John!' It was like the Beatles. There was this crunch. He got completely separated from Dinkins. A cheese display went flying at one point, and a big tough cop said, 'It's a bloody lox riot!' We had to get him out of there. There was flying Brie. People wanted a piece of him. It was wild."

Although Dinkins subsequently lost his reelection bid to Rudolph Giuliani, he had only positive memories of John. "He had tremendous magnetism," said Dinkins. "He could have had a successful political career, if that's what he'd wanted. He was enormously modest. I'm reminded of an occasion several years later when, presented with the prospect of being bestowed an honorary doctorate from a distinguished American university, he graciously declined the honorary degree . . . with the explanation that he had not *earned* the honor."

It was in the fall of 1993 that John encountered Princess Diana. Richard Wiese, who happened to be with him at the time, recalled that they'd been talking about Marilyn Monroe. "John had just seen *Some Like It Hot,* starring Marilyn, and he was extolling her beauty and sexiness. He said something like, 'She's some kind of babe.' Given his father's history, I thought his comment a bit odd. I said, 'Well, obviously some people thought so.' We were in the hotel Carlyle, where President Kennedy and Marilyn were supposed to have shacked up. We were in the elevator going to visit someone. In walked Princess Diana, who'd come to the U.S. on a visit. She was with a security guard. She recognized John and became flustered. She began fumbling with some papers she was holding. The elevator stopped and off she went. Despite countless newspaper and gossip column items linking John and Diana romantically, this marked their sole meeting."

Another encounter, though with somebody of less regal rank, took place at a Manhattan hot spot called Café Un Deux Trois. It involved John Jr. and 1980s supermodel Janice Dickinson whose sexual conquests (according to her tell-all autobiography) included Mick Jagger, Warren Beatty, Jack Nicholson, Sylvester Stallone, Liam Neeson, Dolph Lundgren, and Kelly LeBrock, ex-wife of Steven Seagal. Dressed in a to-kill-for black Valentino, Dickinson met John at the restaurant on a blind date she claimed had been arranged by New York hairstylist Frédéric Fekkai. Intrigued by the history of her dinner partner, Janice asked John: "So, what's it feel like to be Jackie O.'s son?" He barely responded. She proceeded to fire off several other questions about John's mother, then explained that while growing up, Jacqueline Kennedy Onassis had meant "everything" to her. "John was magnetic and spiritual, but I couldn't stop obsessing over Jackie," said Dickinson. "Throughout dinner I kept asking questions about his mother's wardrobe. He sat back in his chair and became dejected. I grew shy and stopped talking. Finally, I excused myself and went to the ladies' room. When I came out, he was standing there, waiting for me. He grabbed me and slammed me against the wall. He began kissing me. We made out for about five minutes. The only thing I could think of during our little session was the blood-spattered Chanel suit Jackie wore when she stepped off Air Force One in Washington in 1963 after the assassination in Dallas of President Kennedy. I realized that for me this wasn't about John—it was about Jackie and *her* fame. When you're in love with the mother, the son has no place."

John evidently reached a similar conclusion. Without accompanying his date back to the table, he made a beeline for the exit and left.

In October 1993 the FBI contacted Jackie with the unsettling news that they had uncovered another abduction plot with John Jr. earmarked as the potential victim. Jackie notified John Viggiano, a former Secret Service agent she hired from time to time for security purposes, and asked him to keep an eye on John. Several days later a Colombian drug dealer was apprehended in Los Angeles and charged with both possession of narcotics and plotting to kidnap JFK Jr. According to FBI files, the dealer wasn't prosecuted but was eventually deported to South America.

In November 1993 John and his friend Billy Way drove from New York to St. Coletta's, a Catholic home for the mentally disabled in Jefferson, Wisconsin, to visit Rosemary Kennedy, the firstborn daughter of Joe and Rose Kennedy. In 1941, without consulting or informing his wife, the paterfamilias authorized a physician to perform a lobotomy in the hope of ameliorating what he considered his daughter's unmanageable behavior. The surgical procedure left Rosemary profoundly retarded and partially paralyzed. Her father made immediate arrangements to have her institutionalized in rural Wisconsin, where she remained for the rest of her life, visited regularly by her sister Eunice Shriver. Rosemary's tragedy had led to the Kennedy family's charitable interest in mental retardation.

"John had met his aunt only once before," said Way. "She'd been brought to Rose Kennedy's Palm Beach estate one Christmas. The Kennedys had donated millions to St. Coletta's and had built a private cottage on the grounds for Rosemary. I don't think she recognized John or knew who he was. 'It doesn't matter,' he said, 'I'm doing this purely for myself.' He very gently stroked her hair and held her hand. She had the mind of a three-year-old. It was depressing, but it revealed a side of John I'd never seen before."

It was the thirty-year anniversary of JFK's assassination. As in years past, Jackie, Caroline, and John Jr. chose to ignore the public observances of the event in favor of a private family Mass at St. Thomas More Church. A day before the Mass, a stranger called the senior pastor, Monsignor George Bardes, and asked which Kennedys would attend. Alarmed by the caller's tone, the pastor notified the police. On the morning of the ceremony, a New York City Police SWAT Team was posted around the church. The Mass went as planned, but the police presence must have reawakened in the family the painful memory of John F. Kennedy's assassination.

The mystery caller was soon revealed to be Gary Lee Higgins, a thirty-two-year-old unemployed salesman from Indiana who was arrested outside Jackie's house in Bernardsville, New Jersey, and charged with criminal possession of a weapon: a .44-caliber handgun. A police report indicated that Higgins had wanted to give Jackie a hundred-page handwritten novella in which he depicted himself as a soldier in an intergalactic paramilitary organization. He apparently meant no harm. Nevertheless, it was revealed that he had been trying to contact Jackie for weeks. He hoped that she could convince Doubleday to publish his manuscript.

Two additional events took place that month. The *Bridgewater Courier News,* a New Jersey newspaper, broke the story on November 26 that Jackie had just sold her Bernardsville home to Caroline and John Jr. for "$100 or less." Doubtless, as part of Jackie's shrewd estate planning, the transfer of property was done to protect her children from unnecessary inheritance taxes. The house and ten-acre tract of land, purchased twenty years earlier for $200,000, was assessed in 1993 at more than $900,000.

The second incident ensued only days later at the Piedmont Club in Haymarket, Virginia. Attempting to clear a formidable stone wall at full gallop, Jackie's mount—a gray gelding named Clown—stumbled, pitching its rider to the ground. Jackie lay semiconscious for twenty minutes before an ambulance arrived and rushed her to Middleburg's Loudoun Hospital Center. She told doctors there that she'd been feeling tired and weak and had lacked the strength to maintain her balance on the horse. She remained overnight for observation and then returned to New York, shaken but with no visible injuries.

At the beginning of December, she noticed a swelling in her right groin. Suspecting an infection, her New York physician prescribed antibiotics, and the swelling subsided. Hoping that the sun and sea air would restore her vigor, Jackie and Maurice spent the Christmas holidays of 1993 aboard his yacht on a leisurely cruise of the Caribbean. But she soon began to complain of flulike symptoms: a persistent cough, swollen glands in her neck, and extreme cramps in her abdomen. Her physician recommended that they cut their vacation short and return home.

An examination and CAT scan revealed swollen lymph nodes in her neck and armpits; additional swollen lymph nodes were located in her chest and deep within her abdomen. Finally, a biopsy of one of the neck nodes determined that Jackie had non-Hodgkin's lymphoma, a cancer of the lymph system. A pathologist further concluded that the cells were anaplastic, or primitive, indicating that the disease was highly malignant and likely to spread to other organs.

Caroline and John Jr. were shocked by the news. To be nearer his mother, JFK Jr. moved temporarily into the Surrey Hotel on East 76th Street. John Politidis, proprietor of the Lenox Hill Grill on Lexington Avenue and 77th Street, recalled John dropping in for breakfast several times during this period, sitting quietly at the counter and reading *The New York Times.* "He usually ordered Special K," said Politidis. Caroline visited Jackie daily, often bringing along her children. Maurice accompanied her to New York Hospital–Cornell Medical Center, where she embarked on a painful series of chemotherapy treatments. To help protect her privacy, some outpatient care was administered in her home. When Jackie went in for treatments—shrouded in a cloak and under an assumed name—Maurice posted himself as a sentry to make certain that only properly certified personnel saw her. He also made the rounds of cancer specialists to gather information on the latest treatment alternatives.

Although outwardly optimistic, Jackie was fully aware of the grim prognosis facing those who suffered from her particular subtype of lymphoma. She couldn't forget the final agonizing months of her half-sister, Janet Auchincloss Rutherfurd, who had succumbed to cancer in 1985, as well as the dementia suffered by her mother as a result of Alzheimer's disease. Determined to command her own fate, Jackie exercised a living will. She didn't want extraordinary steps taken to prolong her life should the illness leave her in any way debilitated or mentally impaired.

As rumors of her ill health quickly spread, Jackie appeared less and less frequently at her Doubleday offices. Her workload was shifted to another editor. She reluctantly gave up a lifelong habit of chain smoking, an obvious concession to the disease. And she now took her customary walks along the cinder path around the Central Park Reservoir with Maurice or John, concealing her bloated appearance—a reaction to the cancer-fighting drugs being administered—with oversized coats and long, woolly scarves draped around her fast-balding head. She later took to wearing wigs.

Early in February 1994 Caroline and John Jr. stood in for their mother at a New York Democratic Party fund-raiser for Ted Kennedy. Caroline brought her husband, while JFK Jr. went with Daryl Hannah. Jackie greeted the "heavy hitters" at her apartment, professing to be suffering from "a bad cold." About this time, *New York Post* columnist Cindy Adams noted in print that Jackie's face appeared "puffy and splotchy," a common side effect of certain cancer drugs. "I lived in a building next door to Jackie on Fifth Avenue," said Cindy. "I used to see her coming and going. One day in early 1994, I saw her step out of a cab. That's when I noticed the telltale signs of illness."

Once the Cindy Adams story broke, Jackie had no choice but to go public. On February 11 friend and spokeswoman Nancy Tuckerman, responding to "speculation and rumor," confirmed that Jackie was indeed suffering from non-Hodgkin's lymphoma. "She's doing very well," Tuckerman informed the press. "She's maintaining her schedule. There's an excellent prognosis. The doctors are optimistic." The terse announcement stunned Jackie's friends and relations. Asked about it by one of his college buddies, John Jr. said, "If my mother can get past the first year, she'll be over the hump."

The public revelation that Jackie was battling a disease known to ravage its victims brought out the paparazzi. A doorman at 1040 Fifth Avenue recalled having "to chase off photographers every time I went out there to hail her a cab. It got so bad that she began taking the service elevator to the basement and exiting the building out a side door."

John Davis termed his cousin's illness "the ultimate cruelty." George Plimpton recalled that Jackie tried hard to keep up appearances, perhaps for the sake of her children and grandchildren. "One winter morning," he said, "she went off for a romp in Central Park with Rose and Tatiana, and they had a kind of snowball fight—Jackie versus the girls. On other days she took walks with Caroline, Ed, and the children. She and Maurice Tempelsman went to several films, including Steven Spielberg's *Schindler's List.* I visited with her one day and we walked up Fifth Avenue to the Guggenheim Museum. 'This illness is a kind of punishment for my hubris,' she told me. 'I've always been proud of keeping so fit. I diet, I swim, I exercise, I do my push-ups, and walk around the reservoir—and then this happens.' I imagine for somebody like Jackie who'd always been obsessed with her health and physical appearance, the realization that she was seriously ill must have been difficult to accept."

Art Russell, a former bookstore owner, first met Jackie in 1965 shortly after she and her children moved to New York. "I'd known her for years, but I didn't really know her," he said. "I met her while running around the reservoir. I was a regular, and so was she. And that's where we'd socialize. We spoke mostly about books and literature. I recall some fellow runners stopping her once to ask for her autograph. She politely declined. She never gave out her autograph. She found it odd, in fact, that strangers would even want her autograph. She always seemed very adept at handling people. She'd give you a smile and a brush-off at the same time. By the time you realized you'd been had, she'd be gone."

Russell remembered the last time he saw Jackie. "It was the winter of 1994," he continued, "and she and her daughter, Caroline, were walking slowly around the reservoir. I bumped into them, and Jackie invited me to join them. It was a bright, chilly day, and Jackie talked about the coming spring. Caroline, whom I'd never met before, seemed very much like her mother—informed, conversant, kind of preppy. That day she talked about her children. I'd read about Jackie's illness. She looked a bit pale and somewhat strained, but she maintained an extremely positive attitude. As we neared the exit to Fifth Avenue, Jackie paused and said to me, 'Let's trot next time we meet.' Then she and Caroline headed home."

It was in 1994 that the Schlossbergs paid $982,000 for a weekend house at 500 Sagaponack Road in Sagaponack, Long Island. Built in 1986, the two-story, shingle-style residence on 3.2 acres (including a tennis court and small swimming pool) contained five bedrooms and four bathrooms. The couple invested another $57,000 in renovation costs and in addition paid more than $10,000 per year in real estate taxes.

"Their house looked expensively decorated but not ostentatious," said George Plimpton. With their three children in tow, the couple often visited the various wildlife and nature preserves in the area. In Bridge-hampton, close to where they lived, the Long Pond Greenbelt offers a six-mile trail, treading past a chain of ponds and wetlands. Rich with bird life, it's popular with the locals.

Ed Schlossberg, several of whose cousins also lived in the area, often shopped for essentials at the Sagaponack General Store. The store took up one-half of an old wooden building, with the local post office occu-pying the other half. Tom Wolfe, Kurt Vonnegut, Roy Scheider, Sarah Jessica Parker, and her husband, Matthew Broderick, were among the store's regular customers. Caroline preferred a nearby catering and gour-met food shop called Loaves & Fishes. For larger quantities of food, they went to the shopping center in Water Mill. They often bought fresh fruit and vegetables at the produce stands that lined the roadside during the summer and fall. As for restaurants, they enjoyed the Palm in East Hamp-ton, the American Hotel in Sag Harbor, and Alison's, a local French bistro surrounded by potato fields. The children's favorite was the Bridge-hampton Candy Kitchen, best known for its homemade ice cream and classic-style soda fountain treats.

Without making their membership known to the general public, the Schlossbergs joined the Georgica Association, a highly selective, ultraex-pensive private beach and tennis club in Wainscott, five minutes from Sagaponack. Located on a private road and guarded by a high-powered security firm, the century-old club, with its clubhouse and cabanas, is open predominantly to old money and generational families whose parents and grandparents preceded them as members. Ed and Caroline Schlossberg were the exception. Their money, though plentiful, was more nouveau than old; and the Kennedys, though politically powerful, were hardly of high Boston Brahmin origin.

"One of the unwritten laws," said an anonymous member, "is that you don't discuss the club or its membership. If you do, you're ostracized. I belong because my parents belonged before me. It's even more selective and snooty and harder to get into than the venerable Maidstone Club in East Hampton. And within this enclave of selective privacy, you will find some of the wealthiest families in America. It's very old school, very classic—lawyers, physicians, financiers, and investment bankers. I'm probably biased, but the Georgica Association beach is arguably the prettiest part of Long Island. It's gorgeous, and it's unpopulated. Caroline Kennedy and her family are associate members, because they don't live within the geographic boundaries of the association. They list their address but not their home telephone number in the club directory. In other words, they're more private than most. My sister once babysat for their children. And my mother has met them. In the summer, I see them on the beach. They keep pretty much to themselves. They rarely attend functions. I've never spoken to Ed Schlossberg, but I've heard he's extraordinarily guarded—not at all talkative. Of the two, Caroline is more outgoing—and that's not saying very much."

Ed Schlossberg's penchant for privacy occasionally bordered on the rude. Stanley Mirsky, a leading New York physician and diabetes specialist with a weekend home in the Hamptons, once encountered Schlossberg in Bridgehampton. "I'd been fashion designer Willi Smith's doctor," said Mirsky. "Willi, a close friend of Schlossberg's, had died from some rare influenza he picked up while in India looking at fabrics. Everyone thought he died of AIDS, but that's not the case. At any rate, I saw Ed Schlossberg walking down the street, and since I'd been Willi's personal physician, I went up to him to introduce myself. Schlossberg gave me one of the most hostile looks I've ever seen, and without so much as an acknowledgment crossed the street to avoid conversation."

Raymond Cox, a former salesclerk in a Bridgehampton clothing store, recounted a similar incident. "Ed Schlossberg," said Cox, "used to come into the store to buy informal outdoor gear—sweatshirts, athletic socks, T-shirts. He must have shopped with us a half-dozen times or more. He certainly knew me by sight. One day I ran into him in a Bridgehampton luncheonette. He was by himself, so I went over to his table to say hello. He barely lifted his head. I began to explain who I was. Without a word, he rose and rushed off to the men's room. I never saw him in our store again."

Perhaps such slights were inadvertent. After all, Ed Schlossberg also had his share of defenders. Freelance photographer Bettina Cirone, who'd been tracking the Kennedys since the 1970s, thought him "a really decent chap. Caroline scored big when she married him. He was always nice to me. I'd show up at an event with my camera and he'd say, 'How're you today?' He'd stare into the lens and let me take the shot. It was Caroline who was unpredictable. I attended a party in New York organized by Jacqueline Kennedy. Caroline and Ed were there. At party's end, I found myself standing next to the couple in the hallway, waiting for the elevator. It was kind of awkward, so I said to Caroline, 'You're wearing the same coatdress as your mother, only yours is navy and hers is green.' She just looked at me and said, 'Oh, wow!' Her words dripped with sarcasm, as if to say, *What a trite comment.* Ed gave me a sympathetic look."

Caroline accorded the photographer a warmer reception the next time they crossed paths. "We were at an American Ballet Theatre gala," said Cirone. "She was with her husband. I'd seen her a few weeks before at the Tribeca Film Festival with her kids, so I asked what they'd seen. 'We saw *Star Trek,*' she said. 'Did you like it?' I asked. 'I loved it,' she responded, 'and so did my children. Yeah, we really enjoyed that film.' Then she said, 'I'm here to balance things out.' In other words, she wanted me to know that she was multicultural, but at least she was cordial about it. As I say, you never knew what to expect with Caroline, whereas Ed Schlossberg was always friendly."

Meanwhile, the purchase of their home in Sagaponack turned into a financial bonanza for the Schlossbergs. By 2006 Sagaponack's 11962 postal zone ranked first on *Forbes* magazine's annual survey of the five hundred most expensive ZIP codes, based on the previous year's median house prices, with a median sales price of $2.8 million. In 2005 the

Schlossberg residence was assessed at a value of $4.8 million. According to the *New York Post*, they sold it in 2006 for $5.75 million, nearly six times what they paid for it.

John Jr. became involved in his own real estate ventures. In 1994 he leased a Victorian-style house on Bluff Road in Amagansett, Long Island, at the same time purchasing a condominium apartment, paying $700,000 for a ninth-floor, 2,400-square-foot loft at 20 North Moore Street in TriBeCa, between Hudson and Varick streets, not far from where he'd rented before. The new North Moore Street apartment had twelve-foot ceilings, hardwood floors, and a view of the city from three directions. Subdivided into several sections, the loft contained a large closed-off bedroom and a second room (not closed off) that he used as a combination study and den. There were storage and living areas. He spent approximately $100,000 on extensive renovations for architectural, detail, plumbing, electrical, painting, and glasswork, a portion of it going into the modernization of an open kitchen area, which was separated from a wooden dining table by a long, stainless steel food-preparation counter. He purchased a new queen-size bed for the bedroom and constructed a small library, its bookshelves filled with biographies as well as volumes devoted to history, political science, and New Journalism, including the works of Hunter S. Thompson, Norman Mailer, and Tom Wolfe. A vintage photograph on the wall showed two bare-fisted boxers squaring off in an outdoor ring. "It symbolized John's competitive drive," said Billy Way. Also in the library stood a large metal box that contained his father's scrimshaw collection, one of the few samples of Kennedy iconography in the apartment. The walls of the loft were covered throughout with native handmade masks that JFK Jr. had picked up on his various journeys to Africa and the Far East. He redid the loft's two bathrooms, installing a whirlpool bath in one and a stall shower in the other. His maintenance fee on the apartment came to $1,900 per month. The ten-story, ten-unit, brick and stone building, with its tall, unpainted double steel doors, was largely indistinguishable from others in the vicinity.

Maury Blaustein, owner of a plumbing and heating contracting firm located half a block from John's house, worked on the steam pipes in his apartment and recalled it as "spare, not very decorated or elaborate. John himself was a wonderful and kind guy with a quick smile and a friendly manner."

Blaustein's sentiments were echoed by nearly all of John's neighbors. Bill Brand, a resident of TriBeCa and a documentary filmmaker, thought it a good neighborhood for John. "It's a semianonymous place," he said, "which is why celebrities like it down here. The apartments and lofts tend to be spacious and nobody bothers you. John fit in. He was a popular neighborhood figure. After it became known that he lived here, the paparazzi began to show up. So did the tourists. They'd ask me to point out John's building. Now when they come down here, they ask me to show them where the World Trade Center once stood."

"He was a regular guy," said Jason Sachs, a TriBeCa picture framer who first encountered John at the Square Diner on Leonard Street. "The first time we met he was eating breakfast and reading the *New York Post*. We began talking about the New York Yankees. He was an easy conversationalist. We remained friendly. It didn't matter who you were—he was always cordial. He'd stop you on the street and ask how you were doing. I had a dog, a mixed breed, and he loved to play with it. This was before he acquired Friday, his own little dog. John was always up and around. You'd see him on his bike, a big steel chain wrapped around his jacket. He was very neighborly. He used to hang out at Socrates, a nearby Greek coffee shop, and he'd practice his Greek with the owner of the place. I guess he knew a smattering of the language from his days with Aristotle Onassis. I once bumped into him in a local hardware store. He'd bought a sponge mop and a broom, and he'd taken out his credit card to pay. The store clerk looked at the card and then looked at JFK Jr. 'Aren't you the son of President Kennedy?' he inquired. John hesitated a moment, then smiled. 'Guilty as charged,' he retorted. It was a cute response, particularly as he'd worked in the DA's office."

One of John's favorite local establishments was the New York Nautical Instrument and Service Corporation, a store that featured antiquarian novelties such as boat models and decorative maps. There he often shopped for Christmas gifts. One time he bought a small brass tabletop telescope. Another time he paid $1,000 for a miniature antique wooden sailboat. Along with such celebrities as Harvey Keitel and Diane Keaton, he was a regular at Bubby's, a bar-restaurant at the corner of North Moore and Hudson, whose menu included such "down-home" selections as barbecued chicken and fried catfish. Puffy's Tavern, at 81 Hudson Street, was another of JFK Jr.'s choice haunts. "He felt comfortable at Puffy's because he could blend in," said Carlo Gilko, a longtime bartender at Puffy's. "He slipped in below the radar. Nobody bothered him. Nobody got in his face. People looked him over, but nobody gave him a hard time."

Such anonymity did not come easily to John. In *Symptoms of Withdrawal,* Chris Lawford wrote: "It always amazed me when I went places with my cousin John how any room would just tilt toward him when he walked in. Everyone's conversation and attention narrowed to the vortex where he stood. He handled it all with a lot of grace. John had all his mother's grace."

In addition to grace, John possessed a trusting—perhaps overly trusting—nature. Carlo Gilko recalled an anecdote involving a friend who lived next door to John in TriBeCa. "My friend is a runner," said Gilko, "and one day after he finished his run he was resting on his stoop. A cab pulls up, and John gets out with a lot of stuff—he'd been on a trip. He had backpacks, suitcases, and skis. He started carrying the gear into his building, one suitcase at a time, leaving the rest on the sidewalk. My friend is sitting there, not paying much heed to what's going on. John says nothing to him. He makes four or five trips in and out of the building. The whole process takes maybe ten minutes. After he gets the last item inside, he comes out again and says to my friend, 'Hey, thanks for watching my stuff.' It wasn't said in jest—he just assumed my friend was looking out for him."

Meyer Yudell, another TriBeCa neighbor, remembered the night in the winter of 1994 when he first "ran into John—or rather, he ran into me. It was around 8:00 p.m., and I was heading home after work. I guess I was sort of weaving back and forth a bit. Somebody came running up behind me. I must have accidentally stepped into his path, because he gave me a hard shove. 'You son of a bitch!' I yelled. He kept going. He had on a jogging suit. I yelled again: 'You son of a bitch!' This time he turned around. I instantly recognized John Kennedy Jr. He gave me the finger and shouted 'Fuck you!' About two hours later, I went to Bubby's for a beer. John was sitting at a table with some friends. When he saw me he got up and walked over. 'Are you the guy I nearly ran over on the street?' he asked. 'That's right,' I answered. 'I'm sorry about that,' he said. 'I owe you an apology. Can I buy you a drink?' He bought me a beer, and we shook hands. Considering that awkward initial moment on the street, he couldn't have been more gracious. I was truly impressed."

Because of her illness, Jackie saw John's North Moore Street apartment only once, while he was still negotiating its price. After the visit, she and Maurice Tempelsman went to a restaurant in the West Village to eat dinner. Mary Zeller, an X-ray technician, sat at the next table. "I don't remember the name of the place—it's no longer there," she said. "I was dining with my husband. I kept looking over at Jackie. She looked familiar, but I didn't recognize her at first. She just didn't look grand enough to be the former First Lady. I didn't realize that she had cancer. She and her companion looked like any ordinary couple having a meal together. Nobody else in the restaurant seemed to recognize them. A not very well made-up young lady with dirty blond hair and a bit of a horsey face soon joined them. She resembled Caroline Kennedy, but again I couldn't be sure. A few minutes later the door opened and in walked one of the most attractive young men I'd ever seen. There was no doubt as to the identity of the newcomer. It was John F. Kennedy Jr. Everyone in the restaurant recognized him, and everyone stopped talking and simply gawked at him."

While still formulating plans to launch a new magazine, John accepted an offer to narrate a six-part documentary, *The Heart of the City,* to be broadcast over WNYC-TV. Dealing largely with the underprivileged neighborhoods of New York, the project was the brainchild of executive producer Jacqueline Leopold. "When first approached, John turned us down," said senior producer Carolyn Kresky. "Then one day he called up and said, 'Hi, this is John Kennedy. You know, I might be interested. Can we get together and talk?' Jackie Leopold and I had lunch with him at a restaurant in SoHo. We chatted about the project, and John agreed to work with us. We had a limited budget, but we arranged to pay him $7,000, which he donated to charity. I wrote the script and then rewrote it because John wanted it to be more low-key and to contain more about the history of New York. We went with the second version. I taught him how to use the teleprompter. He'd never used one before. His acting ability helped him put emotion into the narration, which consisted of forty-five-second introductions before each segment."

John would show up for the shoots on his bicycle, invariably followed by a pack of paparazzi. "Among other sites," continued Kresky, "we shot in the South Bronx, Chinatown, Harlem, Washington Square Park, and under the Brooklyn Bridge. Onlookers constantly approached him. In Harlem people came up to him and said, 'Oh, we adored your father. What a great man!' Given his range of experiences and the way in which he was raised, my impression was that John lived in another dimension compared to the rest of us. He maintained a certain distance, though he was always polite and friendly. He enjoyed the camaraderie of the film crew—the cameramen, the soundman, director, producer, and personal assistants. There was a kind of boyishness about him. He was forever losing or misplacing his personal belongings.

"One day we did a shoot under the Brooklyn Bridge. We'd arranged to have breakfast for everyone at the River Café. Afterward I was working with the director and crew, setting up cameras, when a woman approached me and said, 'Hello, I'm Daryl Hannah.' She was there in support of John. And she was doing some of her own film directing at the time. So now I had Daryl Hannah and John Kennedy on the set. The two of them were all over each other that morning. They were both quite demonstrative."

In spite of their seeming closeness that day, John—perhaps out of deference to his ill mother—continued to pull away from the actress. Later that spring when John attended a big party in New York for the Grateful Dead, he went by himself. In addition to Jackie's fading health—her failure to respond to chemotherapy—other issues complicated the relationship between John and Daryl.

Suzanna Bowling recalled meeting John for the first time at a party in TriBeCa. "I was hanging my coat, and he walked in with Daryl Hannah, and they were arguing. I knew Daryl from Los Angeles. She was very manipulative and clingy. She was ditzy—in fact, she was nuts. I never knew her to be straight. She was always on something—she mixed pharmaceuticals with alcohol. When I saw them at the party, they were already at odds. And that was because she was so crazy. She was beautiful, truly beautiful, but she was also extremely vulnerable. She reminded me of Zelda Fitzgerald, the wife of F. Scott Fitzgerald. Daryl had too much energy. She inhabited a publicity-mad world. She was warm, even passionate, but also suffocating. Her demeanor must have become wearying for John."

More than wearying, the relationship with Daryl had begun to grind at John. Not that he and Daryl didn't have certain traits in common. "They were both exceedingly immature," said California journalist Bonnie Robinson, whose explosive profile of Daryl (in the November 1993 issue of *Women's Day*) sent shock waves through Hollywood. Based largely on a protracted interview with Natalie Cross, the actress's girl Friday for more than two years, the article depicted Hannah as nothing less than a hyped-up, sex-crazed screen queen. "John and Daryl were cases of arrested development—they were like children," continued Robinson. "When Daryl lived with Jackson Browne in Santa Monica, she installed a swing set and a teeter-totter in back of their house. She liked to be pushed back and forth in the swing. I once bumped into John and Daryl at Skaties, a bike and skate shop in Marina del Rey. He was *GQ* perfect in shorts and an unbuttoned, formfitting shirt. Daryl was carrying on like a ten-year-old, trying on every pair of Rollerblades in sight. Evidently Daryl and John had a sexual routine that included all sorts of childlike games. They'd jog, and then they'd play tag, and then they'd blade, and finally they'd go upstairs and fuck like bunnies. And then they'd start all over again. Daryl was dying to become Mrs. JFK Jr., just dying. She was crazy about him. She'd tell Natalie Cross how much she loved him. She was obsessed with him. She dated him while living with Jackson Browne, a situation so anxious-making that she became addicted to sedatives. She referred to them as her 'night-night' pills, and although she later beat the habit, it evidently hampered her short-term memory."

In Robinson's *Women's Day* profile, Natalie Cross repeatedly refers to another of Daryl's purported sex partners, namely her old friend Hilary

Shepard-Turner, with whom she appeared in an HBO movie, *Attack of the 50 Ft. Woman.* Natalie, who later worked in the advertising department at *People* magazine, noted that Daryl and Hilary, clad in T-shirts (and little else), frequently slept in the same bed. They also enjoyed "steamy shower sessions" together. They dressed alike, wore each other's clothes, and were overly affectionate. "Jackson Browne hadn't a clue," said Robinson, "but John knew about it, because Daryl told him." According to Cross, Daryl complained that she and Browne were sexually incompatible, whereas she and John meshed beautifully together.

Whether Daryl and Hilary were actual lovers isn't known. The charge seems to fall into the same category as those levied against John in terms of his own suspected bisexuality. Daryl Hannah's apparent instability and her close association with Hollywood and the world of cinema represented obstacles more difficult to overcome. "If John Jr. hadn't been who he was," said Bonnie Robinson, "he and Daryl might have had a chance. But because of who he was, John had a standard imposed upon him, something he always had to live up to. At times it must have been difficult for him. Win, lose, or draw, most people get to make their own decisions. John didn't have that privilege. The struggle between who he was and who he wanted to be marked the contours of his life. It was only *after* his mother died that he became his own master, but being a Kennedy, being *the* Kennedy, he still had certain constraints."

Sensing that their relationship had reached an impasse, Daryl took the initiative, demanding that they either marry or break up. According to JFK Jr. biographer Chris Andersen, "Daryl got down on one knee and proposed." John snapped back. "Don't push me," he snarled. "I don't like ultimatums."

On one of their last public outings in New York, John and Daryl were spotted at a dingy East Village pizzeria. When they left, JFK Jr. recognized a hot dog vendor he'd often seen near Washington Square Park. The two men did a little jig around the vendor's cart, after which John paid him for a bottle of water. Jack Donahue, a New York City cabdriver, never forgot the time he drove the couple from TriBeCa to Grand Central. "They were both dressed in grungy clothing topped by baseball caps," he said. "They looked like they were on food stamps. They argued the entire trip. It had something to do with Daryl not wanting to accompany John to a political fund-raiser of some sort. By the time we reached Grand Central, they were literally shouting at each other. JFK Jr. must have felt lousy about it, because he gave me a $10 tip."

That they were having problems in their relationship was common knowledge by now. Late night television talk show host David Letterman, having recently switched from NBC to CBS, featured Daryl and John in one of his "Top Ten" routines. "What," he asked, "are the top ten signs of trouble in the Daryl Hannah–JFK Jr. relationship?" Of the ten responses, the one that elicited the loudest laughter from the studio audience went something like: "All of a sudden she doesn't want to wear the mermaid outfit in bed."

Chapter 17

♦

DEATH BE NOT PROUD

Bᴇ ᴇᴀʀʟʏ Aᴘʀɪʟ 1994, Daryl Hannah had vacated her Manhattan residence and returned to California, settling into a house in Malibu and a condominium apartment on Wilshire Boulevard in Beverly Hills. Although John briefly visited her in Los Angeles in late April, he'd already begun to date other women. *Esquire* magazine reported that he and high-fashion model Claudia Schiffer were seeing each other. *The Washington Post* linked him with actress Sharon Stone. The *National Enquirer* had it that he was in "torrid" pursuit of model Elle MacPherson. "It's impossible to say what was true and what wasn't when it comes to John's dating habits," said Richard Wiese. "I introduced him to a *Sports Illustrated* cover girl named Ashley Richardson. She looked a bit like Daryl Hannah: tall, angular, and blond. They dated for a while. It was clear by then that John and Daryl weren't going to make it."

It was also during this period that John became involved with Wilhelmina model Julie Baker. Upset and saddened by his mother's deteriorating health, John consoled himself by spending time with Julie, whose sultry, brunette good looks were reminiscent of Jackie at her best. According to Christy Orr, Julie's roommate, John spent a lot of time at their Greenwich Village apartment, bringing Julie a bouquet of flowers whenever he visited. Julie and John watched television, talked, took long walks, and only occasionally ventured out to clubs and parties. "John was also nice to me," said Orr. "I was going on a trip to Latin America, and he told me what vitamins I should take while I was down there." Having been a friend long before she became John's lover, it's no surprise that Julie remained his friend after they broke up. She, in fact, became one of his closest confidantes. Protective of their tender moments together, Julie described John as "my dear, dear, dear, very close friend. Our friendship was a very private, sensitive thing for me. I still can't talk about it."

It was an extremely difficult period in both Caroline's and John's lives. The chemotherapy sessions Jackie was enduring weren't working. Magnetic Resonance Imaging—commonly known as MRI—revealed that while there were no longer visible signs of the lymphoma in her neck, chest, or abdomen, it had spread to the membranes surrounding the heart and spinal cord. Radiation therapy was now being administered to these vital areas.

Jacqueline remained outwardly composed, determined to live each day as fully as possible. She continued to work on a project or two for Doubleday, but did her editing at home. Maurice Tempelsman set up a makeshift office for himself in Jackie's apartment so that he could be with her round the clock. On April 13 she met Oleg Cassini for lunch to discuss a book he wanted to write on fashion designers. "Except for an obvious wig and a bandage on her cheek, she looked fine to me," said Cassini. "She seemed cheerful. We spoke more about her children and grandchildren than we did about the book, but the luncheon went fine. When we were done, I offered to pay. 'Don't be silly,' she said. 'As implausible as it seems, I still have my expense account with the publisher.'"

A day later Jackie collapsed in her apartment and was rushed to New York Hospital–Cornell Medical Center, where she underwent emergency surgery to repair a perforated ulcer in her stomach, a frequent complication of the steroid drugs that were part of her cancer treatment. Most of the time Maurice Tempelsman sat by her bedside, holding her hand. When she felt up to it, he read to her and helped go through the stacks of mail she received. Caroline and John Jr. also visited for long hours. The gravity of Jackie's illness was beginning to show on the strained faces of all three.

Yet after her discharge from the hospital, everyone—especially Jackie—remained quietly optimistic. "I visited her one day toward the end of April," said John Kenneth Galbraith, the economist who'd served as ambassador to India during the Kennedy administration. "John Jr. came by with his guitar and sang some Spanish songs to his mother, which I thought was a touching gesture on his part. When he finished, we all applauded. Marta Sgubin whipped up some lunch. After lunch, Jackie said she'd seen Christina Haag, John's former girlfriend, in a made-for-television movie. 'She did remarkably well,' added Jackie. John smiled. Then Jackie asked, 'Where's Daryl these days?' 'We're on the downswing,' replied John. 'She's living in California. We still communicate, but it's not the same.' Jackie remained silent."

Galbraith came away from his visit convinced that while Jackie presented a brave front, she knew she was dying. John Loring, head of Tiffany & Co., felt the same way. "In keeping with her characteristic style, Jacqueline wanted you to feel good," he said. "She didn't want anybody to worry about her."

The cancer in Jackie's brain and spine soon grew worse. On May 1, with Maurice, Caroline, and John in attendance, she underwent a complex procedure whereby a tube was inserted in her brain to deliver a powerful surge of cancer drug. The lymphoma failed to respond. Caroline and John took turns looking after their mother. They helped her reach the lavatory, the examination room, and the hospital chapel to pray. Along with Maurice, they held her hand, caressed her cheek, and mopped her brow. All three tried, through love and devotion, to minimize her discomfort and the indignities of the medical process.

On Sunday, May 8, Jackie was seen strolling slowly in Central Park, supported by Maurice and accompanied by Caroline and her one-year-old son, Jack. Jackie appeared dignified in tan slacks and a pink sweater adorned by a silk scarf, but also frail and, for the first time, old. In halting steps, she could walk only a short distance before having to return home. Tempelsman, looking tense, angrily chased away photographers who threatened to intrude upon this brief moment of peace. In recent days, Jackie's speech had slowed, and she seemed less alert; she required assistance to walk. A full-time nurse had been hired to help look after her.

About this time a lesser drama insinuated itself into the picture. While on his bicycle one afternoon, John Jr. encountered Carolyn Bessette, whom he had stopped dating two years earlier when he and Daryl Hannah became re-involved. That evening he visited Carolyn in her East Side apartment. According to Billy Way, John unburdened himself by speaking to Carolyn about his mother's deteriorating condition. He feared she was dying. He also spoke to her about Daryl. There had been too much pushing and pulling—their relationship was coming to an end. He was supposed to have gone to Los Angeles to attend a Pink Floyd concert with Daryl as well as John Perry Barlow and Barlow's girlfriend, Cynthia Horner, a twenty-nine-year-old psychiatrist from Vancouver. Because of his mother's illness, John had refused to go. To add to the drama, Cynthia had just suffered what appeared to be a heart arrhythmia while flying from Los Angeles to New York and died on the plane. The only detail John omitted was that he and Cynthia's younger sister had also become sexually involved.

"John was mixing and matching all these women at the same time," said Billy Way. "I suspect it had something to do with the anxiety he felt over his mother's suffering. Cynthia's death upset him nearly as much as it upset John Perry Barlow. He regarded it as a kind of foreshadowing of his mother's death."

Caroline visited with her mother every afternoon. Having endured her father's death, the thought that her mother might die must have been particularly terrifying for her. John, too, had begun to mourn her absence before the fact. He arrived at his mother's house every evening, stayed until she became tired, then alternated between visits with Julie Baker and Carolyn Bessette, both of whom were secure enough as individuals to serve as his sounding boards.

On May 16 Jackie's condition took a perilous turn. She began shaking with chills and had trouble breathing. She returned to New York Hospital with Maurice and her nurse. Doctors diagnosed pneumonia and treated her with massive doses of antibiotics, which were administered intravenously. She rallied slightly, but then her condition worsened. On Wednesday, May 18, a CAT scan revealed large amounts of lymphoma in her liver, and a biopsy confirmed that it was anaplastic non-

Hodgkin's lymphoma. Surrounded by Maurice, Ed Schlossberg, Caroline, and John, she received the grim news from doctors. There was nothing more they could do to fight the cancer except continue the chemotherapy. It was up to Jackie. Resigned to her fate and unwilling to subject herself to what she realized had become a futile effort to prolong her life, she refused. After her physicians left the room, Jackie and her family broke down, alternately hugging and weeping. A nurse's aide reported seeing John and Caroline waiting for the hospital elevator a bit later, their faces streaked with tears.

Within an hour, Jackie was on her way home to 1040 Fifth Avenue. She traveled by ambulance, with a somber Maurice Tempelsman gently stroking her hand and a nurse at her side. Ambulance attendants carried her through a side entrance to the building, into the service elevator, and up to her fifteenth-floor apartment. An intravenous morphine drip to reduce pain was affixed to her arm. In keeping with her living will, she refused all other means of medical treatment or intervention. She had been tortured enough.

That evening, scores of reporters and photographers, the curious and the faithful, began to gather in front of 1040 Fifth Avenue and had to be restrained by police barricades. The following morning, May 19, Nancy Tuckerman informed the press that Mrs. Onassis "is fighting another phase of her illness with great fortitude." But the crowds grew, fanning across Fifth Avenue into Central Park, closing streets in every direction, while a steady stream of relatives and old friends continued to enter the building throughout the day to pay their final respects to the former First Lady.

John Jr., Caroline, Ed Schlossberg, and Lee Radziwill were the first to arrive. Jackie had been propped up on plush feather pillows in her exquisitely appointed bedroom so she could savor the familiar vista of her cherished world, with its beloved photographs, bound volumes of poetry, and priceless objets d'art. Monsignor George Bardes of St. Thomas More Church arrived to perform the last rites and administer Holy Communion, which Jackie insisted on "getting out of the way." He found John drifting about the apartment, while Caroline sat on the bed in what had been her childhood bedroom. Her eyes were shut, and she was weeping.

Although John opposed the idea of administering last rites on the grounds that his mother might live, he posted himself in the foyer to let in the caterer and greet visitors as they stepped off the elevator into the apartment. Too upset to talk, Caroline remained out of sight. At one point she was spotted on a couch in the living room, crying softly on her husband's shoulder.

With Maurice Tempelsman and her children in the room, Jacqueline greeted one or two visitors at a time: Senator Edward Kennedy and his wife, Victoria Reggie; Yusha Auchincloss; sisters-in-law Ethel Kennedy, Jean Kennedy Smith, Patricia Kennedy Lawford, and Eunice Kennedy Shriver; Sargent Shriver; and Kennedy nieces and nephews—among them Joseph Kennedy II, Robert Kennedy Jr., Douglas Kennedy, Christopher Lawford, Anthony Radziwill, and William Kennedy Smith. Other visitors included a number of her friends, such as Bunny Mellon, George Plimpton, Carly Simon, and Jayne Wrightsman. Jackie received visitors until early that evening. Several dozen familiar figures came and went, their faces etched in pain. Although many of them had known that her cancer was aggressive, they seemed shocked by her rapid decline. They stood in the elegant rooms of her apartment, joining one another in quiet conversation and silent prayer. Some cried, others keened. All were dazed.

By early evening, Jackie remained alone with Maurice and her children. Her main concern at the end had been to avoid pain. Aristotle Onassis had taught her about *thanatos*—the Greek word for death without suffering. When she heard that her case was hopeless, she chose to go home rather than linger in a hospital bed. At home, the management of her pain could be more easily regulated according to her desires and needs. At home, the reporting requirements were less stringent. Jacqueline was well aware that the medication to control pain—especially narcotic analgesics—can depress breathing, particularly when the patient is critically ill, and as a result quicken the onset of death. She was also well aware that a merciful death in a hospital setting with physicians and registered nurses in attendance would be difficult to achieve. In the privacy of her bedroom, with only her loved ones as witnesses, she could regulate her intake of morphine simply by depressing the lever that controlled the intravenous flow.

John Jr., Caroline, and Maurice sat with Jackie in the gathering dark, reading poems, sharing treasured memories and coveted secrets. Tears were shed. Jackie drifted in and out of consciousness. A round-the-clock nurse waited in another room, occasionally looking in, then leaving again. Maurice left Jackie's bedside to get a cup of ice. John and Caroline repaired to Jackie's library in search of several additional volumes of their mother's favorite poetry. When they returned a few minutes later, Jacqueline had drifted into a coma. A doctor was called. She was pronounced dead at 10:15 p.m. on Thursday, May 19, 1994. At age sixty-four, she was far too young to die.

The following morning, dressed in a tailored blue suit, a grieving but remarkably polished John Jr. appeared under the green canopy at 1040 Fifth Avenue and spoke to the press and public alike about his mother's death. "Last night, at around ten-fifteen, my mother passed on," he said. "She was surrounded by her friends and family and her books and people and things that she loved. And she did it in her own way, and on her own terms, and we all feel lucky for that, and now she's in God's hands . . ."

Family and friends assembled at the apartment a few hours later to make arrangements for Jackie's funeral and interment. A dispute arose between Caroline, who favored a private, family funeral, and Ted Kennedy, who argued for a large public observance. John Jr., Ed Schlossberg, and Maurice Tempelsman helped Caroline prevail upon her uncle. Her one major concession to history was that she agreed without hesitation that her mother should be buried next to the late president at Arlington National Cemetery, an irony in that a woman who sought privacy her entire life should be interred in so public a place. John and his sister, accompanied by Maurice, later visited the Frank E. Campbell funeral home on Madison Avenue to select a coffin, which was brought to 1040 Fifth Avenue. Jacqueline was embalmed at home, and her closed mahogany coffin was draped with a delicate antique bedspread. The coffin was subsequently decorated with a blanket of white flowers and green leaves.

Hearing of Jackie's death and perhaps envisioning it as an opportunity to get back in John's good graces, Daryl Hannah boarded a plane and flew to New York, arriving in time to be present at Jackie's wake. Attended by some 150 mourners, the wake took place on May 22 in the former First Lady's apartment. Maud Davis, Jackie's aunt, had made up with her niece the year before and was invited to attend. "I would never in a thousand years have expected Jacqueline to predecease me," she said. "But there she was in a coffin in the middle of her living room. It was hard to believe. Jacqueline seemed almost indestructible. In that respect, her death was all the more difficult to accept, especially for Caroline and John. But in a strange way, their mother's death, after so much suffering, must have come as something of a relief."

John Davis also attended. "The mood in the apartment was somber," he said, "but nobody broke down. It was a simple affair. I suppose we were all in a state of shock, because Jackie's death came so quickly."

The wake—which actually had been Teddy's idea—was ultimately marred by one particularly inglorious moment. Reported by Ed Klein in his book, *Farewell, Jackie,* the incident involved a contemptuous Ed Schlossberg and a contrite Carly Simon. Carly, it seems, had come to the wake armed with several presents she wished to place on top of Jackie's coffin, including a scroll containing the lyrics to a song she'd written with the former First Lady in mind. When Schlossberg saw the scroll atop the casket, he gave Carly a stern lecture. "We're very angry with you, Carly," he said. "You have to take that scroll off the casket. It's only for the grand-children." Caroline's husband didn't stop there. He told the singer she'd been "intrusive" and had committed a "faux pas," causing discomfort among the other guests and reducing Carly to tears. Her intentions had been pure—she merely wanted to pay homage to her good friend.

Following Schlossberg's unfortunate outburst, John Jr. emerged on the apartment balcony with Daryl Hannah. In a gesture that recalled his mother's majesty, he waved to the thousands of well-wishers still keeping vigil on the street below. They, in turn, responded warmly with a refrain of "glory, glory, hallelujah" from "The Battle Hymn of the Republic." Earlier, John and Daryl surprised everyone by Rollerblading out of the building's side entrance—in their running clothes—and gliding down Park Avenue. Their capricious expedition was reported on the front page of the *Daily News. The New York Times* labeled it an attempt on John's part "to intentionally flout decorum." In reality, it was nothing more than a way for him to blow off steam. Hundreds of bouquets of flowers, many from strangers, arrived at Jackie's apartment building and were taken to the basement, where Bunny Mellon and another friend attempted to work them into funeral wreaths. There were occasional skirmishes in front of the building as reporters, photographers, and onlookers attempted to break through the white-and-blue wooden barricades to catch a glimpse of celebrities leaving the wake. As Maria Shriver and Arnold Schwarzenegger slipped into their limousine, several policemen grabbed an encroaching photographer and wrestled him to the pavement, shattering his camera.

At 10:00 a.m. on Monday morning, May 23, eight pallbearers came out of 1040 Fifth Avenue and lifted Jacqueline's coffin—covered with lilies of the valley in the shape of a cross—into a waiting hearse. The pallbearers included Jack Walsh, the Secret Service agent who'd been assigned to guard Jackie's young children following the president's assassination, and seven family members: Edward Kennedy Jr., Robert F. Kennedy Jr., Christopher Lawford, Anthony Radziwill, Lewis Rutherfurd Jr., Timothy Shriver, and William Kennedy Smith (still known to reporters, despite his acquittal, as "the rapist"). With an extended police escort, the limousine carrying Caroline, John, and Maurice Tempelsman followed the hearse three blocks to the seven-hundred-seat Church of St. Ignatius Loyola on Park Avenue and 84th Street. As an infant, Jacqueline Lee Bouvier had been baptized in this same church, and as a teenager she had been confirmed there. John and Caroline, their heads bowed, accompanied the pallbearers as they shouldered the coffin up the stairs of the neoclassic limestone structure, paused in the bright sunlight, then carried the coffin through the arched entranceway into the house of worship. Fifth, Madison, and Park avenues had been closed off, creating gridlock and traffic jams throughout the city. Sound trucks, police vans, and press vehicles of every description filled the streets. Hundreds of New York's finest were posted on street corners, many on horseback. Dozens of highly visible Secret Service agents whispered furtively into their walkie-talkies. In addition to honoring Jackie, they had been dispatched to protect First Lady Hillary Clinton, who'd flown from Washington to attend the funeral. Thousands of teary-eyed spectators, some armed with signs and placards, stood behind police sawhorses, straining for a view. Millions watched on television. New York and New Yorkers had rarely, if ever, seen a funeral of this magnitude.

The church itself was packed with seven hundred "by invitation only" mourners from every nook and cranny of Jackie's life, including Bouviers, relatives of President Kennedy and many of his White House aides, members of Congress, artists, writers, performers, socialites, media moguls, and a number of her children's friends. Hillary Rodham Clinton wore a strangely inappropriate pink suit (with a carnation in her lapel) that reminded many mourners of the outfit Jackie had worn in Dallas on the day of JFK's assassination. Rose Kennedy, Jackie's aging mother-in-law, had been too weak to come from Hyannis Port and instead watched the color commentary on television. Although television cameras weren't permitted inside the church, loudspeakers had been set up outside St. Ignatius Loyola for the benefit of the gathered masses.

John Jr. began the service with a reading from the book of Isaiah, chapter 25, noting that in choosing the readings for the service, "we struggled to find ones that captured my mother's essence." Three attributes, he noted, came to mind again and again: "her love of words, her love of home and family, and her spirit of adventure."

Ted Kennedy gave the main eulogy, exalting Jackie's "deep and unqualified" love for Caroline and John, her place in American history, her valor in the days following her husband's assassination, her uniqueness and individuality. Choking back tears, Caroline read one of her mother's favorite poems, "Memory of Cape Cod," by Edna St. Vincent Millay. Maurice Tempelsman recited "Ithaka," by the Greek poet C. P. Cavafy, following it with words that sounded somewhat stilted: "And now the journey is over. Too short, alas, too short. It was filled with adventure and wisdom, laughter and love, gallantry and grace. So farewell, farewell." Mike Nichols spoke of his friendship with Jackie, Tina Radziwill presented a short reading, and soprano Jessye Norman sang "Ave Maria." Wallace Modrys delivered the Roman Catholic Mass. The Twenty-third Psalm was read by writer Jayne Hitchcock, who was there with journalist Jim Hoagland, and then came the final prayer: *Our sister Jacqueline has gone to Christ. May Jacqueline be at peace, may she be with the immortal God.*

Curiously, the name of Aristotle Onassis hadn't been mentioned during the service. In the end, the Kennedys had successfully reclaimed the one person who had fought so hard to maintain her independence from them. Outside the church, the solemn-faced members of the family gathered on the steps, waiting for the coffin. John Jr. placed a protective arm around his sister. Aware of the historic importance of the moment, the various Kennedy family members stared at the crowds and into the cameras. "All I remember is that there were blocks and blocks of reporters," said Chris Lawford. A fleet of minibuses had lined up behind the hearse to take select members of the funeral party to LaGuardia Airport for the short flight aboard a chartered Boeing 737 jet to Washington, D.C. At National Airport in Washington, President Clinton met the flight, joining the mourners on the motorcade to Arlington National Cemetery. Fewer than a hundred people gathered at the eternal flame that Jackie had lit for JFK more than three decades before. The private burial service for Jackie, led by the Reverend Philip M. Hartman, the retired Roman Catholic archbishop of New Orleans, was modest and brief.

With Hillary standing by his side, President Clinton gave a curtailed summation of Jackie's life: "God gave her very great gifts and imposed upon her great burdens. She bore them all with dignity and grace and uncommon common sense . . ." John Jr. and Caroline read short passages, the U.S. Navy Sea Chanters chorus intoned a hymn, and sixty-four bells rang out from the tower of the Washington National Cathedral across the Potomac River.

At the conclusion of the service, John and Caroline knelt one after the other and kissed their mother's coffin, before it was lowered into place beneath a magnolia tree. As Caroline joined her husband, John walked over and gently touched the graves of his father and his two-day-old baby brother, Patrick, as well as that of the unnamed baby girl who had died at birth. Then the family moved the short distance to visit the grave of Robert F. Kennedy. As they left the area, Caroline's face was lined with grief and pain; in a heartwarming final gesture, she reached over and wiped away several tears from her brother's cheek.

Caroline and John returned to New York. A day after the funeral, John and his friend Richard Wiese met for dinner. "It was a nice night," recalled Wiese, "so we sat in the outside part of a restaurant on Columbus Avenue. John was definitely down, and people tried to be respectful. They weren't staring at him. Everyone knew that his mother had just died. But then this photographer showed up and started taking pictures. He wouldn't go away, just stood there on the sidewalk, unabashedly snapping away. John finally lost it. It was the first time I'd ever seen him lose his cool. He started yelling at the guy: 'Leave me alone, will you!' The veins were popping out of his neck. The photographer said something like, 'You're not inside the restaurant—you're in front of it.' 'Are you telling me I can't sit out here without having to put up with you?' said John. I thought he might actually belt the photographer, but the fellow finally packed it up and left."

In the weeks that followed, Caroline grieved her mother's death inwardly, rarely mentioning her. "John spoke of her all the time," said Billy Way. "He and I went out drinking one night, and he began telling me how different his mother was from everyone he'd ever known. She didn't look like anyone else, didn't talk like anyone, wasn't at all like anyone in her family. He went on from there. He must have done a half-hour soliloquy on his mother. It was all positive and full of love."

Two weeks after his mother's death, JFK Jr. sent Bill and Hillary Clinton a handwritten letter. "I wanted you both to understand how much your burgeoning friendship with my mother meant to her," he wrote. "Since she left Washington, I believe she resisted ever connecting with it emotionally—or the institutional demands of being a former First Lady. It had much to do with the memories stirred and her desire to resist being cast in a lifelong role that didn't quite fit. However, she seemed profoundly happy and relieved to allow herself to reconnect with it through you. It helped her in a profound way—whether it was discussing the perils of raising children in those circumstances (perilous indeed) or perhaps it was the many similarities between your presidency and my father's."

At the time of her demise, Jackie's estate had accrued into a fortune estimated at well over $200 million. Her thirty-six-page will, dated March 22, 1994, with Maurice Tempelsman and her lawyer Alexander Forger named as co-executors, was filed at Surrogate Court in Manhattan on June 1, 1994. It stipulated that Caroline Kennedy Schlossberg and John F. Kennedy Jr. were to receive the bulk of her estate, including $250,000 each in cash; the principal on several trusts; bank accounts; an immense personal portfolio of stocks, bonds, and limited partnerships; the Manhattan apartment; the estate (and assorted realty) on Martha's Vineyard; and all of Jackie's "tangible personal property," such as books, letters, papers, documents, audio tapes, photographs, and films, as well as furniture, antiques, rugs, tapestries, artwork, silver, objets d'art, china, crystal, jewelry, and clothes. A number of bequests went to friends, family relations, and longtime retainers. Lee Radziwill's children, Anthony and Tina, for example, each received $1 million; Nancy Tuckerman was left $250,000; Marta Sgubin got $125,000. Others received varying amounts and an assortment of personal objects. The will directed that any remaining assets be used to establish a trust, the C&J Foundation (named for Caroline and John), which allocated annual profits to sundry philanthropic organizations, the trust to be dissolved after twenty-four years and the principal to be divided among Jackie's grandchildren.

At the same time that Jackie had worked out the tenets and conditions of her last will and testament, she had penned separate letters (on her standard pale blue stationery) to each of her children, to be presented to them following her death. To Caroline, she wrote: "The children have been a wonderful gift to me, and I'm thankful to have once again seen our world through their eyes. They restore my faith in the family's future. You and Ed have been so wonderful to share them with me so unselfishly."

To John, she wrote: "I understand the pressure you'll forever have to endure as a Kennedy, even though we brought you into this world as an innocent. You, especially, have a place in history. No matter what course in life you choose, all I can ask is that you and Caroline continue to make me, the Kennedy family, and yourself proud . . ."

Jackie's final request of Caroline and John appeared in the will itself. Having bequeathed them the preponderance of her personal possessions and papers, she wrote: "I request, but do not direct, my children to respect my wish for privacy with respect to such papers, letters, and writings and, consistent with that wish, to take whatever action is warranted to prevent the display, publication, or distribution, in whole or in part" of this material. Her defensive mode with respect to such matters was predicated on her conviction that deeply personal matters should never be aired in public and particularly not within earshot of strangers.

One of Jackie's last verbal requests of John, according to his friends, was that he never again take piloting lessons—too many tragedies had already befallen members of the Kennedy clan. Although he vowed to honor her deathbed wish, it was a promise he knew he could never keep. By the same token, Caroline seems to have violated the spirit of her mother's written instruction that her privacy and reputation be protected at all costs. Not only did she eventually print several of her mother's personal jottings, Caroline's 2001 publication of a best-selling poetry anthology, *The Best-Loved Poems of Jacqueline Kennedy Onassis,* clearly exploited Jackie's name, as did a number of her other future ventures, many of which were quite lucrative for Caroline. At heart, she was truly her mother's child—in all the best and worst ways.

Part VI

———————◆———————

———————◆———————

Chapter 18

PASSING THE TORCH

O N AUGUST 17, 1994, New York mayor Rudolph Giuliani signed into law a bill designating that the Central Park Reservoir be renamed in honor of Jacqueline Kennedy Onassis. John Jr. had originally suggested that they rename Grand Central Terminal after his mother, but upon further reflection he decided that the reservoir might be a more fitting tribute. Jackie had helped save Grand Central Terminal from demolition, but her daily jaunts around the reservoir had become an integral part of her legendary existence. When asked his opinion concerning the name change by a reporter for *The New York Times,* a foreman supervising the repair of the running track remarked that it seemed totally appropriate. "Like Jackie," he said, "the Central Park Reservoir gives an impression of stillness, as if it harbors its own secrets."

By mid-August Caroline Kennedy had begun to come to grips with her mother's death. She completed her book (with Ellen Alderman) on the right to privacy and helped to organize her mother's vast inventory of personal possessions. Although she maintained a low profile, Caroline took on a more public role, doing things that Jackie would have done, such as chairing a gala for the American Ballet Theatre. Attending opening night with husband Ed Schlossberg, she wore her mother's best pair of diamond earrings. She raised funds for the Municipal Art Society, whose meetings John Jr. began attending as well. She organized fundraisers for the John F. Kennedy Library and continued as a trustee for the Joseph P. Kennedy Jr. Foundation. She became a trustee at Brearley, which her daughters attended, helping direct school policy and writing articles for a parents publication that came out quarterly. Interviewed by *Ladies' Home Journal* regarding her newfound public role and what it entailed in terms of personal exposure, Caroline gave the kind of ambiguous response Jackie would have given under similar circumstances. "The press has a job to do, and as a lawyer I'm aware of that," she said. "I have a husband and three children, and I'm very happy."

Late that summer Ed and Caroline attended the wedding of Anthony and Carole Radziwill at the Most Holy Trinity Church in East Hampton. John Jr. served as best man. Also at the wedding was Maurice Tempelsman, who had stayed on in Jackie's apartment at 1040 Fifth Avenue. Encouraged by Caroline, John Jr. later spoke to Tempelsman, informing him that he and his sister intended to sell the apartment and that he would have to leave. It went on the market in early 1995 and was purchased later that year by industrialist David Koch for $9.2 million, many times what she had paid for it thirty years earlier.

Aware that Caroline and Ed Schlossberg were in the process of acquiring title to their weekend house at Sagaponack, Jackie had assumed that John Jr. would make greater use than his sister of the estate on Martha's Vineyard. To compensate—and to save on inheritance taxes—Jackie had placed the $1.6 million Hyannis Port house in Caroline's name. With its fifty-three ponds and sprawling acreage, Red Gate Farm served as John's second home. He loved the fresh sea air and the sound of ocean waves pounding in the distance. John eventually moved from his own smaller residence on the property to the main house, taking over the master bedroom suite, continuing the annual Memorial Day weekend parties he'd always given for his friends. Because of his mother's death, he gave the 1994 party over the Fourth of July weekend, thereafter visiting Gay Head—with friends—practically every weekend. One of his more frequent Martha's Vineyard houseguests noted that the refrigerator was always fully stocked with fresh fruit and vegetables, ginseng, and six-packs of Beck's beer; he kept the beer mugs in the freezer. The same houseguest recalled that after Jackie's death, John moved a long uphol-stered sofa and several traditional cushioned chairs from Red Gate Farm into his North Moore Street loft. The loft likewise contained one of his mother's antique coffee tables, which he covered with candles and a choice selection of her large-format art books.

Not long after Jackie's death, Caroline arranged through family back channels to have Ed Schlossberg deliver the keynote speech at NewCon, the annual Chicago Merchandise Mart office-furnishings extravaganza. Following his address, he sat down with Barbara Sullivan, a reporter for the *Chicago Tribune*. Recently described by *The New York Times* as "eva-sive," Schlossberg informed Sullivan that he would grant her "a short in-terview," but that he wouldn't talk about the Kennedys. Noting that Schlossberg appeared "uncomfortable" and that he "fidgeted" through-out the interview, Sullivan elicited mostly one-word answers. "Do you enjoy being a father?" she asked him. "Of course," he responded. When asked what qualities he tended to admire in people, Schlossberg retorted that he admired people "who'd mastered one skill and then gone on to something else." Sullivan later interviewed Chris Kennedy, Bobby and Ethel's son, an executive vice president of Merchandise Mart Properties Inc., who used the familiar term "Renaissance man" to describe Schloss-berg, going so far as to compare him to Ben Franklin. "To a lot of people," said Chris Kennedy, "Ed comes across as quiet and shy, but he's actually much the opposite when you know him." Extolling Schloss-berg's "genius," Chris Kennedy remarked, "It's impossible to plumb the depths of his intellect. In Jackie's apartment, the spaces of prominence were reserved for Ed's works."

A number of Ed's works of art went on display at the Ronald Feldman Gallery in Manhattan, where Schlossberg had exhibited twice before. Somewhat later another retrospective of his conceptual artwork went on display at the National Arts Club in New York. When a reporter for *The New York Times* approached Caroline Kennedy for a comment, she blithely referred to her husband's work as "stuff." The National Arts Club retrospective took place at roughly the same time as his design project for HBO of a nationwide interactive television game as well as an interactive program commissioned by the John F. Kennedy Space Center in Florida. The only member of his immediate family who remained unconvinced of Ed Schlossberg's divine genius was JFK Jr.

Although Caroline and her brother were closer than ever, John had long since become disillusioned with his brother-in-law. "I don't think there was ever much love lost between them," said Billy Way, "but after the death of his mother, John's enmity toward Schlossberg finally surfaced. They were so different. Schlossberg lived in his head, and John was physical. He loved Caroline, and he adored her children, but he couldn't stomach Schlossberg. 'He's a smug asshole, a real creep,' he once said to me. His condemnation of Schlossberg was noteworthy insofar as he so rarely bad-mouthed people." John Perry Barlow was similarly aware of their differences. "John certainly wasn't one of Schlossberg's great admirers," he said. Marta Sgubin, having gone to work for Caroline following Jackie's death, recalled a note John wrote to his sister. "I read the note," recalled Sgubin. "The note began, 'Dear Caroline, Marta, and Edwina.' I thought, 'Who's Edwina?' Well, Edwina was Ed Schlossberg. I took it as a practical joke."

It was no practical joke. The feminization of Ed's name reflected the degree of disdain in which John held his brother-in-law. After Jackie's death, the two men rarely saw each other. John preferred to meet alone with Caroline. They often dined together, usually at San Domenico or at Coco Pazzo, two of their favorite restaurants. Marisa May, daughter of Tony May, owner of San Domenico, recalled that John, Caroline, Jackie, and Maurice Tempelsman had been frequent dinner guests in her family's restaurant. On one occasion, John's bike had been stolen from where he'd left it in front of the upscale Central Park South eatery. On another occasion, John and his mother were eating lunch there, and he was being insolent and a bit defiant—he began using his hands rather than a fork and knife. Jackie chastised him so abrasively for his lack of table manners that a newspaper columnist at another table overheard them, and an item appeared a few days later in the *New York Post*. "John and Caroline continued to come in long after Jackie's death," said May. "They usually sat at a secluded table in an alcove toward the rear of the restaurant. They stayed for hours, chatting and laughing. They came in several times a week. They also came in separately—John with his girlfriends, Caroline with her husband. When Ed and Caroline dined with us, they often sat at a table near the front of the restaurant. I can't say I remember ever seeing John come in with Ed Schlossberg. It may have happened, but I don't recall it."

"No matter how bad things got," said George Plimpton, "Caroline could always make John laugh. And vice versa. I don't believe I ever knew a brother-sister team that got along better. They complemented each other. Caroline tended to see the foibles in people, whereas John looked for more positive traits. Caroline could cut people down with a few trenchant words; John built them up. She had a dark sense of humor, a rapier wit; his was effervescent. She trusted nobody, he trusted everyone. The only person he didn't trust was Ed Schlossberg. I believe he thought Schlossberg used the Kennedy connection simply to advance his career, that in actuality he didn't care a whit about the family."

John's negative reaction to Schlossberg came to a head in the late summer of 1994. "Caroline's husband," wrote Rob Littell, "became involved in a project for the JFK Center for the Performing Arts in Washington to make a film honoring JFK's contribution to the arts. John, hearing of Ed's efforts thirdhand, got angry. He felt Ed should have consulted him first." John told Ed as much. The two of them argued. John evidently called the center, and the project was canceled.

In all fairness to Ed Schlossberg, his role as Caroline's husband could not have been easy. A report prepared for the family by a private security firm indicated that Schlossberg had received a series of telephone calls at work from an unnamed "Brooklyn man" who claimed that he was secretly married to Caroline. A second anonymous individual informed Schlossberg that he'd been married to Jackie and that Caroline and John were really his children. Still another instance involved the forgery by a third party of Caroline's signature to a deed for a New York City–owned property at 210 West 50th Street in Manhattan. Such incidents were almost commonplace in the Schlossberg household and included overt and constant threats against the Schlossberg children. Both Ed and Caroline worried endlessly about the ever-present danger of evolving kidnap plots. With Caroline's newfound public visibility, the frequency of plots and threats was on a consistent upswing. Even if none of them ever materialized, they engendered an ongoing state of extreme anxiety.

In the course of her daily activities, Caroline Kennedy managed to create her own set of detractors. "It was a question of attitude more than anything else," said Cynthia Windland, an employee at the Thomas Morrissey Salon, where Caroline customarily had her hair done. "Jackie had been a client, and so had Lee Radziwill. Caroline came in regularly for a cutting, styling, and coloring, which back then cost in excess of four hundred dollars. It was one of the most expensive hair salons in New York. She sometimes brought along her two daughters. She'd arrive and immediately be ushered into a private room—no waiting. On several occasions she asked me to go out and buy her a box of Godiva chocolates. It wasn't my job, but I did it for her. A small box in those days cost five dollars. When I returned with the chocolates, she handed me a five-dollar bill. No tip. Other times she asked me to get her a soup and sandwich. At the very most, she'd give me a dollar tip. When she left the salon, she'd grab her own coat out of the cloakroom to avoid having to tip anyone. She was amazingly cheap. At the time of her mother's death, she seemed extremely remote and withdrawn. But she was never very friendly. She answered questions with either a 'yes' or a 'no'—she never said 'please' or 'thank you.' She was particularly unpleasant to the hired help and the support staff. She simply had no use for us—and she let us know it."

By mid-1995 Caroline had left Thomas Morrissey and was using hairstylist Kevin Marcuso at the Peter Coppola Salon. When word of her switch appeared in the press, the Coppola hair salon suddenly became one of the most popular in town. She subsequently switched again, this time to Joseph Spadaro, who occasionally came to her apartment to cut Caroline's hair. From a frizzy-haired, sloppily dressed teenager, Caroline had emerged into a well-coiffed, carefully dressed middle-aged Park Avenue princess.

Following Jackie's death, John Jr. embarked on a whole new trajectory. For one thing, he became involved in community politics. When he heard that a real estate developer had sought permission from the Landmarks Preservation Commission to tear down a warehouse across the street from his North Moore Street apartment building to make way for a multiplex movie theater, he joined other local residents in opposition to the project. He donated funds to hire a real estate lawyer and went before Community Board 1 to argue that a commercial multiplex would ruin the character of the neighborhood. In the end, the real estate developer abandoned his plans, and the warehouse remained intact. It was eventually transformed into an apartment dwelling similar in design to others on the block.

John's involvement in the defeat of the multiplex project coincided with the ultimate dissolution of his relationship with Daryl Hannah, whose presence at Jackie's funeral served as an epilogue to their increasingly explosive liaison. According to Rob Littell, there had been a final blowout between them, a bitter exchange at JFK Airport over John's reawakened interest in Carolyn Bessette. John left Daryl at the airport and never saw her again.

"I loved them both," said John Perry Barlow, "but by the end their relationship had become very aggressive. In fact, I advised them both to end it. Because they were both so passionate, I just felt they were going to make each other suffer. It wasn't anybody's fault. They were both wonderful people in their own way. But the chemistry had broken down. Relationships have their own internal mysteries. The dynamics get set up, and nobody really understands the rules. That's not to say that there wasn't some lingering bitterness. John might have been willing to continue the friendship without the romance. Daryl didn't want it. She was angry. She felt she'd been inappropriately hoodwinked—she'd been manipulated. Right or wrong, that's how she saw it. In addition, there was John's relationship with Carolyn Bessette. It wasn't possible for him to have any contact with Daryl because Carolyn was rather controlling. He knew that I continued to see a fair amount of Daryl, so from time to time he'd ask me wistful questions about how Daryl was doing. He'd always be very solicitous. He'd ask me to convey his fond regards. I had the feeling with John that once he loved somebody, he always loved them."

In the summer following Jackie's death, John traveled to Boston and was mauled by the public while campaigning for Joe Kennedy II, a candidate for reelection to Congress. Boston journalist Laura Raposa, whom

John knew by name, asked him how he dealt with all the attention, especially the middle-aged and older women who wanted to touch him and talk to him about his father. "It doesn't bother me," replied John. "I'm used to it by now."

When he returned to New York, he decided to buy a dog. He paid $500 for Friday, a black-and-white Canaan puppy that went everywhere with his master. Tina Flaherty, who lived in the penthouse at 1040 Fifth Avenue, recalled John talking and playing with her dogs whenever she bumped into him in the lobby of the building. "He loved dogs," she said. "He once asked me if I thought it was fair to keep a dog in a New York City apartment. I told him that my dogs—all six of them—were very happy. It was soon after this conversation that he acquired his dog."

Efigenio Pinheiro, Jackie's Portuguese butler, now employed by John to run errands and help out around the house, took on the added responsibility of looking after Friday at those times John was unavailable. The only other caretaker he trusted with the newest member of his household was Carolyn Bessette, who owned a cat named Ruby and was often photographed walking Friday around TriBeCa.

Carolyn Jeanne Bessette was born in White Plains, New York, on January 7, 1966, the youngest of three sisters. Lauren and Lisa, "the Bessette twins," were born in July 1964. Their father, William Bessette—tall, lanky, and fair-haired—was an architectural engineer and cabinet designer who opened his own cabinet refinishing shop in White Plains. His wife, Ann Marie, was a schoolteacher and elementary school administrator. When Carolyn turned four, her parents separated and soon divorced, and Ann moved with her daughters to Hartsdale, New York, where the girls attended Juniper Hill Elementary School. Several years later, Ann married Richard Freeman, a well-to-do orthopedic surgeon with three daughters of his own. Ann and her children left Hartsdale and moved to Dr. Freeman's house on Lake Avenue in Greenwich, Connecticut. After two years at the Old Greenwich School, Carolyn went on to St. Mary's, a private coeducational Catholic high school in Greenwich. She graduated in 1983 and enrolled at Boston University—her mother's alma mater—where, in January 1988, she earned her BA in elementary educa-

Caroline and Edwin Schlossberg on their wedding day, July 19, 1986. (Russell Turiak)

John Jr. with devoted girlfriend, actress Christina Haag. They were schoolmates at Brown University. (Russell Turiak)

Aerial view of Red Gate Farm. John Jr. and Caroline inherited the vast seaside estate from their mother following her death in 1994. (Witt Vince/CORBIS SYGMA)

John Jr. and Madonna jogging in Central Park. Their relationship was nearly consummated in a clandestine rendezvous at a seedy Chicago motel. (Rex Features USA)

John Jr. preferred riding his bike to any other mode of transportation in New York City, although he often rode the subway to work. (Alex Oliveira/CORBIS SYGMA)

John Jr. consoling Caroline after the death of their mother in 1994 from non-Hodgkin's lymphoma. Also in the photo are Ed Schlossberg and Jackie's live-in companion, Maurice Tempelsman. (AP/ Wideworld Photos)

John Jr. with girlfriend Julie Baker, a fashion model and jewelry designer, who remained a close friend after he was married. (Russell Turiak)

Daryl Hannah sports a black eye, which, according to press accounts, she received during an argument with boyfriend Jackson Browne. John Jr. went to L.A. and brought her back to New York City. (Russell Turiak)

Some of John Jr.'s friends believe that he might have been happier marrying Daryl Hannah than Carolyn Bessette. (Alex Oliveira/ CORBIS SYGMA)

John Jr. at a press conference launching his magazine, *George,* in 1995. (Ron Galella)

"The Sexiest Man Alive." (SIPA)

Even during their courtship, John Jr. and Carolyn Bessette had their share of arguments. (Paul Adao/ New York News Service)

John Jr. and Carolyn on their honeymoon in Istanbul, Turkey, in 1996. (Russell Turiak)

When he began experiencing problems with *George,* John Jr. consulted his friend Donald Trump. (Davidoff Studio)

John Jr. in TriBeCa with his beloved dog Friday. (RICKERBY/SIPA)

John Jr. and Carolyn sailing off the coast of Hyannis Port. (Boston Herald/Rex Features)

John Jr. with his first plane, a single-engine Cessna 182. (Steve Connolly/Liaison)

From left, Ed Schlossberg, Caroline, John Jr., and Carolyn. Although the two couples rarely socialized together, here they attend a gala for Jackie's favorite project, Grand Central Terminal. (Sonia Moskowitz/Globe Photos, Inc.)

Ed Schlossberg, Caroline, and their children (from left) Jack, Rose, and Tatiana. (Laura Cavanaugh/Globe Photos, Inc.)

Carolyn Bessette and her sister Lauren, who worked at Morgan Stanley Dean Witter as a financial consultant. Both perished in the fatal plane crash of July 16, 1999. (Bibeiro Luiz/CORBIS SYGMA)

John Jr. crashed his Buckeye ultralight Memorial Day 1999 and broke his left ankle six weeks prior to his death. (Chris Howard/AP/Wideworld Photos)

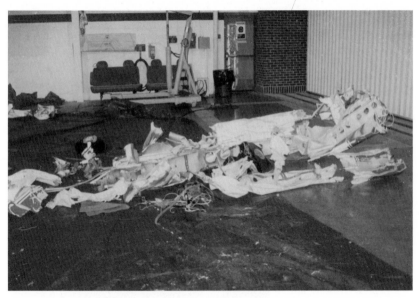

John F. Kennedy Jr., 1960–1999. The wreckage of the Piper Saratoga II HP airplane in which John Jr. and Carolyn and Lauren Bessette died on July 16, 1999. The plane crashed seven and a half miles off the coast of Martha's Vineyard. (CORBIS SYGMA)

Caroline's three children (from left), Rose, Tatiana, and Jack, represent the next generation of Kennedys. (AP/Wideworld Photos)

tion. It is said that she considered a career as a social worker rather than as a teacher or school administrator, both of which would have required her to go for a master's degree.

Linda Bemis, an art teacher at Juniper Hill Elementary School, recalled Carolyn as "a rather shy, but otherwise ordinary child. Her mother was a substitute teacher in the same school. After Carolyn married John Kennedy Jr., the school invited her to come up and read a story to the younger children, which is something a lot of our former students liked to do. She never responded. We assumed it was because she preferred to be identified with Greenwich rather than the less affluent village of Hartsdale."

Mary Lou Darkenwald, Carolyn's third-grade teacher at Juniper Hill, described the young girl in more positive terms. "Carolyn was a very bright, confident, attractive child," she said. "She was outgoing, but in a quiet way. Located in the Greenburgh school district, Juniper had a diverse, integrated student population. Carolyn fit in nicely. She wasn't at all prissy. She was the kind of child you wanted in your class. Once you provided her with a framework for a particular subject—reading, writing, or math—she took off on her own. Carolyn was never a problem child at any time. She was well behaved, polite, and well brought up. She was active and had a number of girlfriends in class. Carolyn's mother came in for regular teacher-parent conferences. Her greatest concern was that Carolyn wouldn't be adversely affected by the divorce, that she didn't experience issues or problems because of it. I don't know what role Mr. Bessette played in Carolyn's upbringing—he evidently paid maintenance and child support for his three daughters. I think he saw them from time to time. At my last conference with Carolyn's mother, she informed me that they were resettling in Greenwich. Once Carolyn married John Kennedy Jr., her years in Hartsdale were rarely mentioned in the press. And when she failed to respond to Juniper's invitation to return, there were some hard feelings among the members of the community."

Despite Carolyn's move to ritzy blue-blooded Greenwich, her upbringing remained less privileged than that of her future husband. Attractive, vivacious, and witty, she formed a number of friendships at St. Mary's. In her senior year, her classmates voted her "the Ultimate Beautiful Person." Outgoing and unspoiled, she had a smile and a kind word for everyone. "You're in a class by yourself," a friend wrote in her high school yearbook.

Following her marriage to JFK Jr., one of Carolyn's high school boyfriends told a tabloid reporter that their relationship had been "hot and heavy." Eugene Carlin, another of her boyfriends, described her as a "fun" lady—"she liked to dance and hang out." Deborah Lamoureux, a classmate of Carolyn's and valedictorian of their graduating class, said, "Carolyn liked to kid around and be a little rowdy at times, but we were all like that."

"She definitely had a naughty side," said Suzanne Ruddick, who knew Carolyn from the age of thirteen. "She and I attended different high schools, but we became friends because we dated some of the same guys. We were teenage girls growing up in one of the wealthiest suburbs in the country. We thought we knew it all. We did pot and drank beer. Carolyn was tall—nearly five feet ten—and stunning. She had large hands and feet, sort of like Jackie Kennedy. Like Jackie, she had a superb sense of style, even as a young girl. Fashion-wise it can be said that she was a kind of successor to Jackie. Her early interest in fashion may have been inspired by an afterschool job she took at Threads & Treads, a chic Greenwich clothing boutique. Over Christmas holidays, she worked behind the jewelry counter at a more downscale Caldor's outlet. Carolyn had a couple of steady boyfriends in high school, but then began going out with guys from Yale. She had a motto: 'Date them, train them, drop them.' When it came to men, she tended to be fickle. She knew instinctively how to play them. 'Never return a man's phone call,' she once said. She could have written *The Rules,* a best-selling primer on how to land Mr. Right. Early on she developed an intangible mystique, a spiritual femininity. It helps, of course, when you possess natural beauty, which she did. She was always trim, always fit, the perfect size 6. She could eat like a horse and never gain an ounce. Carolyn didn't just play hard to get. She was."

One key to Carolyn Bessette's character was her solid inner core. If she played down her early years in Hartsdale, she made no secret of her familial ties to Brooklyn. Maureen Seaberg, a New York journalist, recalled the time Carolyn admitted to nurses at Staten Island University Hospital (where Anthony Radziwill was undergoing radiation treatment for cancer), "I have a little Italian grandmother with a hair growing out of a mole on her face." Carolyn went on to tell the nurses the story of how her grandmother Jenny Messina, as well as her mother, had once lived in Bensonhurst, Brooklyn, and spent their summers at the beach resorts of Staten Island. As a child, Carolyn attended a slew of baby showers and weddings of cousins who still lived in the outer boroughs. One of her favorite Staten Island cousins was a New York City cop who supplemented his income by moonlighting as a limousine driver.

Chris Hudson, a friend of Carolyn's when she attended Boston University, remembered her regaling him with long, drawn-out tales of her "low-end, trailer trash Brooklyn and Staten Island relatives. Concomitantly, she had this very regal, almost aristocratic quality to her. It was the combination of the two that made her so special."

Carolyn's friends at BU described her as incredibly bright, extremely funny, unbelievably cool, and fun to be around. She was also very enterprising. When her mother blocked her cash flow because of excessive spending, she took a job working nights as a cocktail waitress. In her junior year, she received a tuition stipend by serving as a student teacher. She babysat for the children of several of her professors. Something of a "club rat," she spent her leisure hours at such nightspots as Cici and Axis. While in her senior year at BU, she began working for Patrick Lyons, director of the Lyons Group, Boston's major nightclub-management firm. Employed in the corporate sales division, she arranged parties and social functions for local companies and businesses. Jonathan Soroff, a nightlife reporter for the *Boston Herald*, befriended Carolyn soon after she began her new job. "Carolyn and I spent a lot of time together," said Soroff. "She was smart about people and relationships. In fact, she coached me through my first serious romantic breakup. She warned me, 'If you ever feel like calling your ex at 4:00 a.m.—*don't!* Dial my number instead. I don't care what time it is.' She was a together person—kind and fair, and a good and trusted friend to her best buddies. She was very natural, not at all calculating, which is something she and John Jr. evidently had in common. She was a wonderful schmoozer and had formidable social skills. She was always at ease. She possessed a good mind for business, though business per se didn't turn her on. She was secure and strong, exceedingly sure of herself. She didn't take shit from anyone. In other words, it wasn't possible to intimidate her. She always stood up for herself. If she felt she was being spoken to in a disrespectful manner, she'd say, 'Excuse me, please don't talk to me like that.'"

At BU, Carolyn dated Canadian-born Tom Cullen, captain of the ice-hockey team and a future NHL star, whose heart she reportedly broke by simultaneously carrying on with his friend and teammate, Chris Matchett. Among others, she also dated Italian fashion-empire scion Rocco Benetton. Guys constantly hit on her. She had magnetic sex appeal. In photographs, she appeared slick and aloof, but in person she was just the opposite. She was warm, engaging, and caring. One of her defining characteristics was her capacity for joy. She was the life of every party. She had enormous presence, the ability to entertain a group or an individual on a one-to-one basis. She looked you right in the eye when she spoke to you. She was spontaneous. She attained a reputation as the "campus man-eater," gorging on all the best-looking men, spitting them out, and going on to the next course. Colleen Curtis, a friend and classmate at BU, recalled that Carolyn "loved to laugh—hers was an unforgettably contagious belly laugh. She was always ready with a wisecrack. She greeted friends with a big hug. You never doubted her sincerity."

If after marrying JFK Jr. she suddenly grew camera shy, she had a somewhat different mind-set in college. She appeared as the cover girl for a 1988 *Girls of Boston University* cheesecake calendar. She subsequently posed for fashion photographer Bobby DiMarzo. The shots—Carolyn seated on a hay bale and strutting the streets of Boston in cowboy boots and a motorcycle jacket—appeared in the October 8, 1996, issue of *Globe*. Viewing them, a friend said, "She looks more like a refugee from a Van Halen video than the wife of John F. Kennedy Jr." *Playboy* purportedly offered her (when she became Mrs. John F. Kennedy Jr.) $1 million to pose in the nude; unlike Daryl Hannah, she turned them down.

After her graduation, Carolyn moved into her own apartment in an old brownstone off Newbury Street in Back Bay. She'd parlayed her part-time job with the Lyons Group into a full-time position. "She did her job well, but I had the impression she wasn't crazy about it," said Jonathan Soroff. "When another opportunity arose, she grabbed it." The new opportunity consisted of a retail sales position at the Calvin Klein boutique in the Boston suburb of Chestnut Hill, a stepping-stone job that would soon lead her to corporate headquarters in New York. Long an avid reader of *Vogue* and *WWD*, Carolyn had a nose for fashion and a style of her own. "I met her at a social gathering in Boston," said Oleg Cassini. "This was shortly after she began working for the Calvin Klein store up there. She was still young, but she already had a very pronounced look. It was almost extreme—the sharp features, alabaster skin, bright fire-engine red lipstick, long blond hair pulled tightly back, simple jewelry, little makeup other than the lipstick. It was very spare, the look of the future, a kind of WASP-patrician appearance, the sort of thing that appealed to Calvin Klein. She had expressive eyes and a fetching way of moving her head and smiling. It was a time when everyone wore black or white. Later Carolyn began playing around with her hair color, got it down to a whitish yellow. Her appearance made a statement—the vibrant big-city female professional. I read someplace that it took her all of five minutes to get dressed. Like Jackie, she could have been a fashion icon, if that's what she'd wanted. I don't know if she had the discipline Jackie did to reach such lofty heights, but with her clean silhouette and striking good looks, she was the perfect Calvin Klein girl."

"Carolyn was perfect for her job at Calvin Klein," said Jonathan Soroff. "She oozed charisma and looked great. She could have been a highly successful model, but modeling didn't interest her. I later read about all these drugs she supposedly did—I never once knew her to do drugs. She didn't even drink very much—an occasional cocktail or glass of wine. She had a way of putting people at ease. She was totally real, a no-bullshit person—unruffled, unfazed, unimpressed by celebrity."

It was Soroff who introduced Carolyn to Marci Klein, the daughter of Calvin Klein. "Marci was living in Boston at the time," remarked Soroff. "She and I were good friends. After Carolyn began working at the Chestnut Hill boutique, I told Marci about her. I said, 'There's a girl working in Chestnut Hill I think you ought to meet. She's going to end up working for your father in New York, dressing girls like you.' So they met, and they hit it off."

Marci Klein evidently mentioned Carolyn to her father. Calvin Klein dispatched a traveling sales coordinator to Chestnut Hill, who in turn recommended Carolyn to Susan Sokol, a Calvin Klein executive whose equally glowing report set the stage. Paul Wilmot, senior vice president for the firm, followed up by inviting Carolyn to New York for an interview. Duly impressed, he offered her a position as head of "personals." "Personals," said Wilmot, "referred to the fashions shown on the runway—they were available primarily to VIPs and celebrities. It was by invitation only. She became a personal shopper for high-profile clients, such as Blaine Trump and Diane Sawyer. One of the perks of the job was that Carolyn had a wardrobe allowance. She looked great in the clothes. She looked like a mannequin, but she was also extremely personable. Her manners, the quality of her conversation, far exceeded her years. She was elegant, self-aware, and well spoken. She was a knockout, a real stunner. In addition, she was a warm person. She would touch your arm, your hand, when she spoke to you. Calvin *loved* her. He wanted to promote her. After a while he moved her into public relations. This was after I left the firm. But while I was still there, she became friendly with Kelly Rector Klein, Calvin's wife from 1986 to 1996. Kelly was a talented fashion designer and a kind of muse to Calvin. She was a catalyst in getting John Jr. and Carolyn together. She knew John and asked him to some charity function and then invited him to the showroom for some suits, and that's apparently how he and Carolyn met."

Once the press got wind of the relationship between John and Carolyn—the fact that she'd become Daryl Hannah's successor—they descended upon the Calvin Klein employee like a pack of wolves. "She told me," said Wilmot, "that one morning as she walked out of her East Village doorman building—on Second Avenue between 10th and 11th streets—to catch a cab to work, she suddenly found herself surrounded by camera crews. It was her first exposure to this sort of thing, and it became a real problem. When she met with fashion editors of various news-papers and magazines to discuss Calvin Klein, they only wanted to know about John. When he began appearing at the shows to support Carolyn, the press went crazy. There was this terrible frenzy. They began hanging out in front of our offices. At night Carolyn had to take a circuitous route out of the building to avoid the press. She once asked me, 'When will all this press business end?' I told her, 'It'll end when you and John get married.' That turned out to be a bit of very bad advice—if anything, it got worse."

Lynn Tesoro became Carolyn's supervisor at Calvin Klein after the de-parture of Paul Wilmot. In addition to working together, the two forged a close friendship. They went out together the last week of Carolyn's life. "Carolyn was one of the brightest and funniest people I've ever known," said Tesoro. "Although she worked in public relations—and did a great job—I don't think that's what she wanted to do in terms of a career. Car-olyn became an important influence in Calvin Klein's career, as impor-tant as anyone." Stephen Fairchild, former design director for menswear at Calvin Klein, cited Carolyn's modernity and urban chic as key factors in the company's success. "Carolyn had her own eclectic style," said Fairchild. "It wasn't necessarily limited to Calvin Klein fashions. Calvin took elements of her style and incorporated them into his signature look." As early as 1992, *WWD* named her an "up-and-coming fashion star." *Newsweek* proclaimed her the epitome of "throwaway chic." She turned down an invitation to be on the cover of *Harper's Bazaar*. Anna Wintour, then editor of *Vogue*, felt that she had "the look." Oscar de la Renta noted that she was the "incarnation of modern style." "Everything that she wore looked fashionable on her," said Karl Lagerfeld. She was the perfect "Bergdorf blonde," if ever there was one. Regularly seen at Prada and Barneys, Carolyn influenced Calvin Klein, his designers, and even a number of the women employed in the firm, many of whom be-gan imitating her in dress and manner. At night she'd take them to her regular haunts—the MercBar, MK, and the Buddha Bar—and tell them what shade to color their hair. When she began wearing her hair in a ponytail, the others followed suit. She gave out samples of a distinctive oriental scent that she'd picked up for a few dollars from a street vendor.

Carolyn continued to work for Calvin Klein until 1996. Six months prior to her marriage, she left the job. The onslaught of personal publicity made it impossible for her to work.

Other than John F. Kennedy Jr., Carolyn Bessette's most publicized relationship involved an actor and male model named Michael Bergin, whose 2004 memoir, *The Other Man,* purports to trace the details of their romance. The bare details, according to the book, are that Bergin, raised in the blue-collar town of Naugatuck, Connecticut, the son of a policeman and a hairdresser, arrived in New York armed with a Click Model Management contract, rented a room in the East 90s, and took a job as a doorman at the Paramount Hotel in midtown Manhattan. In the late summer of 1992, at age twenty-three, he met Carolyn Bessette at Joe's Café, an Upper East Side singles bar. It was the same summer Carolyn and John had their first go-round. When John dropped her in favor of Daryl Hannah, she began an affair with Bergin, who in December 1993 became Calvin Klein's underwear model, his bulgy crotch appearing on billboards and buses across America. *Sex and the City* author Candace Bushnell commemorated a short-lived Bergin fling of her own by writing him into her novel, dubbing him "the Bone," and depicting him as a well-ripped, pseudo gay, wannabe actor cum underwear model.

Bergin's memoir, chock full of inaccuracies, distortions, discrepancies, and unsubstantiated claims, is further hindered by the almost total use of pseudonyms and a fault-ridden timeline. Unaware that Carolyn had already met and had a romance with John Jr., Bergin admits early in his account that he is a cocaine abuser and a gay tease. Nowhere, however, does he mention that his nearly nude likeness was (and is) a mainstay on a number of pornographic gay websites.

Other than that she smoked cigarettes and referred to past boyfriends merely as "friends," Carolyn remains a mysterious figure in Bergin's book, prone to depressions and angry outbursts. We also learn that the walls of her East Village apartment were covered with empty picture frames, and that (like Elizabeth Taylor) she loved mashed potatoes and "everything" bagels. We find out that she liked to "meow" at her lovers and kept a copy of the JFK Jr. "Sexiest Man Alive" *People* magazine issue under her kitchen sink. In various interviews conducted with Bergin in connection with the publication of his book, he insisted that Carolyn "still" loved him even after she married John Jr., a self-serving statement wildly at odds with the sentiments of Carolyn's closest friends. "I knew Carolyn was in love with me," Bergin writes. "It wasn't that she told me so . . . It was more about the way she looked at me."

According to Jennifer Axelrod, a friend of hers from Boston, "Carolyn was attracted to Bergin but never loved him, not even when John wasn't in the picture. She was three years his senior, far more intelligent, mature, and sophisticated. She used to deride him behind his back. 'He's good in bed but dumb as an ox,' she'd say. Although he reports in his book that they were 'inseparable,' she never dated him exclusively—she went out with two or three other men at the same time. Soon after she and John Jr. became re-involved, she dumped Bergin like a ton of bricks. Then there's his weird claim in the book that before they broke up, he impregnated her. All I can say is that she always used birth control pills and was extremely careful about taking them. Bergin was either an incurable romantic or a complete liar—or both. So far as Carolyn Bessette was concerned, he created a mythology, a piece of pulp fiction that bears no resemblance to reality."

At the beginning of his memoir, Bergin provides the reader with what appears to be the book's main underlying motif. Arriving in New York, he tells us he suddenly realized that "Bullshit . . . was a big part of life." At another juncture in the book, he proclaims: "Lying is so much easier than the truth." It is this philosophy and belief system that underscores Bergin's approach.

The book's title and pivotal point hinge on the author's contention that he and Carolyn continued their sexual relationship *after* she and John married in 1996. Having moved to Los Angeles to embark on an acting career and landing a role as a lifeguard on television's *Baywatch*, Bergin writes that in "late June or early July [1997], Carolyn came to L.A. . . . Carolyn had become one of the most photographed women in America, and we couldn't risk being seen—so [she] took a cab to my place. When I heard [her] pull up, I rushed out to meet [her]. Carolyn was already out of the cab, and she was almost unrecognizable. She had a baseball cap pulled low on her forehead and wore dark sunglasses." Married for nearly a year at this point, Carolyn—according to the text—"threw her arms" around Bergin's neck and gave him "a big kiss on the lips." The opportunity for Carolyn's visit, Bergin tells us, occurred because "John was . . . off in Iceland, kayaking with a group of friends. He would be gone for at least two weeks."

Three days after Carolyn's arrival, writes Bergin, the two "realized we weren't going to be able to resist each other." Six days into her supposed stay with Bergin, the couple rekindled their long-dead romance and for the next five days lived like husband and wife: "At night, we'd order in, or I'd run around the corner for sushi. We'd feed each other. We'd make love. And everything remained unsaid. It was killing me, and I imagined it must have been killing her too." Bergin draws the curtain on the scene by insisting that Carolyn delayed her return to New York because "she couldn't leave" him, suggesting that she was prepared to stay with Bergin forever. It "was almost more than I could handle," writes Bergin. "She was married, for God's sake. What were we doing? What were we thinking?" All told, Bergin claims that he and Carolyn spent eleven days together in California and that their "affair" continued for months to come.

Bergin's tale contained but one minor glitch. Between late June and early July 1997, when Carolyn purportedly visited Bergin in Los Angeles, she was actually at Martha's Vineyard with John. JFK Jr.'s kayak expedition to Iceland took place not in June or July but in mid-August. Moreover, he remained in Iceland for only five days and not, as Bergin would have it, for "at least two weeks." News of John's sojourn appeared in *Morgaunbladid,* Iceland's leading newspaper. Dated August 20, 1997, the article, by Halldor Sveinbjornsson, began: "John F. Kennedy Jr., son of former U.S. President John F. Kennedy, made a five-day trip around Iceland last week with three of his friends . . . Their trip was organized by the travel service Ultima Thule in Reykjavik, which provided them with the necessary equipment and travel plans . . ." For the record, the director of Ultima Thule confirmed the accuracy of the newspaper report, adding that John and his friends "came and went on direct flights from New York aboard Icelandic Airlines."

Michael Bergin's defense would no doubt be that he erred concerning the dates of Carolyn's visit and the length of her stay. Such a defense, however, would be unsupportable. In mid-August 1997, while John was off in Iceland on his five-day trip, Carolyn remained in New York and was joined there by Jennifer Axelrod, a friend from Boston. "I stayed with Carolyn at 20 North Moore Street," said Axelrod. "John called in every morning and every night. Poor Michael Bergin! The one time in his book that he attaches a date to an event, it turns out to be wrong. The only period John and Carolyn were separated that summer were the five days in mid-August that she spent with me. Since she couldn't possibly have been in Los Angeles and New York simultaneously, his entire story falls apart. Carolyn never went out with him after she and John married. Among other things, Carolyn was much too smart to risk her marriage by sleeping with an underpants model, a guy of only tangential interest to her. That simply wasn't her MO. What's amazing is that despite all the hype surrounding that stupid book—all those television appearances and newspaper accounts—not one reporter bothered to investigate the veracity of Bergin's implausible version."

When asked whether there were "holes" in *The Other Man,* Lynn Tesoro, Carolyn's close friend at Calvin Klein, responded: "*Holes* is an understatement. Michael did not have any contact with Carolyn during the last three years of her life. John was the love of her life—once he entered the picture, nothing else mattered."

Clifford Streit, Michael Bergin's former manager, who first met the model-actor (as well as Carolyn Bessette) in November 1993 at a birthday party for Kelly Klein, maintained that "the part about his having an affair with her after she married John Jr. was total horsecrap. Michael and I often discussed Carolyn after she married John, and it's simply not true that he slept with her after she got married. They may have spoken on the phone a few times, but that's about it.

"Michael Bergin was a good-looking, naive little kid with a small-town background. When I met him he'd left the Click modeling agency and signed on with Wilhelmina. I told him he'd signed an onerous contract with Wilhelmina, that he was practically an indentured servant. As for his romance with Carolyn Bessette, the two of them never had a classic boyfriend-girlfriend relationship. There's no question that they had a strong physical attraction to one another, but the connection was nebulous. There was no real commitment, at least not on her part. After she dropped him for John, I tried to console him. 'You can't compete with him,' I said, 'because you're competing against history. John's the most glamorous child of one of the most glamorous couples in history.' Of course Michael was upset. He loved Carolyn. Frankly, I can't blame him. I got to know her. She was spectacular. She was beautiful, bright, demanding, vulnerable, kind, and very appealing on many different levels. She was tough but feminine, an iron fist in a velvet glove. In those days Michael was one of the most sought-after male models in New York, but John Kennedy Jr.'s power transcended all that. He was revered. He was the world's most famous bachelor. When Michael announced his intention to write the book, I advised him to end it with Carolyn's marriage to John. I have no idea what possessed him to do what he did. He was basically a decent guy, so I don't know what happened. I don't know if it was a question of money or hurt pride at having lost Carolyn in the first place."

On April 11, 2004, in conjunction with the publication of *The Other Man,* Michael Bergin conducted a reading and book signing at the West 8th Street Manhattan branch of Barnes & Noble. Alexandra Speck, a literary researcher, approached Bergin after the reading and asked him point-blank if he could provide the name or names of anyone who could confirm his claim that he and Carolyn Bessette had been intimate following her marriage to JFK Jr. After a bit of hemming and hawing, Bergin responded, "You know what—I don't feel like I need to provide a name. In time, I'm sure people will step forward." To date, nobody—not a single soul—has materialized.

In the late summer of 1994, John brought Carolyn Bessette to Hyannis Port and introduced her to Ted Kennedy. After their marriage, Teddy told the press: "You could tell right away that there was something special between the two of them. They're both obviously very deeply in love." The television tabloid show *A Current Affair* ran footage of John and Carolyn on a boat at Martha's Vineyard. A newspaper photo showed them sitting on a curb watching the New York City Marathon. Magazine photographs revealed them kissing in Central Park. John introduced her to his sister, his sister's husband, and their three children. She had a way with kids. She did less well with Caroline Kennedy, who reacted to Carolyn much as the Kennedy clan had initially reacted to Jackie. The group spent the day at Georgica Association, the private beach club to which the Schlossbergs belonged, Carolyn seated on a bath towel under a beach umbrella, while the rest of the family swam and played Frisbee. Never much of an exercise buff, Carolyn once told a friend that she didn't see the point of it. There was no evidence to support the premise that working out extended one's life span. Never a proponent of sunbathing, she observed that too much sunlight was a direct cause of skin cancer.

"Caroline Kennedy perceived herself as her brother's keeper, particularly after Jackie's death," observed Jennifer Axelrod. "She was the gardener, and he was the flower. She cultivated and protected him, although obviously not enough, because he'd begun taking flying lessons again. He also went on a brief but dangerous kayak trip off Alaska. Of course, once his mother died, he felt a sense of freedom that probably nobody, not even Caroline Kennedy, could control. His sister undoubtedly recognized Carolyn Bessette as competition for her brother's affection. Carolyn was a formidable woman. She possessed a multitude of attributes, and Caroline knew it. 'Caroline Kennedy is frightening,' Carolyn said to me. The two women never liked each other. They were night and day, oil and water. To Carolyn's credit, she never tried to come between John and his sister. She steered clear of Caroline, the same way John steered clear of Ed Schlossberg. John and his sister maintained a closeness that precluded everyone around them."

In an effort to introduce Carolyn Bessette to some of his friends, John brought her along to a few of the Saturday afternoon touch football games they played in Central Park every fall. They played a form of the game called Razzle Dazzle, which allowed forward and backward passes on kickoffs. Like Jackie at the Kennedy family compound football games

418 C. David Heymann

in Hyannis Port, Carolyn soon lost interest. She found them overly competitive and at times brutal—and nobody was more brutal or competitive than John. Charlie King, John's former classmate at Brown, recalled a play in which John "just knocked the shit out of me. I felt like all the bones in my body had been shattered. John was driven to win."

"We'd play into the winter months," said Richard Wiese, "and we'd play no matter how cold it got. John and I usually organized the games. For the most part, the teams consisted of friends—his, mine, and ours. I think I remember seeing Carolyn Bessette on the sidelines once or twice with John's dog, Friday. She never attended after they got married. We certainly didn't want to draw attention to ourselves. The last thing we wanted was the press. It wasn't a media event, just a bunch of guys playing football in the park."

Richard Wiese played quarterback for one team and Michael Bush, an attorney, quarterbacked the other. "John always played his heart out, but he was a gentleman about it," said Bush. "After the games, we'd go to this low-key coffee shop on Madison Avenue, and we'd order burgers and milk shakes. We'd sit around and chat, usually about ten of us. It was like being back in college. It was a liberating experience. One thing that struck me about John was that he never spoke ill of anyone, ever."

By late 1994 and early 1995, John and Carolyn were seeing a good deal of each other. One day, returning by car from Boston to New York, they were pulled over by a state trooper on the Massachusetts Turnpike. "John and Carolyn had been doing pot," said Jennifer Axelrod, "and the cop practically swooned when he detected the scent. Fortunately, he recognized JFK Jr. and let him go with nothing more than a 'how do you do.' Carolyn was amazed. John told her that Ted Kennedy had gotten away with involuntary manslaughter in Massachusetts, a reference to Chappaquiddick. 'There's an unwritten law in Massachusetts,' he said, 'whereby members of my family can commit murder and mayhem, and nobody bats an eye.'"

John told Billy Way that he thought he was falling in love with Carolyn. "Getting to know her again," he said, "is as pleasant as slipping into a warm bath. I can't believe I let her go the first time around."

"John realized," said Way, "that Carolyn was fairly high maintenance, but it didn't bother him. He regretted that he'd never introduced her to his mother. Carolyn, like Jackie, was Catholic and the product of divorced parents. They both had a smart, minimalist look and sexiness. Carolyn wasn't exactly the girl next door, but she also wasn't a spoiled, preening film star or fashion model. She seemed very New York, the quintessential Downtown Girl. It happened that she changed her look at this point. She did Botox, got her eyebrows trimmed to a wisp, and had her hair tinged a few shades lighter. She and John made few public appearances, because any function they attended automatically assumed the proportions of a major event. When they did appear in public, John took it upon himself to protect her. I once accompanied them to a large benefit dinner, and he was seated at a separate table from us. He came over every ten minutes to make sure that all was well. On another occasion, we decided to eat dinner at Il Cantinori, in Greenwich Village. Somehow the press found out about it. As we stepped out of the restaurant after dinner, they were on top of us. Usually John posed for a shot or two, and they'd go away. This time, probably because of Carolyn, they kept shooting. They followed us down the street until John finally turned and said, 'If you don't stop, I'll never pose for you guys again.' They stopped."

Since they were reluctant to be seen together at plays and movies, John and Carolyn decided to join a private book club that had been organized by Michael Mailer, the son of Norman Mailer. John's friend Karen Duffy belonged to the same reading group. "The first rule of the club," she wrote in *Glamour* after John's and Carolyn's deaths, "was that whoever chose the book title had to host the dinner and lead the discussion about the book. The second rule was the discussion of the book was shelved until after dinner." When John's turn came, he chose *Neuromancer,* a science fiction novel by William Gibson. Although Karen Duffy wasn't at that particular meeting, she heard that John had prepared a feast that "went on forever." By the end of the meal, the members of the club were too tired to discuss the book. The book club buzz had it that John, having never read the novel, had conceived the endless repast so he could "weasel out of leading the discussion."

Over Thanksgiving vacation of 1994, eight members of the same club—including John and Carolyn—went on a scuba diving trip to Guatemala and Honduras. Carolyn and Karen Duffy's future husband were the only members of the group who weren't certified scuba divers. To become certified they took a course at the Honduran resort where the group was staying. After becoming certified, they joined the group at a 100-foot-deep shipwreck site. To everyone's amazement, including John's, Carolyn performed brilliantly, "She was game and excited about diving," wrote Duffy. "She impressed the others with her skill and bravery."

Carolyn demonstrated less enthusiasm when it came to John's latest endeavor: the Buckeye. John had learned about the ultralight powered parachute, manufactured by Buckeye Aviation, from one of his flight instructors, who thought it would help him master the rudiments of piloting a regular plane. John contacted Frank Evans, owner of Buckeye Sales in Charlton, New York, and purchased a one-seater. He later bought a two-seater for himself and Carolyn.

"The Buckeye might look a bit frightening," admitted Evans, "but it's easy to fly. It's not like an airplane, where you have rudders and so forth. The Buckeye is simple—you fire up the engine, and you steer it down the runway. You increase the power to go up, decrease it to go down. It only takes a couple of hours of ground training, which includes watching a forty-five-minute video. The rest you learn once you're airborne by talking to your instructor over a two-way radio. Or, if it's a two-seater, the instructor goes up with you the first time and shows you what to do."

John's single-seat Buckeye arrived by plane at a small airport in Saratoga, New York. Involved in his initial training sessions were Frank Evans's partner John Murphy, and Lloyd Howard, national director of the firm. "I wanted to be involved," said Howard, "because with a high-profile person like John Kennedy Jr., if something went wrong, it could have been disastrous for the entire company. So, anyway, we made arrangements with him, set a date to train him, then met him at the airfield in Saratoga. After we showed him the ropes, he jumped into the seat, and we buckled him in. Pretty soon he was in the air. He did extremely well for a first-timer. In fact, he didn't want to come down. He was up there for quite a while. It was getting dark. I thought we might have to shoot him out of the air to get him down."

Lloyd Howard and John subsequently became friends. "I got to know him pretty well," continued Howard. "He came out to visit my family at our home in Argos, Indiana. The main reason for the visit was that he wanted to trade his single-seat Buckeye for a two-seater. Before he arrived, he asked me *not* to notify the press. He asked if he could bring along a buddy. Well, the 'buddy' turned out to be Carolyn Bessette. Our corporate lawyer, Chuck Thomas, picked them up at an airport in Chicago and flew them to Plymouth Airport in his private plane. John came straight at me and gave me a big hug. He was wearing a flannel shirt and sweatpants. 'Lloyd,' he said, 'I want you to meet someone.' Carolyn was right behind him. She gave me a hug. 'Lloyd,' she said, 'I've heard so much about you.' They were a very loving couple. And Carolyn had a great comic sensibility. She had us rolling on the floor. She loved to banter and kid around. I think they enjoyed being out of the spotlight for a change. We went to a local restaurant for dinner. Everybody recognized them, but nobody bothered them. John had on this black wool knit cap, which his mother had given him shortly before she died. He misplaced it in the car and became distraught. To everyone's relief, Carolyn found it. The next morning about a dozen of us went out for a big country breakfast. That night we ordered a pizza delivery. John asked a lot of questions about the farms in the area. He was like a reporter gathering information. We talked about John's childhood days in the White House. He didn't remember much, but there was no denying that he intended on going into politics, running for president one day—he said his father would have expected it of him."

During the visit, Lloyd Howard's youngest son, Christopher, took Carolyn for a flight in a two-seat Buckeye. "They were up there for about twenty-five minutes," said Lloyd. "John seemed a bit nervous, because he didn't know how Carolyn would react to the flight, whether she'd like it or not. When they landed, and she removed her helmet, she had a big smile on her face. He went running over to her and said, 'You liked it, didn't you?' She said she did. And that's when he decided to trade in his single-seat Buckeye for a two-seat Dream Machine—the idea was for her to join him on future flights."

Jeff Jenson, a Buckeye flight instructor and salesman from Lynch-burg, Virginia, who met John and Carolyn during their Indiana visit with Lloyd Howard, recalled that John had a cast on his hand. "According to the tabloids," said Jenson, "he'd broken his hand smacking Carolyn around. It was such garbage. He hurt his hand playing football. After they got the two-seater, I went up to Martha's Vineyard to upgrade it, put in better instrumentation. They housed me at Red Gate Farm, even gave me permission to use their car. They were a lovely couple. I was surprised when, shortly before his death, John broke his ankle flying the Buckeye. Such accidents are rare. Just as when he crashed his Saratoga, it was a question of pilot error, though I'm not quite certain what went wrong."

Following the delivery of his two-seat Dream Machine, JFK Jr. also invited Frank Evans and John Murphy to Martha's Vineyard for additional Buckeye training. John Murphy brought along his sister. "Even though John Jr. was most definitely a down-to-earth, regular person," remarked Evans, "I'm afraid I can't say the same for Carolyn. She became exercised because John Murphy's sister began taking photographs. She took several shots of JFK Jr. and Carolyn. When she put down the camera, Carolyn grabbed it and took out the film. This happened more than once. She clearly didn't like having her picture taken."

"I live more in five minutes on the Buckeye," John Jr. once told George Plimpton, "than most people live in a lifetime."

In 1998, two years after he and Carolyn had gotten married, the tabloids began carrying stories emphasizing their supposed marital problems. "There were reports in the press that they were on the verge of divorce," said Lloyd Howard. "I couldn't believe it. I called Carolyn, and I just bluntly asked, or I said, 'Carolyn, you know the tabloids have it that you two are having problems and your marriage is not working well. Is that true?' And she said, 'Lloyd, it's not true. There's always something going around about us. They'll write anything to make money.'

"I fully believed her. From what I could discern—and I spoke with them frequently—they were very much in love. As a matter of fact, I spoke to them shortly before they died. Believe it or not, they were planning on coming out here again for a big midwestern air show. They'd agreed to work the Buckeye Aviation exhibition booth with us. Tragically, it never came to pass."

Chapter 19

✦

LOVE'S LABOUR'S LOST

ON JANUARY 24, 1995, Carolyn Bessette accompanied John Jr. to Boston to attend the funeral services at St. Stephen's Church for his grandmother, 104-year-old Rose Kennedy. It marked Carolyn's first appearance at a major Kennedy family event and signaled the important role she would soon assume in John's life. By the late summer of that year, she had sublet her East Village apartment to Gordon Henderson, a friend and former Calvin Klein designer, and moved into John's loft at 20 North Moore Street. She brought along a virtual warehouse of clothes, a set of her grandmother's dishes, and her cat Ruby. John's dog and Carolyn's cat didn't get along and had to be quartered in separate rooms.

John and Carolyn celebrated their new domestic partnership by attending the Westbury Music Festival to see David Crosby and Graham Nash in concert. They were regularly seen at Asia de Cuba as well as at Michael Schwimmer's Mudville Night Salon, the same dive bar he'd often frequented with Daryl Hannah. Restaurant owner Drew Nieporent attended a dinner party at the Tribeca Grill with John and Carolyn, where they served osso buco (braised veal shank). When the party was nearly over, JFK Jr. discreetly asked the waitress to wrap up the bones for his dog. He asked if he could have extras. John and Carolyn left with a huge doggie bag in tow. The couple dropped in at Gallagher's for cocktails one evening but left when hyperventilating female patrons of the famous Manhattan steak house kept brushing up against JFK Jr. at the bar. When Carolyn became angry, John said to her: "This is the only life I've ever known." Carolyn accompanied John to a fund-raiser given by the Advisory Committee for Mental Retardation, which JFK Jr. had joined at the behest of President Clinton. Again they were forced to depart, this time because photographers clustered around them and refused to leave. They went on an all-too-infrequent double date with Ed and Caroline Schlossberg and attended a huge bash in the Hamptons sponsored by Sony. According to another guest at the party, the two couples barely exchanged glances. "As usual," said the guest, a friend of Caroline's, "John and Ed had nothing to say to each other."

Celebrity photographer J. D. Ligier videotaped John and Carolyn as they emerged late one night from the Bowery Bar in lower Manhattan. Carolyn, holding a newspaper in front of her face, ducked into a waiting car. "Not you again!" John growled at the photographer. Ligier had been stalking them for weeks, paying off informants to disclose the couple's latest whereabouts.

One morning as they went for a walk with John's dog, the couple heard the familiar clicking sound of cameras, then spotted a gaggle of photographers following them down West Broadway. They quickened their pace. One of the photographers, Peter Zola, overheard John say to Carolyn, "Just give them what they want, and they'll go away." "I'm not giving them anything," responded Carolyn. The photographers raced after them for several blocks. Finally John whirled around and approached one of the photographers. "They went eyeball-to-eyeball," said Zola. "Carolyn began to cry. John yanked the camera out of the photographer's hands and yelled, 'Why don't you leave us the fuck alone?' He gave the camera back, but he then flagged down a passing patrol car, and the police chased us away. I'd been photographing him for several years without a single incident. The pressure of being with someone who couldn't deal with the press had begun to tell on John. What did Carolyn Bessette expect? She was dating the most famous celebrity in the country, if not the world. She would later marry him. How bizarre of her to think that we would all simply vanish. If you can't take the heat, get the hell out of the kitchen."

Boston Herald columnist Laura Raposa similarly took note of the change in John Jr.'s attitude toward the press after he and Carolyn began living together. "In former days," said Raposa, "he went out of his way to accommodate journalists and press photographers. Once he became involved with Bessette, he took a complete turn. At Hyannis Port, strolling around in a blue sweat suit with a Walkman draped around his head, he once threw a bucket of water at a news photographer, something he wouldn't have dreamed of doing previously. He later bought the fellow a new camera. Carolyn was a fruitcake—she didn't want anyone from the press within a hundred yards of her. I saw John and Carolyn at a White House correspondents' dinner. It's an event at which a celebrity or two share a table with a group of journalists. I asked him, 'Who's at your table, John?' 'Just myself and Carolyn,' he responded. 'Is that the best you can do?' I said. I was kidding, of course, but John went off like a rocket. 'That's the rudest thing I've ever heard!' he screamed. 'I was just kidding, John,' I told him. 'I don't give a damn!' he thundered. And he kept at it for another five minutes. He did all this for her benefit, a demonstration of his devotion.

"What bothered me about her was that here's a woman who bags the world's most eligible bachelor, and every time you saw her she looked miserable. She made an awful fuss whenever anyone tried to photograph her. If I'd been fortunate enough to bag JFK Jr., I would've been out of my apartment every day with a big smile on my face, waving at the paparazzi. You glut the market with photos, and they go away, because the photos aren't worth anything anymore. Wave and smile at a photographer, and he'll run in the opposite direction. The worst thing you can do is to hide or play hard to get—they'll come after you every time."

Carolyn Bessette's antipathy toward the press won her few friends. Photographer Bettina Cirone never quite considered John's future wife the epitome of style or an icon of fashion. "Carolyn was highly temperamental," said Cirone. "She was on drugs. Everybody knew about it. She was heavy into cocaine, at least during the period she still worked for Calvin Klein. She wasn't always all there. She was manipulative. She rid herself of Michael Bergin and traded up for John Jr. With that bleached blond, chemical-laden mane of hers, she looked absolutely plastic. She was so unlike John. I never understood their relationship. Whatever Carolyn looked like on the outside, she had an ugly-duckling personality that came out in smirks and scowls. It was a tragic and volatile coupling. Whenever I photographed them together, she'd walk with her head down. I always thought it a pretense of shyness. John was not a volatile man, but he became one in her presence. She provoked him. I suppose what energized him about the relationship, at least in the beginning, was that it was so different from what he'd known in the past. John was naive. In many respects, he was still a little kid. His mother wasn't there to protect him, and his sister wasn't about to mother him. Carolyn Bessette succeeded in souring his sweetness."

Photographer Rose Hantman first encountered Carolyn Bessette at a fall 1992 party celebrating the publication of *Pools*, a coffee-table book of swimming pool snapshots by Kelly Klein. *Vogue* magazine sponsored the event, which took place at a health-spa swimming pool in an exclusive East Side apartment building. JFK Jr., having ended his first go-round with Carolyn Bessette, made a brief appearance, staying long enough to be photographed with both Calvin and Kelly Klein. "Carolyn Bessette was there, doing PR," said Hantman. "She was impossible—very annoyed-looking and cold." Several years later, after John and Carolyn had reunited on a permanent basis, Hantman spotted them entering the side door of the Armory to attend a charity event. "As I tried to photograph them," Hantman continued, "Carolyn looked at me like a deer caught in the headlights. She seemed very unhappy. More than once she'd been quoted as saying how much she detested the press. She also appeared to be nervous about the crowds, about being set upon by hordes of people. If she could have somehow made us all disappear, she would've been glad to oblige."

Publicist R. Couri Hay had an even more negative take on Carolyn, insisting that John should never have married her. "The only thing Carolyn Bessette brought to the equation was a sense of drama," said Hay. "John loved drama. He was like a Greek mythological hero whose life consisted of euphoric highs and tragic lows. Carolyn was a huge mistake. She lacked the essential qualities needed to handle the lifestyle he offered her. He was headed for the public arena—the Senate and then the presidency. Carolyn had a near breakdown just living in TriBeCa. How could she possibly have handled being a politician's wife, or residing in the White House? She got what she wanted when John married her, but then she promptly fell apart. She was attractive and chic, but also skittish and erratic. The very sight of a camera sent her scurrying. She wasn't an asset."

Whether out of loyalty or because they truly were impressed, John's friends painted a substantially different picture. Richard Wiese, who knew Carolyn before John did, termed her an "extraordinary woman in that if you were in conversation with her, she would completely lock herself into you. You felt you were the only person in the room, and this could be very provocative. Although I never experienced it personally, I heard that Jackie Kennedy had the same effect on people. After John went back to Daryl Hannah in the late summer of 1992, he continued to show interest in Carolyn. He asked me about her all the time. He had nothing but positive things to say about her. Then, of course, they resumed their relationship. Carolyn had immense confidence, and she challenged people. For a guy like John, who was so used to having people all over him, Carolyn presented a welcome challenge. He wasn't used to people saying 'no' to him. If their relationship was somewhat tempestuous, it was no more so than his romance with Daryl Hannah. John enjoyed the give and take—as a matter of fact, he thrived on it. They had problems, but they were working them out."

John Perry Barlow shared Richard Wiese's opinion of Carolyn Bessette, and for some of the same reasons. "Jackie Kennedy could be talking to a half-dozen men simultaneously," said Barlow, "and have every one of them convinced that he was the only one she was talking to. Carolyn had the same capacity. She was really good at that sort of thing. Like Jackie, she was genuinely interested. It wasn't simulated. She wasn't just a flirt. She was a flirt to the level that it was a holy undertaking. At the high end, flirtation is a holy communion."

Chris Overbeck presented the most balanced appraisal of John and Carolyn's relationship. An investment banker, John's friend from Brown had married and moved to Greenwich, Carolyn's hometown. According to Overbeck, John "was engaged by intelligence and mystery in a woman, rather than pure classic good looks. Interesting and complex women intrigued him—like the two women (his mother and sister) to whom he felt closest. Carolyn was both complex and attractive. She had an aggressive side—if she wanted something, she would find a way to get it. She was very strong and powerful, yet feminine. John was very masculine. He liked to argue, though in his heart he was sweet and affectionate. Carolyn was the tougher of the two. There was an intensity of masculine-feminine attraction between them, although they also embodied fundamental differences. Carolyn had a lot of guile and used it to forge the relationship."

The two couples—John and Carolyn, Chris and his wife, Lizzie— occasionally got together for dinner. "I'd invite them up to Greenwich," remarked Overbeck, "but Carolyn always refused. She'd say, 'I'm not going back to Greenwich.' So we'd meet at restaurants in New York. In her mind, I think she associated Greenwich with her past. She was on an upward path. John was already there. He'd always been there. He was born there. But at some point he began to question himself. He realized he had it all, but one day he asked himself: 'What am I doing with it?' I'm happy to report he found answers in Carolyn Bessette and in *George,* the political magazine he launched in late 1995."

After John's July 1999 death, Pete Hamill wrote a piece for *The New Yorker* recalling the days when he and Jackie Kennedy dated. In the article he describes a walk he took through Central Park with John Jr., then still in his teens. John asked Hamill numerous questions about journalism and the craft of reporting. "You mean you go, say, to a murder scene, and you make your notes, and then you go back to the paper and write the story?" inquired John, demonstrating an early interest in what would later become his profession, presumably en route to a career in politics. Jackie Kennedy had expressed surprise over her son's declared intentions, asking him if he expected to produce a politicized version of *Mad* magazine. Considering that he'd always been on the other side of the camera, it seemed an odd choice for him. He discussed the matter at length with his sister, who was less dubious and more supportive than their mother had been. It was she who encouraged her brother to take a weekend seminar at the New School on "How to Start Your Own Magazine."

John and his partner in the endeavor, a friend he'd known since 1983 named Michael Berman, had previously toyed with the possibility of starting a customized kayak company ("Random Ventures Inc."), one of several businesses JFK Jr. had considered before settling on the idea of a magazine. Kennedy and Berman, who had earlier founded a public relations firm called PRNY, envisioned a publication that would do for politics what *Rolling Stone* had done for rock. The political magazines already on the market were ideologically based; the concept for *George*— named after George Washington—was nonideological. Instead it would focus on the people and personalities that impacted the world of politics, intertwined with strands of pop culture.

After fleshing out their concept and deciding on a business plan, Kennedy and Berman each contributed equal funds to hire consultants and conduct a direct-mail market survey. Once the results were in, they began talking to people. At first they hoped to raise the necessary funds themselves, but when they realized the enormous cost of such an undertaking—at least $30 million, if not more—they turned to various elite publishing firms for financial help. *Rolling Stone* president Jann Wenner was the first magazine magnate to turn them down. Despite his prior friendship with John's mother and sister, he failed to see the potential in a glossy periodical largely devoted to politics. "Politics doesn't sell," he said. "It's not commercial."

They consulted with David Kuhn, a literary agent and former magazine editor, whom John had known since his senior year at Andover. "I became acquainted with John through my friendship with Jenny Christian, his girlfriend at the time," said Kuhn. "Jenny and I both attended Harvard. John and I became old but not close friends. He and Michael Berman contacted me when they were formulating plans for *George*. I brainstormed with them, gave them some ideas, discussed overall concepts and strategies, and introduced them to some people in the magazine business. It was all rather informal. I felt the magazine had a real chance. By virtue of his background and upbringing, John had a true sense of 'the story behind the story.'" Kuhn characterized John as possessing keen insight into people, being able to "read" them quickly and easily—essential gifts in running a successful magazine, or any other enterprise, for that matter. "John had a built-in bullshit meter," continued Kuhn. "He could generally tell when people were posturing or pulling his chain."

Kennedy and Berman approached Steve Florio, CEO at Condé Nast, an ardent JFK Jr. admirer. "John was smart and loved to laugh," said Florio. "He showed tremendous promise as a magazine editor and publisher. He had a point of view. Here's a guy who played in the White House as a kid and had known some of the top political dogs of the day. He understood the nuances of American politics. I wasn't convinced that *George* was the right vehicle for John or for us, but he was certainly the kind of person we wanted in the organization. I discussed the situation a number of times with Si Newhouse, the chairman of Condé Nast. Newhouse wasn't convinced either, but he agreed that John would be a great addition to the firm. 'Maybe he'll want to do a political column for *Vanity Fair* or *The New Yorker*,' he said. John might've agreed, but what he really wanted was to find a backer for *George*. Without making a firm offer or fully turning him down, we left everything open for further discussion. He ultimately found another backer. When the backer began to lose faith because the magazine wasn't succeeding, he came back to us. That was shortly before he died."

John turned to Pierre Salinger for advice. They met in Georgetown during one of Salinger's trips to the United States. "John brought Carolyn Bessette along," recalled Salinger. "I was impressed by how dedicated they both seemed to the prospect of producing a political lifestyle magazine. John had never seemed particularly assertive, but he'd suddenly become a panther on the prowl, ready to pounce on anything. What he lacked in experience, he made up for in enthusiasm. Carolyn appeared just as gung ho as John. Frankly, there are a lot easier ways to put your toe in the political water than to start a publication that has a 99 percent chance of failure. I say this because so many magazines get started and then crash within a short period of time. It was a brave undertaking, especially when you're John Kennedy. He could have done a lot of other things—he could've run somebody's campaign, worked in Ted Kennedy's Senate office, run for office himself. He could have done anything he wanted in that area. *George* represented an awfully public trial. On the other hand, because of who he was, John had a unique advantage. He had name recognition and entrée to practically anyone in the world. Living in Paris at the time, I recommended that he contact Hachette Filipacchi, the French magazine conglomerate. I told him to call David Pecker, the then head of operations for Hachette in the States. The Kennedys are revered in France, largely because of Jackie, and I thought it would be the right fit."

John telephoned David Pecker in New York and made an appointment to see him. "I'd met John on several previous occasions via charitable organizations and fund-raisers," said Pecker. "We got together over lunch, and he and Berman presented their concept. I immediately saw its potential and recognized John's passionate commitment to the project. It was solely my decision to go forward. In fact, when the magazine began to stumble, the Hachette ownership actually asked me if John was essential to the magazine and if we could continue without him. I told them I didn't think we could."

Largely because of John's involvement, the magazine's initial hype was thunderous. To prepare for the media blitz, John hired Michael Sheehan and Paul Begala, both of whom had helped organize Bill Clinton's publicity campaign during his first run for the presidency. Before the publication of *George*'s 280-page premiere issue, Michael Berman sold enough advertising space to fill eight issues—the first five were bimonthlies; thereafter the magazine emerged on a monthly basis. Carolyn Bessette carried around a dummy of the first issue and showed it to everyone she knew; John's sister did the same. Ted Kennedy spread the word among members of Congress. John cut back his personal commitments, rose early, worked out in the gym for an hour in the morning, then biked uptown to the magazine's new offices at 1633 Broadway, carrying his bicycle with him in the elevator. For the first two months he put in twelve-hour days, seven days a week. His business card had neither an *F.* nor a *Jr.* on it. He and Berman traveled across the country, meeting with corporate heads in an effort to sell additional advertising space. In the first of what would soon become a huge promotional package for the magazine, John appeared as himself in a one-and-a-half minute scene in the eighth-season premiere of Candice Bergen's CBS sitcom, *Murphy*

Brown, which shot in the summer and aired in September 1995. In the scene, John gave Murphy a birthday present—a gratis subscription to *George.* Commenting on John's appearance on her show, Bergen told *TV Guide,* "I haven't heard so many women screaming since the Beatles." Under the watchful eye of Carolyn Bessette, John became a clotheshorse in his own right, matching her wardrobe by purchasing a line of executive business suits at $3,000 apiece—he kept three of them in his office. When David Pecker appeared in his office one morning and informed him that Hachette was thinking of changing the name of the magazine to *Criss-Cross,* John took out a paper bag and pretended to retch. Richard Wiese advised him to call it *John Kennedy Loving*—like *Martha Stewart Living*—and fill it with compromising photographs of himself.

Much of JFK Jr.'s and Michael Berman's time was spent interviewing and hiring future staff members, all of whom were asked to sign confidentiality statements agreeing not to talk to the press about the magazine or about John. Eric Etheridge, formerly at *Harper's, Rolling Stone,* and *The New York Observer,* became executive editor—he was later fired, presumably for signing John's name (without his permission) on hundreds of mailings that went out to practically every congressional press secretary in Washington. Matt Berman—no relation to Michael—became the magazine's creative director, though he boasted he'd never in his life finished reading a book. Elinore Carmody, a feisty, fast-talking blonde with experience in advertising and magazine sales, assisted Michael Berman in running the business end of *George.* Elizabeth "Biz" Mitchell, a chain-smoking Brown graduate formerly employed at *Spin,* was hired as managing editor; she subsequently succeeded Eric Etheridge as executive editor, failed to prove herself, and soon followed in Etheridge's footsteps. Thirty-year-old Richard Blow (who has legally changed his surname to Bradley as of 2004), former editor of *Regardie's,* a Washington-based business magazine, began as a senior editor and eventually took over for Biz Mitchell as executive editor. Gary Ginsberg, a lawyer who had gone to Brown with John, came on board as a senior editor and served as the magazine's acting attorney.

There were numerous others, most of them under thirty, few of them with experience in either magazine publishing or politics. The most visible and audible of the lot was RoseMarie (Rose) Terenzio, John's personal assistant, who, according to Richard Blow, cared little about journalism but was evidently fascinated by celebrity. A poor typist, she was loyal, savvy, and given to outbursts of profanity. John appreciated her because she guarded him with the ferocity of a Doberman, slamming down the telephone receiver on anyone she considered objectionable. She also "aggressively" pursued a friendship with Carolyn Bessette, "wearing her designer castoffs to the office" and dying her hair blond. Ultimately, as one staff member put it, "Rose was one of John's biggest hiring mistakes."

If Carolyn Bessette gave her used clothes to select female staffers, JFK Jr. performed a similar service for the men, handing them expensive ties, sweaters, and dress shirts that came in on a regular basis from various fashion designers eager to court John. At Christmas, John and Carolyn gave each staff member a personal present, ranging from engraved cuff links to silk scarves, which Carolyn would pick up at stores like Hermès and Henri Bendel. John frequently let his staffers use his season tickets to Yankees and New York Knicks ball games. At other times he took the staff on weekend excursions into the country. On one such trip—to an inn in the Catskills—he told Richard Blow that he and Carolyn were thinking of buying a house in the Hudson River Valley. John could take a boat to work every day—that, at least, was the fantasy. Tom Karon, an early *George* copy editor, reported that while things at *George* tended to be chaotic, John had a way of defraying tension. "Hey," he'd say, "let's all go out and play touch football in the park tonight." "That was the spirit of the place," noted Karon. "John had a sense that people should have fun while they worked."

John had requested an interview with former Alabama governor George Wallace to appear in the first issue of *George*. Wallace agreed. Accompanied by Gary Ginsberg, JFK Jr. flew to Montgomery, Alabama. They checked into a local hotel and the next afternoon began the first of three consecutive days of interviews with Wallace. Hard of hearing and no longer healthy, the former governor made a poor interview subject. John and Gary ended each day with a game of tennis on the hotel court. After one particularly arduous volley, John paused, reached into a pocket, and produced a small jewelry box. Inside the box was an emerald-and-diamond engagement ring.

"When we get back to New York, I'm going to ask Carolyn to marry me," said John, "but you can't tell anyone."

Gary Ginsberg, this time in company with Richard Blow, returned to Montgomery to interview Governor Wallace yet again in an effort to improve on the original Q & A. John, meanwhile, popped the question and to his utter dismay was partially rebuffed.

"Can I think about it?" asked Carolyn.

Dana Strayton, a Boston University pal of Bessette, contended that while "Carolyn was excited by John's proposal, she wanted to make sure it was the right decision."

Dejected by Carolyn's seeming reluctance, John flew to the West Coast with Michael Berman to conduct an interview with Oliver Stone, ostensibly for the second issue of *George. Nixon,* Stone's latest film, would soon be released. Eric Etheridge had encouraged John to interview Stone. They met for dinner at Rockenwanger, a restaurant in Santa Monica. In the course of the meal, Stone began interrogating John, asking him question after question about the assassination of his father, a subject that had long consumed the Hollywood filmmaker. More than once Berman attempted to intervene. Stone responded by probing even deeper, eventually asking John his opinion of the grassy knoll and the second-gunman theory. John excused himself and left the table. The Stone interview was canceled and replaced by an interview with Warren Beatty. Returning to New York, John apologized to Etheridge for failing to follow through with Oliver Stone. "I just couldn't sit across a table from that man for two hours," said John. "I just couldn't."

One week prior to the September 7, 1995, unveiling of *George,* Carolyn Bessette accepted John's marriage proposal. She had kept him waiting nearly three weeks. Attending the opening press conference in the rotunda of Manhattan's Federal Hall (where George Washington delivered the first inaugural address), she heard her fiancé tell a gathering of more than 160 reporters and press photographers that he hadn't seen so many journalists in one place at one time since the announcement of the results of his first bar exams. "*George,*" he announced, "doesn't just cover politics, it celebrates it." Asked why they'd put Cindy Crawford (dressed as George Washington but with her bare midriff showing) on the cover of the first issue, JFK Jr. quipped, "We thought of posing Alan Greenspan in Speedos—fortunately, Cindy Crawford won out." He continued fielding questions from the press, the majority related to his relationship with Carolyn. His answers were terse but funny: "Yes. No. Maybe. We're only good friends. She's actually my cousin from Connecticut." A reporter at the press conference, having once covered President Kennedy in the White House, remarked that John's offhanded sense of humor reminded him of JFK.

The inaugural issue of *George* (October-November 1995) included the interview with George Wallace, a tongue-in-cheek essay by Madonna ("President Madonna"), a feature on the FBI, another on leaks in the Clinton White House, a report on "the New Divas of Politics," an article ("The New American Revolution") by novelist Caleb Carr, and a smattering of miscellaneous columns and stories. *George* had an initial print run of 500,000 copies (subscription and newsstand sales) and went back to press for an additional 100,000 copies.

To celebrate the magazine's launch, John threw a small party for friends and family at Asia de Cuba. The same restaurant served as the site for a large first-anniversary bash a year later, featuring a star-studded guest list that included such diverse names as Lee Radziwill, Ian Schrager, Donald Trump, Larry Flynt, Conan O'Brien, and Al Sharpton. Dressed in a long black Yohji Yamamoto dress and ebony polished-calf Manolo Blahniks, Carolyn stood with John at the party's entrance for nearly two hours meeting and greeting the invitees. She had a word for everyone— even seventies rocker Ted Nugent, an avid hunter, who walked in wearing a Ducks Unlimited cap. "Don't be too hard on those ducks," she teased. A few hours later, watching Carolyn work the room, John went over to her and said, "How're you doing, honey-bunny?" When asked by the press whether she was surprised her brother had gone into magazine publishing, Caroline Kennedy, while at the party, said: "I'm not, but others might be. Everybody recognizes John, but few people know him." The same could have been said for Jacqueline Kennedy.

To further publicize the new venture, JFK Jr. went out on tour, participating in numerous radio, television, and print-media interviews, taking on everyone from Larry King to Howard Stern, who appeared on the cover of *George*'s April-May 1996 issue. While being interviewed by Stern, JFK Jr. admitted that he'd lost his virginity "somewhere in high school" and had indeed been "in love" with Daryl Hannah. A year after the magazine's maiden appearance, he was still making the rounds. In August of 1996 he attended the Republican National Convention in Santa Monica, which Norman Mailer covered for *George*. Journalist Laura Raposa encountered John at a party hosted by the magazine. Raposa went up to him, and he looked at her and said, "What're you doing here?" "I'm just doing what I'm doing," she responded. "He was drunk—he was plowed," said Raposa. *George* also threw a party that month at the Democratic National Convention in Chicago. Held at the Art Institute of Chicago, the event drew more than 1,500 guests, including Hillary and Chelsea Clinton. While still in the Windy City, John agreed to be interviewed by Oprah Winfrey. When she asked him how he wound up being so normal, he said, "I feel this is a segue leading to talking about my mother somehow."

Larry King was also duly impressed by JFK Jr.'s "normalcy" and "unspoiled attitude" and often spoke of his appearance on *Larry King Live,* noting that when they were done with the interview he offered John, Michael Berman, and Carolyn Bessette access to a car service to be driven wherever they wanted to go. "John politely declined," said King. "The three of them simply hiked three blocks from the CNN studio in Washington to Union Station, bought tickets, and took the next train back to New York. No muss, no fuss. John was like that—he was a great guy. He used to walk around New York carrying a backpack. Everyone loved him."

Although *George* showed commercial promise at first, it soon began to run into trouble. There were essentially two schools of thought on the subject. One was the magazine didn't have enough gravitas, the other being that the magazine wasn't light enough. It sat uncomfortably between two seats, satisfying neither serious readers nor those that sought to be entertained. It seemed as if the editorial board couldn't make up its mind what sort of magazine to publish. There were die-hard politicos who thought the magazine was rubbish. Tabloid readers found it dull. The admixture of politics and entertainment was something new in the world of magazine publishing, but the world wasn't ready for it.

"Politics are a hard sell, and the magazine industry is a tough, unforgiving business," said Michael Berman. By early 1997 Berman and JFK Jr. found themselves at loggerheads, locked in a power struggle that on at least one occasion led to violence when John grabbed Berman and ripped his shirt. Several days later John sent his publishing partner an expensive new shirt and a note of apology. Mostly their altercations resulted in loud screaming, slammed doors, and angry threats. They were still friends, which made the situation even worse. Both were strong-willed and inflexible. Eighteen months after helping John get *George* off the ground, Berman bowed out. Hachette asked him to stay on as head of its film and television department. John never replaced Berman, opting instead to take over the business end of the publication, adding it to his existing responsibility as editor in chief. Although the magazine had begun to flounder commercially while Berman was still there (contributing to their adversarial relationship), it declined with ever increasing speed after Berman's departure.

"*George* went into decline," claimed David Pecker, "because John refused to take risks as an editor, despite the fact that he was an extraordinary risk taker in other areas of his life. He understood that the target audience for *George* was the eighteen-to-thirty-four-year-old demographic, yet he would routinely turn down interviews that would appeal to this age group, like Princess Diana or John Gotti Jr., to interview subjects like Dan Rostenkowski or Vo Nguyen Giap, an obscure North Vietnamese general. The monthly interview constituted a mainstay of the magazine and could've been a real boon, just as it is in *Playboy.* It was a sad commentary on the editorial content when a research study we conducted showed that the most read feature was John's 'editor's letter' at the beginning of each issue, while the rest of the magazine's content did poorly. In his favor, I have to say that John was one of the finest extemporaneous speakers I've ever heard—he never wrote out his speeches beforehand. I also enjoyed watching the effect he had on others—he had an aura about him unlike anyone else. When we established the *George* offices on the forty-first floor of our building, all the women on the other floors would look for excuses to use the copy equipment on John's floor. This went on all the time. Although John never directly said so, I felt he was using *George* to an extent to launch his political career. Had he lived I feel he would have run for senator or governor and then gone for the presidency at some point."

John's problems with David Pecker were similar to those he encountered with Michael Berman. Simply put, he had difficulty dealing with assertive men in positions of power. This may in part have been the result of growing up without a real father figure in his life. Whatever the case, he tended to ignore Pecker's editorial recommendations. Considering that he had access to almost anybody, for example, JFK Jr.'s selection of interview subjects was indeed questionable. Names like Gary Hart, Cokie Roberts, Billy Graham, Dan Quayle, and New Jersey governor Christine Whitman held little interest for a younger reading audience. And the more intriguing personages, such as Fidel Castro and the Dalai Lama, tended to say little of interest to anyone. John spent four days in Havana waiting to meet Castro for dinner, and what might have been a cutting-edge interrogation fell far short of the mark. Castro provided John with little more than platitudes, self-serving blandishments, and a scattering of banal observations about nothing in particular.

"*George* turned out to be a wasted opportunity, an interesting failure," said Oleg Cassini. "It wasn't hard-hitting enough. It was flaccid and unfocused. It covered nothing and everything. John had a point of view, but his magazine didn't. It lacked a guiding philosophy. It was a hodge-podge, a stew—half fish, half fowl. Even the lighthearted material fell flat. For instance, I recall a cover shot [September 1996] of actress Drew Barrymore dressed as Marilyn Monroe with a caption that read, '*Happy Birthday, Mr. President!*' This very obvious reference to the night MM serenaded JFK at Madison Square Garden might have been interesting had it alluded to the liaison between Marilyn and his father. Without it, the reader is left to wonder what it all meant. Nor did John have anything to say about the White House scandal involving Bill Clinton and Monica Lewinsky. I heard James Rubin, Christiane Amanpour's husband, warned him that if he commented on the subject, his critics would retaliate by bringing up President Kennedy's White House indiscretions. As a result, he wrote nothing."

In fact, the Drew Barrymore/Marilyn Monroe cover succeeded only in angering Caroline Kennedy. Despite her original enthusiasm for the magazine, she became increasingly unhappy with the results and while content to let the matter rest, she felt personally offended by the "Happy birthday, Mr. President" reference. Appearing in the *George* offices one day, she reportedly berated her brother for his bad taste. John defended himself. "If I don't find it crass," he told her, "I don't know why anyone else should." Although John told friends that he considered the Clinton-Lewinsky affair "nobody's business but the president's," he refused to tackle the issue head-on in print. Instead, the March 1998 issue of *George* ran a profile of Clinton pal Vernon Jordan—"Sex in High Places"— accusing Jordan of having "talked sex" with Lewinsky over dinner in a local Washington restaurant. Written by serial fabricator Stephen Glass, the article turned out to be full of half-truths and outright lies. Assuming full responsibility for the erroneous piece, JFK Jr. wrote an apology to Jordan, who embarrassed John further by leaking the contents of the letter to *The Washington Post. George*'s editor in chief considered it a betrayal since his correspondence had been personal and private.

Aside from John's monthly "editor's letter" (which appeared at the beginning of each issue), the most invigorating aspect of *George* might well have been its cover art, usually a photograph of an instantly recognizable celebrity. Besides Drew Barrymore, the VIP list included such names as Robert De Niro, Christie Brinkley, Demi Moore, and Barbra Streisand. Streisand refused to pose unless John agreed to accompany the magazine's photographers to her house in Malibu. In anticipation of his arrival, she instructed her gardener to plant several rows of roses and tulips. She purchased a new wardrobe and made herself up to the hilt. She fawned over John as if he were visiting royalty. For his part, John could not have been less impressed or more bored. In the middle of the shoot, he excused himself, donned a bathing suit, and went swimming in the Pacific.

Evidently Carolyn Bessette likewise had her say as far as the magazine's covers were concerned. In *American Son,* Richard Blow's account of the essential *George* experience, the author details Carolyn's frequently "distracting" presence in the magazine offices. Carolyn, he writes, "remained a behind-the-scenes influence; John passed along [her] advice on [which] photographers and models to use." Carolyn once nixed a cover with model Gabrielle Reece because, she told Matt Berman, Reece was passé.

Beyond his inability to formulate a sound editorial policy at *George,* John retained on staff a number of editors and writers simply because they amused him. His loyalty to friends often took precedence over his business judgment. Toward the end of his life, he had begun to make adjustments in this area, but at its height the magazine was jammed with extraneous employees, adding to the periodical's rapidly escalating operational costs while ad revenues continued to plummet. Whenever David Pecker raised the issue, he elicited little more than a blank stare from John. Overemployment remained a stumbling block into early 1999, when Pecker left Hachette to assume ownership of the *National Enquirer* and *Star.*

"Despite the problems," said Pecker, "John and I parted on good terms. After I left Hachette, he sent me a very, very nice note wishing me luck. His letter contained an amusing aside about looking forward to reading about himself in my new publications in the near future. I thought that was really sweet considering he'd been tabloid fodder for so many years."

"*George* was a silly magazine," said JFK Jr.'s pal John Hare. "Who cares what Madonna thinks of our missile defense system? What mattered is that for John the entire venture constituted a learning experience. It humbled him. Here he was, at the end of his rope, going around the country on his hands and knees begging people for money to salvage the magazine. And people are actually saying no to him. This is a guy who grew up with everything handed to him on a silver platter. In the context of a longer life, John's experience at the magazine would have provided an enormously valuable lesson. For once, he was like everyone else in the world. He'd always been humble by choice rather than necessity. Had he lived, the failure of *George* would have proved invaluable to his inner development. And on the other hand, he deserves credit for having taken a huge risk in starting his own magazine. He could have easily waltzed into an editorial position at some high-priority magazine that already existed. If he failed in his endeavor, he most certainly failed on his own terms."

From the beginning, John's relationship with Carolyn Bessette had its problematic moments, some marked by altercations and the need to spend a day or two apart. On those occasions, Carolyn remained behind at 20 North Moore Street while JFK Jr. spent the night at the New York Athletic Club on Central Park South, where he maintained a membership. After *George* opened a business account at the Stanhope Hotel on Fifth Avenue, John would stay there. Fortunately, such blowups were rare, and when they did occur, they were always quickly resolved. On the whole, their union was no less complex than that of any young and successful couple. The main obstacle, as far as Carolyn could tell, was the nonstop scrutiny of the press, the tendency on the part of mass-market media to confabulate stories purely to sell newspapers or television and radio airtime.

Santina Goodman, JFK Jr.'s theater buddy from Brown, recognized the symptoms of strain endured by Carolyn in attempting to adjust to the onslaught of publicity and, at the same time, fitting in with John's social circle. "His friends seem *so* normal," Carolyn commented, comparing them to her more artistic fashion-industry friends and acquaintances. A member of John's set, Santina took the pronouncement more as a challenge than an insult. She and Carolyn developed a jocular rapport, enabling them to bridge the gap. Santina told Carolyn that if she "didn't behave," she would have to introduce John to an African-American princess who would look after him. "I also told her," said Santina, "that when she and John had their first baby, I would be the black governess. We used to jibe back and forth like that. Carolyn loved the give and take. So did John. I began to understand how and why they got along." The degree of closeness achieved by Santina Goodman with JFK Jr. and his future wife can be measured by Caroline Kennedy's asking her to speak at John's memorial service, following the couple's death. And it was Santina who later inherited Ruby, Carolyn's five-year-old cat.

SoHo artist Terry Fugate-Wilcox and his live-in companion, art

dealer Valerie Monroe Shakespeare, became acquainted with John as a result of their friendship with his cousin Michael Kennedy. "We knew
John before he became involved with Carolyn," said Terry. "Later we got
to know them as a couple. John and Carolyn came to one of our Halloween parties disguised as George and Martha Washington in honor of
their magazine. They'd dressed John's dog in orange—he came with
them—and they called him 'Pumpkin' all night. John seemed a bit shy at
first. He was polite and gracious. I asked him, 'How is it the Kennedys all
look alike?' 'Same hairdresser, same dentist,' he answered. Carolyn kept
saying, 'It's not true about George [Washington] and Betsy Ross—they're
just good friends.' Neither John nor Carolyn said anything of a highly
personal nature. They laughed and joked a lot, but they also erected a
kind of wall beyond which you knew not to tread. They usually let down
their hair only in the presence of trusted friends. Once we grew closer,
they began to relax. We saw them at other people's parties as well as our
own. We had a mutual friend, Terry Ward, who lived at the National Arts
Club and knew a number of the Kennedys. He had a brother, Kevin
Ward, who was also a Kennedy family friend. Terry got us invited to
some of their homes. We attended a party at the Mount Kisco home of
Bobby Kennedy Jr. When we arrived at the front door in our old jalopy,
the security guards were convinced we were part of the family. The
Kennedys are notorious for their collection of junky automobiles."

According to Valerie, John took two subjects very seriously: politics
and *George*. "Politics are too important to be left up to the politicians,"
he once said. "John thought he could change the world," observed Valerie. "But unlike Bobby Kennedy Jr., who would take on anyone for any
reason at any time, John didn't shove his ideas down your throat. To draw
him out you had to demonstrate interest in what he had to say. He wasn't
perpetually trying to sell you a bill of goods."

Although he never purchased artwork from Valerie's SoHo gallery,
John always saw to it that Carolyn sent a thank-you note following their
appearance at any of the couple's parties. Caroline Kennedy had steered
her brother to Dempsey & Carroll, a stationery store at the corner of
Madison and 80th Street. Place cards and thank-you notes were a courtesy Caroline and John had both inherited from their mother.

Terry Fugate-Wilcox recalled still another get-together. John brought Tom Hanks, and Hanks kept insisting he was somebody else. "Oh, everyone thinks I look like the actor," he said. Terry also recounted the night at his house when Eric Douglas, the youngest son of Kirk Douglas, walked over to John and impishly said, "Do you know where you are tonight and how lucky you are to be here?" John handled Douglas in a gentlemanly fashion, smiling at him and walking off. Then there was the gathering at which John, Michael Kennedy, and their friend Larry Spagnola got drunk and held a "pissing contest" on Terry and Valerie's fire escape. "They'd had a lot of beer," said Terry. "It was really late, and the party was breaking up."

Terry and Valerie lived not far from John's TriBeCa loft. One evening they spotted John and Carolyn pull up in their car in front of 20 North Moore Street. A dozen or so photographers, obviously waiting for them, popped out of the shadows, surrounded the car, and started snapping away with their cameras. John just posed for them. He had this "just-get-it-over-with-and-leave-us-alone" attitude. Carolyn, on the other hand, squirmed and cringed in her seat. Her discomfort only energized the paparazzi. "They went crazy," said Terry. "They were bobbing and weaving and circling the car. You had to feel sorry for the girl."

Assessing the relationship between JFK Jr. and Carolyn, Valerie concluded that Carolyn "seemed ecstatic about John—she was always very happy, and he was the way he'd always been. He didn't gush over her—no baby talk—and he wasn't particularly demonstrative. She was the more expressive of the two. But it wasn't difficult to tell that he was deeply in love. You could see it in his eyes."

In *American Son,* Richard Blow presents an altogether different picture. Whenever Carolyn visited the magazine offices, John stopped working and attended to his future wife, touching her, running his fingers through her hair, stroking her arms. Carolyn, as Blow portrays her, accepted John's attentions but rarely reciprocated. "John was the more openly affectionate one," writes Blow. To this he adds that whenever she was there, you never wanted her to leave—"she was a more vivid creature than any of the other models in *George's* advertisements."

The conflicting accounts of Carolyn and John's public displays of affection may in part be owing to the varying degrees of comfort each felt among different friends and acquaintances. Another *George* staff member recalled returning to the forty-first floor one evening to retrieve a book he'd left behind, only to find John and Carolyn "making out" in his office, the door wide open. "John's office," said the employee, "reflected his field of interests. Near his desk, he had a large painting of George Washington by an unknown artist. Mounted against another wall were miniature portraits of the presidents and a silk screen of his father. A photo of Carolyn and Friday that he had taken himself decorated another wall. On a small corner table he had a military flight helmet that had belonged to Joe Kennedy Jr., the uncle who'd died during World War II. His desk was usually littered with flight training manuals and lists of story ideas for future issues of the magazine."

Privately, Carolyn left little doubt as to her feelings about John. Returning to New York from a business trip with JFK Jr. and several *George* editors, she told Richard Blow: "Sometimes I look at John when he's sleeping, and he's so beautiful, I can't believe he's really human."

At a Valentine's Day benefit for the Naked Angels Theater Company, a group long supported by John, he and Carolyn gave a somewhat more public display of their mutual attraction. As reported in the *Times-Union,* a newspaper published in Albany, New York, the two were inseparable: "They drank. They danced. They smooched. By the end of the night, they had snuck off to the darkened bar, where Carolyn Bessette coquettishly climbed into her suitor's lap." They repeated their performance at a benefit hosted by George Plimpton at the Russian Consulate in Manhattan for *The Paris Review,* and held hands at a Municipal Art Society function honoring I. M. Pei. Caroline Kennedy attended the Pei ceremony and evidently became annoyed that her brother had brought his girlfriend along.

Richard Johnson, editor of the *New York Post*'s Page Six, first met John in the mid-eighties when both were weekend houseguests of Alfonso Telese, a wealthy Italian businessman who owned "the Castle," a large estate in Garrison, New York. "Additionally, John and I had several mutual friends," said Johnson. "Andre Balasz had gone on a rafting trip with him to Costa Rica. John Mosley played touch football with him in Central Park and at one juncture had been a roommate of Julie Baker's, John's erstwhile girlfriend. My impression of him was that he had charisma up the ying yang and enjoyed being in the spotlight. I felt *George* was only a pit stop for him on his way to political office. What truly amazed me was how women reacted to him, even after the announcement of his engagement to Carolyn Bessette. I remember being at a garden party with him in the West Village, and every woman there had her eye on him. They jumped at the opportunity to talk with him. He acted in a very cool manner, almost blasé, which only added to his appeal."

On February 25, 1996, John and Carolyn became involved in a much-publicized fight having to do precisely with JFK Jr.'s "appeal" to women, particularly those other than Carolyn. As luck would have it, photographers Ken Katz and his associate Angie Coqueran captured much of the sequence on film. "It was a Sunday morning," said Katz, "and John and Carolyn had gone to the Tribeca Grill for brunch. They had Friday with them. When they emerged from the restaurant, you could see and hear Carolyn bitching at John. She went on and on. Among other things, she was saying how cold she felt. So he told her to go home and get another jacket. He waited for her with the dog in front of the restaurant. She must have been gone for a good half hour. When she returned, she was wearing his jacket. He started in on her, wondering what had taken her so long. They hopped in a cab and headed up to Central Park. We followed the cab and caught up with them in the park. Once there, they appeared to have calmed down. They were talking back and forth when Carolyn suddenly ran off, leaving John with the dog. He looked pissed, but he followed her into an open field. They were talking again and then, without warning, she belted him with a closed fist. She hit him somewhere between the chest and shoulder. She tried to sort of jump on him. He went nuts. He totally lost it. I don't think he knew what he was doing. He grabbed her by the throat. He then grabbed her hand and pulled the engagement ring off her finger. He stormed off with the ring, but he turned around, returned to her side, and began yelling again. Carolyn looked dazed. They walked a bit and reached a park bench. They sat down. She was crying, and he was shaking his head back and forth. They sat there in the cold for maybe twenty minutes."

Ken Katz and his associate followed the couple out of the park. "They were talking again," continued Katz. "They crossed the street, and evidently JFK Jr. realized he'd somehow broken the engagement ring. He sat down on the curb and started to cry. She bent over to console him, and she was crying as well. He gave her back the ring. They stood up and walked down the street together, hugging and holding each other. They then hailed a cab and went home."

Ken Katz learned that John often went to newsstands in search of tabloid articles about himself—when he located something, he'd buy the publication. "I heard," said Katz, "he hated the shots we got of him crying. The others—the altercation itself—didn't please him either, but the shots of him crying bothered him the most. On the other hand, he wasn't like his mother or sister. He didn't mind the tabloids or the gossip columns. He basically laughed at them. He didn't take them seriously. If anything, he probably derived some secret pleasure from seeing his name and photo in print."

The Ken Katz shoot consisted of both photographs and a video, portions of which aired on the CBS-TV magazine show *Day & Date* as "Sunday in the Park with John." The altercation, JFK Jr. told friends, stemmed from Carolyn's suspicion that he'd been having an affair with another woman, namely fashion model Claudia Schiffer, one of many with whom he'd been associated in the press. "I don't even know the woman," John protested. The couple made up. In early March 1996, about the time Carolyn left her job at Calvin Klein, the couple traveled to Italy. In Milan, John met several of Carolyn's relatives. They attended fashion shows and went shopping for gifts. Although Carolyn would be forced to sign a prenuptial agreement, John had started an independent checking account in her name, and gave her a set of credit cards and an ATM debit card. They dined with Mariuccia Mandelli, founder of the Italian fashion firm Krizia, whom Carolyn had known from New York. Mandelli found John "absolutely charming." The couple rounded out their stay in Milan by attending a soccer match. From Milan they went to the Lake Como estate of Gianni Versace. "I was a little envious of

Carolyn—who wouldn't be?" said Donatella Versace, Gianni's sister. While there, Carolyn told their hosts, "I'm never going to give up my friends, but at the same time, I will be the best wife for John." Continuing her appraisal, Donatella remarked that John seemed totally entranced by his partner: "He had a completely open mind about Carolyn's fashion friends, who were different from his friends. He adored her personality, her outlook on life." One night they all attended a dinner party at the home of a Versace friend. "You couldn't smoke inside the house," said Donatella, "so Carolyn and I went upstairs and smoked on the balcony, and then we couldn't get back in. The door had locked behind us. John finally came by looking for us and let us in. After they were married, Carolyn occasionally came by my shop on Fifth Avenue. I had never seen her more happy. I made fun of her. 'Carolyn,' I said, 'what do you do all day, sit at home just waiting for the next party? That's not like you.' She said, 'Just you wait and see.'"

John and Carolyn ended their Italian sojourn in Rome, where they dined with Valentino, whose business partner, Giancarlo Giammetti, arranged a dinner party for them. Unaware that they were engaged, Giammetti invited some of Rome's greatest beauties to the dinner. John had eyes only for Carolyn. "He didn't care about the others," said Valentino. "He didn't so much as look at them. He told me he was in love."

When they returned to the States, they gave a *George* party in Washington, D.C. Held at the home of socialite Peggy Cafritz, the sixty-person guest list included George Stephanopoulos, Secretary of Commerce Ron Brown, and Secretary of Health and Human Services Donna Shalala. At one point John and Carolyn slipped away and went for a walk in the moonlight. Richard Blow saw them kiss, and "they didn't return until the party was winding down, and when they did, smiles danced around their faces like waves lapping at the edges of a pool."

Several weeks later JFK Jr. met Rob Littell at the Downtown Athletic Club in Manhattan for a game of racquetball. When they were done, John told his old friend that he and Carolyn were planning to have a small and secret wedding. Above all, they both wanted to avoid a circus. They were looking at out-of-the-way places. "Carolyn's the best shot I've got," said John.

. . .

With John busy running his magazine, it remained for Caroline Kennedy to organize the material contents of Jackie's estate in anticipation of a multisession Sotheby's auction to begin April 23, 1996, the proceeds to be evenly distributed between John and Caroline. Originally appraised to be worth in the neighborhood of $6 million, Jackie's possessions (which included numerous JFK items) ultimately brought in $34.5 million. Little of this staggering sum went to charity. Accused by the press of "cashing in" on her mother's memories, Caroline pointed out that many items from Jackie's estate had gone to the John F. Kennedy Library and Museum, among them 4,500 photographs, 38,000 pages of documents, 200 works of art, and Jacqueline's wedding gown.

Despite these donations—a case of the rich giving to the rich—the public's perception of the event remained decidedly negative, especially when Kennedy family lawyers began quibbling with the IRS over estate taxes accrued as a result of the auction. Possibly the most pernicious example of Caroline Kennedy's money lust involved her stance with regard to private collectors of JFK and Jackie memorabilia, whose valuables were on the block at another Manhattan auction house. When Caroline learned of this development, she and other members of the family instigated legal action against several of the other collectors. In no uncertain terms, she claimed that many of the items in private hands actually belonged to the family and should therefore be returned.

Chief among her targets was Robert L. White, a Maryland businessman who had amassed the single largest collection of Kennedy memorabilia in the world. His assemblage consisted of some 25,000 pieces of correspondence and items of Camelot chattel, among them Kennedy wallets and passports, reading glasses, rocking chairs, and lockets of hair. The collection had expanded because of White's friendship with Evelyn Lincoln, JFK's former personal secretary. Following her death in 1995, he inherited thousands of items that she had gathered during her association with JFK.

"The Kennedys made my life miserable," said Robert White. "I tried to appease them by offering the JFK Library and Museum a number of these items. But that didn't satisfy them. They wanted everything. Ted

Kennedy led the charge, but there's no question that Caroline Schloss-berg was behind it all. Evidently $34.5 million wasn't enough for her. It's like the more money she had, the more she wanted."

After Robert White's death in 2003, his brother William remarked, "The Kennedys were major assholes. After the assassination of President Kennedy, Jackie gave many of these items to Evelyn Lincoln, and she left them to my brother. The items included a portable record player and forty to fifty Irish records that JFK liked to play while traveling. There was a coffee table on which he supposedly screwed Marilyn Monroe. Evelyn took the stuff because it was given to her. Now the Kennedy children started coming after my brother, claiming all the presidential bric-a-brac belonged to the estate. They didn't have a legal leg to stand on, because the material in dispute was clearly the property of my brother. It pissed them off. My brother spent nearly a million dollars in legal fees. He held a sale of his own in New York to help pay his legal fees, and they were all over him, accusing him of this and that. They impugned Evelyn Lincoln's reputation as well, practically accusing her of having stolen the material. They brought the National Archives into the battle. My brother finally died of a heart attack and left the collection to his widow, Jacqueline White. The Kennedys started in on her. They had the means to keep the case going forever."

Relentless in her pursuit of what she considered historically relevant documents and memorabilia, Caroline persisted. In July 2005 a settlement with Robert White's widow was brokered whereby thousands of items were returned to the family, much of it eventually finding its way to the JFK Library. Jacqueline White retained other items—those deemed less valuable—and in December 2005 sold them at an auction of her own.

Over the years, Caroline's demands often seemed petulant and pee-vish. When Yusha Auchincloss decided to auction off various furnishings and objects formerly housed at Hammersmith Farm, Caroline insisted that neither JFK's nor Jackie Kennedy's names be used in conjunction with the sale, though Jackie had grown up at Hammersmith Farm and Jack Kennedy had been a frequent visitor. Yusha complied with Caroline's wishes, causing the Auchinclosses to lose thousands of dollars in the sale.

Mindful of the probability that her brother would one day give up his magazine and embark on a political career, Caroline took it upon herself to do the family's bidding. JFK Jr., meanwhile, continued his work for Reaching Up, a charitable organization he had founded some years earlier, and took time off from *George* to foster philanthropic events and raise money for the needy. Despite the existence of television footage showing him on the verge of throttling his fiancée, his public persona remained largely intact. He rode his bike and took the subway to work. He played touch football with old friends in Central Park. He spent time with his nephew and nieces. He had become the heir apparent to the Kennedy empire, a sure bet to run for political office and eventually the presidency. He was Prince Charming, the Hunk, and an American Son all rolled into one.

On May 17, 1996, John took the subway and ferry to the Hungerford School, an institution for children with special needs in the Clifton section of Staten Island, where he served as "Principal for the Day," placing a ring on the finger of each of the graduating members of the senior class. Dr. Mary McInerney, full-time principal of the school, remembered John staying far beyond the one hour he'd originally allotted for the visit. Not wanting to publicize the occasion, his sole demand was that the media not be informed of his presence. "He was extremely warm and modest," said McInerney, "and let me tell you—that boy sure could hang a jacket. I'm a shoulder kind of gal myself, and he certainly had a pair."

"JFK Jr.'s beauty was internal as well as external," said Lowery McClendon, an adjunct lecturer in composition and English literature at CUNY. "In the mid-nineties I worked as a waiter at E.A.T., and John came in on a regular basis. Everyone there liked him. He seemed like a nice, good, kind human being, full of compassion. I don't want to overly romanticize the guy, but he had a certain grace, just the way he always carried himself. He realized that he commanded attention. I remember once there were some teenaged girls from France in the restaurant, and one of them moved in on him and started taking pictures of him with her camera. He didn't acknowledge her presence or acknowledge her taking his picture, and there was something very graceful in the way he handled it, not really complying but also not complaining. Another time a waiter named Lee, an older fellow, took his order. Lee didn't recognize him. He brought several dishes at the same time, including a platter of pancakes. The pancakes sat there for about fifteen minutes, while John chomped away at something else. When he finally got around to them, he called Lee over and said, 'You know, my pancakes are cold.' And Lee growled: 'Yeah, that's because they've been sitting on your table!' John just looked at Lee, shrugged his shoulders, and said, 'All right.' And he took the pancakes and ate them. He could have bitched about it and demanded to have them heated up or remade, but he didn't. That's pretty remarkable behavior considering his father was John F. Kennedy. Most of the celebrities that come in are spoiled silly."

McClendon recalled times when John came in with his sister: "Caroline Kennedy was always the one who directed the conversation, and he would sit and listen. She seemed to be a quietly strong person whom he greatly respected. It has been said before, but they appeared to be very close, closer than most siblings."

And then there was Carolyn Bessette, who came in with John one morning several months before they were married. "She wasn't wearing makeup," remarked McClendon. "From what I could see, she was in a foul mood. My first impression was, 'I know who's sailing this boat.' John appeared to be the type of man easily drawn to a very strong, dominating woman, somebody who would take charge in the relationship. Carolyn looked bitchy—very, very bitchy. It brought to mind John Lennon and Yoko Ono. JFK Jr. felt abandoned by his mother's death, and he needed to replace her. That's why it worked."

---◆---

Chapter 20

WEDDING OF THE DECADE

On July 4, 1996, while celebrating Independence Day at Hyannis Port with Carolyn Bessette and assorted members of the Kennedy clan, JFK Jr. received bad news. Billy Way, his thirty-five-year-old friend from Andover and Brown, had been struck and killed by a cab the night before as he crossed Madison Avenue after dining at Nello, in the East 60s. In addition to Billy's death, John was faced with the realization that Anthony Radziwill, his favorite cousin, though presently in remission, was suffering from a potentially fatal form of cancer. The two in tandem—Billy's death and Anthony's illness—had come at a crucial point in John's life: He had launched a new magazine and was about to get married and slowly start a family of his own. He was also halfway through a difficult program at Vero Beach in flight instruction, learning to pilot his own plane. In conversation with photographer Jacques Lowe, he confessed to once again having second thoughts about the flight lessons.

"How does Carolyn feel about it?" asked Lowe.

"She's not afraid of anything," responded John. "She doesn't like flying commercially any more than I do. Whenever we go anywhere, the press is always there to greet us."

"Well, then, you've answered your own question," said Lowe.

Besides Billy Way (and David Kennedy, who'd overdosed some years earlier), John had experienced the loss of another contemporary. Mike Motta, CEO and president of Plus One gyms, recalled that in 1991 JFK Jr.'s personal trainer at Plus One, Chris Meaee, had died in a motorcycle accident. "Chris and I cofounded Plus One," said Motta. "John had been training with him since 1983. When we opened the Crosby Street studio in SoHo in 1986, John began training with him there. He also trained with Radu and worked out at La Palestra, Pat Manocchia's gym. But Chris was his main man, and over the years they developed a tight friendship. After Chris's death, John spent more time at our gym in the Waldorf-Astoria. I suppose he became more aware of his own mortality. He didn't say much, but you could tell he was upset about it."

By March 1996 John had convinced Carolyn Bessette—a confirmed nonexercise buff—to join Plus One and embark on her own training program. She occasionally joined JFK Jr. at the Crosby Street and Waldorf locations, but usually she went by herself to Plus One's installation at the World Financial Center. In mid-June, having shed ten pounds, Carolyn contacted fashion designer Narciso Rodriguez, whom she'd befriended at Calvin Klein, and asked him to meet her for drinks at Odeon, where they discussed her plans to marry John and her need for a wedding dress. At the time a designer with the fashion house of Nino Cerruti in Paris, Rodriguez expressed an interest in taking on the assignment. Over the next three months, Carolyn made two trips to Paris for couture fittings. Said to be worth $40,000, the fluid bias-cut, floor-length wedding gown designed by Rodriguez was made of pearl-colored silk crepe and came with a short train, long white gloves, and a veil of silk tulle. Rodriguez agreed not to charge Carolyn for his work, a wise concession considering his as yet unrealized reputation. She asked her friend Gordon Henderson to design John's wedding outfit. Henderson produced a traditional blue wool business suit, augmented by a white pique vest and pale blue tie. John added to the ensemble by donning one of his father's shirts, his father's watch, and a pair of cuff links he'd received from his mother on his thirtieth birthday.

According to insiders, Calvin Klein became enraged at Carolyn for having bypassed him in choosing Rodriguez to design her wedding dress.

He felt the same way regarding her choice of Henderson to design John's suit. "She's the most ungrateful person I've ever known," Klein told an associate. He never spoke to Carolyn again. As for Narciso Rodriguez, he credited Carolyn with having helped him establish his reputation as a leading fashion designer. When she died in 1999, he reportedly had her initials—*CBK*—tattooed to the inside of his biceps.

In arranging their wedding, John and Carolyn set in motion a covert operation of monumental proportions, demanding signed statements of confidentiality from everyone connected to the event, starting with waiters hired for the meals and ending with ferrymen needed to transport the forty select guests to remote Cumberland Island, forty-five minutes by boat off the southeast coast of Georgia. The unspoiled eighteen-mile-long island—which John and Carolyn had visited on two previous occasions—had no bridge access, no telephone lines, no paved roads, and no accommodations other than a handful of scattered campsites and two dozen small rooms at the Greyfield Inn, a nineteenth-century Carnegie family residence, where the wedding guests would be housed and the reception held. Invitations to what the press later billed as the "Wedding of the Decade" went out only days before the ceremony, scheduled for Saturday, September 21, 1996. The invitations didn't disclose the location of the wedding, only that the guests would be flown in a chartered plane to a final destination.

The fifty-member team hired by John and Carolyn to facilitate and manage the island affair cost in excess of $250,000. Their efforts commenced long before "D-day," as John labeled the event. A private security squad coordinated efforts with state troopers, the police, and the National Park Service. Beaches and marinas within a fifteen-mile radius of Cumberland Island were contacted, and all boats and visitors bound for the island were turned away. John and Carolyn hired Ted Kennedy's brother-in-law, Denis Reggie, of Atlanta, to be their wedding photographer—the well-connected Georgian had photographed a number of Kennedy weddings, including Caroline and Ed Schlossberg's. They asked Mary Jo Ferguson, operator of the Greyfield Inn, to arrange for caterers and a band. They commissioned Janet Ferguson, an artist and Mary Jo's sister-in-law, to design the wedding bands. Bunny Mellon selected the flowers for the occasion. Carolyn Bessette's guiding strategy throughout the planning stages was to minimize public exposure by handing out assignments only to those they felt they could trust.

On his sister's recommendation, John had cleared the way for the Georgia marriage by requesting a special letter from Father John A. Boehning, of St. Thomas More Church in New York, stating that there was no objection to his wedding ceremony being held outside his home diocese.

A week before the ceremony, Carolyn signed a prenuptial agreement stipulating that in the event of a divorce within the first three years of her marriage to John, she would receive a settlement of $3 million. Additional contingencies called for other financial arrangements on a sliding-scale basis. Had JFK Jr. predeceased his wife, for example, she would have received a $5 million settlement.

Five days prior to the wedding, the prospective bride flew to Georgia to fill out preliminary wedding documents. By coincidence, she found herself seated on the plane next to Shirley Wise, chief clerk of the Camden County Probate Court, which had jurisdiction over Cumberland Island, owned at the time by the federal government and operated by the National Park Service. Not recognizing Carolyn, Wise began a conversation, learned that her fellow passenger was flying down to fill out marriage papers, and innocently asked what her surname was going to be. When Carolyn told her she wanted to be called "Bessette-Kennedy," Wise's mouth fell open. "What's wrong?" Carolyn asked. Wise replied with an astonished smile: "Well, now I know who's getting married."

Carolyn begged Wise not to discuss the wedding for fear that the clandestine nuptials would be found out by the media. "That's why we're doing it on Cumberland Island," she added. "We want it to be small and intimate—just a few friends and family members."

On Wednesday, September 18, Carolyn saw her hairstylist, Brad Johns ("Mr. Johns"), at his Fifth Avenue salon. Carolyn had been his customer since her first days in New York. He'd given her the "buttery chunks of blond" look that soon caught the attention of the fashion world and later became a vogue. "Natural is not the point," said Johns, "fabulous is the point. Hair color is a beautiful accessory."

On Thursday evening, Carolyn returned to Georgia and was met at the St. Marys, Georgia, airstrip by Shirley Wise and Alice Hughes, a lab assistant in charge of administering blood tests for Camden County marriage licenses. To avoid publicity, Probate Judge Martin Gillette authorized the two women to meet privately with the couple. An hour after Carolyn's arrival, John Jr. landed in a separate plane with his sister and her three children. Wearing a baseball cap, jeans, and a T-shirt, John appeared excited about the wedding. "I can't believe you ladies would come all the way out here for us," he said. The blood tests and marriage license were completed aboard Carolyn's plane.

At the following night's rehearsal dinner, all the toasts—according to Rob Littell—were "boisterous and light," with the exception of Ann Freeman's toast. Carolyn's mother expressed reservations over the union, implying it might not be "in the best interest" of her daughter. Carolyn, after all, had always been a private individual; marrying a public figure would be tantamount to being thrust under a microscope—every aspect of her personal life would be explored and exploited by the media. And who knew what else might come of it? John was visibly shaken by his mother-in-law's remarks. Rude as they were, Ann Freeman's concerns would come back to haunt her, and in ways she could never have imagined.

Later in the evening there was a big bonfire at the beach, an open bar in the gazebo, and dancing until dawn. On Saturday morning the men played Frisbee and touch football in the surf. In the afternoon John invited several of his pals to his suite—the only one at the inn—and presented each with a wedding party gift: a pair of navy blue boxer shorts with his initials ("JFK") embroidered on the right leg and theirs on the left. Handing them out, John quipped, "Wear them well, my friends. Think of me when you wear them."

At 6:00 p.m. a fleet of four-wheel-drive vehicles carried the wedding guests over rutted paths, through the woods, to the northern end of the island where, in a clearing, stood the First African Baptist Church, a white clapboard chapel built by former slaves in 1893. Illuminated by candles and kerosene lamps (installed by Efigenio Pinheiro), the ceremony had a quaint, old-fashioned quality to it. Carrying a bouquet of lilies of the valley, her hair pulled back and held in place by a comb that had belonged to Jackie—a gift from Caroline—the bride looked (said John Perry Barlow) "like some beautiful ghost as she entered the church." Anthony Radziwill served as best man. Caroline Kennedy was matron of honor. Her daughters, Rose and Tatiana, were the flower girls. Three-year-old Jack Schlossberg, Caroline's son, was the ring bearer. Other guests included Ed Schlossberg; Lee Radziwill; Ted and Victoria Kennedy; Bobby Kennedy Jr.; William Kennedy Smith; Dr. Richard Freeman; Sasha Chermayeff; Billy Noonan; Christiane Amanpour; Maurice Tempelsman; and Lisa Bessette and her husband, Michael Roman. Lauren Bessette, working for Morgan Stanley Dean Witter in Hong Kong, didn't attend.

Forced to use a flashlight to read the service, Reverend Charles J. O'Byrne, a Jesuit deacon from St. Ignatius Loyola in Manhattan, conducted the ceremony, the candles in the church casting long, flickering shadows against the walls. Gospel singer David Davis sang "Amazing Grace" and "Will the Circle Be Unbroken." As the newlyweds left the church, John paused to kiss Carolyn's hand, a gesture of respect that would have done Cinderella proud. To marry John F. Kennedy Jr. must have been the fantasy of every other young woman in the country. Rosie O'Donnell made currency of the moment with this joke: "When John F. Kennedy and his girlfriend got married, it was an uneventful ceremony. Except when the preacher asked if anyone objected to the union. Half the women in America yelled out, 'I do!'"

It was Patrick Kennedy, campaigning in Cleveland for Dennis Kucinich, who became the first Kennedy to officially confirm the news of the marriage. Standing before a bank of television cameras on the day of the wedding, he conceded that his cousin and Carolyn Bessette were about to tie the knot. The only detail he omitted was the location of the ceremony, sparing the newlyweds a last-minute invasion by the media.

As a light rain fell on Cumberland Island, the wedding party congregated on the enclosed porch of the Greyfield Inn for a Saturday night reception and dinner. As waiters finally rolled out a three-tiered vanilla butter-cream wedding cake, Ted Kennedy raised his champagne glass, read a poem, and remarked: "Jack and Jackie would have been very proud of you and full of love as you begin your future together." Caroline Kennedy gave a tearful toast, followed by John Jr.'s heartfelt send-off:

"I am the happiest man alive." After Carolyn removed her crystal-beaded satin sandals, she and the groom danced to the strains of Prince's "Forever in My Life."

George Plimpton, unable to attend the wedding because he was out of the country, spoke to John soon afterward. "I finally did it!" John told him. "It seemed an idyllic union," said Plimpton. "John was thirty-five, and she was thirty. They were both bright and beautiful. If Carolyn had the public persona of a vaguely soulless mannequin, it was because she loathed the press. Privately she exuded the profound femininity of a Jackie Kennedy, with the same toughness and sense of humor. Although they weren't given to using baby talk, I once heard her call him 'Mouse,' while he called her 'Catty Cat.' They were truly in love. They were soul mates."

Oddly enough, there was an unmistakable note of similarity between John Jr.'s marriage to Carolyn Bessette and his father's betrothal to Jacqueline Bouvier. The French name *Bessette* lent the same veneer of sophistication to Carolyn's image that the name *Bouvier* had given to Jackie's. And, indeed, both ladies, whatever their respective failings, were certainly sophisticated.

On Sunday John and Carolyn were taken to the St. Marys airstrip to begin their honeymoon. David Sayre, a charter pilot and Janet Ferguson's husband, had been hired to fly the couple to Miami, where they would board a private jet and be flown to Istanbul, a city John had once visited with his mother and Aristotle Onassis. Jackie had returned to Turkey in 1985 and had told John that if he ever married, it was an ideal place to honeymoon. Sayre's plane, a single-engine Beech 18 from the 1940s, sat by itself at the end of the field. Circling the aircraft on foot, JFK Jr. oohed and aahed, noting that it looked like something Amelia Earhart might have flown. "Let's hope we do better than she did," said Carolyn. Noticing that they were alone, John asked Sayre, "Where are all the photographers?" By this point, John was evidently ready to have some pictures taken. "He loved the plane, the whole scene," recalled Sayre. "He wanted to have a record of it."

Traveling as "Mr. and Mrs. Hyannis," Mr. and Mrs. John F. Kennedy Jr. arrived in Istanbul and checked into their $4,500 per night penthouse suite atop the five-star Ciragan Palace Hotel, a former sultan's palazzo on the shores of the Bosporus. Christiane Amanpour, having once stayed at the same hotel, had recommended it to her friends. "I knew the manager," she said, "so I called him and requested that John and Carolyn be extended every possible courtesy. I expressed the need for privacy. I asked him to place a basket with Turkish bread, honey, and fruit in their suite. Bread and honey are the traditional components of a postwedding breakfast in Turkey. As far as the hotel is concerned, it's one of the most luxurious in the world, even by Kennedy standards."

Upon arriving, the couple hired a cabdriver to give them a guided tour, visiting the Blue Mosque, the Hagia Sophia Church, and the Grand Bazaar, where John bought Carolyn a jewelry box. That evening they dined on the patio at the Tugra, one of several chic restaurants owned by the Ciragan Palace. After breakfast the next morning, they walked around, stopping at stalls along the Bosporus to sample the wares. They stopped at a café for honey cake and cups of Turkish coffee. At lunchtime they dropped into a local McDonald's for a taste of home. Looking like typical American tourists, they went largely unnoticed and unrecognized except by other American tourists. When a busload of midwesterners saw them walking down the street and began yelling at them out the windows, they vanished into a crowded clothing store. Here and there a local merchant recognized them. A sidewalk vendor of rugs called him John-John and asked if he wanted to buy a carpet. "No thanks," said John.

That afternoon, while Carolyn napped, JFK Jr. lounged next to the hotel's outdoor swimming pool soaking up the sun. Opening his eyes, he saw a familiar face. *Globe* had dispatched New York photographer Russell Turiak to Turkey in search of the newlyweds. He found them.

"I suppose somebody tipped off *Globe* to the fact that they were honeymooning in Istanbul," said Turiak. "They put me on the next plane, and I'd just arrived at the hotel. I was just looking around when I chanced upon John Jr. at the swimming pool. He recognized me from New York. He gave me a look as if to say, 'Could that be you?' I ducked back into the hotel, where I met up with John Bell, a British guy who headed up *Globe*'s European bureau. There was also someone from Paris named Paul Cooper. We sat down and discussed strategy. An hour later we caught a real break. We were looking at brochures near the travel agent's office in the lobby, and we saw JFK Jr.—he was standing there talking with the agent. They were going over his travel itinerary. So John Bell innocently strolled into the agent's office and overheard their conversation. We now knew where John and Carolyn were headed after Istanbul."

That evening the newlyweds dined at Körfez, a restaurant located on the Bosporus, and afterward went to a nightclub to watch a performance of the whirling dervishes. Emil Gabron, manager of the club, sent the couple a complimentary bottle of champagne. "They were both very sweet," said Gabron. "I told Carolyn that it's all right for a Turkish woman to go 'crazy' two months during her life—the month after her wedding, and the month after the birth of her first child. She said American women didn't require special occasions to go crazy. 'We're always considered nuts,' she remarked. She had an excellent sense of humor. We exchanged telephone numbers. A few months later when I vacationed in New York with my wife and children, John and Carolyn invited us to their house. They confessed that before leaving Istanbul, they went to a tattoo artist who plastered their respective behinds with shamrocks. John offered to show me his, but I told him I preferred to see hers."

Early the next day, Russell Turiak positioned himself in front of the Ciragan Palace. "John and Carolyn came out at about 10:00 a.m.," recalled the photographer. "He was wearing shorts and a baseball cap. She had on dark glasses, like a movie star. The bell captain put them in a cab, and off they went. I managed to get a few shots but nothing spectacular. John Bell said to me, 'Get a cab and go after them.' By the time I climbed into a cab, they were long gone, and I had no idea where they were headed. 'Where do the tourists go?' I asked the driver. 'The old part of the city,' he said, so I told him to take me there. I walked around the Bazaar for a while, past a lot of historic sites. Istanbul is a big city, and I'd just about given up hope when I spotted them coming out of a mosque. John had a sort of built-in antenna developed after years of being stalked by the press. He saw me standing on the other side of the street. I followed them around, snapping pictures. And then he stopped. He took Carolyn's hand, and he kissed it, a replica of the shot of them emerging from the little church on Cumberland Island after they were married. He held her hand to his lips for a few seconds, and I took the shot. It was a fabulous picture, and he knew it. He basically posed for me. And at this point he shot me a glance, like, 'Okay, I gave you the shot. You've got it. Now get lost.' So I gave him a little sign, like 'Bye-bye.' And that was it, at least for the day."

Aware of John's itinerary, Russell Turiak and the rest of the gang from *Globe* were at the airport in Istanbul when John and Carolyn arrived to begin the second leg of their honeymoon—a sojourn to the Aegean Sea. Unseen by the newlyweds, the *Globe* crew huddled at the rear of the plane. Less than an hour later, they landed at İzmir. John and Carolyn climbed into the backseat of a Mercedes. A car driven by a *Globe* reporter picked up Turiak and the others, and the gang of four proceeded to follow the Mercedes.

"I don't think they knew they were being tailed," said Turiak. "Their driver certainly didn't know. After about an hour, the Mercedes stopped. John and Carolyn stepped out and strolled to a nearby café. They sat outdoors and had coffee and cakes. We were parked across the road, and I took some 'tender moments' shots. They got back in their car, and we followed them to Ephesus. They drove slowly, sightseeing along the way. And then they suddenly pulled over and stopped. We pulled over as well. John stepped out of the car and folded his arms. He glared at us. The reporter at the wheel of our car also clambered out, went over to him, and said, 'Can you give us a comment and pose for a photo?' John wasn't pleased. 'Look,' he said, 'I'm on my honeymoon. I'm not going to do this.' I got out of the car and walked over to them. 'How about a picture?' I asked. 'You again,' he said. He got back in the Mercedes, and they drove away. So now the jig was up. He realized we'd picked up his itinerary at the travel agent's office in Istanbul. They'd be sure to be on the lookout for us. We followed them into a parking lot at Ephesus. Other cars pulled in behind us. When they saw that we were boxed in, they turned around and sped out of the lot. We remained in Ephesus a few more days but never saw them again, so we decided to call it quits. We'd gotten what we came for—some exclusive footage of John and Carolyn gallivanting around Istanbul. It filled the next two issues of *Globe*."

John and Carolyn spent the remainder of their honeymoon cruising the Greek Isles. Sixteen days after their wedding, they returned to New York. As their cab pulled in front of 20 North Moore Street, a horde of reporters jumped out at them. "Did you enjoy your honeymoon?" asked a reporter. "Very much," said JFK Jr., struggling to remove their luggage from the trunk of the cab. Carolyn pushed her way past press photographers, their cameras flashing in her face. A few minutes after disappearing into the building behind his wife, John returned to the street. Addressing the media, he said: "Getting married is a big adjustment for us, and for a private citizen like Carolyn even more so. I ask you to give her all the privacy and room you can."

The press paid little heed to John's request. The day after they returned, Carolyn went shopping for groceries. Turning up in front of 20 North Moore Street, she slipped and fell—cans and containers spilled across the sidewalk. Instead of helping her up, photographers began taking pictures. A few days later, on October 10, Ed and Caroline Schlossberg threw a party for the newlyweds in their Park Avenue apartment. As usual, the mostly Kennedy crowd had to run a gauntlet of photographers. Among the guests were Ted Kennedy and Victoria Reggie; William Kennedy Smith and his mother, Jean; Maria Shriver and Arnold Schwarzenegger; Pat Kennedy Lawford and two of her children; Ethel Kennedy and a number of her children. JFK Jr. and his bride arrived separately. Clad in a tuxedo, John rode his bicycle nonchalantly past photographers into the marble lobby of the building, straight into the wood-paneled elevator. By the time the press realized it was JFK Jr., he was safely inside. They were better prepared an hour later when Carolyn pulled up in a taxi. Dressed in a long, clingy black dress, black shawl, and pearls, her blond tresses pulled back in a bun, she could barely move forward as the paparazzi closed in on her. "Please, I can't see," she complained, trying to reach the building entrance. A journalist subsequently identified her dilemma as "paparazzi blindness." The party itself went poorly. Angry that Carolyn had arrived late, Caroline Kennedy spoke only in passing to her sister-in-law. And there was visible tension between John and Ed Schlossberg.

The couple's first official appearance as husband and wife went no better. In early November they attended a thirtieth-anniversary benefit ball for the Whitney Museum of American Art. His mother having cochaired the museum's opening ceremony in 1966, John volunteered to serve as cochairman of the 1996 event. Awaiting the couple's entrance, the press (including Ron Galella) had gathered early behind police barricades set up outside the museum. Arriving late, John and Carolyn rushed inside without pausing to pose or even smile. In a simple black calf-length gown, accompanied by a slim Prada coat, Carolyn led the way. "John!" the photographers pleaded. "Please!" When the couple kept going, the photographers started to jeer. "We'll see you outside your building in TriBeCa tomorrow morning!" one yelled.

Covering the benefit for *The New York Times,* Bob Morris wrote: "Inside, things were more civilized, although many of the city's most-watched citizens found themselves in the odd position of watching rather than being watched." Seeing the couple move from the cocktail hour in the lobby to a sit-down dinner on the third floor, Anna Wintour was overheard (by Morris) saying to her husband, Dr. David Shaffer, "Well, we saw them. Should we go home now?"

Surrounded by the crème de la crème of New York society, Carolyn appeared ill at ease and out of her element. Evelyn Lauder (of Estée Lauder cosmetics), whose husband, Leonard, served as chairman of the museum, tried to comfort John's bride. "You mustn't be unnerved by all this," she said. While some of the guests, such as Flora Miller Biddle, a granddaughter of the museum's founder, Gertrude Vanderbilt Whitney, seemed impressed by Carolyn ("She's as graceful as a swan . . ."), others seemed far less impressed.

"She doesn't look any different than twenty-seven other blondes in this room," shrugged designer Arnold Scaasi. Ingrid Sischy, the editor of *Interview* magazine, who sat next to portrait photographer Richard Avedon, was quoted in the *Times*: "Jackie as a bride was a myth. And as a couple, she and John Kennedy were a fairy tale . . . But with these two here, we know everything about them already. And personally, I'm trying to forget some of it."

After the Whitney extravaganza, Carolyn went through a period of self-imposed isolation. She rarely left the loft except for her daily walks with Friday (and, sometimes, John) and occasional visits to her husband's office. One day after jumping into a cab to be driven uptown, she observed a car full of photographers in close pursuit and, becoming unnerved, insisted the driver take her home again. A similar occurrence took place while Dan Samson, JFK Jr.'s friend, was staying at the loft. Dan and Carolyn were in a cab on their way to an antiques store on Madison Avenue when a car pulled abreast and two photographers started taking pictures. Panicked, Carolyn began barking orders at the driver, ordering him to "step on it" and drive through red lights. Instead of the antiques store, they wound up at John's office. Sympathetic to Carolyn's dilemma, JFK Jr. arranged to have the Empire Executive Car and Limousine Service, used by members of the *George* staff, permanently placed at his wife's disposal. Although she utilized the service to join her husband at *George*-related events, more often than not she used it to go shopping, for which the press likewise took her to task. "What did that woman do with the enormous opportunity presented to her as the wife of John F. Kennedy Jr.? She did nothing," said columnist Camille Paglia.

Paglia's quick dismissal of Carolyn typified the press's reaction to the woman Maureen Dowd—of *The New York Times*—labeled "Our New Obsession." The media constantly commented on every detail of Carolyn's life, invariably casting her in the worst possible light. Tabloid stalkers picked through her black plastic garbage bags. Photographers and rumors followed her everywhere. Her appearance at any public function only stirred the pot anew. When designer Tommy Hilfiger offered her some Goobers (chocolate-covered peanuts) at a party following the movie premiere of *Air Force One,* she declined, insisting that if she were seen eating sweets, the press would assume she was pregnant. "Are you pregnant?" queried Hilfiger. "Absolutely not," she responded. When she lit a cigarette at another party, she looked up and with a wry smile told other guests, "I guess you know this means I'm not pregnant."

Carolyn's failure to immediately become pregnant set off all kinds of alarms in the press. Either there had to be massive problems in the marriage, or John had to be sterile and was consulting with a fertility specialist. Another possibility was that Carolyn, supposedly prone to acute bouts of depression and outrageous temper tantrums, had suffered a miscarriage with John, followed by a nervous breakdown. Still another theory had it that Carolyn, resentful of the amount of time John spent at *George,* refused to have children, though he in fact had already chosen the name Flynn for his firstborn son. When John once sported a bandage on his right hand, having cut it while slicing an onion, the press reported he'd injured it by striking his wife. That purported imbroglio had induced her to stop sleeping with her husband. The rumor mill never stopped churning. "You had to feel sorry for the girl," said Jacques Lowe. "Every move she made—and every move she didn't make—provided the press with yet another story. It mattered little to them whether they were true or false. You wondered how and when it would ever end."

Jenny Messina, Carolyn's grandmother, visited her granddaughter at 20 North Moore Street in December 1996. She wasn't impressed. "So you married this famous man, and you're in every newspaper," she said, "and this is where you live? You must be kidding." She remained equally unimpressed when Carolyn headed the "Best Dressed" list for 1997. "Is that a good or bad thing?" she asked.

Jenny's visit improved Carolyn's disposition. The reluctant hermit came out of hiding. She made a number of public appearances supporting Kennedy-backed groups and organizations, including the Parsons Dance company, of which Lee Radziwill was a supporter. She and John attended an event for the Breast Cancer Research Foundation. Arriving with Bobby and Maria Shriver at the Fire and Ice Ball benefiting the Revlon/UCLA Women's Cancer Research Program, she joked, "I've been waiting a long time for a date with my cousin Bobby." She demonstrated a detailed and concise knowledge of the world of big business. At an event for *George,* the name Galen Weston cropped up in conversation. When she realized John had never heard of Weston, she patiently filled her husband in on the Canadian billionaire's various holdings.

Carolyn's reemergence in the public eye again brought out the "stalkarazzi," as John called them. Seeing Ken Katz in front of 20 North Moore Street one morning, JFK Jr. asked him if he was looking for a fight. Another time he confronted a tabloid photographer who'd been lurking in the shadows outside his residence. "Hey, guy with the green jacket!" he said. 'You're here all the time. You're looking for a harassment lawsuit." He began videotaping the license plates of the lensmen's cars apparently to document their constant presence outside his house, though he never filed an official complaint against anyone.

One evening when Carolyn joined her mother for dinner at Asia de Cuba, they were followed by a horde of photographers. The group waited for them outside the restaurant. As they emerged and began walking down the street, the photographers went after them. "I don't know how you put up with this," Ann Freeman was overheard saying to her daughter. "I don't care how much you love him—it's just not worth it."

Joanna Molloy, of "Rush & Molloy," the New York *Daily News* gossip column, was a TriBeCa neighbor of John's and Carolyn's. "I used to see her around the neighborhood with her sister Lauren," said Molloy. "She'd float by without cracking a smile. John was just the opposite. I'd see him at the Socrates Diner, at the local dry cleaner, and at Nobu (the restaurant). He'd hang out with Fred and Mary, who owned the neighborhood newspaper store. He'd sit there and sip wine with them. There was an anonymous Thai restaurant on 46th Street and Ninth Avenue, near the *George* offices, where he'd often go for lunch. He couldn't walk three feet without some New Yorker saying, 'Hi, John. How's it going?' He always smiled. He was as nice as Carolyn wasn't. She hypnotized John with her beauty. He loved her Romanesque look and aquiline nose. The kindest thing you can say about her is nothing can prepare you for that level of fame. But if you marry John Kennedy and then act surprised at all the attention you're getting from the press, you must have fallen off the turnip truck."

Joanna Molloy's hard-edged response to Carolyn came about after covering an event attended by the couple. Approaching Bessette, the reporter said, "That's a beautiful dress—may I ask who designed it?"

"She looked right through me—right in the eye with such daggers that John noticed it," said Molloy. "She shot ice right through me. She pointedly turned and walked off in a huff. John leaned over, put his arm around me, and whispered the name of the designer in my ear."

John and Carolyn spent New Year's at the Big Sky ski resort in Bozeman, Montana. Paul Boisie, a ski instructor in the area, met them on New Year's Day at the Half Moon Saloon. "They had a kind of break-up-to-make-up romance," he said. "They argued one minute and kissed the next. I had the feeling that's how they stimulated each other sexually. A good row is sometimes a great aphrodisiac—it's a form of foreplay."

Chapter 21

◆

PARADISE LOST

IN EARLY 1997, John and Carolyn invited Condé Nast CEO Steve Florio to their home to look at wedding pictures. "I knew Carolyn from when she worked for Calvin Klein, and I always liked her," said Florio. "I joined them on the floor of their TriBeCa loft. Their dog, Friday, camped out in my lap, and we sorted through the photographs. There was Uncle Teddy doing the macarena. It looked like any Irish family wedding. Everybody was drinking, dancing, and looking happy. I saw that wonderful picture of John kissing Carolyn's hand. They were so beautiful. She was a riot. John adored her. It's such bullshit that she had an affair on him. Did they bicker from time to time? Well, *hello.* You're damn straight they bickered, just like I've been bickering with my wife for thirty-two years—we're still battling it out. I'd be finished without my wife. I know John felt the same way about his. And Carolyn felt the same way about him. I never met or knew a married couple that didn't argue now and again."

JFK Jr. and Steve Florio shared a love of the sea. They often spoke about sailing. That evening, after looking at wedding pictures, John said to his friend, "You like boats. I want to show you something." He led Florio into his library and took out a photo album. He showed his guest the original picture of him as a small child hiding underneath his father's desk in the Oval Office. He then produced the famous photo taken at JFK's funeral, where he solemnly salutes his father's flag-draped coffin. Finally, he took out a lot of boat pictures, including several of the *Honey Fitz,* the presidential yacht named in honor of President Kennedy's maternal grandfather, Boston mayor John F. Fitzgerald.

"My God," said Florio. "Every once in a while I have to remind myself that you're the son of an American president. My grandfather came to this country with five bucks in his pocket and a bag of carpentry tools."

With a big smile, John Jr. said, "That's why you're here, my man. That's why you're the CEO of a major company. It's because your grandfather got on a boat and said, 'I'm going to find a better place.'"

Then John broke it up. "I have to walk the dog," he said. "He's got to take a dump. Come with me."

As they walked the dog, John talked about a two-week trip he'd made years earlier with a buddy to Vietnam. They'd crawled through miles and miles of tunnels built by the Vietcong. Florio suddenly changed the subject. "So what was it like to sleep with Daryl Hannah?" he asked.

"Fuck you, Steve!" shouted John. "I'm married now. Are you nuts?"

"Just testing," said Florio.

Steve Florio's favorite "John" story involved a call he received from JFK Jr. to meet and discuss some of the problems he'd encountered at *George* with respect to diminishing circulation and sales. They met for lunch at a Village restaurant called Da Silvano. John showed up wearing a beret and sunglasses. Florio cracked up. "We're in a little Italian restaurant in Greenwich Village, and you come in looking like the Pink Panther. Ditch the hat and glasses, will you?"

John looked at Florio and said, "Steve, we will not be able to get through lunch. Trust me. You think you know a lot of famous people? Nobody ever stops you from eating your lunch."

"Bullshit!" snapped Florio. "Get over yourself."

Florio reached over, took the beret off John's head, and put it on. John laughed. He slipped off his sunglasses and sat down. The waiter came over. "Mr. Kennedy," he said, "could you please sign the menu?"

"May I see one first?" responded John. "I'm really pretty hungry."

Then the owner came over to the table, followed by the owner's mother, an old Italian woman, who said she had two velvet pictures in her living room—one of Jesus and one of John's father. "Your father was a Catholic," she said. "God bless him."

John looked over at Florio and smiled.

"He didn't say it, but I could tell what he was thinking," remarked Florio, recalling the meeting. "*Don't say I didn't tell you.* It was incredible. People passing by the restaurant looked in and saw the buzz. They recognized John and came in. 'Can I please take your picture?' said a girl with a camera. I apologized to John and suggested we change places. 'Put your back to the window,' I said. We barely got through salad and pasta. We walked outside. 'Told you,' said John, playfully punching my arm. 'Told you, told you.' He was right, and I was wrong. If I hadn't seen it, I wouldn't have believed it. I realized this was something he had to put up with every day of his life."

On another occasion, while recuperating from open-heart surgery at St. Francis Hospital on Long Island, Steve Florio received a visit from John. "I'd had the surgery two days earlier," said Florio, "and I was experiencing a great deal of pain. I heard a commotion in the corridor outside my room. I looked up, and John was standing in front of my bed. 'You look like shit,' he said. 'Look,' he added, 'I brought my cousin along. He had the same operation as you. He had his valve repaired. He said it's a bitch and it hurts like hell, but six weeks from now you'll be fine. He wants to come in and meet you.'

"In walked Arnold Schwarzenegger. He looked me over and said, 'I know, man. It hurts like shit. I couldn't believe it—it hurt so much, I wanted to cry. But don't worry, after a while the pain goes away.'

"John's visit cheered me no end. He was a great guy. As he walked out, I heard him tell the nurse, 'Mr. Florio's my buddy. You better take care of him.'"

In January 1997, encouraged by his sister and Uncle Ted, JFK Jr. informed New York Democratic Party chairwoman Judith Hope that he was considering running for New York senator Daniel Patrick Moynihan's seat, though at this point, entering a major political race still seemed only a distant possibility. To his surprise, however, he found an unexpected supporter in the person of New York real estate developer

Donald Trump. "JFK Jr. was a friend of mine," said Trump. "He was worried about *George,* so he asked me to come to the office and speak to his staff. I did, but at the same time I told him, 'Magazines are a killer business. You don't need it. Stop the magazine silliness and run for office. The public loves you. You appeal to the everyday man and woman. You'll win any political race you enter.' Over the last three years of his life, I must have told him this at least fifty times. We used to go to New York Knicks basketball games together, and I'd keep harping on the subject. He knew he could trust me because I was one of the few people around him who didn't want something from him. One day he said to me, 'Yeah, I think I will run.' But that was the last I heard of it from him."

In February 1997 John and Carolyn visited Donald Trump at Mar-a-Lago, his lavish oceanfront estate in Palm Beach. "I didn't find Carolyn Bessette as attractive as everyone else did," continued Trump. "She had great style and a good body, but she wasn't my type. Hey, that's why they have menus in restaurants. To John, she was beautiful. Most people considered her a great beauty. I constantly heard these rumors about them—they were on the verge of divorce; they were having extramarital affairs. There was that absurd Michael Bergin rumor. It never happened. She dumped Bergin like a bag of dirt to be able to go with John. He never touched her again. Bergin's an absolute sleazebag. I know other girls who have gone out with him—he's a fucking loser! John and I confided in each other. He talked candidly with me because he knew I wasn't going to the press. So one day I asked him, 'What's with all these rumors—is there anything to them?' 'Donald,' he said, 'Carolyn's my absolute best friend in the world. I've never had a better relationship with anybody. That stuff in the press is total bullshit.' I'll never forget that he said 'absolute best friend in the world.' I asked him again. I said, 'So it's all bullshit?' And John replied, 'I'd tell you if it weren't. I trust you.' He admitted that she was difficult. She was demanding. But that only kept him on his toes."

In the early spring of 1997, after attending the White House correspondents' dinner at the Washington Hilton, John and Carolyn traveled to Boston to host a benefit at the John F. Kennedy Library. Jonathan Soroff, Carolyn's journalist friend from her Boston University days, had been assigned to cover the event for *The Improper Bostonian.* "I hadn't spoken with Carolyn since she left Boston for New York," said Soroff. "I'd once seen her from afar on the beach near the Kennedy compound at Hyannis Port when a photographer started taking her picture. She hid behind a towel. John told the guy that he was trespassing on private property. The guy finally went away. I supposed she might be skittish since I was press, and the press was all over her. But when she saw me at the JFK Library, she came right over and gave me a big hug and kiss. 'What're you doing here?' she asked. We launched into a lengthy conversation, catching up on old times. We spoke about Marci Klein, who'd become the talent coordinator for *Saturday Night Live*. Then John Kennedy Jr. joined us and Carolyn said, 'I want you to meet my husband.' 'Nice to meet you,' I said. After he left, we continued talking. I asked her if she was working. 'Right now,' she said, 'I really can't. I'd love to have a job, but it's impossible.' I asked her why. 'Think about it,' she said. 'If I take a job, everyone will say I got it because of John. There's no way around it.' I told Carolyn the whole situation was so weird for anyone who knew her before she got married. 'Tell me about it,' she laughed. 'My life has become surreal—sometimes I'm overwhelmed by it myself. It's an odd way to live.'"

John returned and announced that they were about to serve dinner. Soroff had to cover another function and wasn't staying, so he asked if he could take Carolyn's picture.

"Do you have to?" she asked.

"No," responded Soroff. "Besides, everyone knows what you look like."

Carolyn gave Soroff a farewell hug and started to leave. Then she stopped and turned. "Wait a second," she said. "Every day I'm besieged by complete strangers with cameras. Why should I say no to an old friend?"

She posed, and Soroff took her picture.

Thinking about it afterward, Soroff concluded that Carolyn "must have really loved John to put up with her new lifestyle. She wasn't impressed by his fame or money, and she'd always dated good-looking guys. Not that John wasn't handsome, but that alone wouldn't have been enough. She truly loved him for him."

In mid-May 1997 John and Carolyn returned to Italy, visiting Milan, Florence, and Rome. In Milan, attending an Italian fashion industry dinner, John told guests: "Let me use the same phrase that my father did when he went to Paris with my mother thirty-five years ago. My name is John Kennedy, and I am the man who is accompanying Carolyn Bessette. I am honored to tell you she is my wife." Returning to the States, they took over Jean Kennedy Smith's Long Island house on Ocean Road in Bridgehampton for a week. Named American ambassador to Ireland, Smith had invited them to spend the summer, but once the press learned of their presence, they were forced to move out. George Plimpton recalled going to dinner with them at the Water Mill branch of Carolyn's favorite New York restaurant, the Independent. "She ordered chicken and spinach without the side of mashed potatoes," said Plimpton. "Just as it arrived, the door opened, and in marched a half-dozen paparazzi, their cameras blazing. We took the food away in doggie bags."

In June, while John published an article in *The New Republic* on former African leader Mobutu Sese Seko, Carolyn Bessette's picture appeared in practically every newspaper in town. *WWD* praised her eye for "proportion"—her skirts were always *just* the right length. A *Washington Post* reporter elicited a rare response from Carolyn when he asked her why she hadn't pursued a career in her college major: teaching. "I felt a little underdeveloped to be completely responsible for twenty-five other people's children," she responded. "And to a large extent, I felt it wouldn't be provocative enough for me."

The "career" Carolyn did pursue as the wife of the most watched and photographed man in America eventually proved too "provocative." On August 31, 1997, when Princess Di perished in an automobile crash in Paris pursued by paparazzi, Carolyn became even more wary of the press. Her reaction, as expressed to John, was: "There by the grace of God go I." Her obsession with the media, while understandable, placed a major roadblock in the path of her marriage. Perhaps her mother had been right after all; perhaps John had been the wrong choice as a lifelong partner.

It was George Plimpton who advised John to seek counseling for his wife. "The temptation to say 'Get over it—get past it,' is far too simplistic," said Plimpton. "I know people who'll take a train or bus from New York to California simply because they're scared to death of flying. A mental block isn't something you can wish or reason away. The ordinary person suddenly thrust into the limelight is bound to become neurotic about it. The only problem with the situation was that John, given his birthright, wasn't about to become an obscure and forgotten figure. Among other things, he had political aspirations. In addition, her fear of the media as well as crowds impacted on her desire to have children. So I recommended John send her to a shrink. Is there anyone in New York who hasn't at one time or another been in therapy? John went to the same shrink I'd seen for a while. And he was still in therapy, though with somebody else. Carolyn began therapy in the summer of 1997 and continued for two years, until the end of her life. The psychiatrist put her on antidepressants. She wasn't really a depressive. What saddened her, I believe, was her sense that she was letting John down. That alone didn't exactly qualify her for commitment to a funny farm. Had they lived, I have no doubt she would've learned to cope. They would have had children. He would have run for political office. They would have lived happily ever after, or something like that."

John and Carolyn celebrated their first anniversary in late September at a rustic hotel in Big Sur, California. Their four-day getaway gave rise to a spate of rumors in the press, predominantly of a negative nature. *Boston* magazine, quoting an "eyewitness," reported that the couple had feuded nonstop aboard a twelve-passenger commercial flight from Newark Airport to Martha's Vineyard.

"Maybe we should get divorced," John supposedly told his wife. "We fucking talk about it enough!"

"Oh, no," Carolyn is said to have responded. "We waited for your mother to die to get married. We're waiting for my mother to die to get a divorce."

Jealousy was similarly cited as a common cause of discord. The couple reportedly fought when Carolyn, spending a weekend in New York, learned that Daryl Hannah was on Martha's Vineyard at the same time as John.

"If such were the case, they certainly didn't see each other," commented John Perry Barlow.

Jealousy and divorce were among the more common themes played up in the press's ongoing coverage of the couple. One rumor had it that

Carolyn, in an effort to collect on their prenuptial agreement, had contacted a divorce attorney. Another rumor had it that she'd hired a private investigator to follow her husband, presumably to catch him with another woman. "None of this ever happened, of course," said George Plimpton, "but it made for enticing newspaper copy. The problem is that each story only added to Carolyn's fear and loathing of the media."

Although Carolyn periodically suspected John of seeing other women, she neither hired a private investigator nor consulted with a divorce lawyer. For the most part, their altercations had to do with control issues. One squabble involved Brad Johns, Carolyn's hairdresser. John accused the man of flaunting Carolyn's name in the press in order to promote his hair salon. Perturbed, he telephoned Johns and asked him to stop. When the stylist persisted, JFK Jr. suggested that his wife find another hairdresser. They debated the point for a week before Carolyn finally gave in.

With the passage of time, their disagreements became less frequent. Suzanne Ruddick, a friend of Carolyn's from Greenwich, visited the couple in New York in early October 1997. "Carolyn and I went shopping in the Prada department at Barneys, and she bought a black gabardine jacket," remarked Ruddick. "She said John was both generous and supportive of her. He didn't mind being written up in the gossip columns, but it irked him when they picked on her. 'John's nicer than I am,' she said. I discerned absolutely no friction or tension between them. Quite the opposite—whenever I looked, they were either nuzzling or kissing. One evening he gave her a deep blue cashmere sweater with a note that read, 'To match those matchless eyes.' Before I left, Carolyn reaffirmed her attachment to John. She talked a bit about the Kennedys. There was evidently some feud going on between John and two of his cousins—Michael and Joe. She felt that John was absolutely in the right. According to Carolyn, the two cousins were horrendous."

It was in the September 1997 issue of *George* that JFK Jr. took on Michael and Joe for behavior that had become standard operating procedure among the Kennedys. "Two members of my family chased an idealized alternative to their life," read John's editor's letter that month. "One [Joe II] left behind an embittered former wife [Sheila Rauch]." The other, Michael, had been caught having an affair with his children's fourteen-year-old babysitter and currently faced statutory rape charges in Massachusetts. As JFK Jr. put it: "[Michael] fell in love with youth and surrendered his judgment in the process." Both cousins "became literally poster boys for bad behavior."

To add to the controversy, the same issue of the magazine contained a partially obscured nude photograph of John, an apple suspended overhead to suggest the theme of temptation.

Having previously announced his candidacy for governor of Massachusetts, Joe Kennedy now held a press conference in which he struck back at John. "Ask not what you can do for your cousin," he said, "but what you can do for his magazine." Less than two weeks later, at a second press conference, Joe announced his withdrawal from the gubernatorial race. He blamed John for his troubles.

Egregious as Joe Kennedy's deportment had been, thirty-nine-year-old Michael Kennedy set a new standard for poor behavior, bringing embarrassment and shame to a clan already burdened by an overflow of negative press coverage. Having taken over for his brother Joe as head of the nonprofit Citizens Energy Corporation, it emerged that Michael had set aside a huge salary for himself, nearly $350,000 in 1996 alone. In addition, although married to Victoria Gifford Kennedy—they had three children—Michael had amassed a long list of extramarital affairs, mostly with underage girls. He had, as one of his other cousins noted, "a pee-pee problem."

The prime witness to Michael's infidelities was Michael Skakel, a nephew of Ethel Kennedy, whose 2002 conviction for the 1975 murder of a neighbor, fifteen-year-old Martha Moxley, earned him a lengthy prison sentence. Prior to his conviction, Skakel produced a book proposal, *Dead Man Talking: A Kennedy Cousin Comes Clean,* which unsuccessfully made the rounds of New York publishing firms. Although never picked up, the proposal provides a searing view of a highly dysfunctional family, concentrating on the author's closest Kennedy relations. The group included Chris Lawford, Bobby Kennedy Jr., Max Kennedy, and Michael Kennedy, all of whom were in a twelve-step drug and alcohol rehabilitation program with Skakel.

Regarding Michael Kennedy's proclivity for teenage girls and his affair with Marisa Verochi, the fourteen-year-old babysitter (whose father was a key Massachusetts Democratic politician and friend of the family), Skakel writes: "Everyone knew it, but no one said anything about it. I didn't either. But even Michael's children were aware of what was going on. It was obvious. Once, on a rafting trip, we were all sitting around the fire preparing dinner when Michael and Marisa suddenly emerged from the woods. Somebody yelled out, 'Where have you two been?' Marisa turned to Michael, winked, and said, 'Yeah, where have *you* been?' Everyone laughed. My eyes met Michael Jr.'s. He was not laughing, and the depth of pain and confusion in his eyes frightened me. What a burden for a thirteen-year-old kid to have to carry. What does he do, I thought, when he gets home, and his mother [Victoria] asks him if he had a good time with his dad and babysitter?"

The same book proposal recounts a three-way that Michael had with his secretary and the wife of one of his Kennedy cousins. It also details a telephone call received by Skakel from a young Kennedy-family campaign worker who "claimed to be pregnant with Michael's child. I convinced her to have an abortion. I got money for the abortion— $2,000—from Michael. Later she decided to have the child. Michael demanded his money back."

Scandal soon evolved into travesty. On December 31, 1997, while state authorities continued to investigate the statutory rape charges they intended to bring against him, Michael Kennedy perished in a skiing accident while vacationing with friends and family members in Aspen, Colorado. Michael's death, vividly documented in the media, provided still another example of Kennedy bravado and hubris. Michael died while playing a version of "ski football," wherein a small projectile is tossed back and forth from one player to another while the participants ski without poles or helmets down a difficult run. Michael had just caught a pass when he smashed headfirst into a tree.

R. Couri Hay was one of the friends who'd gone skiing with Michael that day. "I must have been four feet away from him when he crashed into the tree that killed him," said Hay. "I knew immediately he was dead. There was no blood. He went totally white. It was one more tragic act on the part of a Kennedy. The entire affair disgusted JFK Jr. He attended Michael's funeral along with Carolyn Bessette and the rest of his family. His cousins all went limp in his presence. He was the clan's big man, and they were all second bananas. His beauty awed them. His success in the world impressed them. Michael's death only heightened his star power."

On their way home from Michael's funeral, while waiting at Hyannis Airport for a flight to New York, John and Carolyn were approached by the paparazzi. When Laura Cavanaugh, a photographer for *Globe,* came within a foot of the couple, Carolyn told her to back off. Losing her composure, she then spit in the woman's direction. "Why can't you just leave us alone?" said an exasperated JFK Jr. "We're returning from a family funeral."

A day after their return to New York, as John and Carolyn walked the dog, they were again set upon by paparazzi. "When is this going to stop?" John said to one of the photographers. "Calm down," said the photographer, "you're upsetting the dog." "Why are you so concerned about my dog?" asked John. "Why aren't you concerned that you're upsetting my wife?" The photographer pointed out that she was merely doing her job. "You're both celebrities, and you both live in the heart of TriBeCa," she said. "So what do you expect?" To which John responded, "Well, we're not going to move."

Michael Kennedy's senseless death distressed John to the extent that though he'd just passed a flight physical and an FAA written exam, he opted to take a three-month hiatus from his piloting lessons at Flight-Safety International in Florida. He'd contemplated doing the same following Billy Way's untimely demise. Hardly enthusiastic about her brother's flying adventures, Caroline Kennedy hoped the decision would become permanent. When John resumed flight school in late March 1998, his sister resigned herself to the fact that she could do little to stop him. On April 22 he fulfilled the requirements for a private pilot's license and soon purchased his first plane, the Cessna 182. Caroline Kennedy consoled herself by insisting only that he exercise extreme caution. "After all," a friend overheard her say to him, "you're no longer alone—you have a wife to worry about."

"The comment didn't convey her true feelings," said the friend. "In reality, Caroline thought John's wife too self-serving and unstable for her brother. 'John's got to spend all his downtime cajoling and soothing Carolyn,' she complained. 'She's a total head case.' At the same time, she recognized that he was crazy about her. 'Whenever she's around,' said Caroline, 'he's got that goofy, fool-in-love expression on his face.' The only thing I couldn't understand about Caroline was her lack of sympathy for her sister-in-law's fear of the paparazzi, particularly since Caroline couldn't abide them herself."

For Caroline's fortieth birthday—November 27, 1997—the family had put together comic sketches, and Ed Schlossberg had organized a touching slide show of private family photographs. The party featured background music from *The Sound of Music,* one of Caroline's favorite movies. Guests were impressed at how compatible and comfortable with each other Ed and Caroline seemed to be.

In his own fashion, Ed Schlossberg did for Caroline what Maurice Tempelsman had done for Jackie. He created a sanctuary, a safe haven for his wife. Outside the confines of his career, he had little interest in the limelight and even less interest in the myriad philanthropies and charitable organizations whose social functions Caroline so often attended. He accompanied her to the major events but otherwise preferred remaining at home with the children. In that sense, he and Caroline pursued separate lives. Yet despite his lack of enthusiasm for the media, he could cope with it in a way that Carolyn Bessette couldn't.

If Caroline Kennedy proved ineffectual in curbing her brother's appetite for flight school, she showed herself to be more influential in rousing his desire to eventually enter the political arena, hammering away at him to form an unofficial task force to explore the possibility. Publicly he maintained a stance of indifference, insisting that his present occupation as editor in chief of *George* provided the opportunity to comment on politics without becoming directly involved. The closest he came to making a public announcement of his interest in pursuing office came during a televised interview on the occasion of what would have been his father's eightieth birthday. "There are some members of my family that have gone directly into public life," he said. "For me, that's a very loaded situation. It's not a situation that one should step into casually, and you better be ready for it."

In private he told friends and colleagues that the prospect interested him, that sooner or later he intended to make the transition from magazine editor to political hopeful. Carolyn Maloney, New York Democratic congresswoman for the 14th District, heard that when John learned of Hillary Clinton's interest in entering the senatorial race in New York in 2000, he polled for Maloney's seat. He considered several other possibilities as well, among them the race for governor of New York. When Ted Kennedy suggested he consider running for office in Rhode Island, he responded, "That'll put me in the same boat as Hillary—I'll be regarded as a carpetbagger. I might as well run in Arkansas." "Don't be silly," said Ted Kennedy. "Bobby was accused of being a carpetbagger when he ran for the Senate in New York in the mid-1960s. It didn't stop him from winning."

Despite his family's connection to the Clintons, JFK Jr. greatly resented Hillary's political intervention in what he considered his home state. When he read in *The New York Times* that Hillary intended on making an appearance in Binghamton, New York, he said to Richard Blow, "Can you believe this? Since when does the First Lady have to travel to Binghamton?" According to Blow, JFK Jr. wanted to write an op-ed piece for the *Times* accusing Hillary of abusing her position. In the end, he opted not to write the article. He feared that by attacking her, he might jeopardize his magazine's ability to cover her campaign should she decide to run. He nevertheless bridled when his sister presented Hillary with the Arts Advocacy Award during the annual National Arts Awards dinner at Lincoln Center in 1998.

Aside from Hillary Clinton, the main obstacle John faced with regard to his political aspirations had to be Carolyn Bessette. Despite her commitment to therapy, she hadn't yet become immune to the constant pressure exerted by the press, a process that obviously took time. "Carolyn used to hang out at her sister Lauren's house in TriBeCa and bitch about the invasion of her privacy," said family friend William Peter Owen. "She'd stay late. John would return to 20 North Moore Street, and she wouldn't be there for him. This happened on several occasions. One night he came over, and the four of us stayed up all night chatting. Carolyn feared he might abandon his magazine and enter politics without first consulting with her. He said he wouldn't, and I believed him. As I understood it, he planned on a political career, and she intended to support him. She had a similar block against having children. She felt a child would be subjected to the same public scrutiny that she suffered. I'd say that had they lived another year or two, she'd have been both a mother and the wife of a senator."

Carolyn's misgivings about the press supposedly contributed to her most serious vice: drug addiction. Such, at least, is the charge levied against her by author Edward Klein in *The Kennedy Curse,* a 2003 book filled with insinuations and allegations. Rob Littell confirmed that John and Carolyn both used drugs but only in moderation. The stories that periodically surfaced in the tabloids—and later in Klein's book—were, according to Littell, "wildly exaggerated. Carolyn definitely partied, sharing a joint and an occasional line of cocaine, but I saw no evidence that she had an addiction. Nor did she drink very much. I never saw her intoxicated from alcohol or incapacitated from drugs, and I'm certain John would have told me if there had been a problem, or if she'd done hard drugs like heroin or crack."

None of John's other friends, including Richard Wiese, Chris Overbeck, John Hare, or John Perry Barlow, ever encountered Carolyn on a drug binge. Carole Radziwill, one of Carolyn's closest companions, dismissed Edward Klein's "unscrupulous" assertions as "sheer nonsense." In an October 2003 letter to *Vanity Fair,* which had previously published an excerpt from *The Kennedy Curse,* she asked: "Who is this group of anonymous friends of John and Carolyn's who were so helpful in writing Klein's book? No one in the Bessette or Kennedy family spoke to him, and I have spoken to many of Carolyn's closest friends—none of us were asked to cooperate." To this she added: "[Klein's] assertion of 'street drug' abuse (on Carolyn's part) is ludicrous. In the ten years that I knew Carolyn, I never once saw her use drugs. She was as much a 'cokehead' as Klein is a biographer."

Though not herself a direct witness, journalist Annette Witheridge claimed to "know somebody" who'd been present when John Jr. returned home one evening only to find his wife and several of her friends lazing around in a daze, "wiped out" on cocaine. The same "unnamed" source remembered seeing Carolyn at Chaos, a downtown club, "with a ring of white around her nose." JFK Jr.'s acquaintance Richard duPont recalled bumping into John at a TriBeCa bistro called Walker's. "John began questioning me about how I'd recovered from my alcohol and cocaine addiction," said duPont. "He wanted to know about certain rehab clinics, such as Sierra Tucson and the Betty Ford Center. How did it work? What did they do? And so on. I didn't attach much importance to the conversation at the time, but afterward it occurred to me he might have been making inquiries because of Carolyn, though, to be fair, he never mentioned her by name."

Benjamin Turpin, a British photojournalist who knew Carolyn Bessette from her tenure at Calvin Klein, contended that she used cocaine "more frequently before her marriage than after. It's the drug of necessity in the fashion trade. I remember seeing her in 1998 at a renovation benefit for Grand Central Terminal. She was standing there with John Jr. and his sister, who'd taken over the campaign for her mother. Lee Radziwill, Patricia Lawford, and Eunice Shriver were present, as were all sorts of celebrities, from Donald Trump and Brooke Astor, to Tommy Tune and UN Secretary General Kofi Annan. Caroline Kennedy read a passage from a 1975 letter her mother had written about preserving Grand Central to former New York mayor Abe Beame. Carolyn Bessette spotted me and came over. 'Hi, hon,' she said. 'Do you know where I can score some coke?' 'You must be kidding,' I responded. 'I am,' she said with a wink. She had that kind of sense of humor."

The summer of 1998 found Caroline Kennedy and John Jr. locked in a bitter legal dispute with Sheldon Streisand, the older brother of Barbra Streisand, based on a real estate investment partnership that Jackie Kennedy and Sheldon Streisand had set up some twenty years earlier. Caroline and John sued Streisand for turning over his interest in the partnership to his wife without their permission. Accusing Streisand of "blatant and deceitful . . . partnership pilfering," John and Caroline sought to have the matter presented to a court-appointed arbitrator; Streisand

484 C. David Heymann

denied their accusation and opposed their request. Though the case was eventually settled out of court, JFK Jr. took a potshot at Barbra Streisand, condemning her in *George* for "going too far" by urging voters to support Democratic Party congressional candidates simply because of her "blind faith in President Clinton."

No doubt angered by the lawsuit against her brother and still smarting from the way JFK Jr. had dismissed her during his previous visit to her Malibu house, Barbra responded to John's editorial: "The next time you write something, it would be good to check your facts, not to mention the Constitution. Who could have imagined that in this day and age, journalists would question a person's right to express his or her views? So much for freedom of speech."

Despite their lawsuit against Sheldon Streisand, John and his sister were clearly never burdened by financial problems. The Kennedy family had recently sold its interests in the Chicago Merchandise Mart to Venedo Inc. for $625 million, plus preferred stock options in the corporation. John and Caroline each received in excess of $38 million for their share of the proceeds. An examination of the family's financial papers indicates that the Kennedy-controlled Park Foundation still retained substantial real estate holdings in Illinois, Texas, Massachusetts, Florida, and New York. The Kennedy clan remained high on the *Forbes* list of the country's 500 wealthiest families.

The acquisition of his private pilot's license represented the fulfillment of a personal dream for John Jr. It afforded him a certain freedom from the press, freedom from pressures, freedom from people wanting autographs and their photographs taken with him. "Now whenever we want to get away," he said, "we can just climb in a plane and fly off." Yet while certain problems seemed to resolve themselves, others persisted.

Anthony Radziwill's health continued to decline. Early that summer he underwent strenuous sessions of stereotactic body radiosurgery at Staten Island University Hospital. Dr. Gil Lederman, head of the treatment team, said of Carolyn Bessette's frequent appearances at Anthony's bedside: "I will never forget her kindness, her graciousness, and her compassion." John Jr.'s presence was equally important in helping Anthony to rally. One time he sang a nursery rhyme to his bedridden cousin that

Jackie had sung to them both when they were young. Despite his efforts, John remained fully aware that his cousin was slowly dying.

Nor did the press evaporate simply because JFK Jr. and Carolyn Bessette willed it so. In early August 1998, when they flew to Rome to attend the wedding at Lake Bracciano of Christiane Amanpour and James Rubin, they were joined on board the transatlantic airliner by a horde of paparazzi. In mid-October, while visiting Ted Kennedy and Victoria Reggie at Hyannis Port, they were chased around town by another set of photographers. One of the most flagrant violations of their privacy took place over Halloween of 1998.

Invited to attend a Halloween party thrown by the Women Model Management Association of New York, John and Carolyn dug out their George and Martha Washington costumes and prepared to go. At the last minute, Carolyn received a telephone call from her sister Lauren—their grandmother, Jenny Messina, had been hospitalized while vacationing in Florida.

While the sisters flew south, John attended the party alone. The tabloid press, unaware of the circumstances, jumped on the story. "JFK Jr.'s marriage is falling apart because John is spending time with other women," read a report in the *New York Post*. "On Halloween, he left Carolyn at home while he dressed up as George Washington and went to a party attended by Naomi Campbell, Kate Moss, and other leading supermodels. Indications are that his marriage is in trouble." *Star* ran an even more incendiary piece, ending with the line: "Do you think the Hunk showed Naomi Campbell and Kate Moss his Declaration of Independence?"

The Halloween story was followed by several others that ran in the tabloids over the next month, one of which concerned a visit John paid to Republican National Committee chairman Haley Barbour, whom he wanted to profile in *George*. "Although he's married, JFK Jr. remains a heartthrob," reported the *Post*. "According to . . . Haley Barbour, female staffers were coming up with the lamest excuses, like 'Just checking the paperclip supply,' to get a peek at the scion of America's most illustrious family of Democrats." Another story, this one in the London *Daily Mail,* linked John with Paula Barbieri, an actress and model perhaps best known as being O. J. Simpson's ex-girlfriend.

The articles set in motion a whole new spree of arguments between John and Carolyn. Once again she accused her husband of seeing women behind her back. "The situation upset John as well," said Rob Littell, "because he was determined not to publicly humiliate Carolyn as his mother had been by revelations of President Kennedy's womanizing." John and Rob had discussed marriage and fidelity on a number of occasions. It remained clear to Littell that John hadn't cheated on his wife and had no intention of doing so.

John and Carolyn ended the year on a positive note. They had Christmas dinner with Anthony and Carole Radziwill. Though it was clear that Anthony was still ailing, they vowed to make the meal an annual tradition—just the four of them.

Photographer Ken Katz recalled an unpleasant confrontation between John and Angie Coqueran that took place in early 1999. "John and Carolyn spotted Angie, my photo partner, in her parked Jeep not far from their house. John snapped. He leaped on the hood of her car and started shouting, 'I'm going to get you! I'm going to get you!' Angie rolled down her window and asked him to get off her car so she could leave. He grabbed hold of her coat through the window. Carolyn tried to pull him off, but couldn't. I came along. Carolyn started crying. 'Why the hell don't the two of you leave us alone,' said John. I apologized, and we left."

That evening John and Carolyn dined at Rao's, an impossible-to-get-into-unless-you're-a-Kennedy East Harlem restaurant, and when they came out, they were besieged by photographers. Yoel Katzavman, one of their regular Empire Car Service drivers, sped downtown via the East River Drive to lose their pursuers. The next morning JFK Jr. called Pete Olsen, his personal attorney, to complain about the ongoing interference from the press. Olsen, whose clients included the Clintons as well as Caroline Kennedy, told John that short of suing half the world's press corps, little could be done.

In early March the couple went to Italy on what had become an annual sojourn, visiting Milan and Florence, where they were taken on a private tour of the Uffizi Gallery. When they returned to New York, John did an interview with Steve Brill for *Brill's Content* magazine, and then attended a reception with his sister Caroline in honor of Rachel Robinson, the widow of baseball legend Jackie Robinson. Later that month John and his wife were seen arguing over a steak dinner at Smith & Wollensky. The topic of debate, according to a waiter, was when to have children.

It was in late March 1999 that John and Carolyn began marriage counseling. Except for one or two major blowups, the sessions reportedly went well. During their third meeting, when the subject of drugs arose, Carolyn stormed out of the room but returned fifteen minutes later. The marriage counselor suggested that John and Carolyn temporarily table their immediate concerns—starting a family and the presence of the press—and concentrate on spending more leisure time together.

In April they traveled to Vero Beach and stayed in a house owned by financier Pete Peterson while JFK Jr. took additional flying lessons at FlightSafety International. During their stay, John introduced Carolyn to John McColgan, a former air force pilot and longtime flight instructor who had tested Kennedy on his certification run. "He did a good job," McColgan told Carolyn. "He deserved to pass." The couple took their meals at C. J. Cannon's, the sole restaurant at the academy's airport. Lois Cappelen, a waitress at the restaurant, described them as looking "extremely happy" together.

That same month they hosted the newly created *George* awards for Corporate Philanthropy held at the Alexander Hamilton U.S. Customs House in lower Manhattan. By way of contrast, they similarly spent time with porn king Larry Flynt, a First Amendment hero of John's. "I'd met John and Carolyn two years earlier at an anniversary party for *George,*" remarked Flynt. "During that trip, I spent a whole night talking to them. We spoke mostly about magazine publishing. We also discussed politics. John seemed quite aware of his legacy and left little doubt in my mind that he eventually intended to run for the Senate. 'I'm not sure I have enough experience,' he said. 'But it's in your blood,' I told him. 'You ought to run.' They were a charming couple. I asked Carolyn if it was true that she'd been made pregnant by space aliens. She got a big laugh out of it. She had a great sense of humor. Like John, she commandeered a room when she walked in. She was the only real successor I ever met to Jacqueline Onassis."

Larry Flynt was John's guest in May 1999 at the annual White House correspondents' dinner in Washington. "That was the last time I saw him," said Flynt. "We were supposed to see each other again on July 21 of the same year. We'd agreed on a meeting in New York. But obviously it didn't turn out that way. He and Carolyn died five days earlier."

John Perry Barlow also saw John and Carolyn for the last time that May. "They invited me to a political dinner in New York," said Barlow. "John kept telling me how much I'd like hip-hop impresario Puff Daddy [Sean Combs], so he sat me next to Combs on one side and former Republican senator Alfonse D'Amato on the other. And of course he knew full well that I would hate Puff Daddy and love D'Amato. So John sat across the table and watched me interact with those two guys. And he had this growing sly smile on his face. Meanwhile, D'Amato and I were like arm in arm. We began trying to convince John to run for mayor of New York—as a Republican. And John actually seemed to be half considering it. It would have been a great joke on the world. Carolyn Bessette sat on the other side of D'Amato. I don't think she liked the idea very much. But she and I were great pals. After the dinner, the three of us went out to Odeon and hung out real late. We kept in touch by phone and e-mail, but it was the last time I saw either of them in person."

John and Carolyn attended a private dinner party thrown by one of Carolyn's fashion-world friends. Present at the same function was the well-known photographer Bruce Weber, who later told *WWD* that Carolyn was "beautiful and so natural. She looked almost like a cowgirl that you would see at the rodeo. She had the look of a cowgirl who accidentally got thrown into a dress. She had that charm and that grace. Like a horse suddenly jumping up in the air. She was iconic."

The couple went to a JFK Library function in mid-May. It was clear to journalist Laura Raposa that "something had changed. Carolyn behaved different from her usual difficult self. We have pictures of her smiling. She even tweaked John on his ass. They were being very physically playful with each other. I'd heard that they were seeing a marriage counselor. It had evidently worked."

Christa D'Souza, a reporter at London's *Daily Telegraph* and a friend of John's from Brown, had first met Carolyn at Christiane Amanpour's wedding in Italy. D'Souza would later report that toward the end, after starting marriage counseling, Carolyn made tremendous progress in her personal life and was coming around to the idea of starting a family. She questioned the prospect of raising children in New York, but was rapidly getting used to the idea. Carolyn expressed a similar feeling to Evelyn Lauder, whom she'd originally met at the Whitney Museum in late 1997. Discussing the future, Carolyn reflected on her desire "to do what was best for both of them. She was very strong on her own, but it was important to her that the time would be right for John to have a family." This was not to say that she didn't still have reservations—there were moments of trepidation when the thought of having children frightened her, a result perhaps of growing up in a broken home. But her doubts, when they did occur, were less trenchant and gnawing than they'd been in the past.

John and Carolyn spent their weekends at Hyannis Port and Martha's Vineyard, befriending actor Harrison Ford and his wife, Melissa. Like John, Ford was an amateur pilot who kept his plane on the Cape. Carolyn and Melissa frequently joked about having to take piloting lessons themselves in case their husbands should lose control of their aircraft while they were flying with them.

In mid-May John addressed the class of 1999 at Washington College in Chestertown, Maryland, telling them: "You have accomplished something the great man George Washington never did—you are college graduates. And believe it or not, he went on to do great things in politics without ever having to become a lawyer."

On May 25 JFK Jr. and Carolyn took a commercial airliner to San Francisco. That night they dined with Steve Jobs, of Apple Computer, and his wife. The following day John spoke at a luncheon meeting of the 700-member San Francisco Advertising Council. *George* needed high-tech advertisers, but selling a political magazine to tech people wasn't easy. Asked whether he intended to run for the Senate in 2000, he responded, "The big question is whether Hillary will run for the Senate and if it is unacceptable for someone born in Illinois who lived in Arkansas to run in New York . . . It's sort of as acceptable as someone who was born in Washington, D.C., coming to San Francisco to get you to buy an ad in a New York magazine."

Joined by Richard Blow and Michael Voss, *George*'s new marketing director, they flew from San Francisco to Seattle, where they met with executives from Microsoft. John hoped to convince Bill Gates to partner with *George* on a series of online "fireside" chats with prospective presidential candidates in the coming election. The chats—or interviews—would take place before live audiences at the Kennedy School of Government at Harvard. In exchange for control of the project, Microsoft would fund the events and advertise them in *George*.

Although Microsoft ultimately rejected his pitch, John had devised the idea of linking his magazine and high-tech multimedia as a way to keep *George* going. He discussed the possibility of starting a company devoted to just such an enterprise with Dan Samson. He also consulted Arnold Schwarzenegger, whose business advice he always valued. Caroline Kennedy thought it a promising venture and suggested her brother talk to her husband about it. "I'd rather commit hari-kari than discuss my plans with Edwina," John told George Plimpton.

Hari-kari is practically what John committed when he crashed his Buckeye at Martha's Vineyard over Memorial Day weekend, soon after their return from the West Coast. Rob Littell was there with his wife and two children, as were Sasha Chermayeff, her husband, and their children. Several other friends had also joined the group. "The first day," said Littell, "we swam, water-skied, biked, hiked, played touch football, and Frisbee, all the usual Kennedy activities. John expressed concern over his cousin Anthony Radziwill's terminal cancer. Radziwill and his wife were going to spend part of the summer at Red Gate Farm—no doubt, John suggested, Anthony's last summer. The situation troubled John. As Carolyn put it, 'Anthony was the brother John never had.'"

The following day John crashed his Buckeye, breaking his left ankle. He underwent surgery at Lenox Hill Hospital in New York. When patients and hospital attendants gawked at him as they wheeled him through the corridor on a gurney, Carolyn rebuked them: "What's the matter with you—you've never seen anyone with a broken ankle?"

The accident marred John's summer. He'd sold his Cessna and bought the Piper Saratoga and had eagerly anticipated flying the plane back and forth every weekend from Essex County Airport to Martha's

Vineyard. Now, instead of accumulating solo flight time, he and Carolyn were dependent on making the trip with flight instructors at the wheel. John's role was severely reduced.

"Carolyn felt terrible for John," said Suzanne Ruddick. "She realized how much he'd looked forward, now that he had his private pilot's license, to flying his own plane. Personally, I admired her courage. She had great faith in John's aviation abilities. She had no qualms about flying with him. All that posthumously published jazz about her supposed fear of flying was sheer dribble. She loved it, maybe even more than he did."

In a strange way, the Buckeye accident brought John and Carolyn even closer. "With his leg in a cast," continued Ruddick, "Carolyn used to bathe him. She bought a plastic stool, and John would sit on it in the bathtub. She wrapped his cast in vinyl so it wouldn't get wet. Then she'd spray him down with a rubber-hose shower attachment and scrub his back with a soap-lathered washcloth. It was a hot summer, so she did this twice a day—morning and evening. She spent hours talking with him about the financial problems he was having at *George*. She placed phone calls for him and went to several business meetings in his stead. She seemed very attentive to his needs. During most of June, he went to his office, but they spent their evenings at home. On weekends they flew up to Martha's Vineyard and spent time with Anthony and Carole Radziwill. It was a difficult period for John. He couldn't pilot his own plane, his cousin was dying, his magazine was in trouble. Carolyn held the household together. I asked her how (with his broken ankle) they managed their sex life. 'Very simple,' she said. 'I get on top and do all the work.'"

In mid-June Carolyn flew to London by herself to discuss *George*'s future with several Fleet Street publishers. She was in an upbeat mood. She attended a dinner party given by Ralph Lauren in his plush London townhouse. After dinner she urged her tablemates to go out and have fun. "You can be boring at home," she implored. "Let's hit the road."

During Carolyn's absence, Richard Blow and John traveled by Metroliner to D.C. on *George*-related business. As the two took the federally mandated handicapped elevator to the departure gate at Penn Station, John quipped, "Thank God for big government."

On June 18 an Empire Car Service driver took John to Essex County

Airport in Caldwell, New Jersey, where John watched while an FAA official conducted a mandatory annual safety inspection of his Saratoga. To
John's delight, the plane passed with flying colors.

A week later John met with Jeffrey D. Sachs, a Democratic Party political adviser, to discuss the possibility of entering the "field of his calling." Sachs opined that if Hillary entered the senatorial race in New
York, her "name recognition" would afford her a huge advantage. Of
course, John also possessed vast name recognition, though more as a personality than a political operative. Sachs suggested John delay making
any final decision. In early July JFK Jr. went to a small party at David
Kuhn's house in the West Village, wearing a pair of lemony pants that
had belonged to his father and which he'd had retailored. Carolyn met a
friend for drinks that evening and decided not to go. "I remember the occasion very well," said Kuhn. "It wasn't a formal dinner or anything, just
a few old friends getting together at my place. Sasha Chermayeff brought
along Jenny Christian, John's girlfriend from Andover. It was a lovely and
warm and relaxed gathering, almost nostalgic in a way. John and Jenny
hadn't seen one another in quite some time. Jenny lived in North Carolina and didn't come to New York very often. She and John had been in
touch now and then over the years. They had a special bond. Jenny was
an incredibly smart, funny, vivacious woman, and I think John really respected and appreciated her lack of pretense, her integrity, and her free
spirit. That night John talked a bit about his ongoing efforts to save
George. He ventured that perhaps he'd been too easygoing with Hachette.
He complained about all the tedious meals he'd endured with potential
advertisers—and in the end their ads ran not in *George* but in other Hachette publications. He felt Hachette had used him."

John's mood on that evening, according to Kuhn, was "pensive,
slightly distracted, but cordial and amusing, as he almost always was in
the company of a small group of friends. He seemed particularly pleased
to see Jenny."

At the same gathering JFK Jr. again condemned Hillary Clinton not
only for organizing a political campaign in New York but for promising
to do an interview with *George,* then rescinding her offer and instead

doing the interview for the first issue of Tina Brown's ill-fated *Talk* magazine.

Primarily, John seemed concerned with Anthony Radziwill's illness. He had begun writing his cousin's eulogy and was consumed with capturing his essence in only a few pages. "How do you summarize somebody's life," he asked, "in five hundred words?"

In the last days of his own life, John was preoccupied with several issues. Besides Anthony Radziwill, there was the interminable question of what to do about *George.* He told a friend that he didn't want to let down his employees—if the magazine folded, a lot of people would be out of work. He was determined to solve the problem either by working it out with Hachette or finding another publisher to take Hachette's place. On July 11, flying back from a meeting with prospective investors in Toronto, he misplaced his American Express card. It was the third time that year he'd lost it. He blamed the loss of the card on stress.

Efigenio Pinheiro, having spent part of the summer at Red Gate Farm helping to look after Anthony and Carole Radziwill, returned to New York on July 12 and brought with him *The Philosophers in 90 Minutes,* a fifteen-book set by Paul Strathern, which John and Carolyn had received as a wedding present from Rob Littell. While never before particularly enthused by the subject of philosophy, JFK Jr. had read and reread the collection. He wanted the books with him in the city. "One of John's favorite philosophical ideas," said Littell, "was that people spend most of their lives trying to get to a 'promised land,' when in fact we're already there."

John admitted to Richard Blow that he'd been thinking about death a lot lately. Anthony Radziwill's condition had been weighing on him. Carolyn told *George*'s Gary Ginsberg that John could handle Anthony's approaching death.

When Donald Trump's father passed away at that time, JFK Jr. wrote him a letter. "In the letter," said Trump, "he talked about the relationship between fathers and sons and how difficult it is to lose a parent. I was touched. He had such a gracious way about him, the knack for knowing what to say in a difficult situation. It was the last thing I read as I went out the door on a business trip. And then a few days later I heard about John's plane going down. It made his letter all the more meaningful."

He would send John Perry Barlow a similar communication, expressing sorrow over the death of Barlow's mother. "It was as if he sensed something," said Suzanne Ruddick. "Perhaps he had a premonition of something he couldn't otherwise explain. He was a risk addict, so death was never a very distant entity."

On July 14, two days before JFK Jr.'s fatal flight, Richard Blow overheard a loud telephone altercation between John and Carolyn. "The wall separating our offices at *George* was thin, but not *that* thin," wrote Blow. "In startling, staccato bursts of rage, John was yelling. His yells would be followed by silences, then John's fury would resume. At first I couldn't make out the words. Then, after a particularly long pause, I heard John shout, 'Well, goddammit, Carolyn, you're the reason I was up at three o'clock last night!'"

JFK Jr. spent the next two nights at the Stanhope Hotel wrestling with profit-and-loss statements in preparation for a July 16 meeting with Jack Kliger, Hachette's new CEO, after which he, Carolyn, and Lauren Bessette planned on flying to Martha's Vineyard and then on to Hyannis for Rory Kennedy's wedding. According to Sasha Chermayeff, John was tired of Carolyn "coming at him, telling him endlessly about their problems." But in reality, John and Carolyn had gotten past the brunt of their problems. His self-imposed retreat had more to do with a desire to work unencumbered on his prospective plans for *George*. He needed a moment of peace. Then, too, he wanted to be near Lenox Hill Hospital, where his orthopedist would remove his CAM Walker and grant him final clearance to begin using his broken ankle. In addition, Carolyn and Lauren were spending both nights together discussing their own plans to approach William Bessette. They wanted to begin to heal their long-fractured relationship with their father.

On July 16 Richard Blow noticed that John seemed tired as they arrived for lunch at Trionfo, located in the same building as *George*'s offices. It was just the two of them. Relieved to be free from the trappings that had anchored his left leg for the past six weeks, John was nevertheless in pain. When he told Blow he was flying to the Cape later that day for

Rory's wedding, the editor glanced down at John's leg and gave him a skeptical look. "Don't worry," said John, "I'm flying with an instructor."

"Just don't crash, okay?" responded Blow. "Because if you do, that speech about all of us having jobs at Christmas goes right out the window."

John had informed nearly everyone, including members of his family, that he would be bringing along an instructor on the flight to Martha's Vineyard. His orthopedist, in fact, had pointedly instructed him *not* to fly by himself for at least two weeks. But neither the doctor's warning nor the cautionary utterances of friends would deter him from embarking on his latest (and last) high-risk venture. John had made up his mind. He would pilot his own plane. Nothing could change that.

The meeting with Kliger that afternoon went better than expected. John emerged with Kliger's reassurance that though certain changes would be made, Hachette intended to finance the magazine for at least another year.

Alone in his office on a late Friday afternoon waiting to meet up with Carolyn and Lauren Bessette for their flight aboard the Saratoga, John F. Kennedy Jr. tied up some loose odds and ends. He made telephone calls, shuffled papers, and checked his schedule for Monday morning. He then took out a pad with some writing on it. It was his still-in-progress eulogy for Anthony Radziwill. These days he carried it with him wherever he went, but on this day he would leave it behind in his desk. It was merely a draft. John spent his spare time editing and refining it. The draft he left behind began: "A true gentleman, he was humble, decent, charming, and down to earth. He had humor, intelligence, and a heart as big as an ocean. You couldn't help but love him." He ended the draft with the words: "Good night, sweet prince."

Part VII

———————◆———————

Chapter 22

KEEPER OF THE FLAME

On July 17, 1999, a day after the disappearance at sea of John Kennedy Jr.'s aircraft, Anthony Radziwill told the press, "If he's out there somewhere, hanging on to a sinking plane, he'll find a way to get out. He possesses the will to survive, enough will for all three of them."

On July 21 divers located the wreckage of the Saratoga. Near the twisted, broken fuselage, they found the bodies of Carolyn and Lauren Bessette. John's body was discovered still trapped in the pilot's seat. He was thirty-eight at the time of his death. The paradox of the tragedy was that now, America and Americans would never know him in his middle years, would never learn to what extent he would (or could) have fulfilled the promise of his heritage. In his own fashion, he had figured it all out. It had taken him a long time to find a way both to be a Kennedy, to live up to society's expectations of him, but also to forge an identity distinctly his own.

John Jr.'s last will and testament, signed on December 19, 1997, stipulated that his personal belongings, property, and holdings were to be evenly distributed among Caroline Kennedy's three children. As in his mother's case, he also made bequests to relatives, friends, longtime family employees, and charities. There were fourteen beneficiaries in the will, including Kennedy's two godchildren (the son and daughter of Sasha

Chermayeff); family retainers Marta Sgubin and Efigenio Pinheiro; Rose-Marie Terenzio (his personal assistant at *George*); Peter Olsen, his attorney; Robert F. Kennedy Jr.; and Rob Littell. He left funds to two nonprofits, Reaching Up and the John F. Kennedy Library Foundation in Boston. The only specific item mentioned in the will was "a scrimshaw set previously owned by my father," which he left to his nephew, Jack Kennedy Schlossberg. Tim Shriver had been named executor of JFK Jr.'s estate, estimated to be worth between $100 million and $200 million. His first choice for executor had been Anthony Radziwill, but Anthony died of cancer on August 10, 1999.

Had Carolyn Bessette Kennedy survived her husband, in addition to funds set forth in their prenuptial agreement, she would have received his "personal effects" and the loft on North Moore Street in TriBeCa, which in the days following their death became a living memorial laden with flowers, photographs, signs, relics, rosary beads, handwritten prayers, candles, and works of art. "It seemed," said one visitor, "that half of New York flocked by that building to pay their last respects." Caroline Kennedy eventually sold the loft to actor Ed Burns for an estimated $2.1 million.

Friday, John's dog, wound up with Efigenio Pinheiro. Soon after JFK Jr.'s death, Pinheiro retired to Portugal and took the dog with him. Ruby, Carolyn's cat, was first taken by Marta Sgubin and then given to Santina Goodman, John's friend, with whom Ruby still resides today.

John Jr.'s interests in *George* were taken over by his sister. Never particularly enthused by the magazine, she released her share (for an undisclosed sum) to Hachette Filipacchi. With Richard Blow at the helm, Hachette kept the struggling publication in print through March 2001, dedicating its farewell issue to its founder.

The deaths of her daughters—thirty-three-year-old Carolyn and thirty-four-year-old Lauren Bessette—changed Ann Freeman's life forever. Caught by television cameras, she looked forlorn clearing out the contents of her daughters' apartments, later selling Lauren's White Street residence for $1.7 million. In the fall of 1999 William Smith College (in Geneva, New York), which Lauren attended as an undergraduate, commemorated the student by establishing a scholarship fund in her honor.

As the executor of both estates, Ann filed preliminary papers pursuant to a personal injury and wrongful death lawsuit against the estate of John F. Kennedy Jr. The suit was bolstered and supported by the National Transportation Safety Board's findings that the Piper Saratoga had performed flawlessly and was in perfect working condition up to the point of the crash. Its report attributed the cause of the accident solely to "pilot error."

Caroline Kennedy represented her brother's estate in the Freeman lawsuit. John had carried a maximum flight liability of $5 million for bodily injury and property damage, subject to a limit of $1 million per passenger, hardly sufficient considering the egregious nature of Ann Freeman's loss. Had it been litigated, the case could well have exposed John as not only extraordinarily reckless but also as having possibly been semi-inebriated at the time of the fatal crash. To protect her brother's reputation, Caroline settled the matter out of court. On July 30, 2001, ten days prior to an initial hearing, Caroline agreed to pay Ann Freeman $15 million in full consideration of her claims over the July 16, 1999, accident.

The outcome of the case hardly assuaged the grieving mother. Moving with her husband into an exclusive oceanside community in Greenwich, Ann became a virtual recluse. Once active in a charity called Kids in Crisis, she soon cut off from the group and only rarely socialized with friends. Lisa Bessette, the sole surviving sister, moved to Europe with her husband. Carolyn and Lauren's grandmother Jenny Messina died in Florida in 2003. No member of the Bessette, Freeman, or Messina families ever granted an interview or issued a telling public statement, not even following the publication of books like *The Other Man* or *The Kennedy Curse,* which depicted Carolyn as a caricature and in the most uncomplimentary vein.

"Jackie Onassis was lucky," said a friend of Ann Freeman. "She was already dead when the accident occurred. Ann has to live with her loss for the rest of her life. No amount of money can change that. She's extremely bitter. It's safe to say that she harbors great resentment against the Kennedys, particularly John Jr."

William Bessette, the birth father of the Bessette girls, while not party to his former wife's lawsuit, likewise grieved and was similarly bitter over the loss of his two daughters. When journalist Maureen Seaberg attempted to interview him in his White Plains cabinet shop in 2003, he practically threw her out on the street. "He stiffened the minute I mentioned Carolyn by name," said Seaberg. "Tears came to his eyes. He told me to get out. Frankly, I couldn't blame him."

"After her brother died, Caroline tried to refrain from crying in front of her children," said Bettina Lowell, a friend of the family. Maura Moynihan recalled how difficult the first year had been for John's sister. "Caroline was carrying a great emotional burden that needed time to heal," she said. "She was in mourning, but she had to be there for the kids and help them through this. Caroline had endured so much already—the assassinations of her father and uncle, the deaths of her cousins, Jackie's death. And now she had to deal with her brother's tragic end."

With her brother's death, Caroline had suddenly become the keeper of the flame, the sole surviving member of the John F. Kennedy branch of the family. It was a position that didn't altogether fit her personality. Yet the feeling among family and friends was that she would slowly grow into the role. Bandleader Peter Duchin described her as "very together and very much in control of herself. She hadn't always been that way. After her father's assassination in 1963, she crawled into a cocoon and remained there for much of her childhood. But she had long since emerged. She became a well-balanced and psychologically secure woman. She has a great reserve of strength, which she evidently inherited from her mother. She became an inspiration for everyone around her. She was bereaved, but she did her mourning in private. She was first and foremost a mother and a wife."

If Caroline provided her children with the strength to overcome their uncle John's untimely death, it was Uncle Teddy who helped Caroline. She called him "the Pied Piper," and in mid-November 1999, at a fundraiser for Ted, she told a *New York Times* reporter, "Without Teddy, I don't think I could have made it through the past few months." Liz Derringer, a public relations specialist, recalled Teddy telling some "sizzling political stories. He was very entertaining. He was also very devoted to

Caroline. He kept going over and checking on her. As for myself, I spoke only briefly with her that day. I offered her my condolences over John's death. I told her I'd seen him at a benefit aboard the *Intrepid* two weeks before he died. She thanked me but didn't say much."

The Schlossbergs spent a good deal of time in their house at Sagaponack. In the wake of her brother's death, Caroline often took her children to the Holy Rosary Church in nearby Bridgehampton. She celebrated her forty-second birthday in late November 1999 at a small family party; her birthday cake had but one candle on top. One weekend she drove her children to Maryland and joined the family of Kathleen Kennedy, lieutenant governor of the state, on a tour of Civil War sites. Another weekend she went horseback riding with her children in Middleburg, Virginia, her mother's former haunt. Like John Jr., Jack Schlossberg was allergic to horses.

Caroline kept her public appearances to a minimum. She attended the twentieth anniversary of the JFK Library in Boston, where guest speaker Colin Powell referred to John Jr. by saying, "I feel his presence here tonight—he dedicated himself to the proposition that we owe so much to our country. Let us keep that legacy alive." On December 7, 1999, she took her brother's place at a benefit for the Robin Hood Foundation at Tavern on the Green. "John worked very hard for this foundation," she told the gathering, "but as much as he gave, I know he received even more in return." She ended her talk with the words: "He was determined to set his own course and live his own life, and I think this is one of the qualities that people most admired about him."

By the year 2000, Caroline began to emerge from her shell. Having sold her mother's weekend retreat in New Jersey for well over $1 million, she invested a small portion of the proceeds in a new speedboat. On March 2 she attended a reception at Cipriani on 5th Avenue for Mike Nichols. According to a guest at the same affair, "Caroline ate like a horse! She practically closed the place down without missing a bite." In early May she and Tipper Gore, the wife of Vice President Al Gore, attended the opening of the American Ballet Theatre at the Metropolitan Opera House in New York. At a postballet dinner party, she sat next to society columnist Aileen Mehle, better known as "Suzy." With a wry smile, Caroline said to Suzy, "Next to mine, which is the most beautiful dress in the room?"

The keeper of the flame presided over a two-day Ernest Hemingway conference in the Hemingway Room at the JFK Library. Angela Hemingway, Ernest's daughter-in-law, found her "bright and eloquent. I'd met John Jr. and Carolyn Bessette in early 1999. John was more outgoing than his sister, but he lacked her depth and sensitivity."

One of Caroline's most touching gestures in memory of her brother occurred at that year's Profile in Courage awards ceremony at the JFK Library, which in the past John had always attended with his sister. Both sat on an eleven-member board that chose recipients of the award. An empty seat between Caroline and her uncle Ted Kennedy served to symbolize JFK Jr.'s absence.

Aware that John Jr.'s death marked a halt to the Kennedy family's hopes of one day regaining the political power base it once possessed, Uncle Ted presently sought to cast Caroline in the role he had previously mapped out for her brother. In August Caroline, Bobby Jr., and Kathleen Kennedy accompanied Ted to the Democratic National Convention in Los Angeles, the same city where the Kennedy dynasty had started forty years earlier. Introducing her uncle at the convention, Caroline paraphrased her father's inaugural "ask not" summons to sacrifice. Her rendition took account of America's prosperity under the Clinton administration. "Now, when many of us are doing so well, it is time once again to ask more of ourselves," she said.

Although she may have lacked her brother's outward confidence and charisma, Caroline spoke with a refreshing directness and candor. Asked if she envisioned a future for herself in politics, she replied, "I'm not sure my personality is well suited for a political career. I'll have to see how it goes before I make any decisions."

Back in New York, she attended fund-raisers for Gore, first at Radio City Music Hall and then at Elaine's. With her husband and children, she spent Thanksgiving that year at Ted Kennedy's home in Hyannis Port. The Schlossbergs next went to Martha's Vineyard, where they were in the process of spending $1.5 million to renovate Red Gate Farm. They built an outdoor swimming pool and razed the silo that had served as John Jr.'s bachelor quarters. Inside the main house, they tore down walls and enlarged the size of certain rooms. They completely redid the kitchen. They opened up some areas of the house and closed others. One of the workmen on the job pitched pennies with Caroline and her children during his lunch break. Maurice Tempelsman, visiting friends on the island, passed by the house. According to the workman, he didn't look altogether pleased that the Schlossbergs were changing things around.

In early 2001 *New York* magazine ran a piece on Ed Schlossberg ("The Family Man"), detailing his newest and most ambitious project to date, the American Family Immigration History Center at Ellis Island, an interactive-media display of forty-one computer stations and a website. Linked to an extensive database of more than twenty-two million people who passed through the island from 1892 to 1924, the website traced the history and lineage of each and every Ellis Island immigrant.

Ever the workaholic, Schlossberg had several projects going at once. He had recently completed work on a series of displays for the Pope John Paul II Cultural Center in Washington, D.C. He was currently developing an interactive display for the Children's Museum of Los Angeles, and a permanent exhibit called "Unwavering Spirit" for St. Paul's Chapel across the street from where the World Trade Center had once stood. A monument to the 9/11 rescue workers, the exhibit was subtitled "Hope and Healing at Ground Zero." His other work-in-progress was a $20 million, 7,000-square-foot, video-screen billboard for the Times Square offices of the Reuters news agency. Ed's "design dream" was to build an "immense game area in the middle of Times Square" where hundreds of people playing together would engage not only with the game but with one another.

"I never set out to be a designer," Schlossberg told the magazine. "What I was doing was thinking. Suddenly people began to pay for my thoughts."

For all the media attention, Schlossberg's image remained essentially that of the "mystery man" fortunate enough to have nabbed the only daughter of Jack and Jacqueline Kennedy. By no small coincidence, people began paying him for his "thoughts" starting in 1986, the year he and Caroline married. They evidently paid well. According to Dun & Bradstreet, ESI Design had thirty-six employees and did $2 million in sales in 2001. Other business reports listed the corporation as having fifty employees and doing $6 million in sales. Schlossberg was also about to move his offices from 641 Sixth Avenue to the 19,000-square-foot top floor of 111 Fifth Avenue, a classic nineteenth-century building in the Gramercy Park area.

Following the appearance of the *New York* magazine profile, Schlossberg submitted himself to a Q & A with *New York Times* reporter Robin Finn. Commenting on an interactive website he'd recently designed for the Chicago Symphony Orchestra, he conceded that the only musical instrument he played was "the stereo." The remainder of the interview amounted to little more than an exercise in pulling teeth:

"How did you end up designing museum exhibits?"

"I don't know."

"Is there any ambivalence on your part about being married into the Kennedy family?"

"Nope."

"Do you consider yourself a lucky man?"

"Yep."

"Is your work—and maybe your life—all about making improbable connections?"

"Exactly."

Obviously a man of few words, Ed Schlossberg had even less to say than usual when the tabloids ran a series on Caroline's supposedly failing health—how her arthritic hands required repeated shots of cortisone; how she'd nearly keeled over after shedding some twenty unwanted pounds and going from a size 12 to an 8, despite the fact that she regularly shopped for rich desserts in the back room at La Maison du Chocolat. When asked about his wife and children by a Page Six reporter, Schlossberg responded, "They're off limits. My lips are sealed."

In 2001 Caroline published *The Best-Loved Poems of Jacqueline Kennedy Onassis,* replete with a cover photo of the former First Lady reading to her then three-year-old daughter. Capitalizing on her mother's name (the one thing Jackie didn't want her children to do), Caroline produced an anthology crammed with lyrics by Edna St. Vincent Millay, Emily Dickinson, Robert Louis Stevenson, Robert Frost, Homer, Shakespeare, and other immortals. The volume, which became an instant *New York Times* bestseller, contained a scattering of Caroline's notations, among them: "Both my parents loved reading Shakespeare."

In 2002 Caroline again used her family name in a second anthology, *Profiles in Courage for Our Time,* a collection of essays on select winners of the Kennedy clan's Profile in Courage award. Predictably, the volume included articles by such journalists as Bob Woodward, Pete Hamill, and Anna Quindlen.

Hyperion (owned by the Walt Disney Company), the publisher of both volumes, launched the *Profiles in Courage* project by throwing a book party on the second floor of Tiffany & Co. on Fifth Avenue. Invoking yet another family name, Caroline informed the press that she and her late brother had planned on putting out the latter anthology together. In his absence, she had taken the initiative. The same jewelry store was the setting for an award ceremony at which a new line of Tiffany Mark watches was presented to each of five individuals for their "charitable work and community service." The winners included Bette Midler, Candace Bushnell, and Ed Schlossberg. In his acceptance speech, Schlossberg said: "I don't wear a watch, but I will now. I thought it was an interesting social thing to ask someone what time it is." Bette Midler stole Schlossberg's thunder by slipping the new watch onto her wrist and then quipping, "It's about time, darling!"

Perhaps the most blatant example of Caroline's exploitation of her mother's name and reputation occurred when she (and the Kennedy Foundation) sanctioned the licensing of Jackie's valuable jewelry collection to Camrose and Kross, a New Jersey corporation that later sold inexpensive replicas of the originals on QVC, a cable television home-shopping network. The so-called Jacqueline Kennedy Collection consisted of inexpensive reproductions of some forty items, including rings, bracelets, necklaces, earrings, and pins. Instead of diamonds, rubies, pearls, and emeralds, the manufacturer substituted materials of lesser quality. No single item sold for more than $100, allowing every woman in America to become a Jacqueline Kennedy ready-made clone.

Despite Caroline's commercial reliance on Kennedy family ties, she took exception to anyone else's contributions to the Camelot-crazed marketplace. She became enraged when the Turner Broadcasting System (TBS) announced its intention to air a two-hour biopic, *America's Prince,* based on John Jr.'s life. The Fox network followed with its own JFK Jr. television biography, angering her further. It bothered her to learn that a former Kennedy retainer was auctioning off swatches of JFK Jr.'s baby blanket on eBay. Ditto the sale of a toy rifle John had received as a third-birthday present, but which Jackie had kept from him because of President Kennedy's assassination. Richard Blow suspected that Caroline played a more direct role in attempting to halt the 2002 emergence of his unauthorized memoir, *American Son: A Portrait of John F. Kennedy, Jr.,* originally slated for publication by Little, Brown and Company. Although Blow lacked tangible proof that Caroline tried to keep his book from being published, he believed she "exerted influence in subtle ways." In the end, the book was canceled. William Morris, Blow's literary agency, resold the book rights to Henry Holt and Company. Caroline's opposition to the memoir only aided its climb up the bestseller list.

For better or worse, Caroline also appears to have been involved in some behind-the-scenes manipulations with respect to Ed Klein's *The Kennedy Curse,* which had been sold to Hyperion. It came as no surprise to publishing insiders when at the last minute Hyperion, having in the interim become Caroline's publisher, canceled its contract with Klein, forcing him to take the book to St. Martin's Press.

Whatever the extent of her sub-rosa efforts to protect the reputation of her dead brother, Caroline Kennedy Schlossberg remained a popular and sympathetic public figure. Her popularity rose even further when news broke in mid-2002 that still another stalker had been arrested for harassing Caroline. Sidney Waite, thirty-nine, a former mental patient from Richmond, British Columbia, had bombarded Caroline with some forty packages and letters over a ten-year period. Claiming that he was a "long lost" Kennedy relative, he repeatedly requested sums of money from Caroline. He'd written to Ted Kennedy as well. When he turned up in the lobby of 888 Park Avenue, Ed and Caroline's apartment building, the doorman called the police, and he was apprehended. Criminal Court

Judge William Harrington ordered Waite, who pleaded guilty to aggravated harassment, to return to Canada and issued a three-year order of protection, prohibiting the stalker from approaching Caroline or any other member of her immediate family.

The incident, coupled with others of a similar nature, added to Caroline's ongoing obsession with privacy. Alexander Denisow, a young university student from Germany and a collector of Kennedy memorabilia, visited the United States in the fall of 2002 with the hope of meeting Caroline. "I read in the newspaper that she was doing a book signing at the JFK Library," recalled Denisow. "This was shortly after a ceremony at the library to commemorate the fortieth anniversary of the Cuban Missile Crisis and the completion of the Nuclear Test Ban Treaty. She and Sergei Khrushchev, son of the late Russian premier, had given a joint presentation, dedicating new papers and documents to the library. I showed up for the signing event. I had all four of Caroline's books. I wanted to have my picture taken with her, so I brought along a camera. I stood near the end of the line. When I finally reached her table, she signed the books. I asked if we could have a picture together. She told me to step into an adjacent room until she was done. I waited, but she never appeared. When I went to look for her, they told me she'd left."

The year ended on a sour note. Bobby Kennedy Jr. attempted to initiate an intervention to get Ted Kennedy to commit himself to an alcohol rehabilitation program. A wealthy family friend offered to pay off a $2.1 million campaign debt for Ted, provided that he sign into a rehab facility. The senator turned down both offers.

On December 11, 2002, readers of the New York *Daily News* opened their newspaper to a story that all but announced the termination of the Ed Schlossberg–Caroline Kennedy marriage. "Ed Schlossberg and Caroline Divorce Rumor" read the bold headline. The article had it that Schlossberg—"the man who wasn't there"—hadn't accompanied his wife and children to Hyannis Port that November to celebrate Thanksgiving with the rest of the Kennedy clan. Nor had he been with Caroline at any of the more recent colloquiums or meetings she'd attended at the JFK Library. The paper illogically—but sensationally—concluded that the relationship was therefore at an end. It had the familiar ring of the reportage that had forever dogged John Jr. and Carolyn Bessette. Although the Schlossberg rumor proved false, its appearance upset Caroline because it was accessible to her children and her children's schoolmates. In truth, the Schlossberg marriage remained constant and strong.

In late 2002–early 2003, New York City Schools Chancellor Joel Klein, a personal friend of Caroline's, asked her to serve as chief fund-raiser for the New York City Department of Education. The specific title of her position was chief executive, Department of Education—Office of Strategic Partnerships. Working out of a third-floor cubicle at the Tweed Courthouse, 52 Chambers Street, the Department of Education's new headquarters in Manhattan, Caroline received the inglorious salary of $1 a year for her services. The only condition attached to her post was that, unlike every other New York City employee (including the mayor), she would not have to divulge or reveal any of her personal financial records or income tax returns. It was a unique arrangement and one that angered a number of city government leaders and employees. When Joanna Molloy of the *Daily News* asked Caroline's staff if she could photograph Caroline receiving her annual check for $1, she was summarily turned down.

Klein, a political appointee of Mayor Michael Bloomberg with no discernible background or experience in teaching or school administration, defended his selection of Caroline on the basis of her vast network of contacts and connections in every field and at every level. The school system, with a $15 billion budget and 1.1 million students, received over $100 million a year in donations. Klein felt Caroline "would be able to increase this amount substantially."

Caroline's first fund-raising venture—"the Penny Harvest"—involved the collection of loose change from students, parents, and assorted members of the community. "It was a virtual joke," said a high-ranking city official. "It raised almost nothing. In fact, it wasn't even an original concept. Penny harvests—or crusades—had been going on in the public school system since the 1950s and were usually conducted by young schoolchildren. The fallacy of the program is that students and teachers don't have much spare change. A large percentage of New York City schoolchildren live in the projects and don't have lunch money. Caroline's kids went to Brearley and Collegiate. She had no experience working in the public school system and had no idea of the degree of poverty that exists among inner-city families."

A fast learner, Caroline quickly enlisted the help of other high-profile individuals. She convinced Sarah Jessica Parker, one of her brother's ex-girlfriends, to help run a "tag sale" in Central Park with merchandise donated by New York stores and corporations. AOL sponsored a Dave Matthews Band performance in Central Park that raised more than $2 million for a music education program in the schools. Caroline got Sean "Puffy" Combs to donate $2 million to a separate school-sponsored program. Bill Gates allocated $51.2 million in grants to create sixty-seven small theme-based public high schools in New York. Caroline turned to Wall Street and private industry. Merrill Lynch gave $1 million, as did Verizon. *Reader's Digest* pledged $15 million, and Time Warner gave $5 million. "It's difficult to turn down Caroline Kennedy when she asks you for money," said one major contributor. She conceived a novel program called "Adopt a School" in which individual corporate enterprises donated funds and other resources to a school of their own choosing. Still another concept involved the hiring of New York City public high school students as trainees and interns by various media groups, including city-based radio and television stations. She raised a total of $156 million during her first year on the job, and far more in subsequent years.

Louis Liciardi, a public school art teacher, organized a show of student artwork in the Tweed building. "When Caroline saw the work," he said, "she seemed truly impressed. I had the feeling she meant it. She wasn't just spewing verbiage. She was hands-on. She came around to art classes and helped raise private funds for the program. Afterward she sent me a personal letter expressing her gratitude for revealing the value of the program to her. There are so many people at the Board of Education who don't really care. It's just a job for them. Caroline Kennedy did care. She worked hard to raise funds, and she inspired others in the system to do the same."

On Memorial Day 2003, Hyperion published Caroline's latest written work, *A Patriot's Handbook,* 663 pages of songs, poems, stories, and speeches by Americans, from colonial days to the present. Caroline credited her daughter Tatiana with providing the anthology's title. Intended as a kind of literary response to the war in Iraq, the tome included selections from such personages as Mark Twain, Woody Guthrie, William Faulkner, Martin Luther King Jr., Robert Frost, and the inevitable inaugural address by John F. Kennedy. Although it appeared on the *New York Times* bestseller list, it received decidedly mixed reviews. In short, the volume, for all its heft (and perhaps because of it), did little to elucidate or give shape to those qualities that defined the American character and spirit.

Regardless of her seeming lack of prowess as an anthologist, Caroline remained the best and brightest of her generation of Kennedy offspring. When Kerry Kennedy, the wife of Andrew Cuomo, former secretary of the U.S. Department of Housing and Urban Development (HUD), and the son of Mario Cuomo, former governor of New York, splashed onto the front page of tabloids because of her affair with a married polo player, the family turned to Caroline for advice. Caroline's jocular recommendation to Kerry: "Get a divorce; it will legitimize the affair."

On November 22 Caroline and Ted Kennedy went to Arlington National Cemetery to mark the fortieth anniversary of JFK's death. In December she and First Lady Laura Bush discussed public school education on NBC-TV's *Meet the Press*. During the same month, Caroline appeared on CBS-TV as hostess of the Kennedy Center's annual awards ceremony for excellence in the performing arts. Looking stiff and uncomfortable, she nervously read her opening remarks and rigidly smiled as the center honored Loretta Lynn, Carol Burnett, James Brown, Mike Nichols, and Itzhak Perlman. She played the role of hostess with greater confidence in future years. Caroline didn't object to being in the public eye, so long as she controlled the circumstances.

Despite her sporadic flirtations with the media, primarily when publicizing a book or appearing on behalf of a Kennedy-related project, Caroline remained essentially a private citizen. If John Kennedy Jr. was a one-man publicity magnet, if he good-naturedly parried with the press and accepted the lunatic excesses of public adulation and even, at times, enjoyed the attention, his sister preferred a quieter (and saner) existence. If anything, the death of her brother made her quest for privacy tougher.

As the sole survivor of the Camelot mystique, she became the focus of a nation consumed with the passing of the torch.

The press sought out and found Caroline at intermittent events throughout 2004. Along with Bette Midler, Barbara Walters, and Katie Couric, she attended a public school fund-raiser at the Rainbow Room. Mayor Bloomberg invited her to an educational symposium at Gracie Mansion. She appeared at a benefit for the NAACP Legal Defense and Education Fund, for which she served on the board of directors. She was seen at a Waldorf-Astoria benefit for Carnegie Hall. She joined Eunice and Maria Shriver at an affair for the Special Olympics. Maria and her mother were among those in the family that encouraged the press-shy daughter of the late president to run for political office. But it was Arnold Schwarzenegger, Maria's husband, and not Caroline who ran for office, winning the race for governor of California. Caroline provided Schwarzenegger with much-needed advice on statewide educational policy. When Schwarzenegger's political opponents leaked tidbits of his past marital indiscretions, Caroline counseled her cousin not to comment publicly.

The press made much of the fact that style-wise Caroline was no Jackie Kennedy or Carolyn Bessette. *WWD* pointed out that she'd "been spotted wearing the same pantsuit three times in two weeks." She wore the black two-piece suit trimmed with silver beads to the Rita Hayworth Gala (for Alzheimer's disease) and the next night donned the same outfit for the opening of business executive Steve Roth's One Beacon Court, where the Municipal Art Society honored MOMA Chairwoman Emeritus Agnes Gund. She had it on once more at a Yo-Yo Ma concert at Lincoln Center. "The whole town is talking about it," snipped one Upper East Side dowager. "Let them talk," responded Caroline.

She remained a strong and active supporter of Democratic Party politics, attending the opening in Little Rock, Arkansas, of the William J. Clinton Presidential Library and Museum. She joined the Commission on Presidential Debates and appeared with numerous other Kennedys at the Democratic National Convention in Boston in the summer of 2004. In the fall she campaigned for Senator John Kerry in New York and Wisconsin. When President George W. Bush invoked the name and words of her father, John F. Kennedy, in his campaign speeches, she attacked him.

"It's hard for me to listen to President Bush invoking my father's memory to attack John Kerry," she said. "My father inspired and united the country, and so will John Kerry. President Bush is doing just the opposite."

In late 2004 she mysteriously left her post at the Department of Education, but soon returned and resumed her activities with renewed gusto.

Besides the inevitable *National Enquirer* stories—all apocryphal— "revealing" that JFK Jr. had sired a "love child" while visiting Italy in 1997, Caroline had to deal with a new indignity, the emergence of a video game (on November 22, 2004), the object of which was to "assassinate" President Kennedy with three shots in a limited amount of time. "People never cease to amaze me," Caroline told a friend. "You have to be demonic to manufacture a game of that sort, and even more demonic to buy it."

The Schlossbergs celebrated New Year's at Sun Valley, attending an ice-skating party hosted by former Los Angeles mayor Richard Riordan. Others at the gathering included Arnold Schwarzenegger; Maria Shriver; Senator John Kerry; his wife, Teresa Heinz; Clint Eastwood; Tom Hanks; and astronaut Buzz Aldrin. Sharon Tibbs, a cocktail waitress at the get-together, recalled "somebody coming up to Caroline Kennedy and telling her that Michael Moore, the documentary filmmaker, had said he hoped she would consider running for president in 2008."

It was at the party that Maria Shriver, currently California's First Lady, approached Ed Schlossberg to discuss the possibility of his being involved in the creation of a California Women's History Museum. When word spread that she had commissioned him to head the design of the project without taking competitive bids, the press accused her of nepotism. It would not have been the first time for Schlossberg, many of whose assignments had come about because of his marriage to Caroline Kennedy. Unwilling to sully her husband's reputation as governor, Maria insisted she'd never hired Schlossberg. "He didn't receive a penny," she told the *Los Angeles Times*. "I only asked him to come out to Sacramento and have a look around."

• • •

The new year—2005—brought with it a new slew of rumors, including the usual whispers of an impending Schlossberg divorce. When reporters spotted Caroline Kennedy eating lunch with Maria Shriver and Jann Wenner at Michael's, they somehow assumed that the three were plotting Caroline's dissolution of her marriage. When Caroline went to Park Slope in Brooklyn to visit Rory Kennedy, the press concluded that she wanted to buy a brownstone and move out of Manhattan. When the Schlossberg residence at Sagaponack went on the auction block, the tabloids began to buzz. When Kevin Mancuso, Caroline's latest hairstylist, gave her a new look, lightening her hair color a shade or two, the press decided that she had a secret lover.

"I don't get it," said Maura Moynihan. "Ed and Caroline aren't glued together, but it's a wonderful match—and always has been."

Rose, Tatiana, and Jack Schlossberg remained the focus of their conjoined lives. Roberta Fineberg, the mother of a young teenage boy who played in the same baseball and basketball league as Jack Schlossberg, frequently encountered the couple at games. "It's an afterschool and weekend program for public- and private-school kids in Manhattan," said Fineberg. "My son's the same age as theirs, so they played together but on opposing teams. Ed and Caroline would cheer for Jack from the sidelines. I remember seeing them at the championship basketball game at a public school gym on West 70th Street. They were informally dressed. Caroline wore a powder blue denim jacket and jeans. Ed also wore jeans. Rose and Tatiana were with them. Jack played forward for his team. Caroline was the official team photographer and took pictures she later sent home to each child. Ed Schlossberg was assistant coach. He was subdued but friendly and looked like a typical middle-aged father, with strong facial features, a slight paunch, and gray-white hair. Caroline looked thin and had good bones. After the game, Caroline left with her daughters, but Ed joined his son at the postgame pizza party in the school cafeteria."

Fineberg saw the couple at league baseball games as well, which for the most part were played early mornings in Central Park. "The kids rotated positions," she continued. "Jack caught and played first base. He owned all of the requisite catcher's equipment, which he readily shared with other members of the team. He was a good athlete and a team player. There were some other eleven-year-old boys from Collegiate on the team, but Jack was popular with everyone. My son accused me of liking Jack too much. Admittedly I developed an appreciation for him. He appeared to be the product of excellent parenting, and it was clear that his parents enjoyed a close relationship with each other and with him. They are a loving couple, and it was obvious from observing them in conversation with each other that they had a strong bond. Once when Caroline left the game early, she gave Ed a tender good-bye kiss on the lips. It was brief but sweet. Clearly they enjoyed their anonymity and the ease of just being parents at their son's weekly baseball game. Nobody gawked, nobody whispered, nobody bothered them."

For all her anonymity at Jack's sporting events, Caroline's appearances—almost anywhere—were reported in the press, particularly because of her status as sole surviving member of her branch of the family. *The New York Times* covered a Marc Jacobs spring fashion show merely because Caroline attended with Rose and Tatiana. The same paper detailed her attendance at a lunchtime debate (sponsored by the mayor's office) over public school education at Michael Jordan's The Steak House N.Y.C. in Manhattan. The *New York Post* covered her three-day jury service at a civil trial involving the collision of two taxicabs. The *Daily News* ran an item on her eating burgers with her children at a Jackson Hole on Madison Avenue. Both the *Post* and *News* carried stories on her forty-eighth birthday celebration at Michael's with Esther Newberg (her literary agent) and several close friends. Then there was *The New York Sun* story concerning a claim she'd made during a television interview that the New York City Department of Education had run out of money. The paper pointed out in an answering editorial that the Department of Education had more than sufficient funds—the funds simply weren't being properly allocated.

The deaths of her brother and parents had left Caroline and her immediate family with a fortune worth well over $400 million. Despite her wealth, Caroline seemed to have inherited her mother's ell-documented money lust—an insatiable desire to accumulate even greater riches. In this spirit, she decided to conduct a second auction of Kennedy family belongings and memorabilia. The auction, held at Sotheby's in mid-February 2005, had been marred some months earlier by the announcement that Patrick Gallagher, a longtime auction-house employee, had stolen a number of JFK Jr.'s personal effects from a Sotheby's warehouse on East 110th Street. Among the thirty-five missing items was a 1963 Father's Day card John Jr. had made for his dad; a copy of *John Brown's Body* inscribed by Jackie Kennedy; a letter from Queen Elizabeth to Jack and Jackie congratulating them on the birth of their son; and a draft of President Kennedy's inaugural speech valued at more than $100,000. Gallagher had taken the items and then sold them to a friend for $5,000, apparently to settle a gambling debt.

The auction, which included some of the recovered JFK Jr. items, consisted predominantly of old furniture, furnishings, chinaware, bric-a-brac, trinkets, artwork, artifacts, toys, photographs, and throwaways—all the keepsakes and heirlooms that Jackie had kept in her various homes and which hadn't been unloaded in the 1996 auction of her possessions. The second sale, which netted more than $5.5 million, was seen in certain quarters as nothing less than an act of avarice on Caroline's part. London art dealer Alan Jellinek said of the auction, "Only the Kennedys could hold a garage sale at Sotheby's. It was just a collection of old junk, half of which probably never even belonged to the family. I lost all my respect for Caroline Kennedy. She sold everything but her mother's bloomers."

Another moneymaking proposition was Caroline's 2005 publication of *A Family of Poems,* an anthology of poetry for children with illustrations by Jon J. Muth. Dedicating the volume to her son, Jack ("I thought of you the whole time I was putting this book together, and I hope you always love poetry"), Caroline begins the anthology with a by now familiar-sounding introduction reiterating the same themes and thoughts presented in her previous anthologies: her parents loved poetry; her parents read poetry to her as a child. Although ostensibly intended for children, *A Family of Poems* includes all the same poets anthologized in *The Best-Loved Poems of Jacqueline Kennedy Onassis:* Edna St. Vincent Millay, Emily Dickinson, Robert Frost, Shakespeare, and others.

Once again utilizing the family name and image, the cover of the anthology is illustrated with White House pictures of Caroline when she was a young child reading from a book to a teddy bear on a seat next to her. If this doesn't tug at the heartstrings, the back book cover will. It contains a short poem by A. A. Milne with a drawing of a tousled-haired John-John-esque young boy wearing a raincoat and galoshes, turned away so his face can't be seen. But it is very clearly a rendering of Caroline's brother. The final touch is provided by the inclusion in the anthology of a poem by Jacqueline Kennedy Onassis. Titled "Thoughts," it begins: "I love the Autumn / And yet I cannot say / All the thoughts and things / That make me feel this way . . ." If nothing else, the book sold like few other anthologies of children's poetry, reaching the top of the *New York Times* bestseller list and remaining there for months.

Unquestionably the most negative publicity generated by Caroline in 2005 involved Marta Sgubin, who in 1998—with the family's permission—penned *Cooking for Madam,* an innocuous memoir of her years as the children's governess and Jackie's chef. The book included Jackie's favorite recipes and a lighthearted foreword by JFK Jr. After Jackie's death, Sgubin moved permanently into apartment 7C at 929 Park Avenue, between 80th and 81st Streets, a two-bedroom co-op owned by both Caroline and JFK Jr. The two had occupied the apartment from time to time during their single days. After John's death, Caroline assumed sole ownership of the residence. The building's co-op board, while sympathetic to Sgubin, ruled that unless she owned the apartment herself, she would have to move out. Although Sgubin still looked after the Schlossberg children, Caroline refused to sell her the apartment. To avoid a legal conflagration, the board asked Sgubin if she possessed the means to purchase the co-op—she did, and she was willing to buy it from Caroline.

The incident gave rise to a mountain of bad press. Susan Thomases, chairwoman of the building's board and a close friend of Bill and Hillary Clinton, was quoted as saying: "Caroline refuses to sell the apartment . . . It is a matter of 'control' on her part. Caroline neither wants to sell it nor give it to Marta. And we cannot force her. No one wants to see Marta leave the apartment."

The matter created such havoc that Ed Schlossberg felt compelled to step in. In mid-2005 Caroline transferred title of the apartment to Marta Sgubin. "We gave it to her," Caroline's husband told *The New York Times*. "It was a gift."

"She's stubborn as hell and has a bad temper, but otherwise she's great," David Kennedy had said of Caroline when she was sixteen. She hadn't changed. Considering the tragedies she'd endured in her lifetime, she was remarkably well adjusted. As time passed, it seemed increasingly unlikely that she would ever run for elected office. To do so would require a complete makeover of her personality. On October 15, 2005, while appearing on the WOR-AM "Morning Show," she was asked whether she would ever consider running for political office. "I won't rule politics out in the future," she said, "but I like what I'm doing." "Spoken like a true politician," responded the interviewer. It was similar to the answer her brother had so often provided when asked the same question.

"Caroline could certainly succeed in terms of a political future," said Christopher Lawford. Family friend and biographer Burton Hersh felt "Caroline could probably do well in national politics, but she doesn't need it. She's too bright, too clever, to expose herself to that kind of lifestyle."

Caroline remained ambivalent about politics. Her deeply held desire to remain semi-anonymous and private conflicted with her wish to facilitate social change by way of a political career. As her brother's friend Suzanna Bowling put it, "Caroline found her way in the world. She carved a safe niche for herself. John had it worse. That picture of him as a little boy saluting his father's coffin forever marked him as his father's successor."

In 2006 Caroline once more hosted the Kennedy Center's awards program. Among the honorees were Dolly Parton, Steven Spielberg, and Andrew Lloyd Webber. Bedecked in a floor-length evening gown, Caroline wore no jewelry save a pair of pearl earrings. In the same year she augmented her role with the Department of Education by becoming involved with the Fund for the City of New York. On March 15 she and Mary McCormick, head of the fund, were joined on a bus by civic and organization leaders as they drove around to greet the winners of the 2006 Sloan Public Service Awards, given each year to six New York City employees chosen for their outstanding contributions. Caroline had served as cochairwoman of the selection committee.

"Caroline was very unassuming, very down to earth," said an administrator for a public health program. "One of the award recipients was a schoolteacher. When we reached her class, we noticed that all the children had brought their cameras. They wanted their picture taken with Caroline. 'They don't even know who I am,' she said. She posed. Next we headed for a hospital to greet a public hospital administrator. On the elevator, a red-haired hospital worker noticed a bandage on the back of one of Caroline's hands. 'What happened?' he asked. 'I had a little growth removed,' she said. The hospital worker went on to explain how he'd once had a growth removed from his nose. Caroline smiled. 'It's the curse of the Irish,' she said. 'We don't do well in the sun.'"

That evening Caroline and Mayor Bloomberg attended the official Sloan Awards ceremony at Cooper Union in downtown Manhattan. She spoke briefly about the value her father had attached to public service. She handed out checks in the amount of $7,500 to each of the award recipients. When the ceremony ended, she slipped into a North Face ski parka and walked out into the night to catch a taxi home.

With the exception of Caroline's accomplishments, it wasn't the best year for the Kennedy family, particularly for Senator Ted Kennedy. Because of the clan's various trusts (many designed to dodge inheritance taxes) and its lucrative oil holdings, Teddy was described in the press as an "environmental rapist, tax cheat, and oil profiteer." Although he openly opposed windfall profits on the part of huge energy companies, he waged a one-man war against the use of windmills to harvest energy in his home state, evidently because the installation of windmills would have obscured the view from his Hyannis Port home. One gaffe led to another. During confirmation hearings for Supreme Court nominee Samuel A. Alito Jr., Kennedy took Alito to task for belonging to an alumni association that had lobbied to admit fewer women and minorities to Princeton University. A week after opposing Alito, it emerged that for fifty-two years Kennedy had belonged to the Owl Club, an elitist all-male social group composed of Harvard University graduates. So embarrassing was the club to Harvard that it severed its ties to the organization in 1984. Teddy, however, remained a dues-paying member through 2006.

At seventy-four Ted Kennedy had seen better days. His smallest deed seemed fraught with problems. In 2006 he wrote a children's book, *My Senator and Me: A Dog's Eye View of Washington, D.C.,* narrated by his real-life Portuguese Water Dog. Kennedy named his canine Splash, because "the dog loves hanging out in the water for hours." When Caroline Kennedy arranged for Ted to read his book to a class of third-graders at P.S. 11 in Chelsea, Andrea Peyser, a columnist for the *New York Post,* pointed out the folly of the situation. "Splash can stay in the water for hours," she wrote. "What a lucky break for anyone that hangs out with the Kennedys." The unspoken reference to Chappaquiddick was all too apparent.

Teddy's lack of judgment seemed minor compared to that of his son Patrick Kennedy. In recent years, the Rhode Island congressman had added to his previous record of ignominious behavior. In 2000 he damaged a rented yacht, amassing $28,000 in repair expenses. Thereafter he scuffled with a female airport security officer in Los Angeles, incurring a personal lawsuit. Becoming inebriated during a political rally in Washington, he mounted a stage and proceeded to make a spectacle of himself. In April 2006 he had a traffic accident in Rhode Island. On May 5 at 3:40 a.m., he smashed his car into a police barricade while speeding through the deserted streets of Washington. Claiming he had no memory of the second automobile accident, he blamed his troubles on pain pill addiction and binge drinking. Without subjecting him to a sobriety test or issuing a summons, the District of Columbia police simply drove him home. He subsequently spent thirty days in a drug-and-alcohol rehabilitation program and declared himself cured.

"What can you say to that kind of behavior?" remarked newspaper columnist Cindy Adams. "It's incredible. He's high as a kite behind the wheel of a car, and the cops do nothing. It's the old Kennedy shuffle. If it had been you or me, we'd be in the slammer. But not the Kennedys."

The Kennedys were expert by now at downplaying their calamities. In reality, Ted Kennedy had become little more than a senatorial court jester, a limousine liberal whose congressional recitations provided late-night television talk show hosts with all the humor they needed for their opening monologues. As for Patrick Kennedy, his was just one more in an endless litany of ludicrous, self-destructive incidents that seemed to follow him around. "How many times can Patrick make the same mistake?" Caroline Kennedy supposedly asked a friend. The keeper of the flame appeared to be more determined than ever to shield her own privacy, making herself available to the media—and thus the public—only when it suited her. At all costs, Caroline was determined to avoid the pratfalls that had ensnared so many of her Kennedy relatives.

In June 2006 Ed Schlossberg received an honorary Doctor of Humane Letters from the New York City College of Technology. Addressing an auditorium filled with graduating seniors, he discoursed on the future of interactive tools and displays. In July he and Caroline vacationed in Turkey, staying at the same Istanbul hotel where John Jr. had honeymooned with Carolyn Bessette. The Schlossbergs returned to spend part of August with Rose, Tatiana, and Jack at Martha's Vineyard. On August 26 the family of five settled in front of a television set at Red Gate Farm to watch an NBC filmed documentary in celebration of the fiftieth anniversary of the publication of President John F. Kennedy's *Profiles in Courage.* The program, narrated in part by Caroline, saluted the winners of the award named after the book.

Several days later Caroline drove her thirteen-year-old son to the public beach at Gay Head to take part in a volleyball game with other kids from Martha's Vineyard. Mary Rachel Sullivan, a vacationer on the island, saw Caroline sitting on a beach blanket watching the contest. Originally from Newton, Massachusetts, Sullivan had always been an admirer of the Kennedys. "I took the liberty of going over and introducing myself," said Sullivan. "Caroline was very gracious—I can't say otherwise. I told her how much her father had meant to the country, and how I'd once seen her mother at a Democratic Party fund-raiser in Manhattan. I suppose she'd heard all this a million times, but she seemed to appreciate it. We made small talk. She recommended the names of several local restaurants and nightspots. At this point there was a short break in the volleyball game. Her son came running over. Caroline reached into her beach bag and handed him a bottle of water. He took a drink, gave it back, and returned to the game. 'Is that Jack?' I asked. 'It is,' she replied. 'That's Jack.' I told her I thought he resembled a youthful version of her father, the president. 'Really?' she responded. 'I think he looks more like my mother's side of the family. He looks a little like my brother.' There was a pause. Then I said, 'Well, no doubt he'll be president of the United States someday.' Caroline smiled. 'You think so?' she asked. 'I hope not. Then again, you never know.'"

ACKNOWLEDGMENTS

THIS BOOK would not have been possible without the help of a number of individuals and institutions. First, acknowledgment must go to my literary agent, Owen Laster of the William Morris Agency, and to my editor, Emily Bestler. I would also like to thank Mel Berger at the William Morris Agency, and Sarah Branham at Atria Books/Simon & Schuster. With her photo-editing skills, Lewanne Jones proved an invaluable addition to the project. I must thank Joseph Leach, James Kozack, Bill Hughes, and Steve Khosrova for their expertise in computer and office machine services. Sidney Schwartz helped procure Kennedy family memorabilia from eBay auction sites. Dan Holtzer, an investment broker at Morgan Stanley Dean Witter, provided copies of several rare Kennedy books and materials. Alma Schieren provided typing and secretarial services. George Brown, Nina Hein, and Juliane Locker set up a streamlined filing system for a mountain of secondary source materials gathered during the research process. I am indebted to Svanhildur Thorvaldsdotter for her translations of Icelandic newspaper articles on JFK Jr. into English. In addition, I am immensely grateful to a large staff of researchers and interviewers, including Colette Boudreau, Stephen Distinti, Roberta Fineberg, Cathy Griffin, Alex Halpern, Veronica Ikeshoji-Orlati, Sasha Jackinson, Clancy A. Nolan, Mark Padnos, Ryan Rayston, Tinker Ready, Maureen Seaberg, Alexandra Speck, Aileen Torres, and Abe Velez. Special mention must be made with reference to four others. Gerry Visco, a graduate of the Columbia University School of Journalism and a freelance writer, was a mainstay researcher and interviewer who also helped proofread and line edit sections of the manuscript. Barbara Fleck, currently a Washington-based attorney with the State Department, prepared reports and conducted interviews; more important, her familiarity with the mysterious interworkings of the FAA and NTSB resulted in the release of previously withheld John F. Kennedy Jr. files from both agencies. I must thank my mother, Renee Heymann, simply for being my mother, and Bea Schwartz (to whom this book is dedicated) for being Bea Schwartz.

Numerous organizations, institutions, and groups provided documents, correspondence, oral histories, and miscellaneous material. Included among their ranks are the following: Franklin D. Roosevelt Presidential Library and Museum; Harry S. Truman Presidential Museum and Library; Dwight D. Eisenhower Presidential Library; John F. Kennedy Presidential Library and Museum; Lyndon B. Johnson Library and Museum; Richard Nixon Library and Birthplace; Gerald R. Ford Presidential Library and Museum; Jimmy Carter Library and Museum; Ronald Reagan Presidential Library; George Bush Presidential Library and Museum; William J. Clinton Presidential Library and Museum; Library of Congress (manuscript division); New York Public Library system; New York Society Library; Boston Public Library system; New-York Historical Society; City of New York Department of Commerce; Boston Historical Society and Museum; Newport Historical Society; Palm Beach Historical Society; Martha's Vineyard Historical Society; Georgetown Historical Society; Historical Society of the Town of Greenwich (Connecticut); White House Historical Association; Municipal Art Society of New York; U.S. Secret Service (archive division); Federal Bureau of Investigation; U.S. Department of Justice; National Archives; National Geographic Society; Metropolitan Museum of Art; Sotheby's (New York and London); Andy Warhol Museum; State University of New York at Stony Brook Library Services (department of special collections); University of Texas at Austin Libraries (rare books and manuscripts); Georgetown University Library; Houghton Library at Harvard University; Bronx Community College Library; New York University Law Library; New York State Bar Association Library; Columbia University Law School Library; Columbia University Library Services (manuscript division); UCLA Library Services; Brown University Library Services; Boston University Library; Real Estate Board of New York; New York Athletic Club; St. David's School library; Collegiate School library; Phillips Andover Academy library; Brearley School library; Concord Academy library; Concord Academy Alumni Association; Stanhope Hotel (public relations department); hotel Carlyle (public relations department); British Information Service; Grand Central Terminal (public relations department); the Louvre; Alexander Onassis Foundation; Greek Tourist Board; Robin Hood Foundation; Federal Elections Commission; New York State Democratic Committee; John F. Kennedy School of Government (Harvard University).

Also helpful and worthy of mention are a number of newspapers and magazines whose archives yielded a wealth of backdated material. Among these are the following: *The New York Times; The Wall Street Journal; New York Post;* New York *Daily News; The Village Voice; Newsday; The Washington Post; The Washington Times; USA Today; The Boston Globe; Boston Herald; Los Angeles Times; Women's Wear Daily; The East Hampton Star; Dan's Papers; Chicago Tribune; International Herald Tribune; Le Monde;* London *Times;* London *Daily Mail* and *Sunday Mail; Spy* magazine; *Esquire; Vogue; Harper's Bazaar; Elle; Atlantic Monthly; Us Weekly; Brill's Content; GQ; Cosmopolitan; People* magazine; *Time; Life; Newsweek; Vanity Fair; The New Yorker; New York* magazine; *Star* magazine; *National Enquirer; Globe; Rolling Stone; Boston* magazine; *Paris Match; Hello; Redbook; McCall's; Good Housekeeping; Ladies' Home Journal; TV Guide.*

Finally, I must thank those individuals who agreed to be interviewed for this book or who answered specific questions (occasionally in writing). While a handful of the interviewees requested anonymity, most did not. It should be noted that several of these interviews were conducted for previous Kennedy biographies by the author. The complete list of those interviewed reads as follows: Richard Aaron, Susan Abbot, Jack Abel, Bess Abell, Cindy Adams, Charles Addams, Bill Adler, Jim Adler, Jerome Agel, Joseph Alsop, Susan Mary Alsop, Benny Alvarez, Christiane Amanpour, Jan Cushing Amory, Paul Anastasi, Jack Anderson, Florinda Arnold, Agnes Ash, Phil Auburn, Hugh Dudley (Yusha) Auchincloss III,

Jamie Auchincloss, Janet Lee Bouvier Auchincloss, Jennifer Axelrod, Dick Baker, Julie Baker, Letitia Baldridge, Jim Balinson, Tom Bannon, Keith Bardilini, John Perry Barlow, Charles Bartlett, Sam Bassett, Nancy Bastien, Betty Beal, Bouvier Beale, Edith (Little Edie) Beale, Peter Beard, Linda Bemis, Jon Bennett, Gordon Bensley, Frank Berardi, Michael Bergin, Michael Berman, Lillian Biko, K. LeMoyne (Lem) Billings, Sally Bitterman, Sylvia Whitehouse Blake, Peter Blanchard, Maury Blaustein, Al Block, Richard Blow, Paul Boisie, Joseph Robert Bolker, Michael (Miche) Bouvier III, Suzanna Bowling, Joan Braden, Antoinette Pinchot (Tony) Bradlee, Bill Brand, Geoffrey Bride, Harry J. Brown, J. Carter Brown, Katie Brown, Lucia Brown, Marcus Brown, Evangeline (Vangie) Bruce, Jessica Bruno, Art Buchwald, Barbara Burn, Michael Bush, Brian Calcagne, Mortimer Caplin, Truman Capote, Miguel Carcona, Ed Carington, Igor Cassini, Oleg Cassini, Sharon Churcher, Bettina Crone, Bridie Clark, Garry Clifford, David Cohen, Roy Cohn, Margaret Louise Coit, Bob Colacello, Barbara Coleman, David Patrick Columbia, Steve Connelly, Raymond Cox, Susan Crimp, Mimi Crocker, John Cronin, John Crouse, Kent Cunow, Leo Damore, Mary Lou Darkenwald, Fred Davenport, Lester David, John H. Davis, Maude Davis, Maude Bouvier Davis, Jane Dawson, Philipe de Bausset, Mary De Grace, John Dempsey, Alexander Denisow, Liz Derringer, Barbara Deutsch, Tracey Dewart, Marilyn (Missy) Chandler DeYoung, C. Wyatt Dickerson, Nancy Dickerson, Janice Dickinson, David Dinkins, Rod Dinkins, Jack Donahue, Eleanor Doyle, Elizabeth Draper, Peter Duchin, Michael Dukakis, Ralph Dungan, Richard duPont, Cindy Epson Edwards, Steve Eichner, John Emigh, Jane Engelhard, Edward Enick, Alexandra Eno, Deborah Enoch, Frank Evans, Peter Evans, Stephen Fairchild, Pat Fenton, Andy Ferguson, Roberta Fineberg, Tina Flaherty, Barbara Fleck, Catherine Flickingen, Steve Florio, Larry Flynt, Doris Francisco, Sanford Fredman, Chuck Freed, Orville Freeman, Sanford (Sandy) Friedman, Francine Fromm, Terry Fugate-Wilcox, Emil Gabron, Helene Gaillet, John Kenneth Galbraith, Batty Galella, Ron Galella, Mary Gallagher, James C. Garriott, Thurston G. Gauleiter, Terry Gelfenbaum, Carl Gilko, Roswell Gilpatric, Ina Ginsburg, Eugene Girden, Mary Gluck, Judy Golden, Marjory Goldman, Santina Goodman, Richard Goodwin, Tom F. Grace,

Constatine (Costa) Gratsos, Jay P. Greene, Robert Greene, Roosevelt (Rosey) Grier, Cathy Griffin, Michael Gross, Lloyd Grove, Thomas A. Guinzburg, Christina Haag, Halston, Nigel Hamilton, Alexa Hampton, Mark Hampton, Rose Hantman, John Hare, Pamela Harriman, Jacques Harvey, Leonard Haskins, R. Couri Hay, Debbie Hecht, Russell D. Hemenway, Angela Hemingway, Deirdre Henderson, Burton Hersh, Anne Hickory, Tommy Hilfiger, Jacqueline Hirsch, Marjorie Housepian Dobkin, Lloyd Howard, Chris Hudson, Denise Hughes, John G. W. Husted Jr., Ruth Jacobson, Thomas E. Jacobson, Margaret James, Peter Janney, Jack Jason, Jacob Javits, Alan Jellinek, Jeff Jenson, Brad Johns, Richard Johnson, Steven Johnson, Alex Jones, Baird Jones, Jeffrey Jones, Lewanne Jones, William Joyce, James Kalafatis, Ken Katz, Mimi Kazon, David Kennedy, Robert F. Kennedy Jr., Albert (Al) Khafif, Carl Killingsworth, Walter Kilroy, Larry King, Jack Kliger, James Kozack, Carolyn Kresky, David Kuhn, William M. Kunstler, Eleanor Lambert, Theresa Landau, Ida Large, Jane Larson, Christopher Lawford, Lilly Lawrence, Louis Licciardi, Doris Lilly, Evelyn Lincoln, Peter Lisagor, Robert (Rob) Littell, Leon Lobel, John Loring, Jacques Lowe, Ivo Lupis, Renee Luttgen, Christos Malacrinos, Carolyn B. Maloney, William Manchester, Mariuccia (Krizia) Mandelli, Peter Manso, Carol S. Martin, Langdon P. Marvin, Christopher Mason, Jean Christian Massard, Paul Mathias, Marisa May, Lowery McClendon, Godfrey McHugh, Mary McInerney, F. Kenneth McKnight, John J. McLaughlin Jr., Betty McMahon, Robert S. McNamara, Aileen (Suzy) Mehle, Jacques Melki, Johnny Meyer, Stanley Mirsky, Bambi Mitgang, Joanna Molloy, Delores Morris, Mike Motta, Maura Moynihan, Michael Musto, Ken Nedeau, William Nelson, Larry Newman, Martin Nordquist, Nora Nordquist, Murray Steven Nussbaum, Susan Ober, Lawrence (Larry) O'Brien, Kenneth (Ken) O'Donnell, Jerry Oppenheimer, Deirdre O'Rorke, Chris Overbeck, Stuart Owen, William Peter Owen, Mark Padnos, Vanessa Palo, Mark Pardue, Estelle Parker, Endicott Peabody, David Pecker, Claiborne Pell, Nuala Pell, Lester Persky, George Plimpton, Lisa Fair Pliskin, John Politidis, Susan Pollock, Dave Powers, Meredith Price, Lilly Pulitzer, Michelle Bouvier Putnam, Carole Radziwill, Harrison Rainie, Juan Ramos, Laura Raposa, David Ray, Ryan Rayston, Scott Reeds, Denis Reggie, Conrad Rehling,

Maxine Rehling, Cary Reich, Janet Reno, Abraham (Abe) Ribicoff, Roger Ritchie, Larry Rivers, Bonnie Robinson, Franklin D. Roosevelt Jr., Jonathan Rosenbloom, Carol Rosenwald, Tommy Rowles, Suzanne Ruddick, Ron Rudolph, George Rush, Jay Ruskin, Art Russell, Gene Russianoff, Peter Jay Russo, Jason Sacks, Pierre Salinger, Rami Sambath, Brent Saville, Philip Scher, Paul Schlamm, Arthur Schlesigner Jr., Rose Schreiber, Beatrice Schwartz, Maureen Seaberg, Josh Seftel, Marta Sgubin, Valerie Monroe Shakespeare, John Shaw, Tony Sherman, Aaron Shikler, "April Showers," Alex Siegal, Susan Sklover, Eileen Slocum, George Smathers, Amanda Smith, Earl E. T. Smith, George Exley Smith, Liz Smith, Lynn Alpha Smith, Tony Smith, Jonathan Soroff, Charles Spalding, Joel Spalding, Steve Spivek, Sara Stanfill, Ted Stanley, Jessie Stearns, Alexander Stille, Roy Stoppard, Cecil Stoughton, Fred Stover, Clifford Streit, Marianne (Mimi) Strong, Mary Rachel Sullivan, Jonathan Tapper, Radu Teodorescu, Lynn Tesoro, Sharon Tibbs, Mary Tierney, Peter Tollington, Stanley Tretick, Donald Trump, Matt Truro, Russell Turiak, Benjamin F. Turpin, Mike Tyson, Jayda Uras, Jack Valenti, Peter Valiantis, Marty Venker, Liz Villard, Gerry Visco, Frank Waldrop, Hilary Waleson, Bill Walton, Frank Wangler, Andy Warhol, Roma Washburn, Bill Watson, Billy Way, Daryl West, Zella West, Jim Wetteroth, John White, Robert L. White, William M. White, Charles Whitehouse, Les Whitten, Richard Wiese, Nancy Wild, Manfred Willoughby, Don Wilmeth, Paul Wilmot, Cynthia Windland, Annette Witheridge, Stanley Witt, Donald H. Wolfe, Holly Woodlawn, Jayne Wrightsman, Meyer Yudell, Stewart Zak, Larry Zarrow, Mary Zeller, Peter Zola, and David Zucker.

CHAPTER NOTES

◆

When and where possible, the author has provided source notes within the body of the text. The following chapter notes are intended to supplement the textual references as well as to provide the reader with specific secondary source information. Although the following is not necessarily a complete list of sources, it provides the interested reader with a sense of the author's methodology. Because this biography is not meant to be an academic treatise, the author has deviated slightly from the conventional presentation of source notes—key phrases are used as opposed to numbered notes. In large measure the author depended on original interviews rather than already existing secondary sources.

Chapter 1: THE FALL OF ICARUS (1)

3. "Jacqueline Kennedy: The White House Years" was the title of a seventeen-page, illustrated pamphlet prepared by the JFK Presidential Library and Museum, Boston, Massachusetts. Its text described in detail Jackie's fashion needs during her days as First Lady. The public relations department at the Louvre provided a transcript of Caroline and Ted Kennedy's opening remarks at the Jacqueline Kennedy exhibition in Paris.

5. *caravan of reporters:* See *The East Hampton Star,* July 20, 1999.

6. *"If anyone can make it":* The Boston Globe, July 18, 1999.

6. *Harold Anderson:* See *USA Today,* July 22, 1999.

6. *the only person willing to fly: USA Today,* May 25, 1998. JFK Jr. expressed the same sentiments in conversation with the author, particularly the invocation of Charles Lindbergh. From 1990 to 1999 the author both met with and telephoned JFK Jr. on a number of occasions. Although his name is not included in the list of interviewees, anecdotal information imparted by him has been incorporated into the book.

6. *"To the bravest person":* A variation of this inscription is quoted by Edward Klein in "Secrets and Lies," a *Vanity Fair* (August 2003) excerpt (with additional text) from his controversial book *The Kennedy Curse.* The *Vanity Fair* article is more balanced and measured than Klein's book, which contains dubious charges and claims, many of them contested by Kennedy insiders.

6. *Tommy Hilfiger:* JFK Jr. to Hilfiger, May 27, 1998.

9. *"Pinky":* Records released by the Department of Transportation in February 2007 reveal that shortly after 10:00 p.m. on July 16, 1999, Adam Budd, a twenty-one-year-old college student employed at the Martha's Vineyard Airport, placed a call to the FAA's Automated Flight Service Station in Bridgeport, Connecticut, inquiring as to the whereabouts

of JFK Jr.'s plane. An operator at the FAA station told Budd he had no information on the flight.

9. *Carole Radziwill:* For further information on Carole Radziwill and the role she played following the disappearance of JFK Jr.'s plane, see *What Remains,* her memoir on the relationship between John and Anthony Radziwill.

11. *Phil Enright:* Among other sources (including *People*), see Chris Andersen, *The Day John Died,* p. 12.

13. *Teddy cradled her in his arms:* Confidential source.

13. *FlightSafety International:* Located in Vero Beach, Florida, FSI became notorious several years later for inadvertently having given flight lessons to two of the terrorists involved in the events of 9/11.

14. *Mike Tyson:* Mike Tyson interview. See also Chris Andersen, op. cit.

19. *"If you get pregnant":* Christiane Amanpour interview. See also Laurence Leamer, *Sons of Camelot.* Amanpour and husband James Rubin did in fact have a son. Darius John Rubin was born in 2000, a year after John Jr.'s death. The couple named him after JFK Jr.

21. *Graves' disease:* Several previously published reports insist that JFK Jr. began suffering from Graves' disease in 1995. According to his medical reports—made available by a confidential source—he actually began suffering from the ailment in 1990.

24. *fielding his angry wife's telephone calls: George* telephone logs, confidential source.

25. *Julie Baker:* Andersen, op. cit., pp. 21–22.

26. *Christopher Kennedy Lawford:* According to *Symptoms of Withdrawal,* a memoir by Lawford, he encountered John Jr. at the Kennedy family offices on July 16, the day of JFK Jr.'s death. Lawford further claims that he and John partied the night before in Greenwich Village. On page 337 of his memoir, Lawford maintains that John had "a broken foot" and that when he saw him, his foot was in a cast. In fact, JFK Jr. had broken his left ankle, not "a foot," and his cast had been removed two weeks before the date Lawford states he saw John. The dates provided in this chapter by the author for JFK Jr.'s meetings with Lawford are derived from John's business calendar at *George,* which were provided by a confidential source.

26. *Steve Florio:* Steve Florio interview. See also Klein, *Vanity Fair,* August 2003.

28. *William (Billy) Sylvester Noonan:* In 2006 Noonan published a slim memoir, *Forever Young,* based on his friendship with JFK Jr.

29. *Sterling Lord:* Andersen, op. cit., 27.

29. *having a pedicurist match:* Klein, op. cit.

30. *Roy Stoppard:* For the record, it should be noted that "Stoppard" is a pseudonym chosen by the interviewee to "avoid being dogged by the media for the rest of my life." It should also be noted that Stoppard was never interviewed by the FBI for the NTSB report issued a year after JFK Jr.'s death. "They never approached me," said Stoppard, "and it never occurred to me to go to them. Some things are perhaps better left unsaid. Not enough time had elapsed for me to step forward and report the opened bottle of wine. And I have no way of knowing what effect his drinking might have had on his ability to fly that day. Certainly it couldn't have added to his powers of judgment."

While he was by no means an alcoholic, JFK Jr. nevertheless drank heavily while a student at Brown and in the immediate years that followed. Robert Littell, his closest friend, describes John's early drinking habits in his memoir, *The Men We Became.*

Chapter 2: THE FALL OF ICARUS (2)

35. *Cellular phone records:* Verizon Wireless records provided to the author by a confidential source.

36. *took off at 8:38 p.m.:* Initial news and media reports regarding JFK Jr.'s route from Essex County Airport to Martha's Vineyard were incorrect. Evidently, depending on these early press reports, a number of journalists repeated the error in their writings. The error again crept up in an E! network cable television documentary on JFK Jr.'s life broadcast on November 1, 2004. Not required to do so, John didn't file a flight plan prior to departure, which no doubt added to the confusion. On this occasion, the route he followed took him north along the Hudson River, across Westchester County, to the Connecticut coastline. An alternate route, which he flew periodically, took him over the Long Island Sound directly into Connecticut. The latter route, though slightly shorter, would have brought the plane into contact with far more air traffic from both LaGuardia and JFK airports. One reason for the initial erroneous report may in part have resulted from a media interview conducted a day after the fatal flight with a private pilot who purportedly told reporters that he thought he saw John's plane fly off in the direction of Long Island Sound. Since it was nearly dark by the time of JFK Jr.'s departure, it seems unlikely that anyone on the airport tarmac could have determined the plane's exact route simply by visual means. According to one Essex County Airport official (not present at the time), "it's possible John headed for the Sound, then turned away and headed for the Hudson."

41. *("little black box"):* The majority of small private planes do not come equipped with such a device. For some unknown reason, John had one installed after purchasing the plane. It did not survive the crash.

41. *Coast Guard officials:* According to a U.S. Coast Guard report (issued on December 16, 1999), JFK Jr. made radio contact with FAA personnel several minutes prior to the plane crash. The report proved inaccurate and was later revised.

46. *Dennis Canfield:* Canfield, still with the NTSB, was reached by telephone at his current office in New Jersey by C. David Heymann researcher Barbara Fleck. Questioned as to the toxological report of August 6, 1999, Canfield refused to comment. Although rendered under the auspices of the NTSB, the toxological tests were conducted at FAA laboratories. The toxological report is currently available from both FAA and NTSB record archives and is classified as an NTSB-FAA coventure. Spokepersons for both agencies insist that the report was always available and that no coverup was perpetrated. In any event, it is apparent that Canfield had nothing to do with a coverup. Rather, it was perpetrated at higher levels.

46. *James C. Garriott:* Garriott was interviewed over the telephone by the author. He took several days to consider the figures provided by the NTSB report of August 6, 1999. In order to avoid swaying Garriott's interpretation of the toxological figures, the author did not send him an actual copy of the report, preferring that Garriott respond to an oral presentation of the report. It should be added that two other toxological experts contacted by the author, both of whom wished to remain anonymous, agreed with Garriott's interpretation.

49. *"We aren't exactly cursed":* George Plimpton interview.

Chapter 3: "GOOD MORNING, MR. PRESIDENT"

54. *Lorraine Rowan:* See Lorraine Rowan Cooper oral history at University of Kentucky Library (John Sherman Cooper Collection), Louisville, Kentucky. Quotes by Lorraine Rowan Cooper in this and other chapters also based on letters from Lorraine Rowan Cooper to Evangeline Bruce, courtesy of Evangeline Bruce.

56. *incapable of childbearing:* Jackie's concerns regarding childbearing related to author by Truman Capote (August 1975). Capote was at one time a close friend of both Jackie Kennedy's and Lee Radziwill's.

59. *An earlier, unexpurgated draft:* The earlier draft of Maud Shaw's *White House Nanny* was provided the author via a confidential source. It is a more candid version than the published book, which was heavily edited. Unless otherwise noted, Maud Shaw quotations in this and subsequent chapters are derived from the first, unedited draft of the book.

60. *"proper pose":* JFK in conversation with LeMoyne Billings. Related to author by LeMoyne Billings.

61. Life *magazine asked him:* James Spada, *John and Caroline: Their Lives in Pictures,* p. 5.

61. *Jackie finally relented:* Pierre Salinger interview.

61. *The April 21 cover:* Spada, op. cit.

65. *"Now that I'm on the stump":* Jackie in letter to Evangeline Bruce, February 2, 1960. Courtesy of Evangeline Bruce.

69. *"I worked as an inquiring photographer":* Reported to author by Pierre Salinger.

Chapter 4: 1600 PENNSYLVANIA AVENUE

72. *"This is it!":* Related to author by John White.

72. *Transitory quality:* Joan Braden interview.

72. *"There are always loopholes":* Secret Service subject files, John F. Kennedy, n.d.

74. *"If you arrest him":* Secret Service subject files, Jacqueline Bouvier Kennedy (Onassis), November 26, 1960.

76. *Eleanor Roosevelt:* Eleanor Roosevelt to Jacqueline Bouvier Kennedy, December 1, 1960. Franklin D. Roosevelt Presidential Library and Museum, Hyde Park, New York.

79. *The inaugural address:* Thurston Clarke, "Ask How," *The New York Times,* op-ed section, January 15, 2005.

85. *threatening kidnap letter:* FBI files, JFK/children kidnap.

89. *a written list of demands:* List provided by confidential source.

89. *knocked out one of his front teeth:* Secret Service subject files, Jacqueline Bouvier Kennedy (Onassis), no date.

90. *Angier Biddle Duke:* Angier Biddle Duke Papers, Duke University Library (special collections), Durham, North Carolina.

90. *Baltimore Zoo:* Secret Service subject files, Jacqueline Bouvier Kennedy (Onassis), no date. The same Secret Service notation makes reference to "John-John's red velvet-cushioned high chair," an indication of the luxury in which John and Caroline were raised.

102. *"the one blow":* William Manchester's unpublished notes for *The Death of a President,* Manchester Papers, Boston University Libraries, special collections.

Chapter 5: CAMELOT AT DUSK

105. *"Jackie, do you know":* Pierre Salinger interview.

105. *JFK had heard that Lee:* Many of the details regarding Jackie's cruise aboard the *Christina* are derived from Heymann, *A Woman Named Jackie.*

108. *"I knew I was back":* Evangeline Bruce interview.

109. *Supreme Court Justices:* According to witnesses, including journalist Jess Stearn, who was present that evening, the White House reception of November 20, 1963, was the occasion of a sub rosa physical altercation between JFK and Jackie, most probably over his ongoing affair with Mary Pinchot Meyer and the recent disclosure that he had contracted chlamydia, a sexually transmitted disease.

110. *Bob Foster:* The scenes describing Maud Shaw's conversations with Foster and her actions in the aftermath of the JFK assassination are derived primarily from the first draft of *White House Nanny* as well as from Secret Service subject files.

114. *"Your Daddy has gone"*: The first edition of *White House Nanny* erroneously attributes these words to Maud Shaw. Later editions correctly identify RFK as the speaker.

114. *Nor did the handwritten letters:* Copies of LBJ's handwritten notes to Caroline and John can be found at both the LBJ and JFK presidential libraries. To Caroline he wrote: "Your father's death has been a great tragedy for the Nation, as well as for you, and I wanted you to know how much my thoughts are of you at this time. He was a wise and devoted man. You can always be proud of what he did for this country." To John he wrote: "It will be many years before you understand what a great man your father was. His loss is a deep personal tragedy for all of us, but I wanted you particularly to know that I share your grief—You can always be proud of him."

115. *Overtired and full of medication:* Information based on William Manchester's unpublished notes, Manchester Papers.

124. *"She reacted to my rather humble request"*: George Plimpton later revised the article and, with Jackie's blessings, published it in *Redbook* (November 1988).

124. *Jacqueline Hirsh:* Jacqueline Hirsh Oral History, January 17, 1966, JFK Presidential Library and Museum.

125. *"My mother cries all the time"*: Chris Andersen, *Jackie after Jack*, p. 95.

127. *"Ho Chi Minh"*: RFK borrowed this line from Richard Goodwin, who used it to describe RFK's chances of being chosen by LBJ as a running mate.

128. *"Guess what?"*: Shaw, first draft of *White House Nanny.*

Chapter 6: NEW YORK, 1964–1968

132. *Michael O'Connell:* John Freeman Gill, "Bellman to the Stars," *The New York Times,* July 16, 2006.

135. *"Compared to the school"*: Jacqueline Bouvier Kennedy Onassis letter to Evangeline Bruce, n.d. Courtesy Evangeline Bruce.

137. *Erik Erikson:* Ed Klein, *Just Jackie,* pp. 27–39.

138. *"I had planned on going to England"*: Maud Shaw letter to Evelyn Lincoln, March 22, 1965, LBJ Library and Museum.

138. *"You brought such happiness"*: Shaw, *White House Nanny* (published edition), p. 1.

140. *"I'm a bit worried"*: Jan Pottker, *Janet and Jackie,* p. 242.

140. *"a pledge of loyalty"*: Jacqueline Bouvier Kennedy Onassis letter to Maud Shaw, confidential source.

140. *"I feel I have done"*: Maud Shaw letter to Evelyn Lincoln, February 28, 1966, LBJ Library and Museum.

141. *"Hello, Mr. Clifton"*: Jim Dwyer, "Above Everything, a Special Mother," *Newsday Magazine,* May 20, 1994. All references to Peter Clifton in this section of the chapter derive from the Dwyer article.

144. *"Your father's dead"*: Reported to author by Truman Capote, at whose house in Brooklyn Heights Jackie spent the night of November 22, 1966, the third anniversary of JFK's assassination.

150. *"might be the sweetest fellow"*: Pierre Salinger interview.

Chapter 7: RICH AS CROESUS

153. *"The Catholic Church is best"*: Heymann, op. cit., p. 485.

154. *"I hate this country"*: Ibid., p. 486. Both this and the "Catholic Church" quote will be familiar to followers of Jackie's life story.

155. *"Maybe you can woo me":* Pierre Salinger interview.
162. *"I could care less":* Jacqueline Bouvier Kennedy Onassis letter to Bill Walton, November 1, 1968. Courtesy of William Walton. Walton, a close friend of Jackie's, was likewise very friendly with Mary Pinchot Meyer, President Kennedy's last mistress. Walton frequently escorted Mary to the White House, thus bearding for the President in what can only be seen as deceitful behavior toward Jackie.
163. *Bruce Breimer:* Online entry—John F. Kennedy Jr.com.
163. *"You had to feel sorry":* JFK Jr. to author, May 1998.
165. *"You'd better rent":* George Plimpton interview.

Chapter 8: RITES OF PASSAGE

181. *When Rose Kennedy heard:* Heymann, op. cit., p. 527.
182. *"most boring woman":* Pierre Salinger interview.
182. *"The greatest form of child-abuse":* Costa Gratsos interview.
184. *snake hunting expedition:* Peter Beard, "John F. Kennedy Jr.—Images of Summer," *Talk,* Sept. 1999. Author also interviewed Beard for *A Woman Named Jackie.*
186. *"People already think of me":* Author interview with George Plimpton.
188. *"could no longer communicate":* Author interview with Larry Newman.
193. *prolific abuser of pot:* Author interviews with various associates of JFK Jr.
193. *Wilson McCray: People* commemorative issue, summer 1999.
194. *by his own admission:* See Christopher Lawford, *Symptoms of Withdrawal,* for an in-depth look at Lawford's descent into alcoholism and drug addiction.
197. *Barbara Gibson:* See Barbara Gibson, *Life with Rose Kennedy,* pp. 205–208.
197. *Hyannis Port kitchen:* Rose Kennedy to Caroline Kennedy, n.d. Confidential source.

Chapter 9: A GREEK TRAGEDY

198. *called Ari an ingrate:* George Plimpton interview.
198. *last will and testament:* See Heymann, op. cit., p. 554.
199. *"I would pay a king's ransom":* Pottker, op. cit., p. 291.
202. *Christos Kartamos:* Elaine Landau, *John F. Kennedy Jr.,* p. 273.
204. *"I so love that child": Paris Match,* July 30, 1975.

Chapter 10: FIRST LOVE

211. *Sarah Bradford:* Sarah Bradford, *America's Queen,* pp. 211–212.
214. *"You must think you're Aristotle Onassis":* Andy Warhol interview.
215. *New England Baptist Hospital:* Andersen, *Sweet Caroline,* p. 194.
216. *"I wish I could wake up":* Ibid., pp. 196–197.
218. *Newspaper saga:* Bill Adler, *The Kennedy Children,* p. 74.
219. *Rick Leicata:* Andersen, op. cit., p. 200.
219. *"got absolutely smashed":* Kitty Kelley, *Jackie Oh!,* pp. 337–338.
223. *Rabinal, a Guatemalan:* Wendy Leigh, *Prince Charming,* p. 195.
223. *Party in the Hamptons:* George Plimpton interview.
226. *Jenny Christian:* See Stephen Spignesi, *JFK Jr.,* pp. 45–47. Spignesi, in turn, attributes his Jenny Christian quotations to Wendy Leigh, *Prince Charming.*
226. *John Travolta:* Leigh, op. cit., p. 202.
232. *Maureen Lambray:* Andersen, op. cit., p. 207.
232. *"Half the men in America":* George Plimpton interview.

232. *Kevin King:* See Kevin King—Manhattan Criminal Court Records Archive, New York, NY. Also see *The New York Times* and *The Washington Post,* October 17, 1981.
234. *Filled with news photographers:* Andersen, op. cit., pp. 213–215.

Chapter 11: BROWN

236. *breaking with tradition:* At the time, the only other family member to attend Brown was Kerry Kennedy, who went from 1975 to 1977 and purportedly didn't care for the university.
236. *"You have to be suspicious":* JFK Jr. to author.
238. *"too busy socializing":* New York Post, November 15, 1979.
239. *John Hare:* John Hare interview. See also Emily Gold, "JFK Jr. Through the Eyes of Those Who Knew Him," *Brown Alumni Magazine,* July–August 1999.
239. *Rick Moody:* Rick Moody, "The Actor," ibid.
240. *Robert Reichley:* Leamer, op. cit., p. 283.
240. *His first college paper:* Emily Gold, op. cit.
241. *"Whatever you decide to do":* George Plimpton interview.
241. *"Boys will be boys":* Ibid.
242. *"Hi, I'm John's mother":* Magazine interview with Charlie King, "Tribute to JFK Jr.: His Life in Pictures," *People,* commemorative issue, summer 1999.
244. *"John had an annoying way":* Leamer, op. cit., p. 287.
249. *"as a dyslexic":* George Plimpton interview.
249. *"which is the reason":* George Plimpton interview.
249. *"I couldn't sit down":* Leamer, op. cit., pp. 292–293.
250. *"Miss Crazy":* Robert Littell interview. See also Robert Littell, *The Men We Became,* pp. 40–44.
251. *A male classmate of John's:* John's "unnamed" classmate was interviewed by Howard Stern on "The Howard Stern Show," K-Rock FM, January 10, 1996.
252. *"Even on the scale":* Brown University Bursar's Office, Brown University, Providence, RI.
253. *"She wasn't hard":* Online entry—www.Balganarchive.org.
253. *"I was always stunned":* New York *Daily News,* March 22, 2004.
255. *Robert De Niro:* Rick Moody, op. cit.
256. *Dan Samson:* Leamer, op. cit., p. 291.
259. *"We stayed for days":* Littell, op. cit., p. 76.
259. *Todd Murphy:* Magazine interview with Todd Murphy, *People,* commemorative issue, summer 1999.

Chapter 12: MAURICE AND ED

265. *Johnson Hill Road:* Ed Schlossberg sold his house in 2002 for a purported $500,000.
267. *completion of his doctorate:* Schlossberg's PhD dissertation at Columbia—an imaginary dialogue between Albert Einstein and Samuel Beckett.
269. *Herbert Randall Gefvert:* Caroline Kennedy FBI files, January–June 1984, Washington D.C.
271. *Black-and-yellow silk pajama suit:* Sharon Churcher and Ellen Hawkes, "Wedding of the Summer," *Ladies' Home Journal,* August 1986.

Chapter 13: WINNERS AND LOSERS

274. *"a herd of yaks":* Michael Gross interview.
277. *turned up in Madonna's dressing room:* Leigh, op. cit., p. 251.

278. *Museum of the Moving Image:* Andersen, op. cit., p. 260.
284. *"Sympathy for the Devil":* This was evidently one of JFK Jr.'s favorite rock numbers. According to Leamer, in *Sons of Camelot,* he sang it on a canoeing trip with friends.
284. *"Stripped down to his briefs":* Lester David, "JFK Jr.," *McCall's,* November 1988.
285. *Carolina Herrera:* Carl Sferrazza Anthony, *As We Remember Her,* p. 315.
291. *"Caroline seems to have":* Edward Klein, *Farewell, Jackie,* p. 105.

Chapter 14: BABIES, BOOKS, BOYS, AND NEW GIRLFRIENDS

298. *"Caroline wasn't sick":* Lester David, "A Girl for Caroline," *McCall's,* September 1988.
300. *Rudolf Nureyev:* Diana DuBois, *In Her Sister's Shadow,* p. 370.
304. *Alec Baldwin:* Magazine interview with Alec Baldwin, *People,* commemorative issue, summer 1999.
306. *"Jack, I'm going to tell you something":* Darrell M. West, *Patrick Kennedy,* p. 35.
309. *Shelley Shusteroff:* Andersen, op. cit., pp. 236–237.
313. *Pamela Harriman:* When JFK Jr., at age three, stayed in the Harriman residence with his mother and sister, it belonged to Averell and Marie Harriman. Pamela, previously wed to Randolph Churchill and Leland Hayward, married Averell following Marie's death in 1970. She continued to reside in the Georgetown house following Averell's death in 1986.
313. *George Wayne:* Online entry—the Mail Archive, CTAL.com.
318. *Naomi Campbell:* Spignesi, op. cit., pp. 44–45.
318. *who'd just overcome a drinking problem:* DuBois, op. cit., pp. 290–293.
321. *Olympia & York:* "Works in Progress; Play's the Thing," *The New York Times,* June 26, 1988.
325. *Stanley Chess: Newsweek,* May 14, 1990.

Chapter 15: THE BEST AND WORST OF TIMES

331. *"An interactive computer program":* The Boston Globe, January 22, 1992.
331. *burst of hyperbole: The Washington Post,* November 5, 1988.
332. *Karen Duffy:* Karen Duffy, "John & Carolyn, the Spell They Cast," *Glamour,* October 1999.
333. *bachelor party:* Littell, op. cit., p. 123.
333. *Paul and Eva Font:* Sally Bedell Smith, *Grace and Power,* p. 460.
334. *"superior intelligence and iron will":* Mary Kerry Kennedy, who served as director of the RFK Memorial Center for Human Rights, was overheard discussing Caroline Kennedy's attributes at a 1992 Memorial Center fund-raiser. The comments were reported to the author by Juan Ramos, a Memorial Center guest.
339. *"I never doubted":* Magazine interview with Robert Morganthau Jr., *People,* commemorative issue, summer 1999.
340. *"working hunk":* Michael Gross, "Citizen Kennedy," *Esquire,* September 1995.
340. *Xuxa:* Spignesi, op. cit., pp. 62–63. Footage of the JFK Jr.–Xuxa luncheon ran on *A Current Affair,* February 14, 1992. Among Xuxa's other dubious accomplishments, she appeared as a centerfold in an issue of the Brazilian edition of *Playboy* and, according to a biographical online site, allegedly appeared in a "porn" flick. The author has been unable to confirm the facts behind the latter online assertion.
341. *Owen Carragher Jr.:* Magazine interview with Owen Carragher Jr., *People,* commemorative issue, summer 1999.
345. *August 29, 1990:* Leigh, op. cit., p. 285.
345. *Natalie Cross:* Andersen, op. cit., p. 262.

346. *dozens and dozens:* Leigh, op. cit., p. 289. According to Leigh, JFK Jr. sent Daryl Hannah a thousand roses; newspaper clips of the day place the number at several hundred.

346. *"April Showers":* "April" worked for various escort services in the Los Angeles area from 1987 to 1998. Currently a resident of Las Vegas, she is the food and beverage manager of a midsize hotel. For obvious reasons, she didn't want to be identified by her real name.

347. *personal memoir about John:* Littell, op. cit., pp. 230–235.

348. *two-way mirror:* Andersen, *Sweet Caroline,* p. 477.

348. *secretly videotaped:* Ibid.

349. *"You wouldn't mistake":* Ibid.

349. *Peter Gethers:* Jennifer Frey, " "Defense of Privacy," *People,* November 27, 1995.

350. *"I was washing dishes":* Carole Radziwill, *What Remains,* pp. 91–96.

351. *A "foolish" move:* Billy Way interview.

Chapter 16: JOHN AND DARYL

352. *"adrenaline junkie":* Billy Way interview.

352. *Natalie Cross:* Bonnie Robinson interview. Also see Bonnie Robinson, "Daryl's Nude Romps," *Women's Day,* November 1994.

353. *"It is untrue":* Spignesi, op. cit., p. 52; see also Mark Bego, *Jackson Browne.*

355. *Sugar Rautbord:* Spignesi, op. cit., pp. 53–54.

356. Sweet Caroline: Andersen, op. cit., pp. 218–219.

356. *Rob Littell recalled spending:* Littell, op. cit., pp. 140–142.

357. *Frank Mankiewicz:* Doug Wead, *All the Presidents' Children,* p. 214.

357. *In the Baltic:* Ibid.

358. *"Make up your mind":* Andersen, *The Day John Died,* p. 370.

360. *"Caroline is one of the few":* Hillary Clinton, *Living History,* pp. 180–191.

361. *Doris Kearns Goodwin:* Heymann, op. cit., p. 649.

361. *Interview published in* Vogue: William Norwich, "Prize Partnership," *Vogue,* June 1993.

362. *"Doesn't your girlfriend":* George Plimpton interview.

362. *Three and a half years later:* "Kennedy's Stolen Vehicle Is Recovered," *The New York Times,* November 27, 1996.

363. *Zabar's:* David Dinkins interview; see also magazine interview with Ken Sunshine, *People,* commemorative issue, summer 1999.

366. *Monsignor George Bardes:* Klein, op. cit., p. 24.

366. *Gary Lee Higgins:* Heymann, op. cit., p. 652.

372. Forbes *magazine's annual survey:* Forbes, May 2006; see also *New York Post,* May 25, 2006.

373. *$5.75 million:* Page Six, *New York Post,* May 8, 2006.

373. *Large metal box:* A detailed description of JFK Jr.'s North Moore Street loft can be found in Littell, op. cit., pp. 191–192.

375. *"It always amazed me":* Lawford, op. cit., p. 376.

378. *Hilary Shepard-Turner:* Magazine interview with Hilary Shepard-Turner, *People,* commemorative issue, summer 1999.

379. *According to JFK Jr. biographer Chris Andersen:* Andersen, op. cit., p. 293.

380. *"Top Ten":* Late Show with David Letterman, CBS-TV, October 19, 1993.

Chapter 17: DEATH BE NOT PROUD

381. *Julie Baker:* Leigh, op. cit., pp. 299–300.

385. *Drifting:* Klein, op. cit., p. 175.

388. *contemptuous Ed Schlossberg:* Ibid., pp. 183–185.

391. *At the conclusion of the service:* Jackie was the second former First Lady to be buried at Arlington National Cemetery. The first was Mrs. William Howard Taft.
392. *"I wanted you both to understand":* Hillary Clinton, op. cit., pp. 356–357.
393. *she had penned separate letters:* Jackie's last letters to John Jr. and Caroline can be found at the JFK Library. They are also quoted in Klein, *Farewell, Jackie.*

Chapter 18: PASSING THE TORCH

397. *come to grips with her mother's death:* Alfred Schlossberg, Ed's father, died on December 29, 1995. He was eighty-seven.
398. *"The press has a job to do":* Myrna Blyth, "The Right to Privacy," *Ladies' Home Journal,* November 1995.
398. *$9.2 million:* In May 2006 David Koch sold what had been Jackie's apartment for more than $33 million.
399. *Barbara Sullivan:* Sullivan's interview with Ed Schlossberg appeared in the *Chicago Tribune,* July 26, 1994.
399. *"stuff":* The New York Times, September 27, 2001. The article refers to a 1996 National Arts Club exhibit of Ed Schlossberg's work.
401. *"Caroline's husband":* Littell, op. cit., p. 169.
401. *series of telephone calls:* Andersen, *Sweet Caroline,* p. 194.
401. *forgery by a third party:* City of New York Department of Finance, document #2397PG 1448.
403. *Multiplex movie theater:* John Seabrook, "Talk of the Town," *The New Yorker,* August 2, 1999.
406. *Deborah Lamoureux:* Online entry—"Carolyn Bessette Kennedy in Remembrance," www.Geocities.com.
413. *"I knew Carolyn":* Michael Bergin, *The Other Man,* p. 21.
413. *he suddenly realized that:* Ibid., p. 46.
413. *"Lying is so much":* Ibid., p. 195.
414. *In "late June or early July":* Ibid., pp. 208–209. Further notations by Bergin on Carolyn Bessette Kennedy's apocryphal visit appear on pp. 210–212 of *The Other Man.*
414. *eleven days:* "The Other Man," *Variety,* March 29, 2004.
415. *Clifford Streit:* Clifford Streit interview. See also "Affair Tale Unlikely," UPI, March 31, 2004.
416. *Alexandra Speck:* Speck conducted her interview with Bergin on behalf of the author. After the publication of his book, Bergin continued to have problems. On September 14, 2004, he was charged with one felony count of DUI causing injury and one misdemeanor count of driving with a blood-alcohol level of more than the legal limit of 0.08 percent. According to various newspaper accounts, including the *Los Angeles Times,* Bergin was released on $5,000 bail. He was arraigned in connection with a July incident in West Hollywood in which a professional in-line skater was struck and seriously injured by a car. The final disposition of the case is not known to the author.
418. *Charlie King, John's former . . . :* Magazine interview with Charlie King. *People,* commemorative issue, summer 1999.

Chapter 19: LOVE'S LABOUR'S LOST

424. *Asia de Cuba:* There were rumors that JFK Jr. was a partial owner of this chic Murray Hill restaurant. The restaurant's current owners deny that such an affiliation existed, stipulating only that John was a regular customer.

424. *Drew Nieporent:* Magazine interview with Drew Nieporent, *People,* commemorative issue, summer 1999.

425. *J. D. Ligier:* New York *Daily News,* October 15, 1995.

429. *Pete Hamill:* Pete Hamill, "Coming of Age in Public," "Talk of the Town," *The New Yorker,* August 2, 1999.

430. *"Random Ventures Inc.":* JFK Jr. and Michael Berman retained the name of their kayaking enterprise as the corporate name for *George.*

430. *"Politics doesn't sell":* Gross, op. cit.

433. *future staff members:* See Richard Blow, *American Son,* for a more in-depth account of individual *George* staffers. In addition, the author interviewed Blow for this book.

434. *in the Catskills:* A more detailed account of this weekend can be found in Richard Blow, ibid.

434. *Tom Karon:* Magazine interview with Tom Karon, *People,* commemorative issue, summer 1999.

434. *George Wallace:* Leamer, op. cit., pp. 162–163.

435. *Dana Strayton:* Magazine interview with Dana Strayton, ibid.

435. *Oliver Stone:* Blow, op. cit., pp. 77–78.

436. *"We thought of posing":* Andersen, *Sweet Caroline,* p. 261. See also Richard Blow, *American Son,* as well as various newspaper accounts for details of the press conference.

436. *"Yes. No. Maybe":* Andersen, *Sweet Caroline,* p. 261.

438. *John grabbed Berman:* Blow, op. cit., pp. 197–198. In addition, author interviewed Berman for this book.

440. *angering Caroline Kennedy:* Andersen, op. cit., p. 124.

440. *Vernon Jordan:* Blow, op. cit., p. 266.

441. *Gabrielle Reece:* Ibid., pp. 88–89.

444. *Whenever Carolyn visited:* Ibid., p. 59.

445. *"Sometimes I look":* Ibid., p. 199.

448. *Donatella Versace:* Online entry —www.carolynbessettekennedy.com. ("Carolyn Bessette Kennedy in Remembrance—What Others Say").

448. *Valentino:* Ibid.

448. *saw them kiss:* Blow, op. cit., pp. 117–118.

448. *"Carolyn's the best shot I've got":* See excerpt of Littell's *The Men We Became* in *Redbook,* June 2004. Reiterated to the author by George Plimpton.

Chapter 20: WEDDING OF THE DECADE

456. *Shirley Wise:* New York *Daily News,* September 25, 1996. Contrary to the *Daily News* article, *Time* (November 6, 1996) reports that the Carolyn Bessette conversation with Wise took place when Carolyn and JFK Jr. were having their blood tests. Wise could not be reached for comment.

457. *according to Rob Littell.* Littell, op. cit., p. 196.

457. *navy blue boxer shorts:* Ibid.

459. *David Sayre:* Magazine interview with David Sayre, *People,* commemorative issue, summer 1999.

463. *"Getting married is a big adjustment":* New York *Daily News,* October 7, 1996.

464. *Bob Morris:* Bob Morris, "A Debut of Sorts," *The New York Times,* November 10, 1996.

465. *took place while Dan Samson:* Leamer, op. cit., pp. 443–444.

466. *"So you married":* Periodical interview with Carolyn Bessette, *WWD,* December 14, 1996.

467. *"stalkarazzi":* New York *Daily News,* November 18, 1997.

Chapter 21: PARADISE LOST

474. The New Republic: See John F. Kennedy Jr., "Mobutu: A Legend in Winter," *The New Republic,* June 9, 1997.

479. *Laura Cavanaugh:* New York *Daily News,* January 8, 1998.

480. *"There are some members": The Kennedy Legacy: A Conversation with John F. Kennedy Jr.,* History Channel, June 2, 1997.

481. *When Ted Kennedy suggested:* Conversation between JFK Jr. and Ted Kennedy provided by confidential source.

482. *"wildly exaggerated":* See excerpt of Littell's *The Men We Became* in *Redbook* (June 2004).

483. *Sheldon Streisand:* Author interview with Barbara Fleck. See also Andersen, op. cit., pp. 274–275.

484. *"Now whenever we want to get away":* New York *Daily News,* May 19, 1998.

484. *Dr. Gil Lederman:* Tony Brenna, Paola Leva, and Tom DiNardo, "Carolyn Bessette's Jekyll-and-Hyde Lifestyle," *National Enquirer,* July 19, 2004.

485. *"JFK Jr.'s marriage":* New York *Post,* November 2, 1998.

485. *"Do you think":* Star, November 7, 1998.

485. Haley Barbour: *New York Post,* November 20, 1998.

486. *"The situation upset John":* Littell, excerpt of *The Men We Became* in *Redbook.*

486. *called Pete Olsen:* Confidential source.

487. *marriage counseling:* Ibid.

487. *financier Pete Peterson:* Online entry—www.flightsafetyinternational.com.

488. *Bruce Weber:* WWD, July 19, 1999.

488. *Christa D'Souza:* "Rush & Molloy," New York *Daily News,* July 20, 1999.

489. *Evelyn Lauder:* Magazine interview with Evelyn Lauder, *People,* commemorative issue, summer 1999.

489. *Washington College:* Office of public relations, Washington College, Chestertown, Maryland.

489. *commercial airliner to San Francisco:* Blow, op. cit., pp. 273–275.

490. *Microsoft:* Ibid.

490. *Memorial Day weekend:* Rob Littell interview. See also Leamer, op. cit., pp. 520–521.

491. *"You can be boring at home":* WWD, July 19, 1999.

491. *"Thank God for big government":* Blow, op. cit., p. 287.

492. *Jeffrey D. Sachs:* Confidential source.

492. *At the same gathering:* Leamer, op. cit., p. 457.

493. *"One of John's favorite philosophical ideas":* Rob Littell interview. See also Littell, excerpt of *The Men We Became* in *Redbook.*

493. *John admitted to Richard Blow:* Blow, op. cit., p. 301.

494. *Rory Kennedy's wedding:* Rory finally married boyfriend Mark Bailey at the beginning of August 1999. In order to avoid publicity, they had a small private wedding ceremony in Greece.

494. *"coming at him":* Leamer, op. cit., p. 485.

495. *"I'm flying with an instructor":* Blow, op. cit., p. 307.

495. *His orthopedist:* Confidential source.

495. *"A true gentleman":* Ibid.

Chapter 22: KEEPER OF THE FLAME

499. *"If he's out there":* Anthony Radziwill quoted by Reuter's News Service, July 17, 1999.

499. *It had taken him a long time:* Michael Gross interview.

502. *Bettina Lowell:* Andersen, op. cit., p. 283.

503. *"John worked very hard":* New York *Daily News,* December 7, 1999.

503. *"Caroline ate like a horse!":* Boston Herald, March 3, 2000.

504. *Aileen Mehle:* "Caroline Kennedy Update," *People,* May 29, 2000.

504. *"I'm not sure":* The Associated Press, August 16, 2000.

505. *a piece on Ed Schlossberg:* Jeffrey Hogrefe, "The Family Man," *New York* magazine, April 30, 2001.

505. *"immense game area":* Steven Heller, "Big Fun Cool Things," *Metropolis* magazine, May 2002.

506. *Robin Finn: The New York Times,* April 27, 2001.

509. *an intervention:* Confidential source.

512. *"Get a divorce":* Confidential source.

513. *"been spotted wearing":* Online entry—www.MYSA.com, October 18, 2004.

514. *"It's hard for me":* The New York Times, October 28, 2004.

515. *Roberta Fineberg:* Fineberg is the mother of fourteen-year-old Paris Fineberg-Heymann, currently a student at the Hunter School in New York. He is the son of the author of this book.

517. *Patrick Gallagher:* "JFK Jr. Items Stolen," *New York Post,* April 14, 2004.

518. *Susan Thomases:* Online entry—Claudia Bertollini-Ciano, "Caroline Versus the 'Nanny,'" www.Lavox.com. See also "A Generous Gift for a Loyal Friend," *The New York Times,* April 10, 2005.

520. *It wasn't the best year:* Caroline's aunt Patricia Kennedy Lawford, eighty-two, died on September 18, 2006, from complications of pneumonia. Caroline attended the funeral.

520. *"Environmental rapist":* New York Post, January 5, 2006.

521. *Andrea Peyser:* Andrea Peyser, *New York Post,* June 14, 2006.

BIBLIOGRAPHY

◆

Aarons, Slim. *A Wonderful Time: An Intimate Portrait of the Good Life.* New York: Harper & Row, 1974.

Abbe, Kathryn McLaughlin, and Frances McLaughlin Gill. *Twins on Twins.* New York: Clarkson Potter, 1980.

Abernathy, Ralph. *And the Walls Came Tumbling Down: An Autobiography.* New York: Harper & Row, 1989.

Acheson, Dean. *Power and Diplomacy.* Cambridge, Mass.: Harvard University Press, 1958.

Adams, William Howard. *Atget's Gardens.* Garden City, N.Y.: Doubleday, 1979.

Adler, Bill. *The Kennedy Children: Triumphs & Tragedies.* New York: Franklin Watts, 1980.

———, ed. *The Eloquent Jacqueline Kennedy Onassis: A Portrait in Her Own Words.* New York: HarperCollins Publishers, 2004.

Agel, Jerome, and Eugene Boe. *22 Fires.* New York: Bantam Books, 1977.

Aikman, Lonnelle. *The Living White House.* Foreword by Nancy Reagan. Washington, D.C.: White House Historical Association of the National Geographic Society, 1982.

Alderman, Ellen, and Caroline Kennedy. *In Our Defense: The Bill of Rights in Action.* New York: William Morrow & Co., 1991.

———. *The Right to Privacy.* New York: Knopf, 1995.

Alexander, Lois K. *Blacks in the History of Fashion.* New York: Harlem Institute of Fashion, 1982.

Alexander, Shana. *When She Was Bad: The Story of Bess, Hortense, Sukhreet & Nancy.* New York: Random House, 1990.

Alphand, Hervé. *L'étonnement d'être: Journal, 1939–1973.* Paris: Fayard, 1977.

Alsop, Susan Mary. *To Marietta from Paris, 1945–1960.* Garden City, N.Y.: Doubleday, 1975.

Amory, Cleveland. *Who Killed Society?* New York: Harper & Brothers, 1966.

Andersen, Christopher. *The Day John Died.* New York: William Morrow & Co., 2000.

———. *Jackie after Jack: A Portrait of the Lady.* New York: William Morrow & Co., 1998.

———. *Sweet Caroline: Last Child of Camelot.* New York: HarperCollins, 2003.

Anderson, Jack. *Washington Exposé.* Washington, D.C.: Public Affairs Press, 1967.

Angeli, Daniel, and Jean-Paul Dousset. *Private Pictures.* New York: Viking, 1980.

Anger, Kenneth. *Hollywood Babylon.* San Francisco: Straight Arrow, 1975.

———. *Hollywood Babylon II.* New York: E. P. Dutton, 1984.

Anson, Robert Sam. *"They've Killed the President!"* New York: Bantam Books, 1975.

Anthony, Carl Sferrazza. *As We Remember Her: Jacqueline Kennedy Onassis in the Words of Her Family and Friends.* New York: HarperCollins, 1997.

Ardoin, John, and Gerald Fitzgerald. *Callas*. London: Thames & Hudson, 1984.

Aronson, Steven M. L. *Hype*. New York: William Morrow & Co., 1983.

Astor, Brooke. *Footprints: An Autobiography*. New York: Doubleday, 1980.

Auchincloss, Joanna Russell, and Caroline Auchincloss Fowler. *The Auchincloss Family*. Freeport, Maine: The Dingley Press, 1957.

Bacall, Lauren. *By Myself*. New York: Knopf, 1978.

Bacon, James. *Made in Hollywood*. Chicago: Contemporary Books, 1977.

Bair, Marjorie. *Jacqueline Kennedy in the White House*. New York: Paperback Library, 1963.

Baker, Carlos. *Ernest Hemingway: A Life Story*. New York: Scribner, 1969.

Baker, Robert Gene. *Wheeling and Dealing: Confessions of a Capitol Hill Operator*. New York: W. W. Norton & Co., 1978.

Baldrige, Letitia. *Letitia Baldrige's Complete Guide to Executive Manners*. New York: Rawson, 1985.

———. *Of Diamonds and Diplomats*. Boston: Houghton Mifflin, 1968.

Baldwin, Billy. *Billy Baldwin Remembers*. New York: Harcourt Brace Jovanovich, 1974.

Baldwin, Billy, with Michael Gardine. *Billy Baldwin: An Autobiography*. Boston: Little, Brown and Company, 1985.

Barrow, Andrew. *Gossip: A History of High Society from 1920 to 1970*. New York: Coward, McCann & Geoghegan, 1978.

Bayh, Marvella. *Marvella: A Personal Journey*. New York: Harcourt Brace Jovanovich, 1979.

Beaton, Cecil. *Self Portrait with Friends: The Selected Diaries of Cecil Beaton, 1926–1974*. Edited by Richard Buckle. New York: Times Books, 1979.

Bego, Mark. *Jackson Browne: His Life and Music*. New York: Citadel Press, 2005.

Bergin, Michael. *The Other Man: John F. Kennedy, Jr., Carolyn Bessette, and Me*. New York: ReganBooks, 2004.

Beschloss, Michael R. *Kennedy and Roosevelt: The Uneasy Alliance*. New York: W. W. Norton & Co., 1980.

Best-Loved Poems of Jacqueline Kennedy Onassis, The. Selected and introduced by Caroline Kennedy. New York: Hyperion, 2001.

Bevington, Helen. *Along Came the Witch: A Journal in the 1960's*. New York: Harcourt Brace Jovanovich, 1976.

Birmingham, Stephen. *Jacqueline Bouvier Kennedy Onassis*. New York: Grosset & Dunlap, 1978.

———. *Real Lace: America's Irish Rich*. New York: Harper & Row, 1973.

———. *"The Rest of Us": The Rise of America's Eastern European Jews*. Boston: Little, Brown and Company, 1984.

———. *The Right People: A Portrait of the American Social Establishment*. Boston: Little, Brown and Company, 1968.

Bishop, Jim. *A Day in the Life of President Kennedy*. New York: Random House, 1964.

Blackwell, Earl. *Earl Blackwell's Celebrity Register*. Towson, Md.: Times Publishing Group, 1986.

Blair, Joan, and Clay Blair Jr. *The Search for JFK*. New York: Berkley, 1976.

Blakey, George Robert, and Richard N. Billings. *The Plot to Kill the President*. New York: Times Books, 1981.

Blow, Richard. *American Son: A Portrait of John F. Kennedy, Jr.* New York: Henry Holt and Co., 2002.

Boller Jr., Paul F. *Presidential Anecdotes*. New York: Oxford University Press, 1988.

———. *Presidential Wives*. New York: Oxford University Press, 1988.

Bouvier, Jacqueline, and Lee Bouvier. *One Special Summer*. New York: Delacorte Press, 1974.

Bouvier Jr., John Vernou. *Our Forebears.* Privately printed, 1931, 1942, 1944, 1947.

Bouvier, Kathleen. *To Jack with Love: Black Jack Bouvier, a Remembrance.* New York: Kensington, 1979.

Bradford, Sarah. *America's Queen: The Life of Jacqueline Kennedy Onassis.* New York: Viking, 2000.

Bradlee, Benjamin C. *Conversations with Kennedy.* New York: W. W. Norton & Company, 1975.

Brady, Frank. *Onassis: An Extravagant Life.* Englewood Cliffs, N.J.: Prentice-Hall, 1977.

Bragg, Rick. *All Over but the Shoutin'.* New York: Vintage, 1977.

Branch, Taylor. *Parting the Waters: America in the King Years, 1954–63.* New York: Simon & Schuster, 1988.

Brauer, Carl M. *John F. Kennedy and the Second Reconstruction.* New York: Columbia University Press, 1977.

Bray, Howard. *The Pillars of the Post: The Making of a News Empire in Washington.* New York: W. W. Norton & Company, 1980.

Brenner, Marie. *Great Dames: What I Learned from Older Women.* New York: Three Rivers Press, 2000.

Brolin, Brent C. *The Battle of St. Bart's: A Tale of Heroism, Connivance and Bumbling.* New York: William Morrow & Co., 1971.

Brown, Coco. *American Dream: The Houses at Sagaponac: Modern Living in the Hamptons.* Essays by Richard Maier and Alastair Gordon. New York: Rizzoli, 2003.

Brown, Gene, ed. *The Kennedys: A New York Times Profile.* New York: Arno Press, 1980.

Bruno, Jerry, and Jeff Greenfield. *The Advance Man.* New York: William Morrow & Co., 1971.

Bryan, J., III, and Charles J. V. Murphy. *The Windsor Story.* New York: William Morrow & Co., 1979.

Bryant, Traphes, and Frances Spatz Leighton. *Dog Days at the White House: The Outrageous Memoirs of the Presidential Kennel Keeper.* New York: Macmillan Publishing Co., 1975.

Buchwald, Art. *The Establishment Is Alive and Well in Washington.* New York: Putnam, 1968.

Buck, Pearl S. *The Kennedy Women.* New York: Cowles, 1970.

Burns, James MacGregor. *Edward Kennedy and the Camelot Legacy.* New York: W. W. Norton & Company, 1976.

———. *John Kennedy: A Political Profile.* New York: Harcourt Brace Jovanovich, 1960.

Bushnell, Candace. *Sex and the City.* New York: Warner Books, 1996.

Cafarakis, Christian, with Jack Harvey. *The Fabulous Onassis: His Life and Loves.* New York: William Morrow & Co., 1972.

Cameron, Gail. *Rose: A Biography of Rose Fitzgerald Kennedy.* New York: Putnam, 1971.

Capote, Truman. *Answered Prayers: The Unfinished Novel.* New York: Random House, 1987.

———. *A Capote Reader.* New York: Random House, 1987.

———. *Music for Chameleons.* New York: Random House, 1975.

Caroli, Betty Boyd. *First Ladies.* New York: Oxford University Press, 1987.

Carpozi Jr., George. *The Hidden Side of Jacqueline Kennedy.* New York: Pyramid Books, 1967.

Carter, Ernestine. *Magic Names of Fashion.* Englewood Cliffs, N.J.: Prentice-Hall, 1980.

Carter, Rosalynn. *First Lady from Plains.* Boston: Houghton Mifflin, 1984.

Cassini, Igor. *I'd Do It All Over Again.* New York: Putnam, 1977.

Cassini, Oleg. *In My Own Fashion: An Autobiography.* New York: Simon & Schuster, 1987.

Celebrity Homes: Architectural Digest Presents the Private Worlds of Thirty International Personalities. Edited by Paige Rense. New York: Viking Press, 1977.

Cerf, Bennett. *At Random: The Reminiscences of Bennett Cerf.* New York: Random House, 1977.

Chellis, Marcia. *Living with the Kennedys: The Joan Kennedy Story.* New York: Simon & Schuster, 1985.

Cheshire, Maxine. *Maxine Cheshire, Reporter.* Boston: Houghton Mifflin, 1978.

Childs, Marquis William. *Witness to Power.* New York: McGraw-Hill, 1975.

Churcher, Sharon. *New York Confidential.* New York: Crown Publishers, 1986.

Churchill, Sarah. *Keep On Dancing: An Autobiography.* New York: Coward, McCann & Geoghegan, 1981.

Clift, Eleanor, and Tom Brazaitis. *Madam President: Women Blazing the Leadership Trail.* New York; London: Routledge, 2003.

Clinch, Nancy Gager. *The Kennedy Neurosis.* New York: Grosset & Dunlap, 1973.

Clinton, Bill. *My Life.* New York: Knopf, 2004.

Clinton, Hillary Rodham. *Living History.* New York: Simon & Schuster, 2003.

Colby, Gerard. *Du Pont Dynasty: Behind the Nylon Curtain.* Secaucus, N.J.: Lyle Stuart, 1984.

Collier, Peter, and David Horowitz. *The Kennedys: An American Drama.* New York: Summit Books, 1984.

Concise Compendium of the Warren Commission Report on the Assassination of John F. Kennedy, A. New York: Popular Library, 1964.

Condon, Dianne Russell. *Jackie's Treasures: The Fabled Objects from the Auction of the Century.* Foreword by Dominick Dunne. New York: Cader Books, 1996.

Cooney, John. *The American Pope: The Life and Times of Francis Cardinal Spellman.* New York: Times Books, 1984.

———. *The Annenbergs.* New York: Simon & Schuster, 1982.

Cooper, Lady Diana. *The Rainbow Comes and Goes.* Boston: Houghton Mifflin, 1958.

Coover, Robert. *Sesion de cine o Tocala de neuvo, Sam.* Traduccion de Mariano Antolin Rato. Barcelona: Editorial Anagrama, 1993.

Cormier, Frank. *Presidents Are People Too.* Washington, D.C.: Public Affairs Press, 1966.

Coulter, Laurie. *When John and Caroline Lived in the White House.* New York: Hyperion, 2000.

Coward, Noel. *The Noel Coward Diaries.* Edited by Graham Payn and Sheridan Morley. Boston: Little, Brown and Company, 1982.

Cowles, Virginia. *The Astors.* New York: Knopf, 1979.

Curtis, Charlotte. *First Lady.* New York: Pyramid Books, 1962.

———. *The Rich and Other Atrocities.* New York: Harper & Row, 1976.

Cutler, John Henry. *Cardinal Cushing of Boston.* New York: Hawthorne Books, 1970.

Dallas, Rita, and Jeanira Ratcliffe. *The Kennedy Case.* New York: Putnam, 1973.

Damore, Leo. *The Cape Cod Years of John Fitzgerald Kennedy.* Englewood Cliffs, N.J.: Prentice-Hall, 1967.

———. *Senatorial Privilege: The Chappaquiddick Cover-Up.* Washington, D.C.: Regnery-Gateway, 1988.

Dareff, Hal. *Jacqueline Kennedy: A Portrait in Courage.* New York: Parents' Magazine Press, 1966.

David, Lester. *Joan—The Reluctant Kennedy: A Biographical Profile.* New York: Funk & Wagnalls, 1974.

David, Lester, and Irene David. *Bobby Kennedy: The Making of a Folk Hero.* New York: Dodd, Mead, 1986.

Davis, Deborah. *Katharine the Great: Katharine Graham and the Washington Post.* New York: Harcourt Brace Jovanovich, 1979.

Davis, John H. *The Bouviers: A Portrait of an American Family.* New York: Farrar, Straus & Giroux, 1969.

———. *The Kennedys: Dynasty and Disaster, 1848–1983.* New York: McGraw-Hill, 1984.

Davis, L. J. *Onassis: Aristotle and Christina.* New York: St. Martin's Press, 1986.

Davis, William, and Christina Tree. *The Kennedy Library.* Exton, Pa.: Schiffer Publishing, 1980.

Davison, Jean. *Oswald's Game.* New York: W. W. Norton & Co., 1983.

Deaver, Michael K., with Mickey Hershkowitz. *Behind the Scenes.* New York: William Morrow & Co., 1988.

De Combray, Richard. *Goodbye Europe, A Novel in Six Parts.* Garden City, N.Y.: Doubleday, 1983.

de Gaulle, Charles. *Lettres, Notes et Carnets, Janvier 1964–Juin 1966.* Paris: Plon, 1987.

Delany, Kevin. *A Walk through Georgetown: A Guided Stroll That Details the History and Charm of Old Georgetown.* Illustrated by Sally Booher. [Washington ? 1971].

Demaris, Ovid. *The Last Mafioso: The Treacherous World of Jimmy Fratianno.* New York: Times Books, 1981.

De Massy, Baron Christian. *Palace: My Life in the Royal Family of Monaco.* New York: Atheneum, 1986.

De Pauw, Linda Grant, Conover Hunt, and Miriam Schneir. *Remember the Ladies: Women in America, 1750–1815.* New York: The Viking Press, 1976.

De Toledano, Ralph. *R.F.K.: The Man Who Would Be President.* New York: Putnam, 1967.

Devi, Gayatri, and Santha Rama Rau. *A Princess Remembers: The Memoirs of the Maharani of Jaipur.* Philadelphia: J. B. Lippincott, 1976.

Dherbier, Yann-Brice, and Pierre-Henri Verlhac. *John F. Kennedy Jr.: A Life in Pictures.* New York: powerHouse Books, 2005.

Dickerson, Nancy. *Among Those Present: A Reporter's View of Twenty-five Years in Washington.* New York: Random House, 1976.

Dickinson, Janice. *Everything about Me Is Fake . . . and I'm Perfect.* New York: ReganBooks, 2004.

———. *No Lifeguard on Duty: The Accidental Life of the World's First Supermodel.* New York: ReganBooks, 2002.

Donovan, Robert J. *PT 109: John F. Kennedy in World War II.* New York: McGraw-Hill, 1961.

Drosnin, Michael. *Citizen Hughes.* New York: Holt, Rinehart and Winston, 1985.

Druitt, Michael. *John F. Kennedy Jr.: A Life in the Spotlight.* Kansas City: Ariel Books, 1996.

DuBois, Diana. *In Her Sister's Shadow: An Intimate Biography of Lee Radziwill.* Boston: Little, Brown and Company, 1995.

Dumas, Timothy. *Greentown: Murder and Mystery in Greenwich, America's Wealthiest Community.* New York: Arcade Publishing, 1998.

Eban, Abba. *Abba Eban: An Autobiography.* New York: Random House, 1977.

Eisenhower, Julie Nixon. *Pat Nixon: The Untold Story.* New York: Simon & Schuster, 1986.

Englund, Steven. *Grace of Monaco.* Garden City, N.Y.: Doubleday, 1984.

Epstein, Edward Jay. *Inquest: The Warren Commission and the Establishment of Truth.* New York: Viking, 1966.

———. *The Rise and Fall of Diamonds: The Shattering of a Brilliant Illusion.* New York: Simon & Schuster, 1982.

Evans, Peter. *Ari: The Life and Times of Aristotle Onassis.* New York: Summit Books, 1986.

———. *Nemesis: The True Story of Aristotle Onassis, Jackie O, and the Love Triangle That Brought Down the Kennedys.* New York: ReganBooks, 2004.

Evans, Rowland, and Robert Novak. *Lyndon B. Johnson: The Exercise of Power.* New York: New American Library, 1966.

Evica, George Michael. *And We Are All Mortal: New Evidence and Analysis in the John F. Kennedy Assassination.* West Hartford, Conn.: Evica, 1978.

Exner, Judith. *My Story.* New York: Grove Press, 1977.

Fairlee, Henry. *The Kennedy Promise: The Politics of Expectation.* New York: Doubleday, 1972.

Fay, Jr., Paul B. *The Pleasure of His Company.* New York: Harper & Row, 1966.

Finsterwald, Bernard J. *Coincidence or Conspiracy.* New York: Zebra Books, 1977.

Fisher, Eddie. *Eddie: My Life, My Loves.* New York: Harper & Row, 1981.

Flaherty, Tina Santi. *What Jackie Taught Us: Lessons from the Remarkable Life of Jacqueline Kennedy Onassis.* New York: Perigree, 2004.

Folsom, Merrill. *More Great American Mansions and Their Stories.* New York: Hastings House Book Publishers, 1967.

Fontaine, Joan. *No Bed of Roses: An Autobiography.* New York: William Morrow & Co., 1978.

Four Days: The Historical Record of the Death of President Kennedy. Compiled by United Press International and *American Heritage* Magazine. New York: American Heritage Press, 1964.

Frank, Sid, and Arden Davis Melick. *Presidents: Tidbits and Trivia.* Maplewood, N.J.: Hammond World Atlas Corp., 1986.

Franklin, Marc A., David A. Anderson, and Fred H. Cate. *Mass Media Law: Cases and Materials.* 6th ed. New York: Foundation Press, 2000.

Fraser, Nicholas, Philip Jacobson, Mark Ottaway, and Lewis Chester. *Aristotle Onassis.* Philadelphia: J. B. Lippincott, 1977.

Friedman, Stanley P. *The Magnificent Kennedy Women.* Derby, Conn.: Monarch Books, 1964.

Fries, Chuck, and Irv Wilson, with Spencer Green. *"We'll Never Be Young Again": Remembering the Last Days of John F. Kennedy.* Los Angeles: Tallfellow Press, 2003.

Frischauer, Willi. *Onassis.* New York: Meredith Press, 1968.

Fuhrman, Mark. *Murder in Greenwich: Who Killed Martha Moxley?* Foreword by Dominick Dunne. New York: Cliff Street Books, 1998.

Gabor, Zsa Zsa. *Zsa Zsa Gabor, My Story.* Written by Gerold Frank. Cleveland: World Pub. Co., 1960.

Gadney, Reg. *Kennedy.* New York: Holt, Rinehart and Winston, 1983.

Gage, Nicholas. *Greek Fire: The Story of Maria Callas and Aristotle Onassis.* New York: Knopf, 2000.

Gaines, Steven, and Sharon Churcher. *Obsession: The Lives and Times of Calvin Klein.* New York: Carol Publishing Group, 1994.

Galbraith, John Kenneth. *Ambassador's Journal: A Personal Account of the Kennedy Years.* Boston: Houghton Mifflin, 1969.

Galella, Ron. *Jacqueline.* New York: Sheed and Ward, 1974.

————. *Off-Guard: Beautiful People Unveiled before the Camera Lens.* New York: McGraw-Hill Education, 1976.

Gallagher, Mary Barelli. *My Life with Jacqueline Kennedy.* New York: David McKay Co., 1969.

Gardiner Jr., Ralph. *Young, Gifted and Rich: The Secrets of America's Most Successful Entrepreneurs.* New York: Simon & Schuster, 1984.

Gatti, Arthur. *The Kennedy Curse.* Chicago: Regnery, 1976.

Getty, J. Paul. *As I See It: The Autobiography of J. Paul Getty.* Englewood Cliffs, N.J.: Prentice-Hall, 1976.

Giancana, Antoinette, and Thomas C. Renner. *Mafia Princess: Growing Up in Sam Giancana's Family.* New York: William Morrow & Co., 1984.

Gibson, Barbara, and Caroline Latham. *Life with Rose Kennedy.* New York: Warner Books, 1986.

Gibson, Barbara, and Ted Schwarz. *The Kennedys: The Third Generation.* New York: Thunder's Mouth Press, 1993.

————. *Rose Kennedy and Her Family: The Best and Worst of Their Lives and Times.* Secaucus, N.J.: Carol Publishing Corporation, 1995.

Gingras, Angèle de T. *"From Bussing to Bugging": The Best in Congressional Humor.* Washington, D.C.: Acropolis Books, 1973.

Gold, Arthur, and Robert Fizdale. *Misia: The Life of Misia Sert.* New York: Knopf, 1980.

Goldman, Eric F. *The Tragedy of Lyndon Johnson.* New York: Knopf, 1969.

Goodwin, Doris Kearns. *The Fitzgeralds and the Kennedys: An American Saga.* New York: Simon & Schuster, 1987.

Goodwin, Richard N. *Remembering America: A Voice from the Sixties.* Boston: Little, Brown and Company, 1988.

Granger, Stewart. *Sparks Fly Upward.* New York: Putnam, 1981.

Gray, Earle. *Wildcatters: The Story of Pacific Petroleum and Westward Expansion.* Toronto: McClelland and Stewart, 1982.

Greenberg, Carol, and Sara Bonnett Stein. *Pretend Your Nose Is a Crayon: And Other Strategies for Staying Younger Longer.* Boston: Houghton Mifflin, 1991.

Grier, Roosevelt. *Rosey, An Autobiography: The Gentle Giant.* Tulsa: Honor Books, 1986.

Grobel, Lawrence. *Conversations with Capote.* New York: New American Library, 1985.

Guiles, Fred Lawrence. *Legend: The Life and Death of Marilyn Monroe.* New York: Stein and Day Publishing, 1984.

Gulley, Bill, and Mary Ellen Reese. *Breaking Cover.* New York: Simon & Schuster, 1980.

Guthman, Edwin. *We Band of Brothers: A Memoir of Robert F. Kennedy.* New York: Harper & Row, 1971.

Guthrie, Lee. *Jackie: The Price of the Pedestal.* New York: Drake Publishers, 1978.

Halberstam, David. *The Best and the Brightest.* New York: Random House, 1972.

Hall, Gordon Langley, and Ann Pinchot. *Jacqueline Kennedy: A Biography.* New York: Frederick Fell, 1964.

Halle, Kay. *The Grand Original: Portraits of Randolph Churchill by His Friends.* Boston: Houghton Mifflin, 1971.

Hamilton, Ian. *Robert Lowell: A Biography.* New York: Random House, 1982.

Harris, Bill. *John Fitzgerald Kennedy: A Photographic Tribute.* New York: Crescent, 1983.

Harris, Fred R. *Potomac Fever.* New York: W. W. Norton & Company, 1977.

Harris, Kenneth. *Conversations.* London: Hodder & Stoughton, 1967.

Harris, Warren G. *Cary Grant: A Touch of Elegance.* Garden City, N.Y.: Doubleday, 1987.

Healy, Diana Dixon. *America's First Ladies: Private Lives of the Presidential Wives.* New York: Atheneum, 1988.

Heller, Deanne, and David Heller. *A Complete Story of America's First Lady.* Derby, Conn.: Monarch Books, 1961.

———. *Jacqueline Kennedy: The Warmly Human Story of the Woman All Americans Have Taken to Their Heart.* Derby, Conn.: Monarch Books, 1963.

Hemingway, Mary Walsh. *How It Was.* New York: Knopf, 1976.

Herbert, David. *Second Son: An Autobiography.* London: Owen, 1972.

Hersh, Burton. *The Education of Edward Kennedy: A Family Biography.* New York: William Morrow & Co., 1972.

Hersh, Seymour M. *The Dark Side of Camelot.* Boston: Little, Brown and Company, 1997.

Heymann, C. David. *American Aristocracy: The Lives and Times of James Russell, Amy, and Robert Lowell.* New York: Dodd, Mead, 1980.

———. *The Georgetown Ladies' Social Club: Power, Passion, and Politics in the Nation's Capital.* New York: Atria Books, 2003.

———. *Poor Little Rich Girl: The Life and Legend of Barbara Hutton.* Secaucus, N.J.: Lyle Stuart, 1984.

———. *R.F.K.: A Candid Biography of Robert F. Kennedy.* New York: Dutton, 1998.

———. *A Woman Named Jackie: An Intimate Biography of Jacqueline Bouvier Kennedy Onassis.* Secaucus, N.J.: Carol Communications, 1989.

Hibbert, Christopher. *The Royal Victorians: King Edward VII, His Family and Friends.* Philadelphia: J. B. Lippincott, 1976.

Higham, Charles. *Marlena: The Life of Marlena Dietrich.* New York: W. W. Norton & Company, 1977.

———. *Rose: The Life and Times of Rose Fitzgerald Kennedy.* New York: Pocket Books, 1995.

———. *Sisters: The Story of Olivia de Havilland and Joan Fontaine.* New York: Putnam Publishing Group, 1984.

Hohenberg, John. *The Pulitzer Prizes: A History of the Awards in Books, Drama, Music, and Journalism, Based on the Private Files over Six Decades.* New York: Columbia University Press, 1974.

Holland, Max. *The Kennedy Assassination Tapes.* New York: Knopf, 2004.

Honan, William H. *Ted Kennedy: Profile of a Survivor.* New York: Quadrangle Books, 1972.

Hosmer, Charles Bridgham. *Preservation Comes of Age: From Williamsburg to the National Trust, 1926–1949.* Vol. II. Charlottesville: University of Virginia Press, 1981.

Hurt, Henry, *Reasonable Doubt: An Investigation into the Assassination of John F. Kennedy.* New York: Holt, Rinehart and Winston, 1985.

Huste, Annemarie. *Annemarie's Personal Cook Book.* London: Bartholomew House, 1968.

Isaacson, Walter, and Evan Thomas. *The Wise Men—Six Friends and the World They Made: Acheson, Bohlen, Harriman, Kennan, Lovett, McCloy.* New York: Simon & Schuster, 1986.

Jackson, Michael. *Moonwalk.* New York: Doubleday, 1988.

Jamieson, Katherine Hall. *Packaging the Presidency: A History and Criticism of Presidential Campaign Advertising.* New York: Oxford University Press, 1984.

JFK, Jr.: The Untold Story (periodical). *Fifth Anniversary Issue.* New York: American Media Mini Mags Inc., 2004.

Joesten, Joachim. *Onassis: A Biography.* New York: Tower, 1973.

John F. Kennedy Library. *Historical Materials in the John F. Kennedy Library.* Compiled and edited by Ronald E. Whealan. Boston (Columbia Point, Boston 02125): The Library, 2000.

Johnson, Lady Bird. *A White House Diary.* New York: Holt, Rinehart & Winston, 1970.

Johnson, Lyndon Baines. *The Vantage Point: Perspectives of the Presidency 1963–1969.* New York: Holt, Rinehart & Winston, 1971.

Johnson, Sam Houston. *My Brother Lyndon.* New York: Cowles, 1969.

Josephson, Matthew. *The Money Lords: The Great Finance Capitalists, 1925–1950.* New York: Weybright, and Talley, 1972.

Kane, Elizabeth. *Jackie O.: A Life in Pictures.* New York: Barnes & Noble Books, 2004.

Kantor, Seth. *The Ruby Cover-up.* New York: Kensington, 1978.

Kearns, Doris. *Lyndon Johnson and the American Dream.* New York: Harper & Row, 1976.

Keenan, Brigid. *The Women We Wanted to Look Like.* New York: St. Martin's Press, 1978.

Kellerman, Barbara. *All the President's Kin.* New York: The Free Press, 1981.

Kelley, Kitty. *Elizabeth Taylor: The Last Star.* New York: Simon & Schuster, 1981.

———. *His Way: The Unauthorized Biography of Frank Sinatra.* New York: Bantam Books, 1986.

———. *Jackie Oh!* Secaucus, N.J.: Lyle Stuart, 1978.

Kelly, Tom. *The Imperial Post: The Meyers, the Grahams, and the Paper That Rules Washington.* New York: William Morrow & Co., 1983.

Kennedy, Caroline. *A Family of Poems: My Favorite Poetry for Children.* New York: Hyperion Books, 2005.

Kennedy, Edward M., ed. *The Fruitful Bough: A Tribute to Joseph P. Kennedy.* Privately printed, 1965.

Kennedy, John F. *As We Remember Joe.* Privately printed, 1945.

———. *Profiles in Courage.* New York: Harper & Row, 1964.

———. *Public Papers of the Presidents of the United States: John F. Kennedy, 1961, 1962, 1963.* 3 vols. U.S. Government Printing Office, 1962, 1963, 1964.

———. *Why England Slept.* New York: Wilfred Funk, 1940.

Kennedy, Robert F. *The Enemy Within.* New York: Harper, 1960.

———. Edwin O. Guthman and Jeffrey Shulman, eds. *Robert Kennedy in His Own Words: The Unpublished Recollections of the Kennedy Years.* New York: Bantam Books, 1988.

———. *Thirteen Days: A Memoir of the Cuban Missile Crisis.* New York: W. W. Norton & Company, 1969.

———. *To Seek a New World.* Garden City, N.Y.: Doubleday & Company, 1967.

Kennedy Jr., Robert F. *Crimes against Nature: How George W. Bush and His Corporate Pals Are Plundering the Country and Hijacking Our Democracy.* New York: HarperCollins Publishers, 2004.

Kennedy, Sheila Rauch. *Shattered Faith: A Woman's Struggle to Stop the Catholic Church from Annulling Her Marriage.* New York: Henry Holt and Company, 1998.

Kern, Montague, Patricia W. Levering, and Ralph B. Levering. *The Kennedy Crisis: The Press, the Presidency, and Foreign Policy.* Chapel Hill: University of North Carolina Press, 1983.

Kessler, Judy. *Inside People: The Stories behind the Stories.* New York: Villard, 1994.

King, Coretta Scott. *My Life with Martin Luther King, Jr.* New York: Holt, Rinehart & Winston, 1969.

King, Larry, with Peter Occhiogrosso. *Tell It to the King.* New York: G. P. Putnam's Sons, 1988.

Klapthor, Margaret Brown. *The First Ladies.* Washington, D.C.: The White House Historical Association, 1975.

Klein, Edward. *Farewell, Jackie: A Portrait of Her Final Days.* New York: Viking, 2004.

———. *Just Jackie: Her Private Years.* New York: Ballantine Books, 1998.

———. *The Kennedy Curse: Why Tragedy Has Haunted America's First Family for 150 Years.* New York: St. Martin's Press, 2003.

Knight, Frank Kenneth. *Frank-ly McKnight: A Mini-Autobiography.* Laguna Hills, Calif.: McKnight Enterprises, 1992.

Knightly, Phillip, and Caroline Kennedy. *An Affair of State: The Profumo Case and the Framing of Stephen Ward.* New York: Atheneum, 1987.

Konolige, Kit. *The Richest Women in the World.* New York: Macmillan, 1986.

Koskoff, David E. *Joseph P. Kennedy: A Life and Times.* Englewood Cliffs, N.J.: Prentice-Hall, 1974.

Kramer, Freda. *Jackie.* New York: Award Books, 1975.

Krock, Arthur. *In the Nation: 1932–1966.* New York: McGraw-Hill, 1966.

Kwitny, Jonathan. *Endless Enemies: The Making of an Unfriendly World.* New York: Congdon & Weed, 1984.

Lamarr, Hedy. *Ecstasy and Me: My Life as a Woman.* New York: Bartholomew House, 1966.

Lambro, Donald. *Washington—City of Scandals: Investigating Congress and Other Big Spenders.* Boston: Little, Brown and Company, 1984.

Landau, Elaine. *John F. Kennedy Jr.* Brookfield, Conn.: Twenty-First Century Books, 2000.

Lane, Mark. *Rush to Judgment: A Critique of the Warren Commission's Inquiry into the Murders of President John F. Kennedy, Officer J. D. Tippit and Lee Harvey Oswald.* New York: Holt, Rinehart & Winston, 1966.

Lanham, Robert. *The Hipster Handbook.* New York: Anchor Books, 2003.

Lash, Joseph P. *Eleanor: The Years Alone.* New York: W. W. Norton & Company, 1972.

Lasky, Victor. *J.F.K.: The Man and the Myth.* New York: Macmillan, 1963.

Latham, Caroline, and Jeannie Sakol. *The Kennedy Encyclopedia: An Illustrated Guide to America's Royal Family.* New York: NAL Books, 1989.

Lawford, Christopher Kennedy. *Symptoms of Withdrawal: A Memoir of Snapshots and Redemption.* New York: William Morrow & Co., 2005.

Lawford, Lady May. *"Bitch!" The Autobiography of Lady Lawford.* Brookline Village, Mass.: Branden Books, 1986.

Lawford, Patricia Seaton, with Ted Schwarz. *The Peter Lawford Story: Life with the Kennedys, Monroe and the Rat Pack.* New York: Carroll and Graf Publishers, 1988.

Lax, Henry. *Sidelights from the Surgery.* London: Pallas, 1929.

Leamer, Laurence. *Fantastic: The Life of Arnold Schwarzenegger.* New York: St. Martin's Press, 2005.

————. *The Kennedy Women: The Saga of an American Family.* New York: Villard Books, 1994.

————. *Make-Believe: The Story of Nancy and Ronald Reagan.* New York: Harper & Row, 1983.

————. *Sons of Camelot: The Fate of an American Dynasty.* New York: William Morrow & Co., 2004.

Leaming, Barbara. *Mrs. Kennedy: The Missing History of the Kennedy Years.* New York: The Free Press, 2001.

Leary, Timothy. *Changing My Mind, Among Others: Lifetime Writings, Selected and Introduced by the Author.* Englewood Cliffs, N.J.: Prentice-Hall, 1982.

————. *Flashbacks: An Autobiography.* Los Angeles: J. P. Tarcher, 1983.

Lee, Martin A., and Bruce Shlain. *Acid Dreams: The CIA, LSD, and the Sixties Rebellion.* New York: Grove Press, 1985.

Leigh, Wendy. *Prince Charming: The John F. Kennedy, Jr., Story.* New York: Signet, 1994.

Lerner, Max. *Ted and the Kennedy Legend: A Study in Character and Destiny.* New York: St. Martin's Press, 1980.

Lifton, David S. *Best Evidence: Disguise and Deception in the Assassination of John F. Kennedy.* New York: Macmillan, 1980.

Lilienthal, David E. *The Journals of David E. Lilienthal. Volume V: The Harvest Years, 1959–1963.* New York: Harper & Row, 1972.

Lilly, Doris. *Those Fabulous Greeks: Onassis, Niarchos, and Livanos.* London: W. H. Allen, 1971.

Lincoln, Anne H. *The Kennedy White House Parties.* New York: Viking Press, 1967.

Lincoln, Evelyn. *My Twelve Years with John F. Kennedy.* New York: David McKay Company, 1965.

Littell, Robert T. *The Men We Became: My Friendship with John F. Kennedy Jr.:* New York: St. Martin's Press, 2004.

Logan, Joshua. *Movie Stars, Real People and Me.* New York: Delacorte Press, 1989.

Louchheim, Katie. *By the Political Sea.* Garden City, N.Y.: Doubleday, 1970.

Lowe, Jacques. *Kennedy: A Time Remembered.* London: Quartet Books, 1983.

————. *Remembering Jack: Intimate and Unseen Photographs of the Kennedys.* Boston: Bulfinch Press, 2003.

Lowell, James Russell. *Selected Literary Essays from James Russell Lowell.* Introduction by Will David Howe and Norman Zoerster. Boston: Houghton Mifflin, 1914.

Lowell, Robert. *History.* New York: Farrar, Straus & Giroux, 1973.

MacMahon M.D., Edward B., and Leonard Curry. *Medical Cover-ups in the White House.* Washington, D.C.: Farragut Publishing Company, 1987.

Macmillan, Harold. *At the End of the Day, 1961–1963.* New York: Harper & Row, 1973.

MacPherson, Myra. *The Power Lovers: An Intimate Look at Politicians and Their Marriages.* New York: Putnam, 1975.

Maier, Thomas. *The Kennedys: America's Emerald Kings.* New York: Basic Books, 2003.

Mailer, Norman. *Marilyn.* New York: Grosset & Dunlap, 1973.

———. *Of Women and Their Elegance.* New York: Simon & Schuster, 1980.

———. *The Presidential Papers.* New York: Putnam, 1963.

Makower, Joel. *Boom! Talkin' about Our Generation.* Chicago: Contemporary Books, 1985.

Manchester, William. *Controversy and Other Essays in Journalism, 1950–1975.* Boston: Little, Brown and Company, 1976.

———. *The Death of a President: November 1963.* New York: Harper & Row, 1967.

———. *One Brief Shining Moment: Remembering Kennedy.* Boston: Little, Brown and Company, 1983.

———. *Portrait of a President: John F. Kennedy in Profile.* Boston: Little, Brown and Company, 1962.

Manso, Peter. *Mailer: His Life and Times.* New York: Simon & Schuster, 1985.

Marsh, Lisa. *The House of Klein: Fashion, Controversy, and a Business Obsession.* Hoboken, N.J.: Wiley, 2003.

Martin, John Bartlow. *Adlai Stevenson and the World: The Life of Adlai Stevenson.* Garden City, N.Y.: Doubleday and Company, 1977.

Martin, Ralph G. *Cissy: The Extraordinary Life of Eleanor Medill Patterson.* New York: Simon & Schuster, 1979.

———. *A Hero for Our Time: An Intimate Story of the Kennedy Years.* New York: Ballantine Books, 1983.

Maxwell, Elsa. *The Celebrity Circus.* New York: Appleton-Century, 1963.

———. *R.S.V.P.: Elsa Maxwell's Own Story.* Boston: Little, Brown and Company, 1954.

May, Ernest R., and Philip D. Zelikow, eds. *The Kennedy Tapes: Inside the White House during the Cuban Missile Crisis.* Cambridge, Mass.: Belknap Press of Harvard University, 1997.

McCarthy, Dennis V. N. *Protecting the President: The Inside Story of a Secret Service Agent.* New York: William Morrow & Co., 1985.

McCarthy, Joe. *The Remarkable Kennedys.* New York: Dial Press, 1960.

McConnell, Brian. *The History of Assassination.* Nashville: Aurora Publishers, 1970.

McMillan, Priscilla Johnson. *Marina and Lee.* New York: Harper & Row, 1977.

McTaggart, Lynne. *Kathleen Kennedy: Her Life and Times.* Garden City, N.Y.: Dial Press, 1983.

Means, Marianne. *The Woman in the White House.* New York: Random House, 1963.

Meneghini, Giovanni Battista. *My Wife Maria Callas.* New York: Farrar, Straus & Giroux, 1982.

Meyers, Joan, ed. *John Fitzgerald Kennedy . . . As We Remember Him.* New York: Atheneum, 1965.

Michaelis, David. *The Best of Friends: Profiles of Extraordinary Friendships.* New York: William Morrow & Co., 1983.

Miers, Earl Schenck. *America and Its Presidents.* New York: Grosset & Dunlap, 1959.

Miller, Alice P. *A Kennedy Chronology.* New York: Birthdate Research, 1968.

Miller, Arthur. *Timebends: A Life.* New York: Grove Press, 1987.

Miller, Hope Ridings. *Embassy Row: The Life & Times of Diplomatic Washington.* New York: Holt, Rinehart & Winston, 1969.

———. *Scandals in the Highest Office: Facts and Fictions in the Private Lives of Our Presidents.* New York: Random House, 1973.

Miller, Merle. *Plain Speaking: An Oral Biography of Harry S. Truman.* New York: Berkeley Publishing Corporation, 1973.

Miller, William, and Frances Spatz Leighton. *Fishbait: The Memoirs of the Congressional Door-keeper.* Englewood Cliffs, N.J.: Prentice-Hall, 1977.

Montgomery, Ruth Shick. *Flowers at the White House: An Informal Tour of the Home of the Presidents of the United States.* New York: M. Barrows, 1967.

———. *Hail to the Chiefs: My Life and Times with Six Presidents.* New York: Coward-McCann, 1970.

Moon, Vicky. *The Private Passion of Jackie Kennedy Onassis: Portrait of a Rider.* New York: ReganBooks, 2005.

Mooney, Booth. *LBJ: An Irreverent Chronicle.* New York: Crowell, 1976.

Morella, Joe. *Paul and Joanne: A Biography of Paul Newman and Joanne Woodward.* New York: Dell, 1988.

Morella, Joe, and Edward Z. Epstein. *Forever Lucy: The Life of Lucille Ball.* Secaucus, N.J.: Lyle Stuart, 1986.

Morrow, Lance. *The Chief: A Memoir of Fathers and Sons.* New York: Random House, 1984.

Morrow, Robert D. *The Senator Must Die: The Murder of Robert Kennedy.* Santa Monica, Calif.: Roundtable Publishing, 1988.

Moutsatsos, Kiki Feroudie. *The Onassis Women.* New York: G. P. Putnam's Sons, 1998.

Mulvaney, Jay. *Kennedy Weddings: A Family Album.* New York: St. Martin's Press, 1999.

Nicholas, William. *The Bobby Kennedy Nobody Knows.* New York: Fawcett Publications, 1967.

Nin, Anais. *The Diary of Anais Nin (1947–1955).* New York: Harcourt Brace Jovanovich, 1974.

Niven, David. *The Moon's a Balloon.* New York: Putnam, 1972.

Nixon, Richard. *RN: The Memoirs of Richard Nixon.* New York: Grosset & Dunlap, 1978.

Nizer, Louis. *Reflections without Mirrors: An Autobiography of the Mind.* New York: Doubleday & Company, 1978.

Noguchi, Thomas T., with Joseph Dimona. *Coroner to the Stars.* London: Corgi Books, 1983.

Noonan, William Sylvester, with Robert Huber. *Forever Young: My Friendship with John F. Kennedy, Jr.* New York: Viking, 2006.

Nowakowski, Tadeusz. *The Radziwills: The Social History of a Great European Family.* New York: Delacorte Press, 1974.

Nunnerley, David. *President Kennedy and Britain.* New York: St. Martin's Press, 1972.

Oates, Stephen B. *Let the Trumpet Sound: The Life of Martin Luther King, Jr.* New York: Harper & Row, 1982.

———. *William Faulkner: The Man & the Artist.* New York: Harper & Row, 1987.

O'Brien, Lawrence F. *No Final Victories: A Life in Politics—from John F. Kennedy to Watergate.* New York: Doubleday, 1974.

O'Donnell, Kenneth P., and David F. Powers with Joe McCarthy. *"Johnny We Hardly Knew Ye": Memories of John Fitzgerald Kennedy.* Boston: Little, Brown and Company, 1970.

Onassis, Jacqueline Kennedy, ed. *In the Russian Style.* New York: The Viking Press, 1976.

———. *The Last Will and Testament of Jacqueline Kennedy Onassis.* New York: Carroll & Graf Publishers, 1997.

O'Neill, Tip, with William Novak. *Man of the House: The Life and Political Memoirs of Speaker Tip O'Neill.* New York: Random House, 1987.

Osmond, Humphry. *Predicting the Past: Memos on the Enticing Universe of Possibility.* New York: Macmillan Publishing Company, 1981.

Paper, Lewis J. *The Promise and the Performance: The Leadership of John F. Kennedy.* New York: Crown Publishers, 1975.

Parker, Robert, with Richard Rashke. *Capitol Hill in Black and White.* New York: Dodd, Mead, 1987.

Parmet, Herbert S. *Jack: The Struggles of John F. Kennedy.* New York: Dial Press, 1980.

A Patriot's Handbook: Songs, Poems, Stories, and Speeches Celebrating the Land We Love. Selected and introduced by Caroline Kennedy. New York: Hyperion, 2000.

People Weekly: Private Lives. By the editors of *People.* Birmingham, Ala.: Oxmoor House, 1991.

Persico, Joseph E. *The Imperial Rockefeller: A Biography of Nelson A. Rockefeller.* New York: Simon & Schuster, 1982.

Peters, Charles. *Tilting at Windmills: An Autobiography.* Reading, Mass.: Addison-Wesley, 1988.

Peyser, Joan. *Bernstein: A Biography.* New York: Beech Tree Books, 1987.

Phillips, John, with Jim Jerome. *Papa John: An Autobiography by John Phillips.* Garden City, N.Y.: Doubleday, 1986.

Phillips, Julia. *You'll Never Eat Lunch in This Town Again.* New York: Random House, 1991.

Political Profiles: The Johnson Years. New York: Facts on File, 1976.

Political Profiles: The Kennedy Years. New York: Facts on File, 1976.

Potter, Jeffrey. *Men, Money & Magic: The Story of Dorothy Schiff.* New York: Coward, McCann & Geoghegan, 1976.

Pottker, Jan. *Celebrity Washington: Who They Are, Where They Live, and Why They're Famous.* Potomac, Md.: Writers Cramp Books, 1995.

———. *Janet and Jackie: The Story of a Mother and Her Daughter, Jacqueline Kennedy Onassis.* New York: St. Martin's Press, 2001.

Powers, Thomas. *The Men Who Kept the Secrets: Richard Helms and the CIA.* New York: Knopf, 1979.

President's Commission on the Assassination of President Kennedy, The. (The Warren Commission) *Hearings and Exhibits.* Vols. I–XXXVI. Washington, D.C.: U.S. Government Printing Office, September 1964.

Profiles in Courage for Our Time. Introduced and edited by Caroline Kennedy. New York: Hyperion, 2002.

Profiles in History: Catalogue 4. Beverly Hills, Calif.: Joseph M. Menddalena, n.d.

Rachlin, Harvey. *The Kennedys: A Chronological History 1823–Present.* New York: World Almanac Books, 1986.

Radziwill, Carole. *What Remains: A Memoir of Fate, Friendship, and Love.* New York: Scribner, 2005.

Radziwill, Lee. *Happy Times.* New York: Assouline, 2000.

Rainie, Harrison, and John Quinn. *Growing Up Kennedy: The Third Wave Comes of Age.* New York: Putnam Publishing Group, 1983.

Randall, Monica. *The Mansions of Long Island's Gold Coast.* New York: Hastings House, 1979.

Rapoport, Roger. *The Super-Doctors.* Chicago: Playboy Press, 1975.

Rather, Dan, and Gary Paul Gates. *The Palace Guard.* New York: Harper & Row, 1974.

Rather, Dan, and Mickey Herskowitz. *The Camera Never Blinks: Adventures of a TV Journalist.* New York: William Morrow & Co., 1977.

Rattray, Jeannette Edwards. *Fifty Years of the Maidstone Club, 1891–1941.* Souvenir publication privately printed for members of the club (1941).

Reeves, Richard. *President Kennedy: Profile of Power.* New York: Simon & Schuster, 1993.

Reeves, Thomas C. *A Question of Character: A Life of John F. Kennedy.* Rocklin, Calif.: Primay Publishing, 1992.

Reich, Cary. *Financier: The Biography of André Meyer: A Story of Money, Power, and the Reshaping of American Business.* New York: William Morrow & Co., 1983.

Report of the Warren Commission on the Assassination of President Kennedy. New York: Bantam Books, 1964.

Rhea, Mini. *I Was Jacqueline Kennedy's Dressmaker.* New York: Fleet, 1962.

Riese, Randall, and Neal Hitchens. *The Unabridged Marilyn: Her Life from A to Z.* New York: Congdon & Weed, 1987.

Romero, Gerry. *Sinatra's Women.* New York: Manor Books, 1976.

Roosevelt, Felicia Warburg. *Doers and Dowagers.* Garden City, N.Y.: Doubleday & Co., 1975.

Rowe, Robert. *The Bobby Baker Story.* New York: Parallax Publishing Company, 1967.

Rush, George. *Confessions of an Ex–Secret Service Agent.* New York: Donald I. Fine, 1988.

Rust, Zad. *Teddy Bare: The Last of the Kennedy Clan.* Boston: Western Islands, 1971.

Salinger, Pierre. *P.S.: A Memoir.* New York: St. Martin's Press, 1995.

———, ed. *"An Honorable Profession": A Tribute to Robert F. Kennedy.* Garden City, N.Y.: Doubleday, 1968.

———. *With Kennedy.* Garden City, N.Y.: Doubleday, 1966.

Saunders, Frank, with James Southwood. *Torn Lace Curtain.* New York: Holt, Rinehart & Winston, 1982.

Scheim, David E. *Contract on America: The Mafia Murder of President John F. Kennedy.* New York: Shapolsky Publishers, 1988.

Schlesinger Jr., Arthur M. *The Cycles of American History.* Boston: Houghton Mifflin, 1986.

———. *The Imperial Presidency.* Boston: Houghton Mifflin, 1973.

———. *Robert Kennedy and His Times.* Boston: Houghton Mifflin, 1978.

———. *A Thousand Days: John F. Kennedy in the White House.* Boston: Houghton Mifflin, 1965.

Schoenbaum, Thomas J. *Waging Peace & War: Dean Rusk in the Truman, Kennedy & Johnson Years.* New York: Simon & Schuster, 1988.

Schoor, Gene. *Young John Kennedy.* New York: Harcourt, Brace & World, 1963.

Schwartz, Charles. *Cole Porter: A Biography.* New York: Dial Press, 1977.

Sciacca, Tony. *Kennedy and His Women.* New York: Manor Books, 1976.

Sealy, Shirley. *The Celebrity Sex Register.* New York: Simon & Schuster, 1982.

Seaman, Barbara. *Lovely Me: The Life of Jacqueline Susann.* New York: William Morrow & Co., 1987.

Searls, Hank. *The Lost Prince: Young Joe, The Forgotten Kennedy.* New York: World Pub. Co., 1969.

Sgubin, Marta, and Nancy Nicholas. *Cooking for Madam: Recipes and Reminiscences from the Home of Jacqueline Kennedy Onassis.* New York: Scribner, 1998.

Shannon, William V. *The Heir Apparent: Robert Kennedy and the Struggle for Power.* New York: Macmillan, 1967.

Shaw, Mark. *The John F. Kennedys: A Family Album.* New York: Farrar, Straus, 1964.

Shaw, Maud. *White House Nanny: My Years with Caroline and John Kennedy, Jr.* New York: New American Library, 1965.

Shepard Jr., Tazewell. *John F. Kennedy: Man of the Sea.* New York: William Morrow & Co., 1965.

Shriver, Maria. *What's Happening to Grandpa?* Illustrated by Sandra Speidel. Boston: Little, Brown Young Readers, 2004.

Shulman, Irving. *"Jackie!": The Exploitation of a First Lady.* New York: Trident Press, 1970.

Sidey, Hugh. *John F. Kennedy, President.* New York: Atheneum, 1964.

Sills, Beverly, and Lawrence Linderman. *Beverly: An Autobiography.* New York: Bantam Books, 1987.

Silverman, Debora. *Selling Culture: Bloomingdale's, Diana Vreeland, and the New Aristocracy of Taste in Reagan's America.* New York: Pantheon Books, 1986.

Slatzer, Robert F. *The Life and Curious Death of Marilyn Monroe.* New York: Pinnacle House, 1974.

Smith, Amanda, ed. *Hostage to Fortune: The Letters of Joseph P. Kennedy.* New York: Viking, 2001.

Smith, Jane S. *Elsie de Wolfe: A Life in the High Style.* New York: Atheneum, 1982.

Smith, Liz. *Natural Blonde: A Memoir.* New York: Hyperion, 2000.

Smith, Malcom E. *John F. Kennedy's 13 Great Mistakes in the White House.* Smithtown, N.Y.: Suffolk House, 1980.

Smith, Marie. *Entertaining in the White House.* Washington, D.C.: Acropolis Books, 1967.

Smith, Sally Bedell. *Grace and Power: The Private World of the Kennedy White House.* New York: Random House, 2004.

Smolla, Rodney A. *Suing the Press.* New York: Oxford University Press, 1986.

Sommer, Shelley. *John F. Kennedy: His Life and Legacy.* Introduction by Caroline Kennedy. New York: HarperCollins, 2005.

Sorensen, Theodore C. *Kennedy.* New York: Harper & Row, 1965.

Sotheby's Catalogue: *Property from Kennedy Family Homes: Hyannisport, Martha's Vineyard, New Jersey, New York, Virginia. New York Tuesday, Wednesday, & Thursday, February 15, 16, & 17th, 2005.* New York: Sotheby's, 2005.

Spada, James. *Grace: The Secret Lives of a Princess.* Garden City, N.Y.: Doubleday, 1987.

———. *John and Caroline: Their Lives in Pictures.* New York: St. Martin's Press, 2001.

———. *Peter Lawford: The Man Who Kept the Secrets.* New York: Bantam Books, 1991.

Sparks, Fred. *The $20,000,000 Honeymoon: Jackie and Ari's First Year.* New York: B. Geis Associates, 1970.

Spender, Stephen. *Journals 1939–1983.* New York: Random House, 1986.

Speriglio, Milo. *The Marilyn Conspiracy.* New York: Pocket Books, 1986.

Spignesi, Stephen. *J.F.K., Jr.* Secaucus, N.J.: Carol Publishing Group, 1999.

Stack, Robert, with Mark Evans. *Straight Shooting.* New York: Macmillan, 1980.

Stassinopoulos, Arianna. *Maria Callas: The Woman behind the Legend.* New York: Simon & Schuster, 1981.

Steel, Ronald. *Walter Lippmann and the American Century.* Boston: Little, Brown and Company, 1980.

Stein, Jean. *American Journey: The Times of Robert Kennedy.* Edited by George Plimpton. New York: Harcourt Brace Jovanovich, 1970.

———. *Edie: An American Biography.* Edited with George Plimpton. New York: Knopf, 1983.

Steinem, Gloria. *Outrageous Acts and Everyday Rebellions.* New York: Holt, Rinehart & Winston, 1983.

Storm, Tempest, with Bill Boyd. *Tempest Storm: The Lady Is a Vamp.* Atlanta: Peachtree Publishing, 1987.

Stoughton, Cecil, and Chester V. Clifton. *The Memories: JFK 1961–1963.* New York: W. W. Norton & Company, 1973.

Straight, N. A. *Ariabella: The First.* New York: Random House, 1981.

Strait, Raymond. *The Tragic Secret Life of Jayne Mansfield.* Chicago: Regnery Co., 1974.

Suero, Orlando. *Camelot at Dawn: Jacqueline and John Kennedy in Georgetown, May 1954.* Photographs by Orlando Suero; text by Anne Garside. Baltimore: Johns Hopkins University Press, 2001.

Sullivan, Gerald, and Michael Kenney. *The Race for the Eighth: The Making of a Congressional Campaign: Joe Kennedy's Successful Pursuit of a Political Legacy.* New York: Harper & Row, 1987.

Sullivan, William C. *The Bureau: My Thirty Years in Hoover's FBI.* New York: W. W. Norton & Company, 1979.

Sulzberger, Iphigene Ochs. *Iphigene.* New York: Times Books, 1987.

Summers, Anthony. *Conspiracy.* New York: McGraw-Hill, 1980.

———. *Goddess: The Secret Lives of Marilyn Monroe.* New York: Macmillan, 1985.

Summers, Anthony, and Stephen Dorril. *Honeytrap.* London: Weidenfeld and Nicolson, 1987.

Susann, Jacqueline. *Dolores.* New York: William Morrow & Co., 1976.

Swanberg, W. A. *Luce and His Empire.* New York: Charles Scribners Sons, 1972.

Swanson, Gloria. *Swanson on Swanson.* New York: Random House, 1980.

Sykes, Christopher. *Nancy: The Life of Lady Astor.* London: William Collins, Sons & Co., 1972.

Sykes, Plum. *Bergdorf Blondes: A Novel.* New York: Miramax, 2004.

Taraborrelli, J. Randy. *Jackie, Ethel, Joan: Women of Camelot.* New York: Warner Books, 2000.

Taylor, Roger. *Marilyn Monroe in Her Own Words.* New York: Delilah-Putnam, 1983.

Teltscher, Henry O. *Handwriting, Revelation of Self: A Source Book of Psychographology.* New York: Hawthorn Books, 1971.

Ten Year Report 1966–1967 to 1976–1977. Cambridge, Mass.: The Institute of Politics, John Fitzgerald Kennedy School of Government, Harvard University, 1977.

Teodorescu, Radu. *Radu's Simply Fit.* New York: Cader Books, 1996.

ter Horst, J. F., and Ralph Albertazzie. *The Flying White House: The Story of Air Force One.* New York: Coward, McCann & Geoghegan, 1979.

Teti, Frank. *Kennedy: The New Generation.* New York: Delilah, 1983.

Thayer, Mary Van Rensselaer. *Jacqueline Bouvier Kennedy.* Garden City, N.Y.: Doubleday, 1961.

———. *Jacqueline Kennedy: The White House Years.* Boston: Little, Brown and Company, 1971.

Theodoracopulos, Taki. *Princes, Playboys & High-class Tarts.* Princeton, N.J.: Karz-Cohl Pub., 1984.

Thomas, Helen. *Dateline: White House.* New York: Macmillan, 1975.

Thompson, Hunter. *Fear and Loathing in America: The Brutal Odyssey of an Outlaw Journalist.* Foreword by David Halberstam; edited by Douglas Brinkley. New York: Simon & Schuster, 2000.

Thompson, Jim. *The Grifters.* Berkeley, Calif.: Creative Arts, 1975.

Thompson, Josiah. *Six Seconds in Dallas: A Micro-study of the Kennedy Assassination.* New York: Bernard Geis, 1967.

Thompson, Lawrence, and R. H. Winnick. *Robert Frost: The Later Years, 1938–1963.* New York: Holt, Rinehart & Winston, 1976.

Thompson, Nelson. *The Dark Side of Camelot.* Chicago: Playboy Press, 1976.

Thorndike Jr., Joseph J. *The Very Rich: A History of Wealth.* New York: American Heritage, 1976.

Tierney, Gene, with Mickey Herskowitz. *Self-Portrait.* New York: Wyden Books, 1979.

Travell, Janet. *Office Hours: Day and Night—The Autobiography of Janet Travell, M.D.* New York: World Publishing Co., 1968.

Trewhitt, Henry L. *McNamara.* New York: Harper & Row, 1971.

Triumph and Tragedy: The Story of the Kennedys. By the writers, photographers, and editors of the Associated Press. New York: William Morrow & Co., 1968.

Troy, Ann A. *Nutley: Yesterday–Today.* Nutley, N.J.: the Nutley Historical Society, 1961.

Truman, Margaret. *First Ladies: An Intimate Group Portrait of White House Wives.* New York: Random House, 1995.

———. *Harry S. Truman.* New York: William Morrow & Co., 1972.

———. *The President's House: A First Daughter Shares the History and Secrets of the World's Most Famous Home.* New York: Ballantine Books, 2003.

Trump, Donald. *The America We Deserve.* Los Angeles: Renaissance Books, 2000.

Ungar, Sanford J. *FBI.* Boston: Little, Brown and Company, 1975.

United States Senate. *Final Report of the Select Committee to Study Governmental Operations with Respect to Intelligence Activities.* Book V. *The Investigation of the Assassination of John F. Kennedy: Performance of the Intelligence Agencies.* Washington, D.C.: U.S. Government Printing Office, April 23, 1976.

Valentine, Tom, and Patrick Mahn. *Daddy's Duchess: The Unauthorized Biography of Doris Duke.* Secaucus, N.J.: Lyle Stuart, 1987.

Vanden Heuvel, William, and Milton Gwirtzman. *On His Own: Robert F. Kennedy 1964–1968.* Garden City, N.Y.: Doubleday, 1970.

Van Riper, Frank. *Glenn: The Astronaut Who Would Be President.* New York: Empire Books, 1983.

Vickers, Hugo. *Cecil Beaton: A Biography.* Boston: Little, Brown and Company, 1985.

Vidal, Gore. *The Best Man.* Boston: Little, Brown and Company, 1960.

———. *Homage to Daniel Shays: Collected Essays, 1952–1972.* New York: Random House, 1972.

———. *Julian.* Boston: Little, Brown and Company, 1964.

Vreeland, Diana. *Allure.* Garden City, N.Y.: Doubleday, 1980.

Walker, John. *Self-Portrait with Donors: Confessions of an Art Collector.* Boston: Little, Brown and Company, 1974.

Wallace, Irving. *The Sunday Gentleman.* New York: Simon & Schuster, 1965.

Warhol, Andy. *Andy Warhol's Exposures.* Photographs by Andy Warhol, text by Andy Warhol with Bob Colacello. New York: Andy Warhol Books/Grosset & Dunlap, 1979.

Warren Report, The. New York: Associated Press, 1964.

Watney, Hedda Lyons. *Jackie.* North Hollywood, Calif.: Leisure Books, 1971.

Wead, Doug. *All the President's Children: Triumph and Tragedy in the Lives of America's First Families.* New York: Atria Books, 2003.

Weatherby, W. J. *Conversations with Marilyn.* New York: Ballantine Books, 1977.

Weberman, Alan, and Michael Canfield. *Coup D'Etat in America: The CIA and the Assassination of John F. Kennedy.* New York: Third Press, 1975.

Weisberg, Harold. *John F. Kennedy Assassination Post Mortem.* Frederick, Md.: Self-published, 1975.

———. *Whitewash.* Vols. I and II. New York: Dell, 1966; vols. III and IV, self-published, 1967.

Weiss, Murray, and Bill Hoffman. *Palm Beach Babylon: Sins, Scams, and Scandals.* New York: Carol Publishing Group, 1992.

West, Darrell, M. *Patrick Kennedy: The Rise to Power.* Upper Saddle River, N.J.: Prentice-Hall, 2001.

West, J. B., with Mary Lynn Kotz. *Upstairs at the White House: My Life with the First Ladies.* New York: Coward, McCann & Geoghegan, 1973.

Whalen, Richard J. *The Founding Father: The Story of Joseph P. Kennedy and the Family He Raised to Power.* New York: New American Library, 1964.

White House Historical Association. *The White House: An Historical Guide.* Washington, D.C., 1979.

White, Ray Lewis. *Gore Vidal.* New York: Twayne Pub., 1968.

White, Theodore H. *In Search of History: A Personal Adventure.* New York: Harper & Row, 1978.

———. *The Making of the President 1960.* New York: Atheneum, 1961.

White, William S. *The Professional: Lyndon B. Johnson.* Boston: Houghton Mifflin, 1964.

Wicker, Tom. *On Press.* New York: Viking, 1975.

Wills, Garry. *The Kennedy Imprisonment: A Meditation on Power.* Boston: Little, Brown and Company, 1982.

Wilroy, Mary Edith, and Lucie Prinz. *Inside Blair House*. Garden City, N.Y.: Doubleday, 1982.

Wilson, Earl. *Show Business Laid Bare*. New York: G. P. Putnam's Sons, 1974.

———. *The Show Business Nobody Knows*. New York: Cowles Book Co., 1971.

———. *Sinatra: An Unauthorized Biography*. New York: Macmillan, 1976.

Winter-Berger, Robert N. *The Washington Pay-Off*. New York: Dell, 1972.

Wirth, Conrad L. *Parks, Politics, and the People*. Norman: University of Okahoma Press, 1980.

Witnesses, The. Selected and edited from the Warren Commission's hearings by *The New York Times* with an introduction by Anthony Lewis. New York: McGraw-Hill, 1964.

Wofford, Harris. *Of Kennedys and Kings: Making Sense of the Sixties*. New York: Farrar, Straus & Giroux, 1980.

Wolff, Perry. *A Tour of the White House with Mrs. John F. Kennedy*. Garden City, N.Y.: Doubleday, 1962.

Youngblood, Rufus W. *20 Years in the Secret Service: My Life with Five Presidents*. New York: Simon & Schuster, 1973.

Ziegler, Philip. *Diana Cooper: A Biography*. New York: Knopf, 1982.

INDEX

Onassis, Aristotle (*cont.*)
  on 1963 Greece cruise with Jackie,
    106–8
  physical appearance of, 107, 156, 262
  son's death and, 190–92, 198, 199
  as stepfather, 155, 157–58, 159, 161,
    165, 166–68, 169, 173–74, 177,
    182, 191, 199, 202, 209, 228, 374
  troubles in Jackie's marriage to, 168,
    169–71, 178, 180, 181–82, 187,
    189, 190–92, 198–200, 203
Onassis, Artemis, 106, 157, 169, 200, 202,
  212
Onassis, Athina "Tina," 106, 156, 179,
  199–200, 205
Onassis, Christina, 149, 161, 168, 169,
  174, 179–80, 182, 199, 202, 203,
  204–5, 212, 214
  Jackie disliked by, 157, 160, 177,
    199–200, 201, 204–5
Onassis, Jacqueline Bouvier Kennedy, 9,
  15, 19, 25, 42, 81, 135–36, 152–53,
  176, 211, 215, 217, 220, 221, 237,
  255–56, 257, 258, 266, 274, 283,
  288, 319, 321–22, 325, 331, 364,
  375, 389, 418, 421, 428, 430, 454,
  458, 459, 464, 487, 505, 522, 523
  affairs and relationships of, 14, 148–51,
    153, 218, 230, 235, 261–64, 269,
    271, 282, 299, 321, 322–23, 324,
    349, 360, 367, 368, 369, 376, 382,
    383, 384, 385, 386, 398, 400, 429,
    480; *see also* Tempelsman, Maurice
  alcohol use by, 140
  Aristotle Onassis and, *see* Onassis,
    Aristotle
  cancer of, 281, 366–70, 376, 381,
    382–87
  Caroline's wedding and, 285, 286, 287,
    289
  celebrity and popularity of, 63, 121–23,
    127, 155, 163, 165, 217, 331–32,
    344, 369, 388–90, 432, 474; *see also*
    media and press
  children kept grounded and unspoiled
    by, xi, 66, 83, 89, 90, 132–33, 141,
    142, 178, 195–96, 322, 437
  children's privacy guarded by, xi, 61, 64,
    69, 80, 83–84, 86–87, 91, 124, 126,

    146, 155–56, 174–75, 180–81,
    186, 192–93, 210, 299
  children's romantic relationships
    and, 227, 230, 231, 232, 235, 270,
    277, 281, 302, 321, 346, 356, 362,
    379
  Clintons and, 360–61, 389, 390, 391,
    392
  as critical, controlling, and demanding,
    13, 16, 84, 88–90, 100, 123, 177,
    188, 189, 192, 200–201, 211, 214,
    225, 228–29, 238, 240, 241, 243,
    260, 270, 277, 280, 282, 300, 307,
    311, 321, 332, 336, 345, 355,
    362–63, 379
  Dallas trip and, 108, 109
  death and funeral of, 3, 48, 323, 345,
    387–92, 397, 400, 402, 403, 417,
    452, 502, 518
  as devoted mother, xii, 61–62, 69,
    90–91, 96, 97, 99–100, 104, 106,
    108, 113, 119, 136, 142, 144,
    165–66, 169–70, 174, 178, 222,
    229, 243, 400, 454, 508
  education of, 3, 15, 54, 209
  extravagant spending of, 69, 70, 131,
    148, 149, 154–55, 156, 157, 161,
    162, 170–71, 173, 187, 189, 191,
    516
  fashion and personal style of, 3, 68, 69,
    75, 109, 165, 216, 287, 341, 359,
    364, 368, 383, 397, 402, 406, 409,
    513
  father's death and, 58, 59
  Fifth Avenue apartment of, 3, 131,
    132, 146–47, 161, 164, 165, 172,
    174–75, 181, 184–85, 223, 230,
    242, 262, 274, 318, 360, 368, 385,
    398, 399
  financial worth of, 131, 147, 158, 204,
    322–23, 366, 449
  Georgetown years of, 54–55, 57, 60,
    61–62, 68, 69, 72–73, 92, 96,
    120–28, 134, 313
  as grandmother, 300, 321, 324, 330,
    331, 333, 359, 367, 369, 382, 383,
    393
  historical preservation work of, 188,
    397, 483

Russo, Peter Jay, 26
Rutherford, Janet Jennings Auchincloss,
    103, 287, 367
Rutherford, Lewis, Jr., 143, 389

Sachs, Gunther, 214
Sachs, Jason, 374
Sachs, Jeffrey, D., 492
Saex, Robin, 279–81
Sagaponack, Long Island, 5, 12, 350, 352,
    370–73, 398, 503, 515
St. David's School, 141–42, 146, 147, 163,
    165
St. Jacques, Sterling, 218
St. James, Susan, 319
St. Louis Post-Dispatch, 80
St. Paul's Cathedral, 505
Salinger, Pierre, 56, 64, 78, 80, 81, 84, 86,
    91, 93, 94–95, 101–2, 117, 120,
    126, 150, 151, 154, 169, 180, 181,
    183–84, 192, 215, 289, 304, 332,
    355, 431–32
Saltonstall, Leverett, 89
Saltonstall, Mrs. William, 89
Samson, Dan, 28, 256, 307, 465, 490
Saturday Night Live, 330, 473
Saville, Brent, 268
Sawyer, Diane, 322, 410
Sayre, David, 459
Scaasi, Arnold, 464
Schiffer, Claudia, 381, 447
Schlesinger, Arthur M., Jr., 44, 97, 153,
    287, 289
Schlossberg, Alfred, 266–67, 288, 289, 300
Schlossberg, Caroline Bouvier Kennedy,
    vii, xi–xii, 24, 45, 108, 225, 239,
    255, 258, 264, 280, 284, 292, 297,
    315, 318–19, 322, 324, 326, 332,
    356, 360, 376, 417, 427, 430, 432,
    440, 457, 471, 486, 487, 499
  acts of rebellion by, 186–87, 270
  adolescence of, 168–70, 171–79,
    180–81, 182–88, 189, 190, 191,
    196–97, 200–201, 202, 203–4, 519
  affairs and relationships of, 212–15,
    216, 219, 229–32, 270–71
  alcohol and drug use of, 186, 201, 211,
    219, 296, 334
  Aristotle Onassis's strained relationship
    with, 155, 157–58, 159, 160, 161,

    166–67, 168, 169, 173–74, 182,
    191, 202
  athletic pursuits of, 94–95, 100, 132,
    136–37, 166, 167, 172, 173, 180,
    230, 266, 333
  attempts to block JFK Jr. bios by, 508
  birth and baptism of, 58–60
  board memberships and organizations
    backed by, 188, 203–4, 271, 303,
    330–31, 334, 344, 359, 397, 480,
    483, 503, 513, 514, 519–20
  books published by, 301, 329–30,
    348–49, 394, 397, 506–7, 509,
    511–12, 517–18
  car bomb incident and, 211–12, 214
  Carolyn Bessette disliked by, 417, 445,
    464, 479–80
  celebrity of, xi–xii, 81, 121–22, 155,
    216, 217, 286, 301, 344; *see also*
    media and press
  charitable donations and fund-raising
    by, 187, 216, 303, 334, 397, 480,
    510, 513, 514, 519–20
  childhood of, xi, 59–60, 61–62, 63–66,
    68, 69, 70, 71, 73, 75, 77, 79–85,
    86–89, 90, 91–92, 93, 94–98,
    99–101, 102, 103, 104, 106, 108,
    109–11, 112–16, 117–26, 127–28,
    131–41, 142–46, 150, 151, 152,
    154, 155, 156, 157–58, 159–61,
    162, 164, 166–67, 177, 313, 502,
    518
  courtship and marriage of, *see*
    Schlossberg, Edwin "Ed"
  David Kennedy's death and, 270
  diet and weight issues of, 172, 177,
    186, 188, 200–201, 211, 215, 230,
    270–71, 333
  divorce rumors and, 509–10, 515
  education and schooling of, 83–84,
    121, 124–25, 135–36, 137, 142,
    146, 158, 171–72, 174–75, 185–
    88, 200, 203, 216–18, 219, 220,
    229–31, 235, 239, 271, 282, 283,
    290, 291, 293, 359
  in Education Department, 514, 516,
    519
  exercise program of, 300–301
  exploitation of family name by, 506–8,
    518

ABOUT THE AUTHOR

---◆---

C. David Heymann is the internationally known author of such *New York Times* best-selling books as *A Woman Named Jackie: An Intimate Biography of Jacqueline Bouvier Kennedy Onassis, Poor Little Rich Girl: The Life and Legend of Barbara Hutton,* and *Liz: An Intimate Biography of Elizabeth Taylor.* Three of his biographies were made into major award-winning NBC-TV miniseries. A three-time Pulitzer Prize nominee, Mr. Heymann lives and works in New York City.